CLOCKWORK DOMINION

Creator: Zeke Coughlin

Developers: Zeke Coughlin & Nathaniel Dean

Writers: Zeke Coughlin, Nathaniel Dean, Brent Concilio

Editors: Dr. L. Coughlin, Kyle Barrett Friesen, Doug Hagler

Fiction: Brent Concilio, Dirk Manning, Jess Shively

Graphic Design and Page Layout: Adam Jury

Cover Artwork: Raven Mimura

Interior Artwork: Cathrine Langwagen, Helen Mask, Raven Mimura, Michelle Mullen, Ameen Naksewee, and Luke Santiago

Additional Artwork and Design: Brian Crick, Clarence D. Meriweather

Consultants and Contributors:
Brent Concilio, Dr. L. Coughlin, Doug Hagler, Will Harrison, Michael McLaughlin, The Rev. Brian Riddle, Jess Shively

Closed Playtesters:
Christopher Block, Juliet Brownell, Scott Coniam, Stephanie Dierker, James Fisher, Justin Frey, Jack Graham, Aaron Grossman, Melody Hadap, Dr. Matthew Hare, Will Harrison, Rachel Jagielski, Adam Kunst, Tony Lee, Michael McLaughlin, Jessica Noble, Kyle Northrop, Matthew Slavik, Rick Slavik

Public Domain Artwork

Much of the public domain artwork that appears in this book is courtesy of Liam at fromoldbooks.org and William A. Mays from The National Police Gazette. We offer our gratitude for their help in beautifying this book.

Thanks to everyone whose time, effort, and dedication helped make this game a reality: our spouses, whose generous support was invaluable—Lisa, Sarah, and Chelsea, we can't thank you enough; the friends, playtesters, and editors who worked through the many iterations of the rules and helped us apply the final polish and make the game shine; a special debt of gratitude to the many who backed this project on Kickstarter—without you, it would have been a much longer and much harder road to bring this book to production; to everyone through the years who helped us discover and maintain our love of gaming; and everyone reading this book, this book is for you. Enjoy it.

RELIQUARY GAME STUDIOS

Reliquary Game Studios is
Zeke Coughlin, Nathaniel Dean, and Brent Concilio
reliquarygamestudios.com   aclockworkworld.com

TABLE OF CONTENTS

Character Creation 107

SANCTION

Arthur Wescott struggled towards the small farmhouse, desperately trying to keep his heir's intestines from spilling down his blood-soaked arms. The house was less than a hundred paces away now, which prompted him to call out to anyone who might be within.

Elizabeth and Mary had just finished their prayers and started their dinner when they heard the screaming from outside. Their eyes met and they stood without a word. They knew what to do. Elizabeth grabbed the lantern from the table and rushed to the front door in case it was someone in need of their help. Mary hurried to the back of the house to fetch her father's shotgun in case it wasn't.

As the door opened, Wescott cried out again. He stumbled towards the woman framed in the doorway and illuminated by lantern light, carrying his bleeding son in his arms. Whoever this woman was, she had to be able to help them. There was no other option if Ethan was to live.

As the stranger entered the house, Elizabeth could see the child was badly wounded…mutilated, really. His arms hung limply and his head rolled and lolled about with every step the man took. Praying that the beast that did this was not pursuing them, she urged them inside. "Quickly! In here!" She stepped forward to help carry the grisly burden, but she drew up short when she saw the sickly green discoloration on the boy's arm. Hoping to mask her unwillingness to carry the boy, she instead rushed to clear the table. "Here, lay him here."

As the man entered the room, Mary set the shotgun against the wall and rushed forward to help, but Elizabeth quickly stepped between the man and her daughter, "Mary! Go… go fetch my supplies from the barn." Mary looked back at her mother, visibly shaken by the scene before her. "Wh… which ones?" She stammered.

"All of them," she replied.

Elizabeth had a moment to consider the strangers while the man laid the boy gently on the table. Both were dressed in fine modern suits that lacked any sign of wear outside the wash of blood which covered them. The Season had just ended, so this was likely a pair of well-off Londoners looking to take in the clean air now that Parliament had concluded for the summer. What he was doing here without an entourage, she didn't know. She did know that this man had brought death right to her door, and that she must be careful if she was to escape the doom that stalked him.

After a few moments staring at the stricken boy, Wescott gathered himself, wiped his face, ceremoniously pulled down his tie and turned to face the woman of the house. "I am Arthur Wescott," he said with the slightest inclination of his head, the most minimal of bows.

"Elizabeth Caufield, sir. The girl who just left is my daughter, Mary." She spoke without looking up as she circled the boy on the table, observing, but unwilling to touch him. "I will do the best I can to help you with your son." Elizabeth paused before trying to deliver her next words quickly and carefully, especially since she could already hear Mary returning. "You are aware, sir, that this is most likely the result of a… chimera."

Wescott glared at Elizabeth. Both his gaze and his tone were steely and cold. "This is not the time to entertain superstitions about the Pontus. My son is dying."

"There are blankets in the parlor, sir," she said to Wescott. "Please help yourself to as many of them as you may need to bind the boy's wounds."

At that moment, they were interrupted by Mary's return. The red-haired girl entered the room overburdened with a bag filled with well-used tools. Elizabeth began to take the implements and set them down near the table.

"I owe you an apology, madam. I did not take you for a doctor."

"Doctor?" Elizabeth sputtered. "I am no doctor, sir."

Wescott looked down at her with calm, analytical eyes. "You possess the tools of a doctor, do you not? Why else have them here?"

"I merely assist those within traveling distance with their sick or wounded livestock. Damages of this extent, to a person, are beyond the scope of my experience. I can help guide you to do what I think is best, sir, but—"

Wescott had heard enough. "Guide me? You can fulfill your Christian duty, madam, by ending your prattling and helping me bind Ethan's wounds so

we—together—can stabilize his condition. Then we can send for a doctor." Wescott thrust a blanket towards her.

As Elizabeth reached out to take it she could see a single drop of blood on the back of her hand. Despite all her efforts to avoid direct contact with the body, it hadn't been enough. Her fate was sealed. Now, she could only do her best to deny the Pontus another victim tonight. "Of course. I'll always do what I can to help a child."

She turned to her daughter, trying not to betray any emotion. "Mary, I want you to run and get your father. Tell him to bring Dr. Grafton."

Mary looked up "Papa is at the Ackermans' farm. That will take hours!"

"Then we don't have time to waste. Go, Mary! Run!" The girl hesitated for a moment, then nodded, took a lantern, and hurried out the front door.

After seeing her daughter leave the house, Elizabeth turned to the dying boy on the table and spent a few moments in silence assessing the injury. The boy's belly was ripped open and several loops of intestine had spilled out. With steel in her voice she said to Wescott, "All we can do right now is to clean the wound and try to close up the worst of the bleeding. You keep pressure here with the blanket; I'll get water and linens, wash the wound out, and start stitching." With that, she set to work.

***

It was fully dark when Mary reached the edge of their farm and the rutted lane that would take her to the Ackermans. She stopped when she saw lights in the distance, approaching from the same direction the city man and his wounded son did half an hour earlier. The lantern lights danced across the field, bobbing up and down, showing their bearers to be on horseback. The color was wrong for kerosene, though. The light of these lanterns was stark and sickly. They bore the unique, unnatural gleam of alchemically transmuted metals trapped in glass orbs…

Mary turned on her heel and began running back to the house.

***

The bleeding was finally slowing, and it seemed the boy still clung to life. As she moved on to start another set of stitches Elizabeth spoke, mainly to cover the sound of Ethan's slow, ragged breathing. "Were you near the ruins by the loch?"

Wescott took one of the blood-soaked sheets and unceremoniously wrung it out on the bare wooden floor next to the makeshift operating table, then returned to gently pressing on the stitches still oozing blood. "Yes. I was showing him the original family seat. My father did the same for me as a boy. Ethan was running about exploring and I lost sight of him…then I heard him scream. When I arrived I found him lying next to a large burrow in the ground…must have been a badger den. We originally rode up, but something had spooked the horses and they fled…and…so I had to carry him. I saw the smoke from your home, thank God, and here we are."

Elizabeth sighed. "It was no badger, sir. Indeed, it was no natural thing at all."

Wescott looked up, his eyes flashing anger. "Do I strike you as a fool? Do you expect me to believe the stories about aberrations and chimera hiding behind every rock? That the world is broken and crumbling at its foundations? Yes, I've heard all that nonsense before. You forget that the purpose of the Empire is to hold the chaos of the Pontus at bay. We are in England, the heart of the Empire, on lands my family has owned for hundreds of years. If it is not safe here, then it is not safe anywhere. No, it must have been a badger."

If Elizabeth was doomed, she at least wanted the harbinger of her fate to understand his guilt. "No, I do not take you as a fool, sir. I take you for a rationalist. One who can survey a situation and come to the truth from all facts and evidence. You cannot deny the strange events that transpire with greater and greater frequency around the world and, yes, here in Britain that—."

Wescott cut her off. "Around the world, to be sure… but not here. Not at home."

"Very well then, explain away the discoloration on your hands and face, or your son's body. Explain why the same discoloration has been found on dead sheep and deer up by the ruins for a week now, or how it spreads through contact?"

Wescott looked at his hands. Beneath the blood, there was some other discoloration. "A sickness. Contagion is well known." And yet, the merest edge of doubt crept in.

He pushed past Elizabeth to scrub his hands furiously. As the blood came off, it revealed an unhealthy sheen of a deep and damning green. Wescott jabbed an emerald-bright digit towards Elizabeth. "If what attacked my son is a chimera thrown up by the Pontus, then it is only because you yokels are not living according to the laws of God and the Queen!"

Elizabeth refused to rise to the bait, and returned to doing what she could for Ethan. There was no point in saying anything further. The green on her hand was already beginning to spread. From experience, she knew even cutting it off would do no good.

***

The awkward silence was violently interrupted as Mary stormed through the back door and into the room. She was pale, wide-eyed, and mute; it was as if she had seen a ghost.

Elizabeth immediately interposed herself between her daughter and the body on the table. "Mary, what are you doing here!?"

"Lights…" Mary gasped, not sure how to properly impart the urgency of what she had just seen across the way. "Witchfinder lights!"

Elizabeth's face fell and she turned to Wescott who was now smiling. "Finally," he said, "civilization has arrived."

His words were interrupted by the front door splintering as it was battered off its hinges. Five men strode through the debris dressed in black leather longcoats and tall, flat-peaked hats like something out of another time. Everything about them exuded the power and privilege that came from royal patronage, right down to the beautifully-engraved revolvers holstered at their sides. Three of them drew their pistols to cover the occupants of the room.

"Gentlemen," Wescott said with a confidence he did not feel, "thank goodness you are here. My son…"

The man who seemed to be in charge held out a hand to silence Wescott, as his colleague in the rear stepped forward with an outstretched palm. Floating above his hand was a small metal rod, something like an arrow. It remained pointing in the same direction into the room even as its bearer circled his brethren to stand beside their leader. The arrow pointed at the boy.

Wescott stepped forward. "I don't understand what's going on here, but..."

Completely ignoring Wescott, one of the Witchfinders turned to their leader and said, "Orders, sir?"

The man in charge rested his right hand on the large basket hilt of the archaic backsword at his belt. He took in the blood that soaked the table, floorboards, and people in the room, and his eyes rested on the discoloration that was spreading down the boy's arm. They then flicked to Wescott's face and to the outstretched hands of Elizabeth as she interposed herself between the men and her daughter. He sighed heavily, "Full quarantine."

Everyone was silent. Two of the men behind him hurried out of the room. The youngest of them stepped forward towards their leader. His eyes rested on the willowy young girl who stood mortified behind her mother. "Sir?!" was all he could muster. His question was punctuated by the sound of splashing, as his newly returned fellows had begun dousing the floor in kerosene.

The leader took one last look at the people in the room and then turned to his subordinate, "Do it."

Four gun shots echoed through the night air as the leader knelt down to pray in front of the house. He crossed himself and stood, watching sadly as the flames consuming the home lit up the area. He turned to his men, "We can't lose anymore good people to this thing."

"What now?" the youngest among them asked.

The leader turned to the Witchfinder holding the small floating arrow, "Canon Solus, have you the trail?"

"Yes, sir."

"Then we hunt."

WELCOME TO THE CLOCKWORK

The Magisterium taught us that we live within the Great Clockmaker's orderly creation, an intricate world which shows the glory of the Divine in its perfect symmetry. Science has taught us to understand this creation and harness its power through steel and steam, creating the majesty of civilization, a clockwork of our own. The alchemists taught us that the very fabric of creation could be broken down and reformed in ways limited only by our imaginations. Explorers have mapped the globe, and spiritualists have mapped the realms beyond it. Yet, however bright the light of human accomplishment can shine, the shadow it casts still hides what most refuse to see: this Clockwork, so diligently created by God and man, was constructed from chaos … and the chaos wants it back.

THE DOMINION OF GOD AND MAN

At the beginning of time, the Clockmaker came upon a formless void, a primordial nothingness we have since named the Pontus. From chaos, He crafted our beautiful world. Now we, the inhabitants of this magnificently designed Clockwork, must live to maintain the orderly intentions of our Maker. The world turns in accordance with the divine will, moving ever forward toward the culmination of its design.

Everything and everyone has their place, like a cog in a magnificent machine. The role of each individual, animal, institution, and even object must be fulfilled if the Clockwork is to follow its intended path. Thus, each man and woman has a role to play in the grand unfolding of history. Their very essences were designed and created for these roles. To act against them would mean folly for both the individual and the portions of the Clockwork with which they interact. Orderly society is designed to nurture people within their assigned roles, to help them accomplish their ends, and when necessary, to force them back into place. Thus, civilization is both a reflection of the divine intention and the backbone of the Clockwork.

The Clockwork world turns around its hub: the British Empire. In 1896, the Queen's lands house over three-hundred-million subjects, six-million of whom live in Greater London alone. The Crown's domain stretches from London to Lagos, from Delhi to Hong Kong, and across the Atlantic to Montréal. The Empire is so vast and global that the sun never sets on its soil. She controls the mightiest military in human history, the seat of global culture and civility, and the greatest educational and industrial institutions known to man.

Imperial civilization is a beacon in the darkness, giving light and direction to an otherwise lost and decaying world. The Empire illumines the dark corners of the Earth, gives order power over chaos, and ensures safety for humanity. The Clockwork is stabilized by creating, sustaining, and spreading orderly society to those who, by no fault of their own, are lost amid the very chaos that is consuming the world. Thus, the Clockwork can be saved by expanding the Imperial borders and indoctrinating others into the British way of life. It is the will of both the Maker and the Queen, and the bounden duty of all who fall under their authority to meet the call to order and stability mandated by the divine will. All people under the auspices of the Empire must work together, each performing their own individual role, to build and sustain the dominion of God and man.

The higher classes are the well-bred social elite, born with the gifts to govern the Empire. They are nobles and statesmen who oversee and maintain order. The middle classes form genteel society, educated and refined individuals who govern the use of land, promote education through schools and universities, and guide the advancement of science and discovery. They are professors, physicians, priests, scientists, lawmakers, and other highly educated individuals with the skills and means to keep the Clockwork turning. The lower classes work in trade, and perform the manual labor that provides the goods and services that sustain the temporal needs of humanity. These three tiers of society interact and interconnect to bolster the Clockwork and protect its people. If this delicate balance were to fail, the Maker only knows what would happen to the Earth.

THE PONTUS: A CRUMBLING FOUNDATION

Had each person always fulfilled the roles intended for them by the Clockmaker, perhaps the world would have already come to its perfection. However, they did not. From the beginning, people have turned against the will of the Clockmaker and against each other. Adam and Eve ate of the apple. Cain killed Abel. Humanity sinned and fell, and the angels themselves thereafter. Now, history is rife with the result of these transgressions: wars, slavery, injustice, suffering, and chaos. Each strain and crack in the Clockwork allows the primordial chaos to seep in, further eroding the stability of the world. Like a poison, the Pontus emanates both from the depths of the Earth and from the hearts of men, slowly reclaiming the Clockwork and unmaking creation itself. The Pontus is only now becoming a recognized force at work throughout history—perhaps too late to be stopped. Those who study its effects have found a dramatic increase in the scope and severity of Pontus events in recent generations. There is a rot in the foundation of the world, but too little concern as to when this corrosion will cause the whole of reality to collapse.

For all the stability the Empire brings, it can only seem to slow this process. It is simply not the panacea it claims to be. Its far-flung territories are restless, and chafe under British rule. It is becoming apparent that the wonders and achievements of science and technology call for people of brilliance, rather than those of particular birth, to lead. The veneer of safety and calm has lulled the politicians and the indolent rich into a drowsy complacency, leaving them unconcerned with the casual suffering endured by common citizens. Other global powers, jealous of the Empire's reach, increasingly contest with it for territory and control. The great bulwark against the Pontus is failing, and as the Empire falls, the Pontus rises.

Humanity looks on as the very fabric of reality frays and tears. Across the globe, the skies rain down frogs or blood. Fish swim through the morning mists. Such freakish occurrences remind humanity that chaos is taking hold in the world. Other times the manifestations of the Pontus are more devastating. In 1692, the Jamaican city of Port Royal was swallowed by the earth. An outbreak of walking dead attacked Vicksburg, Mississippi on June 17, 1863. These and even more horrifying events were at one time very rare, but now occur with increasing frequency.

Those in power argue desperately in support of their own visions of perfection, in the hope that they can achieve the culmination of the Clockwork before all descends into ruin. Yet, in truth, we do not even know what the Clockwork was meant to become. Although the Clockwork was built to fulfill the divine plan, the Maker is silent as to how His plan was meant to unfold. Humanity is left to discern both the will of the Maker and how to bring it to fruition before we all are destroyed. What will move us toward this goal is unknown and is a matter of endless debate. Those who see what is coming must find a way to save the Clockwork from a slow disintegration into oblivion.

Perhaps we are doomed. Perhaps civilization itself is a product of the fall from grace. After man was exiled from the Garden, what were we to do but build a Clockwork of our own? It seemed the only thing humanity could do to protect itself from the Pontus. Yet today, the same society that allows the righteous to acquire great wealth and power to nurture and protect also allows the wicked to exploit those under their authority. The same traditions that define orderly society, and inform each person of their role within it, restrict the free will instilled in man by his Maker. In some ways, the dominion of man is as much the problem as it is the solution.

Only one thing is certain: unless something is done, the Pontus will devour everything.

Corruption in the Blood

Sometimes social progress and compassion can also add to the frailty of our world. It is estimated that ninety-eight in one-hundred Imperial citizens are pureblooded mortals. The others are products of corrupted blood, beings who descend from a supernatural ancestor. Changelings carry the blood of the fey: strange,

WHAT IS A TABLETOP ROLEPLAYING GAME?

A tabletop roleplaying game is an interactive storytelling game that takes place around a table or similar in-person venue. The game is played primarily through the words and imaginations of the players. One player, the Narrator, provides the plot of the story and the remaining players create the characters that play it out. Much like the narrator of a book, the Narrator of the game will describe the scene, the minor characters and antagonists, and the events that take place around them. The players will playact their characters, describing their actions and speech. The game provides rules to determine if a character succeeds at what they try to do, whether that be defending themselves, making a convincing argument, or understanding the importance of a clue.

Together, everyone can be surprised by what happens, and watch their characters deepen and develop as the story unfolds. The adventure, beyond what anyone might have planned, comes to life at the table as you play.

If you are new to the tabletop roleplaying hobby, there are many places you can go to learn more about how these games are played. There are countless websites that discuss how to start roleplaying, but we recommend http://learntabletoprpgs.com. A quick internet search can uncover dozens of alternatives. Also, as millions of people love this hobby, chances are that you know someone who roleplays already. As tabletop roleplaying involves getting a small group of players together, talking to friends is a great place to start!

The Clockwork Roleplaying Game requires friends, writing utensils, paper, and one deck of Clockwork Cards to be shared among all players. The cards are used for skill resolution, determining action order, and to provide many other random elements within the game. An artless copy of these cards is available within the free Quick-Start Rules, downloadable from our website. Beautiful full-art versions of these cards are available from DriveThruRPG.com or your local game store. Character sheets can be copied from the back of the book and are also available for free download on our website: AClockworkWorld.com.

otherworldly creatures who have no natural place in the Clockwork. Nephilim carry the blood the Grigori, the fallen angels who long ago abandoned the service of the Clockmaker to live and pursue their own ends in the mortal world. Then there are the beastfolk, an unfortunate lot whose blood is not corrupted by an ancestor, but by science. These poor creatures are the product of horrible surgical experimentation that blend the bodies of human and animal.

More and more members of these three corrupted bloodlines enter Imperial borders each year, as the discrimination they face in civilized lands is a better fortune than the murderous violence that often awaits them elsewhere. Tolerance of their presence is a testament to the enlightened society of the Empire, but a mark against its purity. Some decry this tolerance as misplaced; an invitation to *Corruption* and decadence masquerading as acceptance. Others argue that a society that can accept such difference and find a place for those of unusual bloodlines is stronger and more stable than one that cannot. They say integration and unity are a surer bulwark against the Pontus than division and fear. Opinions on both sides are strong, and since none can truly claim to know the will of the Maker, the argument continues.

Denial

There is a vocal minority who say that the Clockwork has held strong since time began; how could anything unmake it? These dissenters believe that no action from a mere human being could ever affect something so vast, and they proclaim that the Clockwork will hold strong as it always has. To them, the Pontus is a fairy tale to explain odd but unrelated events. Meanwhile they undermine the stability of society for financial gain, selfish lusts, and personal amusement. Parliamentarians are quickly seduced by prospects of immediate wealth, power, and lesser battles that seem worthy in the here and now. Nobles are too quick to cast aside their obligations to protect others and provide the stable leadership that keeps the Pontus in check. Instead, they would rather spend their time and efforts on self-serving indulgences, disregarding the unwashed masses whom they were meant to serve and protect. These choices create discontent and suffering that become footholds for the Pontus to crawl into our world.

The Pontus rises at a ponderous rate. It first manifested at the fall of humankind, and has been with us ever since. The great glory of the Clockwork is turning to ruin so slowly it frequently goes unnoticed, and much of humanity views the Pontus as a threat too slow to merit concern. To them, Pontus events are unintelligible supernatural occurrences that foreshadow a possible catastrophe that might come long after they are dead. If the Clockwork is doomed to dissolution, it is the shortsighted who will have served as the vanguard of oblivion.

The World Turns
The Empire Falls
The Pontus Rises
Welcome to the Clockwork

ONE STEP FROM REALITY

In the pages of this book you will find a fictional world inspired by the historical Earth of 1896. The British Empire under Queen Victoria is at its apex. It is a time of etiquette and gentility; a time of war and colonialism; a time of science and discovery. Yet the Clockwork world makes slight deviations from its historical analog, taking things "one step from reality." Rather than creating a game world of fantasy birthed completely from the imaginations of its creators, the Clockwork is instead a product of extensive research used to craft a historically feasible steampunk world peppered with supernatural elements based on the beliefs of the time.

This world does not contain much technology that didn't exist in our own world in 1896. We needn't speculate what would happen if Charles Babbage completed his room-sized mechanical computer, because Swedish inventor Per Georg Scheutz created a table-sized working difference engine in 1843 and his model was improved upon by his contemporary Martin Wiberg in 1875. We simply take this rare computational marvel and ask what would the world be like if it was more ubiquitous. To create a believable steampunk world, we take this and many other technological advancements that were rare or unique and spread them throughout the Clockwork world and imagine the impact they would have on society.

Some technologies that seem fantastical are not as unrealistic as one might think.

In 1845, Joseph Faber exhibited his "Wonderful Talking Head," a stationary automaton capable of fully synthetic speech. In 1893, George Moore invented a steam powered automaton in the shape of man that could stand upright and run at speeds in excess of five miles per hour. Putting these extant technologies together with Wilberg's computer and some of the sensor and communication devices invented by Alexander Graham Bell allows for plausible clockwork automatons that can walk, talk, and perceive. Many of the more outlandish technological devices in the Clockwork are simply the combination of this sort of extant technology, or a slight fast-forward in its development.

Similarly, the supernatural elements of the Clockwork are not invented whole-cloth by the authors, but are based on myth, religion, and unexplained phenomenon reported in newspapers and in popular belief at the time. We draw heavily from Victorian fiction, folklore, Abrahamic holy texts, and popular apocryphal religious texts that were in circulation during the Victorian era. You will see biblical citations within the descriptions of the nephilim, magic, and the cosmology of the Clockwork. You will read snippets of ancient alchemical texts as translated by Sir Isaac Newton. You will see references to the Brothers Grimm and to other historical fiction and folklore when reading about the fey and the myths that surround them.

The Victorian era, for all its achievements, was also a high point for many forms of social injustice and reaction against it. As such, it saw the beginning of many movements for greater equality and freedom. For players that want to explore social themes, the Clockwork world portrays these movements as more vocal and more widespread than in actual history. The advances in technology—especially in communication—and differences in metaphysical belief about the workings of the world have likewise made social debate more active.

All efforts have been made to stretch circumstance, history, and myth minimally to create a believable fantastic world. We hope this allows players to immerse themselves into the Clockwork and that it provides a suitable stage for any stories they wish to tell. What we present in this book is a broad view of the Clockwork world, and we encourage players to draw on their own knowledge and enthusiasm for the Victorian era to explore it, adapt it, and make it their own.

STORIES IN THE CLOCKWORK

CONFLICT: ORDER VERSUS CHAOS

In the beginning, the Clockmaker gave form to the formless by crafting the Pontus into the Clockwork. Akin to this magnificent work of the Clockmaker is the work of the Empire. The dominion of man actualizes the dominion of the Maker, bringing it back to what it was meant to be before the sin and disorder of humanity fell short of the divine plan. Order must be maintained, for if the dominion of man falls, so too will the dominion of God.

Stories within the Clockwork often embrace this conflict by introducing an agent of chaos that must be confronted and overcome. This can be anything from a socially destructive debutante ruining the lives of others to alleviate her boredom, to a secret cabal playing with dangerous powers in a corrupt magical rite. At its most simple, the conflict of order against chaos pits the players against such an agent. The heroes of the story fight against the agent of chaos so that order might be restored and the Clockwork might be strengthened.

It is important to realize that order and chaos are not the same thing as good and evil. There are many societal structures within the Clockwork that rely on sexism, racism, the wildly unfair distribution of wealth, and other vile inequalities. The unjust nature of these structures does not make them less orderly. Just as a flawed foundation may still hold up a wall, such institutions still offer stability. Will players choose to uphold the status quo to bolster the stability of the Clockwork, or will they do what they think is right and hope that any disruption caused by the change they bring to the world will be justified by the good they hope to achieve? Can civilization survive a cultural revolution, or would the justice that such innovations bring come at the cost of the world itself?

MYSTERY: PULLING BACK THE VEIL

Much of what is wrong with the Clockwork lies hidden beneath a veil of normalcy. People are generally aware that the Pontus is tearing apart the world, but are more than happy to overlook any strange phenomena that may occur at the periphery of their lives. It is only when the Pontus brings daily life crashing down around them in a frightening or lasting way that they are forced to face the threat it poses to their reality. It could be said that many citizens of the Empire treat the Pontus the way some people in our modern world treat climate change: until your own island nation needs to relocate due to being swallowed up by the ocean, it's seen as a threat too slow or nebulous to be of concern.

Some citizens of the Empire see beyond this short sightedness, and others are forced to confront the Pontus against their will. These men and women seek out the cosmic truths that lie beneath the veiled world that others are happy to inhabit. Some become alchemists or magi. Others become investigators of the unknown, scientists, inventors, or explorers. By means of choice or circumstance, these individuals delve into the shadows others fear and discover truths others barely dream about.

Stories that focus on pulling back the veil can do so in several ways. Players may cooperate with characters in organizations such as the Witchfinders, Inquisition, or police. Adventures involving these individuals revolve around them receiving orders or missions that they must undertake, even if they don't fully understand the nature of their work. Any group of individuals could be subject to a Pontus event that brings them together and causes the curious among them to investigate why it occurred. Even a story that doesn't focus on the supernatural can still have one or more installments where mystical phenomena refuse to be ignored. No matter the tale being told, there is always room for mystery and the potential for new understanding of the world.

GOTHIC

Stories that take place in the Clockwork are meant to capture the feel of Gothic literature. The origin of this genre is attributed to Horace Walpole with his 1764 novel *The Castle of Otranto*. Walpole's work was a mixture of thematic courtship, melodrama, human relationships, and personal horror. As the genre grew it came to focus on mysterious supernatural phenomena, the plight of the oppressed, unfair social systems, massive and anachronistic architecture, love, and terror. Gothic fiction maintained immense popularity throughout the eighteenth and nineteenth centuries and included such renowned authors as Mary Shelley, Bram Stoker, and Edgar Allen Poe.

Stories in the Clockwork can touch on any Gothic elements that the players wish to explore. Some groups will embrace melodrama and the epic and sometimes tragic romance of Gothic literature as it plays out in Victorian culture. Other groups may have little interest in love, and will instead focus on supernatural mystery and gloomy antagonists. Whatever your group decides, the Narrator should set the mood of a Gothic world: highlight the injustice of corrupt institutions, the fragility of innocence, the extraordinary reality that lies just beneath the surface of the mundane, and the extreme joy, love, and terror that these things can produce. These are the hallmarks of Gothic literature, and no matter what your story involves, they can provide for memorable games.

STEAMPUNK

At its most basic, steampunk has two elements: steam and punk. *Steam* speaks to a Victorian world of speculative fiction where advanced technology appears or historical technologies are put to new and more extreme uses. *Punk* brings a focus on unjust social systems and those people who fight against them or step outside their rules. This is similar to all of the *punk* genres, including cyberpunk and dieselpunk, which highlight anachronistic technology and the human condition in their respective eras. Where cyberpunk focuses on supercomputers used by powerful and unjust megacorporations, and dieselpunk focuses on over-engineered mechanical marvels juxtaposed with noir crime and poverty, steampunk focuses on the wonders and opportunities of technology like steam engines, electricity, and magnetism and how technology offers change in a world of rigid class structures that keep the highborn wealthy and the lowborn disenfranchised. The tension between the disruptive potential of new technologies and the aesthetics and culture of high society lies at the heart of the genre.

Capturing the feel of steampunk involves more than just including clockwork automatons and noblemen in your story. There is an aesthetic to the steampunk genre that can be difficult to put into words. Visually, it involves stylized Victorian elements including fine clothing, top hats, and sword canes. Socially, it both embraces and criticizes aristocratic hierarchy. Viscerally, it involves a certain degree of hope. Unlike the cyberpunk genre that warns of the dangers of advanced technology, steampunk embraces a retrospective hope that advanced technology could have made the world a better, more exciting place. New inventions and new science could have brought about an age of achievement that maintained and spread the best ideals of high society. Steampunk invites us to imagine a world that could have been and revel in it, including high adventure, fantastic technology, and, yes, a good pair of goggles now and then.

YOUR STORY

These components will balance differently in every group of players, offering a complex setting for three dimensional stories with three dimensional characters. Order and chaos battle alongside justice and oppression. A world of hope and progress is contrasted against a Gothic mood of catharsis and terror. The Clockwork is merely your stage. You decide what kind of story to tell.

USING THIS BOOK

All the information players and Narrators will need to know to play *Clockwork: Dominion* is contained within this core rulebook. This first chapter should be enough to allow players to hit the ground running with a very basic understanding of the setting. *Chapter 2: Clockwork Society* expands on the intricacies of Victorian culture and daily life. *Chapter 3: Cosmology* informs players of the reality beyond everyday life and all the wonderful and terrible things that reside in the Clockwork universe. *Chapter 4: Rules & Systems* contains the core rules of the Clockwork Roleplaying Game and all players will want to familiarize themselves with these before game play. *Chapter 5: Character Creation* provides players with the tools to design the extraordinary characters they will portray within the stories of the game.

Chapter 6: Accoutrements & Technology explores the products and lifestyles available to characters, and includes a flexible item creation system that allows characters to create fantastical steampunk inventions of all types. *Chapter 7: Transcendent Powers* explores those abilities that reach beyond the mundane into the supernatural. The final two chapters—*Chapter 8: Narrating the Story* and *Chapter 9: Allies & Antagonists*—contain information and guidance for Narrators to plan adventures, populate them with interesting friends and foes for the player characters, and tips on how to run an exciting game.

Now you have everything you need to begin. Welcome to the Clockwork.

In the soft gaslight of a Mayfair Ballroom, the shadows of dancing couples flitted over a grey-eyed governess who had once been beautiful. Over her silk slip she wore a gown of lace because Charlotte has insisted she *must* look especially pretty for the dancing. The sweet foolish girl. Even at eighteen, Charlotte still had a way of willfully overlooking the social shortcomings of those she liked. Just last Christmas she had inquired why Tom, the recently-widowed coachman, could not join them for the family celebration.

It had been this same simple-hearted generosity that provoked Charlotte to demand that Eanid have a silver bracelet for her wrist and a blue feather for her hair, just as Charlotte did. His Lordship indulged this request because, like all governesses, Eanid came from a good family and therefore was not beneath such ornaments even if they were wasted on her, which they were. Nobody was looking at Eanid, but it seemed that *everyone* was watching Charlotte.

Charlotte Blackwood waltzed with paradoxical elegance; she moved with the mechanical precision of a clockwork toy, turning and bobbing in perfect time, and yet there was a warmth to her gestures that was unmistakably human. Her smooth cheeks had the red flush of life, and her smile promised each man who received it that Charlotte Blackwood thought him every bit as handsome and charming as he wished himself to be. The blond-haired officer dancing with Charlotte looked to Eanid as if he were more than half in love already.

"In my day, the waltz was considered too lewd for well-brought up young ladies," said a papery voice beside Eanid. "A girl needed special permission to be held so close to a man, especially one wearing regimentals. But times change, I suppose."

Eanid turned to find the aging Baroness Hood, whose keen-eyed gaze put the governess in mind of the raptors her father had kept when she was a child in Wales.

"Your Ladyship," Eanid said with a curtsey.

"Young Charlotte is looking well."

"Your Ladyship is kind to say so."

Lady Hood watched Charlotte and the young officer for two more turns before she said, "Captain Hill is a lovely boy, but poor as a church mouse I'm afraid. His father and my husband went to Harrow together, but… times change. Still, he is a lovely dancer. It puts one in mind of one's own first Season *out*."

Eanid too had been thinking of her first Season. And her second. And her third, and the others that came and went until she was too old to marry despite her respectable dowry and good family name. She lifted a hand involuntarily towards the tips of her pointed ears. If Lady Hood remembered Eanid's own time on the marriage market, she was too polite to remind her of it.

"You've done well by the Blackwoods, Eanid. Perhaps if I'd had someone like you to guide her, my Celia wouldn't be married to that ill-bred oaf of a banker." The governess did not know how to respond, but it didn't matter. Baroness Hood had always been adept at keeping up both sides of a conversation.

"Some advice: if you want to do young Charlotte a kindness, see if you can prompt that pasty looking boy by the punch bowl to ask you for an introduction." Eanid followed the Baroness's gaze to a thin framed young man standing so close to the wall that he almost looked like a footman at attention.

"Percy Seymour? I was under the impression that his was a cadet branch of the family." A Seymour would make Charlotte a respectable match, but such a girl as she could reasonably hope for someone titled.

"His great uncle is the Duke of Somerset, and the Duke's son is tragically ill. My physician assures me the poor boy won't live out the year."

"I'm not sure I take your Ladyship's meaning," Eanid lied.

"It means, Eanid, that willowy little Percy Seymour is the most eligible bachelor in the room, but even *he* doesn't know it yet. Best lay a claim before—Oh my—look at *this*…"

A new family had just entered the ballroom, and their arrival sent a shockwave through the gathered socialites. Whispers of "Scotland" and "Lord Hamilton" echoed on every side of Eanid. It was rare for a Scottish family to come south for the English Season, as they had their own Society that they rarely left unless driven from it by scandal or to find a spouse for an unmarriageable child.

In the entryway stood a gentleman and lady in their middle years. The lady wore a fine gown of green tarlatan, her hair done up in the English fashion. Her husband had left the kilt and sporran of his native land behind and wore instead a newly cut tailcoat and dark waistcoat indistinguishable from those of the English gentlemen around him. No amount of pandering to Southern styles, however, could obscure what stood between them. Their daughter had hair the colour of spun silver and ears so sharp and long they were like nothing human; her eyes were so green that they blazed like cut-glass from across the ballroom. She was as beautiful as she was alien.

"Well in all my years…" said the Baroness, "I can't say I've ever seen one quite so touched as that."

"Who is she?" Eanid asked.

"Mary Hamilton, I think—her father is the Earl of Orkney, but I'm afraid the girl won't have any more luck in England than she did in Scotland, poor thing." Lady Hood reddened a little when she looked back at Eanid, suddenly realizing the delicacy of the situation.

"If you will excuse me, my dear." Eanid curtsied again as Lady Hood glided towards a clutch of gossiping dowagers near the tipsy cake.

For a moment, Eanid felt like she was falling. She experienced it all again as though for the first time: how her father's countless invitations were rejected, how her mother's face tightened at the evasive courtesies of women who once called themselves her friends, how the word that was never spoken within her hearing hung over her nevertheless, like the industrial smog that blighted this ancient city: *unsuitable*. She was too unsuitable for a titled husband, too high born for her father to allow any other marriage. And so she became a governess.

It took every ounce of will Eanid possessed to push these thoughts away, to suffer her passions to be ruled by reason, that she might do her duty. She found the Seymour boy, not far from where he had been, feigning interest in a vast painting of Egdon Heath, too shy to seek an introduction to any of the eligible young ladies on the dance floor.

"Pardon me, Mr. Seymour? I'm Eanid Flint. We met two years ago when your family visited Blanely Castle on your way to Southampton."

"Oh…em…yes, how nice to see you again Ms. Flint."

"I was wondering if I might have the pleasure of providing you with an introduction to a certain young lady."

He blushed so red that Eanid could not help feeling a little sorry for him, despite his impending good fortune. *He has kind eyes; he will be good to her.*

"Oh, I, I, well um, yes…are you still governess to Lord Rutherford's daughter?"

"I am, but the young lady I have in mind is Lady Mary of Orkney." He was surprised to be sure, but there was a boyish eagerness that was unmistakable.

"Are you…acquainted with Lady Mary?"

Eanid had never met the Lady Mary, never been to Scotland, and as far as she knew the Flints and the Hamiltons shared no earthly blood, so she told him the truth.

"She is my cousin, and I know her as well as I know myself."

CLOCKWORK SOCIETY

The year is 1896, and the world is a vast network of interconnected metropolises; its center, London. Here, clock towers and church steeples stab upwards into the leaden sky, where airships hasten through the industrial fog on tight schedules. Were it not for the thick haze, the pilots might look down on the black network of railways spreading from London to the surrounding towns, each city center a cog in the machine of progress, each back roadway a fuel line feeding the dark majesty that is the engine of civilization herself.

In the cobblestone byways below, gentlemen in tall hats help ladies into elegant carriages that will soon make their way to West End homes, where even now the ballroom floors are being swept for the evening's reveries. In a few short hours, young ladies will bob, curtsy, and smile coyly at proud young men whose fathers are rumored to have ten thousand a year. Tables are being set with silver and crystal, the violins tuned to lead lines of dancers in graceful geometric patterns.

A few miles away, in the industrial slums of St. Giles, a cacophony of factory bells releases hordes of soot-stained laborers into the stinking streets. Men and women who work the cranks and gears of industrial machinery wend their way to tenement apartments, where they spoon gruel into the mouths of hungry children whose tongues have never tasted meat.

Nevertheless, these children are not without hope of a better life. Perhaps some will one day leave the factory walls behind and join the regimental lines of her Majesty's armed forces, bringing order and enlightenment to still uncivilized corners of the globe. Through them, chaos and barbarism will be driven back by the rhythmic thunder of musket and cannon.

The dark streets outside the tenement walls writhe with the nocturnal activities of those who live beyond the governed order of society. Gangs of orphans rifle through the pockets of drunken sleepers, while syphilitic prostitutes twitch and jabber to themselves like broken automatons in the darkness. Cutpurses, killers, and resurrection-men haunt the narrow alleys where the halos of gas lights illumine the industrial fumes that we call "London Fog," an acrid haze that obscures the worst of what walks the city streets.

Its putrid murk hides things that wriggle through the rent fabric of reason and into the dark foundations beneath our cities. These shadows remind us that as the world turns, the Pontus rises. Order and hierarchy, the Empire, are all that stand between civilization and that black tide of madness and unmaking.

THE HIERARCHY OF CLOCKWORK SOCIETY

One need look no further than the machinery of nature to see that ours is a world of order and hierarchy. The motion of the planets, the rhythm of the tides, and the cycle of the seasons all attest to the order that governs the Clockmaker's creation. At the pinnacle of the earthly hierarchy is man, who throughout the ages has worked tirelessly to bring order and civilization to the part of the Clockwork that is his to govern.

There is no doubt that of all the accomplishments which provide the scaffolding to man's illustrious history, the greatest of these is the creation of our Empire. Our universities have produced the greatest scientists, our aristocracy has bred the greatest political and military minds, and our shires and cities have brought forth poets, writers and musicians whose words and songs are the light of civilization. Ours is the continuation of the greatest human activity: the long proud march from barbarism to enlightenment. It is in recognition of this fact that when we speak of the Clockwork, we refer not only to the majesty of our Maker's design, but to the grandeur of the British Empire itself.

The foundation of Imperial Britain is our class system, which is as hierarchical and nuanced as the Clockmaker's own masterwork. At the top of this hierarchy is the royal family. Immediately beneath these revered personages are the two hundred or so noble families whose eldest sons will inherit titles such as Duke, Earl, or Baron. They control vast political and financial power, and provide the social models that the middle classes seek to emulate. These middle classes are composed of country gentlemen and respectable professionals who in turn inspire a working class of laborers who drive the economy. At the very bottom of the hierarchy are those indigent persons who rely either on charity and the workhouses, or theft and scavenging to survive.

THE ARISTOCRACY

"If there is anything good about nobility it is that it enforces the necessity of avoiding degeneracy."
—Boethius

Royalty (Class 5)

Our sovereign, Queen Victoria, and her immediate family are the pinnacle of our society; merely to be in the presence of their majesty is an honor that can be overwhelming for all but the highest aristocracy. The Queen and her family embody the raw essence of our Empire's noblest qualities. As such, the royals usually invite only the most well-bred and accomplished of their subjects to attend them at court.

Nobility (Class 4)

The most revered class of people, apart from the royal family, are the hereditary peers who bear the titles of Duke, Marquess, Earl, Viscount, or Baron. They are guaranteed seats in The House of Lords, which together with the House of Commons and the Monarch constitutes the supreme legislative body of the British Empire. Hereditary peers inherit not only titles, but also impressive fortunes and vast estates appropriate to their roles as civic and social leaders. It is typical for each of these noble families to own tens of thousands of acres and to be attended by dozens of servants.

To the more plebeian subjects of Her Majesty, the grandeur of these aristocrats can be so dazzling that distinguishing between them is like trying to differentiate the magnitude of equally blinding stars. Amongst their own kind, however, nobles are keenly aware of the differences in rank between a duke and a baron, and families that have been part of the nobility since William the Conqueror are held in much higher esteem than those recently elevated to the nobility. Those wishing to mix with aristocratic personages should know that a duke outranks a marquess, a marquess outranks an earl, an earl outranks a viscount, and a viscount outranks a baron. In the case of two equally ranked aristocrats, precedence is determined by which has the older patent of nobility.

While many members of the upper classes are quite rich, some are not, and a moderately wealthy earl is a far greater personage than an industrialist who may have ten times the earl's fortune.

As with all great societies, we recognize that an educated man or woman of good breeding and accomplishment is made no less noble by relative poverty, nor is a rat ennobled by the acquisition of riches. That said, as Mr. Thackeray reminds us in *Vanity Fair*, "A Countess living at an inn is a ruined woman."

THE MIDDLE CLASSES

Whenever Richard Corey Went to Town
We people on the pavement looked at him:
He was a Gentleman from sole to crown,
Clean favored and imperially slim.

And he was always quietly arrayed,
And he was always human when he talked;
But still he fluttered pulses when he said,
"Good-morning," and he glittered when he walked.
—Edwin Arlington Robinson

Gentry (Class 3)

Just as there are gradations of rank within the upper classes, so too with the middle classes. The most prestigious members of the middle classes are those families who have held the same significant parcel of land for generations. Like their upper class counterparts, these families draw income from tenants on their estates. But while upper class landowners may own fifty thousand acres of land including a dozens villages, these upper middle class landowners are more likely to have between one and three thousand acres, and a single village. The income from their tenants is generally enough to provide for the maintenance of a small manor house and enough servants to spare members of the immediate family the indignity of having to do any sort of manual labor. These landed families are the gentry and compose the most respectable tier of middle class society.

Although generally not titled, a small handful of these families may have a patriarch who enjoys the hereditary title of baronet or has been awarded a knighthood. Baronets are not lords and do not serve in Parliament, but they are addressed with the style "Sir," as knights are. Because baronetcies are hereditary and knighthoods are not, baronets are slightly more prestigious than knights, who are the only other titled members of the middle class. Any landowning patriarch of the gentry may adopt the courtesy title "squire", which although informal does confer an elevated level of respectability.

Another important designation among the middle class is the term "gentleman," which implies a man has the appropriate education, social graces, good character, and financial resources. Legally speaking, a gentleman is an individual who is wealthy enough to avoid any sort of trade or professional occupation while enjoying a middle-class lifestyle. In practice, any university educated man with genteel manners and a respectable occupation might call himself a gentleman without raising too many eyebrows. Nevertheless, doctors and lawyers who refer to themselves as gentlemen, but who own no land and require the income from their professions to make ends meet, may occasionally elicit sardonic smiles from wealthier members of the upper middle class.

Educated Professionals and Business Owners (Class 2)

The lower middle class is composed of individuals who must work in a profession to supplement whatever income they may have from investments or entitlements. The most respectable are barristers, clergyman, military officers, and academics. Physicians are less respected because they accept payment directly from clients, akin to a tradesman. At the very bottom one finds solicitors, clerks, and school teachers who are middle class only by virtue of their education, social graces, and the fact that they do not perform manual labor. Most middle class families enjoy comfortable accommodations and the attention of at least one servant, often a maid who cooks and cleans for the family. Having at least one domestic servant is usually a minimum requirement for middle class status.

Many of these lower middle class professionals eagerly await opportunities to brush shoulders with the gentry and actively seek invitations to balls, dinner parties, and country houses; the majority, however, exist in a community of their own, largely separate from the 10,000 or so individuals who make up what is commonly referred to as Society. Nevertheless, the education, professional activities, and level of comfort enjoyed by these smartly dressed Britons earns them the respect and deference of the working classes, who look up to them as gentleman even though members of the landed gentry might not always share that opinion.

THE LOWER CLASSES

'You call these men a mob…Are you aware of your obligations to a mob? It is the mob that labour in your fields and serve in your houses, that man your navy and recruit your army, that have enabled you to defy the world, and can also defy you when neglected and calamity have driven them to despair…do not forget that a mob too often speaks with the sentiments of the people…" —Lord Byron

The lower classes include both the working class and the poor. The working classes are mostly composed of manual laborers and individuals who are "in trade," a term that refers to merchants and craftspeople. Like in higher echelons of society, the gradations of rank within the working class are considerable. In general, skilled tradesmen like metalsmiths, carriage-makers, and tailors occupy a higher place than semi-skilled laborers like chandlers (shop-keepers), costermongers (street vendors), and carriage drivers (despite the fact carriage drivers are better paid than most skilled craftsmen). These semi-skilled laborers and small shop owners outrank the factory workers, sanitation workers, and agricultural laborers whose work is considered "unskilled."

Working class Britons generally have enough to eat and can even afford a few luxuries. Although the nature of their work, as well as their manners and speech patterns, prevent them entering the middle classes, they are proud subjects of Her Majesty who do their part for the Empire.

The poor occupy a position firmly beneath that of the working class. These individuals are either unemployed, or earn so little from their factory or unskilled jobs that they cannot hope to meet their own basic needs without supplementation by theft or the charity of others. Many live in squalor, and most have a grievously short life expectancy.

Laborers (Class 1)

Among the most prestigious working class jobs are those of high ranking domestic servants like butlers, valets, and ladies' maids whose daily contact with the upper classes enobles their own manners and bearing. It is important to note that this only applies to those serving great houses. A Viscount's personal valet is a person deserving of respect, while a housemaid in the service of a typical middle class family ranks roughly in the middle of the working class. Although high-ranking servants often command respect, they are not necessarily envied by other members of the working class who are able to earn considerably more money and enjoy a much easier work schedule as skilled artisans.

In the city, the highest ranks of the working class are merchants and industrial overseers, who may be in charge of hundreds of workers themselves. Although their lack of formal education and manners, as well as their coarse speech might prevent them from mingling as equals with the middle classes, those who rise high enough can amass considerable fortunes that allow them to live an economically middle class lifestyle and provide their children with the education necessary to climb into the ranks of middle class professionals.

In the countryside, the highest ranking members of the working class are the yeoman farmers with close to a thousand acres, but no tenants and too few laborers to avoid working hard themselves. Although technically part of the working class because they make their living doing manual labor, the wealthiest among them might enjoy many of the trappings of middle class country life: a drawing room with a piano forte, handsome clothes, and inclusion in the local fox hunt. If they are able to provide their children with middle class educations and marriages, they can sometimes climb into the lower levels of the gentry.

For the majority of working class individuals, however, slipping down into the poverty is more likely than rising into the middle classes. In the city, shopkeepers and tradesmen must manage their money carefully to ensure that their families can afford their small tenements, plenty of food, and occasional small luxuries like fine cloth to sew a dress, or a faux oriental tea pot.

In the countryside, the working class is mostly composed of tradespeople and tenant farmers who occupy thatched or slate-roof cottages that typically have between two and four rooms. Many of these cottages have gardens, or perhaps a few acres where cottagers can grow their own food and keep a few animals. In some ways their lives are easier than those of their counterparts in the city who have to contend with urban crime and pollution. In other ways, they are more limited. Their social circles consist only of people from a few nearby villages, which is especially limiting when it comes to marriage. Those in the country also live under the authority of the landed gentry who serve both as landlords and justices of the peace.

The Poor (Class 0)

When my mother died I was very young,
And my father sold me while yet my tongue
Could scarcely cry " 'weep! 'weep! 'weep! 'weep!' "
So your chimneys I sweep & in soot I sleep. —William Blake

These are the lowest ranking members of the segment of society that the late Lord Lytton dubbed "the great unwashed." Their ragged ranks are composed of unskilled factory workers, itinerant laborers, rat-catchers, dustmen, crossing sweepers, mudlarks (children who wade barefoot through the putrid muck of the waste-ridden Thames to scavenge objects of trivial value), as well as crawlers—the elderly or infirm members of the working class who have no family able or willing to care for them. Those born into this class often do not live past their early twenties. Despite their high mortality rate, these unfortunates constitute approximately a quarter of the population of Britain.

Those who cannot find jobs in the factories might apply to work houses, which are not unlike prisons. Men, women, and children are separated from one another and given striped uniforms. They labor ten hours a day breaking stones, crushing bones to make fertilizer, or removing oakum from tarred ropes. As horrid as this is, these circumstances are still better than those of many who live in the disease-ridden alleyways of industrial London.

In the slums of St. Giles, families huddle ten to a room in basement tenements, ragged and filthy, breathing coal smoke and going hungry more often than not; and yet these unfortunates are still better off than those who live in literal holes in the ground hollowed out next to the basement foundations of the buildings on Dudley street. When the inhabitants of these dark pits climb out to gulp the comparatively clean air of the London slums, they blink like miners at even the muted light filtering through the industrial smog. These men and women are so fouled with filth and misery that it is is difficult to determine whether they are in their twenties or their fifties. Although their wretchedness makes them hard to look on, it is important to treat these poor fellows with compassion, they too have a place in the Clockmaker's design.

The rural poor tend to be itinerant farm-hands, drifting from place to place seeking wages or charity from those who already have little to spare. Others may be widows or elderly persons who are no longer able to perform the working class jobs that once sustained them, and who have been left by circumstance without family or friends who are willing to provide their support.

CRIMINALS AND ROOKERIES

For those who are brave, foolish, or desperate enough, there are a variety of ways to make a living outside of the law. The industrial slums, colloquially called "rookeries," are home to numerous territorial gangs. Most engage in a variety of criminal activities including pick-pocketing, burglary, and prostitution.

GANGS

Gang members, both male and female, are called "scuttlers" or "hooligans", and often wear distinctive outfits that include colorful scarves and elaborate belt buckles that can be used as weapons in a scuttle (gang fight). These fights are common occurrences, sometimes as the result of a grievance and sometimes as a form of entertainment. Deaths are uncommon, but permanent disfigurement and maiming happen with distressing regularity.

St. Giles is London's most notorious rookery, and its gangs include "The Centre Point Boys," "The Russell Street Gougers," and "The Darlings." Gang-names frequently incorporate the name of the street that anchors their territory. There are even gangs of child thieves, although these are typically run by an adult called a "kidsman."

HIGHWAYMEN

There are also independent operators. The most notable of these are highwaymen; robbers who waylay the wealthy at gun point or sword point to relieve them of their valuables. Because they tend to rob only the rich, some of these highwaymen become local celebrities among the lower orders, although the majority of these glorified individuals end on the gallows.

RESURRECTION MEN

Resurrection men are body snatchers. Before the Anatomy Act of 1832 made it easier for medical schools to obtain cadavers, either donated or unclaimed from the workhouses to use for anatomical teaching, these bold individuals would steal corpses from graves (or create fresh ones) to sell to doctors. The recent return of this criminal profession suggests there is once again a market for human corpses, but it remains unclear who is buying these grisly commodities.

FLASH HOUSES

In cities, criminal elements often congregate in pubs called "flash houses." A flash house is an important resource for criminals looking to trade information, learn new skills, or hire help. Flash houses have their own dialects and social customs almost as nuanced and complex as the upper echelons of society. A member of the gentry unfortunate enough to find herself in one of these establishments would be as out of place as a rookery hooligan would be at a Kensington ball.

Some of these unfortunate individuals manage to escape their poverty. A few do this by joining the army, even fewer by utilizing the services of benefactors as springboards to better jobs. Others try to better their circumstance by becoming involved in criminal activities like prostitution, theft, and body-snatching.

OUTCASTS (CLASS O)

Some of the poorest inhabitants of the British Isles have foolishly elected to reject Clockwork society entirely. In the country, transient peoples including clans of gipsies and tinkers fall into this category, while in London there are also known to be "toshers," colonies of sewer people that inhabit the vast network of sewage, flood, and ancient Roman tunnels that compose the Undercity. Most who live this life are born into it, although there are rumors that increasing numbers of beastfolk can be found amongst those who dwell in the margins of society.

Although poets often romanticize the lives of gipsies and tinkers who wander the British countryside in caravans of colourful wagons, singing, dancing, stealing, and swindling to support themselves, the reality of this existence is anything but romantic. They live out of doors in all seasons, sometimes struggle to find enough food, and are not welcome anywhere. At best these people are tolerated by lords and farmers who might allow gipsies to camp for a few weeks on their land in exchange for cheap labor, but soon it is time to move again.

Although little is known about the sewer people, one can only assume their existence is ghastly. Most live near the surface and survive by selling or trading junk they pull from sewer drains, or bits of copper they strip from the hulls of ships moored in the Thames. Even the rookery gangs look down on the toshers as *almost* beneath contempt. Rumors of elaborate societies that live 24 hours a day in the deep darkness of the Undercity remain unsubstantiated, but are common nonetheless.

THE WORLD TURNS

England is the paradise of women, the hell of horses, and the purgatory of servants.
—Bonaventure Des Periers

THE SEASON

For the fifteen-hundred or so aristocratic and genteel families that constitute London Society, life revolves around an annual migration from the country to the city and back again. A few weeks after Christmas, aristocratic families leave their vast country estates for their elegant homes in the West End of London, so that the peers among them will be ready to take up their legislative responsibilities in Parliament in the spring. Other illustrious but untitled families and the richer families among the gentry also return to the city at this time so that they can mix with the aristocracy at the breakfasts, clubs, balls, and dinner parties that characterize daily life during the Season. This frivolity extends until late June, when most families return to the country to enjoy mounted fox hunting, which lasts until winter.

In addition to providing exciting opportunities to socialize with a wide variety of other people of quality, the Season is essential to the continuance of society in the most literal sense: it is at these events that young women of marriageable age find husbands and young men with high titles but dwindling fortunes find wealthy brides from among the newly rich members of the upper middle class.

DAILY LIFE IN THE CITY

For members of the most privileged classes, a typical day in London begins with an early morning ride in Hyde Park. Although both men and women enjoy this activity, the men stay on a path called Rotten Row, while the women utilize The Ladies' Mile.

After this mounted constitutional, it's back home for breakfast, after which women make calls and go shopping while men go to

the clubs. Making a call involves a lady or small group travelling in her carriage to visit other women at their homes, with the planned stay about 30 minutes. The guest's calling card is offered to the lady of the house, who may then accept and invite in her guest for tea and light edibles such as biscuits or cucumber sandwiches. Conversations tend to revolve around the machinations of society, as well as art, culture, and travel.

If the lady in question is not at home, the guest will leave her calling card behind, which not only includes her name and title on beautifully decorated heavy paper, but possibly her London address. Occasionally short messages indicating regret are written on the backs of these, although it is understood that just because a servant explains that the lady of the house is "not at home," this does not necessarily mean she is not on the premises, only that she is not receiving visitors at this time (or that she is unwilling to receive this particular visitor). If the visitor is a new acquaintance or is beneath the social status of the person on whom she is paying a call, it is expected that a visit would not immediately take place, and instead the visitor's card would be left in the hopes of receiving a card in return, which then indicates a future visit would be acceptable. Aristocratic visitors who are forced by circumstance to call on a person significantly lower in status may refrain from leaving a card for fear that it will be ostentatiously displayed on top of the other cards collected on a silver salver or china bowl in the entryway for any other visitor to see, implying a more significant connection to that great personage than actually exists.

While women make calls, the men of Society spend their time in social clubs. Although there are, as of 1896, nearly two hundred such institutions in London, some applicants may wait more than fifteen years to be admitted to the most exclusive clubs. Membership confers the privilege of socializing and dining at the club itself, which is typically a large and elegantly furnished building generally on St. James Street or Pall Mall. Many of these clubs cater to a gentleman's particular interests. The Athenaeum attracts men of art, science and literature; The Carlton, political conservatives; The United Service Club is for senior level military officers, and so on. Despite these differences, conversations generally revolve around the same topics: politics, finance, culture, and Society gossip.

In the early evening, men and women return home to prepare for dinner, usually around 6:30pm. After dinner, they go to the opera, the theatre, or may attend a private ball. The latter can extend late into the evenings or early hours of the morning, affording relatively few hours of sleep to those who stay until the end, should they plan to be up early for tomorrow's ride in Hyde Park.

Attending Balls

Except among the very poor, balls are the most popular social events in Britain. In addition to London's exclusive invitational balls that are the essential machinery of the Season, there are country balls, servants balls, military balls, fire engine company balls, and so on. In most cases, the attendees of a particular ball are of the same social class, but so long as one is at least working class [*Class* 1] there are balls available to attend.

Balls are formal occasions that require carefully selected attire. Women dress to reflect their social standing, marital status, age, and whether they are in mourning. Young unmarried ladies wear gowns of tarlatan, gauze, lace, or other light fabrics over a silk slip which provide an air of delicacy and comfort while dancing. The hair is worn up, often with flowers or a single feather. Too much jewelry is considered ostentatious, especially for the young. In colder weather, ladies are likely to wear an opera cloak over their gowns for travel.

For men, dressing is a simpler matter. A dark tailcoat, fitted pants of the same color, and a low cut vest called a "waistcoat" comprise the essential elements of the outfit. A black or white cravat, tie or stock, is also worn (this garment should be textured; only vulgar people wear stocks made of silk). Patent leather boots and white kidskin gloves are also traditional. Military men usually wear their dress regimentals. Among working class people and in the country, it is not uncommon for men to simply wear their best clothes, rather than rich garments they cannot afford.

When the privileged attend exclusive balls, it is fashionable to arrive by carriage about an hour late. At any ball, however, those who arrive on time will wait to be conducted into the ballroom by the floormaster, usually the organizer of the affair. The floormaster signals to the orchestra to begin playing and then gentlemen accompany the ladies in the party to their seats first and then acquire programs for each of them; these programs are dance cards that enable ladies to navigate the evening without accidentally promising the same dance to more than one gentleman.

A gentleman begins by dancing with each of the ladies in his party, after which he is free to ask other women, "May I have the pleasure of a dance?" In order to make such a request of a young lady he has never met, a man will require an introduction by someone already acquainted with her. If accepted, he will add his name to her card, bow, and withdraw. It is a considerable insult for a lady to refuse a dance if she is on the floor and does not already have a partner. An exception exists if she has already danced with the gentleman more than once; in fact, it is considered ill-bred for any young woman to dance more than three dances with the same partner, even if she is engaged to him. It is also extremely rude for any husband and wife to dance together.

It is important to remember that the introductions made at balls do not extend beyond the night of the ball. Should a gentleman pass a lady on the street with whom he danced the night before, it would be very rude for him to assume any familiarity with her. At most, he may tip his hat, and he ought not take offense if the young lady is too discreet to return the courtesy.

For those not inclined to dancing, there is still plenty at a ball to keep one occupied. A refreshment room adjacent to the ballroom supplies tea, sandwiches, ices, and pastries. At fancier affairs an entire meal might be laid out including roast fowl, ham,

jellies, trifle, and tipsy cake. However, food is not the only pleasure offered to the non-dancers, and many who are not themselves at the mercy of the marriage-market find it amusing to watch the courtships of the young.

Because overt talk of romance is considered ill-bred in such a setting, much is communicated with subtle non-verbal cues. In recent years, a "language of the fan" has developed that enables young ladies to communicate messages that range from "I hate you," to "we're being watched," and "please proceed," simply from the way they manipulate these oriental accessories. Fortunately, young men can purchase pocket guidebooks to help them navigate these complex signals.

When the festivities are over, hats, canes, and opera-cloaks are retrieved from the cloakroom before gentlemen guide the ladies to their carriages. After especially elegant affairs in private homes, it is considered good manners to stop in during visiting hours the following week to compliment the host on a successful evening.

DAILY LIFE IN THE COUNTRY

For members of the gentry and the aristocracy, daily life in the country is less likely to follow a predictable schedule than when in the city. Both men and women have a variety of activities available to occupy their time. Reading, writing letters, and going riding are entertainments available to both sexes. Men may go hunting, and pheasant, grouse, duck, and goose are all popular quarry. Women may also pass their time with embroidery, while young unmarried women may spend their days working on their accomplishments, which include mastering European languages, singing, playing the pianoforte, and painting. In the evenings, card games like Wist and Lottery are popular. Activities vary depending on the interests, tastes, and talents of individuals and families.

Dinner parties, balls, and making calls are important aspects of country life just as they are in the city, although they happen less frequently than in London. Also, because of the vast distances to be traveled by carriage, there are relatively few "respectable"

families from which to invite dining companions when planning a dinner. As a result, the arrival of a new family in the county is an exciting event, especially for those genteel families not quite rich enough for the annual migration to London.

Visiting

Although making calls to local acquaintances is a frequent country pastime, it is not unusual for friends and relations to travel between more distant country homes and stay for weeks at a time. Although the presence of visitors does not substantially change the rhythm of country life, it can add refreshing new dynamics to conversations and card games. Typically, these visits are arranged by letter ahead of time, although exact arrival and departure dates often remain hazy until the day guests arrive.

Fox Hunting

One extremely popular pastime for members of both sexes is fox-hunting, so much so that Parliament is intentionally scheduled to close before hunting season begins. This sport relies on the indulgence of a local Master of Foxhounds, usually a member of the gentry or the aristocracy who keeps a pack of highly trained foxhounds. Some may also hire a full-time professional huntsman. The Master of Foxhounds invites his neighbors to join him in riding to hounds several days a week from about the middle of summer until the end of fall.

Riders congregate on the grounds of a local estate in the early mists of morning when there is still a chill in the air holding the aroma of the foxes' nocturnal activities close to the ground. Distinguished male members of the hunt wear scarlet jackets called "hunt pinks," while ladies and younger male members wear black. Most riders sport flat-topped black hats; ladies often attach veils to the brim.

For the next several hours the hounds do their best to find and catch a fox, while the riders, called "the field," do their best to keep up with the hounds, although they must never ride past the

field master in their efforts to do so. On good days, this results in several spirited chases with riders galloping at full speed through rolling fields and leaping over hedges, stone walls, ditches and anything else that happens to be in the way.

For those most determined to keep up with the field master, fox hunting can involve a greater element of risk than any other popular sport. It is also the only dangerous activity available to ladies, the more so for them because they jump the hedges and ditches while riding sidesaddle.

ETIQUETTE

Rules of etiquette serve two important functions among the upper classes. They create a clear and orderly framework for every aspect of life, from the way parents and children address one another to the rules by which conflicts are resolved and courtships are conducted. These guidelines enable men and women to strive for aesthetic and moral perfection in every nuance of their lives. The second function of etiquette is that it enables those who understand its subtleties to identify social climbers who are attempting to escape from their proper place in the order of things.

The social norms and codes of behavior that govern interactions among people of quality are so nuanced and complex that complete fluency is virtually impossible for those not raised in the framework. That said, recent years have produced many members of the merchant classes elbowing their way into polite society, thereby diluting the norms and making it more difficult to recognize fraudulent pretensions. Higher members of the aristocracy and gentry can almost always recognize their own from accent and bearing alone. Even if an imposter manages to perfect these, which is not an easy feat, there are a thousand other minute behaviours that can reveal a pretender, from the words she uses to describe a piece of furniture to the way she eats a roll.

Although fraudulently passing for a member of the upper classes is almost impossible amongst real aristocrats, it is usually possible to get by in the middle classes without causing offense simply by showing deference and adhering to the foundational principle of our Empire's social and moral codes: *control the passions*. Emotional outbursts of any kind are evidence of an uncouth, wild sensibility. The emotions are by nature irrational, and it is reason and order that are the foundation not only of our Empire, but of creation itself. The passions are antithetical to reason, and when they become predominant, chaos ensues. Think before you speak. Eat your food slowly. Never lose your temper.

For foreign gentleman and those who have entered the elevated ranks through education and training, the following are a few very basic pieces of advice:

- Dukes and Duchesses are addressed as "Your Grace" by inferiors and "Duke" or "Duchess" by social equals. Other male members of the aristocracy are usually addressed as "My Lord" or "Your Lordship." Women can generally safely be addressed as "My Lady" or "Your Ladyship." If one has been permitted to mix socially with such worthies, it is not necessary to use these titles every time you address those who bear them; only servants do that (further detail can be found in the *Forms of Address* table, p. 159).

- Knights and baronets are addressed as "Sir" followed by their first or given name. Their wives are addressed as "Lady" followed by her surname. Other members of the gentry are referred to as "Mr." unless they have a professional title or military rank.

- Untitled men under the age of eighteen are referred to as "Master" followed by their first name. An untitled and unmarried young woman is referred to as "Miss" followed by her surname if she is the eldest unmarried daughter of her father. Otherwise she is called "Miss" followed by her given name and then surname.

- A gentleman does not introduce himself to a lady, and he will require an introduction by someone already of the lady's acquaintance. The same is true of interactions with one's social betters.

- A gentleman removes his hat in-doors, particularly when in the presence of a lady or his social betters.

- If a lady pretends not to notice a person with whom she is already acquainted she is sending a message that should be respected. This is called "cutting." It is only permissible for a lady to "cut" someone if that person has acted improperly or continually offers unwanted attention.

- An unmarried lady under thirty must not be long in the presence of a man while unchaperoned, unless he is a relation. As such, male cousins of similar age are often a lady's most intimate opposite sex companions. It is not unusual for one of these cousins to eventually become a lady's husband.

- A married lady must not be alone with any man outside of her family, unless it is to discuss business.

- When in doubt about social rank, consult the hierarchy as it is established in a document called "The Order of Precedence." It is particularly useful to foreign dignitaries at court, and ladies of quality who must take care when planning dinner parties not to seat guests in an order that would be offensive. The highest ranking guests enter the dining room first, and then the rest in descending order.

Sex and Sexuality

Sex is not to be discussed in polite company. It is assumed that no man or woman of good breeding would ever engage in sexual behavior outside the bonds of marriage. Violation of this social code is especially frowned upon for women, as the fairer sex is capable of, and therefore expected to show, greater sexual restraint. Men are not believed to be capable of such virtue. Due to their apparent increased sexual desire, it may be overlooked if a man fails to contain his carnal desires before being wed or strays from his marriage from time to time. However, discretion is of the utmost import; public knowledge of such activity would disgrace a man as well as his entire family. An adulterous husband will often keep an affair secret from his wife to protect her from social disgrace rather than to protect her feelings.

SEXUAL AND RACIAL DISCRIMINATION

By 1896, the rights of women were gaining ground against legal inequities, but in many areas women had fewer rights than men. Women could vote in some local elections, but not in national ones. The first female physician opened her practice in 1865, but acting as a magistrate, serving on a jury, and many other professions remained closed to women. The Married Women's Property Acts of 1870 and 1882 allowed for a married woman to retain earned wages, inherited property, and inherited money up to 200 pounds; hold rented properties in her own name; allowed a wife to be sued separately from her husband; made women responsible for their own debts; and created financial obligation to her children.

Ethnic and religious discrimination was pervasive in much of the Empire. Race was viewed as a hierarchy, and the English viewed themselves on top. The English were often disdainful of other ethnicities, especially the Irish, Welsh, Africans, gipsies, and people from southern or eastern Europe. Some "scientific" claims used appearance, skeletal structure, as well as stereotyped behaviors to prove certain peoples were evolutionarily inferior. However, many persons of these origins came to prominence in British society: Mr. Pablo Fanque (born William Darby) was the proprietor of the most popular circus in Great Britain; professional sports players, Andrew Watson and Arthur Wharton; Lady Sara Forbes Bonetta was orphaned in West Africa and was "gifted" by King Ghezo to Queen Victoria—Lady Sara was raised as her Majesty's goddaughter, married Captain James P. L. Davies, and their daughter Victoria was also a goddaughter of the Queen.

It is expected that romantically involved couples be of opposite and clearly defined genders. Obviously relationships and personal expression come in myriad varieties, but society and the law define the roles of the sexes and the relationships between them. The Criminal Law Amendment Act of 1885 extended the definition of buggery to include any sexual activity between males, and is punishable by no less than 10 years in prison. Several famous trials of "gross indecency", including those of author Oscar Wilde, artist Simeon Solomon, and cross-dressers Thomas Ernest Boulton and Frederick William Park, garnered great public attention. Romantic relationships between women are not subject to prosecution under the same laws as men, and couples such as Katherine Bradley and Edith Cooper are locally acknowledged and discreetly accepted. Shifting views toward a more positive understanding of homosexuality have recently been encouraged by publications such as Carl Westphal's *Contrary Sexual Sensations* (1870) and the English translation of Richard von Krafft-Ebing's *Psychopathia Sexualis* (1895). However, while a more sophisticated discussion has begun in academia, most people in the general populace still whisper about homosexuality as a mental illness that requires medical treatment.

Poverty and trickery have pushed many young women into prostitution, and social campaigns have yet to solve this problem. Once a woman enters the sex trade, she is at great risk from violence and illness. Most can only expect to live four to seven years and death is rarely peaceful. Parliament has passed many laws to try to protect women, especially children, from such fates, but has met with mixed results. Working as a prostitute incurs such public shame that some of the most well-intended laws have resulted in almost as much oppression and ostracization as the sex trade itself.

TRANSPORTATION

Our Empire is more vast than any the world has ever known, and yet Imperial subjects are able to travel with ease and speed that would have been unimaginable only a generation ago. Railway lines have spread across the forests and fields of the home counties and beyond, connecting all the principal cities of Britain. Trains can travel from London to Manchester in about eight hours. Steamships travel our oceans and waterways, and airships wander our skies transporting goods and passengers to locations as near as Manchester and as distant as Singapore or Brazil. A zeppelin can travel from from London to São Paulo in three days.

While technological innovation has provided new ways of traversing great distances with speed, the horse is still the primary means of travel within the city and between remote locations in the countryside. Although the riding horse has become almost exclusively an instrument of pleasure rather than necessity, carriages remain essential. While only members of the gentry and aristocracy can afford to keep horses and carriages of their own, hackney carriages are available to others in the city for hire at reasonable sums. Those wishing to travel considerable distances in the countryside can obtain a seat on a mail coach at similarly reasonable rates.

Wealthy individuals with a taste for adventure and a desire to reach exotic locations can hire tramp steamers to take them almost anywhere accessible by water. For those wishing to reach far-flung locations inaccessible by steamer, the other option is by air. An independent airship, called a "rogue wind," can sometimes be hired, but these charters carry significant risk. Such independent airships are technically illegal in the Empire, and likely to be crewed by smugglers or pirates—typically just the sort of people that those with money would prefer to avoid.

COMMUNICATION

The primary mode of communication is the Royal Mail. Within London the mail is delivered five times per day, so it is an extremely efficient means of communication over short distances. Those wishing to have a message delivered immediately can send a servant with a note, or hire a boy in the street.

The most efficient means of communication over long distances is the telegraph machine, a device that sends electrical signals through a wire to a remote location. These signals form a code that can be interpreted by the telegraph operator receiving them, who then writes out the message for the intended recipient. Telegraph wires connect all the great cities of Europe not only to one another, but also to the United States and India. Private individuals wishing to send a telegraph can do so at a commercial telegraph office in any city.

The most instantaneous form of communication is the telephone. This device is used by speaking into a metallic mouth piece that extends from a large wooden desk while simultaneously holding a metal funnel to one's ear. Telephones are usually only found in affluent estates, hotels, gentlemen's clubs, and key civic offices.

GOVERNMENT

Ours is the greatest empire the world has ever known, and its success relies on the machinery of our bureaucracy. At the switchboard of that vast array of institutional mechanisms is the supreme legislative body composed of Parliament and the Monarch. It is the job of Parliament to create laws and budgets, as well as to manage international commerce, diplomacy, and defense. Meanwhile, the Monarch's participation in the opening and closing of Parliament and in the signing of bills, provides an important reminder of our purpose and identity.

PARLIAMENT

Parliament consists of two chambers, the House of Lords and the House of Commons. Both Houses can introduce and debate new legislation, although there are key differences. The most notable of these is that while the Lords are appointed to their position as a result of hereditary or ecclesiastical privilege, members of the House of Commons are elected.

The House of Lords is further divided into two estates: the Lords Spiritual and the Lords Temporal. The Lords Spiritual are all Anglican archbishops or diocesan bishops, while the significantly more numerous Lords Temporal are hereditary peers: titled members of the high aristocracy. In addition to the power to introduce and debate legislation, the House of Lords retains the power to veto legislation that passes in the Commons.

Each member of the House of Commons owes his position to his constituency, a particular geographic region that has elected him to represent their interests in the government. Almost all of these individuals are members of the gentry, and many have knighthoods. General elections occur every five years, at which time men who meet the minimal requirements can vote in their constituencies to elect a representative to the House of Commons. The Representation of the People Act of 1884 act utterly changed Parliamentary elections by establishing the "one man one vote policy." Males over the age of twenty five who own property or rent unfurnished lodgings with a value of at least ten pounds per year are permitted to vote. This constitutes about 60% of adult males and tripled the size of the electorate.

There are two main political parties whose membership spans both Houses, the Liberal and the Conservative Parties. The Liberal Party favors unfettered and unregulated capitalism, arguing for the necessity of free trade; they also favor further limiting the powers of the Crown and the Church so that individual liberty might be increased. A significant number of members even favor granting home rule to Ireland. The Conservative Party, in contrast, favors a strong centralized government and the protection of those powers traditionally enjoyed by the Crown and the Church as essential to the well being of the Empire. The current government has a Conservative majority and is headed by Robert Arthur Talbot Gascoyne-Cecil, the third Marquess of Salisbury.

Whichever political party has a majority in Parliament elects from among its members a Prime Minister, who becomes the head of the government, and is able to appoint other members of Parliament to important cabinet posts. He retains his position until he receives a vote of no confidence, or new elections are held that change the balance of power. The minority party in Parliament also elects a leader who is referred to as the Leader of the Opposition.

RULE OF LAW

As in all great civilizations, the Rule of Law in our Empire is absolute. Nobody, regardless of class or birth, is exempt from the scales or the sword of justice. All subjects of Her Majesty have a right to a trial by a jury if arrested for a felony. Jurors are twelve men chosen from citizens in the community to hear the evidence and pronounce a right judgement, and no one is exempt from punishment if found guilty. Even aristocrats, who cannot be tried in the lower courts, will be tried by the House of Lords should they be arrested in connection with a serious offense.

Enforcement

In London, the Metropolitan Police force is primarily composed of working class constables, nicknamed peelers or bobbies in honor of the Home Secretary Robert Peel whose efforts led to the professionalization and standardization of policing in the 1820s and '30s. Each constable reports to a sergeant, each sergeant to an inspector, and each inspector to a superintendent who reports to the Home Secretary. This newly professionalised police force maintains public order and investigates criminal activities according to the regulations imposed by the law.

In the country there is no salaried police force. Instead, the law is enforced by local Justices of the Peace, members of the gentry and in some cases clergymen, who are responsible for maintaining order in the parishes where they are the chief landholders. Justices of the Peace are more commonly referred to as magistrates, and they are empowered to appoint members of the community as constables when it is necessary to capture an accused person. Magistrates are also responsible for using their best judgement to convict petty criminals without trial and for turning significant offenders over to the higher courts. They only have power to jail such individuals for a few months, but each year they will order the incarceration of tens of tens of thousands of petty ne'er-do-wells; far more people, in some years, than are jailed by the juries of the higher courts.

In order to assure that only men of property, good breeding, and good judgement are given this considerable authority, magistrates in each country are appointed by the Lord Lieutenant of the County. He is usually a member of the aristocracy whose inherent talent for delegation makes it possible to fulfill this obligation without being present in the county for most of the year. Appointing magistrates is among the only duties of a Lord Lieutenant, a position that is largely ceremonial.

Crime and Punishment

We have the good fortune to live in an age of increasingly enlightened attitudes with regard to crime. After the discoveries of Mr. Charles Darwin and Dr. Sigmund Freud, educated persons now understand that the vast majority of those who compose the criminal classes are plagued by behavioral abnormalities that are the result of either genetic defects or dissolute parents. A generation ago, our forebears regarded career criminals as lazy ne'er-do-wells unwilling to do honest labor for honest pay; now we understand that most lawbreakers must be treated with compassion as well as sternness. In today's prisons, psychiatrists have earned a place alongside that of the chaplain in efforts to reform criminals.

In this enlightened era, the death penalty is reserved for those guilty of murder, treason, espionage, arson in the royal dockyards, piracy with violence, and the performance of "maleficium"—any magic that harms another. Lesser crimes are typically punished with fines or imprisonment. Mental infirmity is considered as a factor in determining punishments; that is why Robert Pate, who attempted to kill Her Majesty Queen Victoria, was merely sentenced to seven years transportation to a penal colony.

Those in prison are rarely required to perform unproductive labor on the crank and tread-wheel; instead, prison labor involves productive tasks, like picking oakum (removing usable strands from old tarry ropes and cordage) or manual labor such as working in quarries, docks, or on construction projects. This gives inmates a healthy sense of accomplishment as they make substantive contributions to society.

Perhaps the most progressive development is the establishment of juvenile reformatories for prisoners under the age of twenty-three, where offenders receive education, enjoy the same House system that has long characterized the British school experience, and take long walks in the countryside that help develop their moral spirits.

Resolving Matters Between Gentlemen: Dueling

Personal disputes between gentlemen are rarely dealt with in the courts. Instead, reparations are made with formal apologies, usually in the presence of mutual peers. If no apology is made, or if an apology is deemed unacceptable, the matter may escalate. Such conflicts will cost gentlemen considerable Esteem if their actions are seen as unreasonably aggressive or cowardly by others. Unless the situation can be resolved without either party losing face, a duel may be the inevitable result of any insult, real or imagined.

A gentleman issues a challenge by demanding satisfaction, at which point all direct communication between the two aggrieved parties ceases and future messages are carried by friends designated as seconds. The gentleman who has received the challenge may choose either swords or pistols, after which, a time and place are agreed upon. The delay created by this tradition provides an opportunity for tempers to cool, and mutual friends to encourage the would-be-duelists to resolve matters peaceably. It is important to remember that a gentleman may only challenge a member of his own social class, although in rare circumstances aristocrats might challenge members of the gentry.

Duels are not as common today as they were before 1845, when the practice was made illegal in Britain, but they still occur with some regularity, especially among the higher echelons of society and military men. Authorities will usually turn a blind eye so long as there are no fatalities, thus care is taken to avoid such outcomes. The last reported fatal duel on Imperial soil was fought in 1852. However, it is impossible to know how many non-fatal duels have occurred since.

Fights are always conducted in the presence of the duelists' seconds, who are there to keep the combatants honest, and under the watchful eye of one or two surgeons who can provide immediate medical attention to any injuries. Duels fought with pistols involve each party firing a single shot. Due to the limited accuracy of dueling pistols, it is common for both shots to be fired, neither opponent to be hit, and both parties leave with their honor intact. However, the offended party may always declare that the debt of honor will not be satisfied until blood is spilled, in which case shots continue to be fired until one man is wounded. Duels fought with small swords, epees, or sabers are much more common in recent decades. They are fought either to first blood or until one party is too badly injured to continue and yields. This type of duel rarely results in a fatality.

Witchfinders and the Laws Regarding Witchcraft

The role of magic in society usually falls outside most people's notice. The rites of the Church have become so commonplace that they are rarely thought of as magic by those not deeply educated in the faith, and the threat of Witchfinders forces magi outside the Church to be very secretive about their art. Thus, magic as a mystical art has all but faded from the public mind. Imperial subjects do not disbelieve it so much as they question its morality, its authenticity, and its usefulness in the face of modern science. In the minds of most people, magic is a novelty, an atrocity, or an eccentricity indulged in by the wealthy and the credulous. Those who recognize the true power of magic have made certain that laws were passed to control its use.

Legally, magic is separated into two categories: the rites of the Church, and witchcraft. Ecclesiastical rites are viewed as beneficial to society and were sanctioned by Parliament in the Act of Uniformity of 1662, which produced the current Book of Common Prayer and a list of rites sanctioned for use by the clergy and laity. Witchcraft is a legal term referring to any magic condemned by the state, and specifically includes conjuring or speaking with spirits, magically locating lost objects, provoking involuntary love, harming another person, and desecrating religious artifacts. Within the law, the term 'magus' is used to refer to anyone who practices magic, while 'witch' exclusively refers to those practicing witchcraft or its darker cousin, sorcery. Under King James' Act against conjuration witchcraft and dealing with evil and wicked spirits (1604 1 Jac. I, c. 12), the penalty for witchcraft where non-fatal harm is caused is one year's imprisonment for the first offence, but repeat offenders or those that conjure spirits, kill, or employ any kind of sorcery are sentenced to death by hanging.

Britain's approach of handling witchcraft accusations through normal legal process led to the unmasking of several famously fraudulent accusations, but some mistook this due process for a lack of concern regarding real witchcraft and decided to take matters into their own hands. By 1644, this culminated in the vigilante Matthew Hopkins, the self-titled Witchfinder General, touring England and personally seeing to the prosecution and execution of almost two-hundred witches in three years. Seeing the need for enforcement as well as a need for due process, King James sanctioned an organization called the Witchfinders in 1647. This action placed Matthew Hopkins under the oversight of the crown, and gave both legitimacy and boundaries to his unique skillset.

Two orders of Witchfinders were formed: the Canons and the Stars. The Order of the Star Chamber came first. These men were recruited primarily from the ranks of court officers or the military and were chosen for their experience both with battling the horrors of the Pontus and with tracking down those who broke the law. Later in 1691, in the wake of the Glorious Revolution, the Order of Canons was established by special request of The Most Reverend John Tillotson, the Archbishop of Canterbury. It

was to be funded by the Church and its ranks filled by members of the clergy. Current historians believe that his intention was to add an informed Christian conscience to the Witchfinders to prevent them from becoming a despotic organization. Over time, the Stars came to serve as the Witchfinder soldiers and enforcers while the Canons became its chaplains, scholars, and mystics. Witchfinders began to be deployed in teams with equal parts of both orders to ensure that they were prepared to face both physical and mystic threats.

For the next century, the Witchfinders sought out and arrested those who practiced the occult arts. Their black leather longcoats, tall hats, and archaic Scottish backblades became a symbol of fear to those guilty of magical impropriety. Witchfinders enjoyed unprecedented legal privileges to act with the authority of both the Church and the State, but they were still viewed with fear. For all their good work, and even with the two orders watching each other for excesses, there were those who went too far. Rumors painted them as bogeymen, or blamed them for any questionable individual who went missing during the night. Parliament attempted to curb the power of the Witchfinders with the Witchcraft Act of 1735 (9 Geo. II, c. 5). In response, the Crown extended the authority of the Star Chamber as a court of royal justice. This has enabled the Witchfinders to act as magistrates in matters of magic and witchcraft with little secular oversight. As spiritualism and occultism have gained popularity in recent years, and in the face of the the rising swell of Pontus events, the Witchfinders have again become more active.

Those seeking to indulge their curiosities in magic without attracting the Witchfinders' notice often join secret societies. The most exclusive are large enough and have enough political clout to protect their members. These organizations allow for dabbling aristocrats, professional magi, and even Christian mystics to practice magic unmolested by legal authorities and, if the practitioners are wealthy and powerful enough, the Witchfinders themselves. Certain factions within the Church are fully aware of the origin of magic in the divine plan, and may reach out to protect members of their congregations who practice pure art with good and kindly intent. Solitary practitioners who come to the notice of the authorities often come to an unfortunate end.

RELIGIOUS INSTITUTIONS

The dominant religion within the British Isles is Christianity, and the See of Canterbury is the state-sanctioned Church of the Empire. However, there are many smaller religious institutions that exist on British soil and larger ones that hold sway in more distant Imperial lands. Although Christian evangelism has made a profound impact on India, Hinduism is still the majority faith there. The indigenous religions of Africa are still dominant in the Sub-Saharan region. Islam has a firm hold on the Near East and in Northern Africa. While not dominant, many adherents of these religions have come to England or been converted here.

Religious tolerance as well as interreligious dialogue has become much more common under the rationalism of the modern day. The Roman Catholic Relief Act of 1829 repealed many of the Empire's former proscriptions against members of the Magisterium, granting them franchise and allowing them to take seats in Parliament. In 1858, the same rites were granted to Jewish subjects. In 1893, the Parliament of the World's Religions was held in the American city of Chicago, where respectful conversation was held between members of most of the Earth's monotheistic faiths. Confusion and consternation still reign over the boundaries where foreign religions meet, but there is hope that enlightenment will bring all of the Earth to a fuller understanding of the Clockmaker's divinity and peace between His children.

CHRISTIANITY

Christianity is a faith that reveres the Great Clockmaker through His ancient corporeal incarnation, the Christ. Ideally, it is a faith based on a communal pursuit of truth, peace, and love; but, like most religions, it has been practiced in varying degrees of adherence to its core principles. Organizationally, Christianity began in the first century as a single institution often referred to as the One Holy Universal and Apostolic Church. It remained a single entity until the Great Schism of 1054, when the Eastern and Western Churches split from one another. Subsequent centuries saw further splintering, and now there are several major religious institutions under the Christian umbrella: the Magisterium, the See of Canterbury, the Eastern Sees, and the Denominationalists.

The Magisterium

The Magisterium is the Holy See of Rome. It is the largest surviving remnant of the One Holy Universal and Apostolic Church and the oldest Christian religious institution in the West, encompassing all the faithful that fall under the ecclesial authority of Pope Leo XIII, the bishop of Rome. This includes much of mainland Europe, South America, portions of Africa, and even further reaches. In fact, the Magisterium is so expansive, it is difficult to talk about it as a single ideological entity. Local practices and politics can vary greatly. Despite the best efforts of the Pope, the religious authority of the Magisterium often clashes with the sovereign political authority of the nations under its oversight, and individual countries within the See of Rome can at times been at odds or even at war with one another.

Religious practices center around the Mass, a weekly reenactment of portions of the life and teachings of the Christ. Daily practices include veneration of holy ancestors called saints, particularly the mother of the Christ, and private prayer. Specific beliefs are derived from the writings within the Bible and the oral and written traditions of the Church. Discrepancies in belief are remedied in global conferences referred to as ecumenical councils, which occur once or twice per century. More immediate discrepancies are seen to by the Pope, who is believed to have inerrant discernment regarding these issues while he sits on a throne, physically located over the grave of the Church's mortal founder, St. Peter.

While the spiritual concerns of the See of Rome are overseen by the Pope, its temporal affairs are overseen by the Curia, an administrative council, itself made up of many departments called "congregations." The sometimes competing interests of its branches mix with the varying national allegiances of its members to form a vast bureaucracy whose complexity allows for a great deal of political machination. Much of this is truly done in the best interests of the Magisterium, but a good amount of scheming is performed in pursuit of national or personal goals. The result is an institution where most members are attempting to better the Clockwork, but must often struggle through the bureaucrats and power-seekers in their own institution to do so.

The most problematic congregation within the Curia is the Supreme Sacred Congregation of the Roman and Universal Inquisition. Most of this congregation is composed of dedicated theologians concerned with eliminating harmful teaching within the Church. However, when most people speak of the Inquisition, they most often refer to its most extreme fringes where fanatic Inquisitors hunt down those of corrupt bloodlines, heinous sinners, or those accused of witchcraft or heresy and try them at secret tribunals. These extremists within the Inquisition have come under heavy scrutiny by the papacy and their actions have been made illegal in several nations, but this congregation continues to operate. The Inquisition has garnered the support of a very powerful minority within the Curia, and thus it appears that it will not be dissolved anytime soon.

The See of Canterbury

Most historians will claim that the Church of England began in 1534 when King Henry VIII declared religious independence from the Magisterium and placed himself as the absolute authority over a new English Church. In truth, this simply created a tumult of religious controversy, bloodshed, and war that plagued England for centuries. Peace and unity did not come until the end of the Glorious Revolution in 1689, when the last pro-Magisterium king was deposed. The rise of the See of Canterbury was not a single act of Parliament, but rather a one-hundred and fifty year process that embraced moderation in the face of extremism, solidarity in the face of division, and national identity in the face of mainland European conformity. The result is a truly English expression of Christianity.

Today, the See of Canterbury is the official Church in England, and places much of the Empire under the ecclesial oversight of the Archbishop of Canterbury and the Crown. Doctrinally, differences in belief between the Magisterium and the See of Canterbury are few and far between, but the polity of these two institutions are dramatically different. So long as local expressions of faith do not overtly oppose the *39 Articles of Religion*, discrepancies in belief

and practice are largely overlooked, or sometimes even encouraged. Many practices are labeled as "permissible but not required" and thus minor differences in worship, local customs, and religious discipline are permitted. Canterbury allows for a great variety of religious practices as opposed to the conformity of the Magisterium, an important necessity for an institution that oversees a population who were once willing to kill one another over matters of faith.

There are two major points of contention between the See of Canterbury and the See of Rome. The first is *Apostolicae curae*, the papal bull of 1896 declaring all English ordinations to be "absolutely null and utterly void," publicly declaring that Rome no longer acknowledged the authority of priests under the See of Canterbury. The second is a belief in the Pontus. The Magisterium maintains a belief in *creation ex nihilo*, the belief that the Clockmaker fashioned the cosmos from nothing. The See of Canterbury teaches that the Clockmaker made the word from the substance of the primordial void. This discrepancy makes both sees view the other as misguided, and dramatically affects the way each institution advises their adherents to react to the strange phenomena that seem to be occurring with increasing regularity. While Canterbury treats the Pontus as a supernatural force devouring the world, the Magisterium teaches that the Pontus is just a word used to describe isolated incidents of evil that are consolidated into an idol of fear by the superstitious.

The Eastern Sees

When Christianity split in 1054, many of the most powerful patriarchs were in the East. The Pope in Rome became the head of the Magisterium and each of the eastern patriarchs became the head of their own sees. The eastern patriarchs view each of their sees as parts of a single grander Church, a belief very similar to what was held to be true in the original One Holy Universal and Apostolic Church. Greece, Russia, and much of Eastern Europe fall under these ecclesial authorities. While the East has maintained good relationships with each other, the Magisterium, and with Canterbury, they have not instituted an organization to confront the Pontus. England's Witchfinders and Rome's Inquisition have no equivalent in the East. Thus, there are unsurprising rumors that Eastern Europe is haven to many breeds of aberrations that have been allowed to thrive unchecked.

Denominationalism

In 1517, Martin Luther nailed a list of criticisms (the Ninety-Five Theses) to the door of All Saint's Church in Wittenberg. This act protested many wrongdoings done in Germany by the See of Rome and, perhaps unintentionally, began the Protestant Reformation. Luther's act gave many religious reformers the courage to stand up against perceived moral failings of the See of Rome. Right or wrong, the Western Church splintered into dozens of individual Christian denominations, each stressing how to practice Christianity in a way that made sense to their local customs and culture, or doctrinal differences over the Magisterial stance on particular teachings. The largest denominations include the Lutherans of Germany and the Presbyterians of Scotland. The Puritans are sometimes referred to as a denomination, but they were expelled from Britain in 1662 and most adherents joined other denominations such as the Presbyterians, Baptists, and Congregationalists, or left Britain to settle in America or other colonies.

OTHER ABRAHAMIC FAITHS

In addition to Christianity, four other world religions claim to worship the Great Clockmaker as the God of Abraham: the Bahá'í, the Muslims, and the Jews. To Imperial subjects these are the most socially acceptable minority religious practices. The institutions that form around these faith communities are often politically motivated to secure safety and religious freedom for their adherents. Their success has prompted Parliament to pass many laws to provide protection and, one hopes, to open wide the door of tolerance for these other Abrahamic traditions.

Strong legislation against anti-Semitism in the last century has substantially increased the Jewish population across England, and the London Committee of Deputies of British Jews acts to safeguard a standard of living and worship that is lacking in many parts of mainland Europe. This has led to a massive influx of Jewish immigrants fleeing persecution on the mainland and in Russia, forming large and vibrant communities in cities such as Birmingham, London, Manchester, and Leeds. Today, Jews are accepted and highly respectable members of society, including some who serve in Parliament and even a former mayor of London.

The Islamic faith is dominant in Egypt, India, and other parts of the Empire in Africa and Asia, but its adherents have become more frequent residents of Britain in recent years. The city of Woking is known for its tolerance of foreign religions, and Muslim and Bahá'í faith communities are openly accepted. The first mosque in England was built there in 1889 by the orientalist Dr. Gottlieb Leitner, and hosts Islamic teachers and worshipers from all over the world. That same year, the Liverpool Muslim Institute was opened by converted Englishman Abdullah Quilliam, a man titled the *Shiekh ul-Islam of the British Isles* by the Ottoman Sultan, Hamid II, in recognition of his accomplishments as an Islamic scholar and evangelist.

OTHER RELIGIONS

A wide variety of faiths are practiced within the boundaries of the Empire, but most are not overseen by large religious institutions. Hinduism, for example, is the dominant religion in India, but it is overseen by dozens of local and regional institutions which are not centralized enough to gain attention or speak with one voice on the international stage. Buddhism is likewise a widespread practice throughout much of southeast Asia, but the many different philosophical and practical observances are too decentralized to draw the attention of global powers. With the modern trend towards a slowly-growing religious tolerance and the ever-increasing amount of travel and trade sharing culture around the globe perhaps we will see these different faiths and practices become more well known in the century to come.

GREAT BRITAIN

The term "Great Britain," refers to a union of four nations: England, Scotland, Wales, and Ireland, which together compose the United Kingdom. The British Empire encompasses not only these four nations, but Britain's vast colonial holdings as well.

ENGLAND

England is the political, economic, and social center of the British Empire. Her cities are the industrial engine of the Empire, while her rolling countryside dotted with small villages remains the aesthetic anchor of much of the United Kingdom's history and tradition. Like the rest of the United Kingdom, England is governed by British Parliament, although each of her fifty individual counties are administrated by their own county council. Some counties, like London, consist only of a single city, while others, like Devon, cover over a million acres of countryside.

London

London is the clockwork heart of the British Empire and the financial capital of the entire world. More than a mere industrial centre, London boasts financial houses that drive the international economy and the governmental institutions that shape Imperial policy. Simply put, in 1896 London is the most influential city on Earth.

The wealthiest districts are home to the most privileged and powerful people in the United Kingdom. For decades, London has been the destination for British subjects from throughout the Empire who are eager to climb to the highest echelons of international business or British high society. The Season illuminates the parks, theaters, hotels, and town houses of the great and the good with the latest fashions, most popular performers, and the social elite.

Under the glittering surface, though, many of London's over six million inhabitants live in unimaginable squalor, crammed into tight quarters in the overpacked houses of Shadwell, Whitechapel, and gritty expanse of the East End. The shops and apartments of laborers are cheek-to-jowl with the docks and warehouses vital to shipping, and the winding alleys so loved by criminals. Rookeries, gin sinks, and flash houses sit like cankers throughout the East End and Southwark across the Thames. Many good and honest Londoners call these places home because they cannot afford to live elsewhere, and many criminals prey on them because they

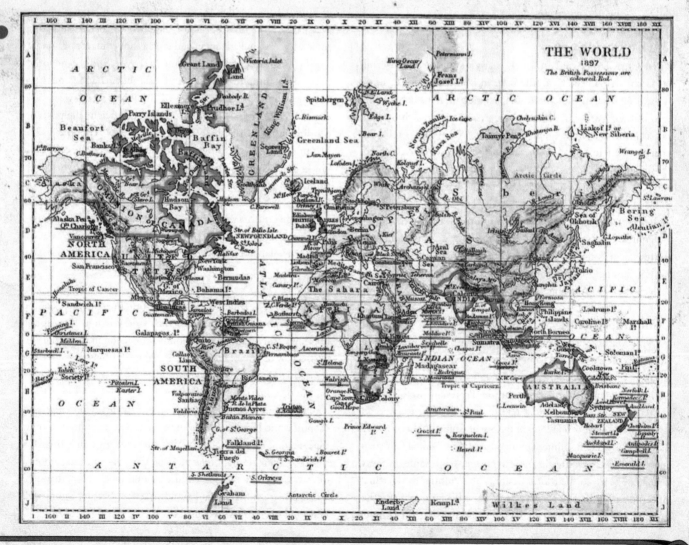

cannot escape. The Ripper murders are a good example of the dangers lurking in the city, but far worse can happen.

It is hardly known to the well-off, but a poorly kept secret among the working poor is that London also hosts a strange and dangerous Undercity. Almost a dozen rivers and tributaries feed into the Thames in channels long ago boarded up and built over. Ancient springs, Roman sewers, the undercrofts of forgotten medieval churches, access tunnels, and the basements and foundations of houses lost to the Great Fire of 1666 all lie beneath the streets, accessible through the sewers and cisterns of the city. The massive projects of the tunnels and earthworks for the Underground cleared space for the rail lines, but also dug mazes of connecting passages or ghost stations that sit abandoned or half collapsed. These places have always housed a hidden population of the truly desperate or deeply strange. The Pontus is strong below London, a rising tide that threatens the city. Many toshers or mudlarks have tales to tell of strange beasts and impossible events they barely escaped, but many more have been lost down there in the dark.

Oxford and Cambridge

For almost 800 years Oxford and Cambridge have been the most important intellectual centers in Great Britain. Each of these ancient research universities is composed of a conglomeration of individual colleges, each with its own grassy quad, library, and elegant dining hall. Despite being no more than eighty miles away from each other, each university prides itself on its unique character.

For generations, the most respectable families in England have sent their children to either Oxford or Cambridge to study alongside the greatest academic minds in Britain and to form social bonds that will be invaluable later in life. Although often associated with privilege, both Oxford and Cambridge offer avenues for intellectually talented students of good character but inferior social connections to attend that they might fully realize their potential in the Clockwork.

IRELAND

Ireland is a large island nation separated from England by the Irish Sea. Its majestic landscape is composed of low-lying mountains that surround a central plain of farmland and navigable rivers. Ireland is often called the Emerald Isle because of its year round temperate climate that allows for an abundance of lush green foliage. In times when it is legal to do so, the natives who speak the ancient language of their people call the island Éire or Airlann. The island often captivates visitors with its beauty, but its history is much more savage.

The story of Ireland contains so many conquests by foreign powers that its formal history is recorded in a book titled *Lebor Gabála Érenn*, the Book of Invasions. Warriors from the Iberian peninsula arrived in the eighth millennium before the Christ, and the subsequent centuries saw nearly every land within reach attempt to take control of Ireland at some point. Even the Tuatha Dé Dannan, a race of feyfolk from the Borderlands, invaded and controlled Ireland for a time. Modern Irishmen are descended from countless generations of invading warriors, making them a fearsome and mystical people.

Foreign control continued until 1348, when the Black Death made its way to Irish shores. The English and Normans who controlled much of Ireland at the time were nearly wiped out, and the native Irish, who suffered much less due to their more rural and dispersed communities, retook much of their country. English culture and authority survived only in a small fortified area around the city of Dublin, a region which came to be known as the Pale. Beyond the Pale, native Irish culture became dominant for the first time in millennia. This truer Ireland lasted for two centuries until the reign of Henry VIII, who undertook a violent and swift confiscation and colonialization of Irish land. English subjects and aristocrats were sent in to "tame" the Irish and culturally retake the island. This led to several quelled rebellions and ultimately to Ireland being absorbed into Great Britain in 1801.

Whatever Ireland was before, it is a different place after the Great Famine. Between 1845 and 1852, one million Irish subjects died of starvation and disease while another million emigrated to other countries. This forever changed the religious and political demographics of the population. England's religious influence on the island nation was greatly strengthened as most of those who fled were adherents of the Magisterium, but England's political

influence was greatly weakened. Many mistakes were made in handling relief to the starving people of Ireland, leaving those who remained with a strong desire for self-rule. There came a yearning to return to a glamorized vision of the self-governed Ireland that existed before the confiscations by King Henry. The Irish Socialist Republican Party formed to support Irish republicanism and independence, and other revolutionaries have taken a more extreme approach than parliamentary politics will allow. Today, many people view Ireland as a political powder keg around which upstarts and revolutionaries are dancing with matches.

The Pale & Beyond

The city of Dublin was settled in ancient times. Since then, It has frequently changed hands as various invaders took control, but usually remained the seat of power for whomever dominated the country. It was given the title 'the Pale,' a word that designated it as a middle ground between the civility of England and the savagery of the lands to the west. The Pale was the land that accepted the culture of its invaders and felt more like home to the foreign nobility that lived there. The land beyond the Pale is a place of tainted blood, a strong presence of the Pontus, and thin places that allow passage into the Borderlands. Mixed with a hatred of oppression born from centuries of invasion, these factors formed a cultural ferocity that made even the Romans think twice about occupation. Even in our modern era, the land beyond the Pale is not to be taken lightly.

Dublin

The earliest record of a settlement in the area of Dublin Bay was recorded in the *Geographia* of Claudius Ptolemaeus in AD 140. It was named Eblana. However, the site of modern Dublin is believed to be built on a Viking colony settled in the tenth century. From these roots, it has grown into a bustling metropolis. Despite its proximity to the wilds beyond the Pale, it is a populous and cosmopolitan city. It is home to many institutions of higher learning such as Trinity College, University College, and the Dublin Institute for Technology. It has been home to great authors such as Oscar Wilde, Jonathan Swift, and Bram Stoker. Dublin is seen as

a bright glimmer of civilization on an otherwise untamable island.

There is a great deal of animosity between the city of Dublin and the Pale. Since the reign of Henry VIII, Dublin has supported the See of Canterbury while beyond the lands beyond the Pale stayed true to the Magisterium. Across Great Britain, Dublin is known for wealth, prosperity, and refinement; while the Pale is at best seen as rustic and at worst, savage. With access to proper aid, Dublin even escaped much of the death and despair of the Great Famine, which earned little love from those who were dying mere miles away. To those beyond the Pale, Dublin is seen as an Imperial city and not the true Ireland. However, despite this antagonism, Dublin has continued to grow as a voice of discontent regarding Imperial rule.

SCOTLAND

No other land is more tightly bound with England by shared history and blood than Scotland. From ancient times, the two nations have fought over culture, religion, land, wealth, and political differences. Beginning with the ascension of King James VI of Scotland to the English throne on the death of his unmarried and childless cousin, Queen Elizabeth, the two kingdoms began to treat more closely with one another and on more friendly terms as they shared a common monarch. A long, slow process of greater trade and social interaction developed under the common rule, and the two countries were formally joined to form the United Kingdom of Great Britain in 1707 with the Acts of Union.

Unification removed the threat of open war and outright hostilities, but it did not end the strife between the two societies. Gaelic identity, culture, and language was deeply foreign to the English, and even those Scots generally supportive of union would sooner die than give up the tartan, Gaelic language, and way of life. It would take nothing less than industrialization, the growth of Empire, and, sadly, persecution to quiet these differences.

The growth of industry brought many country folk into cities. The social tumult of rapid growth, newfound wealth, and an exposure of more Scots to English cultural influences blunted the edge of some differences. More importantly, it shifted the Scottish population out of the glens, valleys, and highlands that were the traditional bases of

power for the Scottish lairds and clan chiefs, weakening their political clout and bleeding away strength from those who still opposed union. At the same time, the growth of industry brought new English, Welsh, and Irish immigrants from other parts of Britain into Scotland, and blended in their own cultures as well. Many Scottish newcomers to cities had to begin speaking and reading English for the first time, and were given their first exposure to a broader British society. Britain also invited the Scottish to play a key role in the expansion of Empire, bringing Scots out of Scotland in droves. The Highland regiments took tens of thousands of young men to Africa and India, and became some of the most decorated and important units in the British Army around the globe.

Sadly, all of these trends were taken advantage of by many unscrupulous landlords throughout Scotland in what came to be known as the Highland Clearances. The rapid growth of industry led to an insatiable demand for wool, and the slight voluntary depopulation from migration out of the country destabilized many established villages and towns. Landlords seized on this weakness and evicted tenant farmers to clear grazing land for massive herds of sheep. Although there was uproar, there was little that the poor could do. The clearances effectively destroyed Gaelic culture, and left behind bitterness against many of the lairds and landowners.

The cultural and emotional upheaval caused by the clearances had dire consequences. The abandoned villages and glens have been plagued by infrequent but very serious Pontus events, and provide a haven for aberrations and chimera that roam the glens and moors. Efforts to re-settle are rare, as the brave homesteaders who try often give up after one harrowing experience too many, or simply vanish altogether. Those who do return tell stories of thin places and unnatural beasts that draw foolhardy explorers, monster hunters, and magicians alike to trek into the highlands for their own purposes.

Despite the challenges of its past, Scotland is now deeply engaged in its role as part of the United Kingdom and the Empire. Edinburgh is nearly as prominent as London as a center of culture, political power, and close association with the Crown. Glasgow is a major port and industrial center as important as Manchester or Liverpool. St. Andrews and Aberdeen host ancient universities on par with Cambridge and Oxford. Industry has raised the standard of living for the laboring and professional classes, and they are becoming more and more important in politics. The Highland regiments maintain an unparalleled reputation for bravery and efficacy around the world. Scottish culture and Gaelic identity have been romanticized, and although it does not replace or excuse prior persecution, it allows for a distinctly Scottish sense of personality and pride that has become part of Britain.

Edinburgh

Edinburgh has always been the seat of royalty, culture, and learning in Scotland, and throughout the 19th century Edinburgh has more fully bloomed as the center of the Scottish Enlightenment. The Royal Mile runs straight through the center of the Auld Toon, and is perhaps one of the most important streets anywhere in the Empire. At its base sits Holyrood Palace—the home of the royal family while they are in Scotland—then it winds its way up the hill, passing the High Kirk of Scotland, St. Giles cathedral, to end at Edinburgh castle. Once falling into disuse, the castle has been revived and now serves as an active royal garrison and parade ground, and also hosts the royal regalia of Scotland and several regimental museums that are open for public visitation. Edinburgh's role as a political and military center makes it the natural social hub of high society, which brings with it a lively selection of salons, theaters, artists, and as many hangers-on and country gentry coming to the city for the Scottish Season as the London Season does for the English upper classes.

No city exists only for the rich and powerful, and indeed Edinburgh is a major center for laborers and professionals. In the last century the New City has sprung up around the ancient borders of the royal burgh, and is on the whole a bright, beautiful, and modern city with a large number of highly educated and skilled professionals that work as merchants, in government, as part of the Church, or in a position at Edinburgh University, the Edinburgh Medical College, or the Bank of Scotland. Even laborers in Edinburgh enjoy better prospects than in many other cities, working in low-level positions in any of the aforementioned institutions, as part of the Edinburgh Police, or with the rail and shipping companies in the city. The people of Edinburgh are generally better-educated than those in other cities, and a preoccupation with Scottish and Imperial politics, civic culture, and local news are all eagerly fed by the city's many newspapers. Indeed, the Edinburgh Evening Post is one of the most widely-read papers in the Empire and can be found in Cairo and Melbourne as easily as on the corner of Prince's street.

For all the promise in Edinburgh, there is still danger lurking underneath. Those unable to find good work survive as best they can in the dilapidated tenements crammed along the edges of the Auld Toon, or huddled in the cellars and forgotten spaces that riddle the hill and form the undercity locally known as the Vaults. Aside from those too poor to live elsewhere, the Vaults have always been home to thieves, prostitutes, resurrection men, and witches. The Witchfinders and police do what they can, but the Vaults are too extensive to ever control or wholly seal up. Though most citizens never know of them, Pontus events are frequent in the Vaults, and from time to time they spit forth some calamity or pack of aberrations and chimera.

Even outside the Vaults, Edinburgh has a bloody history that puts the Ripper murders to shame. Popular memory still recalls the lurid confessions of the witch-covens of Dr. Dee and Lord Nicol, the gruesome murderers Burke and Hare who supplied Dr. Knox with bodies for public dissection, or the sad tale of Jessie King, the murderess and "baby-farmer" hanged just a few years past in 1889. As recently as two-score years past, resurrectionists stole and sold so many of the bodies of the dead that iron coffins, burial cages, and cemetery traps are still widely used by those that can afford them. If Edinburgh is to pursue its bright future, it must carefully guard against its shadowed past.

WALES

Since the the official union in the 16th century, Wales has been subsumed into England, but the differences between the Welsh and their English lords has caused enduring differences that linger to this day. Wales has always remained removed from much of the predominantly English culture now common in the Empire. The Welsh language is still widely spoken, the See of Canterbury has never been especially well received, Wales has long hosted many nonconforming denominationalists, and although trade and wealth flowed out of Wales into the rest of Britain, far less flowed back in. Nobles from English lines hold many Welsh lands and titles, and as a result there is little in the way of Society that stands separate from English centers of culture and political power. The Welsh people do not see themselves as English, do not hold the nobility and Imperial culture in high esteem, and do not pretend otherwise. Many English stereotype the Welsh as unrefined, dirty, and simple, and such condescending attitudes make for chilly social relations in most circumstances.

These real and perceived differences have been accentuated throughout the 19th century. As industrialization swept through Britain it found fertile ground in Wales. The population took to mills, collieries, and newly expanded and increasingly productive lead, copper, silver, and gold mines to fuel the growth of Welsh and British industry as a whole. Unfortunately, the wealth generated by the rush of development only rarely made its way into the hands of those working in the mills and mines, and laborers suffered many indignities and abuses at the hands of the companies so eagerly exploiting their toil. Throughout the century Wales has hosted a dramatic series of worker's movements and uprisings. The "Merthyr Rising" in Merthyr Tydfil in 1831 began the trend, but it has continued ever since. There were raids by police to arrest political firebrands and Chartists in the '30s and '40s, and all manner of labor protests ranging from work stoppages over demands for better pay and safer work conditions, up to full-blown riots. On several occasions the army was called in to forcibly disperse marches, occupations, and protests, and violence ensued. Thankfully none have died in these clashes since '75, but with a series of riots over the last decade, a major hauliers strike in '93, and the beginnings of a regional work stoppage in the mines in North Wales picking up right now, there's worry that the worst may be yet to come.

Building on long-standing grievances against the English and the Empire, a small but growing group of politicians have been openly pushing for separation under the name of Cymru Fydd, "Young Wales." Begun in London, and spreading through other cities with a large Welsh population, the group built on the frustrations in the North and West of Wales and shaped a political coalition calling for self-rule. Their success in areas that have historically had weak ties to England and that have benefited least from the industrial boom gave them enough momentum to form the Welsh National Federation with other political groups in 1895, including organizations like the Women's Liberal Associations that hope a new government could bring broader social reform. However, attempts to garner influence in the South and East have been stopped cold, much to the relief of Parliament. The South Wales Liberal Federation, which covers Cardiff and the more prosperous southeast, just rejected the proposal to join, an unexpected and serious blow to Cymru Fydd. As the opposition was led by Robert Bird, a Cardiff Alderman, and David Alfred Thomas, the MP for Merthyr Tydfil, the separatists claim it is toadyism to England, but more astute political observers believe it is part of a longer play by politicians in the Southeast to make sure that they, and Wales as a whole, have important voices in British government in the years to come.

Cardiff

As the century draws to a close, Cardiff has come into its own as an important Imperial city, rather than just a Welsh city. Its location has long made it an important hub of commerce and communication between Wales and England, but the steady growth of general industry and the development of regional coal production in the last generation has made Cardiff the most populous and prosperous city in Wales. This so-called "Coal Metropolis" has been steadily drawing in new arrivals from the countryside in England and Scotland to find work, and unlike other prominent cities, Cardiff's civic culture focuses on the professional rather than the upper classes. This newfound importance has made it an attractive home for those with strong political views trying to build it up as a bastion for their movements. The various nonconformist denominationalists make noises about disestablishing the Church of England in Wales and preach it to their congregations, various labor groups and left-leaning politicians work to make Cardiff and Wales as a whole into a liberal stronghold to bolster their influence in Parliament, and even socialists like the Fabian society are actively spreading their views and encouraging gradual but sweeping social changes. The political activity in the city is being keenly observed by the government lest Cardiff become the center of any future unrest. For now, at least, nothing is being done, but some conservative newspapers are running more stories detailing any reported Pontus events that occur in the city so these social campaigners can be painted as destabilizing influences on the city.

THE IMPERIAL REACH

The sun never sets on the British Empire. Imperial lands are on almost every continent, and several strong and influential nations fall under the auspices of the Queen. Together with these peoples, the Empire creates a single civilization that helps the world hold back the Pontus.

AUSTRALIA

The continent of Australia is divided into six crown colonies, each of which is ruled by its own representative government, partially elected by the local populace, and partially installed by Britain. The most prominent of these colonies is New South Wales, in the south east, where the cities of Sydney and Melbourne are located. Despite its remote location, Melbourne is a marvel of the modern age, with the same grand architecture, dense development, and industrial infrastructure that are the glory of Her Majesty's Clockwork Dominion. Sydney is the main point of debarkation for those forced immigrants sent to Australia as part of the British policy of Transportation as a sentence for petty crime, which has resulted in a high concentration of those with corrupted blood. Changelings, nephilim, and beastfolk make up slightly over ten percent of this population.

Mid-century Australia experienced an explosion of economic growth, prompted by the gold rush and the ensuing foreign investment, but it has since petered out. At the moment, these colonies are in the midst of a severe economic depression that has prompted the rise of an Australian Labor Party that advocates for workers rights, and a movement seeking to federalize the six colonies into a single nation. So far, the proposed Federation of Australia has tepid popular support, but there have been conventions to draft a constitution, and major politicians like Sir Henry Parkes, the Premier of New South Wales, and the parliamentarian Sir Edmund Barton, have emerged as leaders of the movement. Whether this will be successful remains unclear.

Outside its urban centers and the rail systems that connect them, much of Australia remains a vast wilderness that is known for some of the most potent Pontus activity on the planet. This wild land is inhabited by Aboriginal peoples, many of whom have been displaced by the growth of colonial populations. Although many of these Aboriginals have been obliterated by disease and conflict with Europeans, there are still many hundreds of thousands of them living in the bush. Efforts to convert these tribal peoples to English religion, or to bring them into colonial society have only been partially successful due to the dramatic differences between Aboriginal and Imperial culture. Prominent among them is the Aboriginal belief in the "Dreamtime," a place that exists either outside or alongside the Clockwork. This understanding of a timeless reality beyond the Clockwork informs their spiritual practice and can influence the habits of their daily life. Some are quick to blame Pontus events in the bush on Aborigines who live there, but there are many white outlaws and political dissidents called Bushrangers who choose to live in these regions that might also be to blame. Others claim that the wild Pontus events of the Australian outback have no source in human behavior but are something intrinsic to the land.

Melbourne

Melbourne is a phoenix, brilliant in its activity, and seemingly destined for cycles of death and rebirth. First established on land purchased from the Wurundjeri tribe in 1835, it began as a venture in good faith and cooperation between its white settlers and the Aborigines that agreed to share the settlement. However, within a year of its founding, the site was made the administrative center of the Port Phillip District of New South Wales, the treaty with the Aborigines was annulled by the colonial government, and Aborigines were forcibly dispossessed of their land as Melbourne rapidly expanded. Melbourne grew in size and importance so quickly that by 1851 Port Phillip was carved out into its own distinct colony of Victoria. However, the colony paid the price for its displacement of the Aborigines, as the decade without their presence and assistance managing the lands around the city left it vulnerable to Australia's harsh environment. On the day now known as "Black Thursday"—Feb 6, 1851—more than a quarter of the land area of Victoria covering millions of acres was ravaged by brush fires, including the outskirts of the city. Thankfully there was small loss of life, but it devastated the farms, cattle, and sheep herds vital to the region's food supply and economy. It seemed a deathblow, but almost immediately gold was discovered.

Within a season more than ten thousand newcomers flooded into Victoria, bringing a huge influx of money and demand for land, goods, and services, that Melbourne and Victoria were able to spend their way out of devastation. When the gold began coming out of the mines, it flowed through Melbourne and kicked off a boom of building, banking, and mining innovation. By the 1880s Melbourne was the richest city in the world, a major finance center, home to the tallest building in the world, a telephone exchange that covered most of the city, an extensive electric light grid, street-cars, and every other modern convenience. The mining industry made it a center of mechanical innovation, and the adopted home of some of the first alchemists.

The unprecedented wealth and huge influx of immigration to the city created an unprecedented social environment for a major Imperial city. There were a few old family names and established members of the upper classes that came to Melbourne to promote their interests, but there were far more people of low station that struck it rich with mining claims, or that clawed their way to great wealth and prominence through hard work, shrewd business deal-ings, or outright criminal activity. People of many cultures also set up enclaves in the city—thousands of Chinese, Pacific Islanders, Africans, and Irish flocked to the area. Many changelings, nephilim, and beastfolk have also found a home in Melbourne, because it is a patchwork city where all acknowledge that money and success are far more important than birth and bloodline.

Since 1890 the mines have dried up, more than a dozen banks and land trusts have collapsed, and hundreds of private com-panies have been liquidated. The fall of Melbourne's economic might led to an Australian depression that the colonies have only barely begun to recover from. Now that the aura of prosperity has begun to tarnish and the speed of life has slowed, the cracks in the city's foundation have begun to show. The desperation of the depression years brought many to financial ruin, and crime is very much on the upswing as the city must now deal with a large number of unemployed poor. The city's near-constant growth and upheavals have always led to a high number of Pontus events, but in recent years they have become even more frequent and more severe. Disappearances, aberrant animals, and freak weather occur with increasing regularity. None can say whether Melbourne is in the first throes of a spectacular end, or if it can be stabilized and brought to another rebirth.

CANADA

Canada provides an inviting frontier for those from the heart of the Empire that seek new opportunities in a familiar cultural setting, but have differing religious views from the See of Canterbury, or that are otherwise dissatisfied with life in Britain. The French involvement in Canada's early history allowed the establishment of many denominationalist communities and a considerable Magisterial presence, and has always attracted immigrants of those faiths. When Canada joined the Empire, the pull only increased. Likewise, those with restless natures, or that balked at the position their birth afforded them in Britain, have found some freedom and opportunity to make a new life for themselves in Canada.

The patchwork of different colonies, governments, and communi-ties has always held promise for people of many different beliefs and dispositions, yet over time their idiosyncrasies have developed into a distinct Canadian sense of identity. As calls for self-rule strengthened, there was a brief spasm of violence in the 1830s that made the British government fear they might lose Canada. It was simply too large, too prominent, and too far away to govern efficiently from London. There was significant effort to smooth and improve the relations between colonial and British powers, and a deliberate and thoughtful partnership to slowly increase Canadian autonomy. In 1866, the land was reorganized into four provinces that would join in a federation to govern themselves as the Dominion of Canada.

Since then, Canada has continued to prosper and grow. Many prominent Scottish and several English families have transplanted themselves to Montréal and Ottawa, joining with the most suc-cessful of the older colonial families to establish a small but very influential high society. The expansion of Canadian cities and the development of the eastern maritimes has led to a boom for the railroad and steel industries, and the building trades have created a few very wealthy families as well. These leaders of industry are held up as figures of national pride, and their support has done much to create a proud civic culture. As there is no landed aristocracy in Canada, and only those who have traveled abroad from Britain have titles, society revolves more around wealth and the trappings of aristocracy than it does actual lineage.

Throughout the Empire, Canadians are held up to be bright, hard-working, and loyal subject of the Crown. The success of the Dominion keeps Pontus events to a minimum, and Canada is often pointed to as one of the best examples of the promise of stability brought by the Empire.

Montréal

Montréal has been an important center of trade and travel due to its ideal location along the St. Lawrence river between the Atlantic and the Great Lakes. The commercial opportunities have kept it one of the most populous cities in Canada, and have also led to its unusual and fractious development since becoming part of the Empire. Originally French and Catholic, the city drew so many Scottish and Irish immigrants that it is roughly split between French and English-speaking communities. Even with the inclusion of more British, the religious leanings of the immigrants keep Montréal a major center for the Magisterium in Canada—so much so that it is rumored to be a base for a cell of Inquisitors, but neither the local government or the Witchfinders stationed in the city acknowledge any such presence. Wealth also divides the city. The so-called "Golden Square Mile" in the Mount Royal area is crowded with the recently built, lavish estates of expatriate Scottish aristocrats and the newly-minted magnates of the Canadian railway, shipping and banking families that control almost 70% of Canadian wealth. The old city along the docks and hugging the waterway is crowded with French, Irish, and Italian laborers, mill workers, and small traders and has changed little in the past century. In an echo of London, streets and ethnic enclaves are both preyed upon and protected from one another by gangs. The whole city faces recurring disruptions from the ever-shifting mob of sailors, rivermen, fur trappers, and

vagabonds that move through the city as immigrants and traders. Drunken sprees, dockside fights, and strange wanderers disrupt the routines of daily life, and stir up more Pontus events than in other Canadian cities.

The splits between wealthy and poor, French-Canadian and British communities, those loyal to Britain and those seeking more independence, have made Montréal a hotbed during the rebellion period in the 1830s and 40s, and led to a mob burning down the Parliament buildings in Montréal. This political unrest was a major factor in establishing Ottawa as the political capital of Canada, but Montréal is still the economic and cultural capital of the dominion. Despite its prominence as both a Canadian and Imperial city, Montréal is most concerned with its stature as Montréal.

INDIA

India may be the most important foreign component of our Empire. British interests in India are responsible for a significant portion of our domestic prosperity. And although the East India Company was guilty of some abuses in the first half of the nineteenth century, those peccadilloes were rectified in 1858 when Queen Victoria relieved the East India company of their governmental power in the region and became the Empress of India.

For centuries, India has been divided into several hundred Princely States, each with its own local culture and ancient aristocratic family. Although Her Majesty's government respects the authority of these local Princes in many governmental matters, supreme power to determine national policy in India belongs to the British Crown. The Earl of Elgin rules as Viceroy of India on behalf of the Queen. In demonstrating her commitment to the wellbeing of her colonial subjects in India, Queen Victoria famously declared, "We hold ourselves bound to the natives of our Indian territories by the same obligation of duty which bind us to all our other subjects."

Under British rule, India has enjoyed considerable growth and modernization. It has the fourth largest railway system in the world, and many industrial strongholds that boast production capacities to shame most of our European neighbors. Modern Universities have been created in Madras, Calcutta, and Bombay, wherein Indian nationals can learn from Oxford and Cambridge educated professors.

The result of all of this benevolent management and development by Great Britain is a growing highly educated Indian middle class, and the creation of the Indian National Congress, which supplies middle class Indians with an opportunity to have a voice in Her Majesty's Government. And although most Indians have been slow to accept Christianity (preferring Hinduism, Islam, or Sikhism, to the Anglican tradition), many members of the middle class have embraced cricket, rugby, and the English language.

Of all the colonies, ancient and modern, India maybe the best example of a harmonious and mutually beneficial relationship between the parent nation and her native colonial subjects.

There are more nations at work on the world's political stage than simply the Empire. Smaller countries create great pull both for and against us.

AFRICA

Millennia ago, it was our Eden, but in the last years of this nineteenth century, Africa is vast and dark and dangerous. Perhaps one day it will be covered with railways from horizon to horizon, and vast complexes of factories will provide the native inhabitants with all the comforts of modern European life, but this dream will take decades to realize. Many African societies are hostile to the betterment offered by European colonizers. The Pontus has taken hold of the more remote African territories, which house some of the most terrifying chimera ever seen.

Africa's vast resources of ivory, palm oil, rubber, cotton, gold, and gemstones have made new colonies an alluring prospect for European empires anxious to acquire them in exchange for civilization and order. To better facilitate peaceful colonization of Africa, the continent was divided between European powers at the Berlin Conference of 1885.

Often unwilling to accept their new political identities, the rebellious inhabitants of Africa have fought their colonizers--and one another--almost continuously since European intervention in the region began. In some cases, these conflicts have pitted professional European armies against on-going insurgencies carried out by stateless peoples, while others have involved more traditional wars between colonizers and powerful African monarchies. Our own recently resolved war against the Zulus was such a conflict, as was the war between Italy and King Menelik II of Ethiopia. Menelik II put an end to Italian authority in the region at the Battle of Adowa.

Africa offers special opportunities for young men of good breeding (but no fortune) to make something of themselves. This is especially true for those who have a talent for establishing authority and delegating responsibility. Ivory steamers are in need of captains, mining camps are in need of overseers, and numerous trading companies are desperate for capable representatives. Although such positions would usually go to men of experience, the significant danger posed by disease and the native populations have made these posts undesirable for seasoned bureaucrats. Young men unburdened by moral scruples are especially likely to thrive in such positions.

Lagos

Lagos' history is bound up with the slave trade, and its future is tied to the growth of Africa. Long a center of culture and trade for the Yoruba people, and an important part of Benin, Lagos was seized and long-held as a Portugese colony. Under the Portugese it became the most active slaving port in the world. Once Britain abolished slavery within the Empire, it began using its naval and political might to tackle the slave trade as a whole. By harrying slavers at sea and developing anti-slavery treaties with West African coastal chiefs, it greatly diminished the trade and Lagos became a focus of interest. Britain took on the military protection of Lagos in 1852, and in 1861 took full control of the city under threat of bombardment. Although many still resent the heavy-handedness of British seizure, Lagos has remained largely in control of its own daily affairs. Its history as a major port ensured that there has always been wealth and a well-established African professional and upper class in the city. Lagos is home to many prominent families of the Awori Yoruba and other tribes that are as established and important in West African society as the British gentry and aristocracy are inside Great Britain. Since becoming part of the Empire, the upper classes of Lagos have increased their ties to Britain, sending children for education, visiting London for the Season, and hosting Britons coming to Nigeria for business or pleasure on safari. Trade has continued to grow as Lagos ships out raw materials and gold from the African interior, and takes in British goods and a piece of the taxes and fees from commerce flowing through the port. The wealth has led to development and a steady increase in population though the century.

ARABY

For centuries, not only the Arabian Peninsula but the entire Near East have been the subject of wild tales and romantic conjecture. "Sweet Araby", a land of exotic peoples and mysterious customs often figures in the tales of professional sailors and eccentric travelers, whose stories paint in broad brush strokes images of vast deserts and exotic caravans. The reality of course is that this region of the world is every bit as nuanced and complex as Europe. A confusing history of shifting borders, competing dynastic families, and religious strife has created political and cultural tensions that must be carefully navigated if British interests in the region are to remain secure. Perhaps the most powerful political and military force in this region of the world is the Ottoman Empire, despite having been in perpetual decline for most of the century. Based in Constantinople, the Ottomans, under Sultan Abdülhamid II, control a considerable portion of the Middle East. Although they were our allies in the 1854–1856 Crimean War against Russia current relations are merely polite, and not especially warm.

British interests in the Near East are comprised mainly of a few ports on the Arabian Peninsula that are important stops on the trade route with India, and the Suez Canal in Egypt, which has been in British hands since 1882. Egypt, although technically a tributary state of the Ottoman Empire, is essentially an unofficial protectorate of Great Britain.

FRANCE

Although the rise of Germany has unseated France as the Continent's most important military and economic power, Paris remains the Epicurean capital of the West. For those who have devoted themselves to the arts, food, and sumptuous fashions, this ancient city is irresistible. It is also morally perilous; Parisian culture is founded in French *joie de vivre*, rather than the common decency and simple social codes that are the bedrock of Britain.

There is little doubt that the moral and political decline of France over the last few decades is the direct result of the dissolution of the French Monarchy. Without that guiding light, the French Republic is morally adrift. Sexual permissiveness and scandal abound. The most notable recent example is the Dreyfus Affair, in which a military officer of Jewish descent was imprisoned for treason despite his obvious innocence. The event has split the country along political lines, the liberal supporters of Captain Dreyfus calling themselves "Dreyfusards" and his conservative detractors declaring their status as "Anti-dreyfusards." Gentlemen who choose to visit Paris will hardly be able to avoid the debate.

Despite rampant moral laxity, the Magisterium remains particularly influential in France, where the vast majority of the population consider themselves among its adherents. Many of the bishops and high clergy remain staunch royalists and are important figures in France's conservative movement.

In recent years, changelings and even some beastfolk have begun to gravitate towards Paris, where the socially permissive culture makes it possible for them to lead relatively normal lives.

GERMANY

Twenty-five years ago, Germany was a loosely federated patchwork of provinces ruled by rival noblemen. In 1871, these provinces were unified into a single nation state under Emperor Wilhelm of Prussia, who, with the help of Chancellor Otto Von Bismark, provoked a nine month war with France that made Germany one of the most powerful European nations. Together with the Seven Weeks War that preceded it, this conflict has popularized the idea that quick victories in brief military conflicts may be Germany's best path to ever increasing wealth and power.

Economically, Germany's star is rising. Fierce industrial expansion and thriving coal and steel industries have created an economy that rivals our own. Just this year, the Great Industrial Exposition of Berlin showcased the industrial puissance of Europe's newest power. Among the most notable exhibits were a pair of steam powered automatons that are being developed to one day have military applications.

Despite talk of future tensions between Germany and her neighbors, subjects of Her Majesty need not worry. Queen Victoria is Emperor Wilhelm's grandmother, and should our German neighbors become ill-behaved, there is no doubt our illustrious Monarch will issue whatever reprimands are necessary to prevent conflicts from escalating.

ITALY

Like Germany, Italy has only been a unified nation since 1870, when the Franco–Prussian war destabilized Europe and made Italian *Risorgimento* possible; it was in this year that French troops abandoned Rome and that ancient city once again became the Italian capital. Contemporary Italy is a constitutional monarchy, united under His Majesty Umberto I. Unlike in Germany, Italian unification has not been accompanied by explosive industrial and economic advancement. Only in the last six years have Italians begun building a modern infrastructure of extensive rail systems, and the economic future remains bleak for many who hoped that the dissolution of the old feudal system would bring universal prosperity. Every year, many thousands of Italians emigrate to other nations, often the United States, in the hopes of building a better life.

Despite this new political unification, Italian identity remains fiercely regionalized around particular cities. Rome, Florence, Milan, and Venice each have their own unique cultures, each of which have dazzled visitors from Britain for centuries with their exotic customs and connections to antiquity. Although Rome is no longer the property of the Papal States, the Vatican is still tremendously influential; Italy continues to be the stronghold of the Magisterium.

PORTUGAL

A constitutional monarchy under Louis I, Portugal has been gradually modernizing over the last three decades. Railways and telegraph lines now connect Lisbon, Madrid, and many remote areas within Portugal itself, but similar to the situation in Spain, the social and technological infrastructure are not sufficient to prevent high illiteracy rates and poor services in rural areas.

Portugal is our Empire's oldest and most faithful friend. This relationship was put to the test decades ago when Portugal endured grievous war because she refused to comply with Napoleon's trade embargo against Britain, but where Napoleon failed, Britain and Portugal have endured. We remain committed to this friendship today, but despite the long history of good relations, Britons may encounter a prickly reception in Portugal. Britain's 1890 ultimatum that Portugal give up a significant portion of Africa was not well received, even though Portugal acquiesced to the demand. It should be noted that Portugal was in no position to make use of these lands, whereas our vast Empire is even now bringing order and the light of modernity to these distant corners of the Dark Continent.

RUSSIA

The Russian Empire, under Tsar Nicholas II, is a significant force on the international stage largely because of the sheer size of the Russian population and territory. Unlike most of her European neighbors, Russia is fully autocratic, and serfdom was only abolished in Russia in 1861. As a result, there is significant social unrest in Russia instigated by those who advocate for workers' rights and the establishment of a constitutional monarchy.

Although the largest sector of Russia's economy is still agriculture, it is rapidly industrializing. Should the Russian Empire ever achieve an industrial infrastructure sufficient to modernize its vast territory, it could represent a significant rival to our own Imperial power, especially if its domestic social tensions are resolved. While that might be disturbing to some, it is important to note that the rise of Germany could make Russia a key ally of France, our most important friend on the continent. Despite frequent conflicts of Russian and British interests during the last century, including those that lead to the Anglo-Afghan and Crimean wars, Russia may be an important ally in the coming century.

Although rumors of frequent and significant Pontus events in remote parts of the Russian Empire remain unsubstantiated, it is a matter of public record that several English clergymen known to be experts on such things have been advising their Orthodox counterparts for over a year now. In recent months stories have surfaced of Witchfinders assigned to assist Russian authorities as part of an effort to build greater cooperation between the two Empires.

SCANDINAVIA

Norway and Sweden are peaceful nations that have largely been spared the wars of the 18th and 19th centuries. They share a constitutional monarchy under Oscar II, who resides primarily in Sweden and has presided over a period of relative prosperity and modernization. The Norwegian capital of Kristiana, formally called Oslo, is an important center for international shipping.

Denmark—which also controls Iceland and Greenland—is also a constitutional monarchy currently under Christian IX. Although it lacks the significant natural resources of its Northern neighbor, Denmark has managed to maintain a presence on the world stage by securing key trade unions and developing an advanced telecommunications and rail system. After being badly beaten by Germany a generation ago and losing valuable lands in the South, Denmark has scrupulously avoided foreign military conflict.

Finland is a Grand Duchy of the Russian Empire, presided over by the Russian Tzar who is the grand Duke. The upper classes of Finland are Swedish speaking, but promote Finnish history and culture. The lower classes speak Finnish and have little in common with their Russian rulers.

SOUTH AMERICA

British interests in South America are focused in our colonies of British Guiana, and the recently combined colonies on Trinidad and Tobago. These islands have long been a part of the sugarcane trade that dominates the region, but they also serve as welcome ports for British shipping heading to South America. A century ago, the plantations and shipping had much to do with the slave trade, but the Empire abolished slavery in the early part of the 19th century. The colonies have free subjects now, and are responsible for the introduction of many "Black British" into our Empire. The labor that was once performed by those who suffered under the cruel institution of slavery is now undertaken largely by indentured servants from India. Although these workers are only paid a few cents a day, such wages can amount to respectable sums by Indian standards when they have worked for the five years required in order for them to return to their homeland.

Only British Guiana is on the mainland, and it is dwarfed by the countries that surround it. The majority of the continent is composed of large, recently independent nations. Although each of these states has a large population of indigenous peoples, descendents of Spanish and Portuguese colonists make up the ruling classes. The sugarcane industry drives their economies, and modest factories and railroads have been built to support the plantations. The United States of Brazil might be our most powerful neighbor in South America. Steamships, railways, factories, and telephone service have made it a modern nation, at least in the areas surrounding major urban centers like Rio De Janeiro. Until 1889 this nation was an independent monarchy ruled by the same royal family that holds the throne of Portugal. A republican military coup has resulted in a democratic government with separate executive, legislative, and judicial branches. Most of those in power, however, come from wealthy families connected to the coffee industry.

Venezuela, Chile, and Argentina are also presidential nations, each of which has won independence from Spain. Despite their shared struggles, relations between these nations are not always cordial. Chile and Argentina are locked in a naval arms race and Venezuela has been plagued by the same civil conflict and violent upheaval that has wrought devastation and suffering in almost every American nation. These should serve as an important reminder of the stability and order that the Empire provides.

SPAIN

Like other mediterranean peoples, the Spanish are hot blooded and passionate, prone to turbulent emotional dispositions, which may account for the decades of revolution and political turmoil that have plagued the country. Over the last century, the once formidable Spanish Empire has collapsed as the result of a series of lost wars, internal conflicts, and failures to modernize.

In 1868, Queen Isabella was forced by rebels into Parisian exile. The twenty-four months of anarchy and bloodshed that followed were curbed by the crowning of an Italian prince as King of Spain, who three years later abdicated the throne, declaring the Spanish people to be ungovernable. The current Spanish government is a flimsy constitutional monarchy under Alfonso XIII, currently embroiled in a war with the Spanish colony of Cuba, which is seeking independence.

Although Madrid is a fascinating city filled with architectural reminders of Spain's Imperial and Islamic past, the majority of the country exists in a premodern state. Unlike France, where a vast network of railroads connects the countryside to Paris, much of Spain remains remote, both literally and figuratively. Rail systems are not as elaborate as they are in Britain and France, and rural towns tend to be illiterate, provincial, and superstitious.

THE ORIENT

Although the term "Orient" has had many meanings over the centuries, here we are referring primarily to India and China. These nations have long held a deep fascination for Westerners; we have often found ourselves transfixed by their art and customs, which are as beautiful as they are alien. We see evidence of this fascination in the popular oriental rooms that were such a fad in great houses earlier in the century. We would be remiss not to also mention the role of the Orient in introducing our most popular hot beverage. It is of course trade with India and China that has made us a nation of tea-drinkers.

China

The Qing Dynasty of Imperial China is as old as most European dynastic families. The current Guangxu Emperor is the eleventh to rule China, although it is widely whispered that his sister-in-law, the Empress Dowager Cixi remains the real ruler of this ancient Empire.

After being twice defeated by the British Empire in the Opium Wars in 1840 and 1860, and more recently by Japan in 1894, China has gradually made moves towards modernization; but despite plans to create a railway system and a Western style university in Beijing, this ancient nation remains essentially medieval in its social and technological development. Most of the provinces are peopled with illiterate peasants, hostile to Christianity and Western learning. Their vastly underdeveloped military technology has left them largely unable to resist the interference of Russia, Germany, France, and England, all of whom are eager to help China develop in exchange for robust trade opportunities.

Since the conclusion of the first Opium War, England has had a powerful stronghold in the city of Hong Kong, which became a British colony as a result of the treaty of Nanking. It is from Hong Kong that we manage our political and economic interests in this region of the globe.

THE UNITED STATES

In 1775 this nation was a patchwork of marginally important British colonies. In the century following their violent rebellion against the Crown, the Americans have expanded their borders by exterminating the native populations of the West, and have barely preserved the authority of their central government by waging one of the bloodiest civil wars the world has ever seen. Despite her violent temperament, the United States has built impressive rail and telegraph systems linking the Eastern seaboard to California, and created an industrial infrastructure that may eventually secure America a place on the world stage.

Although the United States is in the midst of a considerable economic depression caused by the Panic of 1893, in which wild investment speculation in the railroads crashed the banking industry, the US has the most productive domestic economy in the world. As a result, it seems inevitable that our American cousins will wield influence in future decades, despite having an army that is only a fifth the size of our own, and barely a tenth of the naval power of Her Majesty's fleet.

The economic growth responsible for America's increasing importance continues to lure many thousands of European peasants to leave the stability of their homelands behind in the hopes of enjoying greater material wealth in America. Because of this wave of immigration, the largest American cities have become riots of discordant languages and customs, places where racial tensions often lead to violence. Despite their hopes, many immigrants still find themselves living with prejudice and poverty. These circumstances sometimes motivate adventurous persons to travel west in search of free land or easy gold; however, these territories remain largely lawless, and what local governments do exist are often dangerously corrupt. For every American who realizes his dream with this migration, there are dozens who find only a new flavor of hardship.

Although America has become ethnically diverse, the ruling class is predominantly composed of white European immigrant families who have been influential for generations. Some of these families have become so wealthy that they compose a *de facto* "American Aristocracy," which is based primarily in eastern cities like New York and Boston. British aristocrats of dwindling fortunes sometimes travel to New England to secure American brides with good families and large dowries. Such a marriage match is the best any former colonial can hope to make.

Amedeo Ortegon awoke locked within a small wooden crate. His last memory was that he had stumbled in his panicked flight from his pursuers. He tripped and fell over the edge of the bluffs in the dark, and the long fall to the sandy beach below must have rendered him unconscious. They must have found him while he was blacked out. Now, terrified, he beat the ceiling of his coffin-like prison with his fists. The only answer was the creak of timbers and the murmurs of the ocean telling him he was on a ship sailing into open waters.

He was going to die. No…not die. Be murdered. Murdered like his mother, who he watched be sealed, brick by brick, behind a cellar wall of an old church and left to claw, cry, and eventually beg for mercy that was never delivered. Murdered like his brother, who was flayed alive with long, curved blades, held by men who ignored his screams, and paused in their work only long enough to awaken him whenever he passed out from pain. On a tide of fear the sound of the sea brought a terrifying realization: he would be murdered as his father was, locked in a steel cage and thrown into the ocean. He was going to be murdered in an endless cycle of drownings on the ocean floor until the seas ran dry.

Amedeo raged, then, but a child of thirteen lacked the strength to break free of a locked crate. After a fit of ineffective screaming and pounding, he ceased and lay still, too tired to carry on. He found himself resigned to his fate. God willing, perhaps his body would at least forever lie near that of his father.

Soon, he heard the sound of others approaching, then felt his prison being lifted and carried above-deck. As the lid was removed from the crate the sunlight nearly blinded both sets of his eyes. The eyes on his face saw the silhouettes of the two men pulling his nearly lifeless body from the box. The eyes on his shoulder blades confirmed that, yes, he was indeed on a ship—sailing away from the rocky coast of Spain, leaving what had been his home far behind.

"Gently, gently…" A distant voice instructed his two handlers. It appeared that, despite their desire to expunge nephilim from creation, the Inquisition still felt that courtesy was next to Godliness.

"My boy, my boy… please… drink…" The voice calmly implored him as he felt a small cup pressed against his lips.

Too thirsty and hopeless to maintain even a pretense of rebellion, Amedeo did as he was told, and found his voice returning to him after several full gulps. *"Why are you doing this…"* He croaked, hoarsely, *"If you're just going to kill me anyway?"* He opened all of his eyes as he spoke, finding that nourishment was already reinvigorating his desire to escape. He hoped his strength would return to him as quickly as his will. He took stock of his captor, an older man with a flowing black leather longcoat and a large, wide-brimmed hat. The man's wise eyes softened and his lips pulled back into a bemused smile as he spoke.

"Kill you?" Dipping the cup he held into a barrel of water, the strange man continued to smile at Amedeo as he spoke. "Contrary to anything you may have heard, the Witchfinders mean none of your kind any immediate or unnecessary harm."

Amedeo's four eyes dramatically widened as he muttered the word that made his heart race: *"Witchfinder…"*

The gentle man smiled again as he held the cup not to Amedeo's lips, but instead towards his chest, inviting him to take it and drink freely. After studying the cup for several moments, Amedeo did just that, slightly nodding his head in a sign of thanks.

"Those shackles…" The gentle man asked, motioning to the iron bracelets that still adorned Amedeo's wrists, "You escaped the Inquisition, yes?"

Amedeo, drinking greedily from the cup, again nodded cautiously.

"You are truly blessed, then, for it is few who escape their wrath once their attention is earned."

"They killed my family." The choked words leapt from Amedeo's mouth before could stop them.

The Witchfinder and the others who lifted him from the crate all let out simultaneous sighs of unmistakably sincere regret. After a few moments, the gentle man took off his hat, lowered himself to Amedeo's level, and spoke to him with quiet conviction. "My child… I do not have the words to console your loss. Clearly you are naphil, but rest assured that neither the Witchfinders nor the See of Canterbury have any unfounded biases against your kind. Your birth, while unnatural, does not define you. It is choice alone that can make men—and nephlim—monsters."

This message of tolerance he had never before heard uttered aloud, yet it was one that he always knew in his heart to be true. Amedeo felt himself on the verge of tears.

"We had a longboat on the shore for our own business and were making ready to leave when we spotted your fall. We came to you with the intention to provide you with the same assistance we would offer any traveler in need and found you unconscious on the beach. Upon seeing you for what you really are—and recognizing that the men coming down the bluffs were most likely coming for you—I decided to sneak you onto our ship rather than let that mob have you. Putting you in the crate was necessary to hide you from their notice, and I am sorry for your discomfort. You're now coming back with us to England."

"You're… not going to drown me?"

The gentle man chuckled too easily. "Oh, no, my child. Not unless your actions make such dramatic measures necessary. On the contrary, we would like to offer you sanctuary… and perhaps, in due time, a job."

COSMOLOGY

In the beginning there was only the primordial void, an endless and formless sea of chaos which we have since named the Pontus. This was the stage upon which the Clockmaker first stepped to utter the words, "Let there be…" Thus creation was made, a masterpiece of precision, complexity and interconnectivity. In just seven utterances, He created the Clockwork and then withdrew to His heavenly throne to rest. From there, He continues to watch as creation unfolds.

When mortals speak of 'The Clockwork,' many are simply referring to the Clockwork in which they live: the Earth. Citizens of the Empire frequently use the term even more exclusively to speak solely of those countries under the Queen's rule. However, the true boundaries of the Clockwork extend much further than the ends of our Empire or even our planet. What was created in the beginning was not simply this Clockwork world, but rather a majestic collection of interconnected realms, each turning like cogs in the Clockmaker's grand design. It includes galaxies and planets, intended and unintended realms, the body and soul of the universe. This vast expanse is what an educated man refers to when he uses the word 'Clockwork.'

It is so splendid a work of order that many have forgotten that it was called into being out of the void. The cogs and gears of the Clockwork were made from the Pontus. This chaos was formed into our ordered universe, but it has not remained as such. Whether it is because of human action or natural decay, the elements of this world are breaking back down into that from which they were made. To all who are willing to observe it, it is obvious that the Clockwork is being dismantled, and the question we are left with is, "Why?"

The ability to answer this question may be all that stands between us and oblivion. While some ignore the problem, seeking their own pleasures, and others engage the problem with violence or intrigue, there are those of us who investigate the Clockwork, trying to determine the nature of its unraveling. If there is any hope left for humanity, it lies in stabilizing this crumbling Clockwork world; and if that is ever to happen, it will be through our efforts. If we fail, the Pontus will devour us all.

THE GREAT CLOCKMAKER

Over the millennia, many poets, artists, and scientists have made careful observations of the mortal world, seeing the image of the Maker in the Earth He created. Beyond the borders of this world, many mystics, prophets, and spiritualists have chronicled encounters with celestial beings and passed down the wisdom they received. From the knowledge and observations recorded by these dedicated individuals, it is incontrovertibly true that there is one true creator God who has made all that was, and is, and is to come. Like deducing the manner of a poet by his words or an artist by her paintings, those with eyes to see can discern the will and nature of the Clockmaker by experiencing direct revelation or encountering His reflection in the Clockwork.

RELIGION

Strangely, the undeniable truth that there is only one God does not mean that there is one religion. Devout believers from many creeds adamantly argue the true nature of our Maker. Yet it cannot be said that one of these faiths is shown preference over another. It has been seen and witnessed that the Clockmaker has bestowed spiritual gifts called charisms upon adherents in several different religions. It has also been observed that some religious practices appear to lie outside the favor of our Maker. However, the line between these categories is not as clear as one might think.

The Christians, Jews, Muslims, and the newly formed Bahá'í make up the Abrahamic faiths. These religions explicitly worship the Great Clockmaker and are bestowed His favor and generosity, though the accuracy of each faith's particular customs will likely not be determined until the culmination of the divine plan. Most scholars and theologians see each of these groups as playing a role in the processes of the Clockwork, even if some of their more vocal adherents are desperately attempting to oppress or kill one another. The relationship of other faith practices to the Clockmaker is much less clear.

Monotheism

It is predominantly held by most liberal scholars and theologians that all monotheistic faiths worship the Great Clockmaker. To the Zoroastrians he is called Ahura-Mazda; to the the ancient Chinese, Shangdi; to the Himba peoples of southern Africa, Mukuru; to the Igbo peoples of Sub-Saharan Africa, Chukwu; to the Sikhs, Ik Onkar, and to those factions of Hinduism that venerate all gods as manifestations of a single Godhead, Brahman. Most educated citizens of the Empire would see such faith practices as legitimate in the eyes of the Clockmaker, even if some of the cultural rites might be viewed as somewhat barbaric and in need of correction.

Polytheism

There is only one true God. Thus polytheistic religions are seen to be, at the very least, confused regarding cosmological truth. Some of these faiths are animistic, venerating the angels that govern nature, calling them "spirits" and making sacrifices to them. Others worship the greatest heroes among their ancestors, praying that they intercede in their lives by granting emotional strength and skill. These forms of polytheism are certainly idolatrous, but largely viewed as harmless. They lack a deeper knowledge of the Maker, but they still live in alignment with the Clockwork. In any case, these types of polytheism are rarer than one might think. Many animistic or ancestor religions venerate a transcendent High God, who, most would claim, is just another way of seeing the Great Clockmaker.

Other forms of polytheism truly worship false gods. Practitioners of these religions make sacrifices to beings of power in exchange for magic, unsavory pacts, and unjust gain. In actuality, these false gods are demons, powerful nephilim, wyldling fey lords, or even the greatest of the fallen Grigori who seek human worshipers to aid them in their escape from the Outer Darkness. These forms of polytheism are not in alignment with the divine plan and are believed to undermine the stability of the Clockwork.

It is the duty of the Empire to eradicate these practices through proper instruction or, if need be, more drastic measures.

False gods grant whatever favors and abilities are within their power to give, but they cannot grant charisms; only the Clockmaker can do that. Thus, the presence of charisms in a community is often used to test the validity of that religion. The logic behind this appears sound to many, but it has caused problems in the past. Some foreign religions are seen as false practices for centuries because no known charisms existed among their adherents. An individual charismatic that surfaces in such a group can be quickly denied and condemned to maintain the status quo. Worse, a truly faithful individual honored by the Clockmaker with spiritual gifts can be treated as a heretic and put to death. Most educated citizens of the Empire attempt to err on the side of polite disapproval, but many Witchfinders and Inquisitors do not feel that acceptance is a luxury they can afford.

CREATION: THE INTENDED REALMS

Only an egotist would claim to fully know the intentions of the Clockmaker. Thus, what may be intentional and what may be incidental is a fierce topic of debate among religious and secular scholars. Still, it is popularly held by both that some realms of the Clockwork were purposefully created by our Maker and others were not. The intended realms are those believed to be a part of the divine plan for humanity and the cosmos. They are what we are trying to preserve as we fight back against the Pontus. It is within them that we will discover the answers and meanings to our lives and the hope of glory in the culmination of the Clockwork. The intended realms are the heavens, the Earth, and the Outer Darkness.

Like all things native to the Clockwork, the intended realms are fully corporeal. Each of the three realms and the lesser domains within them may or may not be physically connected, but all are tangible places with solid ground, foliage, and architecture. Even the throne of the Clockmaker Himself is made of the solid bodies of the angelic cherubim. The living who travel to the intended realms beyond the Earth do so in their mortal bodies, with all the risks that entails.

THE HEAVENS

"And Enoch walked with God: and he was not; for God took him."
—Genesis 5:24

Nearly all of what we know of the heavens comes from the first man to have gone there: Enoch. Almost four millennia ago, Enoch was taken to the heavens by the Clockmaker and transfigured into the Metatron: an angelic guardian of heaven's treasuries, chief of its archangels, and attendant to the holy throne. The Metatron serves as the Clockmaker's mouthpiece to humanity. He is the voice that gave the commandments to Moses, and the Word to the prophets. The revelations regarding himself are recorded in three Books of Enoch which contain all of the reliable information that we have

concerning the heavens. Enoch informs us that there are seven heavenly realms.

The Veil (Vilon)
The first Heaven is the boundary or firmament that prevents normal passage from the world of men to the heavenly realms. It also serves to prevent mortals from viewing or communicating with those who reside within the heavens. Seers and spiritualists have discovered ways to circumvent this barrier through the use of magic, but even with powerful rituals it is a difficult obstacle to overcome. The Veil is overseen by the archangel Gabriel, who is often chosen by the Clockmaker as a messenger to humankind due to his proximity to them.

The Expanse (Rakia)
The second Heaven is the area above the firmament where the sun, moon, stars, and all of the planets follow their courses. Each heavenly body is governed by an angel that assures its proper movement and function. These processes are overseen by the angels Zachariel and Raphael, who sometimes intercede on the behalf of humans, but the other angels of the Expanse are concerned only with their assigned task and rarely involve themselves in the world of men. This does not stop the most ambitious of mystics from seeking them out to learn about the movement of the cosmos, especially astrologers who desire to learn of those heavenly bodies believed to affect the behavior of humanity or to give portents of the future.

Paradise (Shekim)
The third Heaven is that heavenly realm to which the Garden of Eden and the Tree of Life were removed after the fall. Here, animals all speak the Green Language, the lion lies down with the lamb, and no animal feasts upon the flesh of another. It is inhabited by creatures who live in peace as they were intended. It is the

world as it should have been, and may yet become. It is guarded by Anahel, a fierce cherubim who works tirelessly to prevent mystics from achieving the immortality that comes with eating the fruit of the Tree of Life.

The Habitation (Zebul)

The fourth Heaven is the perfect metropolis, extending as far as the eye can see. The souls of the righteous dead live here as they await the coming Day of Judgement when their mortal bodies will be resurrected and their city will become the capital of the Clockmaker's new kingdom on Earth. Until that day, the Habitation rests in the heavens and is neither truly corporeal nor incorporeal. Instead, it is in a constant state of becoming. The souls of the dead interact with their surroundings as though they were embodied, even though in truth their bodies yet lie in the mortal realm. The souls who rest in the Habitation are governed by the angel Zachiel and his two subordinates: Zebul and Sabat.

The Refuge (Ma'on)

The Refuge is the fifth Heaven, and home to the angelic host. It is a magnificent realm of barracks, arsenals, and beautiful gardens. It is governed by Michael the archangel, who is the general of the Clockmaker's celestial armies. From here, battalions of angels are sent to all parts of the Clockwork to war against the most powerful of the Fallen, the fey, and others who would work to thwart the divine plan. However, the primary focus of this vast angelic army is to protect the borders of the higher heavens and prepare for the Great Battle that will occur at the end of the world.

The City (Makon)

The sixth Heaven is home to those angels who serve as scholars, historians, healers, harbingers, and messengers. It is home to the Angelic University, a boundless collection of tomes that contain all knowledge that has ever been recorded or conceived in Heaven, on earth, or under the earth. It is governed by the prophet Elijah, who was taken into heaven by the Maker and transfigured into the angel Sandalphon.

The Desert (Araboth)

The seventh Heaven is a vacuous place without air, earth, or moisture. Here sits the heavenly throne upon which sits the Clockmaker. At His feet, the highest seraphim continually sing His glory. It is rare even for angels to come into the presence of the Great Clockmaker, and only a handful of humans have ever beheld His countenance directly. He eternally sits within the Desert and observes as His divine plan unfolds.

THE EARTH

From a cosmological perspective, it is easy to think of the Earth as the center of the intended realms. However, from a scientific perspective, the Earth is one of several planets that orbit around the star at the center of our solar system. In some ways, science has offered criteria to measure the previously immeasurable supernatural world. However, the science of cosmology is still a nascent field and will certainly need to grapple with many profound questions before it could ever hope to offer a functionally complete understanding of creation. There is so much that science cannot yet measure, and reconciling a mechanistic understanding of the world with a theological one is an ongoing process with no end in sight. Despite these difficulties, newly held scientific belief have told us much about how the Earth fits into the Clockwork.

Ancient theologians with a geocentric worldview may have claimed that the intended realms were composed of different substances and separated naturally as oil does from water. As they comprehended it, Heaven was above the Earth, and the Outer Darkness below it. Modern theologians have a different understanding. Today, it is held that the three intended realms are actually one place, separated only because of the boundaries that prevent passage from one to another. The Veil stands as a barrier to prevent humanity from ascending to the heavens. The Abaddon—a fierce cherub guardian—prevents humanity from descending into the Outer Darkness. These intended realms center on the Earth only from a human perspective. In truth, they are all interconnected pieces of one Clockwork. Perhaps one day we will fully understand the relationship between Heaven, the Earth, and the Outer Darkness. Until then, we expand our understanding through visions, exploration, and discovery.

THE OUTER DARKNESS

The Outer Darkness was not truly created by the Clockmaker. It is not the product of deliberate design by the Maker, yet it was intentionally allowed to remain as it had always existed. Before creation was forged, the Outer Darkness was the oblivion that lay beyond the primordial chaos. There it remains. It is an absolute and empty nothingness, containing only those things which have fallen or been cast out of creation. Its only inhabitants are those placed there by the Clockmaker for crimes beyond imagination.

The Outer Darkness was unapproachable to all but the Clockmaker when the boundaries of creation were drawn. A barrier similar to the Veil separated it from the Earth. However, the destruction of Sheol has left access to this realm open like a wound. It is connected to the world of men through an obstacle called the Pit.

Sheol and the Pit

Sheol was once a realm designed by the Clockmaker as a place for the souls of the dead to rest and await judgement. It was governed by the Abaddon, a cherub guardian. He oversaw these souls as they relived their lives through joyful memories and horrific nightmares, and guided them toward proper repentance and healing. Sheol remained this way until the first century.

The destruction of Sheol is a mystery. The Christians teach that the Christ destroyed Sheol so that all souls would have access to the heavenly realms. The diabolists believe that Sheol was destroyed by the fallen Grigori attempting to make a path back into the mortal world from their exile in the Outer Darkness. Every human religion has its own story. Whatever the cause, Sheol is no more.

What is left in its place is the Pit. When Sheol was destroyed, it could have dissolved entirely and if the souls that slept there had left, this would have occurred. However, many souls refused to leave Sheol, and so, the realm could not be undone. As it no longer served its role in the Clockwork, its remnant began to decay. This rot eventually opened a hole into the Outer Darkness. Thus the Pit was formed and for the first time since the creation of the

Clockwork, beings with enough power could now leave the Outer Darkness and enter the world of men.

Today, the Abaddon is both guardian and threshold to the Pit, acting as the sentinel and barrier preventing the original inhabitants of the Outer Darkness from crossing into the Clockwork. Some spiritualists claim to have journeyed past the Abaddon, and gazed upon the captives of the Outer Darkness: the Grigori, the first generation of nephilim, and the souls of the damned. While the Abaddon is a creature of order, none understand the logic governing which travelers it allows admittance into the Pit and which it rejects.

THE UNINTENDED REALMS

There are two unintended realms the Pontus and the Borderlands, and neither were created by the Clockmaker. Instead, they are the product of creation having gone awry and differ from the intended realms in several ways. The largest difference is that the unintended realms are not "real" as mortals understand. While the intended realms are permanent, material places, the unintended realms are mutable and inconstant. Form, location, and even the passage of time are in flux. In the intended realms, a tree is a plant that will grow from a seed and remain in place until it dies and rots back into the earth; in the Borderlands a tree is a physical manifestation of an intangible stimulus and may well become an elephant the next time it is viewed, or simply vanish. In the Pontus, there is nothing but ceaseless chaos.

THE PONTUS

"In the beginning… the earth was without form, and void; and darkness was upon the face of the deep." —Genesis 1:1–2a

The Pontus is all that remains of the primordial chaos from which the world was made. It is no longer a location, but more an infection that is slowly eating away at the Clockwork. It worms through creation, always in motion, tainting whatever it touches. The Pontus is drawn to places where *Corruption* and sin erode orderly living. Where it settles, it begins to dismantle the laws and systems that govern our reality.

The Pontus manifests in different ways in different times and locations. Cities are chaotic places with shifting populations, crime, and rampant inequality, all of which erode the stability of orderly life. For this reason, the Pontus is a constant presence in most metropolises; however, its manifestations are relatively minor. It is as if the chaotic nature of a city acts as a pressure valve, bleeding off its rising influence and preventing explosive results. The countryside is not so fortunate. While the presence of the Pontus is rare in the almost unchanging rural communities of the Empire, when it does manifest there, it does so violently.

Pontus Manifestations

Efforts to find order and meaning in how and when the Pontus manifests invariably fail. Aside from broad trends of urban manifestations being relatively minor and frequent, and rural manifestations

being rare but more extreme, there is no consistency. It can sometimes be difficult to tell which strange phenomenon are born of the Pontus and which are caused by other means not yet understood by science, but others are clear violations of all known natural laws.

The most common Pontus manifestations are meteorological. Rains of frogs, snakes, or blood are not unheard of, but others are even more striking. In 1869, a giant pillar of living flame set down in Cheatham County, Tennessee, setting fire to dozens of trees, razing a farmhouse, and turning a local river to steam before it vanished. Other, stranger reports of fish swimming through the the morning mists and solid storm clouds shattering against buildings have been reported in England itself.

Disappearances are also frequent, minor manifestation of the Pontus. The ground may open to swallow a person whole, or friends and family witness someone simply disappearing before their eyes. Confirmed reports include James Worson, a shoemaker from Warwickshire, who vanished before two witnesses in 1873; and Orion Williamson, an Alabama farmer whose wife and son watched as he disappeared in 1854, leaving only a scorch mark on the ground. The disappearance of animals is even more common than humans.

Sometimes the Pontus gives back what it has taken, but never as it was. Only horrific hybrid abominations emerge from its depths. Just this year, the Journal of the Royal Society of Antiquaries of Ireland reported a seven-foot man-eating wolf-fish that the locals were calling a Dorraghowor. A sixteen-foot iridescent dragon was discovered in Lake Brosno near Andreapol, Russia in 1854. And in 1883, a gigantic beast over forty feet in length, with three heads and a rhinoceros hide was slain in Bolivia.

As terrifying as these events are, the larger manifestations of the Pontus can make the aforementioned examples seem trivial. Rumors of entire towns being overrun by the undead crop up every few generations. Many thought these to be folkloric explanations for plague until the attack on Vicksburg, Mississippi in 1863, a documented assault by the living dead that lead to the death of over two-thousand Americans. Finds of isolated farming villages full of corpses that have cannibalized each other happens just frequently enough to make rumors of ravenous undead never truly go away.

More unique incidents have included whole villages being swallowed by the ground, cattle developing a hunger for human flesh, and natural and physical laws weakening or fading altogether. Anything is possible when the Pontus rises.

THE BORDERLANDS

The Borderlands are composed of the creative energies that remained unused after the creation of the Clockwork. Some suggest it is a reserve of raw potentiality, building material for the intended Realms purified from the destructive essence of the Pontus. Those who claim to have ventured there state it manifests in forms desired by those with the strongest will in an area. Thus, solitary travelers to remote and unformed areas of the Borderlands will find themselves in a world of their own making, while the more populous areas are formed to the desires and nature of the strongest individual who resides in them. Each such region of the Borderlands is called a domain, and each bends to the will of its creator.

The Borderlands fill the space between the heavens, the Earth, and the Outer Darkness. Thus, this realm is also known as 'the Pale,' 'the Marches,' or 'the Median'—all names that denote 'in the middle.' It is also sometimes called 'the Reach' as it is believed by many to be beyond the Clockwork and therefore beyond the Clockmaker's concern. Since it occupies the space between the intended realms and is not under the protection of the heavenly host, it can be used by mystics and supernatural creatures to move unnoticed from one realm to the next.

There are many beings within the Borderlands. Ambitious (or unwitting) explorers enter them by means of rare but naturally occurring portals called 'thin places.' The souls of the living can slip into the Borderlands while they sleep, and since the destruction of Sheol, the souls of the dead can be trapped there if they cannot or will not ascend to their proper place in the heavens. It is believed that the fey are native to the Borderlands, but their exact nature is not fully understood. It is commonly held that they have some link to dreams, as the manifestations of mortal dreams roam as living beings in the Borderlands until they are forgotten. Beyond these, the Borderlands are home to myriad travelers, who use them to find passage into and out of the Clockwork world.

Thin Places

Any place where the boundaries between the Borderlands and the mortal world are traversable is called a thin place. Thin places occur when the normal order of a location has been undermined. This is usually caused by a Pontus event, fey or mortal magics, or unconsecrated places that have been host to a great many deaths. Thin places do not look any different from the normal world, but will have slightly irregular properties based on the desires and fears of those who enter them. A lover of flowers may find herself walking into a patch of beautiful and oddly placed roses. A arachnophobic might wander into a portion of forest completely covered in spider web. Once within a thin place, any individual who interacts with any aspect of the Borderlands will be unable to step back into the mortal world. There are stories of wanderers who stumble upon feast tables in the middle of forests only to eat of the mystical food and become trapped there, unable to return to the Earth. Even speaking with a native of the Borderlands can be enough to bar a person from returning home. Once this interaction takes place, no matter which way she travels, a person can only move through to the Borderlands domain to which the thin place is connected.

Most thin places are fleeting, and are as likely to be there as not at any given time. However, there are rare thin places that will be present for a lengthy period of time. Some of these were intentional creations by unknown beings of power, and can appear as free standing doors or passageways through trees or architecture. Others are simply the result of the weakening Clockwork and can change in appearance based on the observer. Still others are traps laid by wicked fey and can take the form of enticing illusions or beautiful individuals of the observer's preferred gender. These thin places function in the same way. Once a door knob is touched, an archway is overhead, or words are spoken and heard, there is no turning back.

Domains within the Borderlands

The Borderlands are not a single place, but rather a collection of domains that bleed into one another and into the intended realms. It is not part of the Clockwork, but rather its warped reflection. However it was formed, it now exists to fulfill the wants and needs unmet by the Clockwork. Each need creates its own domain, and each domain is in constant flux as it gives shape to the need that created it. Travelers must move through these domains as they move through the Borderlands.

Annwn, The Lands Beyond the Water

Annwn is the home of the wyldlings, those fey who have no desire to manifest in the mortal world. Rather, they lure mortals to visit their domain through oaths and trickery. Once a mortal eats the food of Annwn or drinks of its waters, she is trapped there. These captives become servants, soldiers, and playthings to the wyldlings, who are known to feed upon the unmet desires of mortals. A few captives are known to have escaped through guile, but they live the rest of their lives horrified by memories of their captivity and yet yearning for the bliss of Annwn. Some even try to return, but it is unknown if any have succeeded.

Annwn borders the Underworld and the Earth. Here, fey society is an anachronistic reflection of human society with kings and courts and wars. The wyldlings divide themselves into two courts: the Seelie, a group of cheerful hedonists; and the Unseelie, a group of malicious sadists. These two factions war with one another and steal each other's captives, but they do so for amusement, not for spite. Their endless dramas and intrigues are the only things that give meaning to their existence, and the constant presence of new captives always gives them pawns with which to play and an audience for whom to perform. It is believed that the wyldlings are dreams seeking dreamers, so it may be true that this constant influx of captives is the only thing that keeps them alive. Without this host of mortals, perhaps Annwn would fade away, but none are brave or foolish enough to attempt to free them all.

The Broken Road

Many righteous souls are retrieved by angels or by loved ones to guide them on the path to Heaven. For whatever reason, some are left without a direct route to the Habitation. These souls must travel through the Borderlands on the journey from Earth to the heavens. The route available to them is called the Broken Road, but is also known as the Golden Road or Purgatory.

It is a well trod path, but it is narrow, arduous, and long. The Broken Road winds through many domains before it reaches the heavens. It is thought that the domains created by the ambient creative energies of the Borderlands have an almost sentient desire to survive, and thus require a route to bring new visitors whose witness and belief will sustain them. While the Broken Road was likely intended to help souls navigate to their proper afterlife, the Borderlands have warped it into a treacherous path of temptation, constantly diverting its travelers into those domains along its route where they may be enticed to step off the safety of the path into an undesirable new home.

Like most things in the Borderlands, the Broken Road is fluid rather than constant, always changing in topography and even in length. Yet it is the largest landmark in the Borderlands and runs through many of its domains. It therefore sees constant use, not only by the souls of the dead, but by any being traveling from domain to domain.

As its length can take decades to traverse, living mortals who explore the Broken Road will often need to leave its safety to find food or supplies, never to return. Others fall victim to the trickery of wyldlings from Annwn who stalk its edges for captives, or to the Fallen who will often claim wanderers for their own dark purposes. The Clockmaker's angels sometimes patrol its length, but their primary function is to guide the souls of the dead, not to enable the arrogance of mystics seeking supernatural knowledge. Make no mistake, this road to Heaven may be the most dangerous place in the Clockwork.

The Dreamscape

While asleep, the souls of the living slip from their bodies and travel to the Dreamscape. The Dreamscape is whatever its current inhabitants dream it to be, and can change violently from moment to moment as one traverses it. It is not bound by logic or continuity, and its power manifests to fulfill the deepest desires or fears of the dreamers it entertains.

While away from their bodies, souls are anchored to their physical form by a silver cord. Whenever a dreamer is about to suffer a fatal wound or dangerous emotional catharsis, the silver cord will pull the dreamer back to her body and often times to consciousness. Those who physically travel to the Dreamscape while awake will not have a silver cord and must face its dangers without this safety.

The most dangerous visitors to the Dreamscape are the wyldlings who frequent this place to feed on the energy produced by the dreams of men, or on any travelers who lack the protection of a silver cord. Here the wyldlings sate their hunger on the chaotic fancies of the mortal subconscious.

Hell

Hell is the realm of the Slanderer, one of the Fallen. He is the great tempter spoken of in many cultures. From Hell, he travels the breadth of creation to purchase or swindle the souls of men, secure the service of other fallen angels, and even seek the oaths of fey. With these stolen lives, he populates his realm and strengthens his host. Prophets have foretold that this army will one day war with the Clockmaker's angels in a Great Battle at the end of days. Until then the Slanderer builds his forces and bides his time.

On Earth, his name is scorned by the faithful and worshiped by diabolists to whom he grants sorcerous powers in exchange for their souls. The Fallen fear both him and the fate that many under his rule will suffer when the Great Battle is fought. His own minions are continually kept in a political and martial struggle to maintain power, or sent out to sabotage the Clockwork and skirmish with the heavenly host. The purpose of Hell and the Slanderer's true intentions are unknown, but there is no doubt that Hell is a thorn in the side of creation and a threat that would still be present even if the Pontus is overcome.

The darkened streets of Hell are cobbled with the bones of the unrepentant and lit with the burning corpses of its betrayers; its buildings are carved from flesh and desire; and its forests are fields of gallows. The strongest of the stolen are forged into the bricks of Pandemonium, the vast and impregnable fortress that stands at the center of the realm. As with most of the Borderlands, it is fluid, but only because of the will and fancy of its master. It appears as an antithesis of Heaven, full of flame and envy. It is a place of hopelessness and despair…and the promise of vengeance.

The Underworld

When Sheol was destroyed, many of the souls of the dead wandered into the Borderlands in search of a place where they might continue to dream. The realm accommodated them by creating the Underworld. It is a grand necropolis where the sleeping souls of the un-judged lie in wait for the end of time. The landscape of the Underworld is largely static and respectfully melancholy, filled with grand cathedrals, tombs, and sarcophagi. Pockets of the underworld live out the muted and solemn dreams of the dead, while other spaces simply house their souls in quiet waiting. This place is frequented by wyldlings, especially those of the Unseelie court. Such grim fey have a fondness for the somber reflections of the dead, untarnished by the hope that so often flavors the dreams of the living.

Other Domains

The expanse of the Borderlands is undetermined. It may extend into infinity in all directions. If there is an end to its purview, or a final domain to be discovered, it has yet to be found. The chaotic nature of the Borderlands places it in a constant state of flux. None can say with certainty whether old domains must be destroyed before new ones can form, or if they are simply lost in a great sea of potentiality. Many a spiritualist has made it their entire life's work to map the Borderlands, only to die frustrated at how little progress they had made. It is unlikely that its expanse will ever be fully explored.

DENIZENS OF THE CLOCKWORK

The realms are full of many fearsome and wondrous beings. Some are the intentions of the Maker, and others are unintended ramifications of misused free will. Each searches for a home somewhere in the cogs of the Maker's Clockwork or in the realms that border it. Some succeed in finding a place to rest their head, while others endlessly wander the realms until they breathe their last.

Natives and Outsiders

All intended creatures have a home in the Clockwork. They are native to the place that was designed for them. However, the moment they leave their intended home, these creatures are considered outsiders. Most of the time this distinction has no effect, but there are situations where natives or outsiders may suffer different consequences from supernatural abilities. Outsiders are generally more vulnerable to such powers, and natives may receive some special protections.

Most beings have a clear place in one or more realms, and it is easy to determine if they are treated as a native or outsider. Purebloods are native to the mortal realm, so a pureblood on Earth is a native, while one traveling in the Borderlands would be considered an outsider. The souls of the dead are intended to move on to the heavens and would be treated as natives there, but a shade clinging to the mortal world is an outsider. Feyfolk are only native to the Borderlands, and are outsiders everywhere else. Other entities can claim multiple homes. Angels are bound to the Clockwork and are native to all of the intended realms, but outsiders in the Borderlands. Changelings are anomalies, native to both the mortal realm and the Borderlands.

Some creatures have no home. The Fallen and their progeny the nephilim betrayed their intended role and have no place in the divine plan. Demons are the souls of the nephilim, and no resting place was prepared for them, so they restlessly wander the earth. Chimera are creations of the Pontus, warped beyond recognition, and do not truly belong anywhere. Mortals or aberrations who gain a total of five ranks of *Corruption* are so tainted that they stand against the order of the world by their very existence. All of these entities have no native realm and are considered outsiders no matter where they travel.

Corporeal and Incorporeal Beings

The Clockwork is a physical place, and every being that was intended to live within it has a body. Even in Heaven, the angels have physical forms and live in a physical realm. All beings with physical forms are corporeal entities. Some entities, however, have lost their physical bodies. These beings are mostly the souls of bodies that have died. Shades are the souls of mortals. Demons are the souls of the nephilim. Fey creatures are a strange anomaly and do not follow the same natural laws as other beings within the Clockwork. Wyldling fey are incorporeal, but no one knows if they ever had a corporeal body. Feyfolk have physical bodies that are not crafted by the Maker and no one really knows how these bodies are formed or from what they were made.

Tethers

Any being that has a mortal body can travel anywhere it likes, even if it crosses the boundaries between realms. However, once an incorporeal being crosses the boundary to leave its native realm, it is an outsider and must have a tether or it will be drawn back to its native realm. Tethers are the supernatural ties that bind an incorporeal entity to something. Most tethers are unnatural fixations or goals that keep an incorporeal entity in a place it is not meant to be. On the Earth, the most common tethers are those born of powerful attachments to objects, people, or concepts that bind shades to the mortal realm. Such entities can remain in a foreign realm as outsiders until the tether is resolved or destroyed. However, beings with no home, who are always treated as outsiders, are drawn to any realm. They restlessly wander and need no tether.

ANIMALS

Animals are any non-sapient creatures that inhabit the forests, seas, and skies of the Earth. This includes beasts, insects, birds, and all animate things that draw the breath of life. Creatures such as man, who were made with a conscience to make moral decisions, are considered mortals, but all other things within the Animal Kingdom are called animals.

The Pontus exists beyond the boundaries of space and time, and thus when it consumes a creature, it may return it to a place it would never have naturally occurred. In minor instances, this has allowed for kangaroos in Hyde Park. In an especially severe anachronism, this has even allowed dinosaurs to wander the wilds of Africa. Despite these creatures being out of their proper place and time, so long as they are whole and natural, they are still animals.

Aberrations

Aberrations are creatures that suffer changes due to exposure to the Pontus. Animals, insects, and even plant life can become aberrant if they reside within a location that has been breached by the Pontus or if they were caught up in an ongoing Pontus event. The severity of effect will depend on the creature itself and the duration of the exposure. Subterranean and aquatic creatures seem to be more susceptible to aberrancy if for no other reason than the Pontus has a stronger presence beneath the surface of the earth and in the deeps. Communal and pack animals are somewhat protected from aberrancy by their orderly behaviors, but a single creature that becomes aberrant can be the source of exposure to the rest of its peers. This process has been known to create entire colonies of aberrant animals, whose exposure to one another continually worsens their aberrancy.

If aberrations of a similar type are able to survive together long enough, breeding is possible. The danger posed by such a population establishing itself is huge, and can become a major threat if left unchecked. Many hunters and others who actively fight manifestations of the Pontus go out of their way to track down, kill, or

CREATURE TYPES

Within the systems of the game, sometimes creature types are used to define the parameters of an ability. For example, an expulsion ritual may be performed against an animal, or a *Banish* charism spoken against an outsider. The headings in this chapter are the creature types used within the Clockwork Roleplaying Game. Major headings are creature types that contain those subtypes listed beneath them. These terms are used consistently throughout this book and the descriptions within this chapter may help reinforce rules described elsewhere.

capture aberrations to prevent them gaining a foothold in the natural ecology.

Aberrations are the most common effect of the Pontus. They are most present in urban areas that contain compromised locations where animals are forced to reside in order to gain access to food, resources, or perceived safety. Thus, sewers, waste dumps, and dead-end alleys are common homes to mild aberrations. (The presence of urban garbage incinerators is largely to prevent the trash dumps that could become havens to aberrations.) The bravery of these creatures often increases as their aberrancies develop, and they can fight and kill their way into better situations. It was recently reported that a pack of aberrant dogs in the city of Lagos killed a human family and took over their home. They had claimed over a dozen domiciles before Witchfinders arrived to deal with the problem.

Mild aberrations are simply normal creatures that adopt erratic or violent behavior. Such animals will lose their fear of humans, act primarily based on an intent to harm rather than to preserve their own life, or simply develop an unquenchable thirst for blood. They are much more likely to attack one another than work together to hunt, and some will die or destroy themselves quickly after being turned. Therefore, the aberrations commonly encountered by humans are of a more cooperative variety. A tell-tale sign of mild aberrations can be the presence of natural enemies working together in a behavioral symbiosis to commit purposeless acts of violence.

Severe aberrations suffer from profound mutations. Common abnormalities include bone spurs that protrude from the flesh, open sores, elongated fangs or claws, joint displacement, and patently unnatural features such as a second mouth or extra limbs.

In extreme cases, qualities have been observed that defy the laws of science such as glowing eyes, unnatural intelligence, or even the fusing of flesh into new and impossible appendages. In addition to these visual markers, severe aberrations are significantly stronger than their mild counterparts and are much more likely to attack on sight and without provocation.

Human aberrations are thankfully rare, but even so, many cases have been recorded. In nearly all instances, aberrancy is mistaken for insanity and the inflicted are placed into asylums or turned over to medical institutions for study. If their condition is discovered before it spreads to the surrounding patients, they are often dealt with quietly and permanently. However, several instances, such as the revolt at Matteawan State Hospital for the Criminally Insane, have ended in dozens of aberrations attacking and killing health workers only to flee into the surrounding community. Despite rumors of exceptional and ancient magical rituals, there is no known cure for aberrancy. All aberrations, including humans, must be killed to prevent the spread of Pontus exposure.

CELESTIALS

The original celestials were the angels made to maintain the Clockwork. These beings were charged with the oversight of both creation and its inhabitants. Over time, this category came to include many perversions. Angels that left the service of Heaven became the Fallen; the children of the Fallen became the nephilim; and the souls of dead nephilim became the demons that plague the earth.

Angels

While technically only the lowest order of these celestial beings are called angels, the term is widely used to refer to all of the Clockmaker's heavenly servants. There are nine choirs of angels, each tasked with a different role in the Clockwork. The nine choirs are again grouped into three spheres, and then ordered from highest to lowest. Angels of the lower spheres have more call to interact with mortals and take on a slightly more mortal appearance. Angels of the higher spheres are abstract in visage and are too alien to properly communicate with humanity. All angels are integrated into the inner workings of the Clockwork and are considered native to all of the intended realms.

The highest sphere contains the seraphim, cherubim, and erelim. The seraph's purpose is to serve the Clockmaker and to eternally proclaim His praises. The cherubim are guardian beings that protect the thresholds over which man is not meant to cross. They guard the pathways to the Tree of Life in the Garden of Eden and the gate to the heavenly throne. The erelim are the secret police: astute advisors and cunning warriors. They subtly work to punish the unjust rulers of creation and to bring justice to the Clockwork through the rise and fall of nations over the grand course of history. Celestials from this sphere are beyond human comprehension, appearing more like events, locations or faceless automatons than individuals.

The second sphere of angels contains dominions, virtues, and powers. Dominions rule over entire nations, yet they themselves act under the direction of the erelim. Virtues govern the movement of celestial bodies and the workings of natural laws throughout the Clockwork. Powers are the keepers of history and conscience who work to distribute authority equally among humanity; it is believed that no power has ever fallen.

The third and lowest sphere contains principalities, archangels and angels. These celestials are the most human in appearance and are the only angels that mortals can hope to directly speak to or reason with. Principalities are the servants of the dominions and virtues, doing their work throughout the Clockwork and speaking with mortals on their behalf. Archangels are messengers, protectors, and warriors who are active in the world of men, but who often go about their work outside the ken of mortals in other realms of creation. Angels are the celestials most concerned with the affairs of mortal lives, often intervening for pious individuals. They are the celestials most understandable in form and appearance, and most likely to be encountered by mortals.

The Fallen

"…and I saw a star fall from heaven unto the earth: and to him was given the key of the bottomless pit."

—Revelation 9:1

Angels are circumscribed beings with a single, eternal role to play, and a single choice: perform their duty or abandon their station and fall. The majority of angels have remained loyal and are content with their role in the Clockwork, but if they ever choose their own designs over the Clockmaker's they will join the ranks of the Fallen. In the instant they choose their own path they abandon their perfect purpose, lose the defining qualities of their former choir and control over their appointed function, and no longer have a place in the Clockwork. Those Fallen that perform deeds abhorrent to the Clockmaker are cast into the Outer Darkness, but those who fall due to an abandonment or neglect of duty may descend to Earth or flee into the Borderlands in search of isolation.

The Fallen are forever without a true home or role, and are thus outsiders no matter where they are found. Each Fallen begins its new existence as an entirely unique being, with no purpose but still retaining the knowledge and much of the power it formerly wielded. As beings with no role in the divine plan, they must either carve a new place for themselves in the Clockwork, flee into the Outer Darkness, or risk succumbing to the dissolution of the Pontus. For this reason, the Fallen typically desire a place of relative safety above all things so they can continue their new, self-serving existence. A few descend to Earth and go into hiding, attempting to find a role in the world. Many pursue their own vision of order in the Borderlands, fulfilling their need for a place by establishing themselves as rulers of their own domains, or at the head of a cult of mortals who worship them as a false god. Most find new motivation in misdirected anger over their fall, and desire revenge upon

the Clockmaker they falsely believe caused their descent. These Fallen find a waiting role in the cruel hierarchies of the courts of Hell. There, the Fallen bide their time ruling over lesser beings, work to thwart the work of loyal angels where they can, and wait until the Great Battle when they can openly war with Heaven.

The Grigori

After the fall of man, the Clockmaker sent angels known as the Grigori to watch over mortals and keep them safe. After seeing the lives of these mortals, the Grigori grew resentful of their own limited role in the Clockwork. Thus, two hundred of these angels descended on Mount Hermon to mutiny, leaving the service of the Clockmaker so they might live like mortals. They remained on the earth, taught mortals the secrets of Heaven, took wives, and began families, birthing the first nephilim.

The Grigori brought to Earth the knowledge taught to the angels by the Clockmaker. Arakiel taught the signs of the earth and how to more effectively till the soil; Gadriel, the art of weaponsmithing, cosmetics, and ornamentation; Chazaquiel, the signs and predictions of weather; and Penemue taught the art of ink and writing. However, not all of this knowledge was innocuous. The angel Baraqel taught men the secrets of astrology and Azazel taught them the arts of magic, sorcery and warfare, sowing the seeds of strife and *Corruption* that have plagued humanity ever since.

For the teaching of these darker arts and for begetting the abominations known as the nephilim, the Great Clockmaker expelled the Grigori into the Outer Darkness. Some fled this wrath and escaped deep into the Borderlands. Those who could not escape damnation await their chance to reenter the world, either by testing themselves against the Abaddon to escape the Pit, through the gathering of human worshippers that could call them back to the world through a magical rite, or by finding a crack in the world formed by the Pontus.

Nephilim

"In those days, nephilim lived on the earth and also afterward, when divine beings and human daughters had sexual relations and gave birth to children. These were the ancient heroes, famous men."

—Genesis 6:4

The children of the Grigori are the nephilim, a race of immortal heroes and men of renown who carried within them the blood of fallen angels. Today, as more mortals cleave to naphil spouses and lovers, the bloodline is thinner and less powerful than it once was, but all nephilim breed true. Even over countless generations, the naphil taint cannot be completely removed. Every descendent of a Grigoros, no matter how distant, is a naphil.

The word nephilim translates to 'he who causes others to sin.' They were called this because of the heinous acts that the first generation of their kind committed. The strength and vile natures of these original nephilim were so destructive that the Clockmaker had the worst of these unrepentant creatures bodily chained in

the Outer Darkness. Many other nephilim fled into the Borderlands where their Grigori parents sought safety from the wrath of the Clockmaker. The remaining nephilim were culled periodically throughout history. The Great Flood came to lessen their numbers, as did the Cleansing when the Israelites took Canaan under the leadership of Joshua and killed the naphil inhabitants of entire cities.

The angelic heritage of the nephilim brings with it a number of physical and spiritual complications. Most recognizably, the physical appearance of a nephilim will change according to her behavior. Those who embrace orderly living will take on a more angelic appearance, while those who embrace chaos will take on a more demonic one. This allows those familiar with nephilim to easily recognize their potential, and demonically manifesting naphil are often presumed to be guilty of terrible things. However, chaotic behavior is not always evil, and this prejudice can often result in wrongful persecution.

The immortal nature of their forebears, the Grigori, continues to an extent in the nephilim: they cannot die by ordinary means. If their physical bodies are killed, they return to life three days later. However, the Clockwork is broken and so mortal blood always plants the seed of death. As for the nephilim, the world itself works to eradicate them: each naphil has an unique Bane, a substance or circumstance that can bring true and permanent death to their physical bodies. Nephilim themselves must be ever-vigilant to keep their Banes secret, and guard against having them discovered. Those seeking to permanently slay a naphil must learn this Bane and use it against them, and through the ages many have.

Despite all this, the nephilim persist. Today, there are at least six known lineages: the Anakim, Rephaim, Emim, Moabim, Zamzummim, and Zophim. Each lineage protects their own and adheres to familial traditions focused on survival and piety. A seventh lineage, called the Sepherim, is a collection of those who have abandoned the traditions of their ancestors and seek their fortune in the world by any means necessary. This group is despised by the others as some of their ranks embody the worst excesses and degeneracy of their ancestors.

Just as the nephilim have endured, so too have the groups that would see them destroyed. The Magisterium's Inquisitors actively hunt them for incarceration or execution. Although the Witchfinders do not do so openly, their agents will often persecute nephilim that have engaged in even the hint of wrongdoing. Witchfinder records estimate that there are currently over half a million nephilim within the boundaries of the Empire (about half a percent of the total population, or one in every 200 inhabitants). While most of these individuals probably bear no ill toward their greater communities, the risk posed by those that do merit all nephilim be diligently watched.

Demons

Nephilim are immortal beings that can only be truly killed by their Banes, those substances or circumstances through which the Clockwork attempts to eradicate them. It is commonly held that when nephilim are so slain, their souls have no place in the Clockwork and thus become the restless and predatory spirits known as demons. Demons have no true home, and are outsiders no matter where they travel.

Regardless of their nature while alive, all demons are wretched beings of want and destruction. They seek to feed on the misery of mortals and to possess their bodies so that they can once again experience the pleasures of living. Demons cannot be killed, only banished into the Outer Darkness. Charismatics with the gift of Exorcism are prized for this purpose, but when they cannot be found, magi with the proper rituals serve as an adequate substitution.

For this reason, those who hunt the nephilim prefer permanent incarceration to execution. At the conclusion of a hunt, the still-living naphil is sealed away, most often in the foundation of a building, buried alive, or weighed down and dropped to the bottom of the sea. Such prisoners are doomed by their own immortality to an eternity of torment as they die and rise every few days, only to die again from suffocation, thirst or starvation, quickly reducing them to insane, broken things.

CHIMERA

Chimera are the hybrid monstrosities that emerge from the Pontus. Sometimes the animals and people swallowed by the Pontus are returned, but only after they are shattered and reassembled in horrifying ways. Chimera may be a blending of animals such as the griffon of Scythia or the centaur of Greece. More often, chimera are ghastly and nightmarish beasts, changed so drastically as to bear no resemblance to anything natural. These chimera are collections of organs and limbs from a plethora of victims, often configured in ways that would prevent any natural longevity. There have been reports of chimera that have died within hours of being spawned because their physical bodies lacked appropriate organs to eat or filter blood. Stranger still, even time seems to matter little to the Pontus, as the body of the Bolivian hydra seems to have come from a brontosaurus.

Chimera are actively hunted down by both Her Majesty's Witchfinders and the Inquisitors of the Magisterium. No quarter is given. Even those chimera that have a slight human visage have proven to be monstrous entities fit only for spreading the influence of the Pontus and wanton destruction. If ever there was a chimera that retained even a portion of its original will or identity, it has never been recorded. Yet, the Pontus is a realm of pure chaos, so it is difficult to say what might be possible.

FEY

Some say that the fey should not even be called creatures. A creature is a being that was created by the Clockmaker as a part of the Clockwork. It seems as though this is not the case with the fey. They have no natural home in the intended realms, nor do they seem to originate from any intended thing. They are alien and unknown. All that can be said with certainty is that they exist and they seem to either desire a place in the Clockwork or to collect its objects and inhabitants.

The Irish say the fey are a group of angels that fell to the Earth, but the fey do not behave like the Fallen. The Britons have a belief that the fey are the dreams of mortals that escape to enter the world of men, but the fey pursue their own agendas beyond mortal ken. The Aborigines of Australia see the fey as part of the Dreamscape, both coming from the past and existing in the present. In Africa, Asia, and the Americas, each culture has their own stories detailing where the fey originated, but many of them create more questions than they answer, and none of them agree. The only things these stories have in common is the powerful illusory magics that the fey seem to possess.

While unpopular with theologians, there is a modern theory that the fey are products of the fallen Grigori who fled into the Borderlands. The Borderlands give shape to desire and dream. When the Grigori fled from the wrath of the Clockmaker and

made their way there, what they desired most was to maintain their families and lands, or at least have some vestige of the Clockwork they were forced to flee. The reactive nature of the Borderlands would have provided manifestations of the wives, children, kingdoms, and servants the Grigori desired. It is very possible that the fey originated as these dream beings, but as the Grigori fled deeper into the Borderlands and fell into madness or introversion, the fey remained as dreams with no one left to dream them.

Without some powerful organizing force the temporary emanations of the Borderlands fall back into formlessness. Fey, bereft of the Grigori, had only two choices: cease to exist or find others to dream them. Thus, some took captives from the mortal world, a collection of willful subjects who would see and believe in them, maintaining them as they were. This group became the rulers of Annwn, the fey domain within the Borderlands. The later, larger group escaped into the Clockwork and manifested in forms that fit the unfulfilled beliefs of mortals.

Whatever their origins, the fey are a strange and manifold race of beings that have lived alongside humanity for ages. The only thing we can say about them is that they seem to be native to the Borderlands, as this is from where they come.

Wyldlings

Wyldlings are the fluid and capricious beings who inhabit the Borderlands and collect mortal servants to live in their domains. The vast majority of these beings live in Annwn, a realm supposedly of their own making, but others have been encountered nearly everywhere in the Borderlands. These beings seem to change dramatically depending on where they are encountered, and can appear as strange almost-humans in Annwn, or as utterly alien creatures in other domains. It has been observed that those with the most captives are the most constant, and those with few are the most fluid. This may explain the craving all wyldlings have to abduct and steal the lives of those they prey upon.

The exact reason wyldlings collect mortal captives is elusive, but it is assumed it has something to do with them increasing the stability of their natures. Those who live in Annwn use their victims to populate their courts, armies, and servants' quarters. Those who wander tend to bring their captives with them where they go. Most of these abductees are living mortals, but some fey seem to prefer the souls of the dead. A few cryptic hints exist in magical writings that especially powerful fey lords in Annwn have even captured lesser angels. Wilder stories circulate amongst the mystics and explorers who traverse the Borderlands. Of all the beings in the cosmos, the wyldlings are those of which we know the least, as there are vanishingly few reliable sources to draw upon.

Feyfolk

The most commonly encountered form of fey are the feyfolk. This term refers to an origin rather than a single type of being. These are wyldlings that search for legends and tales so common that they are believed to be real even though they are not. The weakened state of the Clockwork sometimes allows such belief to create a thin place where the wyldling can cross over into the mortal world. As the wyldling comes over, it becomes an embodiment of the belief, whether it is the monster that lives beneath a child's bed, the rookery criminal with mystical abilities, the troll beneath the bridge, or the witch in the abandoned house. When they manifest, that wyldling becomes a feyfolk.

Feyfolk are not fluid like their wyldling cousins, which are ever-changing in the tenuous domains of the Borderlands. The urge for permanence must be appealing to these beings, as once they take the form of a myth, their transformation is permanent. They become corporeal and must eat, sleep, and breathe. They possess all the strengths and vulnerabilities of the thing they become, and may be killed.

Some feyfolk will manifest as individual beliefs, and these are by far the most common. These beings are unique, even though they may be born from the same legend. Lesser feyfolk of this type can manifest from very small stories, such as those that are only held by a few people. There is tell of a man who fabricated the story of a lover to prevent the jeering of his cohorts only to find her show up at a party to be introduced to them. Othertimes, feyfolk will manifest as anything from sin eaters to tiny elves that repair shoes. The more widespread the belief, the more powerful the feyfolk that it allows to manifest.

There are rarer instances where a belief is held regarding an entire group of beings, in which case many fey can enter the world at once and in force. The Book of Invasions tells tale of a race called the Tuatha Dé Danann who invaded Ireland in the nineteenth century before the Christ. They were beings of great magical power, and were worshipped as gods by the local inhabitants. It is believed that this is the first recording of a massive simultaneous manifestation of feyfolk. Their armies ruled those lands for quite some time before being driven off. The belief that gave room for them to rise also made them mortal, and so they fell prey to death and conquest just the same as others.

The further outside civilized lands one travels, the more common feyfolk become. They are born of misunderstanding and gossip, and thus frequently appear in rural areas where education is rare, and in lands where superstitious beliefs are ubiquitous. Innumerable feyfolk have been recorded, but none can know how many there truly are. So long as the Clockwork is weak and there is belief in the unreal, feyfolk will find new forms to take in our world.

Feyfolk: Nature Spirits

In truth, angels are given governance over mighty forces of nature as befits their role as stewards of the Clockwork. One angel may be set to govern an entire mountain chain, or the movement of a planet through the heavens. Yet many of the faithful in animistic religions believe that all objects, regardless of size or power, have a living spirit. This belief allows for some wyldlings to manifest as the spirits of small things that do not have angels appointed to oversee them. When wyldings do manifest as the avatars of such things, they are known as nature spirits. Although these niches do not allow for great power, they are ever present and easy to acquire. Depending on local beliefs, one could find almost anything—from small forests, or even an individual tree or stream—with its own attendant spirit. Their manifestation often comes with a great deal of knowledge regarding the object or place they govern, and for this reason they are frequently sought out by magi and mystics as oracles and servants.

Unlike other, fully embodied fey, nature spirits are rarely corporeal, and have little or no physical needs. They are instead tethered to the objects or places they are meant to govern, and their power and well-being are intimately linked with the prominence of the thing they represent. Nature spirits that are magically barred from their objects, or whose objects are irrevocably changed or destroyed can be undone entirely.

Changelings

Many feyfolk who have the physiology to make it possible will mate with mortal partners. The charisma, guile, and manipulative powers of the fey often make seduction a simple matter, so it is not uncommon for unplanned children to be born from these encounters. The offspring of these unions are called changelings. The term originates from a belief that many changelings were swapped out for mortal children when the parents were not minding them. In some instances this is exactly what happens when a female feyfolk has birthed a child she has no interest in raising. Swapping such a changeling baby for a mortal one who can be cast aside or traded to the wyldlings of Annwn seems a good option. At other times, this story is to cover up an instance of infidelity that could possibly end a marriage.

Changelings are met with some degree of curiosity by ssubjects of the Empire, but can find true hostility in rural areas or those under the auspices of the Magisterium. Within Imperial borders they make up about two percent of the total population, about the same as identical twins. These numbers may be underreported as changelings of a fairer bearing are generally accepted in society, but those who bear grotesque features are usually hidden from view if they even grow to adulthood. Many changelings also inherit some fey glamours that make them suspect to local authorities and Witchfinders, which is another reason to hide their true nature.

MORTALS

Mortal humans are the intended inhabitants of the Clockwork. The Great Maker made the cosmos and all that is in it for them. The angels maintain the Clockwork for humanity, and the plants, animals, and all other intended creatures were formed to provide for them. Pureblood mortals are imbedded in the Clockwork. The divine ordinance holds a place for each and every mortal that ever was, is, or will be born; a path through life that serves the greater purpose of human history. The way may not be easy, and the value of an individual's role may not always be clear, but so long as these

mortals are not corrupted by outside influence, they retain the favor of both the Clockwork and the Clockmaker.

Free will is the Clockmaker's greatest gift and harshest test. Just as all mortals are born with a purpose that is critical to the ultimate stability of the Clockwork, they are also born with a personal responsibility to rise to meet that purpose. Sadly, humanity's own self-serving tendencies often see us fall short of our true potential, and through an imperfect understanding of the divine plan and our own faults we undermine the perfection and stability of the Clockwork.

There is always the possibility of restoring the order of the world that it may yet achieve its intended perfection. Each person must ever strive to understand their place in the world and work to make the world better, or serve themselves and their own desires, and let the world sink into chaos and dissolution. Ultimately, it is humanity who will save or destroy the Clockwork.

Beastfolk

In 1886, a small collection of ghastly animal-human hybrids floated into the Singapore harbor in a makeshift boat. Their story was appalling. It seems that fringe scientists experimenting in the fields of vivisection and xenotransplantation fled the legal sanction of the British Empire and began to practice their dark sciences in remote locations unhindered by governmental oversight. These mad scientists had been experimenting with replacing human limbs and organs with those of animals for decades. Countless shipwrecked sailors, abductees, and illegal slaves purchased on the Asian market died during these experiments. Those who survived were no longer fully human. They had portions of their body replaced with the parts of animals. Over time, the products of their surgical experimentation escaped from their masters' laboratories to make their way back to civilization. These unfortunate victims were labeled "beastfolk" and the name now applies to all who share their lot.

SOULS

"And the Lord God formed man of the dust of the ground, and breathed into his nostrils the breath of life; and man became a living soul."

—Genesis 2:7

Mortal beings are one part body and one part breath. The body is the tangible substance of life. It is the blood that pumps the chemicals that fuel our emotions, the brain that contains our memories, and the limbs that make us mobile. Yet all of this would be inanimate if not for the breath. The breath is breathed into our bodies by our Maker, and this is what gives us life. When we die, our breath leaves our body, and our bodies become lifeless again. This breath is the soul.

Make no mistake, a whole person is both body and breath. One without the other is incomplete. A body without breath cannot move or live. Breath without a body cannot touch objects in the world, properly feel emotion, or retain real memories. After death, it is not until the Day of Resurrection at the end of time when our bodies and our breath will be reunited and we will become whole once again.

Souls of the Righteous

The souls of the righteous ascend to be near the Clockmaker upon their death, and reside in the fourth Heaven. There they wait until the Day of Resurrection, when they will be reunited with their restored bodies and their ultimate fate will be proclaimed. While within the heavenly realm, they live in a state of semi-consciousness. Often this existence is spent reliving the best moments of their time on earth and praying for those they have left behind. As a soul without a body cannot form new long-term memories, the souls of the righteous have only the vaguest notion that they are dead, but they are able to constantly relive the most blissful moments of their lives. There is little impetus to question this as their surroundings keep them in a state of constant peace and joy until that day when they will be reunited with both their bodies and their beloved at the end of time.

Shades

Shades are the restless souls who refuse to enter an afterlife due to some obsession that tethers them to the mortal world. They strive to fulfill whatever need prevents them from moving on. Some are consumed by love or lust for a person, place, or material possessions. Others—especially the victims of murder or catastrophe—are bound by an injustice that must be corrected or a slight that must be avenged. Some suffer such terror or alienation at their time of passing that they cling to the the familiarity of the mortal world. All these souls develop tethers. It is unknown what will happen to tethered shades on the Day of Resurrection, but it is possible that they will be unable to return to their bodies and be forever lost.

Any soul tethered to the mortal realm is called a shade. The term *shade* is used because this type of soul is a mere shadow of the person from which it comes. As a whole person necessitates both body and breath, a soul is only part of a greater whole. Thus, a shade is trapped in a conscious existence, trying to interact with a world that largely does not even know it exists. It cannot form new memories, and is often driven by the same untempered impulses it had in the moment of death. This existence divorced from reason and clear thought leaves most shades effectively insane. For this reason, they can be very dangerous, manipulative, and fearsome, and should be avoided at all costs.

Souls of the Dead

All souls who are not tethered to mortal concerns will move on to wander the Broken Road through the Borderlands towards Heaven. Those who find the offer of Heaven unappealing may find a place to rest along the way in the necropolis of the Underworld. There they are tethered by their yearning for rest and contemplation.

It is difficult to imagine why any would refuse their heavenly reward, but spiritualists who tell of such things hint that the souls in the Underworld were exhausted by life's burdens, and rest was more appealing to them than bliss. Like all souls, these are incomplete beings who cannot form new memories, but without the all-consuming burden of mortal concerns the souls of the dead spend their afterlife in somber reflection on their lives, or a deep and tranquil rest. Rarely, a reflective soul will come to peace with itself and once more resume the journey along the Broken Road toward Heaven.

Angels will journey through the Underworld in search of souls ready to move on as well as to guard the resting multitudes against depredation. Fey and the servants of darker powers travel the Underworld as well, attempting to deceive or take souls into bondage for their own dark purposes.

Souls of the Damned

There are souls in the Outer Darkness. Some say that the Clockmaker tethers the worst of the unrepentant dead there. Others claim that these souls journey there intentionally or unwillingly, drawn to the fell masters they served in life. Whatever the cause, the damned somehow find their way into the Outer Darkness. There, the luckiest among them are driven mad, while others are consumed by the Grigori, the first generation of nephilim, or even darker things.

To be opened upon the execution of my will:

Enclosed you will find a partial transcript of testimony given by Private "Jack" Canton at his court martial, over which I presided in April of 1881. Private Canton was placed under military arrest, along with Private Gary Irvine and Corporal Ross Duffy, after a prisoner exchange at the conclusion of the Boer War. All three men were observed at some distance bayoneting wounded comrades during the British rout at the battle of Majuba Hill.

Their execution remains the single greatest regret of my career.

In my defense, I can say only that we did not know then what we know now. No man of the court, not even the defendants' own lawyer, believed them. Nevertheless, in light of the events of the last ten years, it seems overwhelmingly likely that Private Canton's testimony was truthful. I leave this record in the hope that something can be done to ensure Canton, Irvine, and Duffy are remembered as casualties of that unfortunate war and not for the alleged treachery and murder with which they were charged.

—Lieutenant-Colonel Graeme Stirling, Surry, 1896

Transcript Excerpted from Field General Court Martial Proceedings, 16th of April, 1881:

Canton: I read in the paper that the soldiers now yell "Remember Mujaba Hill", while they are advancing in the field. But by the body and breath I wish I could forget it.

Prosecuting Officer: Hold to the facts please. Recount for us, if you would, your role in the events that took place on Mujaba Hill, 27th of February, 1881.

Canton: It was nearing midday when the Boer forces took the knoll below us. We could see it happen from the top of the Hill, hundreds of Dutch rebels in faded khakis spread out low in the scrub-growth like native hunters. Just a handful of Highlanders held the summit with no ditches for cover and no artillery support.

You have to understand, the Boers don't open like we do, with volley-fire. Instead, each man picks his target and fires when he's ready. After the battle, while I was a prisoner, I learned that the Boers grow up with their guns, hunting and sporting amongst themselves, shooting eggs at fifty meters—that sort of thing. Half are crack shots before they're grown men. So, that skirmish was over almost as soon as it began. Some of the Highlanders with us on the hill wanted to charge when the Boers advanced on their fellows below, but General Colley gave no orders and so we held.

After the Boers took the knoll, they started moving against our position on Majuba Hill. As I said, we had no ditches because General Colley did not expect to be attacked. We formed firing lines on the ridge, but the Boers were so spread out in the scrub growth that we had nowhere to focus fire.

Our red jackets and white helmets made easy targets against the brown of the hillside—and we had little cover. Men started taking hits and the screaming was soon as loud as the gunfire.

The 92nd Highlanders below us took the brunt of the initial attack, but my unit, the 58th, broke first, streaming down the backside of the hill. Someone next to me was shouting that General Colley was dead, and I saw Captain Bryce take a bullet through the chin. It was a bad rout, worse than anything I saw in the Zulu war.

But there was a group of Highlanders still holding in the center where the fighting was fiercest. I ran down the thirty yards or so to their ragged firing line and threw myself down behind two dead men who had fallen one on top of the other. I wasn't being especially brave or anything, it's just that I'm from Northumberland and I wasn't going to be outdone by a bunch of Scots.

We held there for several minutes firing on the Boers, but our rifles were sighted to 500 yards and they weren't more than 100 yards away, downhill and spread out in the scrub. We didn't hit much, but all around us men continued to die. I could hear round after round striking the corpses in front of me.

That's when it happened. The bodies…they started twitching and flopping as if they weren't dead any more. And I know what I saw. My father ran a slaughterhouse in Tynemouth when I was a boy, and I know when life leaves a body, how it slows down and stops. I know death when I see it, when I smell it. The air stank of iron, gunpowder, and shit, and there were only a handful of us there that still had the spark of life.

I scrambled to my feet to run, but a hand closed on my ankle. At first, I hoped it was some wounded man begging to be carried, but when I looked back it was the dead man I had been using as cover. His face, turned toward me now, was split apart from heavy rifle fire, spilling the contents of his skull. He pulled my feet out from under me as if I weighed no more than a child and reached for me with his other dead hand.

I suppose I must have been screaming, but all I remember is trying to fire my rifle into the thing's body, and the click of the empty gun. I used my bayonet instead, forcing it into the blighter's torso until it stopped moving.

But all around me other dead men were climbing to their feet and laying hands on the surviving Highlanders. I saw one man, a red haired youth who not more than nineteen, grappled from behind by a dead comrade who twisted the boy's head around until the wet snap of the neck stopped his screams.

I rammed my bayonet into the dead Scotsman's flank over and over until he sank back down—and all about me the surviving Highlanders were doing the same, driving their bayonets into the dead men as they rose around us. The corpse-things used no weapons, but they were stronger than any living man I've ever seen—and there were far more dead Highlanders on that ridge than there were living ones, and more and more were being killed and rising again each minute.

While I had my bayonet in the throat of the corpse of a man I had played cards with the night before, two more of the creatures took hold of my arms and began to twist; the pain was like fire in my shoulders and elbows. I dropped my rifle. I was sure I was about to die.

There was an explosion of gunfire all around us, and the corpses jerked and spun, hit from multiple angles. In a moment we were surrounded by the Boers—most were just farm boys, bearded youths with homespun clothes, but when they saw what was happening they saved our lives.

When it was over, Irvine and Duffy and I surrendered. We were the only Britons left alive on the hill. I can't say what we killed that day, but I swear by my body and breath they weren't men, and we committed neither treason nor murder.

RULES & SYSTEMS

At their heart, roleplaying games center around getting together with friends and telling amazing stories. Those stories are enabled by a set of commonly understood rules to regulate play. The rules for *Clockwork: Dominion* provide a robust and flexible system to handle the events of your stories, and create the framework for players and Narrators alike to explore the many facets of the Clockwork. Players will take on the role of the player characters (PCs) and the Narrator will portray Narrator characters (NCs), all of whom are subject to the rules herein. Every player should familiarize themselves with the material in this chapter. Narrators should make sure they thoroughly understand the concepts of narrative time, the mechanics for test resolution, conflict, and the uses for potential before running a game.

NARRATIVE TIME

One of the most popular formats for narrative fiction in the Victorian age was the serial. A serialized publication is a story published in small installments within periodicals over a long period of time, and this fits the structure of a tabletop roleplaying game perfectly. While in the Clockwork, storytellers will manage their own use of narrative time based on this format.

Like a serial, each series told by the Narrator and players is divided into books, scenes, chapters, and installments. Each book is made up of many chapters. Each chapter is made up of several scenes. Each installment of a story is a single gaming session, the narrative length of which will depend on the length of real time the players spend together; it can be of any length from a single scene to a complete book.

Many different abilities and systems use narrative time to establish duration of effects. The Narrator will determine what units of time are required for the story as it's being told using the guidelines below. The Narrator has final say as to when one segment of time ends and the next begins, but any good serialized publication can be used as an example to help determine when these changes should occur. Charles Dickens' *The Pickwick Papers* (1836–37) popularized this format, and it was used by other iconic works such as Alexandre Dumas' *The Count of Monte Cristo* (1844–45) and Sir Arthur Conan Doyle's tales of Sherlock Holmes (1887–1927).

Series

A series is a complete serial story. It is made up of many books, culminating in a grand conclusion. Usually a series encompasses all of the adventurers a person will take in their life, although they can later appear as peripheral characters in a series that spotlights new protagonists.

Book

A book is one complete plot arc. It needn't answer all questions raised within it, and although it often contains situations that lead directly into a subsequent book, the arc of each book should finish with a sense of accomplishment or conclusion. A full series is told across several books. *The Count of Monte Cristo* was told in 18 books, each book culminating in a single grand conclusion that leads directly into the drama of the next. The stories of Sherlock Holmes were told in 56 books, many of which were narratively self-contained, but the characters and their relationships still evolved from book to book.

Installment

Within serialized fiction, an installment is a portion of the story that is released to readers all at once. A periodical might publish one installment of a story each week, and that installment would contain anything from a few scenes to a complete book. At the gaming table, an installment is one session of play. Hence, it can vary in length, as how much story can be told depends on how long the players spend together in real time. Like the installment of a serialized story, each game session should have a clear beginning and ending with enough action and plot to progress the story and capture the interest of the players. The 18 books of *The Count of Monte Cristo* contained 139 installments, each directly leading into the next. The books of Sherlock Holmes were sometimes completed in a single installment, while others took several to resolve. Both approaches have merit, and varying how much ground is covered in a single installment is a good way to add variety and change pacing over the course of a series.

RULES FLEXIBILITY

Some playgroups will want to follow every rule to the letter, while others might only use the conflict mechanics and handle everything else narratively. While every rule covered in this chapter is integrated and flexible enough to cover many play styles, Narrators should feel free to adapt them as needed to make sure their group has a great time. If a question comes up that isn't explicitly addressed by the rules, try to find a way to creatively say yes to the players in a way that keeps the story moving. In the end, a roleplaying game is all about enjoying the stories we explore together: use these rules toward that end.

Chapter

A chapter is a long series of events that usually takes place around a central theme, or regarding a particular event. Within a serial, a grand ball takes one chapter to describe, as does traveling from one town to the next. A good rule of thumb is that a new chapter begins when a new undertaking or social event begins: a dinner party, a journey, or a large scale battle. It concludes when the event or undertaking concludes. Just like in a serialized story, the more eventful a period of time, the more chapters it will take to describe; and just like an author, the Narrator may simply decide to break one series of closely-related events into two or more chapters due to length. For example, *The Count of Monte Cristo* is told in 117 chapters.

Scene

A scene is a more specific series of events tied together by location or mood. While a chapter might encompass the events of an entire ball, the dancing, dining, smoking, and mingling portions of the evening would all be separate scenes. A week-long hunting trip in the Scottish Highlands might be a chapter, while each meal and outing might be individual scenes. Also, if a verbal or physical fight broke out during one of these times, that would create a change in mood significant enough to create its own scene within the current chapter's events. Scenes only need to cover narratively important events, however, and shouldn't walk through unimportant minutiae or the daily routines of the characters that don't affect the progression of the plot.

Sequence & Turn

Sequence and turn are not measurements of narrative time, but rather refer to time increments used in the conflict system. They are mentioned here only because some abilities and effects use these increments for duration. Each is described in much greater detail in the relevant sections below. For now, know that a conflict is a scene that is made up of one or more sequences, and a sequence is made up of several turns. When required to calculate the use of these time increments outside of conflict, treat a sequence as about one minute and a turn as about three to five seconds. This abstraction is useful during play, but the length of sequences and turns in a true conflict will vary widely.

THE CORE MECHANIC: TEST RESOLUTION

As a story is told, characters will want to affect the events unfolding around them. The test resolution system determines if a character succeeds or fails at her undertakings. Use this system as much as it adds to the drama of the game. Routine tasks performed while not under pressure or without consequences for failure should never be tested. Save test resolution rules for conflicts, dramatic situations, and narratively significant tasks whose success or failure impact the story.

CARDS

Running the game requires there be a certain element of unpredictability to represent the vagaries of circumstance and the unknowable influence of the Clockwork, and so randomly drawn cards are used to simulate these factors. The Clockwork Roleplaying Game exclusively uses Clockwork Cards, a specially created deck of 100 unique cards. All players will draw from a single deck to resolve trait tests, determine action order, and to provide many other random elements within the game (see *Handling the Deck*, p. 276). Each Clockwork Card will have the following information:

- **Card Value:** a large print, positive or negative number between +5 and -5. This is used to resolve tests and to determine initiative in conflict.
- **Card Number:** a unique number between 1 and 100 which is used to break ties and provide percentages.
- **Condition:** This is a special circumstance that can be placed on an opponent when an attack achieves a remarkable success (DoS 4+). For ease of reference, the mechanical effect of each condition is summarized at the bottom of the card. The full rules for each condition are given under *Condition Descriptions*, p. 97.

Card Value
Used for initiative
and added to trait tests

Card Number
Used to break ties and to produce
a number from 1–100 for
percentrage tests

Condition Name
The Condition this
card can produce

Condition Text
A description of the
Conditions effects
within the game

Outmaneuvered

Opponents receive a
+1 to all trait tests made
against an
Outmaneuvered target.

TRAITS AND VARIABLE TRAITS

The abilities and properties of objects and people within the game are defined by various traits. Each trait is measured in ranks, generally on a scale from zero (0) to five (5), with zero representing the lowest value and five representing the highest. Aptitudes and skills are traits that define a character's raw and trained capabilities. Potential is a set of three traits that define how much a character aligns to her divinely intended role (*Purpose*), how much she exerts her will to choose her own fate (*Ether*), and how much she is tainted by the insidious influence of the Pontus (*Corruption*). Affinities are traits chosen by the player to represent her character's deepest loyalties and affections, while Reputations are traits chosen by the player to describe how other people in the Clockwork regard her character. Guard and Defense are derived traits used in conflict situations. *Class* and *Means* are status traits that define a character's wealth and social standing respectively.

Some of these are special traits called variable traits, which are pliable and may have their temporary rank value increased or decreased by circumstance or environmental factors. Variable traits are listed on the character sheet with a circle to record their fixed rank and five boxes to record their temporary rank. The fixed rank represents the normal rank of the trait, while the temporary rank represents the current modified rank value of the trait. When a variable trait must be used in a test, use its temporary rank.

ACTIONS & TRAIT TESTS

A narratively significant undertaking is referred to as an action, and whenever the rules or Narrator determine that a character is undertaking such a task, a trait test must occur. To perform a trait test, a character will first add together the value of the two traits most relevant to the situation or challenge. This is almost always an aptitude and a skill. A Difficulty value representing the complexity of the attempted task is subtracted from this sum. Lastly, a card is drawn and its value is added. The total result is the Degree of Success (DoS), a measure of how well the attempt was made. Some cards have negative values that lower the total when added, and may even drop the sum below zero. A negative DoS means that the attempt was not successful, and the lower the negative number the more poorly the attempt was performed.

Trait + Trait – Difficulty + Card Value = Degree of Success

For example, Alix says that her character, Penelope, is trying to climb over a fence. The Narrator decides that this calls for a combination of the traits *Grace* and *Athletics*, and has a Difficulty of 2. Penelope has *Grace* 3 and *Athletics* 2, and Alix draws a card with a value of –1. The math looks like this:

Grace (3) + *Athletics* (2) – Difficulty (2) + Card Value (–1) = DoS 2

Success! Penelope is able to jump over the fence and continue on her way.

Making Trait Combinations

Trait tests require a player to create a trait combination. The skill and special ability descriptions provided throughout this book provide examples of which combinations are used for many tasks (skill descriptions begin on p. 138). The Narrator can also determine which traits to use based on the situation at hand and has the final say to determine all trait combinations not explicitly detailed in the rules.

There are some instances when an action may allow for several possible trait combinations: a character attempting to strike an opponent with a sword may use *Grace + Fencing* or *Grace + Melee*. When more than one combination is available, the player may choose which she wishes to use. The Narrator should describe the action accordingly, including any ramifications for using socially inappropriate tactics (e.g. using *Melee* in a formal duel would be a faux pas).

Sometimes, players will want their characters to do something that the rules don't specifically address. This sort of "outside of the box" thinking is encouraged by the system. In these situations, the player and Narrator cooperatively decide on a suitable trait combination for the desired action. An attempt to pilot an airship would usually use a *Grace + Engineering* combination as defined in the *Engineering* skill. However, if the character wanted to muck up the controls and render them unusable, perhaps *Reason + Engineering* would be more suitable.

Difficulty

The Difficulty of an action is measured on a scale of zero to ten and represents how hard a task is to successfully complete. The target of an action usually determines its Difficulty:

- **Situation**: When a trait test has no specific target, but is made against a circumstance or situation, the Difficulty of the test is assigned by the Narrator. Use the *Situational Difficulties* table as a guide.
- **Object**: When a trait test targets an inanimate object, the Difficulty for the test is based on the traits of that object. The Narrator will decide which of the object's traits is most relevant

SITUATIONAL DIFFICULTIES

Task Type	Difficulty
Simple Task: any task that normally wouldn't require a test, but is being performed in a circumstance where failure would create dramatic effects.	0
Routine Task: the kind of task that would be simple for a trained individual, but an untrained person may find difficult.	1–2
Demanding Task: a task that requires the focused attention of a trained individual. Most professional work falls into this range.	3–4
Challenging Task: a task that forces most trained individuals to push the normal limits of their ability.	5–6
Daunting Task: an undertaking that takes everything the character has, and is often beyond the reach of all but the most gifted individuals.	7–8
Incredible Task: an attempt to push the very limits of mortal ability.	9–10
Impossible Task: In almost all circumstances, any task with a Difficulty higher than ten is impossible and may not even be attempted. Players wishing to take on such tasks are encouraged to find ways to reduce the Difficulty.	11+

to the test. A door's Structure trait may be used in a test to break it down. A lock's Complexity may be used in a test to pick it.

- **Character:** When a trait test targets another character the Difficulty for the test is determined by the traits of the character being targeted. The Difficulty will normally equal the total of an applicable aptitude + skill. Commonly used aptitude and skill combinations are recorded on the character sheet as social Defense and physical Defense scores, and are discussed in more detail in the *Conflict* section (p. 73). In very rare cases, Narrator characters may have Defenses of higher than ten, but characters may still attempt to attack them.

Degree of Success (DoS)

More dramatic effects within the game are attained by meeting certain thresholds of success or failure. The players and Narrator should describe the result of actions according to their Degree of Success, with higher degrees being more elaborate or impressive and lower degrees being more meager or uninspiring. Likewise, a particularly severe failure should be disastrous or comical.

PASSIVE TRAIT TESTS

In narrative play, passive tests can quickly resolve whether a character can be successful at routine tasks that have only marginal impact on the game. Passive tests are made without drawing a card and allow accomplished characters to succeed at simple undertakings without wasting time at the gaming table.

To perform a passive trait test, simply add the character's trait combination together, subtract the Difficulty, and the result is the DoS for that test. If it is positive, the character succeeds. If it is zero or below, the character fails. If a character would fail a passive test, they normally have the option to attempt the test actively instead, which allows them to draw a card as normal.

Some abilities allow a character to make passive tests in conflict. In these instances, passive tests are taken as maneuvers rather than actions, since they do not require a card to be drawn. This allows a character to accomplish more in a single turn (see *The Turn*, p. 77). For example, the *Riding* skill allows a character to make a passive trait test to control her steed. This would allow a character to take a maneuver to manage her horse and take an action to attack in the same turn.

FATE AND DOOM CARDS

Sometimes the gears of the Clockwork align to guarantee or prevent a particular action. It is impossible to know why this occurs: the Clockwork responds to the web of how all things interrelate, rarely focusing on the individual. The subtleties of the Clockwork can seem like a fickle thing, as it seems to prefer the outcomes an action will put into motion, rather than an action itself. Whatever the reason, some things are fated to occur, while others are doomed to fail.

The play deck contains two special cards to represent these occurrences: the Fate card and the Doom card. When a character draws the Fate card, as long as her action is possible, it cannot fail. The Fate card has a value of +5, but the final DoS for a fated action can never drop below 1 and any values or penalties that would reduce the DoS below 1 are ignored. Actions with a Difficulty higher than ten are impossible and the Fate card will not allow them to succeed, it simply prevents any harm befalling the character in the attempt.

FATE, DOOM, & POTENTIAL

Whenever the Fate or Doom cards are drawn and played, no further effects that manipulate cards can be triggered, and no potential can be spent to alter the results or prevent those cards from being played. The Fate and Doom cards represent fixed points in the unfolding of the Clockwork and cannot be resisted in any way.

NARRATING DEGREES OF SUCCESS

DoS	Effect
+8	*Extraordinary Success:* A display of excellence that will be spoken of for some time. At the end of the evening, a slightly drunk wedding guest begins loudly insulting everyone, but does it with such wit and aplomb that the room is taken with laughter. A duelist takes careful aim and places his shot straight through his opponent's chest, gravely wounding him and dropping him with a single shot.
+4	*Remarkable Success:* A good display of skill with a meaningful effect. The groom makes a spontaneous declaration of his love for his new spouse that moves her to tears, and leaves other guests commenting on his sincerity and obvious devotion. One duelist shoots the gun from his opponent's grip and calmly asks him if he'd prefer to concede.
+1	*Success:* A meager victory, successful but not noteworthy. A gentleman attempts to persuade his wife to leave the reception, and she assents. A duelist aims and shoots, wounding his target.
0	*Marginal Success:* The result is not a complete failure, but more action is necessary to complete the action. A young cousin attempts to join in on political conversation with some older, well-connected relatives and only barely manages to keep up, but can't make any meaningful contributions to the discussion. The shooter is able to empty the misfired round from her revolver chamber, but still needs to clear the barrel before being able to shoot again.*
-1	*Failure:* The attempt fails, but there is neither anything redeeming nor embarrassing about the attempt. During dancing, a couple attempts to join in a complicated waltz, but can't quite keep up and must retire from the floor. A duelist takes proper aim and shoots, but fails to hit his foe.
-4	*Remarkable Failure:* The attempt fails badly, perhaps embarrassingly so. When proposing a toast to the bride and groom, Uncle Abernathy's off-color comment about the bride and groom "not having to sneak off to the library together at night anymore" comes off as scandalous rather than as just a tasteless joke. A duelist's pistol misfires, making it useless and leaving him impotent against his opponent.
-8	*Extraordinary Failure:* The failure is catastrophic or humiliating. A best man stands to deliver a toast, but trips, falls onto the head table, and spills food and drink across the wedding party. A duelist shoots himself in the foot.

* In situations where an action must either succeed or fail with no room for narrative middleground, a marginal success (DoS 0) will fail against a target that is actively resisting (treat as a DoS –1) and succeed against a target that is not (treat as a DoS 1). In conflict, an opponent is considered to be actively resisting if she reacts, and not resisting if she does not or cannot do so. Inanimate objects, such as doors or locks, are never considered to be actively resisting.

If a character draws the Doom card, she cannot succeed. The Doom card has a value of –5, but the DoS for a doomed action can never be increased above –1 and any values or bonuses that would increase the DoS above –1 are ignored.

Additionally, whenever the Doom card is played a Pontus event may occur. The severity and nature of a Pontus event triggered in this way depends upon the *Corruption* of the characters and the stability of the environment. Pontus events are discussed in detail in *Chapter 8: Narrating the Story*.

If ever any ability or effect grants the option to use one of several drawn cards and the Fate card or Doom card is among them, the player must choose it. It is the will of the Clockwork. If it happens that a character must choose one card from several, and both the Fate and Doom cards are present, resolve both cards: use the Fate card to resolve the test, and the Doom card to simultaneously trigger a Pontus event.

POTENTIAL

The Great Clockmaker has an intended role for every individual in the Clockwork, but He has also blessed them with free will. For humanity, there is a constant pull between the divine call to embrace our intended place and the divinely granted freedom to choose our own fate. Those who actively pursue their role in the Clockwork will benefit from its support and protection. Those who actively embrace their free will find ways to create and seize opportunities to move according to their own desires. The balance of these two impulses is called a character's potential, and it is measured by two traits: *Purpose* and *Ether*.

These are variable traits and a character may choose to spend points of *Purpose* and *Ether*, lowering their temporary rank by one each time this is done. Doing this can achieve a variety of effects within the game.

A character's potential can also be tainted by grievous sin, causing her to gain ranks in a trait called *Corruption*. Points of *Corruption* cannot be spent; it simply sits within a character, rotting her soul.

Ether

The extent to which someone chooses to step outside the Maker's role for them within the order of the Clockwork is represented by her ranks in Ether. *Ether* can be spent to stretch chance and circumstance to bring about a different result than what was intended. Anytime a card is drawn by a character, she may spend a point of *Ether* to draw a new card to replace it. Likewise, anytime an opponent draws a card to attack or otherwise act against a character, that character may spend a point of *Ether* to have that card redrawn. The new card is used in place of the old card, and only a single card may be redrawn for each point of *Ether* spent. Outside of conflict, a character can spend *Ether* multiple times, redrawing one new card each time. During conflict, a character can only spend a single point of potential each round, and so cannot use *Ether* to redraw more than once.

Purpose

Purpose is an abstracted measurement of the bond a character has to her intended role in the Clockwork. *Purpose* can thus be spent to prevent outcomes that would thwart a character's efforts to fulfill her role. Any time a character would suffer from an attack outcome (Wound, subdual, conviction, or persuasion) or a condition, she may spend one point of *Purpose* to prevent that outcome or condition from being placed on her. The outcome or condition simply does not occur and produces no effect. Only a single outcome or condition may be prevented for each point of *Purpose* spent. Any other effects of the instigating action will still occur.

Purpose also represents the way the Clockwork actively intercedes, not just to protect, but also to aid a character in fulfilling her role in the Clockwork. To represent this, a character may spend a point of *Purpose* to take slightly more control over the narrative in order to cause one helpful and plausible phenomenon to occur. This event must serve the will of the Clockwork and thus cannot produce a situation that would aid the Pontus or cause a character to take *Corruption*. Ultimately, the Narrator decides what changes are allowed, and can disallow any that are innately chaotic, implausible, or that undermine the larger story. Rain beginning to fall is usually quite plausible (especially in England), while snow falling in the middle of August is not. A gentleman having left his sword cane in a cloakroom for a character to grab is plausible, while a loaded pistol lying undisturbed in the middle of Abbey Road is not. In general, anything rational and non-chaotic can occur when a point of *Purpose* is spent. Several examples of how this may play out in your game are provided below.

- **Acquaintances**: The character may establish a casual acquaintance with any character whom she has plausibly met in the past. This acquaintanceship includes minor familiarity with each other, including the character's Reputation, but does not include any owed debts or favors.

  "Rupert, good to see you chap. I was just telling these people about my renown in the regiment for that action in Egypt, but they've never heard of it! Surely you can set them straight."
- **Chance Encounters**: The character runs into the right person at the right time. The timing must be plausible, meaning the event must be something that was already planned by the individuals in question. It is not plausible for police to pick just the right moment to raid a rookery unless they already had plans to do so in place, but it is plausible for a pair of police to show up anytime along their scheduled route.

  "Lady Dalton, I had hoped to see you here! I have someone you just have to meet…"
- **Environmental Changes**: The character may narrate changes to the environment, creating climate effects that take place at the end of the current turn.

  "And then the rain began to fall at just the right moment, otherwise that house would have burnt to the ground."
- **Revising History**: The character may rewrite a small part of a recent occurrence. The rewrite must occur in a plausible fashion sometime in the current installment of the story and not have any ramifications on anything that has been narrated since that time.

  "I know I didn't mention it, but I packed my pistol in my satchel."
- **Scenery Specifications**: A character may describe the scenery of the current scene in any plausible way that does not contradict those descriptions already made. This can include the presence of objects that could reasonably be found in that location.

  "The rope that holds the chandelier to the ceiling has to be tied to the wall somewhere… how about right here? I cut it."

- **Special knowledge**: So long as the character's education makes it plausible, the character may declare knowledge of a unique fact not normally covered by his ability selection. This represents a very limited focus of information, not knowledge of a broad topic or ranks in a particular skill. These declarations become a part of the character's backstory and must remain consistent as the story progresses.

  "I know most academics would be useless in this situation, but I happened to have written my anthropological thesis on the Hungarian Curse of Turan."

Regaining Spent Purpose and Ether

At the beginning of each installment, every character regains one temporary rank of potential, choosing either *Purpose* or *Ether*. Pureblood characters will, in addition, automatically regain one point of *Purpose* due to their bloodline's *Driven* blessing. If a character is already at her fixed rank maximum for *Purpose* and *Ether*, then no potential is regained.

Characters can also regain potential during gameplay when they behave in specific ways. Once per installment, when a character takes a significant and selfless action that bolsters the orderly nature of the Clockwork, or her role within it, she may immediately regain a single point of *Purpose*. Likewise, once per installment, when a character takes a significant and selfless action that introduces or supports change in the Clockwork, she immediately regains a single point of *Ether*. The Narrator alone determines what actions qualify for this award.

Corruption

Corruption measures how far a character has fallen from grace. There are some acts so abhorrent to the Clockmaker that any involvement with them stains the soul and deforms the Clockwork enough that the Pontus leaks in:

- Involvement in the unnatural death of any pureblood, beastfolk, changeling, or angel
- Involvement or complicity in an act of degradation such as slavery or torture, and
- The violation of solemn vows.
-

Whenever a character participates in or allows one of those events to occur because of their own action, inaction, or shortcomings, they immediately gain a point of *Corruption*. If a character's *Corruption* is already at five ranks and she is required to take more, instead of taking *Corruption* she immediately triggers a Pontus event.

Unlike other types of potential, *Corruption* has no use. In fact, it is dangerous. Pontus events are often made more severe when triggered by characters with *Corruption*. A character can only rid herself of *Corruption* by performing sincere and meaningful acts of contrition, receiving absolution from the Church, direct exposure to the purity of the Clockwork, or by triggering a Pontus event. *Corruption* is discussed in detail on p. 280.

CONFLICT

Much of your story in the Clockwork will be told in a narrative fashion. The players and Narrator engage in cooperative storytelling, where the players control and speak for their characters and the Narrator controls everything else in the game. While this is typically very conversational, there will come times when characters don't want to play nice anymore. When the friendly dialogue ends and there comes a need for coercion or combat, a conflict will begin.

While conflict may be primarily physical or social, these conflict types frequently interrelate and overlap. A physical conflict fought with fists, blades, and guns will often include social attacks such as distractions, intimidations, and feints. A social conflict of negotiation or trickery can sometimes come to blows. Characters exploring the Clockwork often require skill in both the physical and social realms of conflict in order to stay alive and achieve their goals.

CONFLICT SPECIFIC TRAITS

There are four traits that are specifically calculated for and only used during conflict: Guard, Disposition, Esteem, and Morale. Guard and Morale are used in physical conflicts; Disposition and Esteem, in social conflicts. When a conflict of a particular type begins, each player should calculate the traits that it will require for her character.

GUARD

Guard = ½ Focus; +1 for weapon

Guard is the ability of a defender to correctly identify and respond to attacks without overextending, losing her balance, or otherwise creating gaps in her defensive posture. The higher a character's Guard trait, the more observant she is while in combat, allowing her to anticipate attacks and knock them aside without significantly diminishing her protective stance. When an opponent successfully attacks a defender, she is able to throw her off balance and reduce her ability to protect herself from further attacks. In a fight, the slow dismantling of Guard is how an attacker manipulates the motion of a defender to open up her defenses and create a hole through which to strike a penetrating blow. Each strike in this series is necessary to win the fight, but only the last one penetrates the Guard and achieves its desired outcome.

At the beginning of a physical conflict, each character begins with a Guard equal to ½ her *Focus* aptitude rounded down. Characters armed with a close combat weapon get an additional +1 bonus to Guard. If a character receiving this weapon bonus is disarmed the bonus is immediately lost. A character's Guard is "up" when she has at least one point of Guard. It is lowered by one for each successful attack or feint made against her. When a character has no remaining Guard, her Guard is "down", and she is subject to penetrating attacks.

Any weapon solid enough to deflect a blow can be used as a parrying weapon, even a ranged weapon such as a rifle. However, a ranged weapon cannot be used simultaneously to grant a bonus to Guard and to attack. It takes one maneuver to alter one's grip on a ranged weapon so that it can be used as parrying weapon, and another maneuver to reorient one's grip so that it can be used for ranged attacks.

Some attacks, such as those using firearms, will ignore the character's Guard. No warrior can block bullets. A character cannot use Guard to protect against any attack of which she is unaware or by which she is surprised.

DISPOSITION

Disposition = Hostile, Guarded, Indifferent, Agreeable, or Favorable

Disposition is the spectrum of emotion covering how a character feels about a topic of discussion or course of action. It will range on a scale of five steps: *Hostile, Guarded, Indifferent, Agreeable,* or *Favorable*. At the beginning of a social conflict, each character chooses their own Disposition toward the relevant topic for the argument. It may be anywhere on the scale the character chooses, but a *Hostile* Disposition may have social consequences.

- **Hostile** indicates a character that refuses to listen to or engage with an argument in any way. In most circumstances, being openly *Hostile* is a social faux pas.
- **Guarded** indicates a character that is mistrustful and will challenge the position, but is willing to listen and may be persuaded with strong arguments.
- **Indifferent** indicates a character that has no strong feelings or conviction to either agree with or oppose the position being argued.

- **Agreeable** indicates a character with sympathy and growing agreement that could come around to the position with some mild persuasion.
- **Favorable** indicates a character who broadly agrees with the position and only needs a bit more certitude to determine how best to put the position into practice.

In social conflict, a character's Disposition is moved one step in the direction of the attacker's choice for each successful social attack made against her. Once her Disposition is *Favorable* toward a line of argument, the next successful attack will penetrate her defenses and create a social outcome (usually a conviction or persuasion, see *Placing Social Outcomes*, p. 90).

ESTEEM

Esteem = Status Trait – Tenor +/– ½ relevant Reputations' rank

Esteem represents how well a character is viewed by others in her current social surroundings, and represents the Disposition of the current social gathering toward her. It is usually calculated the first time it is needed in a scene and persists as long as the social event continues. If a chapter contains multiple linked social scenes as part of the same event, Esteem is not recalculated for each conflict. It will only be recalculated when a new gathering or chapter begins.

Before calculating Esteem, the Narrator must first declare the Tenor for the gathering. Tenor determines what type of status is important to those present and how they will judge others in attendance. Tenor is declared as an assigned rank of either *Means* or *Class*. The status trait used is whichever is most important to those gathered, and the rank will be based on the average of the invited guests (servants and uninvited attendees are not considered when determining Tenor). For example, a formal ball at the manor home of the Earl of Cranbrook might have a Tenor of *Class 4*, as the average attendee belongs to a noble house, and the gathering cares more about family lineage than money. A Friday night at the local pub might have a Tenor of *Means 1*, because the gathering is mostly factory workers of a similar economic station. When choosing which trait to use for Tenor, remember that most lower class gatherings tend to care more about *Means*, while higher class gatherings tend to care more about *Class*.

Once the Tenor of the gathering is chosen, the character's Esteem is determined by how far above or below that Tenor her own relevant status trait falls. A character's Esteem will always start at *Indifferent*. If her status trait exceeds that of the Tenor for the gathering, her Esteem increases by the difference. For example, if the Tenor for a gathering was *Class 2* and a character had a *Class 3*, her Esteem would raise one step from *Indifferent* to *Agreeable*. Likewise, if her status trait is below the Tenor of the gathering, her Esteem lowers by the difference. For example, if the Tenor for a gathering was *Means 2* and a character in attendance had a *Means 0*, that character's Esteem would drop two steps from *Indifferent* to *Hostile*.

Two of a character's Reputations will also affect Esteem: the most advantageous and the most hindering (see *Reputations*, p. 170). Her Esteem will increase by ½ the rank of her most highly regarded Reputation, rounded down. Likewise, her Esteem will be lowered by ½ the rank of her most detested Reputation (if any), rounded down. Only the most advantageous and most disadvantageous Reputations are used in this way. Also, keep in mind that a Reputation that is advantageous in one situation may be disadvantageous in another. For example, if a character with the rank 3 Reputation "*Honorable soldier in Her Majesty's service*" attended a military gathering, his Esteem would raise one step. However, if that same character found himself surrounded by mercenaries or in a den of thieves, his Reputation would lower his Esteem by one step.

The final result is marked on the character's character sheet with a token. It may be raised or lowered throughout the encounter depending on the character's actions. Altering Esteem values is discussed in depth below under *Intrigues*, p. 92.

MORALE

Morale is a trait that measures how confident characters are when entering a conflict and determines how likely they are to keep fighting when things get rough. To track this, Morale is calculated as a character's Disposition towards fleeing or surrender.

Players normally choose their own characters' starting Morale at the beginning of a conflict, and may set it to whatever they wish unless a special circumstance dictates their Morale.

An individual or unit of allies or antagonists will have a Morale based on their Threat, a trait that measures their power and competency in conflict (see *Threat*, p. 293). Each will start with a base Morale of being *Favorable*, which is then shifted one step towards *Hostile* per rank of their Threat. This means that all Threat 1 characters will have a starting Morale of *Agreeable*; all Threat 2 characters, a Morale of *Indifferent*; all Threat 3 characters, a Morale of *Guarded*; and any character with Threat 4 or higher will begin a conflict with a Morale of *Hostile*.

During a conflict, several things will weaken a character's Morale (moving it toward *Favorable*). Whenever a character suffers a Wound or witnesses an allied character flee, surrender, or become *Incapacitated*, the Morale of that character will weaken by one step. An opponent can also directly attack Morale. Usually this is done with a *Presence + Command* attack made to intimidate (see *Changing Disposition*, p. 90). If this is successful, the character's Morale would weaken by one step. Once a character's Morale is pushed to *Favorable*, the next time it would be lowered will instead cause them to flee or surrender.

Characters can also make *Presence + Command* attacks to rally their side: if successful, every allied character will strengthen their Morale and shift their Disposition one step towards *Hostile*.

ZONE OF CONTROL

When in conflict, a character's movement and positioning is governed by the abstract concept of a zone of control. A character's zone of control is a bubble that extends approximately ten feet around her in all directions. That space can easily be covered in a few steps, falls well within the effective reach of most skilled hand-to-hand combatants, and characters within that area can easily be spoken to. Characters are presumed to be aware of and able to interact with other characters and objects within their zone of control.

A zone of control can also be defined by the Narrator based on a physical structure or location. Zones of control may be smaller parts of a larger space that flow into each other—such as an alehouse with one zone of control at the bar and a second zone at the tables—or distinct areas that are accessible from one another but separate—such as a family dining room that is one zone of control and an adjacent kitchen that is another. Whenever conflict begins, the Narrator should take a moment to describe the scene and establish a clear sense of placement for player and Narrator characters, as well as any key features of the environment that may come into play. The Narrator should specify whether the scene is large and open enough that zones of control are centered on characters, or defined by the building or structures of the scene. Knowing who and what is in a given zone of control is very important for understanding where characters can move and with whom they can engage in conflict.

THE INITIATIVE SEQUENCE

Once the relevant conflict traits (Guard & Morale, or Disposition & Esteem) have been calculated and recorded, the initiative sequence may begin. Each initiative sequence will determine the order and number of turns each character receives during that sequence.

Dealing Initiative Cards

An initiative sequence begins by dealing cards to each participating player character and the Narrator. These will serve as their initiative cards for the sequence. Usually, players are each dealt four cards, then discard one of their choice and retain three cards. Some special abilities or circumstances may alter the number of cards dealt or retained, but a player character may never retain more than three cards. For example, Wounded player characters are dealt and retain one fewer card for each Wound suffered (i.e. a character with one Wound would be dealt three cards and retain two, see *Placing Physical Outcomes*, p. 84).

Players show their retained cards face-up on the table next to their character sheets. These are the player character's initiative cards—keep them separate from all other cards that come into play. Player initiative cards are always placed face-up so all players can see them, as this aids the group in tactical decisionmaking and helps represent the awareness the characters have of one another during conflict.

Neither the Fate card nor the Doom card can be discarded if they are dealt as initiative cards. The Fate card is treated as the highest card value in the deck and counts as two cards when seizing initiative (see below). The Doom card is considered the lowest card in the deck. A player may use the Doom card to take a turn normally, but doing so will instigate a Pontus event (see *Triggering Pontus Events*, p. 281).

Using Initiative Cards

After initiative cards are dealt and retained, the character with the highest showing initiative card value may choose to become the acting character. If that character passes, the character with the next-highest card value may choose to be the acting character, and so on. If two players have cards with the same value, the card numbers (the numerals in the upper right corner of each card) decide the play order—the highest card number has the initiative. Once the acting character is chosen, she will take a turn (see *The Turn*, opposite page).

If the activities declared for a turn will not affect another character, the acting player simply flips her highest initiative card face-down and attempts those actions. However, if her endeavors do affect at least one other character, the affected characters may immediately react to her. This elicits an exchange (see *The Exchange*, p. 79). Each reacting character must flip over *any* one of their unused initiative cards—it does not have to be the highest—to participate in the exchange. Once all actions within the exchange are resolved, the next acting character is chosen as described above.

The option to be the next acting character is always given first to the character with the highest showing initiative card value and then in descending order. Thus, it is first available to a player with the Fate card, then to those with card values of +5, +4, +3, and so on. Players do not need to use all of their initiative cards; they may simply pass if they do not wish to act. Characters passing on a possible turn do not flip over an initiative card; this allows them to use their cards later in the sequence when they desire to act.

The initiative sequence will continue in this manner until all players and the Narrator have used all of their available initiative cards, or until all participants decline to act.

Seizing Initiative

At any time during an initiative sequence, any character may flip over two unused initiative cards, or the Fate card by itself, to seize the initiative. The Doom card may not be used for this purpose. Seizing initiative allows a character to interrupt the normal flow of the initiative sequence and take a turn. The current turn is paused regardless of what is being done, and the interrupting player immediately takes a full turn. If multiple characters attempt to seize the initiative at the same time, the interrupt turns are resolved in order of the highest value initiative cards that were flipped. When the interrupt turn is resolved, the initiative sequence resumes as normal.

Surprise Sequences

In situations where the Narrator determines that one side of a fight is caught completely unawares, a surprise sequence will take place. All aware attackers may draw and keep a single initiative card and play out an initiative sequence where only they may act. During this surprise sequence, unaware combatants are not dealt cards and their Guard remains down until the end of the surprise sequence. After all aware combatants take their turn, the surprise sequence is over and the first full initiative sequence begins with initiative cards being dealt normally. Surprise sequences should only be used with ambushes (as created with the *Tactics* skill, p. 153) or in extraordinarily rare and serendipitous moments.

ALLIES AND ANTAGONISTS IN THE INITIATIVE SEQUENCE

The Narrator deals initiative cards to herself a bit differently because she likely controls several characters at once. The Narrator receives a number of initiative cards equal to the total Threat rank of all antagonists participating in the conflict. These cards comprise a single hand for the Narrator, and any card may be used for any antagonist. The Narrator is not required to display her cards face-up on the table as players do, and will normally keep them concealed from the view of the players.

If the Narrator is controlling both antagonists and allies, the allies' initiative cards are dealt as a second hand of initiative cards equal in number to their total Threat. These cards are kept and played separately from the antagonists' cards. Allies' initiative cards should be dealt face up on the table in the same manner as player character initiative cards so the players can plan and coordinate with them effectively. Allies use the cards from their own hand and otherwise follow the same rules as antagonists.

As each of the Narrator characters take a turn, spent initiative cards are placed face-down upon the table in a distinct stack for that character. This allows the Narrator to keep track of how many times each Narrator character has taken a turn. No Narrator character may take more turns in a single sequence than her rank of Threat.

When a Narrator character is Wounded, she loses one of her initiative cards. So long as the character's stack of used initiative cards does not already contain a number of cards equal to her Threat, the Narrator must immediately flip one unused initiative card and place it on the stack for that character. At the beginning of the next sequence, the number of initiative cards dealt to the ally and antagonist hands is reduced by one for each Wound a character of that type has sustained. When an individual Narrator character has Wounds equal to or exceeding its Threat, that character is *Incapacitated* or killed. Rational antagonists will often surrender or flee before this occurs, especially if their Morale is attacked.

Further rules for using Narrator characters are discussed in *Chapter 9: Allies & Antagonists*.

INITIATIVE SEQUENCE

Deal 4 initiative cards to each player (abilities may provide more). Players discard down to three initiative cards.
Deal a hand of initiative cards to the Narrator, one card for each rank of antagonist Threat.
If there are allies, deal a separate hand to the Narrator, one initiative card for each rank of ally Threat.
During play, Narrators may use any card from a hand to play for any character related to that hand.

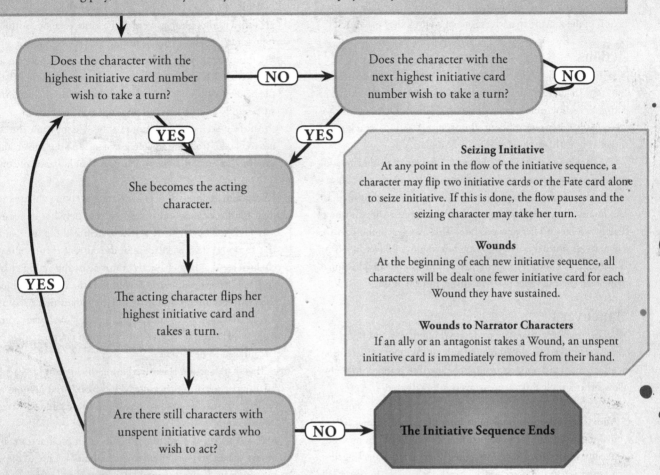

Does the character with the highest initiative card number wish to take a turn? — NO → **Does the character with the next highest initiative card number wish to take a turn?** — NO

YES / YES

She becomes the acting character.

The acting character flips her highest initiative card and takes a turn.

Are there still characters with unspent initiative cards who wish to act? — YES / NO → **The Initiative Sequence Ends**

Seizing Initiative
At any point in the flow of the initiative sequence, a character may flip two initiative cards or the Fate card alone to seize initiative. If this is done, the flow pauses and the seizing character may take her turn.

Wounds
At the beginning of each new initiative sequence, all characters will be dealt one fewer initiative card for each Wound they have sustained.

Wounds to Narrator Characters
If an ally or an antagonist takes a Wound, an unspent initiative card is immediately removed from their hand.

STRIKING AT THE RIGHT MOMENT

By allowing any card to be used for reactions or to seize the initiative, players always have options to join the action as long as they have unused initiative cards. Remembering these options is very important for everyone at the table—both players and Narrators alike—as it is a key feature that keeps conflict in *Clockwork: Dominion* fluid and exciting.

As you become more familiar with conflict over your first few sessions, you will discover many more strategic and tactical options for how and when to use initiative cards. There are times when seizing the initiative aggressively for a quick, decisive strike will win the day, and others where it will be best to conserve your initiative cards while your opponents overextend and leave themselves open to a deadly counterattack. Skills, assets, and other game mechanics can also be leveraged to give you even more options and control over the initiative sequence.

THE TURN

Before a character may take a turn, the player must flip over an unused initiative card. For the acting character, this must be her highest valued initiative card. Reacting characters who wish to take a turn during an exchange must flip an unused initiative card of her choice (usually the lowest they have). During her turn, the acting character may move, maneuver, and act; a reacting character may only move and act.

Moves, maneuvers, and actions are taken at any time and in any order during her turn. However, narrators may require characters reacting to one another to resolve things in a particular order to maintain logical consistency or to clarify the particulars of an exchange.

Move

The character may move about ten feet. In open areas, this allows her to recenter her zone of control on her new location. If zones in the current conflict are defined by location, she may move to an adjacent zone. A character is automatically engaged with other characters in her zone of control. If any part of a move takes place while an opponent is in the moving character's zone of control, they may react.

Actions

Actions allow the character to perform any task that requires a trait test. In conflict, this usually means attacking an opponent or acting to secure some sort of advantage. The character may move freely within her zone of control during her action, attacking or interacting with anything within its boundaries.

A character may also trade her action to perform either an additional move or maneuver during her turn. If a character chooses to spend her action to take a move, she moves an additional 10 feet in any direction she chooses; her zone of control will immediately recenter on her new position. This may be combined with a character's normal move, allowing her to move 20 feet in a turn. If a character chooses to spend her action to take an additional maneuver, she may take two maneuvers instead of one.

Maneuvers

Maneuvers allow a character to do anything that would not necessitate a trait test, but would require at least a moment of attention or effort. Standard options are listed below. The Narrator may also allow other simple tasks as maneuvers at her discretion.

- **Aim:** This maneuver is taken to carefully aim a weapon before making an attack. It can be performed to eliminate an unaimed penalty when using ranged weapons, to prepare an attack against a target, or to more accurately attack a character in cover. All ranged weapons require a maneuver to *Aim* before an attack, otherwise they suffer a –2 penalty on the test. This includes all

firearms and weapons with a Reach of *Short Range* or *Long Range*. Thrown weapons do not need to be aimed. After an *Aim* maneuver is taken to remove the unaimed penalty with a ranged weapon, additional *Aim* maneuvers may be performed to reduce the penalties for firing at a target in cover (see *Cover and Aiming*, p. 82).

While *Aiming* at a target, a character may react to her target's turn as though they were in the same zone of control. This represents the ability of an aiming character to shoot a target the moment they move or attempt an action. So long as the attacker took a maneuver to *Aim* at her target on her last turn, the benefits of aiming will last until the aiming character fires, is successfully attacked, or can no longer see the target.

An *Aiming* character cannot raise her Guard while she continues to benefit from the advantages of an *Aim* maneuver, and she cannot *Aim* at all if an opponent is within her zone of control.

- **Elicit Aid:** Before she acts, a character taking this maneuver may ask one or more other characters to help her in her efforts. Any invited character that agrees to help will flip over an initiative card and then participate in the current turn as a reacting character. All aiding characters must assist the acting character and will make a trait test to accomplish the same goal, however the trait combination may be different than that used by the acting character. The Narrator has final say over what combinations are allowed to render aid in a given circumstance, but is encouraged to be flexible.

This shared action is resolved using the highest DoS achieved by any participating character. However, if the Doom card is drawn, it must be used to resolve the test and will trigger a Pontus event as usual.

If a reaction is made against the attempted action, it will always use a Difficulty equal to the highest Defense of those participating in the instigating action, regardless of who is specifically targeted. Characters assisting one another in this way are considered to use only a single avenue of attack (see discussion of *Physical Avenues of Attack*, p. 82 and *Social Avenues of Attack*, p. 88 and *Multiple Attackers in a Single Avenue of Attack*, p. 88).

- **Interact with the Environment:** Simple interactions—such as opening a door, flipping a switch, pushing a button, drawing or stowing a weapon, or dropping an object —can be accomplished as a maneuver.

- **Passive Trait Test:** Any task a character's abilities allow her to attempt with a passive trait test may be performed as a maneuver.

- **Sidestep:** Remove an avenue of attack from a character until your next action. This may remove an avenue of attack from one's own character by putting her back up against a wall or moving erratically, or it may remove an avenue of attack from a neighboring character by stepping into that character's zone of control and protecting her. If two characters take this maneuver concurrently, they fight back to back and remove an avenue of attack from each other. Remember that if a character reduces her avenues of attack to 0, she will remove her own ability to attack others (see *Physical Avenues of Attack*, p. 82).

- **Take Cover:** If cover is available within the character's zone of control she may take this maneuver to use it to protect herself. This does not remove an avenue of attack, but will grant the character the benefit of whatever type of cover is available (see *Cover and Aiming*, p. 82)
- **Attract:** Only used in social conflict, this maneuver ensures a single character is paying attention to the attracting character. Additional details on *Attract* are discussed on p. p. 88

THE EXCHANGE

An exchange occurs when one character's action directly affects a second character who chooses to react. If any portion of the acting character's turn (move, action, or maneuver) will take place while another character is within her zone of control, the nearby character may choose to react. Any action that directly affects an opponent outside her zone of control, such as targeting a character with a ranged attack, can elicit a reaction from the targeted opponent. Lastly, a character who is actively *Aiming* at a target may react to that target's turn as though the target was in her zone of control. If any characters allowed to react decide to do so, an exchange will begin.

At the beginning of an exchange, all participants will declare what they will do on their turn. If the instigating character has already declared her move, maneuver, or action, these may not be changed. Other participating characters will declare their movements and reactions in response to whatever instigated the exchange—usually to counter-attack or actively defend themselves. Remember that reacting characters do not take maneuvers unless they trade their action to do so.

Attack Priority

Attack Priority dictates the order turns are resolved within an exchange. The character with the most advantageous circumstances will go first, followed by the participating character with the next highest number of advantageous circumstances, and so on. If characters have equivalent numbers of advantageous circumstances, their turns are resolved simultaneously.

Depending on the type of conflict, there are several circumstances that are considered advantageous. In all conflicts, one advantageous circumstance is given to the acting character. In physical conflicts, an additional advantage is given to a character if the Reach category of her weapon is longer than that of her target (see *Reach*, p. 81); and a final advantage to any character who has

THE TURN

Does any portion of your move, maneuver or action take place within another character's zone of control? — **NO** → Does your action directly or indirectly target another character? — **NO** → **This turn does not elicit an exchange.**

Does any portion... — **YES** ↓

Does your action... — **YES** ↓

Does an affected character wish to react to your action? — **NO** → This turn does not elicit an exchange.

This turn does not elicit an exchange. → The acting character resolves her move, maneuver, and action and the turn ends.

Does an affected character wish to react to your action? — **YES** → **This turn elicits an exchange.**

This turn elicits an exchange. ↓

Does a reacting character have a higher Attack Priority? — **YES** → The reacting character with the highest Attack Priority resolves her move and action.

Does a reacting character have a higher Attack Priority? — **NO** ↓

The acting character resolves her move, maneuver, and action. → Any remaining reacting characters resolve their move and action in order of Attack Priority and the turn ends.

Attack Priority
Below are a list of advantageous situations that grant Attack Priority. The character with the most advantageous situations is considered to have the highest attack priority.

- Being the Acting Character
- Longer weapon Reach (physical only)
- Advantageous positioning (physical only)
- Each step of superior Esteem (social only)
- Being host or guest of honor (social only)
- Other factors as deemed appropriate by the Narrator

a tactical advantage such as higher ground, standing while their opponent is prone, or other such circumstance. In social conflict, an additional advantage is given to a character if her Esteem is higher than her target's (see *Esteem*, p. 74), and an extra advantage to any character who is the host or guest of honor at a given event.

Each character participating in the exchange will calculate her number of advantageous circumstances (1, 2, or 3). Resolve the characters' turns in order from most advantageous circumstances to the least. In the case of a tie for the number of advantageous circumstances, or if more than one character has zero advantageous circumstances, the turns are resolved simultaneously. The Narrator has final say over any questions regarding Attack Priority.

Subtle Actions

If the character targeted by an action is unaware that she is being acted upon, the action is considered subtle. Subtle actions do not elicit exchanges, and the targeted character may neither react nor protect herself with Guard. So long as a subtle action is not readily observable and does not create an immediately obvious outcome, it continues to go unnoticed. Physical attacks will always be seen for what they are after they have been made, regardless of whether or not they are successful. Other subtle actions that fail remain unnoticed unless the action suffers a remarkable failure or worse (DoS –4 or –8), in which case the action is seen for what it is.

ENDING AN INITIATIVE SEQUENCE

The initiative sequence ends when all initiative cards are flipped face-down or all participants with remaining face-up initiative cards choose not to become the acting character. If it ever happens that all remaining face-up initiative cards belong to a single player, that player may only take one turn before the sequence will end. The remaining cards have been lost to hesitation.

Temporary conditions inflicted during that sequence end (there are some exceptions to this listed under *Condition Descriptions*, p. 97). In a physical conflict, all characters will refresh a single point of Guard, up to their maximum calculated Guard. Then the deck is reshuffled and either new cards are dealt for the next initiative sequence, or the game returns to non-conflict play and a fresh draw deck is available.

In physical conflicts, sequences will continue until all characters in the scene are unwilling or unable to continue the fight. Social conflicts will only last a single initiative sequence (although the timing of this sequence may take as long as a chapter to complete). If the sequence ends before a character can persuade or convince her opponent of her goal, she is simply unable to do so. Changes in Disposition will remain; although if the players initiate social conflict in a subsequent chapter or scene, all parties may alter their Dispositions as they deem fit. The players and Narrator may interpret the changes in their character's Disposition at their own discretion, bearing in mind that being *Hostile* is almost always a faux-pas. Social conflicts will also end if a physical conflict arises from them.

PHYSICAL ATTACKS

A physical attack is any action made with the intent to Wound, subdue, or hamper an opponent in a physical conflict. Attacks are made like any other trait test, but the importance and variety of attacks merit additional related rules and discussion.

A physical attack is normally made with a combination of the *Grace* aptitude and one of the physical conflict skills (*Firearms, Fencing, Fisticuffs,* or *Melee*) made against a Difficulty equal to the opponent's most relevant Defense. Every attack must have a clear pathway to the target called an avenue of attack. Successful attacks reduce Guard, which is the opponent's ability to defend themselves. Particularly successful attacks will have additional effects. For example, a an attack that achieves a remarkable success (DoS 4+) will place a condition on an opponent, while an extraordinary hit (DoS 8+) will automatically bypass Guard. If an opponent's Guard is already down or the attack bypasses Guard, the attacker may place an outcome on the opponent. This will Wound or subdue an opponent or place a condition of the attacker's choice on her.

PHYSICAL WEAPONS

It's never wise to bring a knife to a gunfight. Needless to say, the weapon a combatant carries can make the difference between walking away from a skirmish or never walking again. In the Clockwork Roleplaying Game, weapons have several traits that reflect their use and effectiveness in conflict: Reach, Potency, Load, and weapon conditions.

Reach

A weapon's Reach is an abstraction of how far a weapon can reach toward a target: if a weapon can reach a target, it can be used to attack. Reach is measured in the following categories: *Touch, Close, Extended, Short Range,* and *Long Range.* Each category reaches further than the last.

- **Touch:** this weapon is made for close combat, but does not add any significant distance to a person's unarmed reach. As long as the attacker can freely move around her zone of control, she may use a *Touch* weapon to target any opponent within it.
  Examples: a dagger, brass knuckles
- **Close:** this weapon increases the unarmed reach of the attacker, but is still intended for close combat. Attackers can strike anything in their zone of control with *Close* weapons.
  Examples: a sword, a walking stick
- **Extended:** this weapon can strike at opponents up to fifteen feet away, allowing attacks against targets both within and adjacent to the wielder's zone of control.
  Examples: a rifle mounted bayonet, most thrown weapons
- **Short Range:** this weapon is made for ranged combat and can hit any visible target within about twenty-five feet. All *Short Range* weapons require a maneuver to *Aim* to avoid a –2 unaimed penalty (see *Cover and Aiming,* next page).
  Example: a revolver

- **Long Range:** this weapon is made for ranged combat and can shoot at any visible target. So long as the attacker can distinctly see the target, she can shoot it. Usually, this is about 250 feet in combat conditions, but many *Long Range* rifles can fire at targets up to 1000 yards away if using a scope to magnify the target and sight the shot. All *Long Range* weapons require a maneuver to *Aim* to avoid a –2 unaimed penalty (see *Cover and Aiming,* next page).
  Example: a rifle
- **Area of Effect:** The term 'area' may be added to any weapon's Reach value. Such a weapon does not target a single opponent, but rather everything within a diameter equal to the Reach. For example, a weapon with an *Extended* Reach area would be able to hit everyone within fifteen feet. Many area weapons are explosives or similar devices that may have the center of their effect be somewhere other than the attacker. If so, they are explained in the weapon's description.
  Examples: a grenade, explosive artillery

Physical Weapon Potency

Potency is an abstraction of the impact a weapon can have on an opponent. This includes its ability to punch through Armor and the extent of physical injury or strain it can inflict with a strike. An attack cannot cause a Wound unless the Potency rank of the weapon is greater than the Armor rank of the target. Also, in a situation where an attack can place a condition, such as with a remarkable success (DoS 4+), the weapon's Potency minus the target's Armor determines the number of cards drawn to choose the condition (see *Placing Physical Conditions,* p. 83). Physical attacks made without a weapon have Potency 1.

Load

Load is only listed for weapons that use ammunition. It measures how many shots may be fired before the weapon is empty. For weapons that shoot more than one projectile per attack, this value is abstracted to show how many turns the weapon may be fired before it is empty.

Physical Weapon Conditions

Many weapons have special conditions to which they always have access in addition to those drawn from the deck. So long as an attacker can draw at least a single card to determine the condition placed by an attack that achieves a remarkable success (DoS 4+), she may choose to apply her weapon's condition to her target rather than the conditions presented to her on the cards (see *Placing Physical Conditions,* p. 83). If a weapon lists multiple weapon conditions, only one may be chosen. If the opponent's Armor reduces her card flip to zero cards, then no condition may be placed. Weapon conditions are listed and described later in this chapter (see *Conditions,* p. 96).

PHYSICAL AVENUES OF ATTACK

A clear path from the attacker to the target is called an avenue of attack. Before a character can make the trait test for an attack, she must first establish that there is an open avenue through which the attack may take place. All attacks, close and ranged, require an open avenue of attack. If there is no open avenue, there simply isn't a way for the attacker to strike at her opponent.

In physical conflict, it is assumed that each individual defender has three available avenues of attack. There just isn't enough space around a character for more than three people to effectively see or strike at her. Any close combat attacker that moves into a character's zone of control will occupy one of these avenues. Ranged attackers who are not within the target's zone of control do not occupy an avenue of attack, and multiple ranged attackers can fire through a single open avenue of attack. Terrain and maneuvers may also occupy or eliminate avenues of attack by limiting the number of attackers who can engage a target. If a defender has no open avenues to her, she may not be directly attacked or attack others.

Mechanically, avenues of attack are conceptual placeholders that are either occupied or open. However, in the narrative of the story, characters are considered to be in constant motion throughout their zone of control. Thus, it can make more sense for Narrators to describe an avenue of attack as an opening that appears during the attacker's turn rather than a static slot through which a character may strike. This is especially true when narrating ranged attacks, where movement can allow a shot to suddenly open up.

Using Maneuvers with Avenues of Attack

Certain conflict maneuvers will change how avenues of attack can be used. It is possible for more than one attacker to share an avenue of attack through use of the *Elicit Aid* maneuver (p. 78). A character may also eliminate a single avenue of attack through use of the *Sidestep* maneuver (p. 78).

Blocking Terrain

Blocking terrain prevents line of sight to the target and automatically occupies an avenue of attack because it prevents any strike from that direction. Any terrain feature that makes it impossible for an attacker to engage or see an opponent will fill one of the opponent's avenues of attack. Unless a target is almost completely surrounded or enclosed, blocking terrain will not fill more than one avenue of attack.

Cover and Aiming

Cover does not occupy an avenue of attack to the target, but rather obscures the target in some way. This can be anything from intervening people, to smaller terrain features, or even darkness. Anything that hinders attacks, but does interfere with a direct line of sight to the target is cover.

There are two varieties of cover: light and heavy. Light cover represents anything that obscures about half of the target. Heavy cover represents anything that obscures about three quarters of the target. When a ranged attacker shoots at a character in light cover, she will draw one additional card and use the lower of the two to resolve her attack. When shooting at a character in heavy cover, the attacker will draw two additional cards and use the lowest of the three to resolve her attack. Additionally, if the attacker fails to hit with her lowest card, but succeeds with her highest card, she will shoot the cover that is protecting her target. This is especially important if the cover protecting the target is another character.

A ranged attacker will always suffer a –2 penalty if she does not take a maneuver to *Aim*, and this penalty applies to all cards drawn to resolve the shot (see *Aim*, p. 78). After a ranged attacker *Aims* to eliminate the –2 penalty, she may make additional *Aim* maneuvers to reduce the number of cards she must draw when resolving an attack against a target in cover. Every *Aim* will reduce the total required draw by a single card. Thus, a ranged attacker firing at a target in heavy cover who takes no maneuvers to *Aim* will suffer the –2 penalty for not aiming and then must draw three cards (one card, plus two cards for the target being in heavy cover). She will use the worst card to resolve her shot. However, if she took two maneuvers to *Aim* before firing, she would receive no penalty and would draw two cards and use the lower to resolve her shot. *Aiming* a total of three times would allow her a shot without penalty and a single card draw. Remember that actions can be used to take maneuvers (see *The Turn*, p. 77).

If an attack or damaging circumstance with an area of effect is able to target someone in cover, extra cards must be drawn to resolve the attack test as described above.

TRAIT COMBINATIONS FOR PHYSICAL ATTACKS

When forming a trait combination for a physical attack, characters will always use the *Grace* aptitude unless a special rule or ability states otherwise. The skill used in this combination will depend on both the weapon and style of combat being used by the attacker. For example, a swordsman may use *Grace + Fencing* or *Grace + Melee*. The former represents a great deal of finesse and traditional forms, while the later represents doing anything it takes to win, including elbowing one's opponent in the face or hitting him in the head with the hilt. In general, *Melee* can be used by almost any close combat attack; however, it lacks any restraint. Thus, any use of *Melee* will shamefully disqualify a character from a formal duel and be seen as a serious faux pas anywhere but a back alley, battlefield, or barroom brawl.

PHYSICAL DEFENSE

As with all trait tests, once the attack's trait combination is chosen, a Difficulty is subtracted from it. All physical attacks made against another character will use that character's Defense value as a Difficulty. A Defense value is a trait combination that will always use the *Vigor* aptitude, but the skill used will depend upon the circumstance. A character may always use a physical Defense of *Vigor + Athletics* and will never lose access to this Defense unless

PHYSICAL ATTACKS

Weapon Used	Possible Attack Trait Combinations
Unarmed Attacks	*Grace + Athletics:* grappling and wrestling *Grace + Fisticuffs:* formal boxing, bartitsu, or other forms of martial art *Grace + Melee:* brawling
Guns	*Grace + Firearms:* firing a gun at a target *Grace + Melee:* using a gun as a club or spear
Improvised Weapons	*Grace + Melee:* using anything at hand in creative violence
Mechanized Weapons, Artillery	*Grace + Engineering:* to shoot a foe within visual range *Reason + Engineering:* to calculate a trajectory to an unseen foe
Swords or Canes	*Grace + Fencing:* for formal fighting using traditional forms *Grace + Melee:* for "anything goes" combat
Thrown Weapon	*Grace + Athletics:* accurately tossing an area of effect object such as a grenade *Grace + Melee:* throwing an object to directly hit a target

UNUSUAL COMBINATIONS

Pontus events, supernatural creatures, and extreme circumstance may all put characters in strange situations where the normal rules don't apply, and Narrators may sometimes call for attack or Defense combinations outside those described above. Narrators always have the final say on what traits are used for tests, but should use such exceptions judiciously. Likewise, they should also be open to clever trait combinations suggested by players.

rendered *Incapacitated*. Other trait combinations will depend on the character's accoutrements. A character must have empty hands to use *Vigor + Fisticuffs* or a sword to use *Vigor + Fencing*. Melee may always be used to calculate physical Defense, and is the only skill allowed to substitute for *Athletics* if an opponent is facing off against multiple opponents. *Firearms* may never be used to calculate Defense.

PHYSICAL ATTACK RESOLUTION

As with any trait test, the attack test resolves by drawing a card from the play deck and adding its value to the current trait combination minus Defense. The result is the DoS of the attack.

Aptitude + Skill – physical Defense + Card Value = Degree of Success (DoS)

If DoS is positive, the attack succeeds. If it negative, the attack fails. A marginal success (DoS 0) will succeed if, and only if, the opponent does not or cannot react. A successful attack can have further effects based on the DoS it achieves. In general, a successful attack will do one or more of the following: lower the target's Guard, place a condition on the target, or place an outcome on the target.

Lowering Guard

Every attack that achieves at least a basic success (DoS 1+) will reduce a character's Guard by one, until the Guard is down. Attacks that succeed when an opponent has no remaining Guard allow the attacker to place an outcome or a standard condition of her choosing on the target (see below). Guard is discussed in detail on p. 73.

Placing Physical Conditions

Attacks that achieve a remarkable success (DoS 4+) will place a condition on the defender. To place a condition, immediately draw a number of new cards equal to the Potency of the attacker's weapon minus the rank of the defender's Armor. The attacker may then place a single condition on the defender, choosing from among those appearing on the drawn cards or from any weapon condition made available by the attacking weapon. The defender immediately begins suffering from the selected condition.

If the defender's Guard is up, the condition is temporary and will be removed at the end of the sequence when cards are discarded and reshuffled. If the defender's Guard is down, the condition is persistent, and is treated as a malady that must heal over time (see *Healing and Recovery*, p. 100). Record persistent conditions on the victim's character sheet.

PHYSICAL DEFENSE

Defending Against	Possible Defense Trait Combinations
Close Combat Attack	*Vigor + Athletics, Vigor + Fencing, Vigor + Fisticuffs, Vigor + Melee*
Close Combat Attack while fighting multiple opponents	*Vigor + Athletics, Vigor + Melee*
Ranged Attack	*Vigor + Athletics*

If an attacker obtains a remarkable failure (DoS –4), the attacker places a condition on herself. Draw a number of cards equal to the Potency of the attack and the Narrator selects which condition to place on the attacker.

Placing Physical Outcomes

A successful strike that hits when the defender's Guard is down is a penetrating attack. Such a hit will place an outcome on the defender. There are three common outcomes that cover most physical conflict situations: Wound, subdue, or inflicting a standard condition.

- **Wound:** A character is expected to get a few bumps and scrapes while fighting, but Wounds are something much more deadly. A Wound represents a shot through the lung, a knife in the gut, fractured bones, or some other debilitating injury. Wounded characters need medical attention quickly, are at risk of going into shock and dying, and will need to spend time recuperating outside of conflict.

  When a character acquires a Wound, she immediately suffers a –2 penalty to all tests and Defenses, is dealt and retains one less initiative card in future sequences, and can no longer perform maneuvers. Each additional Wound inflicts an additional, cumulative –2 Wound Penalty to all actions and the loss of one additional dealt and retained initiative card.

  While Wounded, a character can develop shock from blood loss and trauma until she is stabilized with a successful *Reason + Medicine* trait tests using a Difficulty of her current Wound Penalties (see the *Medicine* skill description on p. 101 and *Healing and Recovery*, p. 100). If she is not stabilized, she will suffer an additional cumulative –1 Wound Penalty at the end of each sequence if in conflict, or five minutes if at rest. If at any time a character's cumulative Wound Penalty reaches –10, she dies.

- **Subdue:** Attacks made to subdue an opponent take the form of wrestling, grabbing, pushing, or tripping. The outcome of

a penetrating attack made to subdue is a grapple, hold, or lock. If successful, the opponent is held in place, must remain adjacent to the attacker, and will have limited options for action. Once an opponent is confined in this way, neither character involved may raise their Guard until they are separated. An attacker subduing an opponent must use future actions to maintain the subdual or attack the subdued target. A subdued opponent can only attack the character subduing her, typically using the *Athletics* or *Melee* skill. All attacks performed by either character are made at a –2 penalty. If a subdued character successfully attacks her subduer, she is released and is no longer subdued.

- **Standard Conditions:** The attacker may choose and apply any standard condition as the outcome of her attack, even if the target is wearing armor that would normally protect her from conditions. For instance, the *Disarmed* condition can render Armor useless or remove a weapon from use. The full list of standard conditions is detailed beginning on p. 97.

- **Other Outcomes:** A Narrator has the freedom to allow any outcome that makes sense for a given attack. However, outcomes can only be created by penetrating attacks. It is highly recommended that players utilize the three detailed outcomes which are provided whenever possible, and other situational outcomes with caution and at Narrator discretion.

Extraordinary Successes

An attack that achieves an extraordinary success (DoS 8+) or extraordinary failure (DoS –8) will place an outcome, regardless of Guard. If an opponent's Guard is up, an extraordinary success (DoS 8+) is still considered a penetrating attack and will bypass the target's Guard to create an outcome. If an opponent's Guard is down, an extraordinary success (DoS 8+) will place the *Incapacitated* condition on the target. If an attack yields an extraordinary failure (DoS –8), the target of the attack may choose to

ATTACKS AND EFFECTS

DoS	Success Type	Target's Guard is Up	Target's Guard is Down
+8	Extraordinary Success	Attacker places outcome on target	Attacker places outcome on target and the target is *Incapacitated* or *Nonfunctional*
+4	–Remarkable Success	Guard –1 and apply a condition	Attacker places outcome and a persistent condition on target
+1	Successful Success	Guard –1	Attacker places outcome on target
0	Marginal Success	Treat as DoS +1 if target reacted, DoS –1 if they did not react	Treat as DoS +1 if target reacted, DoS –1 if they did not react
–1	Failure	No effect	No effect
–4	Remarkable Failure	Defender places condition on attacker	Narrator places condition on attacker
–8	Extraordinary Failure	Defender places outcome on attacker	Defender places outcome on attacker

place an outcome of their choosing on the attacker.

PHYSICAL ARMOR

Armor has two effects: making a character harder to Wound and reducing the number of cards drawn when determining the condition to be placed on an armored character.

Armor will render some weapons useless against it, making the wearer harder to Wound. Armored defenders can only be Wounded by weapons whose Potency rank exceeds the rank of their Armor. An armored character can be subdued and afflicted with conditions, but she is immune to Wounds caused by the inferior weapon, even if her Guard is down. Sometimes the only way to Wound a heavily-armored character is to place the *Disarmed* condition on her, rendering Armor useless.

When choosing possible conditions after an attack achieves a remarkable success (DoS 4+) against an armored character, the number of cards drawn is reduced by one for each rank of Armor worn by the target. If this reduces the number of cards drawn to zero, then no condition is placed—even if the weapon has access to a weapon condition. For example, if an attack yields a remarkable success (DoS 4+) using a blade with Potency 2, normally two

cards would be drawn to determine the condition. However, if the target wore Armor 1, the attacker would draw only one card when determining which condition to place.

Physical armor offers no protections against the effects of social attacks, and does not reduce cards drawn to determine conditions placed by social attacks.

ATTACKING OBJECTS

Characters can also make attacks against objects they are attempting to sabotage, disable, or destroy. An attack made against an object tests the attacker's relevant aptitude and skill combination against a Difficulty equal to the higher of the object's Bulk or Structure. If the targeted object is being wielded or worn by another character, the physical Defense of that character is used as the Difficulty if it is higher than both the object's Bulk and Structure. *Bulk* (p. 185) and *Structure* (p. 186) are listed in item descriptions, and are also discussed in more detail in *Chapter 6: Accoutrements & Technology*.

Objects have no Guard, but the attacking weapon must still overcome an object's Armor in order to make a successful penetrating attack. An object is always considered to possess an Armor

PHYSICAL ATTACKS

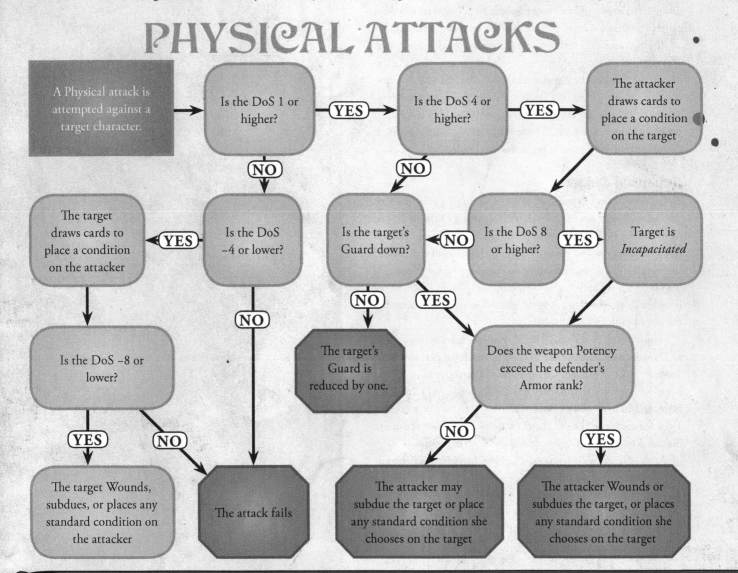

rank equal to one half its Structure, rounded down. This rank is reduced by one for fragile or hollow materials and increased by one if the object is reinforced. Objects with Structure 2 or less are always considered fragile and thus may never have an Armor rank. If the object's Armor is higher than the Potency of the weapon being used to attack, then the attack may still place temporary conditions on the object but will be unable to damage or destroy it.

Objects do not suffer Wounds like living things, so instead, each penetrating attack places a rank of Damage on the object. If a character attempts to use a Damaged object, each rank of Damage inflicts a cumulative –2 penalty when performing trait tests. An object that has taken Damage ranks equal to its Structure automatically suffers the *Nonfunctional* condition. If if the *Nonfunctional* object suffers further Damage, it becomes *Destroyed*. *Destroyed* objects may not be repaired, but can be salvaged as scrap for making, or repairing, other similar items.

Placing Conditions on Objects

If a successful penetrating attack yields a remarkable success (DoS 4+), the player may place the *Nonfunctional* condition on the object. Since objects do not have Guard, this is a persistent condition. The object will no longer be able to perform its intended purpose so long as it suffers from the *Nonfunctional* condition.

The Narrator may also allow the placement of other conditions that she feels are reasonable given the circumstances, such as allowing a torch to place the *Burning* condition. The Narrator may also disallow the placement of a condition if the circumstances of the attack are unrealistic. For example, a pistol could never render a building *Nonfunctional* because the function of a building cannot be compromised by putting tiny holes in its walls.

Repairing Objects

To repair an object, a character must successfully perform a trait test using *Reason* + an applicable skill against a Difficulty equal to the object's current Damage penalties. An object that has suffered Damage may be repaired using the same skill that would have been used to make it (*Artisan*, *Engineering*, or *Science*). If the object would have necessitated multiple skills to make, repair it with a single trait test using the skill in which the repairer has the lowest rank.

A successful repair test (DoS 1+) will remove a single rank of Damage and its associated Damage penalties. A remarkable success (DoS 4+) will remove two ranks of Damage and associated penalties; and an extraordinary success (DoS 8+) will remove all Damage from the object. Each repair test will take one rank of Time for each rank of the object's Complexity. These terms are discussed in detail in *Chapter 6: Accoutrements & Technology*.

At the Narrator's discretion, repairs will require proper tools and replacement parts. If so, each test will require replacement parts that cost one half the total value of the object. *Nonfunctional* objects will lose this condition after a single rank of Damage has been repaired. Damage penalties will be removed with the ranks of Damage that cause them.

SOCIAL ATTACKS

A social attack is any action made with the intent to convince, persuade, or confuse an opponent in either physical or social conflict. Typically a social attack is made by combining the *Presence* aptitude with one of the social conflict skills (*Command, Guile, Parley,* or *Temptation*) against a Difficulty equal to the opponent's most relevant social Defense. Some situations, where etiquette is paramount, may also allow for *Refinement* or *Streetwise* to be used for social attacks.

In social conflict, social attacks are made to alter the Disposition of another character, changing her heart and mind. A single successful attack will shift the Disposition one step toward *Favorable*. Once an opponent's Disposition toward the attacker's argument is *Favorable*, a further successful attack will convince or persuade them.

In physical conflict, social attacks can be made to distract or demoralize. A successful distract attack will confound an opponent and reduce her Guard. Each successful distract attack will lower an opponent's Guard by one. Demoralizing attacks will reduce an opponent's Morale (see *Morale,* p. 74). Each successful demoralize attack will move an opponent's Moral by one step towards being *Favorable* to retreat or surrender.

In all conflicts, attacks that achieve especially high Degrees of Success will have additional effects. For example, a remarkable success (DoS 4+) will allow an attacker to place a condition on her opponent.

SOCIAL WEAPONS: EVIDENCE

In social conflict, evidence is wielded like a weapon. Credible evidence is used to overcome a defender's social Armor that protects her from persuasion. This Armor can come from many sources, including reliable knowledge that shields the mind against misinformation and Affinities that guard the heart against frivolity. With the proper evidence, any person can be convinced or persuaded. Evidence has the following traits: Potency, weapon conditions, and Reach.

Social Weapon Potency

The Potency of evidence is based on its source and the relationship the defender has to it. Basically, if the defender trusts the source of the information, a social attack using this information is more Potent.

Potency can be determined by the Reputation rank of the person from whom the evidence originates. A fact from a book written by a famous scholar with the three-rank Reputation "Knowledgeable Scientist" will be a piece of evidence with Potency 3. If the evidence comes from a source to which the defender has an Affinity, the Potency will be equal to the rank of that Affinity. If there is a situation where multiple sources grant Potency, they are not cummulative; use the highest available rating. Social attacks made without evidence have Potency 1.

Attacks that achieve a remarkable success (DoS 4+) will allow a condition to be placed on the defender. To select this condition, the attacker draws a number of cards equal to the Potency of her

attack minus the opponent's social Armor rank. A condition is then selected from those available on these cards, and then placed on the defender. For example, a character makes a social attack with a Potency 4 piece of evidence and achieves a remarkable success (DoS 4+). Her opponent has social Armor 2. The attacking player would draw only two cards (4 – 2 = 2). The attacker may choose from the two conditions described on these cards, and place the condition she selects on the defender.

Penetrating social attacks can only persuade or convince the defender if the evidence's Potency rank is higher than the opponent's Armor (see *Placing Social Outcomes,* p. 90).

Physical Weapons in a Social Attack

Sometimes a character uses a physical weapon to scare someone rather than hurt them. This is a social attack. If such an attack uses a physical weapon to help provoke fear, the attacker can use the Potency of that weapon for the social attack. The Narrator has the option to reduce or negate this Potency if the weapon is not frightening to the character for some reason, such as her knowing the gun isn't loaded because she removed the bullets. The Narrator may also increase the Potency of the weapon for intimidation purposes if it is coated in blood or otherwise designed to look menacing (see the *Command* skill, p. 142).

Social Weapon Conditions

A piece of evidence can be granted a weapon condition if it is particularly credible. The credibility can be influenced by any Affinity the defender may hold which causes her to be more susceptible to the evidence. A young man is more likely to be persuaded to enlist in Her Majesty's navy if he has an Affinity for "Queen and Country." Such situations grant the *Overwhelmed* condition to the attack. In situations where the evidence is incontrovertible, such as an undoctored photograph or the direct witnessing of an event, the attack is granted the *Undone* condition. These conditions are granted to an attack even in situations where the attack is already receiving a different condition from a skill mastery, transcendent power, or asset. Remember that these are considered weapon conditions and may be selected anytime an attack has the power to place a condition on an opponent.

Social Attack Type & Reach

A social attack must Reach an opponent for her to be aware of the attack and suffer from any of its effects. There are two types of social Reach: spoken and written. A spoken attack is by far the most common and has a Reach of *Audible,* which can affect everyone who hears it, if they are paying attention. In a room with moderate levels of conversation, this is about ten feet in every direction and is capable of engaging everyone in a character's zone of control. Other circumstances—such as speaking to a hushed room of attentive listeners, or trying to relay orders in the midst of an artillery barrage—could expand or reduce this range considerably. In active social scenes or noisy environments it may be necessary to use a maneuver to *Attract* the attention of a particular target.

Written attacks are those made through letters, posters, propaganda, or other textual media. These attacks have a Reach of *Visual,* and can affect everyone who chooses to read them and understands the language in which they are composed. A single piece of writing can make multiple attacks depending on its length, but no single document may ever make more than three. A poster or piece of propaganda can only make a single attack, and usually is made to alter a character's Disposition more than to convince or persuade her. Letters and newspaper articles convey more information, but lack the length and rigor to provide full arguments, and usually make two attacks. By design, a treatise or essay is meant to be a full argument, and thus makes three social attacks against its readers.

When a written social attack is composed, the author makes her attack tests against a Difficulty 0. The DoS for each attack are recorded. When the work is read, apply the attacks to the reader, subtracting her most relevant Defense from the DoS. The result of each attack is then applied to the reader. Keep in mind that a character always has the choice to ignore written material.

SOCIAL AVENUES OF ATTACK

Socially, an avenue of attack is a single line of argument. In social conflict each defender has only one available avenue of attack as an individual character simply cannot meaningfully focus on two or more in depth conversations at the same time. Once this single avenue is occupied, it becomes closed and no longer available for other attackers.

A defender may leave a social conflict at any time. Leaving a conversation may have social ramifications depending on the situation, but it is always an option for eliminating all avenues of attack and ending a conflict. The only time a character may not leave a social conflict is if they are forced to remain against their will, such as an interrogation or other circumstance where they are held captive. Pressing a conversation once a character has attempted to leave is viewed as boorish behavior and very rude, and is always considered a faux pas in polite company.

Multiple Attackers in a Single Avenue of Attack

It is possible for more than one attacker to share an avenue of attack. This is done through the use of the *Elicit Aid* maneuver, and happens in almost every social conflict where more than one social attacker is attempting to convince or persuade a target. The first attacker to act occupies the avenue of attack and may use a maneuver to *Elicit Aid*, inviting other attackers to share her avenue. This represents working together, such as playing off of one another in a "good cop/bad cop" scenario, showing agreement and support to exert peer pressure, or by presenting complementary arguments. All participating attackers make a trait test, but only the highest DoS achieved is used to resolve the attack for that turn.

In polite argument or discourse, the first character to step into a social avenue of attack will occupy that avenue for the duration of the conflict. When that character spends all of her available attacks, she can no longer *Elicit Aid* and her side's role in the conflict is over. However, player characters needn't always be polite. When an opponent is unable to flee from an argument, such as during an interrogation where the opponent is tied up or otherwise restrained, the players may wish to browbeat their social target.

Browbeating is done by "daisy chaining" to fill the avenue of attack. The instigating character will make two attacks and then *Elicit Aid* on the third attack, bringing a new character into the conflict. Then she will step back allowing the newly added attacker to control the avenue of attack in her stead. That new attacker will have two remaining actions. She may make one attack alone, and then *Elicit Aid* on her third attack, inviting a third attacker to occupy the avenue of attack. This can continue until there are no more attackers from which to *Elicit Aid*, and is the only method that will allow more than three attacks from one side in a single social conflict. However, this is in no way a civil discourse and is *always* a social faux pas and frequently seen as rude or even cruel. As most individuals are free to leave a social conflict at any time, few will subject themselves to browbeating. This tactic is only truly useful when the opponent is tied down, *Entrapped*, or otherwise unable to flee. Thus, browbeating is frequently used by interrogators, torturers, and exceptionally petty aristocrats. The Narrator may inflict *Corruption* on players who browbeat frequently through the use of threats and emotional manipulation.

TRAIT COMBINATIONS FOR SOCIAL ATTACKS

When forming a trait combination for a social attack, characters will always use the *Presence* aptitude unless a special rule or ability specifically states otherwise. The skill used in this combination will depend on both the social situation and conversational style being used by the attacker.

Characters aiding one another in social conflicts will frequently employ different trait combinations from one another to best play to their individual strengths. Police officers working on an

SOCIAL ATTACKS

Attack Type	Possible Attack Trait Combinations
Deceit or Trickery	*Presence + Guile*
Emotional Manipulation	*Presence + Temptation*
Factual Debate	*Presence* + related technical or professional skill such as *Science*
Intimidation or Leadership	*Presence + Command*
Negotiation	*Presence + Parley*
Seduction or Temptation	*Presence + Temptation*

interrogation might have one friendly character making *Presence + Parley* tests, while their more aggressive partner uses *Presence + Command* to make threats, but both are working together to extract a confession. A duo of con artists might begin with a honeypot using *Presence + Seduction* to distract their mark and then a hustler using *Presence + Guile* bamboozles him into revealing information they can use later for blackmail. During friendly debate at a social club dinner, one member might lead a discussion using *Presence + Refinement* to enforce proper etiquette while her more ideological friend is making impassioned political arguments using *Presence + Bureaucracy*.

SOCIAL DEFENSE

Once the attack's trait combination is chosen, a Difficulty is subtracted from it. All social attacks made against another character will use that character's social Defense value as a Difficulty. A Defense's trait combination will always use the *Will* aptitude, but as with attacks, the skill used will depend on the situation. A character may always use a Defense of *Will + Composure* no matter what the situation, and will never lose access to this Defense.

SOCIAL ATTACK RESOLUTION

As with any trait test, the attack test resolves by drawing a card from the play deck and adding its value to the current total (aptitude + skill – Defense). The result is the DoS of the attack.

**Aptitude + Skill – social Defense + Card Value
= Degree of Success (DoS)**

If it is positive, the attack succeeds. If it is negative, the attack fails. A marginal success (DoS 0) will succeed, and only if, the opponent does not or cannot react. A successful attack will do one or more of the of the following: reduce a target's Guard (if used during physical conflict), change the target's Disposition, or place an outcome on the target.

SOCIAL DEFENSE

Defending Against	Possible Defense Trait Combinations
Any Situation	*Will + Composure.*
Deceit or Trickery	*Will + Intuition, Will + Composure*
Emotional Manipulation	*Will + Intuition, Will + Composure*
Factual Debate	*Will* + related technical or professional skill such as *Academics*
Intimidation	*Will + Command, Will + Composure*
Negotiation	*Will + Parley, Will + Composure*
Seduction	*Will + Intuition, Will + Composure*

Lowering Guard

Social attacks made during physical conflict can be performed to confuse an opponent. An attacker may feint with her weapon, intimidate the defender into making a mistake, or even just distract an opponent from the task at hand. Such attacks may potentially reduce Guard. These attacks will always use *Presence* in their trait combination, but can use several different skills (including physical skills). A successful attack of this type can reduce Guard by one just like a physical attack. It can even place a temporary condition if it achieves a remarkable success (DoS 4+). However, it can never create outcomes (persuasions, convictions, Wounds, etc.).

SOCIAL ATTACKS IN PHYSICAL CONFLICT

Attack Type	Possible Trait Combinations
Distraction or Trick	*Presence + Guile*
Feint	*Presence + Fencing, Presence + Fisticuffs, Presence + Melee*
Intimidation	*Presence + Command*

SOCIAL ATTACKS AND EFFECTS

DoS	Success Type	Target's Disposition not Favorable	Target's Disposition Favorable
+8	Extraordinary Success	Attacker places an outcome on targeted character	Attacker places an outcome on targeted character and the target gains temporary rank 1 Affinity for the new belief/course of action
+4	Remarkable Success	Attacker moves target Disposition and applies a condition	Attacker places outcome on targeted character and applies a persistent condition
+1	Successful Success	Attacker moves target Disposition	Attacker places outcome on targeted character
0	Marginal Success	Treat as DoS +1 if target reacted, DoS −1 if they did not	Treat as DoS +1 if target reacted, DoS −1 if they did not
−1	Failure	No effect	No effect
−4	Remarkable Failure	Defender moves target Disposition	Defender moves target Disposition
−8	Extraordinary Failure	Defender moves target Disposition, and applies a condition to the attacker	Defender moves target Disposition, and applies a condition to the attacker

Changing Disposition

Working to change an opponent's Disposition is a common use of social attack. Every successful social attack (DoS 1+) against a character can move the target's Disposition one step in a direction chosen by the attacker. A character may even change her own Disposition this way, using a Difficulty equal to her strongest opponent's Defense. This allows her to undo the changes wrought on her Disposition by a socially manipulative opponent.

Attacking to shift a Disposition can be very important in physical conflict as well: this is the primary means of weakening foes' Morale, convincing them to flee or surrender, or bolstering the Morale of allies to prevent them from breaking. Disposition and Morale are discussed in greater detail in *Conflict Specific Traits*, p. 73.

Placing Social Conditions

If an attack achieves a remarkable success (DoS 4+) it will place a condition. The attacker draws a number of cards equal to the Potency of the evidence used in the argument (minus the rank in social Armor her opponent has, if any), chooses a single condition from the newly drawn cards, and then places it on the defender. Depending on the evidence used to make the attack or other special abilities, the attack may include a weapon condition, which would provide an additional choice to the conditions from the drawn cards.

The defender immediately begins suffering from the selected condition. If the defender's Disposition is anything other than *Favorable* before the attack, or if in physical conflict and her Guard is up, the condition is temporary and will be removed at the end of the sequence. If the defender's Guard is down, or her Disposition was *Favorable* before the attack, the newly placed condition is persistent, and is treated as a malady that must heal over time (see *Healing and Recovery*, p. 100).

If an attacker is attempting to change her own Disposition and her test yields a remarkable success (DoS 4+), the condition

is placed on the opponent whose social Defense was used as a Difficulty for the attack.

Placing Social Outcomes

A successful attack on a defender whose Disposition is already *Favorable* is a penetrating attack, and it will place an outcome. There are three common outcomes that cover most social conflict situations: convince, persuade, or any standard condition.

- **Convince:** A successful penetrating attack can convince the opponent to believe the information she is told to be true. She will continue to believe it until she is given reason to doubt.

- **Persuade:** A successful penetrating attack to persuade will cause the opponent to desire to perform an action they did not previously wish to do. She will find the easiest, safest, and most convenient way to enact this intention. If the opportunity to take action does not present itself within the current chapter, the persuaded opponent may have time to think better of the choice (see *Healing and Recovery*, p. 100).

Although player characters may always spend a point of *Purpose* to avoid this outcome, they are encouraged to remember that everyone has momentary lapses of reason, makes errors in judgement, and will sometimes succumb to temptation. A character need not believe she is doing the right thing in order to be persuaded to take an action. The proper motivation or temptation can make many an honest person do dishonest things. Likewise, just because a character is persuaded to take an action does not mean that she won't regret it later.

- **Conditions as Outcomes:** Any standard condition may be placed on an opponent as the result of a penetrating attack. Standard conditions are listed starting on p. 97. Conditions such as *Disarmed* and *Entrapped* are frequently used in social conflicts, as they can make social Armor irrelevant or keep someone from leaving the conversation.

- **Other Outcomes:** A Narrator has the freedom to allow any sort of outcome that makes sense for a given attack. It is highly recommended that players utilize the three detailed outcomes which are provided above, and add other situational outcomes with caution and Narrator discretion.

Extraordinary Successes

An attack that achieves a extraordinary success (DoS 8+) will create an outcome regardless the target's current Disposition. If an opponent's Disposition is already Favorable, an extraordinary success (DoS 8+) will not only place an outcome, but will also so thoroughly sway the target that they gain a temporary rank 1 Affinity related to the outcome. This Affinity will normalize thereafter (see *Healing and Recovery*, p. 100).

Remarkable failures (DoS −4) move the targeted Disposition one step in a direction chosen by the defender. If an attack yields an extraordinary failure (DoS −8), the targeted Disposition will move one step in a direction chosen by the defender and the attacker has so badly bungled the conversation that they suffer a temporary condition. Draw a number of cards equal to the Potency of the attack and have the target choose which condition is applied to the attacker.

SOCIAL ARMOR

Armor is used to fend off social attacks. Social Armor comes in the form of pre-existing knowledge regarding the topic, the known Reputation of the person being gossiped about, or a predisposed opinion caused by an Affinity. Armor ranks are not cummulative. If a character would receive armor from multiple sources, use only the best rank.

Knowledge as Armor

Knowledge can be a powerful defensive tool against being fooled. It is much more difficult to convince a scientist that the basic theories of her field are false then it is to convince her of something about which she knows very little. If an attacker in a social conflict attempts to persuade or convince a character regarding knowledge controlled by a skill in which she has ranks, she may use her ranks in that skill as an Armor rank against the attack. The Narrator has ultimate say in what knowledge skills can be used as Armor in any given situation. The Narrator may also declare certain social attacks to automatically fail based on the incredibility of the information. Skills may only be used as Armor in social conflict.

SOCIAL ATTACKS

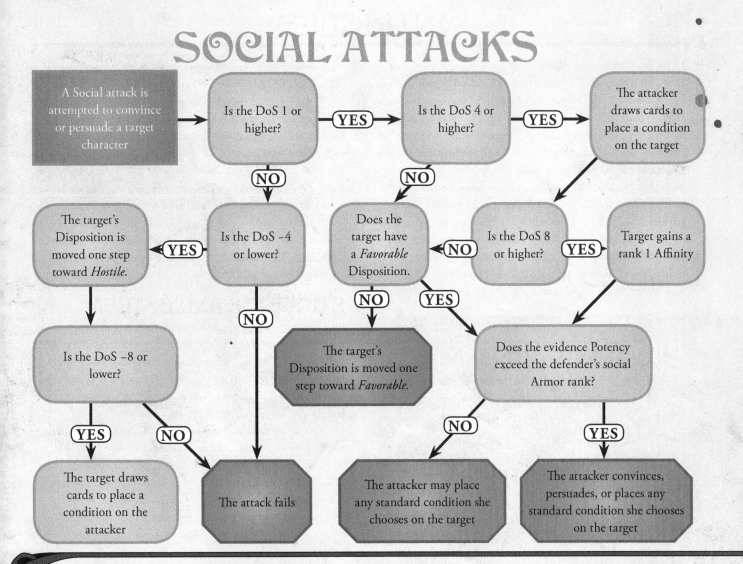

Affinities as Armor

Affinities may play a large role in how difficult a character is to persuade or convince. If an attacker attempts to persuade or convince a character regarding something that would conflict with one of her Affinities, she may use the rank of that Affinity as Armor against that attack.

Reputations as Armor

Gossip can be a vicious thing, but those that have strong Reputations are resistant to the tales that liars tell. When a character's Reputation is well known, people are less likely to believe any information about her which conflicts with that Reputation. If any character is aware of someone's Reputation and another character tries to convince her of something that contradicts it, use the rank of that Reputation as Armor against the attack.

Effects of Armor

Armor has two effects: reducing the number of cards drawn by the attacker when determining what condition is to be placed on the armored character, and making her more resistant to being convinced or persuaded.

After an attack yields a remarkable success (DoS 4+) against a socially armored character and the attacker draws to determine what condition is to be placed, the attacker draws one fewer cards for each rank of the defender's Armor. If this reduces the number of cards drawn to zero, then no condition is placed even if the attack has access to a weapon condition. For example, if a remarkable success (DoS 4+) is made using a piece of evidence with Potency 2, normally two cards would be drawn to determine the condition. However, if the target had Armor 1, the attacker would only draw one card to determine which condition is placed.

Armor will also render some evidence useless, making the armored character harder to convince or persuade. If the Potency rank of the evidence does not exceed the defender's Armor rank then that evidence cannot be used to convince or persuade the defender. Such an armored character may still be inflicted with conditions and have her Disposition changed, but she is immune to all persuasions and convictions. However, even when Armor is social, a *Disarm* condition may still be placed to render the Armor useless. This usually symbolizes second guessing or confusion.

INTRIGUES

Intrigues are more complicated social conflicts that occur over the course of a chapter. They are made to build up or tear down a character's Esteem or Reputation. Each successful intrigue attack shifts a character's Esteem by one step toward *Hostile* or *Favorable*, as chosen by the attacker. If a character's Esteem is elevated to *Favorable*, the next successful intrigue attack made against her will provide her with one rank of positive Reputation. If a character's Esteem is degraded to *Hostile*, the next successful intrigue attack will inflict one rank of negative Reputation on her. Social careers have been bolstered or destroyed by the clever use of intrigues.

Manipulating Esteem during a chapter is an excellent way to create or deny short-term opportunities for social interaction, as a character will behave very differently when the room is *Guarded* against her rather than *Agreeable*. For many, these short-term consequences are an end unto themselves. Such intrigues at parties are a staple of high society events throughout "the Season," as bright young things vie with one another in games of popularity.

Especially savvy or vindictive socialites may take this a step further: once a person's Esteem reaches either *Hostile* or *Favorable*, an attacker can attempt to bolster or damage that person's Reputation. Since Reputations are used to calculate Esteem at the beginning of every new chapter, manipulating them in lasting ways can shift how an individual is respected by others in future social situations. This makes intrigue a key tool in political campaigning, improving one's own social standing, or destroying one's rivals. Those working towards any type of permanent social advancement must often rely on intrigues to improve their station.

ETIQUETTE AND ESTEEM

Intrigues start by targeting a character's Esteem, and Esteem is not a static thing. Esteem is calculated at the beginning of a chapter (see *Esteem*, p. 74), and it may change if the character commits a faux pas or is recognized for a courtesy. A faux pas is an embarrassing misstep in etiquette that lowers one's Esteem, while a courtesy is a praiseworthy act that elevates one's Esteem.

Navigating a social situation with courtesies and faux pas requires the use of etiquette tests. In civil society (*Class* 2+), an etiquette test is performed with *Presence + Refinement*. In social situations involving lower classes (Class 0–1), an etiquette test can be performed with *Presence + Streetwise*. Etiquette tests use a Difficulty equal to twice the Tenor rank for the gathering.

THE ART OF INTRIGUE

As few modern readers are deeply versed in the genteel violence of weaponized etiquette, it may be difficult to imagine the turns of cruelty and brilliance that could build and destroy Reputations in Victorian society. Serious inspiration may be found in the movie *Ridicule* (1996), while a more comical approach can be seen in the *Oscar Wilde* sketch from *Monty Python's Flying Circus* (Episode 39, aired 1973).

INTRIGUE

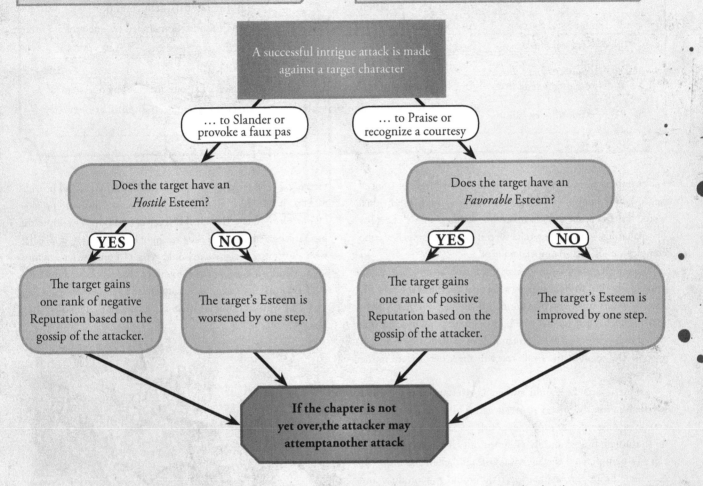

<table>
<tr><td>

Intrigue attacks using Etiquette

Combination: *Presence + Refinement/Streetwise*

Difficulty: Tenor x2

Armor: None

Failure at this test will degrade the attacker's Esteem by one step

</td><td>

Intrigue attacks using Praise or Slander

Combination: *Presence + Refinement/Guile*

Difficulty: Target's Esteem steps (+1 if attacker's Esteem is higher than the target, –2 if lower)

Armor: Target's best relevant Reputation

</td></tr>
</table>

A successful intrigue attack is made against a target character

... to Slander or provoke a faux pas

... to Praise or recognize a courtesy

Does the target have an *Hostile* Esteem?

Does the target have an *Favorable* Esteem?

YES — The target gains one rank of negative Reputation based on the gossip of the attacker.

NO — The target's Esteem is worsened by one step.

YES — The target gains one rank of positive Reputation based on the gossip of the attacker.

NO — The target's Esteem is improved by one step.

If the chapter is not yet over, the attacker may attempt another attack

Anytime a character commits a faux pas, she must perform an etiquette test to pull it off without suffering a loss of Esteem. If she fails this test, her Esteem is moved one step towards *Hostile*. If the character succeeds, her Esteem remains unchanged. What constitutes a faux pas is highly dependent upon the situation, and each play group should decide for themselves how deeply they wish to delve into the depths of Victorian etiquette. Narrators should always warn a character who is about to commit a faux pas if her character would be savvy to the situation (a passive *Reason + Refinement* test can show if a character has this knowledge). *Chapter 2: The Clockwork World*, offers many examples of what is seen as proper in polite society.

Courtesies are not merely well mannered behavior. A courtesy is something that makes everyone at the event take notice: the giving of exquisite gifts to one or more guests, the delivery of a beneficent speech, or a truly generous deed such as forgiving the debt of someone who was about to be placed in prison. Any action that would be a faux pas due to timing or nature can never be a courtesy, even if the character makes her trait test to maintain her Esteem. If a character performs a courtesy, she may make an etiquette test to raise her Esteem by one step. If she fails this test, her Esteem remains unchanged.

INTRIGUE ATTACKS USING ETIQUETTE

This sort of attack can be performed in any way that forces the target to gracefully deal with an impossible situation. The most common usage is to manipulate a situation into one where the target must make a faux pas. For example, giving a rival misinformation regarding proper behavior in a given situation or subtly rearranging their tableware so as to provoke a spill. A more aggressive method involves behaving in a way that demands a response.

INTRIGUE ATTACKS AND EFFECTS

DoS	Success Type	Target's Esteem not *Favorable/Hostile*	Target's Esteem *Favorable/Hostile*
+8	Extraordinary Success	Target's Reputation altered by one rank.	Target's Reputation altered by one rank and she becomes a guest of honor or a pariah for the remainder of the chapter.
+4	Remarkable Success	Attacker moves targeted Esteem one step and applies a condition	Target's Reputation altered by one rank and suffers a persistent condition
+1	Successful Success	Attacker moves targeted Esteem one step	Target's Reputation altered by one rank.
0	Marginal Success	No effect	No effect
−1	Failure	No effect	No effect
−4	Remarkable Failure	Attacker's Esteem decreases by one step	Attacker's Esteem decreases by one step
−8	Extraordinary Failure	Attacker's Reputation diminishes by one rank	Attacker's Reputation diminishes by one rank

For example, the attacker may subtly insult the target in front of her love or employer. In such situations, the aggrieved individual would lose face if she did not retort, but would commit a faux pas by retaliating—forcing an etiquette test either way. Such are the complexities of Victorian social politics.

In such an instance, the attacker must make an etiquette test to provoke her rival without making a faux pas herself. If she fails, her Esteem lowers by one step as normal. If she succeeds her Esteem remains unchanged and her rival is forced to respond in a way that will breach proper behavior, demanding an etiquette test from her as well. The result of the rival's test will affect her Esteem in the same way.

Etiquette attacks should always be relevant to the current social situation. Members of street gangs often make etiquette attacks against one another to establish pecking order, but they do so through brutish insults and posturing. If one gang member cleverly manipulated the silverware of another in the hopes to cost him the respect of their peers, it would not produce any result. Meanwhile, socialites with high ranks in *Refinement* may make much more subtle attacks to harass or embarrass less skilled individuals, removing them from situations of high praise or even eventually branding them as social pariahs.

INTRIGUE ATTACKS USING PRAISE AND SLANDER

Another way to change a character's Esteem is to praise or slander them behind their back. Such an action will use a trait combination of *Presence* + skill, with the skill being whatever is most appropriate to the nature of the attack (usually *Guile* or *Refinement*, but rarer situations may call for any of the social attack skills). The action targets a single character. The targeted character needn't be present, but her Esteem should be calculated as though she were. The Difficulty for this test is based on the Esteem of the target. The base Difficulty is 1 for each step of Esteem currently held by the

target (e.g. a targeted person with a *Hostile* Esteem would provide a Difficulty 1, while one with an *Agreeable* Esteem would provide a Difficulty 4, etc.). The attacker receives a +1 bonus to this test if her Esteem is higher than the Esteem of her target (e.g. a socialite with an Esteem of *Agreeable* would get a +1 bonus when attempting to slander a social opponent with an Esteem of *Indifferent*), or a −2 penalty if her Esteem is lower than than of her opponent (e.g. a socialite with an Esteem of *Guarded* would get a −2 penalty when

attempting to praise a companion with an Esteem of *Agreeable*). Calculate this bonus or penalty during each new attack to account for any changes in Esteem.

$$\text{Presence} + [\text{Guile or Refinement}] - \text{steps of Esteem} + \text{Card Value} = \text{DoS}$$

+1 bonus if the attacker's Esteem is higher than the target, –2 if it is lower

If the test succeeds, the targeted character's Esteem will raise or lower by one step as determine by the nature of the attack. If the test fails, no change is made. Other results are described in the *Intrigue Attacks and Effects* table.

INTRIGUES AND REPUTATIONS

If a target character's Esteem is elevated to *Favorable*, her Reputations can be built up; and if her Esteem is lowered to *Hostile*, her Reputations are vulnerable to damage. When a character's Esteem is *Favorable*, a successful intrigue attack can raise one of her Reputations by one rank or assign one rank to a new positive Reputation. When a character's Esteem is *Hostile*, a successful intrigue attack can reduce one of her Reputations by one rank or assign one rank to a new negative one.

Attacks made to praise or slander will use *Presence + Guile* or *Refinement* against a Difficulty based on the target's Esteem, as described in the previous section. Intrigue attacks using etiquette will use *Presence + Refinement* or *Streetwise* against a Difficulty of twice the Tenor of the current gathering, as described above. So long as the target's Esteem is *Hostile* or *Favorable*, either attack style may be used to alter Reputations. If so, they are considered penetrating attacks and therefore must overcome social Armor.

The target of a slander will receive social Armor equal to the rank of any one Reputation that contradicts the vicious rumors made about her. The target of a praise will receive social Armor equal to the rank of any Reputation that undermines the positive things being said about her.

If the attacker wishes to make a penetrating attack that would affect a character's Reputations (see *Reputations as Armor*, p. 92), she will need evidence (see *Social Weapons: Evidence*, p. 87). The evidence must have a rank equal to or greater than the Armor rank. Successful penetrating intrigue attacks that bypass Armor will alter Reputations.

Permanently Altering Reputations

The effects of intrigues are usually only temporary. Reputations are variable traits, and an intrigue attack can only alter the temporary rank of a Reputation. The fixed rank remains unchanged. Thus, Reputations will then heal over time, eventually returning to the fixed rank (see *Normalizing Reputations*, p. 103).

Before a Reputation's temporary rank returns to its fixed rank, either the target or the attacker may spend experience points to make that temporary value permanent. If this is done, the temporary rank becomes the new fixed rank, preventing any normalization from occurring. The experience point cost to do this is twice the new fixed rank of the Reputation. This can be paid by one character to change the fixed Reputation rank of another character. For example, an attacker reduces her target's Reputation from rank 2 to rank 1. Given the rules for *Normalizing Reputations*, that Reputation will return to rank 2 in three days. Before this happens, the attacker can spend a number of experience points equal to twice the current temporary rank (in this case, 2 x rank 1 = 2 experience points) to make the change permanent. If she does this, the Reputation will remain at rank 1, its new fixed value.

If a Reputation is raised or lowered by more than one rank, each new rank must be purchased separately in this way (e.g. when raising a Reputation from 2 to 4, the character must first buy rank 3, and then rank 4).

This method can only be used to make a temporary value a fixed value. It can never be used to change a Reputation whose temporary and fixed values are the same. A character cannot simply spend experience points to raise her Reputations during character advancement if the story has not given her a temporary change of which to take advantage!

If a Narrator Character desires to negatively affect a character by permanently altering her Reputation, the Narrator will award the targeted character a number of experience points equal to the new fixed value of her Reputation. Note that when receiving experience points from the Narrator for altered Reputations, player characters receive only the new fixed value in points and not twice the fixed value. For example, if a Narrator character reduced a player character's current Reputation rank from 3 to 2, the Narrator may award that player two experience points to change that Reputation's fixed rank to 2 as well. A Narrator only awards experience points if this tactic is used to raise a bad Reputation or lower a good one. A player character is never rewarded for a kind Narrator character ridding her of a bad Reputation or building a good one.

CONDITIONS

The Clockwork Roleplaying Game uses different conditions to represent minor injuries or situational complications that negatively affect a character. While outcomes represent significant danger to a character's health or free will, conditions are the bumps, bruises, surprises, or situations that impede a character's ability to act normally. Conditions are also used to represent the effects of drugs or illness, inclement weather, and minor occurrences that are narratively significant. Outside of conflict, conditions are ignored unless they are persistent. It is assumed that brief complications are minor and fleeting, and lack the strength or staying power to affect a narrative scene.

In conflict, any attack that achieves a remarkable success (DoS 4+) will place a single condition on the target character, which will last until the end of the sequence. If the attack is penetrating, the condition will persist. Persistent conditions are complications and lingering injuries that are treated as maladies, and will heal using the rules for *Healing and Recovery* (p. 100). A few conditions, such as *Burning*, have special rules regarding when they become persistent and how they can be removed. Read the description of each condition for more information on how that specific condition is used within the game.

TYPES OF CONDITIONS

Within the game, conditions are either standard or special. Standard conditions appear on the Clockwork Cards, and each could conceivably occur in any number of ways in both physical or social circumstances. The remaining conditions are special. Special conditions are used for many different purposes in the game, including specialized weapon damage, environmental hazards, illnesses, and other effects. All conditions are used in the same way unless the description specifically states otherwise.

STANDARD CONDITIONS

Standard conditions are applicable to both social and physical conflict and are the most commonly occurring conditions. Within conflict, one may be placed after a remarkable success (DoS 4+) or when chosen to be placed as an outcome (see *Placing Physical Conditions*, p. 83, and *Placing Social Conditions*, p. 90). Outside of conflict, these standard conditions are used alongside special conditions for many different purposes as described below.

ENVIRONMENTAL SEVERITY

Severity	Description and Examples	Difficulty
Moderate	Harsh weather: a midwinter's night in a countryside forest	3
Severe	A hostile climate: arctic, desert, jungle, swamp, tundra	5
Deadly	Life-threatening weather, such as a blizzard, sandstorm, or volcanic ash	7
Hazardous	Environmental hazards: Walking through a burning room, breathing poisonous gas, being submerged in water or other suffocating conditions.	9

WEAPON CONDITIONS

When a character achieves a remarkable success (DoS 4+) on an attack and selects a condition to place on her opponent, her weapon may offer her an additional condition. This weapon condition is always added to the pool of conditions from which a player may choose. Some weapons will provide conditions from the standard condition list, while others provide special conditions.

ENVIRONMENTAL CONDITIONS

While conditions are often used to represent injuries and complications sustained in conflict, they may also be used to represent the effects of harsh environments. Character's can become *Fatigued* while journeying through the heat of a desert or be *Deprived* of water when they are dying of thirst. All of these effects are handled through the use of conditions.

Extreme Environments

Extreme climates or environmental hazards can be very dangerous. A character wandering in the desert or tundra can suffer anything from general malaise to death. A character running into a burning building can suffer from smoke inhalation, heat, or even be burned alive.

ENVIRONMENTAL PREPAREDNESS

Preparedness	Test Frequency
Prepared	No test needed
Ill-prepared	Test each chapter
Unprepared	Test each scene

Any time a character is exposed to an extreme environment, she will need to test *Vigor + Will* or *Vigor + Survival* against a Difficulty set by the severity of the environment. Environments can be moderate, severe, deadly, or hazardous; with set Difficulties of 3, 5, 7, and 9 respectively. If a character fails this test, she immediately receives the *Fatigued* condition. For each *Fatigued* condition, she is dealt one fewer initiative card at the start of conflict, and her travel speed is reduced by one third. Once a character has failed three tests and acquired three *Fatigued* conditions, she becomes *Incapacitated*. Henceforth, anytime she would become *Fatigued* she receives the *Deprived* condition instead. If any test yields a remarkable failure (DoS –4), she immediately receives the *Fatigued* condition and a Wound. If she suffers an extraordinary failure (DoS –8), she immediately receives a Wound and both the *Fatigued* and *Incapacitated* conditions.

Equipment and Preparedness

Proper equipment plays a large role in how well a character can survive in an extreme environment. Preparation will determine how often a character needs to make a test to endure her surroundings. In any extreme environment, a character is considered to be Prepared, Ill-prepared, or Unprepared. She will use her *Survival* skill or rely on that of another character, to determine how prepared she is for the severity of her surroundings.

When time and resources allow a group to prepare supplies and gear before venturing into an extreme environment, a single character (or a group aiding one another) tests *Reason + Survival* against a Difficulty based on the severity of the environment. Success (DoS 1+) means that the characters are Prepared for the environment; failure means that the characters are Ill-prepared; and a remarkable failure (DoS –4) means the characters are Unprepared.

This test assumes the characters have access to proper modern equipment and know the nature of the environment they will be entering. Access to improvised or poor equipment places a –2 penalty on the preparation test. Preparing for the wrong sort of environment reduces the quality of preparation by one step

(Prepared becomes Ill-prepared, Ill-prepared becomes Unprepared). If characters have both improper equipment and attempt to prepare for the wrong environment, they are automatically Unprepared. Likewise if they have no access to gear and supplies, they are automatically Unprepared.

Machines in Extreme Environments

Complicated mechanical equipment such as engines, firearms, or machines with multiple moving parts can also be subject to the dangers of extreme environments. A character wishing to keep such machinery in good working order must make maintenance tests. This will usually be a *Reason + Engineering* test, but other skills can be substituted for *Engineering* if they are directly relevant, such as using *Firearms* to maintain a rifle. Just like a *Survival* test, the Difficulty for any maintenance test is equal to the extremity of the environment, with test frequency determined by the preparedness of the character. Unlike a *Survival* test, maintenance tests can be taken passively if the character is assured success that way. Failure to properly maintain a machine exposed to an extreme environment will give it the *Nonfunctional* condition. This condition may be removed once the machine is repaired (see *Repairing Objects*, p. 86).

Falling & Impact

As a general abstraction, a character falling from any significant height will hit the ground at the end of the sequence. Technically, constant acceleration toward the earth would cause a character to descend more than 10,000 feet during this time, meaning most falling characters would hit the ground almost instantaneously. However, to provide good drama, a character who still has face-up initiative cards when she falls may take her remaining turns before she impacts. Characters falling only short distances may hit the ground much sooner at Narrator discretion.

Treat the impact after a fall as a hazardous extreme environment. The fallen character must test *Vigor + Will*, Difficulty 9. This test is performed for every ten feet fallen.

CONDITION DESCRIPTIONS

The following is an alphabetical list of all the conditions used in the game. Standard conditions are listed in red.

Aggravated

Any single condition on the targeted character now becomes a persistent condition. If the *Aggravated* condition is placed on a character without any current conditions, treat it as the *Dazed* condition.

Bleeding

The character immediately receives a Wound Penalty of –1, and another at the beginning of each sequence until the character is stabilized with a successful *Reason + Medicine* test. If the character

is outside of conflict, this penalty will increase once for every five minutes of light activity. This stacks with all other Wound Penalties. If *Bleeding* is applied as a persistent condition, successfully stabilizing the character stops the bleeding, but the condition remains until removed via physical recovery. If a character takes a Wound or another condition before removing the *Bleeding* condition, she will begin to bleed again.

Blinded

A *Blinded* character cannot see. This means the character cannot use maneuvers to *Aim*, make *Focus* tests that involve sight, and all opponents in physical conflict are treated as having heavy cover.

Burdened

Characters attempting to carry too much weight or too many awkward accoutrements have movement and activity severely limited and must forfeit their free maneuver when they take a turn, even if they are uninjured. A *Burdened* character can take a maneuver is if they use an action to to do so.

Burning

The character is on fire. She receives a cumulative –1 Wound Penalty at the end of each sequence that she remains burning. Extinguishing herself requires one action and requires access to water, soil, room to roll or some other way to suffocate the flame, and can only be taken if the character is not currently engulfed in another source of flame. *Burning* is always a persistent condition, but it is removed when the character is extinguished instead of using the normal recovery rules.

Crippled

A character suffering from the *Crippled* condition loses the use of one sensory organ or limb. The Narrator and player agree on what is lost. If the character receives the *Crippled* condition from an extraordinary attack (DoS 8+) while her Guard is down, one of her limbs or body parts is amputated or crushed beyond natural recovery.

Corrupted

This is almost exclusively used as a weapon condition for the touch of certain chimera and other creatures birthed by the Pontus. The character afflicted with this as a temporary condition immediately takes one point of *Corruption*. If this is applied as a persistent condition, the character immediately gains a point of *Corruption* and cannot lose any *Corruption* until she recovers from this condition.

Damaged

Characters suffering this condition immediately take a physical or emotional Wound. The current context of the character should determine which type of Wound she receives, and the Narrator will decide if it is not obvious. If this is placed as a persistent condition, the Wound may not be healed until the character recovers from this condition.

Dazed

A *Dazed* character has trouble reacting to her surroundings. Reacting requires the use of two initiative cards instead of one.

Delirious

This condition is usually the result of feverous illnesses or drugs that cause paranoia, delusions, and hallucinations. A *Delirious* character suffers a –2 penalty to her *Focus* aptitude. This penalty will affect all combinations and traits that use *Focus*, including Guard. This condition can be acquired multiple times and its effects are cumulative. Additionally, any test using *Focus* that

achieves a remarkable failure (DoS –4) will cause the character to suffer a delusion or hallucination. This may carry with it false sights, sounds, or smells that other characters cannot perceive.

Deprived

This condition is most commonly the result of hazardous environments and lack of access to basic necessities. In the barren wilderness, a person can die from a *Deprivation* of food or heat. When submerged underwater, a person can die from a *Deprivation* of air. A person with a dehydrating disease, or one stranded in the desert can die from a *Deprivation* of water. This condition can apply to any situation where a person is denied access to something necessary for life.

This condition can be acquired multiple times and its effects are cumulative. This represents a continued lack of a life-sustaining necessity, such as air, food, or water. Each instance of the *Deprivation* condition inflicts a –1 penalty to a character's *Vigor* aptitude. These penalties affect all combinations and traits that use *Vigor*, including physical Defense. If a character acquires another *Deprived* condition when her *Vigor* is already reduced to zero, she receives a Wound instead. Any penalties to *Vigor* are removed the moment the character regains access to the necessity she was lacking, but Wounds remain: a character deprived of food recovers from all *Deprived* conditions after her first full meal, but any Wounds sustained from being *Deprived* remain until healed via normal recovery.

The rules for how often a character acquires this condition are listed under the rules for *Extreme Environments*, p. 96

Destroyed

This persistent condition can only be placed by doing Damage to an object that has already been rendered *Nonfunctional*. An object that has been *Destroyed* cannot be repaired, but can be salvaged for half its Cost value in materials. This condition has no effect on living beings.

Disarmed

A character who becomes *Disarmed* loses the use of one weapon, one piece of evidence, her armor, or some other accoutrement worn or carried. This usually represents dropping a weapon or tool, cutting through armor straps to leave an area exposed, or providing an argument that renders a piece of evidence useless. The character loses access to the lost tool until the end of the current conflict or scene. Alternatively, if the object is a hand held tool, the Narrator may allow a character to make a *Focus + Composure* test to find the tool and a maneuver to pick it up. When *Disarmed* is a persistent condition, the object in question takes a rank of Damage and needs to be repaired before it can be used again.

Disoriented

Disoriented characters automatically lose Attack Priority, regardless of all other modifiers. In the case of two or more *Disoriented* characters engaging in an exchange, the actions of all *Disoriented* characters resolve simultaneously after all non-*Disoriented* characters' actions are completed.

Entrapped

When a character becomes *Entrapped*, she is in some way barred from leaving the scene and cannot flee. This usually abstracts being backed into a corner or emotionally captivated. If persistent, this may involve emotional outrage, a sprained ankle, or some other malady that prevents the desire or ability to flee.

Exposed

Normally a targeted character has three available avenues of attack in physical conflict and only one in social conflict. When a character is *Exposed*, an additional avenue of attack is available when attacking her. Perhaps this moves the character to uneven ground where she opens a new angle from which to be struck, or the conversation naturally divides to allow for two lines of argument to convince a single person. However it happens, more characters can attack an *Exposed* target at the same time than would normally be allowed.

Fatigued

When a character becomes *Fatigued,* she immediately loses one unused initiative card. If the *Fatigued* condition is applied more than once, an additional card is lost with each new application. A character who has *Fatigued* as a persistent condition is dealt and retains one fewer initiative cards. *Fatigued* characters also travel much more slowly. For each *Fatigued* condition, a character's travel rate on foot is reduced by one third of their normal rate, and a character with three *Fatigued* conditions is too exhausted to move under their own power.

Incapacitated

A character who receives the *Incapacitated* condition is rendered unconscious. Immediately discard all initiative cards, and do not draw new initiative cards while this condition persists. *Incapacitated* characters immediately drop their Guard. If the condition is temporary, another character may spend an action to stabilize this character, rendering her conscious and removing the condition; becoming conscious does not allow her to gain new initiative cards, but it does allow her to raise her Guard. If left untreated, the condition remains until the end of the sequence. If the condition is persistent, the character is comatose, and cannot regain consciousness until the condition is removed via physical recovery.

Moribund

A character with this severe condition has experienced enough physical trauma that they are at a significant risk of going into terminal shock and dying. While suffering from the *Moribund* condition, the character will die when her Wound Penalties reach –8, rather than the normal –10.

Nonfunctional

An object that receives this condition will no longer perform its intended functions. If placed as a temporary condition, it represents a machine jamming up or otherwise ceasing to work for momentary environmental factors. Usually, *Nonfunctional* cannot be placed as a persistent condition by a penetrating attack, rather such a condition is the consequence of the object receiving a number of Damage ranks that exceeds its Structure. Also, this condition is not removed like other conditions. As soon as a single rank of Damage is repaired, reducing the Damage ranks to below the object's Structure, it is functional again. This condition has no effect on living beings.

Obsessed

This condition is most linked to drug addiction and magically created infatuations. While a character suffers from *Obsessed*, she takes a –2 penalty to all actions during each chapter where she does not indulge in the object of her obsession. So long as the character indulges in her obsession during the current chapter, this condition has no effect other than the consequences created by the object of the character's desire. This condition may not be removed through normal healing if the character has indulged during the recovery period. Also, this condition may be assigned multiple times to simulate depth of obsession and lengthen recovery time.

Outmaneuvered

A character can be outmaneuvered by a deft conversationalist in a ballroom or by a cunning warrior on a battlefield. This represents being manipulated into a disadvantageous position. All opponents receive a noncumulative +1 to any trait tests made against an *Outmaneuvered* target.

Overwhelmed

A character can be overwhelmed by information, emotion, or enemy combatants. When a character becomes *Overwhelmed*, she immediately drops one point of Guard or shifts one step of Disposition to her opponent's advantage. If this condition is persistent, these changes will occur at the beginning of every conflict until the character recovers from this condition.

Staggered

The character is struck so forcefully, or told something so unexpected that she cannot maintain defense of herself or her positions. In physical conflict, a *Staggered* character will not regain a point of Guard at their next normal opportunity to do so (either through direct action or at the end of a sequence). In social conflict, a *Staggered* character will not move her Disposition in the desired direction on her next opportunity to do so (opponents may still change her Disposition to her detriment). After the first missed opportunity to regain Guard or voluntarily change her own Disposition this condition is removed. If *Staggered* is placed as a persistent condition, the character may neither regain Guard nor move her own Disposition regarding the instigating argument until the condition is removed.

Unbalanced

A character can be physically unbalanced from standing on an uneven platform or emotionally unbalanced due to anger, rage, grief, or other strong emotions. If an *Unbalanced* character wishes to take a maneuver on any turn in a conflict, she must flip an additional initiative card to take that maneuver.

Undone

Treat this condition as an additional successful attack of the same type just made that succeeds with a DoS 1. Resolve the second attack and then discard this condition. This condition is never persistent.

HEALING AND RECOVERY

The Clockwork is a dangerous place. People get hurt and Reputations are destroyed. Thankfully, time heals. Characters will naturally recover from physical maladies and social standing will eventually return to equilibrium.

RECOVERING FROM PHYSICAL MALADIES

Physical maladies are Wounds, persistent conditions, or other long term physical afflictions from which a character suffers. Maladies will continue to plague the character until they are healed and removed. Even when a character is fully recovered of all maladies, she still may suffer from pain and discomfort. The removal of maladies simply means that any lingering effects are not severe enough to create mechanical effects within the game. Scarring and other cosmetic ramifications may remain if the Narrator and player agree that it would add to the game. However, these should never give a mechanical disadvantage.

NATURAL HEALING

If the afflicted character avoids infection and other hazards, the human body can do a rather good job of healing itself. Any character who remains mostly inactive with sufficient access to food, water, and shelter will slowly recover from physical maladies. The character may make one healing test after three days; another after one week; and another after three weeks. At each interval, the healing character tests *Vigor + Will* with a Difficulty equal to her current Wound Penalties. Success (DoS 1+) on a healing test removes one malady. A remarkable success (DoS 4+) removes two. The patient may choose which of her maladies she removes when she is allowed to do so. If any maladies remain after this three week healing process, they are beyond the body's natural ability to heal and the character needs to seek medical care.

MEDICAL CARE

Any character with at least one rank in the *Medicine* skill can provide basic medical care. Such a character may test *Reason + Medicine* to Stabilize, Diagnose, or Treat a patient. Each type of test is described below.

Stabilizing a Patient

Anytime a character is suffering trauma, blood loss, or any other kind of accumulating Wound Penalties, she may be stabilized to prevent further penalties. This requires a *Reason + Medicine* test with a Difficulty equal to the patient's current Wound Penalties. If the test is successful, the target character is stabilized. Once stabilized, her Wound Penalties are reduced to –2 per Wound. All additional penalties from trauma and blood loss are removed and she will no longer accrue new penalties unless she suffers further harm. Stabilizing a patient often requires minimal medical supplies such as bandages and antiseptic to prevent infection. If no medical supplies are available, they are subject to the risk of Infection at the Narrator's discretion.

Diagnosing a Patient

A patient's illness can be identified through diagnosis. The diagnosing character tests *Reason + Medicine* against a Difficulty based on the obscurity of the illness. Common issues such as Infection can be diagnosed with a Difficulty of 1, and common diseases can be diagnosed at Difficulty 3. Exotic diseases, which the physician must research, require Difficulties of 5 or higher. Success on this test will identify the illness and determine the best course of treatment. See *Medicines* (below) for the use of medication.

Treating a Patient

Once stabilized, characters who have access to a physician and a clean environment will automatically succeed at all recovery tests. Thus, one malady is simply removed after three days, one week, and three weeks. In addition to this, characters receive the benefit of a physician to make *Reason + Medicine* tests to continue treatment if any maladies remain at the end of three weeks. The Difficulty for this test is equal to the patient's current Wound Penalties. At the end of the three weeks of Wound treatment and care, the physician may test once for each remaining malady. Each success removes one malady. If any maladies remain unhealed, the physician may test again for each remaining malady after every three week interval.

MEDICINES

A character will continue to suffer the effects of persistent conditions and Wounds until they are removed through recovery. However, some medicines can ameliorate these ills. Common anodynes such as laudanum can be used to temporarily reduce Wound Penalties. Cocaine drops are given to teething children as well as to singers and orators to soothe the throat. More specific and expensive medications can ameliorate certain persistent conditions and fight off disease. A list of commonly taken medicines is given on the *Medicines and Drugs* table, p. 193.

Medicines require proper dosing to be effective and not harm a patient. After a successful Diagnosis, performing a *Medicine* test is necessary to determine a safe dosage for a patient to use. The physician tests *Reason + Medicine* against a Difficulty equal to the Strength of the medicine (see *Medicines*, this page). Success (DoS + 1) provides the proper dosage. The proper dose of a medicine produces the drug's Effect, which will last for the medicine's Duration. If the *Medicine* test yields a marginal success (DoS 0), the medicine was underdosed and has no effect. If the test yields a failure (DoS –1), the medicine was over prescribed and produces double its normal Effect and one Side-Effect. If the test yields a remarkable failure (DoS –4), the patient receives an overdose and she suffers all listed Side-Effects without any beneficial effect.

All drugs with the listed side effect *Obsessed* are addictive. As long as a character uses the proper dosage, the medicine will create its desired effect without side effects or risk of addiction.

REWARDING PLAYERS FOR ACCEPTING OUTCOMES

Player characters have the option of spending a point of *Purpose* to avoid a social outcome, or to stop believing in or pursuing something of which they have been convinced or persuaded. However, if they allow their characters to be swayed by discourse in the game and they do not avoid these outcomes they should be rewarded for their good roleplaying. When a player character goes along with being convinced or persuaded and acts on their new belief or course of action in a meaningful way in the game, they receive a single additional experience point for following through on their social outcome. Once the character takes the experience point for this choice, the outcome may never be undone by spending *Purpose*: the only way to think better of their actions is if someone else convinces them they were wrong, or persuades them to act against their new belief. Following through with that reversal does not allow for any additional experience.

Characters with the *Medicine* skill may also self-medicate for medical or recreational purposes. If a character wishes to intentionally take enough of a drug to gain a Side-Effect, she tests *Reason + Medicine* against a Difficulty equal to the Strength of the medicine. If she succeeds, she achieves the level of over-prescription she desires and may choose her Side Effect in addition to double the normal Effect of the medicine. Usually characters choose *Dazed* to represent euphoria. If this test ever fails (DoS –1), the character misjudges the dose and will acquire triple the normal Effect of the medicine and the *Obsessed* condition. The character is now struggling with addiction.

ADDICTION AS A CONDITION

When a character takes a more than the recommended dosage of an addictive medicine or drug, the drug will make an attack on the character. Instead of an aptitude + skill combination, the drug will use its Strength, and will use a Difficulty equal to the consuming character's *Vigor + Will*. If the drug achieves a remarkable success (DoS 4+), it will place the *Obsessed* condition on the character. The object of the character's obsession will be the drug. For the full effects of this result, see the description of the *Obsessed* condition, p. 100.

INFECTION

Any time a character is made to bleed in an unclean environment, there is the risk of Infection. The use of antiseptics in the same scene in which the *Bleeding* condition or Wound was suffered will eliminate all chance of Infection. Otherwise, the character must test Vigor + Will, Difficulty 5 once per day. A remarkable success (DoS 4+) will remove the Infection. Each failure allows the Narrator to assign one of the following conditions: Crippled, Delirious, or Deprived. These are treated as persistent conditions and can be healed as such. Infection can be deadly and is one of the leading causes of death in the Clockwork world.

DEATH AND DYING

If a character's total Wound Penalties ever equal or exceed –10, she dies. The character should be allowed to speak any dramatic last words she wishes, but then will breathe her last and give up the ghost. Sometimes, however, the will to live is just strong enough to let a character cling to life beyond all odds.

Escaping Death

At the moment of death, the Clockwork itself may move to grant one more chance at life so that a character may continue toward her *Purpose*, or a near-miraculous circumstance snatches a character from the jaws of death thanks to an incredible expenditure of *Ether*. If a character is about to die for any reason, they may instead lose one fixed rank of either *Purpose* or *Ether* to escape dying. This loss is permanent and may be performed even if the character has already spent potential during the current sequence. A character who chooses to cheat death in this way avoids the last Wound Penalty, Wound, or other effect that would have killed her, then immediately stabilizes. She refreshes all temporary potential of the same type as the fixed rank that was lost, and may spend potential of that type for the remainder of the sequence ignoring all normal restrictions. Then, she immediately seizes the initiative (even if she has no initiative cards to flip), gaining an immediate interrupt turn with a move, maneuver, and action. During this single turn, she ignores the effects of all wound penalties and conditions.

Escaping death in this way does not remove any conditions, Wounds, or Wound Penalties. Even those that do escape death for a moment are in serious danger, as they are still incredibly vulnerable. Without immediate aid or escape provided by others, a character is likely to quickly succumb to their circumstances.

RECOVERING FROM SOCIAL RAMIFICATIONS

Social ramifications include being convinced or persuaded as well as having one's Affinities or Reputations altered. Dispositions are not included in social ramifications, as they can be changed by characters at the beginning of each new social encounter. Altered Affinities and Reputations require time to recover, and the attendant social ramifications will continue to affect the character until she is restored. Even when a character is fully recovered of all ramifications, she still may suffer from the occasional nagging rumor or jilted acquaintance. The removal of ramifications simply means that their lingering effects are not severe enough to create mechanical effects within the game. Once something is known in society, it is never unknown. However, any continuing fame or scorn is too minimal to create any mechanical effects.

RECOVERING FROM BEING CONVINCED

A convincing argument will hold sway over its target for at least a single chapter. After that the character will maintain their new conviction until evidence to the contrary surfaces. New evidence allows for a new social conflict to occur, which may see the targeted character convinced of a new belief.

RECOVERING FROM A PERSUASION

When a character is persuaded, she will perform the action that she has been persuaded to do at the first convenient and physically safe opportunity. The persuaded character will hold to her new found desire until an opportunity to act presents itself or until the end of the chapter, whichever happens first.

NORMALIZING AFFINITIES

Affinities don't heal, they normalize. Those that have been temporarily elevated beyond their fixed value will fall back to it over time. Those that have been temporarily reduced below their fixed value will raise back to it over time. Affinities that were never chosen by a character, but were placed on her by another character or circumstance, are considered to have a fixed value of 0 ranks. So long as certain conditions are met, each altered Affinity will normalize one rank after three days; another rank after one week; and another after three weeks, and then one more every three weeks following. Once the Affinity's current temporary rank has reached its fixed rank, it is considered to have fully recovered. Characters may normalize any number of Affinities at once. If an Affinity is altered during recovery, its recovery time cycle begins anew.

There are two necessary conditions for the positive normalization of Affinities: positive exposure to the subject of the Affinity and no behavior that would damage it. For example, a man who damaged his Affinity for his wife by cheating on her must have positive exposure to his wife and a lack of exposure to his mistress in order for the Affinity for his wife to normalize. A woman who damaged her Affinity to her personal code of honor by lying must avoid lying and tell the truth. If positive exposure to the subject of the Affinity and a lack of damaging behavior are maintained for the required time, the Affinity will move one rank closer to its fixed value.

Characters can also reduce a temporarily increased Affinity by avoiding it or intentionally acting against it. Normally, avoiding the focus of an Affinity is the best course of action, as enthusiasm can quickly fade. A young gentleman who finds himself too caught up in gambling and carousing may retire to the countryside for a few weeks to clear his head and cool his enthusiasm for reckless living. In other circumstances, directly acting against an enhanced Affinity will reduce it back towards its normal rating. If, rather than leaving the social scene that caused him trouble, the gentleman instead began actively campaigning against the vice of gambling and quit the social club that introduced him to it, he might push down his temporary Affinity more quickly.

Making Altered Affinities Permanent

An Affinity is a variable trait. If an Affinity has been strengthened or damaged by character actions, it will return to normal over time (see *Affinities*, p. 168). However, a character may spend experience points to make the change in rank value permanent, making the temporary value of the Affinity its new fixed rank. These experience points may be spent by the character herself or by someone else. The experience point cost for making an altered Affinity permanent is equal to the newly achieved level.

Sometimes a Narrator character has manipulated a player character into developing a disadvantageous Affinity or decreasing an advantageous one. That antagonist may also make the changes he instigated permanent by spending experience points. If a Narrator character opts to making a change to an Affinity permanent, the Narrator awards the affected character ½ its new fixed value in experience points.

NORMALIZING REPUTATIONS

Like Affinities, Reputations don't heal, they normalize. Those that have been temporarily elevated beyond their fixed value will fall back to it over time. Those that have been temporarily reduced below their fixed value will regain it over time. Reputations that were never chosen by a character, but were placed on her by another character or circumstance are considered to have a fixed value of 0 ranks. So long as certain conditions are met, each altered Reputation will normalize one rank after three days; another rank after one week; and another after three weeks and then one more every three weeks following. Once the Reputation's current temporary rank has reached its fixed rank, it is considered to have fully recovered. Characters normalize any number of Reputations at once. If a Reputation is altered during recovery, its recovery time cycle begins anew.

Altered Reputations are fickle things: they return to normal as circumstances return to normal. If the character lays low, her Reputation will normalize. However, if the character is seen in public participating in actions that support a particular Reputation, the talk will continue and no recovery may occur. Elevated Reputations will always recover at normal recovery intervals unless they are made permanent.

Making Altered Reputations Permanent

If a Reputation has been strengthened or damaged by character actions, it will return to normal over time. However, if a character spends experience points to make the change permanent, she can prevent a Reputation from normalizing. These experience points may be spent by the character herself, or by someone else. The experience point cost for making an altered Reputation permanent is equal to twice the newly achieved level.

Sometimes a Narrator character has manipulated a player character into developing a disadvantageous Reputation or decreasing an advantageous one. That antagonist may also make the changes he instigated permanent by spending experience points. If a Narrator character opts to making a change to a Reputation permanent, the Narrator awards the affected character its new value in experience points.

The slim envelope was light in her hands as Elise shut the door to the small bedroom she shared with her mother at the boardinghouse. Although her heart fluttered like a silk scarf on a Portsmouth pier, Elise did not open the envelope until she had composed herself in front of the vanity. Aside from this single piece of furniture, pride and self-control were among the only things she had left from her life before the death of her father; the entailment had cost her family everything except each other. A single stroke of the bronze letter opener, and she began to read:

My Beloved Sister,

I have treated you very badly in not writing before now, but when you know the reason, I think you will understand my hesitance, even if you are not able to forgive it. Any letters you have sent to Johannesburg have not reached me; I was gone before they arrived. The story that I have to relate is harrowing in places, but keep in mind as you read that I am well and in much better spirits than when we said farewell those many months ago in Portsmouth.

It will not surprise you that I turned out to be a poor fit for mining. The work is tremendously difficult and there is such an enormous deal to be mindful of that accidents happen easily. In my first week, a Dutchman had his leg crushed in a collapse and another man was asphyxiated before we could dig him out. I tell you this only so that when I explain what happened next, you understand how much worse things could have been.

There was an explosion. I will not go into detail, as much for my own sake as for yours, but the fact is my hands were injured quite badly. The surgeon insisted that if both hands were not removed, I would almost certainly die of infection. I told him that without my hands, I would just as certainly die of starvation, having no money and no prospect for work that did not involve the use of tools. I explained that even if I could have afforded the return trip to England, I should not become a burden to my mother and sister.

After hearing my desperate protestations, the surgeon, who was not much older than I am, gave me a long hard look. He said that there might be another way, if I was "an open minded sort of lad who could keep his mouth shut." He had a colleague in Pretoria, a Dr. Standish, who was recruiting patients willing to undergo experimental treatments that aren't strictly legal yet because of some bad business in Singapore a few years back.

In any event, I agreed. What choice did I have? This Dr. Standish had all the appropriate qualifications, trained at the university in Manchester, etc. Best of all, he wasn't concerned that I couldn't pay. He just wanted to see if his treatment would succeed.

I will not bore you with the tale of my journey to Pretoria in the back of a mule cart, nor will I embarrass you with stories of how the surgeon's assistant Heinrich had to travel with me and assist with the most simple of tasks, as my hands were wrapped so completely as to be useless.

When we arrived in Pretoria, the medical facility was neither so modern nor so clean as I had hoped, and Dr. Standish—although older and more experienced than his colleague in Johannesburg—had a wolfish look to him that was unsettling. By the body and breath, I thank the Clockmaker that I had no alternatives at this point other than degradation and starvation, because I am quite sure I should not have gone through with it otherwise. I agreed to allow Dr. Standish to do, "whatever he saw fit," during the operation. He repeated this phrase three times so that I would remember it exactly; it was not until

I woke up after surgery that I understood why.

There was no pain, at least not at first. When I awoke, I was strapped down to the table. Both my hands and feet were wrapped in bulky gauze and I had no feeling below my wrists or ankles, not even when Dr. Standish pricked me through the gauze with a long needle. This did not please him, nor did my questions. "Why," I demanded to know, "had he operated on my feet?" "Because I saw fit," was his only reply.

For three nights and days I remained strapped to that table. His assistant looked after my bodily needs, although this daily humiliation seemed unimportant now, preoccupied as I was with the thought that I had not only lost the use of my hands, but would also never walk.

On the third day everything changed. When Dr. Standish pricked me with the needle in the morning, I felt a dull pain in each extremity. By noon, I could move my hands and feet, although they were sluggish and strange. By evening, I was restored, but it was not until Dr. Standish unwrapped the gauze that I saw how this was possible.

This may be hard for you to read, but I need you to believe with all the fierce faith of our childhood together that what I tell you now is a good thing: Dr. Standish has given me new hands and new feet. I am stronger than I was before; I can do things I had never imagined a human being could do. This is because I have the hands and feet of an orangutan.

You must not be upset, for all is well with me. The only drawback I can see is that not everyone will be as open-minded and understanding as I know that you and mother will be. You have probably heard some of the words they call those of us who have had the treatment; they are not flattering. But since the operation my life has become more exciting than anything I have dared to imagine since boyhood. Despite the prejudices against "beastfolk," it was easy to find work. I can do things no mere human being could even attempt.

I am a crewman now on a rogue wind called the *Lady Stuart's Revenge*. We are in Rome now, but will be gone before this letter reaches you. It turns out being an outlaw can be every bit as romantic and exciting as the storybooks would have you believe; I have never been so happy.

I do not know when I will see you again, but I promise that one day I will come home and we will be together again. Please explain to mother. I trust you to judge which details will put her at ease and which are better left out.

With all my love, your devoted brother-

J.T.

Elise was not sure when she had started crying, but by the time she finished the letter she was blinking through her tears. She fought the revulsion that rose in her throat and hastily set the letter down, wiping her hands as though she could wipe away the feeling of contamination. An outlaw? That could be a matter for forgiveness, but this? How could she forgive anyone for the mutilation of the beautiful boy her brother had been? When she tried to picture his face, all she could see was the foul creature she had observed begging on the docks last June, a thing that was once a man; it had the snout of a dog and the grotesque eyes of some hungry raptor. Such an abomination could never be any kin of hers. She would tell her mother the kindest lie she could; Jonathan was dead after all.

CHARACTER CREATION

The Clockwork is a divinely created, incomprehensibly complex series of systems, ever unfolding toward the culmination of the Clockmaker's plan, and every person that ever existed is a cog in this vast cosmic machine. Those who fulfill their designated purpose in this divine plan support this orderly creation. However, not all of the cogs turn in the manner the Clockmaker intended. While some citizens of the Clockwork adhere to the rules, morality, and structures of orderly society, others reject them. Most people fall somewhere in between. As the Clockwork is all that protects us against the rising Pontus, there is a vital balance to be struck between supporting its machinations by siding with the greater good and following one's own dreams and desires.

In order to enter the Clockwork world, a player must first create a character—a persona to be portrayed within the game. Like all inhabitants of the Clockwork, this character must choose a path between divine order and personal desire. As a character is created, the player must choose aspects of her personality, body, mind, and background. Some choices will actualize her potential and provide a *Purpose*, while others will offer greater freedom but dislodge her from the protection of the Clockwork. All choices define her capabilities within the game.

Mechanically, much of a character is defined by various traits which determine her abilities, desires, and goals. As a character is created, these traits are recorded on a character sheet. Each character's sheet will be referenced throughout the game to remind players of that character's capabilities and passions.

CHARACTER CREATION SUMMARY

CHARACTER CREATION IN TEN STEPS

1 Choose a Bloodline p. 109

Is your character a pure mortal, or does she descend from a corrupted ancestry?

Choose a bloodline, record its bonuses, blessings, and curses.

2 Choose a Pursuit p. 123

How does your character choose to act against the Pontus, and how does that affect her core nature, motivations, and personality?

Choose one pursuit, record its bonuses.

3 Choose a Background p. 130

What trade, lifestyle, or situation of birth influenced your character the most?

Choose a background, record its bonuses.

4 Assign Aptitudes p. 135

What are your character's core competencies?

Assign 5 ranks to aptitudes.

5 Assign Skills p. 136

What skills has your character learned?

Assign 12 ranks of skills.

6 Choose Assets and Liabilities p. 155

Does your character have any special social advantages or disadvantages, fiscal resources or debts, or other benefits or complications?

Choose a number of assets determined by your chosen background. Any character may choose up to two liabilities, gaining an additional asset for each one taken.

7 Choose Affinities p. 168

What are the things, people, or ideologies that drive your character to do what she does?

Place three ranks into at least two different Affinities.

8 Choose Reputations p. 170

For what behaviors, adventures, or events is your character known?

Place three ranks in at least two Reputations.

9 Choose Starting Accoutrements p. 171

What special gear and accoutrements does your character own?

10 Finishing Touches p. 171

Calculate common derived traits and get her ready for play.

ANATOMY OF A CHARACTER

The following terms appear on the character sheet. Here is a quick reference for what they mean and where to find further information on them.

Affinities: These are deep affections and loyalties that motivate a character. See p. 168.

Aptitudes: Broad areas of talent that can be applied to any number of tasks. They are combined with skills to perform trait tests. See p. 135 for aptitudes, and p. 68. for trait tests.

Assets: Atypical talents, possessions, or circumstances that aid a character. See p. 155.

Background: The early life experiences of a character: determines starting *Class*, *Means*, and Assets, and gives bonus ranks in some skills. See p. 130.

Blessings: Special benefits a character receives through her bloodline. Blessings are detailed in the entries for each bloodline.

Bloodline: A hereditary lineage within the Clockwork. Each character must come from one of the four bloodlines: pureblood, beast-folk, changeling, or nephilim. See opposite page.

Class: A character's long-term position in the social hierarchy of the Empire. *Class* is often considered along with Reputations to determine how highly Esteemed a character is. *Class* can only be changed through great effort. See p. 135.

Corruption: One of three types of potential and a measure of the taint in one's soul. It is not assigned in character creation, but rather gained in gameplay by committing heinous sins. See p. 72.

Curses: Special vulnerabilities that afflict a character because of her bloodline. Curses are detailed in the entries for each bloodline.

Esteem: The circumstantial and subjective respect and influence that a character has in social situations. Esteem protects a character from the effects of slander, insults, and social faux-pas. It is derived from a mixture of Reputation and either *Class* or *Means*. See p. 74.

Ether: One of three types of potential. *Ether* represents a character's tendency to change, create opportunity, and disrupt the intended course of events in the Clockwork. See p. 71.

Liabilities: Unusual or circumstantial drawbacks and difficulties that afflict a character. See p. 155.

Means: General resources, property, and reliable annual income; stable material wealth that can only be increased with great effort. See p. 135.

Membership: A character who takes the *Membership* asset (see p. 156) will receive the privilleges of belonging to an organization See p. 160.

Potential: A metaphysical measure of the orderly and disorderly tendencies of a character, and how much *Corruption* taints a character. See p. 71.

Purpose: One of three types of potential. *Purpose* represents a character's ability resist outside influence and participate in the divine plan for the Clockwork. See p. 72.

Pursuit: The fundamental outlook on life that guides a character's actions. See p. 123.

Reputations: The perceptions and expectations that color others' reactions to a character. Combines with *Class* or *Means* to determine Esteem. See p. 170.

Skills: Specialized ability or learning focused on narrow areas of endeavor; combined with aptitudes to perform trait tests. See p. 136.

Transcendent Powers: Various ways to supernaturally affect change in the world. See p. 219.

CLOCKWORK

Name: _____
Pursuit: _____
Player Name: _____

Bloodline: _____
Background: _____

STATUS
Class ○ 1 2 3 4 5
Means ○ 1 2 3 4 5

POTENTIAL
Purpose ○ 1 2 3 4 5
Ether ○ 1 2 3 4 5
Corruption 1 2 3 4 5

Grace
Vigor
1 2 3 4 5
1 2 3 4 5

APTITUDES

Reason
Focus
1 2 3 4 5
1 2 3 4 5

Presence
Will
1 2 3 4 5
1 2 3 4 5

MEMBERSHIPS
○ 1 2 3 4 5

REPUTATIONS
○ 1 2 3 4 5
○ 1 2 3 4 5

AFFINITIES
○ 1 2 3 4 5
○ 1 2 3 4 5

Academics 1 2 3 4 5
Artisan 1 2 3 4 5
Athletics 1 2 3 4 5
Bureaucracy 1 2 3 4 5
Burglary 1 2 3 4 5
Command 1 2 3 4 5
Composure 1 2 3 4 5
Engineering 1 2 3 4 5
Fencing 1 2 3 4 5

SKILLS

Firearms 1 2 3 4 5
Fisticuffs 1 2 3 4 5
Guile 1 2 3 4 5
Intuition 1 2 3 4 5
Investigation 1 2 3 4 5
Medicine 1 2 3 4 5
Melee 1 2 3 4 5
Mysteries 1 2 3 4 5
Parley 1 2 3 4 5

Refinement 1 2 3 4 5
Riding 1 2 3 4 5
Science 1 2 3 4 5
Stealth 1 2 3 4 5
Streetwise 1 2 3 4 5
Survival 1 2 3 4 5
Tactics 1 2 3 4 5
Temptation 1 2 3 4 5
Vocation 1 2 3 4 5

BLESSINGS, CURSES & MASTERIES

SOCIAL CONFLICT
SOCIAL DEFENSE
WILL + SKILL
Composure _____

PHYSICAL CONFLICT
PHYSICAL DEFENSE
VIGOR + SKILL
Athletics _____   Armor

ASSETS, LIABILITIES & TRANSCENDENT POWERS

DISPOSITIONS
Hostile Guarded Indifferent Agreeable Favorable
H G I A F
H G I A F

GUARD
1/2 FOCUS +1 for Weapon
○ ○ ○ ○ ○
WOUNDS ○ ○ ○ ○

WEAPONS & EVIDENCE
Name   Reach Potency Load Weapon Condition

ESTEEM
Indifferent + (Tenor-Status) +/- 1/2 Relevant Reputation
H G I A F

Wound Penalties ☐
Persistent Conditions _____

EXPERIENCE POINTS ☐

BLOODLINES: CHARACTER CREATION STEP ONE

Who a person is begins in the blood. The blood of countless forebears flows in the veins of every human being, fueling their passions, and influencing their thoughts and impulses. It also does much to determine a character's place in the Clockwork, so the first step of character creation is to choose a bloodline. Players choose one of four bloodlines for their characters: pureblood, beastfolk, changeling, or nephilim. Each defines both physical and metaphysical properties of the character, and whether they are natural, corrupted, or have been altered through scientific experimentation.

Census data shows that purebloods make up over ninety-eight percent of the Empire's population, leaving corrupted bloodlines a tiny minority. However, the Empire's tolerance of unnatural bloodlines sees a climbing number of corrupted immigrants due to the threat of death and persecution they face in other lands. Thus, it is assumed that the percentage of corrupted beings on mainland Europe is even less than within the Empire.

Choose a bloodline for your character and record the bonuses it grants on your character sheet. All bloodlines grant a single one-rank bonus to an aptitude and an one-rank bonus to each of two skills. Each bloodline will also provide two ranks of potential, which reflects how that bloodline pushes a character toward order or chaos. All bloodlines also have multiple blessings and curses—special benefits and drawbacks linked to that bloodline alone.

PUREBLOODS

So the Maker created mankind in His own image, in the image of the Maker He crafted them, male and female He created them.

—Genesis 1:27

The Clockwork was created as a place for the Maker's beloved humans to dwell, and in turn humans were meant to be its stewards and the chief participants of the divine plan. They have failed to live up to this duty. From the first errors in judgement made in Eden, and down through the tragic and bloody ages since, humankind has turned from the path laid out for them and brought pain and suffering upon themselves. The selfishness and mistakes of humanity weaken the Clockwork and expose it to the primordial chaos of the Pontus, which spreads through creation like a poison, weakening the fabric of reality and allowing outside influences to slowly contaminate those within it. Those lineages of mortals who have escaped this taint retain their pure blood, while others now descend from corrupted bloodlines.

While there are many purebloods who choose to act against their intended role in the Clockwork, the freedom to so choose seems to be valued by the Maker. No celestial action prevents humanity from suffering the consequences of its decisions—including the ravages of the Pontus—yet there is regular heavenly intervention made to preserve the sanctity of free will. A vanguard of angels patrols the Borderlands to thwart powerful fey or Grigori who seek to gather human worshipers to do their bidding. Heavenly guardians traverse the Broken Road, and watch over those who sleep in the Underworld. Most cosmologists agree that it is the divine hope that pure blooded mortals will eventually learn to use the gift of free will to choose rightly, and bring about the glorious culmination of the Clockwork.

The power and destiny of purebloods is ultimately a matter of choice: live according to a plan we make for ourselves and hope that the world will endure, or strive to fulfill the divine plan and bring the Clockwork to its intended culmination. No mortal knows exactly what the Maker intended for her, but everyone must choose how she makes her way through the world. It is within the power of every pureblood to have a hand in saving the world if she chooses rightly, and the Maker has endowed each pureblood with powerful blessings to help her live up to that potential.

The very gears of the Clockwork turn to protect purebloods and smooth their path through life. The deep and constantly-renewed connection to the Clockwork from their *Purposed* blessing allows all purebloods to face the challenges of life with more certainty and safety. This powerful connection with their intended purpose protects those living uneventful lives, or acts as a shield for those who actively push back against the rising chaos.

Purebloods also enjoy several advantages in dealing with the greater spiritual reality of the Clockwork. Purebloods are the only bloodline that receives charisms, rare and mysterious spiritual gifts bestowed upon individuals by the Clockmaker. The descent of the Maker's Spirit upon a person imbues them with a special mystical power such as healing the sick, banishing demons, or the gift of speaking in foreign tongues. Of the small handful of men and women who receive these gifts, most are pious individuals who live exemplary lives of devotion and prayer before they ever discover their blessing. A tiny handful are people of little or no faith, yet are granted with these abilities without precondition. Perhaps such unexpected gifts are a last chance for the recipient to live a better life than they have, or a last warning before they are crushed by spiritual realities for which they are unprepared. It is also possible that their use of the charisms for what appear to be their own purposes supports the Clockwork in some subtle way. Also, ritual magic was never meant to directly impact humans, so all purebloods enjoy some protection from its workings, and are likewise shielded from the direct activity of angels and the Fallen.

All purebloods are born with an innate talent for a particular area of endeavor. Many discover where their gift lies at a young age and use that ability to help shape their lives. If they choose to devote themselves to developing the skill related to their talent they can become incredibly proficient in its use. So it is that each pureblood is given an opportunity to reach heights of accomplishment that other bloodlines cannot match. Those few who dedicate themselves utterly to their calling are revered as great thinkers, guardians, artists, and leaders whose names are remembered throughout the ages, and whose deeds impact the unfolding of the Clockwork long after they pass.

With these gifts, all purebloods have the capacity and opportunity to be successful stewards of the Clockwork, prepared for greatness and protected from many ills. There have always been those who dedicate themselves to bolstering the Clockwork, exploring its wonders, and improving the lives of their fellows. Millions of purebloods work to fulfill their role in the divine plan and hold the chaos at bay. The efforts of purebloods to better understand the Clockwork and themselves has benefited many through scientific discovery, art, and social progress. Although some disagree on the relative merits of particular advancements, all must affirm that the fruit of human endeavor has enabled the wonders of modern life, and there is a chance to improve the lives of many more with further discovery.

Pure and Corrupted Blood

Purebloods are not the only inhabitants of the Clockwork, and share the world with others that descend from unnatural parentage. The union of humans with the Fallen created the nephilim.

Intermingling with fey beings resulted in the birth of changelings. The excesses of unrestrained science and horrific surgical practices grafted animal parts to human bodies to create a third tainted bloodline called beastfolk. None of these beings were intended to exist, and therefore have no natural niche in the Clockwork, but by their partial human heritage they are born into it. These bloodlines also have free will and can choose to find or build a role for themselves in society and the workings of the world. Some purebloods reject this notion and ostracize those of tainted blood or even work to eradicate them, but a growing majority have come to believe that there is some responsibility to help find a place in the world for all bloodlines. Thankfully, within the Empire, there is tolerance for other bloodlines, even if that tolerance is not always paired with a full measure of respect.

QUALITIES OF A PUREBLOOD

- *Potential:* Every pureblood is purposed with a role in the divine plan, and the Clockwork protects their ability to fulfill it. Beginning pureblood characters receive two points of *Purpose*.
- *Aptitude Bonus:* The free will granted to humanity by the Clockmaker as part of the divine plan manifests in a one-rank bonus to the *Will* aptitude.
- *Skill Bonuses:* Whether they choose to pursue it or not, all mortals are born with a purpose within the divine plan and are gifted with the skills to perform it. At character creation, purebloods receive a one-rank bonus to any two skills of the player's choosing.
- *Blessing—Protected:* A human with pure blood is more fully integrated into the workings of the Clockwork than those of corrupted bloodlines, and the Clockwork protects its own. Supernatural powers are less likely to affect these characters. When targeting any pureblood characters, all ritual magic is performed with a -1 penalty. Likewise, angels and the Fallen receive a -1 penalty when targeting a pureblood with any action, as their being and purpose is bound to magic.
- *Blessing—Purposed:* Pureblood humans refresh one point of *Purpose* at the beginning of each session. This is in addition to the single point of *Purpose* or *Ether* granted to every character at that time.
- *Blessing—Talent:* To aid them in fulfilling their intended role in the Clockwork, purebloods receive a single mastery ability for one skill of their choosing. They need not meet the normal requirement of having a skill at five ranks in order to acquire this mastery (see *Mastery Abilities,* p. 138).

BEASTFOLK

"The most obvious deformity was in their faces, almost all of which were prognathous, malformed about the ears, with large and protuberant noses, very furry or very bristly hair, and often strangely-colored or strangely-placed eyes. … Beyond these general characters their heads had little in common; each preserved the quality of its particular species: the human mark distorted but did not hide the leopard, the ox, or the sow, or other animal or animals, from which the creature had been moulded"

—*The Island of Doctor Moreau*, H.G. Wells

The history of animal vivisection began with the second-century Roman physician Galen, who is said to have fathered the science. This ancient and well-explored practice taught us much about the inner workings of both the animal and human bodies and eventually led to the science of xenotransplantation, the merging of animal limbs and organs to the human body.

Xenotransplantation first came to public notice in 1668 with the reports of a Russian surgeon who repaired a human skull using bone from a dog. By 1670, both France and the Magisterium had declared the practice illegal and immoral. In the years that followed, much of the world came to agree. However, the ostracized practices continued in secluded locations, and came to the world's attention again in 1886 when a handful of ghastly animal-human hybrids washed up onto the docks in Singapore after fleeing those who had created them. These refugees told a story about a mad scientist performing hideous experiments on a remote island somewhere in the Pacific, a story that was eventually fictionalized in *The Island of Doctor Moreau (1896)*, a novel by H. G Wells. The unfortunate victims were labeled "beastfolk" and the name now applies to all who share their lot.

News of the refugee beastfolk made headlines around the world, which unfortunately gave inspiration for others to attempt xenotransplantation. Some surgeons see great promise in using xenotransplantation to rehabilitate those who have suffered major trauma, or were born with severe congenital problems, but for now the Empire and other civilized nations maintain a legal prohibition against the practice. This has not stopped all surgeons, though, and in recent years more and more beastfolk have been discovered, and it appears that rogue science may have opened a new Pandora's box. Introducing animal flesh into the body of a human taints the blood, and is believed to affect personality as well. This does not create drastic change, but tends to exaggerate some behaviors. An augmented man who once tended towards anger may now fly into rages, while someone with a nervous disposition might become skittish. Carriage and attitude can be impacted as well, as confidence may become arrogance, or polite shyness becomes submission. Due to the often shocking physical disfigurements and differences in behavior that result from their augmentations, beastfolk are often subject to fear, scorn, and alienation, all of which leaves them little hope for leading normal lives.

Some two thousand of these poor souls are believed to live within the Empire, but even that number is far from certain. The harsh reactions of others often cause them to be transient, or find a place at the fringes of society, so it is impossible to know how many there truly are. No one can predict how many more might be living in the shadows of other societies, or are suffering on the operating tables of mad surgeons even now to swell their ranks tomorrow.

When creating a beastman, the player must decide whether the character is lightly or heavily augmented with animal features. The primary difference between these two types of beastfolk are how easily they may reintegrate into society and how many beneficial augmentations they have been given. Heavily augmented beastfolk are monstrous amalgamations of human and animal parts, and the bloodline's curses are also more severe for them. Some augmentations are so extensive that they can only be taken by heavily augmented beastfolk. The bestial portions of lightly augmented beastfolk are more localized and easier to conceal.

ABILITIES AND BONUSES

- *Potential:* Lightly augmented beastfolk receive one point of *Ether* and one point of *Purpose*. Heavily augmented beastfolk receive two points of *Ether*.
- *Aptitude Bonus:* Only very healthy subjects survive the surgical processes to become a beastman, thus beastfolk receive a one-rank bonus to the *Vigor* aptitude.
- *Skill Bonuses:* During the first few years of a beastman's transformation, strength of character and a will to survive are often the only things that keep them from death. These skills must be honed in order to escape captivity, survive the journey home, and reintegrate into society as best as they are able. All beastfolk characters begin play with a one-rank bonus to the *Command* and *Survival* skills.
- *Blessing—Animal Augmentations:* Lightly augmented beastfolk receive two augmentations and heavily augmented beastfolk receive three. Augmentations are chosen from the list provided below. Augmentations listed in red text are so extensive that they may only be taken by heavily augmented characters.
- *Curse—Immunosuppressed:* A cocktail of immunosuppressive medication is necessary to force the human body to accept the integration of animal parts. Thus, all beastfolk have a compromised immune system to some degree. Diseases and Infection are considered to have +2 Strength when attacking a beastman, and tests for disease onset happen in half the time. For this reason, beastfolk are sometimes treated as disease vectors.
- *Curse—Monstrous:* The inhuman appearance of beastfolk causes many to view them with scorn or pity. Lightly augmented beastfolk may escape this fate if they successfully hide their augmentations, but they will suffer prejudice from those who know of their true situation. Heavily augmented beastfolk do not have the option of blending in, and their alterations are so extensive that they cannot escape being treated as less than

human. Whenever the majority of people in a scene know that a character is a beastman or their augmentations are readily visible, that beastman will suffer a penalty to Esteem. Lightly augmented beastfolk suffer from a one-step penalty to Esteem, and heavily augmented beastfolk suffer a two-step penalty to Esteem (see *Esteem*, p. 74).

BESTIAL AUGMENTATIONS

Lightly augmented beastfolk choose two augmentations from the following list, and heavily augmented beastfolk choose three. These represent all the significant augmentations that impact what the beastman can do, but do not necessarily represent everything that was surgically altered on a character. Players may decide to have as many cosmetic augmentations as they desire, but these will not grant any mechanical benefits.

Aquatic Adaptation

This beastman has been affixed with webbing between her fingers and toes, and perhaps fins along her extremities. This grants her an additional move when submerged in water and all *Athletics* tests made to swim or move through water may become passive tests.

Connective tissues from other mammals (not necessarily aquatic mammals) are used for this augmentation rather than tissue from fish, as the separation between warm and cold-blooded physiology has, thankfully, not yet been violated. The added skin and cartilage does not require any special care, but is difficult and uncomfortable to conceal. Wearing very loose clothing and shoes can conceal the alterations to limbs and feet, but unless the character's hands are kept completely out of sight, it is impossible to disguise the webbing.

The beastman has also had an additional animal lung grafted into her respiratory system that enables her to hold her breath much longer than a normal human. Instead of automatically receiving the *Deprived* condition after each minute or sequence without air, she may instead test *Vigor + Athletics* against a Difficulty of the number of minutes or sequences she has been without air. She will only receive the *Deprived* condition if she fails this test.

The external signs of this augmentation are large scars around the sternum and abdomen, and a slight distension of the belly when holding her breath or breathing as deeply as she can.

This augmentation is often found in conjunction with *Nictitating Membranes*.

Brachiator

The muscles and flesh of this beastman's hands, forearms, and feet have been replaced or reconnected with animal sinew to increase durability and flexibility so that her body is especially suited for climbing. All *Athletics* tests made to climb may become passive tests and she can climb anything with hand and footholds at her normal movement rate. She only risks falling after suffering a Wound or when the Doom card is drawn while climbing.

This augmentation typically uses tissue taken from primates, and requires extensive surgery down the entire length of the limbs. The scarring and unusual muscle structure is readily visible any time the flesh of the arms or legs is exposed.

Some beastfolk with this augmentation have also undergone the total replacement of their feet as described in *Prehensile Feet*.

Claws

This beastman's fingers, in addition to one or both hands, have been replaced. She now has the digits or entire paw of the large predatory mammal from which they were taken (frequently from a tiger, wolf, or lion). The player may choose whether one or both of her character's hands have been augmented. If the hand(s) were only partially replaced and the character can still manipulate with all the skill of a normal human hand, the claws have Potency 1. If the hand(s) were more fully replaced with a beast's paw, the Claws will have Potency 2, but they are substandard manipulators and cannot properly use tools or weapons. Regardless of the Potency rating, the Claws grant the *Bleeding* condition when used to physically attack an opponent. Short of a character always wearing very large mittens or hiding her hand(s) from view entirely, it is impossible to conceal this augmentation.

Enhanced Smell

The character's nose and nasal cavity have been removed and replaced with the snout of a beast, most likely that of a dog or pig. Although this augmentation is shocking and difficult to hide, cold comfort can be sought in the much more discerning and powerful sense of smell provided by this new feature.

A character with *Enhanced Smell* receives a +1 bonus to all skill tests that use the *Focus* aptitude and relate to the sense of smell. She may also use her sense of smell in remarkable ways. She will remember any scent she has ever smelled. On a successful *Focus + Composure* test, she will be able to identify the scents of familiar people or objects. She can also track people by scent so long as the trail does not cross water or some other scent-destroying substance. On a successful *Focus + Survival* test, she may follow an individual even if there are no other visible signs of passage. If tracking by scent when there are both olfactory and visual cues, she may flip two cards and choose which one is used to resolve the *Focus + Survival* test.

Those with the *Predator's Maw* augmentation often also have *Enhanced Smell,* as the tissue for both augmentations is often transplanted as part of the same surgery.

Echolocation

Those few beastfolk with this odd augmentation have had their ears removed and replaced with those of a large bat or similar animal. Even in absolute darkness, the character can perceive her surroundings using sound. She must use a maneuver to make some sort of noise, and then interpreting the information as it bounces back to her allows her to know the location and approximate size of every solid object within her zone of control. A beastman with *Echolocation* may also test *Focus + Composure*, Difficulty 3 to gather more information, such as specific size, what accoutrements are being carried, or to make a fine distinction between objects that are touching one another, such as how many individual books are in a stack.

Hiding this augmentation is possible through the use of scarves and headwraps, but doing so greatly reduces the clarity of sound and prevents the use of *Echolocation*.

Enhanced Hearing

Beastfolk with Enhanced Hearing have had their ears wholly removed and replaced by those of an animal. Extensive reconstructive surgery must be done around their new animal ears to add muscle and skin to allow them enhanced range of motion. The nature and placement of this augmentation makes it impossible to fully conceal. The new ears often come from large cats, or a few species of foxes because of the sensitivity, size, and positional control that these animals possess. The ear replacement doesn't allow the full range of hearing available to the natural animal since the inner ear and neurological connections are different in humans, but the sheer increase in mechanical capability of the external ears ensures their hearing is far better than any normal human. Beastfolk with this augmentation always benefit from a +1 bonus on all Focus tests with a significant hearing component. The expanded hearing range can also detect sounds slightly above, below, or more faint than un-augmented humans could hear, which may allow them to make Focus tests when others cannot.

Fur

Significant portions of the character's body have been covered with skin grafts from a furred animal. As a result, the character can better survive in cold temperatures and more easily avoid the ill effects of exposure to wind and rain. The character cannot be worse than Ill-Prepared for all cold weather conditions, and for exposure to wind, rain, and other foul weather. Exposure to extreme heat is dangerous and the character cannot be better than Ill-Prepared for hot and desert environments (see *Environmental Conditions,* p. 96). The thick pelt also offers a physical Armor of rank 1, which will not stack with armor worn; if the character is wearing different ranks of Armor only the highest single Armor rating is used.

Hide

The character has received skin grafts over much of her body from an animal with a thick, hardened hide such as a rhinoceros or hippopotamus. This grants rank 2 physical Armor, which will not stack with any other armor worn; if the character is wearing different ranks of Armor only the highest single Armor rating is used.

The new flesh is thick and cumbersome, but in a chilling sign of rationality and planning, whatever misguided genius performed the graft planned the placement of the hide so it wouldn't hinder movement or fine manipulation. This leaves the character's face, hands, and joints relatively untouched, but her back, chest, and limbs have been covered with layers of thick hide. Due to the extent of the replaced skin and the notable bulk of the *Hide,* this augmentation cannot be hidden.

Muscular Structure

The character has undergone multiple extensive surgeries that have dramatically altered her muscle structure. Tendons and ligaments from a variety of animals have been used to replace their human counterparts, and provide additional strength, speed, and range of motion. The character may make all *Athletics* tests related to motion as passive tests, and the Potency of any physical strike she makes is increased by one.

Although less outwardly horrific than other augmentations, this one is perhaps the most disturbing in its implications. Whoever performed such extensive and painstaking surgery was well past the point of experimentation. They were at the point of working on redesigning the human body in a pervasive and specific way, and spitting in the face of the natural order. Although not as outwardly grotesque as other augmentations, the character's skin is a tapestry of scars, and the silhouette of their limbs and the way they move have been noticeably altered. The beastman's nature is apparent to anyone who sees any skin other than their hands and face, and to all who observe the character engaging in any physical activity more strenuous than walking.

Nictitating Membrane

The character has a membrane that slips over her eyes whenever they are exposed to irritants. Closing the nictitating membrane is an automatic reflex and does not require any conscious action. While the membrane is in place, the character's eyes are protected against glare, water, and any airborne environmental conditions that might irritate them such as gas, dust, wind, or precipitation. As a result, the beastman does not suffer any environmental penalties to tests using the *Focus* aptitude in those circumstances. Although the augmentation itself is subtle, the scarring around the eyes, odd fleshiness of the eyelids, and jellied appearance of the eyes when the membrane is in use are all clear markers of this augmentation and will betray their unnatural nature to all who see them in use.

This augmentation is usually paired with either or both of the *Aquatic Adaptation* or *Low Light Vision* augmentations.

Low Light Vision

A sure sign that the surgeon who victimized this beastman was both mad and truly gifted, the character's eyes were completely removed and replaced with those of a large hunting cat or predatory bird. As a result, her new eyes are able to see even when there is vanishingly little ambient light. The character cannot see in absolute darkness, but now benefits from the reflective qualities of the *tapetum lucidum* her human eyes lacked. The character will never suffer penalties or increased difficulties to *Focus* tests due to poor lighting, and although there is no significant drawback to being in bright light, it can be uncomfortable to be exposed to bright light for long periods. For this reason hats or bonnets that provide shade for the eyes are helpful accessories.

The character's pupils will be unnaturally large or slit, and most likely some shade of gold or green depending upon the animal of origin. If the character has her photograph taken it's very likely that the eyes will appear to glow as they reflect the light. Anyone who can see the character's eyes knows her altered nature: only heavy veils or dark smoked glasses could potentially hide her unnatural eyes.

Predator's Maw

The beastman's lower jaw and much of her upper jaw have been replaced with those of a predator. The human tongue and most of the throat musculature was preserved, so she can still talk, albeit unclearly. The lips and teeth of her new mouth were not designed for speech, so it comes out as muttered, lisping, or guttural and can be hard to understand until the listener is familiar with it. The new anatomy provides a fearsome bite attack, and should they be desperate or savage enough to do so, the character can test *Grace + Melee* to use her jaw as a weapon with a Potency of 2 and the *Bleeding* weapon condition.

This augmentation cannot normally be hidden. Due to the interconnected anatomy of the grafted tissue, this augmentation is often taken along with *Enhanced Smell.*

Prehensile Feet

Rare even among beastfolk, some few have had their ankles and feet replaced with the prehensile lower appendages of orangutans or similar apes. Whenever the character has her feet free of all footwear she can manipulate objects with them as she would with her hands. Climbing becomes much easier, and the character gains a +1 bonus on all *Athletics* tests made to climb. This augmentation is often paired with *Brachiator,* and such beastfolk can be incredibly gifted sailors or airmen.

Prehensile Tail

Surgery at the base of the beastman's spine has added a tail taken from a howler monkey or similar animal. The tail is too weak to support significant weight and cannot aid in climbing or acrobatics, but with practice it can be trained into a dextrous and useful appendage. A Prehensile Tail allows the beastman to manipulate objects just as she would with an additional hand. However, the tail cannot lift objects larger than Bulk 2 and any trait tests made to manipulate the object suffer a –2 penalty to due to the lack of fine control. Using the tail effectively requires concentration, so it does not grant any additional maneuvers or actions.

Hiding the tail under clothing is possible, but very uncomfortable if done for more than a scene. When allowed to move freely, the tail will flick and swish idly when not in active use.

CHANGELING

"A certain mother's child had been taken away out of its cradle by the elves, and a changeling with a large head and staring eyes laid in its place."
—*The Elves*, The Brothers Grimm

Feyfolk were never meant to be part of this world. From their origins in unknown realms, each fey is an interloper in the mortal world. They can only find a place in the Clockwork by filling a niche left open by mortal legend and misguided beliefs. Where there is belief but no substance, they may manifest. A child truly believes there is a monster in his closet, and so one emerges. The citizens of London believe there are goblins living in the tunnels under the city, and a colony may manifest. Why fey wish to be here is known only to themselves.

Once in the mortal world, many feyfolk whose physiologies allow for it take what pleasures they can in mortal company. If a child is born from a physical union, it carries the blood of its fey parent and is called a changeling. Most fey lack the constancy to concern themselves with child rearing. The term changeling was coined because fey babies are often swapped with those of mortals. Female fey who find themselves impregnated by mortals will often find an unsuspecting human mother and swap their fey newborn for the mother's natural child. Hence, the changeling is raised by unsuspecting mortals, while their true-born child is often abandoned to die of exposure. Such behavior is common enough amongst fey that even fey-blooded individuals who do not have such a history are still referred to as changelings. Mortal women impregnated by fey are most often abandoned and left to rear the child alone.

Fey Blood

When creating a changeling, a player must decide whether her character is strong or weak-blooded. A strong-blooded changeling is usually the immediate offspring of a fey parent, and clearly manifests her fey ancestry through inhuman features such as disproportionate features or limbs, scales, horns, goat legs or other obvious marks of beauty or terror. Weak-blooded changelings are more distant descendants of a fey ancestor, and are much more human in appearance. These changelings have a beauty or ferocity displayed in simpler and subtler ways, such as unnatural coloration of the eyes and hair, pointed ears, and similar attributes.

Life can be largely normal for those changelings who can pass for purebloods, but their bloodline can sometimes be a dark secret that must be kept for the sake of their survival. On mainland Europe and in many areas under the auspices of the Magisterium, changelings are viewed as abominations that must be hunted down. In rural parts of the British Empire, they are met with the same fear shown toward their fey parents, which is just as likely to end with a sort of reverential isolation as with a grisly misunderstanding involving a length of rope and the nearest tree. Within the more cosmopolitan urban centers of the Empire, high status changelings tend to be treated with dignity and wonder while low status changelings are treated as acceptable oddities.

Fey Lineages

A changeling's appearance and innate abilities are linked to the nature of their fey ancestor. There are dozens of fey "species" and innumerable unique fey beings that have parented half-human children. In general, they can be categorized into three broad lineages: tricksters, brutes, and fairfolk. Each changeling character must be descended from one of these three lines, although how much they resemble their specific ancestry is left to the player to decide.

Tricksters are beings such as gremlins and pixies who survive in the Clockwork through guile and mischief. Their descendents tend to manifest oddly colored skin or hair, horns, claws, fur, and many other features. Changelings of this lineage are descended from cunning feyfolk, and therefore excel at the skills of *Guile* and *Stealth*.

Brutes are feyfolk like ogres and trolls who survive in the Clockwork through strength and intimidation. Their descendents tend to manifest disproportionate bodies, great height or girth, glowing eyes, and other fearsome features. Their size and visage make changelings of this lineage intimidating to strangers, but they can more easily carve a place among those in low places as they excel at the skills of *Command* and *Streetwise*.

Fairfolk are changelings with ancestors such as the sidhe or Tuatha Dé Danann, the ancient fey invaders of the British Isles known for their beauty and cunning. Their descendents are beautiful but unnaturally tall, large-eyed, and lack certain human characteristics like eyebrows or coloration of the lips. Descended from dignified and alluring fey royalty, changelings from this lineage excel at the skills of *Refinement* and *Temptation*.

ABILITIES AND BONUSES

- *Potential:* Weak-blooded changelings receive one point of *Ether* and one point of *Purpose*. Strong-blooded changelings receive two points of *Ether*.
- *Aptitude Bonus:* Changelings receive a one-rank bonus to the *Presence* aptitude to represent the striking appearance and manner of their fey lineage.
- *Skill Bonuses:* A changeling's lineage defines the two skills in which the changeling receives a one-rank bonus:
  - Tricksters: *Guile* and *Stealth*
  - Brutes: *Command* and *Streetwise*
  - Fairfolk: *Refinement* and *Temptation*
- *Blessing—Glamour:* Weak-blooded changelings begin play with two Glamours, and Strong-blooded changelings begin play with three. See the Changeling Glamours table on this page and the complete descriptions of glamours starting on p. 229.
- *Curse—Unnatural:* Weak-blooded changelings have received a degree of social acceptance within the cosmopolitan centers of the Empire, but are still viewed with awe and fear in more rural communities. Strong-blooded changelings are simply too inhuman to be completely accepted anywhere, and their unnatural features and manners cannot be hidden. Strong-blooded changelings suffer from a one-step penalty whenever the character calculates Esteem (see *Esteem*, p. 74). In addition to this, strong-blooded changelings must be careful of where they travel, as they are often persecuted by a variety of religious orders outside the Empire.

CHANGELING GLAMOURS

Glamour	Trait	Page	Description
Awe	Guile 3	(p. 230)	Spend Ether to affect your Esteem or the Morale of friends or foes
Befriend	Guile 2	(p. 230)	Test Presence + Guile to give a target person a rank 1 Affinity for you
Beguile	Guile 3	(p. 230)	Spend Ether to ensure an opponent's Disposition never drops below Indifferent
Captivate	Guile 2	(p. 230)	All your social attacks have the Entrapped weapon condition
Charm	Guile 3	(p. 230)	Spend Ether & test Presence + Guile to give a target person a rank 2 Affinity for you
Curse	Guile 4	(p. 230)	Spend Ether to worsen an opponent's next failed test
Doppelgänger	Guile 5	(p. 230)	Spend Ether to take on the appearance of another person for the duration of one scene
Enthrall	Guile 5	(p. 231)	Spend Ether & test Presence + Guile to give a target person a rank 3 Affinity for you
Fey Stroke	Guile 5	(p. 231)	Spend Ether & test Presence + combat skill to place the Incapacitated condition on a foe
Geas	Guile 5	(p. 231)	Spend Ether to invite or persuade others to enter into a pact.
Hex	Guile 2	(p. 232)	Spend Ether to force an opponent to draw two cards and take the worse to resolve a test
Phantasm	Guile 2	(p. 232)	Subtly test Presence + Guile to make an opponent see a simple illusion
Phantasmagoria	Guile 4	(p. 232)	Spend Ether & test Presence + Guile to make targeted people see a complex illusion
Second Chances	Guile 2	(p. 232)	Whenever you spend Ether to draw a new card during a trait test, always use the best
Weaken Purpose	Guile 4	(p. 232)	Spend Ether & Subtly test Presence + Mysteries to drain points of Purpose from an opponent

NEPHILIM

"And the angels, the keepers of the Clockwork, saw and lusted after them, saying to one another: 'Come, let us choose wives from among the children of men and beget children. So all of them took wives, each choosing one for himself… The women became pregnant and bore the nephilim, great giants who consumed all the acquisitions of mankind. And when men could no longer sustain them, the nephilim turned against mankind and devoured them. They began to sin against all the creatures of the Clockwork. They began to devour one another's flesh and to drink their blood. Then the Clockwork laid accusation against the nephilim."

—Enoch 6:1–3; 7:1,3–6

Nephilim are the descendents of the Grigori, a choir of guardian angels once set to watch over humanity. After seeing the free and varied lives of mortals, the Grigori grew resentful of their own limited role in the Clockwork. They mutinied and began to live among mortals. Angelic power was always intended to be circumscribed, their great strengths tailored but also limited to their narrow roles. When it was joined with the free will and self-determination of mortals and tainted by the selfish and fallen nature of the Grigori, the offspring of their unions became a great risk to the world. This forbidden union blessed the nephilim with incredible gifts, but also made them abominations that had no place in the divine plan.

The features and appearance of a naphil align themselves to the choices she makes. Orderly living manifests the angelic qualities of her ancestors, while chaotic or selfish living causes her to instead manifest demonic features. A naphil may rigorously choose her behavior, but cannot prevent the manifestation her behavior dictates. Any manifestation is plain proof of their heritage, and is likely to get a naphil killed by fear-struck peasants or religious zealots.

Today, most naphil strive to balance their lives and pass for pureblood mortals, but in antediluvian times, the nephilim had no such fear and were a powerful presence in the ancient world. They embraced their natures, allowing them to manifest fully, and gloried in their might. The Clockmaker saw the wickedness that emerged from the great strength of the nephilim and acted to end the threat they posed to the Clockwork. Thus came the Great Flood, a divine act intended to eradicate the nephilim. Yet some nephilim survived the floodwaters and again rose to power, so the Clockmaker sent the prophet Joshua to lead armies against them. Joshua's efforts broke the power of the nephilim and many went into hiding.

Even now, modern nephilim still refer to the genocide of Joshua as 'The Cleansing', and are fearful of what would happen if their natures were widely known. As a result most try to be as inconspicuous as possible, leading reclusive lives and clinging to one another in closely-knit families. Older nephilim instruct their young how to use the gifts of their bloodline carefully and remain hidden. Caution and secrecy allow the nephilim to survive in a world that is hostile to their very existence.

Some few, however, are not so subtle and seek out choices that would allow their angelic nature to fully manifest as in times of old. Ideologues adopt orderly traditions to repent for the sins of their ancestors, live lives of obedience to the Clockmaker, and hope to fully manifest their angelic heritage and reclaim their sacred nature. These nephilim often find a home in the See of Canterbury or the Witchfinders. Others simply revel in the power of their birthright, hoping to go unnoticed by the agents of the Church and avoid the wrath of the Clockmaker long enough to complete their own fiendish apotheosis. All nephilim must choose: suppress their heritage and hide from a world that would see them destroyed, or dare to embrace the power of their birthright in pursuit of becoming something greater than the mortals around them.

NEPHILIM LINEAGES

Though thousands of years of persecution and generations of intermarriage with non-nephilim have lessened their power, the ancient nephilim tribes that survived The Cleansing live on even to this day. The culture of each lineage passes on traditions, beliefs, and behaviors, and their blood influences the specific ways a naphil will manifest their supernatural heritage.

Anakim

"The descendants of Anak come from the nephilim. We saw ourselves like grasshoppers in their presence, and we looked the same to them."
—Numbers 13:33

The Sons of Anak were towering giants and mighty warriors, most notable for their scion Goliath. They once ruled many nations, but their fame and stature made them easily distinguished targets during The Cleansing and in the many hunts that followed.

Anakim are meticulous about keeping themselves on a middle path between order and chaos, lest they manifest the great height and brutish proportions that are the hallmark of their lineage. Even early manifestations could see them standing a head taller than normal humans, with bulky frames and heavy features that are difficult to hide or explain away. Thus, the children of Anak have developed family traditions of meditation and contemplative prayer to balance their natural predilections toward wrath and violence. Those who reject these traditions usually manifest quickly, and are sometimes even hunted down by their loved ones before their size and temperament can bring their family to the attention of Inquisitors or Witchfinders.

Emim

"In the fourteenth year, Kedorlaomer and the kings allied with him went out and defeated the Rephaim in Ashteroth Karnaim, the Zamzummim in Ham, the Emim in Shaveh Kiriathaim"
—Genesis 14:5

The Emim are the most monstrous of the nephilim, and they manifest a horrific appearance. Their bodily changes show eyes and all four angelic faces (human, ox, eagle, and lion). Their lineage is named from the singular *Ema* in Hebrew, which translates as "horror" or "terror." Despite their appearance, most Emim are quite docile, and have been hunted down and destroyed even more thoroughly than other nephilim. As a result of their persecution they have adopted a siege mentality and focus on survival above all else. Their traditions teach them to live on the fringes of civilization in xenophobic communities focused on taking care of their own. Their fear of discovery and destruction is so great that some among them supposedly cleanse their lineage by putting to death any who would threaten the safety and moderation of the whole.

Moabim

"And Benaiah the son of Jehoiada, the son of a valiant man, of Kabzeel, who had done many acts, he slew two of the lionlike men of Moab."
—2 Samuel 23:20

The nephilim of Moab are known as fierce and mighty warriors; almost more animal than man. Their chief physical manifestations are the features of the lion, and they share the ferocity of this beast. Ancient Moabim kept lions as pets, and rumors circulated that these animals were actually their brethren who had fully manifested their power. Moabim traditions teach that the best way to protect their families is to eradicate any threats through merciless violence. Many Moabim still pursue work as soldiers and mercenaries today, as the orderliness of the modern military helps balance the chaos of war. If too much time fighting causes them to begin manifesting, Moabim will often leave the service by letting themselves be "killed" in action before their true nature is discovered.

Rephaim

"Ogias of Bashan was the last king of the Rephaim. His bed was decorated with iron and was more than nine cubits long and four cubits wide."
—Deuteronomy 3:11

The Rephaim were another line of nephilim known for their amazing height. King Ogias was said to be over thirteen feet tall. However, like the Anakim, the tallest of their kind were the most easily discovered and slain. Today, these nephilim stand only slightly larger than most ordinary humans. When they do manifest, their most common manifestations are the features of oxen.

The Rephaim were almost entirely wiped out when their king Ogias went to war against the prophet Moses. Afterwards, the remnants of this proud family kept almost no ties with one another. It is their current belief that small immediate families are less easily noticed by those who might wish to do them harm. Traditions are unique to each individual family unit, but most are based on keeping their presence in society a closely guarded secret.

Sepherim

In Ancient Hebrew, this word refers to the "others." It is not a true lineage, but rather a term used for those nephilim who have abandoned the traditions of their families and struck out on their own. Some Sepherim families develop their own traditions, while others shun other members of their kind. Most of these nephilim live in small transient communities that move from place to place before their secrets can be discovered. Since the blood of the Sepherim is blended from the other nephilim families there is no set pattern in their manifestation.

Zamzummim

"You have been in heaven, but all the mysteries had not yet been revealed to you, and you knew worthless ones, and these in the hardness of your hearts you have made known … and through these mysteries women and men work much evil on earth. Say to them therefore: 'You have no peace.'"

—Enoch 16:3–4

The Zamzummim have always been the most divided of the nephilim lineages. Begun by dissenters from other families who believed that the key to reclaiming their angelic heritage lay in mastering the greater mysteries hinted at by the Clockmaker in the Book of Enoch, they are known for their fascination with magic, but have little else in common with one another. Many Zamzummim pursue their search for secrets alone, but some work their way into positions of influence in religions or cults to access those groups' knowledge. Some Zamzummim are fastidiously careful in their work and only use pure magic to bolster the Clockwork, but others tread the dark path of sorcery and personal power. The factions within this lineage despise one another and actively work to thwart the designs of their rivals, or even kill them outright.

The extremes pursued by most Zamzummim make balance almost impossible, and almost all end up manifesting in an orderly or chaotic way early in their lives. For these nephilim, this usually shows in the feathers and features of the eagle.

Zophim

"And go, say to the Grigori, who have sent thee to intercede for them: 'You should intercede for men, and not men for you'."

—Enoch 16:2

"As for the spirits of heaven, in heaven shall be their dwelling, but as for the spirits of the earth which were born upon the earth, on the earth shall be their dwelling."

—Enoch 16:10

When it was clear that the Clockmaker abhorred the actions of the Grigori, some among their number sought forgiveness for their sins. The prophet Enoch communicated a rebuke from the Clockmaker, but the Zophim believe that it was an opportunity for redemption: they should not ask forgiveness, they should earn it by performing their intended role and reclaiming their position as "spirits of heaven." They hope that they may yet be accepted by

fulfilling the duty their Grigori ancestors abandoned: they watch. Well adjusted Zophim families choose villages, organizations, or generations of pureblood families and take the role of guardian angels. Less functional families become stalkers and obsessives that try to fix what they see are the errors of their unwitting charges.

Zophim acting as watchful angels need not be especially orderly or chaotic to be effective, and many are capable of maintaining enough balance to avoid manifesting, or to only manifest in minor ways. Those who become more pronounced in their manifestation have their bodies covered with eyes, regardless of their orderly or chaotic tendencies.

ABILITIES AND BONUSES

- *Potential:* Naphil characters begin play with two points of *Ether*. Despite this connection to chaos and free will, some nephilim spend their lives working to cleanse what they see as a taint and infuse themselves with *Purpose*, manifesting their angelic heritage and perhaps returning to a state of grace.
- *Aptitude Bonus:* All nephilim are descended from the Grigori, watcher angels charged with the oversight of humanity. They receive a one-rank bonus to the *Focus* aptitude.
- *Skill Bonus:* Angels are the caretakers that keep the Clockwork functional, and the nephilim inherit a limited form of this knowledge. Nephilim characters receive a one-rank bonus to the *Mysteries* skill.
- *Skill Bonus:* The world 'nephilim' can be translated to 'those who cause others to fall.' Nephilim have a natural ability to entice others, even into deep depravity. All nephilim receive a one-rank bonus to the *Temptation* skill.
- *Blessing—Angelic Immortality:* Nephilim will never die of natural means. A naphil that suffers death in any way other than through her Bane will simply reanimate after three sunsets, retaining her Wounds. The fragile state in which a naphil rises may result in an almost immediate return to death if she awakens in a hostile environment such as caged underwater or consumed in flame. Those who hunt the nephilim are willing to inflict such deaths and far worse. Repeated death in such a fashion will quickly drive all but the most indomitable naphil insane.
- *Blessing—Knowledge in the Flesh:* Even in their fallen state, nephilim maintain a degraded benefit of their forebears' power to know the hearts and minds of mortals. Whereas an angelic Grigoros merely had to observe someone to know her thoughts and deeds, a naphil may only temporarily absorb the memories from the minds of those whose flesh they eat or blood they drink. Once per day, a naphil may consume several mouthfuls (approximately 8 oz.) of flesh or blood to activate this ability. After ingesting the blood or flesh, they may choose to either gain a temporary one-rank bonus to any skill that the victim possessed at a higher rank than she, or she may learn a single memory from her victim. The benefits fade at the following sunrise. Nephilim who often use this ability usually keep journals full of stolen memories, and may even develop a taste for human flesh and blood.

BANES

Every naphil has a Bane. A Bane is a single material, fetish (an object with an unusual quality, origin, or manufacture), or circumstance through which the Clockwork is trying to eradicate a particular naphil. Every player making a naphil character must choose a Bane during character creation, and only that single predetermined material, fetish, or circumstance will provide the threat of permanent death.

A naphil's Bane will impact her anytime she is exposed to it, whether she is aware of it or not. However, a naphil can make a *Focus + Intuition* test against a Difficulty equal to the rank of the Bane to instinctually know that her Bane is in her zone of control. A naphil is considered to be exposed to any circumstantial Bane for which she is present or which she can experience. For example, a naphil with the circumstantial Bane "lunar eclipses" is vulnerable during the several minutes of a lunar eclipse that occurs in the night sky above her, whether or not she is outside or if it is overcast. A naphil is considered to be exposed to any material or fetish Bane that touches her, is on her person, or is used to attack her. If a naphil dies while exposed to her Bane, her death is permanent and she will not resurrect via *Angelic Immortality*. Additional effects of exposure are listed below.

Banes are ranked from one to three, representing their strength and rarity. Those of low rank are easy to come by, but have mild effects. Those of high rank are rare, but can have debilitating or deadly effects on the naphil. A player can choose whichever rank she wishes for her character's Bane.

RANK 1

A Bane of this rank causes psychological distress and disorientation. A naphil who is exposed to her rank 1 Bane is immediately inflicted with the *Disoriented* temporary condition. This condition cannot be removed until exposure to the Bane has ended. A weapon made of a rank 1 material or fetish Bane receives +1 Potency against the vulnerable naphil. All attacks made against her during her rank 1 circumstantial Bane will also receive +1 to Potency. If this weapon or attack kills her, the death is permanent.

Examples

- **Common Substance:** iron, granite, bone, linden wood, roses, bay, wheat, alcohol, pork
- **Common Fetish:** virgin's tears, grave dirt
- **Common Circumstance:** the tolling of a church bell, midnight

RANK 2

A Bane of this rank causes physical harm. A naphil who is exposed to her rank 2 Bane will suffer from all of the effects of a rank 1 Bane, and in addition to these, all actions or attacks that are made during the exposure and target her directly will double any positive DoS they achieve. For example: an attack made against a character during her rank 2 Bane circumstance, a lunar eclipse, achieves a DoS of 2. It is instead treated in all ways as having achieved a DoS of 4.

Examples

- **Uncommon Substance:** a mule's jawbone, amber, silver, rubies, crocodile meat, lotus root, fermented mare's milk
- **Uncommon Fetish:** thorns from roses grown on virgin's blood, the hair of a king, metal that hasn't been touched by human hands, the relic of a saint
- **Uncommon Circumstance:** trampled by horses, lunar or solar eclipse, noon on Sundays in Lent, New Year's Day at midnight

RANK 3

A Bane of this rank is rare and very difficult to find, but will cause debilitating pain to the naphil, and any attacks that land will leave mutilating injuries. A naphil who is exposed to her rank 3 Bane will suffer from all of the effects of rank 1 and rank 2 Banes, and in addition to these, all attacks that are made during the exposure and target her directly will inflict the *Incapacitated* weapon condition in addition to any other weapon conditions that would normally apply. If it is a rank 3 circumstance Bane, the naphil is automatically afflicted with the *Incapacitated* condition for the duration of the circumstance.

Examples

- **Rare Substance:** the bone of a dragon, chitin from a giant squid, blossoms of a "corpse flower," liver from a whale shark, Himalayan pink salt
- **Rare Fetish:** a blade used in kinslaying wielded by the kinslayer, a blow struck by someone who has never raised her hand in anger, a piece of obsidian from the lava flow that destroyed Pompeii
- **Rare occurrence:** at the same time a blood relation dies, caught in an avalanche or volcanic eruption, while in the personal presence of an angel or living saint, during a full solar eclipse

- *Curse—Abomination:* Nephilim are weak against magic and the creatures who wield it. A ritual magic test affecting only nephilim will receive a +1 bonus. Angels and Fallen also receive +1 bonus to any test performed against nephilim.
- *Curse—Bane:* The Clockwork abhors nephilim and works to eradicate them from creation. Each naphil has her own Bane: a substance, event, or circumstance that can cause her permanent death. All players making naphil characters must choose a Bane during character creation (see sidebar).
- *Curse—Fluid Mien:* Nephilim are not of this world and are constantly being pulled toward ascendance or damnation. As they choose a more orderly or disorderly life, their physical appearance expresses their decisions. If a naphil strives to return to a place in the Clockwork, she takes on an angelic appearance; however, if she lives only for herself and embraces the rebellious nature of her Grigori forebears, she takes on a demonic appearance. Balancing these two paths retains her human appearance. Mechanically, this is calculated by the balance of a character's potential traits. Subtract the lower of *Ether* and *potential* from the higher. This is a character's manifestation rank. If the character's *Corruption* ever exceeds this rank, use it instead. For example, a character with *potential* 3 and *Ether* 2 would have a manifestation rank of 1. If she somehow accumulated two ranks of *Corruption*, her manifestation rank would increase to 2.
  - Rank 0: The naphil appears completely human.
  - Rank 1: The naphil manifests subtle and easily concealed features such as incredibly smooth skin, skin that is cold to the touch, eyes that are too pale or dark to be natural, or an odd quality to their voice.
  - Rank 2: There are pronounced physical changes that could possibly be concealed or explained away. The skin of demonic nephilim takes on an unnatural hue such as blue or purple, while the skin of angelic nephilim takes on the appearance of

porcelain or a metallic sheen. The eyes become oddly colored or might even glow. Hair pigment is exaggerated or bleached of all color. The naphil becomes at least slightly taller and other features are either idealized beyond human norms or become somehow menacing or dreadful.
  - Rank 3: Previous manifestations intensify and become impossible to fully conceal, and their inhuman nature is readily apparent. The lineage will determine which features manifest most strongly. Small groupings of colored nodules akin to spider or bird eyes appear on the hands, body, and face. Distinctly animal features such as claws, fangs, feathers, and hooves develop. It is almost certain that strongly manifested nephilim will be reported and hunted down by agents of the Magisterium or the Witchfinders, but they are also likely to attract the attention and devotion of certain religious extremists, cultists, or the insane who may wish to serve or venerate them.
  - Rank 4: The naphil now stands a head taller than normal mortals and fully manifests the qualities of their lineage. Their face, chest, and hands show fully functional eyes. Their features have become utterly inhuman: skin takes on vivid and unnatural hues, and feathers grow from the arms. Most mortals will either flee or attack the naphil on sight, but some may fall into fits of ecstasy or worship. Fully manifested nephilim are aggressively hunted by the Witchfinders, Inquisition, and most other religious organizations. There is almost no refuge for such beings.

All manifesting features are cosmetic and grant no inherent mechanical benefit. Manifesting characters may inspire discomfort or fear in others. When a character is recognized as a naphil and the majority of others in the scene are non-nephilim she suffers a two step penalty to Esteem.

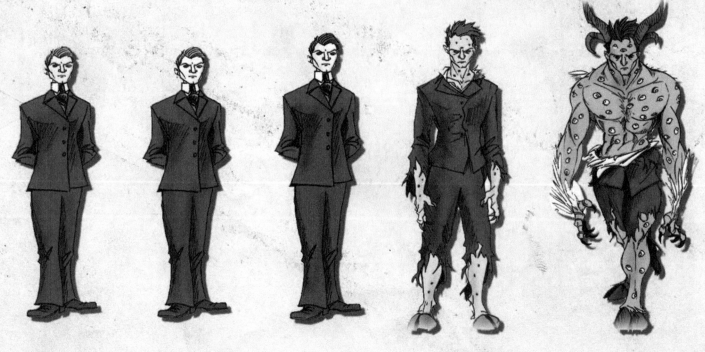

PURSUITS: CHARACTER CREATION STEP TWO

The destabilization of the Clockwork is too complex a problem to be solved by a single ideology or strategy. A multitude of ideologies have arisen concerning how to deal with the Pontus, but in the game these approaches are all distilled into six pursuits: Ambition, Discovery, Dominion, Industry, Faith, and Freedom. Which pursuit a character chooses and how she chooses to act it out could make her either a savior of the Clockwork or one of its saboteurs.

Each player chooses one pursuit for her character. This represents the chief way that her character strives to preserve the Clockwork and her own interests within it. Any pursuit can have positive or negative results depending on the life choices of the character who follows it, but some are more likely to bring about certain results. Those pursuing Dominion, Industry, and Faith, rely on a deep engagement with the world at large, and their actions are likely to bolster the Clockwork in some way. In the case of Discovery, Ambition and Freedom, the pursuits are first and foremost individually-focused, and depending on the priorities of the character her choices can be positive, negative, or both for the Clockwork at large. An Ambitious person working for their own glory, or one striving to express her individual Freedom is just as likely to be a great hero in the fight against the Pontus as she is to be its unwitting advocate.

A character's chosen pursuit provides her with two one-rank bonuses to aptitudes and one point of potential. These represent the innate inclinations and learned abilities that come with the pursuit that character follows. If a character ever changes her pursuit during the course of character advancement, a change in potential will occur, but the aptitude bonuses can never be altered after character creation is completed.

The six pursuits are each described below from the perspective of a man or woman who lives by those ideals. Each also lists short descriptions of several professions that are frequently associated with these pursuits. Professions are not part of character creation and provide no mechanical benefits, but may help players envision what their characters do in the Clockwork.

AMBITION

No, I didn't always look this way. Clever of you to figure that out. This was done to me. I was a sailor aboard the *Irene*, transporting lumber from British Columbia to Fiji. We were a week out from Hawaii when we got hit with a hellish storm. The ship was pulled under, but some of us managed to make it into a lifeboat. We'd no idea where land was, so we set out as best we could to the southeast and prayed for rescue to happen before we died of thirst. After three days we saw a ship and got picked up, but I wish we'd died. We were picked up by pirates, and eventually they sold us to a colony on an island I still can't find on any chart. That's where I met Dr. Carroll.

None of my mates survived what he did to us. I was the only one. Dr. Carroll took out my eyes and tried to replace them with some from a bird. He did it four times before it worked. I spent months sitting in a cell, blind and bleeding. I've got no notion what makes a man want to do that to someone. I never fully recovered. I still get sick all the time, but at least I'm still breathin'.

Eight years I spent on that island. Eight years! Dr. Carroll died. I got no idea whether it was natural or not, but I took the opportunity to steal a boat with some other man-made-monsters, and we fled the island. I'd sooner risk dying on the water than live there another day. This time we got lucky and got picked up by the steamer *Southern Star* headed to Australia. Almost a decade after I was lost at sea, I made it home. It wasn't home no more. "Beastfolk," they called us. A hundred others like us had shown up in Singapore and Parliament was still trying to figure out what to do. Should we be quarantined? Taken to surgeons to be tested and picked apart to see how it was done, or just call us all animals, put us out of our misery and be done? There was no place for me anymore. To some, I wasn't even a man anymore. At least, not like I was meant to be.

You know who wants to hire a beastman? No one. I had to make my living any way I could…still do. Life ain't fair, and if you

PURSUIT SUMMARY TABLE

Pursuit	Potential	Aptitude Bonuses	Professions
Ambition	*Ether*	*Presence, Vigor*	Mercenary, Pirate, Socialite, Thief
Discovery	*Ether*	*Focus, Reason*	Academic, Alchemist, Explorer, Magus
Dominion	*Purpose*	*Presence, Vigor*	Constable, Diplomat, Politician, Soldier, Spy, Witchfinder Star
Faith	*Purpose*	*Focus, Will*	Priest, Tradesman, Witchfinder Canon
Industry	*Purpose*	*Grace, Reason*	Industrialist, Inventor, Politician
Freedom	*Ether*	*Grace, Will*	Activist, Artist, Radical, Unionist

try to live life assuming it will be, it'll get ya. All this talk about how to fight the Pontus, that's talk from those on top trying to hold onto what they've already got. Men of ambition, we worry more about us: how our fortune is to be made, how to find a place to call home, how to get what we want. No time to be concerned with what's gonna happen to the whole world when I need to worry about what's happening to me right now. Some men of ambition stand on the shoulders of the aristocracy and just want more for themselves, while the rest of us are just making ends meet. After all I've survived, I still have to scrape coins together just to eat. Like I said, life ain't fair. Now if you'll kindly hand over your billfold and whatever jewelry is on your lady there, I'll be on my way and no one needs be hurt.

The Mercenary

When money dries up, you got to find it where you can. There are scores of patrons in this world that will pay for all sorts of odd jobs: private security, assassination, smuggling, transport, and just about anything else you can think of. You can scratch out a living if you got the stomach for what needs doing, or the patience to wait for more savory work. Anytime a man of means needs things accomplished and is willing to pay for it, there's someone willing to take his coin.

The Pirate

If you get romantic about it, you could say a pirate's just a soldier who gives his own orders and lives free. If you're a realist, a pirate's just a thief with enough cohorts and equipment to steal on a grand scale. A good crew can aim big, taking cargo out of merchant and military vessels to make their fortunes. Of necessity, a pirate crew is equal, as it only matters how good a man can sail, fight, and steal. If you're worth your salt, there's money to be had, and no one will look down at you for being what you are unless you're fool enough to let them. It's a hard and dangerous life, but for those of us with "corrupt blood" it may be the only place we can find a group that will accept us.

Pirates are mainly on the sea, sailing gunships to capture merchanters or raiding passenger liners. A few use blimps or hot air balloons to take down airships that run cargo overland. Some prefer air piracy due to the lack of canons and the fear everyone has about shooting guns near hydrogen: if you can catch and board an airship, it's usually a short fight with a small crew and the bird is yours. Me, I prefer sea piracy. More cargo, more supplies, and more ransom when things go right, and a shorter fall if things go wrong.

The Socialite

Socialites are the rich folk who are either crawling up the social ladder or trying desperately not to fall off of it. The rock bottom most socialites are trying to avoid is the mountaintop I'm trying to make it to, so they get little sympathy from me. Don't hear me wrong, though, I can respect anyone who sets a goal and does whatever it takes to make it happen. I use a pistol, they use a party. We all care about ourselves first and foremost.

The Thief

If you can avoid being hanged, this is an easy way to make a living. You don't need wealthy patrons to agree to hire you; you don't need a ship or crew to do your work; and you don't need noble blood. All you need is a will to take what don't belong to you and someone to take it from.

DISCOVERY

I was four years old when the newspapers proclaimed that the American inventor, Thomas Edison, had discovered etheric force. I remember my father reading the article to me. "Abigail," he said, "something happened today that will change the world forever." It certainly changed my world forever. I was utterly fascinated with the idea that there was an energy that surrounded and infused all matter. It was like someone pulled aside a curtain to show me the secret workings of the world. On that day, I knew that I would spend the rest of my life trying to understand the complexities of the Clockwork.

At first my passion for study stemmed from my own intellectual curiosity, but as I grew older, I began to understand just how valuable the pursuit of discovery was. All the guns and bombs that man can make might be able to conquer the Earth, but they cannot unravel its mysteries and cannot protect us from the Pontus. We need to first learn how the Clockwork truly operates if we are to have any hope of finding and fulfilling its purpose. Science and exploration give humanity a means to glimpse the divine will that is imbedded in creation, and help us to understand the inner workings of reality itself. It is through learning and making use of the systems that govern our world that we begin to see how to the Clockwork was meant to be, and what we might do to restore it to stability.

As for my role in this pursuit, it was more difficult than it needed to be. I was raised by a liberal father of modern sensibilities, so the idea that my gender would be a hindrance to me in the field of science was never a thought that crossed my mind. That changed when I learned that many higher institutions of learning would not even accept my application. Many colleges for women were little more than finishing schools. My options were limited, but of those schools who would take me, there were still some of note. After much consideration, I applied and was accepted to Lady Margaret Hall, a sexually-segregated but prestigious school on the campus of Oxford University.

After graduation, even though I could not join the ranks of the Royal Society, I discovered the exclusivity of their membership did not extend to their funding. My first grant funded my participation on an excursion to the North Pole to study the effects of the magnetic fields of the pole on alchemical transmutation. Despite it being an adventure I barely survived—a story for another time—I proved to myself and to the public that gaining understanding is worth risking all. Since then, I have made a name for myself in alchemical research with the help of affluent investors and the growing support of the Royal Society. I have made it my life's work to explore the secrets of the world, and if I can help pass on the light of knowledge to others who share my passion, perhaps one day we will understand how the Clockwork can be made stable once more.

The Academic

All the progress humanity has made has depended on the efforts and insights of learned men and women. Scholars and scientists have built the modern world, and new innovations only come from building on the work of the past. Without academics and others who devote themselves to research and experimentation, our society would not exist as it does today.

Perhaps most importantly, those dedicated to their studies can provide us with critical insight about the true nature and workings of the Clockwork, perhaps even to find a way to fight the influence of the Pontus directly. Scientists work to unravel the mysteries of the cosmos, attempting everything from completing Mendeleev's Periodic Table to travelling to Pontus infected lands to study lingering effects. Historians collect and interpret the Pontus events of the past. Sociologists evaluate what cultures and societal behaviors seem to alter the frequency and intensity of Pontus events. If collected and used sensibly, this information could be vital in both fighting the Pontus and moving society towards the intended ideal.

The Alchemist

Etheric Force was the missing variable in thousands of years' worth of alchemical formulae. Edison's discovery allowed alchemy to move from a mystic art to an academic discipline almost overnight. Now, we who practice the New Science are one part mystic and one part scientist, transmuting substances and uncovering the nature of matter itself. Many pursue this discipline simply due to its lucrative nature, but there are a some of us who see the ability to transmute matter as humanity's best hope to repair the Clockwork. Gaining an insight into the deep workings of previously mysterious forces and changing them as suits our needs is the closest humanity has yet come to understanding the mind of the Clockmaker. Such understanding should excite anyone, and I can only approach my work with wonder and humility.

Some academics and many in the Church remain skeptical of alchemy's historical link to both hermetic magic and outright fraud, but the results of the New Science should speak for themselves. Alchemists have already offered much to science and industry, creating new materials and innovations that are invaluable in aeronautics, textiles, and war. Demand for alchemists is so high the classes at Oxford can't produce them fast enough. In time the whole world will recognize just how vital the contributions of alchemists can be.

The Explorer

Even in the modern day, there is still much of the globe that is unknown. Explorers seek to discover lands yet untouched by modern civilization and to uncover the secrets they hold. It is dangerous work, but every newly discovered plant, beast, or culture brings with it new compounds and medicines, new cultures to be brought into the Imperial fold, and more complete maps and data that move us toward a fuller understanding of the Clockwork. The world of exploration changed dramatically when the Royal Geographical Society was granted its charter under Queen Victoria in 1859. This institution for the advancement of geographical science absorbed earlier groups such as the African Association and established itself as a powerhouse of funding and resources for explorers and cartographers who would otherwise lack the means to pursue their own work. Today, the RGS is the largest funder of expeditions and cartography in the Empire, and its financing allows many bold explorers to set off into the unknown. It takes daring and fortitude to make such trips, and I respect anyone who does so greatly, especially after the harrowing events of my own trip into the Arctic.

The Magus

Many subjects of the Empire believe in the power of ritual magic, and so do many governments and religions as attested to by the enduring presence of organizations like the Witchfinders and Inquisition. There is little doubt that magic has power, but is it really worth bothering at this point? Ritual magic is tedious, time consuming, and unreliable when compared to modern medicine, science, and technology. I can see that some of them are kindred spirits working to unravel the workings of the world, but I have difficulty grasping why anyone would dedicate their lives to a discipline that only works some of of the time, and that no one can claim to truly understand.

My own reservations aside, there are still those who dedicate their lives to these arcane studies. Magi claim there are things that can only be learned through the mystic arts. Although the fear of persecution has led many magi throughout history to hoard knowledge in secret, recent decades have seen some arcane researchers begin to share their discoveries with the broader world. Organizations such as the Hermetic Order of the Golden Dawn, Freemasonry, and the Rosicrucians allow for magi to mingle and share ideas with fellow mystics, dabblers, and specialists in other fields of study. One can hope that this growing availability and sharing of knowledge will either lead more people to decide the study of magic is a dead end for meaningful inquiry, or bring about new revelations and insight so that it can find it a home among respected and reliable sciences as happened with alchemy.

DOMINION

I joined the Queen's armed forces at the age of eighteen, and was immediately shipped off to fight the Transvaal Boers in southern Africa. The Dark Continent is far from Britain, and I don't just mean distance. For me, it was a realm of torment. During the day, I watched the Limpopo River turned red from the blood of my brothers who fell there. During the night, I heard the screams as unimaginable creatures feasted upon those who slept at the edge of our encampment. Hell is not near strong enough a word.

Since then, I have traveled the world, expanding the dominion of the Empire. I have poured out my sweat and my blood on three continents. I have seen a nation rise with the first man to take up arms against its governor, and seen one fall as its last man dropped to the ground. My body bears scars from the most savage of men and the most horrific of chimera. I have gazed into the depths of the Pontus and saw it stare back. The academics and businessmen in their ivory towers may proclaim ideologies of peaceful discovery or industry as the best way to hold fast against the madness, but they have not seen what I have seen, and don't know what it means to fight for their beliefs.

Today, I'm a man of thirty-four years. I have a wife and two sons. I have seen the world and all the horror that it can be, and I know what it means to have something worth protecting. The world beyond our borders is terrifying and needs to be conquered, for their sake if not my own. As the Empire expands, it pushes back the Pontus. It is not some alien intelligence we are battling; rather, we subdue those portions of humanity whose ignorance of proper living causes the cracks in the Clockwork that allow the Pontus to enter our world.

Dominion. That's the word they keep saying to us to make us want to wake up each morning to return to the front. The Empire is the dominion of man. As the Empire expands its dominion to the far reaches of the earth, spreading civilization to its darkest corners and stabilizing humanity through the order and hierarchy of refined culture, it thwarts the Pontus and secures the future. The Empire has been given dominion over every living thing on the Earth, and it is therefore our responsibility to protect them… even from themselves. If we truly love humanity, then we must teach them how to live in a way that doesn't bring about the destruction of the world.

In this year of Our Lord 1896, our way of life has made the British Empire the largest political entity in the known world. Our hands stretch across the horizon so that the sun never sets on our soil. As the Maker has commanded so have we done: the Earth is our dominion. For if the Empire falls, the Pontus will rise.

The Constable

The constabulary are like soldiers, but they fight on a different scale. Our regiments protect cities and provinces, while they protect our streets and neighborhoods. Some soldiers look down on them, but the ones that take their work seriously get my respect. We all work for the Crown and get paid to wear a uniform and protect people. They may not see the horrors we see out beyond the borders of the Empire, but they get their own dreck to deal with right there in England. A good man willing to act can solve problems when dealing with outlaws on the streets, but organized crime in the rookeries offers more obstacles than a stout truncheon can overcome. It's a different battlefield, but they're fighting a domestic war against an army of thieves preying on the common man. Most of it is minor action, if dangerous, but there are still stories from time to time of skirmishes with gangs and darker things hiding in back alleys.

The Diplomat

Some us of try to solve the world's problems with guns, others try to solve them with words. Ideally, diplomats are sent in to negotiate long before soldiers are sent in to dominate. These are the men and women who travel to the farthest Imperial borders to try to find peaceful remedies to problems that could, at best, be a severe resource drain on the Empire, and at worst cost much in blood and coin. Truth be told, though, diplomats live and operate in a different world. Their bread and butter is lies, half-truths, false smiles, and secrecy. Anyone who can live with themselves when they might be able to start or stop a war or topple a foreign king over drinks is cut from different cloth than me. We all have our roles to play, and I suppose someone has to have theirs.

The Politician (Conservative)

I don't claim to understand the world of politics. Those dandies roll into London for the Season and attend far more parties than Parliamentary sessions, yet I am not fool enough to believe that the Empire could run without them. If I have to side with one group of fops over another, I throw in with the Conservatives. These men and those who ascribe to their views push for the expansion of the Empire, honor the social hierarchy, and respect the authority of the Queen. The hierarchy of the Empire is civilization itself, and it is held together by adhering to tradition and etiquette, respecting those of higher station and protecting those of lesser means, and everyone performing the role in which they find themselves. So long as there are opportunities for those of spirit and talent to raise their station, the system works. If we allow this structure to be eroded from within by liberal politicians, we may as well just abandon the Empire and give the world over to the Pontus now rather than go the way of the Romans and drag out our decline and fall.

The Soldier

We stand on the boundary between civilization and chaos. Be it in a training garrison in the highlands of Scotland, aboard a zeppelin in the Air Battalion of Royal Engineers, or in the passes of Afghanistan, we hold back both the chaos and disorder of the world that invites the Pontus in. Whether it's pacifying territory or sinking bullets into chimera, soldiers are the ones willing to lay down their lives for the Empire and, by extension, the world. The Empire must expand if it is not to fall, and that depends on our guns, our honor, and our blood.

The Spy

For diplomats and soldiers to do their work, they need information. Correct intelligence can mean the difference between success and failure for delicate negotiations or military invasion. Spies are the men and women who provide this. They infiltrate enemy territory and learn about foreign politics, geography, military strength, and a thousand other things necessary for the Imperial war machine to do what it needs to do. I can't speak to the methods they use, but if someone serves the Empire by passing bribes, lying, stealing, and spending time on their back rather than standing on a firing line, I can't judge them too harshly. All I care about is whether they do their jobs as well as I do mine. My arse has been saved more than once by good intelligence, and I've almost been killed a half dozen times by bad.

The Witchfinder Star

When I was in Afghanistan there was one village we were staying in that became the larder for some fearsome chimera whose appearance led the men to call it the "rhino-bear." I glimpsed the beast once, and its moniker did not disappoint—it looked like a hairy rhinoceros that bled through its pores and shed maggots like sweat. I would have moved the men on, but the village was at the head of a valley pass. We sent word back to command, but were told to hold the position. Over two weeks the damn thing devoured near two score villagers and four of my own men.

When the Witchfinders arrived, there were only two of them. One from the Order of the Canon and the other from the Order of the Star. The Canon spent a lot of quiet time in prayer, while the Star asked countless tactical questions while he loaded the most complicated rifle I'd ever laid eyes on. That's when I recognized him. I knew this Star. I served with him in South Africa against the Boers. We were just boys then. I don't know what he had seen since then, but he didn't look like the same man. His eyes were focused like a hawk when it sees its prey, and his face had aged more than the years that had passed. I remembered him as a promising soldier and a great shot, but I recall thinking that I was looking at two dead men. My own soldiers hadn't been able to even wound the beast, so what could two men possibly do against the monster? I never found out. They took a few locals with them out into the valley to look for the thing, then the next morning the beast's head was laid in the road outside the village. I never saw them or the villagers again.

FAITH

My name is Amedeo Ortegon, and I was raised in the village of Capella in the Aragon province of Spain. It was a miniscule collection of farmsteads in those days, and it was the sort of place where everyone knew everything about everyone else. That meant that my family's secret was not truly a secret so much as it was something no one in the village spoke about. The people of Capella were happier pretending we were normal people.

As you can tell by my appearance, my family was not of pure blood. My ancient ancestor was Arakel, an angel who long ago took part in a mutiny against the Maker. We are nephilim, mortals that carry the blood of fallen angels. No one seemed to take issue with this so long as we all appeared like everyone else. However, it is the curse of the nephilim that our bodies manifest the inclinations of our heart. Those tied to the order of the world appear as angels, those who care only for themselves as monsters. When our behavior becomes too orderly or too chaotic, we manifest. I was thirteen when my body grew feathers and two large eyes opened on the back of my shoulderblades. Hiding that I was a naphil was no longer an option.

The effect in the village was divisive. Some thought that I was suddenly holy, while others thought that I was suddenly hideous. When the villagers came to our door to drive us out, the local priest interceded and helped my family flee to the cathedral of Salvador of Zaragoza to seek refuge with the Church. However, despite the best intentions of our priest, we found no haven there, only the Inquisition. In the months that followed, I saw members of my family bricked into walls, buried alive, and sunk into the ocean. When I finally did escape, I fled alone to the west. Near the crags north of Bilbao I met a man in a wide brimmed hat and a long black coat. He brought me here to Salisbury Cathedral and taught me the difference between the chaos of the Pontus and the Maker's order. More importantly, he taught me how to forgive.

While too many people in this world focus on overthrowing chaos with monumental change and epic battles, whereas we who pursue faith understand the importance of the subtle but constant struggle in everyday life. Fighting the Pontus need not involve expanding the borders of the Empire or some new scientific epiphany. It can be done by each and every human being leading honest and quiet lives, fulfilling their role in the Clockwork, and listening to the will of the Maker that speaks to us through creation. Everyone has a place in the Clockwork. We need only live into our vocations and help others to do the same, and the Clockwork will continue to turn in perpetuity. I learned that in Salisbury.

On the mainland, the Inquisitors of the Holy See of Rome seek to purify its people by eliminating mine. Here, in England, the See of Canterbury has taken me in. The simplicity of my faith has not been changed by the machinations of others. There are those even here in England who would rather see me dead than serving the Maker, but it is no matter. People hold fear in their hearts the world over, and any ridicule I suffer here is better than the execution I would have received in Spain. Now that I am ordained, I serve as a priest and Canon, and try to teach others the lesson that saved my life. I teach them the difference between the chaos of the Pontus and the Maker's order. More importantly, I teach them how to forgive.

The Priest

There are as many different types of priests are there are types of people. There are country parsons, who preach and care for small congregations of farmers; charismatics, who are gifted with divine abilities by the Maker; itinerant clergy, who travel from village to village while ministering to people and facing evil in all its petty forms; and also ritualists who specialize in the rites of the Church and knowledge of the Pontus. All clergy serve under the auspices of a bishop, and all bishops under the Archbishop of Canterbury, but individual priests can be given great autonomy if their skills serve the Church by doing so. Some, like myself, even find their way into the Witchfinders as members of the Order of Canons. I can speak less of other religions, but there are holy men and women who serve the Maker in other faiths and in other forms. The Maker has shown favor to many denominations aside from the Magisterium and the See of Canterbury, as well as to those who practice Judaism, Islam, Bahá'í, and even forms of Hinduism. I dare not claim to speak with absolute knowledge or authority, but I see us all as servants of the Maker.

The Tradesman

It is important not to forget the tradesmen and women who live out their roles within the Clockwork, stabilizing our world through the most powerful means available: doing what they were made to do. Sometimes the tradesmen of this world are the targets of chaos, simply because they are the bulwark that hold up civilization. The importance of their role cannot be overstated, for if these cogs of the Clockwork abandon their post, it is the whole of creation that will suffer. Without the farmers and tailors and factory workers our cities and soldiers would starve, and we would all go bare into the wilderness. Everyone has a role to play in the world, and we are doomed if we ever forget that truth.

The Witchfinder Canon

No one is under any delusion regarding how dangerous the Witchfinders can be. We are an organization given wide authority by both the Church and the Crown. Thus, the necessity of the two orders. While the Order of the Star was created to serve the interests of the monarch and guard the safety of the British people against supernatural threats, the Order of the Canons was created to be the moral compass for an organization that otherwise could have become despotic. It is likely true that we hold each other in balance. Without the Canons, the Witchfinders would become like the Inquisitors of Rome. Without the Stars, the Witchfinders would lack the tactical knowledge and skill to directly fight the things that rise from the Pontus. Together, we fight back the rising chaos so that the subjects of the Empire may live out their lives in peace.

The Canons also collect and keep the substantial magical lore that has been amassed since the founding of the Witchfinders. We undergo training as ritualists to ensure that, when needed, we can call on powers and tools greater than our own mortal skills to face the menace of witches and the Pontus. We Canons must keep a watchful eye over the conduct of our fellow Witchfinders, lest the many powers and horrifying events we face cause any of our number to turn from a path of virtue to one of *Corruption*.

FREEDOM

"Genevieve Beauvoir is no saint in Thaïs" was the headline in the Times, wasn't it? I give a performance that makes the audience gasp, and weep, and demand an encore, and the reviewer spends most of his piece in a fit because he saw a bit of flesh below my shoulders for a moment at the end of Act I, and now I'm somehow a salacious degenerate. That encapsulates so much of what is wrong with this world. The art of my singing, the experience of beauty for the audience, the talent and dedication of those in the orchestra, even the work of the painters and carpenters and ushers that let the theater run, trampled and ignored because some people saw too much of me. Little wonder that London society ogled and

obsessed over Wilde's trial with glee only weeks after selling out shows of his plays.

To those that say the world is changing for the worse, or that society is on the brink of some dissolution because life is different, or stranger, or more daring than it was ten or fifty or a hundred years ago, I say they are fools. People are burdened by decrepit notions of what one's "place in the world" limits them to be. If that was true, or worthy, should I be scrubbing pots in a kitchen? Attendant on the needs of some husband? Stoned or killed or abandoned as a child because the color of my eyes and cast of my features mark me out as an abomination with tainted blood? The woman I am now is the woman I have made myself, in spite of the circumstances of my birth. I am liberated by my own choice, and I travel the world singing because of it. How anyone equates that with the destruction of the world is quite incomprehensible.

How do I threaten the safety of the creation? Does the poet, the painter, the abolitionist, or the suffragette? No. We see a better world, and we must build it ourselves, everyday. We embrace the wonders of the new world we are all capable of creating. Everyone has some gift, insight, or spark of beauty, and the world will be a brighter place when we are free to cultivate those glimmers of potential. If those outlets are repressed, that is the threat to stability. Silenced expression becomes vitriol, unfulfilled aspiration becomes aggression, and violent revolutions eat their heroes and ideals.

So.

I would sooner sing for pleasure than burn the world down with a bit of skin. Wouldn't you?

The Activist

There are always those who see the injustice in the world and act to correct it, and the Empire does, at least, have a strong tradition of people raising their voices in the public square. Quakers were key agitators in the abolitionist movement throughout its history, and the suffragists and moral campaigners carry on that tradition in the fight for broader reforms today. Fighting for the right to vote, for fair treatment for those of every bloodline and race, working against the social ills of drunkenness, the cruel treatment of the orphans and debtors in those workhouses, and a thousand other noble causes requires tireless effort. Although many ladies of high society make a fashion of charitable giving to some of these causes, it is the regular women and men who talk to their neighbors, organize and participate in demonstrations, and vote when and where they can to support those ideas that will help make our society better than it is. I have great respect for their work, and make what contributions I can to their efforts.

Well, aside from the teetotalers. I must confess a glass of champagne after a show is a delight I'm unlikely to give up.

The Artist

The fool and the actor have always been able to hold a mirror to society to exaggerate its flaws or praise its virtues. Sculptors and singers enshrine the ideals of beauty and explore the depths of suffering. Painters literally bring color to the world. At their best, artists and aesthetes can find ways to touch what is truly and beautifully human in all of us. Using those aching insights to sway the hearts and minds of an audience can be a powerful force for change. At their least, they can bring moments of beauty or release. At their best, their truths can change our lives.

Quite aside from the direct impact of our work, artists have always found or made space at the edge of society for our own little refuge from the rules and standards of others. In the back stages of theaters, the little cellars of bars, and sometimes in the parlors or bedrooms of the cream of society, we step away from all the rules we are told we need to follow. We can more easily be who we are, truly, and find others who can love and accept us for it. Life needs such places and such people if it is to mean anything. The breadth of love and beauty is far greater than what is talked about in the high street.

The Radical

Some cannot abide the injustices they see or imagine, and are willing to sacrifice themselves for their cause. It is easy to romanticize or vilify such passion, but most of those who take up arms or resort to violence for a cause do so because they feel there is no other option open to them. The Empire's many military actions in the past few decades have often been the result of harsh governance, or cultural suppression of so-called "barbaric" people, so I fear that the coming years will see more and more radicals—at home and abroad—willing to take drastic measures to fight the domination of the Empire. If there are no options for change and growth, if opposing the status quo can only be done at the end of a gun rather than at the ballot box, we are only setting ourselves up for pain and violence. It all makes for high drama, but I much prefer such deeds be limited to plays and operas, rather than writ large and bloody in headlines of the paper.

The Unionist

Those who are weak alone can be strong together, and the recent success of unionizing common laborers is a hopeful sign that more and more people are realizing this. The dock workers' strike in London in 1889 saw more than 100,000 working poor band together and demand better pay and fairer treatment, and it was one of the first times that public sympathy went with the workers. If the grinding advance of industry can be tempered by more people who believe they can rise and fall together, there is hope that our society might one day stop treating workers as having less value than those born into wealth. Although art has allowed me an escape to a different life, I still care for my fellows and I hope their efforts can secure them a more humane life ahead.

INDUSTRY

My great-grandfather was sold at a slave auction in Lagos. Before he was shipped to the Americas he somehow managed to purchase the freedom of one of his five children, my grandfather. I do not know what happened to great-grandfather or the rest of his family, but my grandfather did not make vain his father's sacrifice. Though a boy, he worked his fingers to the bone, scraping together all the money he could save, even if it meant going without food for himself. Twenty years later he bought his first fishing boat. By the time of his death, he owned nine. His firstborn son, my father, traded the fishing boats for a schooner and began to fish the deeper waters where the threat of the Pontus kept most fishermen away. His success left me a legacy that I have grown into exclusive shipping contracts. Today, if you want silk out of the Port of Lagos, you deal with me. Tomorrow, who knows? Zeppelins seem promising.

In my years as a merchant and businessman, I've learned two very important things. The first is that money can cross bridges that a lack of social status would normally render impassable. Even the most bigoted of buyers will deal with anyone if the price is right and the supply is limited. The second is that there is no limit to what man can achieve. It may take great sacrifice and it may take many generations, but human ingenuity can overcome prejudice, poverty, and even the Pontus.

Man is the cause for the fallen world. Man can also be the source of its rehabilitation. We have been gifted by our Maker with ingenuity and skill. While those gifts can be used to cause great chaos in the world, they can also be used to secure order and safety for humanity. We were given the world; so far we have just managed it poorly. The antiquated institutions of the Empire hold humanity's creativity in check by drowning them in an inflexible structure that was created by us and not by the Clockmaker. If we free ourselves from these hindrances, we can let human ingenuity thrive and allow all people, regardless of birth, to reach the fullness of their potential within the Clockwork. Each man has inherent worth that must be tapped if our society is to thrive. Thus, we must allow each man to follow their chosen path and rise or fall based on their own strength and determination.

Because of the sacrifice of my ancestors, I can now stand proud in British ballrooms. There are many who suffer under the weight of societal impositions who could bolster the Clockwork. If we allow them to find their place in the divine plan, we open a door of possibility. That is how the Pontus is thwarted, not through entrenching ourselves in the institutions of the past, but by embracing the possibilities of the future.

The Industrialist

Industrialists have speckled the landscape of the Empire with factories, and these cathedrals of steel and steam churn out textiles, metalwork, and countless manufactured goods that make modern life possible. Revenue from trade has brought unprecedented wealth into the Empire. Profit from exports alone has quintupled in the last century, to say nothing of the money made from internal trade. Fortunes are there to be made, and a new class of people is ready to seize these opportunities.

Since the birth of England, high society has been governed by nobility and those favored by the monarch. As the nineteenth century comes to a close, we are beginning to see a world where those of intelligence and ingenuity may rise to stations once determined only by birth or some dusty ancestor's ability to swing a sword. Entrepreneurs and businessmen now don the garb of the elite, and what they lack in class, they make up for in means. The stranglehold of old money is coming to a close. Now anyone with the drive and knowledge to become a master of industry can achieve wealth and status, achieving roles within the Clockwork that may have once been denied to them due to the circumstances of their birth.

The Inventor

New technology has changed the world time and again, and we live in an unprecedented era of technological advances. In my own lifetime we have witnessed the arrival of clockwork automatons, flying ships, analytical engines, and even more spectacular feats of human ingenuity. Men like Thomas Edison and Nikola Tesla are household names, inspiring a new generation of inventors to begin shaping the future of our Empire. Truly, it is an exciting time to be alive.

Who knows what technological marvels will be displayed at the forthcoming World's Fair in Paris? Never before has ingenuity been given such a stage upon which to shine, nor has so much attention been paid to the important work of the engineers and innovators. Perhaps the key to unlocking the secrets of the Clockwork or controlling the chaos of the Pontus is already in the mind of the next great inventor and we just need to provide the opportunity for their brilliance to manifest.

The Politician (Liberal)

The Liberals are the saner of the two dominant political parties on the floor of Parliament. These politicians and those who share their views argue for the advancement of privatized industry, the freedom to do business and earn wealth without undue interference from the government, and the slow dismantling of the status quo. Civilization has been held together by an antiquated system of social hierarchy for far too long; now is the time to give opportunity to anyone who has the drive to build themselves up. Although few dare to say so openly, many believe that the class system should be abandoned utterly; let each of us prove our worth and reward those who show themselves worthy.

BACKGROUNDS:
CHARACTER CREATION STEP THREE

A background represents the circumstances of birth, life events, or professional experiences that have shaped a character prior to the time she enters the game. Select your character's background based on the experiences that had the most impact on who she is now.

Backgrounds do not necessarily correlate to a character's current profession or lifestyle. For example, any character who takes the asset for *Membership: London Constabulary* will be a police officer, but one who takes the *Police* background was perhaps raised by a father who was a constable, or was trained from a young age, while someone who chooses the *Criminal* background can be a reformed felon or a crooked cop. Likewise, any character who takes rank 1 of the *Membership: See of Canterbury* asset can be a priest, while one who takes the *Clergy* background was raised in the church and likely went to seminary; while another with the *Soldier* background could be a man who came back from the war to find a religious calling. Different combinations of backgrounds, assets, and professions can create a myriad of different character stories.

After you choose a background for your character, record the rank of potential it assigns, as well as its starting *Class* and *Means* on your character sheet. These represent your character's role in the societal hierarchy and the resources she has available to her. Full descriptions of *Class* and *Means* and what they mean for a character are listed in the next section of this chapter. *Class* and *Means* can also be raised or lowered by taking assets or liabilities in step six, described on p. 155.

Additionally, backgrounds include a list of skills which characters with that life experience would have developed. Each listed skill receives a free one or two-rank bonus (two-rank bonuses are designated with a 'x2'); record these ranks on your sheet. Full descriptions of skills are provided in character creation step five beginning on p. 138. Backgrounds also determine how many assets will be assigned in step six. The *Building a Character* sections under each background offer ideas on how to spend these bonuses in order to create a well rounded and competent character.

AGENT

The powers of the modern world wage wars for resources, over political differences, and to carry on feuds drenched in the blood of the past. You have learned that the world is bigger than any one person, and anyone foolish enough to believe they can face it alone is doomed to failure and ruin. Based on this understanding, you've committed yourself to further the interests of some organization—be it a church, government, conspiracy, or mercantile company—and have learned and benefited from the association. Birth and background are meaningless when wars and fortunes can turn on a smile or a sharp knife at the right time, and you've learned the skills to find and seize the moments to use each.

Building an Agent

Agents represent a powerful organization, so one or more ranks in the *Membership* asset should be taken to gain access to that organization's prestige and resources. Different types of *Agents* will need different skill sets. Politicians and other governmental *Agents* will excel in *Bureaucracy*. Diplomats will take extra ranks in *Parley*, while Spies will take extra ranks in *Guile* and *Stealth* and should develop one or more physical conflict skills. Priests and other *Agents* of the Church, Inquisition, or one of the two Witchfinder orders will most certainly acquire extra ranks in *Mysteries*.

CLERGY

Perhaps you have an undeniable religious calling, a craving for access to secret knowledge, or your family placed you in the care of the Church out of necessity. Whatever pushed you in this direction, you have spent your formative years in institutional religious life. Regardless of denomination or personal belief, the Church has been a home for you, with all the blessings and restrictions that entails. Your upbringing has provided educational opportunities

far beyond those available to most, and perhaps a deeper insight into the mysteries of the Clockwork and the perils it faces.

Building a Cleric

Priests will need to take at least one rank of the *Membership* asset in a religious hierarchy in order to be ordained. Higher authorities within the Church will take more ranks in the *Membership* asset associated with their institution. Witchfinders must take the *Membership: Witchfinders* asset, while those specifically in the Order of Canons must also take one rank in the *Membership: See of Canterbury* asset if they wish to be ordained clergymen. Exorcists, healers, and other miracle workers will need to take the *Charism* asset one or more times to acquire their miraculous abilities. Mystical abilities may also come in the form of the *Magical Word* asset, providing the ability to understand ritual magic. There are also a plethora of character concepts outside the institutional Church, including ecclesial diplomats, tradesmen, artists, and those who abandoned ordained service for reasons of faith or politics.

CRIMINAL

Unless you are one of the lucky few to be born into privilege, the world is a hard and uncaring place. You grew up or spent a significant portion of your life on the streets or in the poor house. You may have willfully thrown off the yoke of law and society to take what you want from others, or perhaps you spent your childhood stealing in order to survive and have come to regret those years. Either way, you have lived on the fringes of society and you had to do what was needed to survive until now. The question is, what will you do tomorrow?

Building a Criminal

A thief may focus on *Burglary* and *Stealth* to make a living as a pickpocket or burglar, or find *Command* indispensable to

BACKGROUNDS SUMMARY TABLE

Backgrounds	Potential	Class	Means	Skill Bonuses	Assets
Agent	Ether	2	2	Bureaucracy, Composure x2, Guile, Intuition, Parley, Refinement	3
Clergy	Purpose	2	2	Academics x2, Composure, Intuition, Mysteries, Parley, Refinement	3
Criminal	Ether	0	0	Athletics x2, Burglary x2, Guile, Melee x2, Streetwise x2	4
Gentry	Purpose	3	3	Academics, Bureaucracy x2, Composure, Refinement x2, Riding	2
Laborer	Purpose	1	1	Artisan x2, Athletics x2, Guile, Vocation x2	4
Peer	Purpose	4	3	Academics, Bureaucracy, Command x2, Composure, Refinement x2, Riding	1
Police	Purpose	1	1	Athletics x2, Command, Composure, Investigation x2, Melee, Streetwise x2	3
Professional	Purpose	2	2	Academics x2, Bureaucracy, Parley x2, Refinement, Vocation/Medicine	3
Rogue	Ether	1	0	Composure, Guile x2, Intuition x2, Parley, Streetwise x2, Temptation x2	3
Scientist	Ether	2	2	Academics x2, Bureaucracy, Composure, Engineering, Science x2	3
Soldier	Ether	1	1	Athletics x2, Command, Composure, Firearms x2, Melee, Tactics x2	3
Vagabond	Ether	0	0	Guile, Streetwise x2, Survival x2	6

lead their own gangs and intimidate victims. Others focus on *Streetwise* and work as fences, lookouts, and information brokers. Mercenaries will take ranks in physical conflict skills such as *Melee* and *Firearms*, and pirates may take *Vocation: Airman* or *Vocation: Sailor*. This background can also be an interesting foundation for those who rise above the circumstances of their birth to become priests, tradesmen, activists, or even police.

GENTRY

You have been born into gentility and privilege. Perhaps your family is a lesser branch of some aristocratic household, or perhaps yours has been the first family in your village for hundreds of years. You are well bred and educated, and it shows in your bearing, speech, and social graces. Your social standing rests above those who must work for a living, as income from investments and rents from tenants are sufficient to cover living expenses. A handful of servants keep your large home running smoothly, including one or more maids or manservants, a cook, and perhaps even a butler. These things afford you a great deal of leisure time to focus on hobbies and accomplishments. Having few necessities to occupy their schedules, a lady or gentleman will often seek out adventure for adventure's sake, spend their days at grand parties, or arranging beneficial marriages for their eligible sons and daughters to keep them from slipping down into the professional classes.

Building a Gentleman or Lady

Aside from the basic requirements of genteel living accounted for by this background's skill bonuses, ladies and gentlemen often pursue hobbies and activities that are meant to show off their accomplishments. Those who fancy fox or bird hunting in the countryside may have ranks in *Firearms*, *Riding*, and *Survival*. Those who have a fondness for gambling may have ranks in *Guile*, while those who find more eccentric hobbies may have ranks in *Vocation*, *Mysteries*, *Engineering*, or other skills. Most *Gentry* are also highly educated, which can be represented by ranks in *Academics*, *Bureaucracy*, or *Science*. Those who focus on the life of a socialite may choose ranks in *Parley* or *Temptation*. All in all, *Gentry* are very open ended characters. Their resources and free time make most any combinations of skills and assets possible.

LABORER

The gears of the world would grind to a halt if it were not for the men and women that work building and maintaining the homes and businesses, or running the machines and mills that make modern life possible. You have been raised in a laborer's household and perhaps spent a fair portion of your years working a trade, developing physical hardiness along with the skills to work in any type of labor. Society makes a virtue of hard work and pats your shoulder with one hand while slapping you in the face with the other for your "simple character" and "crude behavior." One hand has oft been heavier than the other, but your low birth and limited opportunities left you with little choice in your early life. It's up to you to create any change you want to happen, otherwise you and your family will remain as you have been: workers with a job to do.

Building a Laborer

Most player characters will not be tied to workhouses, factories, and apprenticeships. Rather, those with the *Laborer* background are more often skilled tradesmen such as brewers, carpenters, or clothiers whose skills can find use anywhere, or traveling laborers like navvies who work at building railways and canals. The *Vocation* and *Artisan* skills will be the center of any laborer's livelihood, but a successful laborer who advances his station through outwitting his betters will need *Guile*, *Parley*, or maybe even *Temptation*. Those who have left the life of a laborer behind in pursuit of loftier goals can be small scale industrialists, who used their assets to improve their *Class* and *Means*. Laborers who wish to be inventors may also wish to take one or more of the *Inventor* assets, and those who wish to take on the mantle of a unionist or radical may find it useful to build up their *Bureaucracy* and *Parley* skills.

PEER

You are a member of the nobility, the privileged few, who for centuries have dominated the social hierarchy at the heart of the British Empire. Perhaps you are a titled baron, countess, or earl, or maybe you are the son or daughter of one of these celebrated aristocrats. Regardless, your birth provides you access to the most exclusive social circles, and will cause those of lesser status to treat you with deference. At the very least, your family owns a palatial country estate with thousands of acres of land, and an elegant townhouse in London. With privileges, however, come perils. Those with the most wealth and power also have the most to lose, and you must constantly tend to your standing. Do not be surprised to find that despite your many advantages, your entitlements also come with significant responsibilities and expectations.

Building a Peer

Peers that have their hands in running their large family estates and varied business interests must excel at *Bureaucracy*, while those who serve as politicians in the House of Lords should have extra ranks in *Parley*. Those focusing on their accomplishments may find *Fencing* or *Riding* a rewarding pastime, while socialites may benefit from *Guile* and *Temptation*. Some nobles can be appointed as ambassadors and diplomats or high ranking members of one of her Majesty's military branches, and for such roles would be expected to improve their ranks of *Command, Composure, Tactics* as well as the *Membership: British Army* asset.

POLICE

Policing offers important, respectable employment that didn't exist a generation ago. British cities have led the way in reforming the patchwork remnants of city guards, private security, and court officers into coherent constabulary forces that are among the best in the world. The expansion of telegraph service into the countryside has made previously isolated officers extensions of a vast network of communications, and legal reforms from Parliament have shaped coherent standards for public safety. Perhaps for you,

policing is a stable paycheck and a chance at improving your *Class*. Perhaps a history in law enforcement has caused you to be sought by large merchant concerns and shipping houses to secure their goods. Maybe your exceptional detective work has even come to the attention of the Witchfinders who mark you as a possible recruit for the Order of the Star.

Building a Police Officer

Private security is commonly hired by individuals or institutions with something to protect, but characters that hold a formal job with local law enforcement will need the *Membership: Constabulary* asset. Detectives focus on *Composure, Investigation,* and perhaps *Medicine*, while those patrolling the streets may need *Command, Melee,* and *Streetwise*. Rural constables often have ranks in *Ride* and *Survival*. For those very few officers allowed to carry guns, ranks in *Firearms* are vital. Officers may take the *Membership* asset more than once, and may also increase their *Class* and *Means* to reflect their improved lot in life.

PROFESSIONAL

You come from the ranks of the educated men and women that drive culture, innovation, learning, and industry ever onward through their work as doctors, lawyers, academics, and scientists. Although you are able to live in relative comfort and wealth compared to most citizens, *Professionals* must still work for their daily bread. This distinction causes many of the gentry to look at you with pity or snobbery, but you are still invited into the fringes of upper class society. You may aspire to attain a knighthood or some special civic appointment that could help further your ascendance in the social hierarchy, but such rewards only come to the best and brightest. A foot in the door of elite gatherings could also be all that is needed to secure a good marriage that could change the status of your family forever.

Building a Professional

Professional characters will be built differently based on their vocation, and usually take at least two ranks in relevant skills. Physicians need ranks in *Medicine*. Industrialists and businessmen should improve their skill in *Vocation* and *Parley* so they can understand their business and manage their employees. Solicitors depend on high ranks of *Bureaucracy* and *Parley*. Professors will take higher ranks in *Academics*. Any professionals who aspire to participate in high society will benefit from ranks in *Refinement* and may take assets such as *Higher Class, Title,* and *Well-off.*

ROGUE

Where many content themselves with taking only what they've been given, you look to life and take what you damn well please. Less prone to violence than common criminals, you have learned that deception and manipulation of others are the best ways to get what you want quickly and without the toil and strife which hinder others. Your life so far has been spent well past the bounds of the law, and you aren't afraid to risk life and liberty to make your living at the expense of others, but if you're subtle it's possible to maintain a position in society while feeding off it to get by.

Building a Rogue

All *Rogues* rely chiefly on *Guile* to hatch their schemes and manipulate their marks, but different approaches use different complementary skills. Charlatans and confidence tricksters use *Parley* to charm and reassure, seducers use *Temptation* to lead targets into disgrace or blackmail, and bully-boys and bravos use *Command* to intimidate the weak-willed. Highwaymen and others who steal by force will also have skill in *Firearms* or *Fencing*. All *Rogues* can benefit from additional ranks in *Composure* to keep their cool and avoid tripping themselves up in their deceptions, and having a rank or two in *Melee* provides a good backup in case things go wrong.

SCIENTIST

Moreso than any other time in human history, this wondrous age holds knowledge in high regard, and your talents have allowed you to make a place in the world through your intellectual pursuits. You have had educational opportunities far beyond most others, continuing schooling through your teenage years and earning either a degree—or better still, a position—with an institution of higher learning to carry on your work. Through the rigorous application of reasoned inquiry the fundamental workings of the Clockwork itself are slowly being discovered. With enough diligence and investigation you may be the one to discover an important revelation .

Building a Scientist

Researchers and scientists must excel in *Academics*. Those who interact with the academic hierarchy or seek funding sources should increase their ranks in *Bureaucracy* and *Parley*. Those engaged in active experimentation rely on *Artisan, Engineering,* and *Science* along with one or more *Inventor* assets to build and test their designs. Mad scientists willing to push the limits of creativity—and, perhaps, morality—may want to eventually acquire the *Science Mastery: Experimental Biologist* or the *Engineering Mastery: Automata Design*. Those studying alchemy should have at least three ranks in *Science* and take one or more *Alchemical Reaction* assets.

SOLDIER

The Empire has stretched itself across the globe thanks to the blood and honor of its armed forces, and boasts one of the greatest militaries the Clockwork has ever known. Soldiers and sailors like you come from every corner of the world to stand in service to the Crown, and may traverse it several times during a career. Military service can allow even the simplest country lad (and a few lasses in disguise, if songs and gossip are to be believed) a chance to escape anonymity in service to the realm. With enough grit and a little luck, even the lowliest recruit could become a minor officer and make something of himself. Brotherhood, adventure, and peril await any who take the Queen's shilling and raise arms for the Empire.

Building a Soldier

Any character can have a military background, but those who are currently serving must take a *Membership* asset in a branch of the military. Any soldier with extensive field experience might increase ranks of *Athletics, Firearms,* and *Melee*. Scouts would benefit from *Stealth* and *Survival*. Artillerymen will have ranks in *Engineering*. Soldiers, who have elevated themselves through merit to the rank of officer, should represent this by taking additional ranks in *Command* to qualify for the second rank of the military *Membership* asset. If your change in station has carried over to your personal affairs, you could also take the *Higher Class* or *Well-off* assets.

VAGABOND

Your early life was hard, as you had to scrabble and claw for basic survival as one of the destitute poor. What skills you learned were those that let you eke out a life on the edges of society. Others barely acknowledge your existence—even the working poor that are little better off than you—but that anonymity has allowed you to move through the Empire in a way that many do not know is possible. Unrestrained by many of the bonds and obligations that hold others in place, you have had a rough freedom that many will never know. The world has been cruel to you, but you've been hardened and made resolute by your trials. With determination and a little luck, you can still do great things.

Building a Vagabond

Vagabonds are the most varied background. These transient characters make ends meet any way they can, developing a mixture of skills but rarely mastering any. Using assets to take *Skilled* multiple times is a common way to build up the necessary variety. Beyond that, other assets that create personal connections or informal resources outside of *Class* and *Means* are very helpful. Not all those who start as vagabonds finish life that way, and those that have found a place for themselves in society might represent this with the *Higher Class* or *Well-off* assets.

CLASS AND MEANS

CLASS

A character's *Class* is how she fits into society. Upper class characters (*Class* 4 and 5) spend their days learning accomplishments, playing politics, dabbling in science or mysticism, and garnering favor among their peers. Middle class characters (*Class* 2 and 3) work in highly skilled professions or have others who work for them. They may work to either gain a place in higher society or supplant its influence. Lower class characters (*Class* 1) are seen as needed but fungible pieces of a larger world. They often work long hours for little pay or move from job to job across the Empire. The poor (*Class* 0) are often ignored by the other *Classes* and simply try to survive as best they can.

MEANS

Means is a measure of how much wealth a character has accumulated and how much access to goods and services she has through purchase with ready cash or credit. A character's *Means* covers both her standard of living and her discretionary income. Normally, a character may already own or be able to purchase any accessible goods or services she desires so long as its Cost rank is less than or equal to her *Means* rank. Narrators always have final say on what amount of shopping and expenditure a given *Means* can support, and should work with players to ensure they understand the limits of their *Means*.

Further rules for spending wealth, along with a list of available items and accoutrements is detailed in *Chapter 6: Accoutrements & Technology*, starting on p. 183.

CLASS

Class	Station	Notes
0	Pauper	You live at the fringes of society, viewed with contempt or pity by others
1	Worker	You are a tradesman, whose skilled or unskilled labor is vital, if not valued, for the survival of the Clockwork. This is the most common *Class* in the Empire.
2	Educated Professional	You are an educated and genteel member of society who lacks the birth required for higher *Class*. Physicians, lawyers, and industrialists all fall into this stratum of society.
3	Gentleman, Lady	You are a lady or gentleman and you do not work. Rather, you have tenants, land rights, and perhaps even commercial investments that supply your wealth. This *Class* includes the most socially elite of those without formal title and those noble families who have fallen on hard times.
4	Peer, Titled Noble	You are a noble, the true heart of society, and a driving force in the politics and culture of the Empire. This *Class* includes old families surrounded by wealth and clothed in inherited glory.
5	Royal	The apex of society, you are a member of the extended royal family, though not in direct line for the throne.

APTITUDES: CHARACTER CREATION STEP FOUR

Aptitudes are a character's foundational capabilities. Each character has two physical aptitudes: *Grace* and *Vigor*; two mental aptitudes: *Reason* and *Focus*; and two emotional aptitudes: *Presence* and *Will*. For ease of reference, these aptitudes are listed on the character sheet in these pairs.

All characters begin with one rank in each aptitude. Your character's bloodline and pursuit will grant a total of three additional one-rank bonuses to these aptitudes. Make sure these bonuses have been recorded on your character sheet from the previous steps. Finally, distribute five more ranks as you see fit among all six aptitudes.

GRACE

This is a character's elegance and precision in movement. *Grace* is used for all trait tests involving agile maneuvering and the delivery of force based on proper body mechanics. Graceful characters move with a smooth bearing and confident disposition and excel at activities such as dancing, running, and fighting. Characters who lack *Grace* can be perceived as clumsy or awkward, and will fumble complicated physical activities.

VIGOR

This is a character's physical health and brute strength. *Vigor* is used for lifting heavy objects, resisting sickness, enduring hardship, and other robust physical skill tests. Vigorous characters excel at feats of endurance and strength. Characters that lack *Vigor* can seem sickly or frail. *Vigor* is also used to determine how many large accoutrements a character can carry without becoming *Burdened* (see *Optional Rule: Encumbrance,* p. 186).

REASON

This is the power to think, understand, use logic, and make discerning judgements. *Reason* is used for skill tests to remember an event, figure things out through inference or general knowledge, or solve logical problems. Reasonable characters come across as rational and intelligent. Characters that lack *Reason* can be perceived as foolish or ignorant.

FOCUS

This is a measure of mental acuity, including powers of concentration and the use of the senses. *Focus* is used for skill tests to perceive things, or to be selectively aware of specific stimuli under duress. Focused characters are seen as observant and attentive. Characters that lack *Focus* can be seen as easily distracted or flighty.

PRESENCE

This is the power of a character's personality as well as the confidence and ease with which she comports herself. *Presence* is used for skill tests involving social interaction, charisma, and influencing others. Characters with strong *Presence* are seen as magnetic, influential, and handsome or beautiful. Characters without *Presence* are seen as meek, socially awkward and ineffective, or perhaps even submissive.

WILL

This is a character's mental and emotional fortitude. It is her resolve to do as she chooses regardless of physical and emotional urges, or in spite of the manipulation of others. *Will* is used in skill tests to avoid temptation, stay the course, and stay resolute in the face of horrors. Willful individuals are seen as self-assured, dauntless, and having strong character. Weak-willed individuals are seen as credulous, decadent, or unreliable.

Aptitude Values

Rank 0—Afflicted: A character can only achieve an aptitude at rank 0 by taking the *Affliction* liability (p. 165). This represents a severe handicap.

Rank 1—Mediocre: An attribute at this rank is average for the general population or a bit below average for a player character. It represents a standard level of ability that is neither flawed nor noteworthy.

Rank 2—Able: An attribute at this rank is average for a player character or a bit above average for the general population. It represents reliable ability that has been honed.

Rank 3—Gifted: A character with an aptitude at this rank is noticeably talented. Remarkable careers are built on an aptitude of this rank.

Rank 4—Excellent: The best and the brightest have aptitudes at this rank. Truly exceptional individuals make a name for themselves with this level of ability.

Rank 5—Awesome: A character with this awe-inspiring level of aptitude comes along only a few times in a generation and often becomes a household name or the stuff of legend.

SKILLS: CHARACTER CREATION STEP FIVE

At this point in character creation, a character has received skill rank bonuses from step one (choosing a bloodline) and step three (choosing a background). Make sure that these bonuses are recorded on the character sheet.

During this step, every character receives 12 additional skill ranks. These ranks may now be distributed into whichever skills the player wishes up to rank 3. No character may begin the game with a skill above rank 3 unless she takes the *Expertise* asset to specifically allow this.

Skill Values

Rank 1—Competent: Basic concepts and uses are understood, and the character will likely be successful in attempts made to use this skill in routine situations.

Rank 2—Proficient: The character has reliable understanding of all common uses, and is comfortable using the skill regularly. Professionals and tradesmen often make their livelihoods with this level of skill.

Rank 3—Adept: The character has a sophisticated grasp of all areas of the skill. She can adapt the skill to uncommon situations and is likely to succeed in the face of adversity.

Rank 4—Expert: The character is notable for her success with the skill, even when compared to others who use it regularly.

Rank 5—Master: The character is so thoroughly versed in the skill that their success is almost guaranteed, and their deep understanding of the skill allows them to use it in ways that others can only envy.

LANGUAGES

Language Group	Languages in Group
Altaic	Azerbaijani, Mongolian, Osmanli, Turkish
Afro-Asiatic	Egyptian, Somali, and most Northern African languages
Austronesian	Indonesian, Malay, and most Polynesian and Australian languages
Baltic	Latvian, Lithuanian
Basque	Basque (believed by some to be a fey language)
Fino-Ugric	Estonian, Finnish, Hungarian, Lappish
Gaelic	Irish, Scots Gaelic, Welsh
Germanic	Afrikaans, Dutch, English, German
Hellenic	Attic (Ancient Greek), Greek (Modern), Koine (Biblical Greek)
Indic	Bengali, Hindi, Kashmiri, Marathi, Persian, Sanskrit
Japonic	Japanese, Korean, and the Asian Tungusic languages
Niger-Congo	Bantu dialects, Mande, Zulu, and most sub-saharan languages
Romance	French, Italian, Latin, Portuguese, Romanian, Spanish
Scandinavian	Danish, Icelandic, Faroese, Norwegian, Swedish
Semitic	Arabic, Aramaic, Coptic, Hebrew, Moroccan
Sinitic	Cantonese, Katta, Mandarin, Szechuanese
Slavic	Bulgarian, Czech, Polish, Russian, Slovak, Slovenian
Other	Narrators and players are free to research more obscure languages

SKILLS AND LANGUAGES

Skill	Partial Fluencies Gained at Rank 3
Academics	Based on location of the character's education: **Within England:** Attic (Ancient Greek), Latin **Elsewhere:** English, Latin
Mysteries	Students of *Mysteries* receive partial fluency in Enochian, and other languages based on their mystical tradition: **Buddhist or Hindu:** Sanskrit **Christian:** Hebrew, Koine (Biblical Greek), Latin **Jewish:** Aramaic, Hebrew, Koine (Biblical Greek) **Muslim:** Arabic, Persian **Occultist:** Coptic, Latin **Other culture-specific:** Narrator's discretion
Refinement	Based on location of exposure to high society: **Within England:** French, Latin **Elsewhere:** English, Latin
Vocation	Characters involved in trade may take partial fluency in one language spoken by the people with whom the character regularly does business.

MASTERY ABILITIES

Masteries represent special ways of using a particular skill that only characters with advanced training can accomplish. When a character achieves five ranks in a skill, she chooses a single mastery ability in that skill, which represents her area of personal expertise.

Purebloods receive a single mastery ability during character creation due to their *Talent* blessing. They do not need to have the skill at rank 5 to acquire this blessing. However, when that skill is raised to rank 5, they may receive a second mastery in that skill.

LITERACY AND LANGUAGE

There are three levels of language fluency for Clockwork characters: none, partial, and full. A character with no fluency in a language cannot communicate in it at all. A character with partial fluency may communicate with some difficulty, and will suffer a -2 to all social attacks and Defenses if she engages in social conflict. A character with full fluency in a language can communicate perfectly, and suffers no penalties.

A character's native languages depend upon where they grew up. Characters reared in the British Isles are fully fluent in English, while characters from elsewhere are fully fluent in the language their parents spoke to them and partially fluent in English. Full fluency in additional languages can be achieved by taking the *Polyglot* asset or by spending experience points during play (see *Character Advancement*, p. 172). Anytime a character learns a language to full fluency, she also gains partial fluency in the other languages in its language group. For example, full fluency in Spanish would grant partial fluency all Romance languages, such as Italian and Romanian. Native fluency does *not* grant partial fluency in other languages.

A character with at least 1 rank in *Academics* is also literate in all languages in which she is fully fluent. Reading and writing languages she holds partial fluency for is possible but time consuming, and can only be used to communicate simple ideas and information. Accurate translation or writing in partially fluent languages requires a lexicon and at least one scene to do the work.

Some skills have such broad and consistent exposure to certain languages that she will gain partial fluency in one or more languages when she reaches rank 3. Thus, well-bred, well-traveled, and highly educated characters are often versed in multiple languages. If a character is granted partial fluency in a language in which she is already partially fluent, she instead becomes fully fluent in that language. Skills and associated languages are listed below, but Narrators may offer different languages based on their story's particular context.

SKILL DESCRIPTIONS & MASTERIES

ACADEMICS

Although many of the poor are unlettered, most working adults and all those above them in society have at least enough exposure to *Academics* to read and write. The upper classes and those with the spark to study *Academics* are exposed to diverse learning in history, theology, philosophy, literature, art, simple mathematics, and the humanities.

Ranks in *Academics* do not simply correlate to years of study: they represent the depth of learning and what is remembered from that study. While the undereducated will always have low ranks in *Academics*, so will those who spent their university years drinking and carousing rather than studying. *Academics* is combined with the *Reason* aptitude for tests to recall information, or with the *Focus* aptitude for tests to perform research (see sidebar). All characters with at least one rank in *Academics* can read and write the languages they can speak.

Academics Mastery: Linguist

Linguists pick up languages much more quickly and easily than others. They need only spend 1 experience point to achieve partial fluency in any mortal language, and a total of 3 to achieve full fluency (this is opposed to the normal 2 and 5 points respectively). Linguists can also read languages in which they have only partially fluency. They may even attempt broken communication in languages in which they have no fluency, provided they have at least minimal exposure to the language. To do so, the linguist tests *Reason + Academics* once for a scene. If successful, the linguist can follow the basic concept of what's being said, and can respond in basic words or phrases.

SKILL LIST

LIBRARIES AND RESEARCH

With the spread of academic institutions throughout the Empire, almost every city now boasts some university or athenaeum, and well-stocked libraries are always a mark of prestige for the elite. More people than ever before have access to libraries, and these can prove invaluable aids to researchers.

Characters normally rely on their own knowledge when testing *Reason + skill*, with Narrators setting the Difficulty based on the obscurity of the relevant information. Access to a library or special collection allows the character to instead test *Focus + skill*, Difficulty 0 to find relevant information in the library. This makes success far more likely, but the quality of information available is limited to what is contained in the library's collection. Each library has a quality rating for their collection on each topic, and tests made to do research in that topic cannot yield a category of success higher than its rating. Basic collections allow for basic successes (DoS 1–3), remarkable collections allow for remarkable successes of (DoS 4–7), and extraordinary collections allow for extraordinary successes (DoS 8+). Drawing the Fate card allows for any DoS so long as the topic is available in that library, as you come upon a book that is specifically relevant to your query.

A suggested list of topics appears below, and includes the types of information covered by that topic and the skill normally used in the test. Some topics may overlap; in such cases use the highest relevant collection quality.

Occult and religious collections have a chance to contain magical rites, and technical collections may contain alchemical formulae or item designs. At the Narrator's discretion, when players test to use a library, they may have a chance of finding such information. If the research test is successful, check the card number of the card drawn to see if a rite, formula, or pattern is found. Basic collections have a 5% chance (card numbers 96–100), remarkable collections have a 20% chance (card numbers 81–100), and extraordinary collections have a 50% chance (card numbers 51–100).

LIBRARY TOPICS AND TESTS

Collection	Skill Test	Information Available
Classics	*Academics*	Covers all topics from the Greek & Roman period.
Geography	*Academics*	Detailed information for travel planning.
Legal	*Bureaucracy*	Laws, case history, precedent, judicial writings, and civil governmental organization and regulations.
Military History	*Tactics*	Historical accounts, strategic principles & practical tactics.
Medicine	*Medicine*	Historical and current medical knowledge.
Occult	*Mysteries*	Folklore, legends, Pontus events & magical theory. Collections have a chance of containing functional magical rites.
Religion	*Mysteries*	Religious teachings, holy texts, religious history. Collections have a chance of containing actual rites using the *Ban, Commune, Expel, Protect, Restore,* or *Ward* words of power.
Social History	*Parley* or *Refinement*	Books of manners, etiquette, literature, poetry, fashion, and world events.
Technical	*Engineering* or *Science*	Historical and modern mathematical, scientific, and engineering principles and history. Collections have a chance of containing alchemical formulae or item patterns.

Academics Mastery: Theoretical Knowledge

Though not necessarily formally trained, the character is widely-read and possesses enough incidental knowledge and understanding of basic principles in a wide variety of fields that they can attempt to use any skill with at least some benefit to their endeavor. Once per installment, the character may substitute their rank in *Academics* for any other skill called for in a test.

ARTISAN

The *Artisan* skill is used across the strata of society for different reasons. For middle class men and women with creativity and the leisure time to use it, this skill is used to invent all sorts of technological marvels that might find their way into the next World's Fair. However, those aspiring to loftier social status ought be careful, as manual labor is the line that separates "those in trade" from the more educated professionals allowed to participate in high society. For the tradesman, the *Artisan* skill is not a hobby, it is a livelihood. Blacksmiths, coopers, cobblers, carpenters, and craftsmen of all sorts use this skill to produce the goods that are bought and sold across the Empire. For those of lower class, daily life requires the *Artisan* skill to work with one's hands: cooking, cleaning, and mending clothes.

Artisan is combined with *Grace* or *Vigor* to perform basic repairs and maintenance on common objects, and to produce the products of many trades. Testing *Focus + Artisan* is used to evaluate and appraise common objects. Characters who take the *Inventor: Fabricator* asset can use the *Artisan* skill to create their own grand inventions (See *Fabricator*, p. 157 , *Item Creation*, p. 198, and *Repairing Objects*, p. 86).

Artisan Mastery: Expert Production

The familiarity of good habits improves the output of any trade, but those who master *Expert Production* are a cut above others in their field. Characters with this mastery are so focused on consistent quality in their efforts that their work reliably demonstrates superior craftsmanship. All *Artisan* tests to produce items receive a +1 bonus.

Artisan Mastery: Rapid Production

Masters of their crafts can perform their work with an economy of effort and efficiency of process that lesser practitioners can only envy. When working alone (or with up to 4 other people) to produce an item, the Time required to complete the task is reduced by one rank.

ATHLETICS

Sport has always been popular entertainment, but the current era has seen athletic endeavors lifted up to promote health and sportsmanship, and codified to support fair play. In Athens, the ancient tradition of the Olympics is being revived for the modern era, where nations from around the globe will meet in peaceful contest. It is a testament to the stability and progress of the age and the prosperity of the Empire that sports are enjoyed by men and women of all ages and classes, including lawn tennis, football, cricket, croquet, rugby, cycling, and golf.

Athletics is also prized among the constabulary, all branches of the military, and the Witchfinders. For those in dire circumstances, skill in *Athletics* may very well save their lives moving through dangerous terrain, in the thick of combat, or by allowing them to escape the same.

Sprinting, jumping, climbing, swinging, and throwing accurately are tests of *Grace + Athletics*. Tasks that require endurance such as running a marathon, or feats of raw strength test *Vigor + Athletics*. Specialized sports such as fencing, horse racing, polo, harness racing, and shooting fall under the auspices of other skills. Archery is a unique case that can be performed with *Grace* and either the *Athletics* or *Firearms* skill, provided the character is familiar with a bow.

Athletics Mastery: Acrobat

Acrobats are rarely found outside of entertainment venues in the Empire, but some dancers, performers, sailors, and airmen have a preternatural deftness that lets them move about in unusual ways or through difficult physical circumstances. Acrobats treat all *Grace + Athletics* tests related to movement, climbing, leaping, tumbling, balance, and acrobatic performances as passive tests. They may also move at their normal speed when attempting to climb.

Athletics Mastery: Olympian

1896 is the year that sees the rebirth of the ancient tradition of the Olympics. Athletes from around the world will attend to show their prowess in many sports, and doubtless many in attendance will have this mastery. A particular sport or closely related group of track and field events is chosen in consultation with the Narrator. When making a test in their area of expertise, characters with this mastery draw two cards and choose which result to use to resolve the test.

Note that this mastery only applies to sports tested with the *Athletics* skill alone, and does not apply to any uses of the *Fencing*, *Fisticuffs*, or *Firearms* skills.

BUREAUCRACY

Properly maintained institutions are the backbone of civilization. Where would our society be without Parliament, the Church, courts, or hospitals? Londoners would not be receiving mail seven times a day if there were not a well-developed system delivering the post. Bureaucracies are everywhere, sustaining the daily life we've come to expect. However, sometimes laws contradict, paperwork becomes cumbersome, or mechanisms of society do not operate as they should. In these instances, a bureaucrat can navigate the complexities of our society to accomplish things despite these hindrances. When dealing with political, civil, medical, religious, military, or legal institutions, test *Reason + Bureaucracy* to understand and utilize proper procedures, chain of command, paper trails, loopholes, and general methodology. It also covers an understanding of how money, law, and personnel function within these institutions. *Reason + Bureaucracy* tests can also be made to legitimately or illegitimately create legal documents, identification, or official papers. Counterfeit documents may be detected as fraudulent by succeeding on a *Focus + Bureaucracy* test with a Difficulty equal to the DoS of the forgery. When dealing with procedural hurdles, test *Presence + Bureaucracy* to persuade, bluff, or bluster past a procedure that would normally be mandatory. This combination can also be used when attempting to bribe, con, or fast talk past institutional administrators and personnel.

Bureaucracy Mastery: Appeal to Higher Powers

Using deep knowledge of the system and knowing the right names to drop, anyone who knows how to *Appeal to Higher Powers* gets results. Once per installment a character with this mastery may draw two cards for a *Bureaucracy* test and choose which one is used to resolve the test.

Bureaucracy Mastery: Expert Forger

Characters with this ability have honed their ability to create false documentation and records of all sorts—everything from fake certificates and identification to creative accounting in business ledgers to cover up embezzlement. Such reprobates can utilize false and misleading records with great ingenuity. When creating a forgery the character tests *Reason + Bureaucracy* against a Difficulty set by the Narrator based on the importance and complexity of the fraud. If successful, the falsified documents are exceptionally well-made, and will automatically deceive anyone examining them with a passive test. These forgeries can only be discovered as fakes by deliberate, active tests against them by someone who suspects a fraud. Even then, the reviewer must draw two cards for their test and use the worst result to determine the outcome. The Difficulty to detect the fraud is equal to the DoS of the expert forgery success.

Forgery Experts are also adept at detecting others' forgeries and always receive a +1 bonus on all *Bureaucracy* tests they make to detect falsified documents.

BURGLARY

For some, theft is a profession. In the worst city slums, children with aspirations to a lucrative life of crime begin their training at an early age. Petty thieves pick pockets and sometimes rob homes, while more sophisticated criminals work in teams to orchestrate theft from shops, warehouses, and large estates. In addition to blatant theft, skill in *Burglary* also covers sleight of hand, distraction, and reconnoitering. These additional uses make it a popular skill among tinkers, magicians, prostitutes and other unsavory folk of the lower classes.

Testing *Grace + Burglary* is used to palm objects, escape bonds, and pick pockets. The Difficulty to pick a lock or crack a safe is equal to the lock's Complexity. Escaping tied bonds uses a Difficulty equal to the DoS of the test used to tie the knots. Escaping from handcuffs uses a Difficulty equal to the handcuffs' Complexity, so usually a 3.

Focus + Burglary tests are made to perform the role of a "crow" (or "canary" for a female burglar): a lookout who watches out for police and wary citizens. Unlike the more typical *Focus + Composure* test used for general observation, the *Focus + Burglary* test identifies specific threats to the operation. Staking out a location to gather observable information to help plan a theft is also performed with *Focus + Burglary*.

Criminal acts can be planned and judged by testing *Reason + Burglary* to find the best way to break into a secure building, plot escape routes, and appraise common valuables. When formulating a plan for a job, test *Reason + Burglary*, Difficulty 3. For each DoS, players may ask the Narrator to tell them the trait combination and maximum possible Difficulty for one test that will be required during the heist. On remarkable or extraordinary successes the Narrator will make suggestions for how the plan could be altered to improve your chances of success. All such information will be limited to what you already know of the target.

Appraisal of goods also tests *Reason + Burglary*, and is usually a passive test against a Difficulty of 3. Success reveals the *Means* value of an object. Unusual or rare objects require an active test. At the Narrator's discretion, items that are only valuable in a very specific way or to specific people or organizations may require other skill tests to properly evaluate.

Burglary Mastery: Misdirection

Through long practice with graft and deception, it is possible to reliably confuse and confound victims to set them up for the final step in a con or theft. To use this mastery, the character chooses a target she can engage socially and makes a subtle social attack of *Presence + Burglary* against the target's *Focus + Composure*. If successful, place the *Outmaneuvered* temporary condition on the target. *Misdirection* is most often used to allow another to sneak past a distracted watchman, or by the character herself to set up a test to pick the target's pocket or sucker-punch someone at the start of a physical conflict.

Burglary Mastery: Skilled Hands

With a touch of natural talent and many hours long practice, it is possible to become so deft with one's hands that pickpocketing, picking locks, escaping bonds, palming objects, and other feats of sleight-of-hand can become almost effortless. Characters with *Skilled Hands* testing *Grace + Burglary* for any of the listed tasks may draw two cards and choose which is used to resolve the test.

COMMAND

Whether it be a noble overseeing servants, an officer leading troops in the thick of combat, or a street tough bullying the residents of a rookery, those in positions of power project their authority to achieve their ends. The *Command* skill is used to demand obedience and to lead by example, to sow fear, and to build respect. Its diverse applicability to exercise authority spans all classes and cultures; any who desire to lead are well served by this skill.

In social conflict, testing *Presence + Command* attempts to convince or persuade through inspiration or intimidation. In physical conflict, this can be used to improve the Morale of units under a leader's charge, or attack the Morale of opponents to convince them to flee or surrender (see *Morale*, p. 74). Outside of conflict , *Presence + Command* tests are used whenever a character attempts to project power and authority.

Command is a language-dependent skill and even the most basic and bellicose uses to intimidate or embolden require the target to be able to hear and understand the speaker. If a target cannot hear the speaker or is otherwise unable to understand her due to noise or a language barrier, the speaker suffers an automatic -2 penalty to *Command* related tests.

Command Mastery: Cow

Sometimes a few sharp words and a withering glance are enough to stop someone dead for a critical moment. Up to once per conflict, those capable of cowing an opponent may declare a special test of *Presence + Command* as a social attack with a Potency of 3 and the *Fatigued* condition. If the attack is successful, the target immediately loses one unplayed initiative card of their choice. Targets of this ability may choose to spend a point of *Purpose* to avoid the outcome as usual. *Cow* may only be used on a PC or NC with unused initiative cards.

Command Mastery: Iron Morale

The greatest leaders can inspire those under their command to press on in the face of death, terror, and insurmountable odds. While a commander with *Iron Morale* is leading troops, any unit directly under her command does not shift Morale the first time they normally would. Further, the commander is so skilled at stiffening the spine of those around her that when she makes *Presence + Command* tests to improve her own side's Morale, she may draw two cards and choose which one will resolve the test.

COMPOSURE

Composure is the ability both to perceive and make sense of the world and one's experiences in it, as well as a measure of the discipline needed to retain control of oneself in situations that inflame animal passions and instinctual responses. Lack of awareness has its own dangers, and coming off as undisciplined and not in control of one's emotions can be a serious breach of etiquette in the Empire, so almost all subjects have at least one or two ranks of this skill.

Tests of *Focus + Composure* are used for activity related to concentration, perception, use of the senses, or to recall fine detail in memories. Circumstances that challenge self-control and deportment test *Will + Composure*. The same trait combination is used as the default social Defense for characters. The awareness and self-control that comes with high *Composure* is often tested by those gifted with charisms when they use their abilities (see *Charisms*, p. 226).

SOCIAL CONFLICT SKILLS

The social skills a character chooses to develop shape her interactions with others and the way she is seen by society at large, so choose these skills carefully.

Command is blunt and direct: either directions issued from the speaker's real or assumed position of authority, or blatant threats using intimidation.

Guile covers all lies and deceptions that the speaker uses to mislead, confuse, or distract.

Parley is the skill of negotiation, and is applicable to most normal social interactions and any other polite discourse.

Temptation is used when the speaker entices a listener to undertake a course of action for her own gratification, fulfillment, and reward.

Composure Mastery: Palace of Memory

The Clockwork is filled with wonders and terrors, and some have cultivated the ability to almost perfectly recall even the minutiae of passive observation with near-immaculate clarity so they may be savored or studied at their leisure. At the beginning of any scene, a character with *Palace of Memory* may take a calm moment to commit their surroundings to memory. Anytime after this, the character may perfectly recall any detail to which she was exposed and may even make relevant tests regarding sensory information as though she was back in that moment. She may even "recognize" things that she hadn't seen at the time, but has since come to understand.

Composure Mastery: Unsullied Mind

The character is especially resistant to any attempts to control or befuddle her mind, and benefits from a +1 bonus to her social Defense when targeted by a supernatural effect that requires or allows *Composure* as part of the defending trait combination. Further, if the character spends a point of *Purpose* to prevent the effects of such attacks, it does not count towards their limit of spending one point of potential per sequence.

ENGINEERING

Under Victoria's patronage of the sciences, the Empire is enjoying a time of rapid technological advancement. Steamships and zeppelins carry people from London to Indochina; men can speak to each other from opposite sides of the globe by way of telegraph and telephone. Through the utilization of cutting-edge analytic engines, business, science and even war have become the purview of both man and machine. All of these marvels of the Imperial Age are the work of engineers. Today, they continue to push the boundaries of what we think can be accomplished.

The *Engineering* skill may be used to understand a technological device, repair one that has been broken, or even design entirely new items. Operating or repairing industrial machinery, analytic engines, and other advanced equipment is usually performed with a *Reason + Engineering* test. Piloting vehicles such as automobiles or zeppelins tests *Grace + Engineering*. Gauging a machine's function through observation, or attempting to assemble a machine from parts without instruction calls for a *Focus + Engineering* test. Characters who take the *Inventor: Machinist* asset can create new inventions using the *Engineering* skill (see *Inventor*, p. 157 and *Item Creation*, p. 198)

Engineering Mastery: Automata Design

A confluence of technology has allowed for an incredible new field of engineering to open up: automata. Although sophisticated, automata are still incredibly rare, characters with this mastery are among the few minds who have grasped their intricacies. Rather than using the normal list of functions from the item creation system (see *Item Creation*, p. 198) to design automata normally, you instead use the Narrator character build system (see *Creating Narrator Characters*, p. 297) to design them, and can create a creature of up to Threat 3 from the automata template.

Each automaton you create requires a *Power Supply* with a power output equal to its Threat, which is designed separately

PHYSICAL CONFLICT SKILLS: WEAPONS AND STYLES

In *Clockwork: Dominion*, physically attacking an opponent is done using one of the physical conflict skills: *Fencing, Firearms, Fisticuffs, or Melee*. While these skills do control what weapons a character can effectively use, they are more concerned with the style in which a character fights. For example a character with a sword could attack with either *Fencing* or *Melee*. The former would be a very structured attack using a formal dueling style, while the latter might involve striking the opponent in the face with the pommel. The weapons and style used by each skill is discussed below.

- *Fencing* is the regimented art of formal dueling. Fencers are taught to use the foil, *épée*, and saber, but this skill will cover any balanced single-handed weapon such as the back blade and the shillelagh. Combat is highly structured and involves rules of engagement, honor, and etiquette. *Fencing* can be used effectively on the battlefield, but it is more commonly seen in sport or dueling.

- *Firearms* is the dominant focus of military combat training as guns are the weapon of choice in the modern world. The inherent lethality of guns makes this a deadly skill. *Firearms* covers the use of all pistols, rifles, and other personal artillery.

- *Fisticuffs* represents formal training in boxing or some other martial art and covers unarmed combat. Fighting with *Fisticuffs* follows a few rules of good conduct and is often used between gentlemen or those who aspire to be seen as such. It can be used in any combat situation, but is most commonly used to solve disputes between men of good repute.

- *Melee* is no-holds-barred brawling and mass-combat fighting. Combatants using *Melee* will use any method available to survive the fight, including dirty tricks, the scenery, and improvised tools. *Melee* can be used with any weapon with a Reach of *Extended* or less, although it may not use the weapon as intended and often comes across as inelegant. It is also the skill used to attack with thrown weapons. The skill is most frequently used by soldiers, criminals, and brawlers. It can be used in formal duels, but will always be a social faux pas.

according to the normal item creation rules. Producing the automaton requires Time equal to 4 times the Threat, incurs expenses at a *Means* value of the Threat +1, and the test Difficulty is 4 times the Threat. The test Difficulty can be reduced with the *Crew Build, Production: Dangerous, Slow,* and/or *Refined Materials* restrictions (see *Restrictions*, p. 211).

Engineering Mastery: Expert Production

Some characters have a gift when it comes to running a build: their techniques are flawless, and they have an eye for detail that lets them work from even rudimentary or bad designs and turn out good results. Characters with *Expert Production* receive a +1 bonus to *Engineering* tests used for item creation (see *Item Creation*, p. 198).

FENCING

Though guns and cannons are the present and future of war, there is neither elegance nor beauty in their use. Swords are blood and power forged into steel, and those skilled in their use are treated with respect. Skill with blades is both a matter of life and death as well as a mark of status, and training with such weapons has been a hallmark of the elite for centuries.

The *Fencing* skill covers the use of swords and similarly balanced thrusting and slashing weapons in actual combat as well as formalized sport fighting. Everything from sharpened steel longswords to wooden training weapons, from a walking stick to a cutlass, can be used with this skill. Whether used in combat or friendly competition, attackers test *Grace + Fencing* against the target's physical Defense. When engaged in a formal duel, or other one-on-one fighting, a character may opt to use their *Vigor + Fencing* for their physical Defense rather than the default of *Vigor + Athletics*.

Observing someone else using *Fencing* can tell a great deal about her capabilities: success on a test of *Focus + Fencing*, Difficulty 4, while observing another will let a character know the target's current *Grace + Fencing* total, her physical Defense, as well as her current Guard. This check can be made even when not engaged with the target, so long as the observer takes an action and can clearly see her while she is using the skill. A successful *Reason + Fencing* test allows a character to gauge the quality and strength of a weapon.

Fencing Mastery: Flawless Defense

Duelists have long realized that wounding an opponent is worthless if they themselves are injured in the process. Those with *Flawless Defense* exemplify the skill of staying alive through constant, expert use of their weapon to deflect and minimize incoming attacks. Any time a character with this mastery wields a balanced weapon usable with the *Fencing* skill, she has an Armor of 2 against all close-quarters attacks.

Fencing Mastery: Vicious Riposte

Though a subject of much debate among different martial traditions, there are those who insist that the counterattack is the most deadly of strikes, and characters with a *Vicious Riposte* are often cited as exemplars of why this is true. Once per conflict, so long as her Guard is up, a character with this mastery may attempt a *Vicious Riposte* after an attacker has just failed an attack against her. The fencer makes an immediate *Grace + Fencing* counterattack against her aggressor without the need to flip an initiative card.

FIREARMS

Though still primarily the realm of the Army and Navy, the long history of firearms use within the Empire also sees its subjects in possession of guns and having skill therewith. The *Firearms* skill covers all aspects of shooting pistols, rifles, and other small arms as well as basic maintenance for the same. To attack, characters test *Grace + Firearms* against a target's physical Defense. Attacks made with *Firearms* are subject to penalties and restrictions for using the *Aim* maneuver (p. 78) and shooting into cover (p. 82).

Firearms Mastery: Marksman

Whether through military training, long practice, or a natural gift, there are those that can, place shots exactly where they want them.

The ability to place shots with such precision allows them a distinct advantage when shooting against targets in cover, as even small exposures can be targeted reliably. Whenever an *Aim* maneuver is taken to bypass cover, it bypasses both light and heavy cover. This allows a *Marksman* to attack targets in heavy cover much more quickly and reliably than other shooters.

Firearms Mastery: Quick Draw

Though far more common in the lawless regions of the American West, or some of the wilder waters off the Barbary coast, than in the peaceful lands of the Empire, there are those who spend their lives a split second from mortal conflicts. When shooting first can mean the difference between the quick and the dead, quick draw artists are the only ones like to see old age.

A character with *Quick Draw* has achieved blinding speed with sidearms, and can draw any single-handed firearm from a holster or within easy reach as a free action, rather than taking a maneuver to do so as normal. This also enables a character to retrieve a firearm and shoot as part of reaction, even though they do not have a maneuver. Shots fired by the character during a turn when *Quick Draw* is used benefit from two advantageous circumstances when determining Attack Priority (p. 79).

FISTICUFFS

Various established schools of hand-to-hand combat exist around the world, and the use of any such formalized style is covered by the *Fisticuffs* skill. Regardless of the particular techniques and philosophy, structured and stylized fighting is covered by *Fisticuffs* (whereas no-holds-barred brawling and general mob combat is governed by *Melee*). In Britain, boxing and wrestling are the most common forms of this skill, and are popular sports among the lower classes. Since the mid-1800s boxing has become especially faddish, and the wide acceptance of the Marquess of Queensberry Rules since 1867 have regularized the sport and enforced fair play. The growing popularity of Bartitsu is exposing more British subjects to Eastern martial arts, but given the global breadth of the Empire there are practitioners of many styles from many cultures that live under its auspices.

Characters can attempt to grapple, punch, kick, or otherwise strike one another with unarmed attacks by testing *Grace + Fisticuffs* against their target's physical Defense. As a defender, a character may choose to use *Vigor + Fisticuffs* as their physical Defense, rather than the default trait combination of *Vigor + Athletics*.

Evaluating someone else's ability as a fighter can be accomplished by testing *Focus + Fisticuffs*, Difficulty 4. Success lets the observer know the target's total trait combination of *Grace + Fisticuffs*, physical Defense, and current Guard.

Fisticuffs Mastery: Bartitsu

Bartitsu is a martial art that was developed by weapons master Edward William Barton-Wright after living for three years in Japan. It has become popular among gentleman as a trained form of self-defense. Characters who have mastered Bartitsu gain distinct advantages in hand to hand combat. This character may use *Fisticuffs* rather than the *Fencing* or *Melee* skill when using canes or clothing as weapons. Additionally, this character receives a +1 bonus to Guard normally reserved for those with a weapon so long as she has at least one free hand, a cane, or a piece of flowing cloth at her disposal. All of her close combat attacks also gain the *Disarmed* weapon condition.

Fisticuffs Mastery: Pugilist

Whether through practiced skill or brute strength, pugilists hit hard and to great effect. They may choose to use either *Grace + Fisticuffs* or *Vigor + Fisticuffs* when making unarmed attacks. Their

unarmed attacks also gain the *Incapacitated* weapon condition, which allows pugilists to render foes helpless. Additionally, so long as she has at least one free hand at her disposal the character receives the +1 bonus to Guard normally reserved for those with a weapon.

GUILE

Guile is the art of lying. Lies take many forms, from the well-mannered deceptions at the heart of social intrigues to the complex layers of confidence schemes and criminal plots. Since lies and deceptions are so often selfish and socially disruptive, this skill is not viewed favorably by society at large, but it is a polite fiction to ignore the fact that most, if not all, people use it from time to time.

The most common uses of *Guile* are to deceive, confuse, fast-talk, or manipulate others with falsehoods as part of social conflict. Such attacks test *Presence + Guile* against the target's social Defense. *Presence + Guile* tests are also commonly tested by changelings performing various glamours that manipulate their targets (see *Glamour*, p. 229). If given incomplete information about another's schemes, a *Reason + Guile* test can be made to understand their likely intent, or it can be used to convince someone that has been deceived by the use of *Guile* that they have been tricked. In physical conflict, *Grace + Guile* can be used to feint, making attacks that reduce Guard.

Characters familiar with a target can test *Grace + Guile* to mimic their gait and physical manner, or a *Presence + Guile* test to mimic their voice and speech patterns. All such tests are made at Difficulty 0, and the DoS of the test becomes the Difficulty for others to notice the imposture with their own passive tests of *Focus + Composure*. Those who are deeply familiar with the target may receive bonuses to their tests to detect impostors, or succeed automatically, at the Narrator's discretion. When a character attempts to pass themselves off as a non-descript member of an organization—say as a constable in the Edinburgh police rather than the specific person of Sgt. Mathieson—most people will not doubt the impostor enough to make the test unless there is a specific cause for disbelief or concern.

Guile Mastery: Bald Lies

Part mentalism and part inspired lying, some charlatans develop the ability to so convincingly deliver a *Bald Lie* that the target is awestruck and finds it almost impossible to resist, at least for a moment. Once per scene or conflict, the liar may nominate a single *Presence + Guile* attack that is delivering false information as a *Bald Lie*; against that attack the target's social Defense is equal to their *Will* alone. The attack can be used in social conflict to change disposition, or in physical conflict to lower an opponent's Guard through a feint, though in the latter case the lie must somehow convey a credible threat to the target.

Guile Mastery: Expert Impostor

Talented actors are able to capture the feel of a character, but few can capture their essence. By embodying everything from minute physical mannerisms to subtleties of speech and mindset, expert impostors are incredibly convincing. Whenever a character with this mastery tests *Presence + Guile* to present themselves as someone else, whether real or fictional, they may flip two cards and choose which is used to resolve the test.

When impersonating a specific individual that has been carefully studied it can be almost impossible to detect the impersonation. When an expert impostor has observed the target closely in person for at least a scene in the past month, and are able to appear in an appropriate disguise, those trying to detect the deception are subject to a -2 penalty on any test to see through the deception.

INTUITION

Some characters learn to follow their instincts in addition to their rational mind. *Intuition* is the strength of one's gut feeling and use of passive observation to pick up on nuances of emotion, behavior, and awareness. It allows a character to get a sense of what other people are feeling, how they may act, and whether or not they are lying. In situations where a character is exposed to the supernatural, *Intuition* may also be used to "feel" what the normal senses cannot perceive.

The most common use of this skill is to test *Focus + Intuition* against a target's *Will + Composure* to know the basic emotion another character is feeling. The result of a successful test gives a sense of their dominant emotion in broad strokes such as: anger, fear, envy, joy, etc.

Characters that suspect they are being lied to may choose to use *Will + Intuition* as a social Defense against most social attacks; if the attack fails the character will know if *Guile* was used in the attack. A character can also actively attempt to perceive if any character she can hear and see is lying by testing *Focus + Intuition* against a Difficulty equal to the target's *Presence + Guile*. Recognizing that something is a lie does not mean that there is any logical inconsistency in what was said, only that the character has picked up on the body language and demeanor of the target and believes that they are being false.

With the many strange events that occur with the rising of the Pontus and the deceptions of glamours and magical effects, there are times when one's senses cannot be trusted and *Intuition* is all that can be relied upon. A passive *Focus + Intuition* test can tell if there are Pontus-touched creatures (aberrations, chimera, etc.) or outsiders (demons, fey, shades, etc.) in a character's zone of control. This test uses a Difficulty equal to the target's *Will + Composure*. Even though the character cannot see the entities, she will experience a distinct sense of wrongness that could give critical warning, preventing her from being surprised.

Intuition Mastery: Medium

Mediums are particularly aware of the presence of shades and other entities who are trespassing or lingering in the mortal realm. The character cannot see these entities if they are incorporeal, but she can sense when they are around her. Whenever a medium is in the presence of a shade, demon, fey spirit, Pontus event, or she is in a Breached location she automatically makes a passive *Focus + Intuition* test, Difficulty 2. With a marginal success (DoS 0), the medium feels a slight shiver and gets a sense that something supernatural is present but no specific information. A success (DoS 1+) lets her know where the supernatural entity or event is generally located and its dominant emotion, if any. A remarkable success (DoS 4+) tells the medium the type of the entity or creature (e.g. demon, fey, etc). An extraordinary success (DoS 8+) tells her the entity's Threat and whether or not it has any *Corruption*. Those who have this mastery are frequently associated with religious or occult groups, and such a talent is highly prized by the Witchfinders, Inquisition, and cults alike.

Intuition Mastery: Smell a Lie

Most often developed by astute detectives and the parents of many children, there are some who are uncannily accurate at picking out even believable falsehoods. Whenever the character is the target of a *Presence + Guile* test, the attacker must draw two cards and use the worse to resolve her test. Also, whenever the character actively makes a *Focus + Intuition* test to see if they recognize a lie, she may choose to draw two cards and choose which is used to resolve the test.

INVESTIGATION

The *Investigation* skill is a character's ability to collect and interpret clues, rumors, and information in an organized, thoughtful manner. With the spread of organized law enforcement and the birth of forensic science, recent decades have seen Britain take the lead on developing robust methods of analysis and **systematic inquiry**. Unsurprisingly, this skill is prized among police, **but can also be** very helpful for scientists and researchers that **work in the** field, rather than in a laboratory or library.

Different trait combinations are used depending on how a character is investigating. The careful analysis of a crime scene and a search for physical clues tests *Focus + Investigation*. Interviewing witnesses or parsing rumors at the local bar tests *Presence + Investigation*. Cutting edge forensic technology, such as lifting fingerprints or casting molds of footprints tests *Grace + Investigation*. In circumstances where there are multiple pieces of evidence to uncover, the tests are generally made at Difficulty 0, and each DoS reveals one piece of relevant information. The Narrator may set a higher Difficulty for the test at her discretion.

Some Narrators will prefer to give the characters information without a test and let the players deduce what has happened. However, sometimes the players will need a little assistance and clarification. In these situations, all investigating players may aid one another to test *Reason + Investigation* against a Difficulty set by the Narrator to craft a theory. Crafting a theory allows them to ask additional yes or no questions to the Narrator regarding the information they have discovered. For each DoS achieved, players can ask the Narrator one question that can be answered "yes", "no", or "unclear." If a situation is "unclear", the Narrator should tell the player how they could get enough information to achieve a more definitive answer. If the character fails, this effort yields no new information from the Narrator.

Investigation Mastery: Cold Reading

Cold Reading can quickly and accurately piece together likely truths about targets that have only been briefly observed. Similar to Sherlock Holmes, characters with this mastery can often deduce facts regarding a person's history and habits. *Cold Reading* a target tests *Focus + Investigation*, Difficulty 3. For each positive DoS the Narrator provides one specific piece of insightful information about the target such as "That is not dirt under his nails, it is dried blood," or "She has a barely perceptible limp that she has learned to compensate for; it must come from some childhood illness or injury." Failure provides obvious information, and remarkable failures (DoS -4) or worse give the wrong impression, and inflict a -2 penalty on the next test for social interactions made against or with the target in the scene.

Investigation Mastery: Eye for Detail

Even the tiniest detail or subtlest clue can be critical in piecing together information, and characters with an *Eye for Detail* are especially meticulous when searching a scene for useful data. The first time characters with this mastery test *Focus + Investigation* to search an area for clues they may choose to draw two cards and choose which one is used to resolve the test.

MEDICINE

Over the last hundred years, advances in biology, chemistry, and the understanding of human anatomy have completely revolutionized modern medicine. Texts such as *Gray's Anatomy* (1858) and Joseph Lister's *Antiseptic Principle of the Practice of Surgery* (1867) have revolutionized surgery and the understanding of infection. Vaccines now protect against such deadly diseases as cholera, rabies, and typhoid. Antiseptics, analgesics, and anesthetics have changed the way maladies are treated. Inventions such as the stethoscope, x-ray imaging, and the galvanometer for monitoring brain activity have advanced the practice of medicine. Physicians undergo formal training, but a basic understanding of medicine is vital for any who risk their lives in battle or live in remote locations, as without it even simple injuries and infection can quickly become life-threatening.

Training in the *Medicine* skill represents a character's knowledge of practical first aid, ability to diagnose and treat diseases and maladies, and to plan and execute long-term care. *Characters test Reason + Medicine to Stabilize, Diagnose, or Treat a patient.* The Difficulty for a *Medicine* test is usually equal to the current Wound Penalties of the patient. Much more detailed information on the use of *Medicine* is given in the *Healing and Recovery* section starting on p. 100.

Medicine Mastery: Battlefield Medic

The character is well-trained in all manner of first aid, and is familiar with immediate treatment options for almost any injury likely to occur through accidents or physical conflict. Such skill is often hard-won, and this mastery is usually found among military doctors, members of the British National Society for Aid to the Sick and Wounded in War, or physicians working in areas of excessive violence or machinery accidents. Whenever a battlefield medic tests *Reason + Medicine* to provide first aid they may choose to flip two cards and choose which is used to resolve the test.

Medicine Mastery: Gifted Surgeon

The character may perform the most complex surgeries known, including unusual or experimental techniques. While a character with *Gifted Surgeon* is still able to make mistakes, it is almost impossible for them to make things worse. Whenever testing *Grace + Medicine* for surgery, gifted surgeons may choose to draw two cards and choose which one is used to resolve the test. When performing surgery there are no consequences for failure unless the Doom card is drawn, in which case consequences occur based on the final DoS, as normal.

MELEE

While *Fisticuffs* and *Fencing* represent formal methods of fighting with rules and etiquette, *Melee* is the anything goes combat that occurs on battlefields and in brawls. *Melee* can be used to attack with a variety of weapons and is essentially the skill of using anything at one's disposal to win a fight. A man in a melee is just as likely to strike at his opponent with a weapon as he is to grab his opponent and slam his face into the nearest brick wall or hit him with a nearby chair. *Melee* attacks are about brutal efficacy by any means possible.

This is not a skill used by duelists and men of refinement. Rather, it is a skill used by brawlers and anyone who is fighting to survive. *Melee* tactics, if you can call them that, lack the gentility of more "dignified" combat styles. In formal situations under the gaze of dignified men and women, the use of the *Melee* skill is a faux pas. Thankfully, the peace and prosperity of the Empire has freed most of its subjects from any physical struggle for their safety, so those skilled in *Melee* are found primarily among the military, police, or criminals. Sadly, the roughest and least reputable among the working classes may have skill borne of dire circumstance.

A fighter in close combat may test *Grace + Melee* to make any sort of attack, be it stabbing with a blade, throwing sand in someone's face, or punching them with the butt of a rifle. The *Melee* skill can be used with any weapon that has a Reach of *Extended* or less and often uses whatever improvised weaponry is at hand—this covers all weapons not governed by other skills, including archaic weapons such as naval boarding pikes, spears, and greatswords. Characters may choose to use *Vigor + Melee* for their physical Defense against close quarters attacks rather than the default of *Vigor + Athletics*.

If observing a scrum, it is possible to evaluate someone else's skill by testing *Focus + Melee*, Difficulty 4. Success lets the observer know the target's total trait combination of *Grace + Melee*, physical Defense using *Vigor + Melee*, and current Guard.

Melee Mastery: Brawler

Some fighters learn to monopolize on the chaos and confusion of multiple opponents, using some opponents as cover against the attacks of others. Whenever a brawler has two or more opponents in her zone of control, she may designate any one opponent. This need not be one of the opponents in the character's zone of control. When attacking the brawler, the designated opponent must draw two cards and use the worse to resolve her attack. This penalty will remain in effect as long as the brawler has at least two people in her zone of control. At any time, the brawler may spend a maneuver to switch the attacker to which this penalty is assigned.

Melee Mastery: Improvised Weapons

Those who regularly turn workaday objects into tools of violence can become quite creative in their use. Anyone skilled in using *Improvised Weapons* can spend one maneuver to manipulate whatever she has at hand to make it more deadly. Any improvised weapon made in this way will have a Potency of 3 and a choice of the *Dazed* or *Bleeding* weapon condition. This can be as easy as breaking a bottle the right way so it retains an usable cutting edge, getting the ideal grip on a length of pipe to swing it with maximum force, or finding the face of the rock with the nastiest ridge to point towards an opponent.

MYSTERIES

There are many truths that exist beyond science and pure reason, and only through studying *Mysteries* can one hope to deepen an understanding of the Clockwork's theological and magical reality. The physical world is but one aspect of creation, and some have glimpsed what lies beyond its borders: Heaven, the Outer Darkness, the strangeness of the Borderlands, and the depths of the Pontus itself. Peculiar rules govern these places and the behaviors of their inhabitants: angels and their Fallen brethren, shades, wyldlings, and the monstrosities that arise where the Pontus touches creation. Unraveling these *Mysteries* that exist beyond mortal experience may be vital to preserving the world, or may hasten its degradation.

Characters most often test *Reason + Mysteries* to understand religious or cosmological concepts and scholarship, and this skill is used daily by clergy, philosophers, and cultists alike. Less formal uses also cover folklore, superstition, popular spiritualism, and knowledge of supernatural beings such as fey, shades, and chimera. Arguing or preaching religious, spiritual, and cosmological points tests *Presence + Mysteries*, and such tests are often part of heated social conflicts.

Although outside the experience of most lay faithful, the *Mysteries* skill is also intimately connected to the study and practice of ritual magic. If unknown magical rites are found and they are written in a language a character understands, they can be deciphered by testing *Reason + Mysteries* against the Difficulty to perform the ritual. If successful, the reader understands how to perform the ritual, and may attempt to do so if they can meet its requirements (see *Ritual Magic*, p. 233). Actually performing a magical ritual tests *Will + Mysteries* against the Difficulty of the rite. Magic is a dangerous and powerful art, and even the well-informed practice it at some risk.

Mysteries Mastery: Expert Ritualist

Through hard study or perhaps some blessing or curse, there are some who can call upon even the most dangerous and difficult powers more easily than others. Such expert ritualists always receive a +1 bonus when testing *Will + Mysteries* to perform a ritual. This skillfulness can lead to recklessness, though, as overconfidence may tempt her to perform rituals that others would never undertake.

Mysteries Mastery: Scholar of the Profane

The world is beset by all manner of supernatural threats, and a scholar of the profane has dedicated herself to understanding the ways of Pontus-touched creatures (aberrations, chimera) and outsiders to the mortal realm (demons, Fallen, fey, shades, etc.)

so that she may be better prepared to face them. Characters with this mastery always receive a +1 bonus on *Mysteries* tests made to identify such creatures, understand their powers, and learn their weaknesses. Such talent is highly prized by the Witchfinders and Inquisition.

PARLEY

In an ordered society that depends on peoples' ability to have civil discourse, the ability to *Parley* is vital. This skill is used to influence others through polite conversation, debate, and negotiation. *Parley* can be used to haggle, guide the topic of conversation, and otherwise engage in discussions and disagreements with art, poise, and intelligence. *Presence + Parley* is by far the most common trait combination used to convince or persuade in social conflicts.

Parley Mastery: Closing Argument

Mastering powerful *Closing Arguments* is a prized skill for characters who succeed and fail by their words, such as barristers, preachers, and politicians. Whenever a character with this mastery tests *Presence + Parley* against a target that is currently *Favorable* to their line of argument, they may choose to draw two cards and choose which one is used to resolve the test.

Parley Mastery: Silver Tongue

With a smile and a soft word, someone with a *Silver Tongue* can make even outlandish requests or ludicrous suggestions seem like the best course of action. Up to once per scene or conflict, a character with this mastery may nominate one special test of *Presence + Parley* to benefit from the *Silver Tongue* ability. If the test is successful it shifts the target's Disposition by two steps instead of one.

REFINEMENT

The stability and privilege of middle and upper class living (*Class 2+*) requires adherence to strict formalities, with behaviors and standards governed by a complex and rigidly enforced etiquette. Familiarity with such stylized manners is handled by the *Refinement* skill. Those trained in *Refinement* can navigate genteel culture, but those lacking this skill are viewed as unfit to interact with polite society. Those of high *Class* without this skill are considered uncultured boors and suffer social consequences.

Refinement represents a character's ability to follow etiquette and participate in the functions of polite society. Displaying good and proper manners at social gatherings, or breaking such etiquette and getting away with it, tests *Presence + Refinement* against a Difficulty equal to twice the Tenor of the occasion. This combination can also be used as a social attack to trap others into breaching etiquette (see *Intrigues*, p. 92) or to participate in civic occasions such as parades, award ceremonies, and other events in the public eye. Dancing and carrying oneself with noble bearing tests *Grace + Refinement*. Planning and organizing social events tests *Reason + Refinement*. Success on any of these tests indicates the character, performance, or event is well-received. Failure may ruin an occasion or cause embarrassment.

All uses of *Refinement* depend on a deep familiarity with the specific etiquette of a culture. When characters are travelling or otherwise interacting with cultures that are very different from their own, the Narrator may impose a -2 penalty on *Refinement* tests while characters become acclimated. Studying etiquette primers or working with someone to learn the particulars of a foreign culture may avoid the penalty.

Refinement Mastery: Acid Tongue

Manners demand civility, but even the harshest comments and rudest snubs can and often are overlooked if they are delivered with wit or outré ruthlessness that amuses the room. Once per scene, when testing *Presence + Refinement* to avoid committing a faux pas, a character with this mastery may choose to draw two cards and choose which one is used to resolve the test.

Refinement Mastery: Flawless Etiquette

Characters with *Flawless Etiquette* can navigate even the most perplexing requirements and strangest circumstances with little effort, and can plan, host, or attend an event of any type and carry themselves flawlessly. The first time a character with this mastery commits a faux pas in each scene, others are likely to ignore it, and all *Presence + Refinement* tests may be taken passively.

RIDING

Although the steam train revolutionized mass transportation and the automobile is becoming more popular, the horse remains the most common method for personal travel. However, riding is not only a method of transportation, it is also embedded in the culture. A young lady would never dream of trotting down the Lady's Mile in Hyde Park before she could properly handle her animal, nor would she consider accompanying a young man who did not dress his mount with the proper accoutrements. Skill at *Riding* is well respected by the middle and upper classes, while a lack of competence is considered a shortcoming in almost any man or woman with pretensions toward gentility. In rural areas, riding is often the most reliable way to get from place to place and work horses can be used when not occupied with labors.

Each time a mounted character takes a turn during which her mount is moving, the character passively tests *Grace + Riding* against

RIDING DIFFICULTIES

Difficulty	Sample Terrain and Conditions
1–2	Routine Task: Mostly even ground at a pace faster than a walk
3–4	Demanding Task: Broken ground or swamp at a canter or gallop
5–6	Challenging Task: Downward travel on steep slopes at a gallop
7–8	Daunting Task: Broken Ground while under artillery fire on a panicked horse

a Difficulty determined by the current terrain and environmental conditions (remember that passive tests use a maneuver when in conflict). If her skill is not high enough to succeed at a passive *Riding* test or the task at hand is complex (such as jumping a fence, navigating complex obstacles, or avoiding active assailants), this requires an active test as her action on that turn. If a character does not take the action or maneuver to perform a required test or if she attempts the test and fails, she loses control of her mount. On a remarkable failure (DoS -4), she falls off the horse. On an extraordinary failure (DoS -8), she is thrown from her horse and suffers a Wound.

If a mount is untrained for the task at hand—such as dressage, riding in a hunt, or fighting in conflict—all *Riding* tests suffer a -2 penalty.

The *Riding* skill also allows a character to quickly assess the training of another rider or mount. For people, this is useful in discovering not only practical skill level, but also social background. Successfully testing *Focus + Riding*, Difficulty 4 reveals both the target's rank in *Riding* and whether she has been formally schooled, which may imply either military experience or a education of privilege. A successful *Focus + Riding* test may also be used to determine whether an animal is fit for anything beyond basic transportation (e.g. hunting, polo, agricultural labor, carriage driving, or war).

Within the Empire, the *Riding* skill almost exclusively relates to horses, but characters from more exotic locales may receive specialized training with camels, mules, elephants, or other beasts. Characters testing *Riding* on unfamiliar species will generally suffer a -2 penalty on all tests until they become familiar with the new type of mount.

Riding Mastery: Dragoon's Agility

A skill found among the dragoons of the Empire, the plains Indians of the Americas, and some Turkish or Asian nomads, these mounted fighters have developed a technique of riding flush against their mount, or even hanging alongside them in a way that enables the rider to use her mount as cover. While mounted, a character with *Dragoon's Agility* are considered to have light cover any time she wishes. No action is required. Be mindful, though, that in the case of a miss that hits cover, your mount will suffer the effects of the attack.

Riding Mastery: Uncanny Horse-Sense

Anyone with *Uncanny Horse-Sense* can compel horses to do the improbable. With a successful *Presence + Riding* test, characters with this mastery can strongly influence any horse who is near enough to be affected by her touch or voice. Possible uses are quieting someone else's panicking animal with a whisper, convincing a wild animal to accept a halter, or compelling an unfamiliar and unrestrained horse to approach and trust the character. While a character with *Uncanny Horse-Sense* is mounted she can persuade that animal to participate in activities for which it is not trained, like fox-hunting, polo, and conflict without the usual -2 penalty. Additionally, the first time in each scene that you fail a test to control a frightened or panicked animal, you may instead treat it as a marginal success (DoS 0) on any result but a Doom card.

SCIENCE

Characters with ranks in *Science* have formal education in specialized fields of study such as mathematics, physics, biology, and chemistry, as well as experimental procedure and lab work. The Empire and all the great powers of the world actively embrace the development of scientists in their own societies, and many universities and private organizations, like the Royal Society, exist to teach and promote scientific learning.

Performing scientific experiments, analyzing case studies or experimental data, and recalling popularly held theories are tests of *Reason + Science*. The results of such tests can sometimes produce evidence to be used in social conflict (see *Social Weapons: Evidence*, p. 87). Presenting scientific information in an engaging way during lectures or discussions tests *Presence + Science*, while serious, scientific debate and defense of hypotheses requires *Reason + Science*. Depending on the nature of the scene, either or both those combinations might be used in social conflict.

Expanding a scientific understanding of the world and its workings—based on observation, experimentation, and verification—is the surest path to new areas of invention and discovery. The *Inventor: Innovator* asset uses *Reason + Science* tests to produce new creations (see *Inventor: Innovator*, p. 157 and *Item Creation*, p. 198), and the same trait combination is used in *Alchemical Reactions* (see *Alchemical Reaction*, p. 300 and p. 223).

Science Mastery: Experimental Biologist

Through diligent study of surgical techniques, husbandry, and, perhaps, the use of chimerical or aberrant test subjects, it is possible for a daring or depraved *Experimental Biologist* to create unique creatures. This mastery allows a character to alter living things so drastically that she can remake them into beings of her own design using the Narrator character creation system (see *Creating Narrator Characters*, p. 297).

However, experimental biology has its limits, and can only produce creatures up to Threat 3, and only based on the aberration, animal, or beastfolk templates. Performing the necessary alterations requires a *Reason + Science* test at a Difficulty of 4 times the new creation's Threat, but this can be reduced with the *Crew Build, Production: Dangerous, Slow,* and/or *Refined Materials* restrictions. The production Time is equal to 3 times the Threat, and incurs Cost of the creature's Threat +1 (see *Restrictions*, p. 211).

Science Mastery: Expert Alchemist

If a character is deeply dedicated to the study of the New Science she may become an *Expert Alchemist*. Through long practice the necessary calculations have become so deeply ingrained that a character with this mastery can reliably achieve success in even the most demanding transmutations. Expert alchemists receive a +1 bonus to *Reason + Science* tests for alchemy.

STEALTH

Even in the safety and security of Imperial cities, there are still those who make their living through criminal acts. For these people, the ability to hide, sneak, and move about unnoticed is essential. In the country, poachers who hunt for sustenance depend on their ability to remain unseen both by the animals they stalk and the foresters who hunt them.

Whatever the reason, a character with *Stealth* can move unnoticed by testing *Grace + Stealth* against a Difficulty set by the Narrator (usually equal to the *Focus + Composure* of anything actively observing the area). If there is plentiful concealment in the area, the character testing *Grace + Stealth* may receive a +1 bonus, but if there is no cover and good light, she may receive a -2 penalty.

In cities, crowds can hide a character as effectively as shadows. If a character is trying to blend in with a crowd or follow a person in city traffic without raising suspicion, she tests *Presence + Stealth* against the observer's *Focus + Composure*. The composition of a crowd may grant bonuses or penalties as above; a mudlark will go unnoticed on the docks of the Thames, but will look outlandish standing outside Marshall & Snelgrove's on Oxford Street.

Stealth Mastery: Blend into the Crowd

Becoming lost in the throng on the city's streets is among the most effective camouflage available in the teeming metropolises of the Empire, and can be of use to both criminals and those upholding the law. Yet even in small towns or country villages the ability to blend in with the locals can be of use to avoid coming off as an interloper. When a character who knows how to *Blend into the Crowd* tests *Presence + Stealth* to mix into a group she may draw two cards and choose which one is used to determine the result of the test.

Stealth Mastery: Expert Sneak

Military scouts, foresters, criminals, and explorers can all find themselves in dire situations where going unnoticed is vital. The few who have long careers in such roles can come to develop an almost inhuman ability to control their own motion and use their surroundings to move undetected. An *Expert Sneak* attempting to move unseen through her environment may draw two cards when testing *Grace + Stealth* and choose one to resolve the test.

STREETWISE

Beneath the glittering life of polite society and politics, cities teem with the working poor, street urchins, criminals, and toshers. *Streetwise* represents a character's understanding of the geographical, mercantile, and social nuances of this underbelly of society. Most savvy city-dwellers have at least a rank of the skill to ensure they know how to avoid bad neighborhoods, but those who truly spend time in the streets of a city can learn the strange secrets of its hidden places and shadow culture. *Streetwise* is an invaluable skill for anyone exposed to the harsher side of her city—not just the thieves and homeless, or the tradesmen in the tenements, but also the police who keep watch over them.

A *Reason + Streetwise* test can tell a character which neighborhoods are safe at night, which rookeries are controlled by which gangs, or the quickest way to get to any known location in the city. This knowledge also includes the best places to go shopping for whatever she desires, be it fresh produce, opium, or stolen goods. Navigating quickly through the city tests *Grace + Streetwise*. Remarkable successes (DoS 4+) and higher on either type of test might even reveal interesting shortcuts that are not on most maps, although there is no guarantee of safety in such places. Outrunning or evading pursuers in an urban setting may also test *Grace + Streetwise*.

Presence + Streetwise is most often used to engage in the rough pidgin etiquette of lower society. In social settings with low class individuals (Class 0 and 1), *Streetwise* is often used instead of *Refinement* to make etiquette tests and avoid making faux pas (see *Intrigues*, p. 92). *Presence + Streetwise* is also used to spread or gather rumors, or to buy, sell, and haggle over illicit goods.

Streetwise Mastery: Ear to the Street

Most people find the bustle and chaos of city streets to be an annoyance or a source of excitement. A few learn what it really is: a resource to be exploited. A character with an *Ear to the Street* knows how to talk to the mudlarks and prostitutes, street vendors and porters, the petty criminals and bobbies to find out what's really going on. Every city has people who depend on the street for their livelihoods, so this mastery can be used around the world. Anyone with an *Ear to the Street* may passively test *Presence + Streetwise* to collect and spread rumors and gossip, and always receives a +1 bonus on *Presence + Streetwise* tests to follow low *Class* etiquette.

Streetwise Mastery: Home City

When a character immerses herself in a city, can picture every street and alley, church and public house clear as day, and recite the gossip and headlines that made waves in years past, she has found her home city. This mastery reflects an incredible understanding of how all the disparate parts—people, commerce, buildings, and history—come together to make a magnificent whole. A character in her home city never needs to make *Streetwise* tests to safely travel through it. Further, whenever she tests *Presence + Streetwise* for non-conflict social interactions with others of that city she may choose to draw two cards and choose which is used to resolve the test.

SURVIVAL

Beyond the edges of civilization, there are places where people cannot easily obtain the resources necessary to survive. Those that grow up in the wilder parts of the world must anticipate the weather, find food, water, and shelter, as they live without the comforts of modern life. The *Survival* skill is what makes this possible. The typical country farmer or infrequent hunter will likely have a rank of *Survival* and the training to survive a few days in the woods, while Army scouts, explorers, and the indigenous peoples inhabiting the far reaches of the world can survive for weeks or even months in the wild based on their expertise in this skill.

Preparing for time in the wilderness, or trying to make do if one is stranded, tests *Reason + Survival*. If Unprepared or Ill-prepared, a character enduring exposure or deprivation will test *Vigor + Survival*. The full rules for dealing with life in the wilds are covered in *Extreme Environments* on p. 96.

Survival is also used to navigate in the wilderness, track quarry, and to cover one's own tracks. These tasks test *Focus + Survival*, with a Difficulty set by the Narrator based on qualities of the terrain. The character's DoS when hiding her tracks will become the test Difficulty for any pursuers attempting to track her.

Survival Mastery: Rugged Survivor

The worst blizzards, sand storms, and heat waves can barely slow down a rugged survivor, and they know how to prepare for the absolute worst that nature has to offer. A rugged survivor may make passive *Reason + Survival* tests to prepare for an environment, as well as passive *Vigor + Survival* tests to endure an extreme environment.

Survival Mastery: Trapper

Beyond the simple snares typically set for catching small game, trappers can create large, elaborate, and deadly traps capable of wounding or killing large game or people. A character with this mastery can use the item creation system to design traps and even create some poisons using a limited list of functions and restrictions (see *Trapper Designs* sidebar). Producing these items uses a *Reason + Survival* test instead of the usual *Reason + Artisan* (see *Item Creation*, p. 198).

TACTICS

Humanity has spent much of its history embroiled in conflict, and there are many lessons available to those who study its subtleties. An individual trained in *Tactics* can draw upon her knowledge of strategy and military history to anticipate the flow of conflict, and quickly redirect the efforts of her troops to maximize advantageous situations. The ability to visualize potential scenarios is also useful when orchestrating or attempting to spot an ambush. This flexibility makes those with training in *Tactics* strong candidates for promotion in the British military or on metropolitan police forces.

A character may set an ambush using a *Reason + Tactics* test against a Difficulty set by the Narrator based on the availability of terrain in which to hide. The DoS achieved on such a test becomes the Difficulty for an opponent's *Focus + Tactics* test to recognize the ambush. If the ambush is recognized, then the hidden foes are discovered before they attack. However, if the ambush goes unnoticed, the ambushers get to take a suprise sequence (see *Surprise Sequences*, p. 76).

In the thick of combat, a tactician may take an action to provide beneficial commands to those allies that can see and hear her. She selects as many allies as desired and tests *Reason + Tactics* against a Difficulty equal to the total number of unused initiative cards currently held by all chosen allies. If successful, the tactician grants all targets an advantageous circumstance when determining Attack Priority (see p. 79) until the end of the sequence.

Tacticians can also help spur an ally to act by pointing out opportunities for them to seize. A tactician chooses a single friendly character and tests *Reason + Tactics*, Difficulty 0. A basic success (DoS 1+) allows the target to draw two new cards from the deck, and the target may choose to use them to replace any of her unused initiative cards. A remarkable success (DoS 4+) allows the target to draw three cards, and a extraordinary success (DoS 8+) allows her to draw 4. If the target draws the Doom card in this way, it must be chosen to replace one of her unused initiative cards.

Outside of active conflict, *Tactics* can provide insight into the plans and activities of foes. Using recent information about an opponent's tactical decisions, testing *Reason + Tactics* may provide insight into their strategies anticipated actions. A *Focus + Tactics* test allows the shrewd assessment of terrain to understand what impact it might have on troop mobility, the availability and quality of cover, lines of sight, and how best to array troops to attack or defend a given location. Success can tell a character the best positioning for a sniper, the safest place to set camp, or the best route along which to march troops without fatiguing them or opening them up to possible ambush.

Tactics Mastery: Outflank

Even in the heat of combat, keen tactical awareness lets a character with this mastery press her enemies mercilessly. Once per sequence in physical conflict, a tactician with *Outflank* may take an action to test *Reason + Tactics*, Difficulty 0. A basic success (DoS 1+) forces the Narrator to draw two initiative cards and add them to her hand, then discard her two highest unused initiative cards. If the cards that were just drawn are the highest, then those are the ones discarded. A remarkable success (DoS 4+) forces the Narrator to draw three cards and discard her three highest cards, and an extraordinary success (DoS 8+) forces the Narrator to draw four cards and then discard her highest four cards.

The only exception to this mastery is if the Narrator has the Fate card already in hand. Before drawing new cards, the Narrator shows the Fate card to the players and may retain the card. If the Narrator does not show the Fate card to the players before drawing, or if the Fate card is drawn, it must be discarded.

Tactics Mastery: Cunning Strategist

When developing a plan before a physical conflict, a cunning strategist may test *Reason + Tactics*, Difficulty 0. If successful, when dealing initiative cards during the first sequence of the planned conflict, the tactician draws a number of additional initiative cards based on her DoS and may deal them to allies of her choosing. A basic success (DoS 1+) allows her to draw two additional cards. A remarkable success (DoS 4+) allows her to draw three cards, and a extraordinary success (DoS 8+) allows her to draw four. The tactician may give any number of these extra cards to any player of her choice, or retain them for herself. After extra initiative cards are dealt, all characters must discard down to the normal number of retained initiative cards (e.g. three if unwounded). There is no benefit from this mastery in any subsequent sequence of the same conflict.

TEMPTATION

The gentle whispers of temptation have been with man since the serpent first spoke in Eden. A character skilled in *Temptation* can manipulate the weaknesses and desires of others to influence their behavior. She can skillfully sway a young gentleman to spend a night carousing and ignoring an important familial obligation, or more sinisterly draw him into a situation which escalates into excellent fodder for blackmail.

In social conflict any offer of reward, pleasure, or personal benefit can be used in an attempt to convince or persuade another by testing *Presence + Temptation* against the target's social Defense. *Temptation* is most effective when it indulges an opponent's Affinities, so the most successful tempters often spend time learning about what might entice a target before engaging her in social conflict. If a character is able to discreetly observe or otherwise gather information on a target's personality and habits she can test *Focus + Temptation* against a Difficulty set by the Narrator. Success reveals the general strength and concept of the target's strongest Affinity (e.g. an unwavering devotion to family, a lifelong love for the Church, or a convenient sense of duty to some authority).

Temptation Mastery: Forbidden Fruit

The temptation to rebel for the sheer thrill of transgression can be difficult to resist, especially when the normal social expectations on a character are so restrictive. Tempting someone to ignore the heavy obligations of an Affinity can be a potent invitation to sin, and those with this mastery know just how to make it nearly irresistible. If the tempter knows the full description of one of their target's Affinities and is able to couch their temptation as a way to escape or violate that obligation without immediately harming the object of the Affinity, they can add extra allure to their machinations. Once per scene, the character nominates a single test of *Presence + Temptation* as offering *Forbidden Fruit*: the attack gains Potency equal to the rank of the known Affinity and ignores the Armor normally granted by the Affinity.

Temptation Mastery: Seducer

Although Victorian high society shames anyone so bold and louche as to attempt outright seduction, there are many who find benefit in using their physical wiles to manipulate others. During a social conflict a character with this mastery can nominate a single test of *Presence + Temptation* against a Difficulty of the target's *Will* alone. No skills may be included in the social Defense. Seducers must take care, however as such behavior could be a faux pas.

VOCATION

Vocation covers all routine endeavors of a particular occupation. The specific tasks covered by this skill depend on the occupation chosen. *Vocation: Carpenter* covers construction with wood, while *Vocation: Artilleryman* covers the maintenance and firing of military artillery. Almost everyone in the lower and middle strata of society (*Class 0–1*) are likely to have at least a rank in a *Vocation* skill, but those of more prestigious social ranking (*Class 3–5*) would be snubbed by their peers for working a trade.

When a character performs work solely related to her occupation she may choose to passively or actively test aptitude + *Vocation* against a Difficulty set by the Narrator. In cases where *Vocation* is being used to mimic activity usually covered by other skills, *Vocation* can only be used in passive tests and not during adverse circumstances such as being in conflict or under intense pressure. For example, a character with *Vocation: Locksmith* would be able to pick a lock in a situation without significant pressure or distraction. If the same character attempted to quickly pick the lock on a manor gate as part of a break-in, she would need to use the *Burglary* skill. Pharmacists would be perfectly capable of mixing drugs based on a physician's notes using the *Vocation: Pharmacist* skill, but would need to make a *Medicine* test if attempting to diagnose or treat a patient. Soldiers can endure long marches, set up encampments, and reassemble a rifle with *Vocation: Soldier*, but should they try to shoot someone, they would need to make a *Firearms* test. Uses of a *Vocation* skill that do not mimic the primary functions of other skills, such as *Vocation: Artilleryman*'s ability to fire a field gun or *Vocation: Chauffeur*'s ability to drive an automobile, may be used actively in any situation.

Vocations include: Accountant, Airman, Artilleryman, Barrister, Butler, Chauffeur, Coachman, Clothier, Entertainer, Farmer, Footman, Herald, Lawyer, Locksmith, Maid, Mason, Miller, Mudlark, Musician, Navigator, Navvy, Pharmacist, Publican, Ragman, Sailor, Sewerman, Signalman, Smith, Steward, Soldier, Tailor, Teacher, Writer, and any other occupations as allowed by the Narrator.

Vocation Mastery: Related Knowledge

A character with *Related Knowledge* branches out from her main occupation to develop skill in a related field. After taking the mastery, she may also make passive tests in that occupation as though it were her chosen *Vocation* specialty. For example, a character with *Vocation: Navigator* who has served in the Navy could choose *Vocation: Sailor* as a related mastery, and would thereafter use her *Vocation* ranks as part of any passive tests for sailing or performing other work on ships. When taking this mastery, players should discuss their uses and overlaps with the Narrator to ensure a common understanding of how it will come up in play.

ASSETS AND LIABILITIES: CHARACTER CREATION STEP SIX

The Clockwork is filled with unusual circumstances and individuals that are a step outside the status quo, and these special variances and abilities can be explored and reflected as assets and liabilities. Assets are special benefits a character enjoys, and cover everything from transcendent powers to special access to allies and helpful accoutrements. Liabilities are the hindrances burdening a character, and are often the consequences of ill luck or indiscretion.

GAINING AND LOSING ASSETS AND LIABILITIES

A character's chosen background provides her with a number of assets to represent the chances she has had to better herself, noteworthy perks she's inherited, unique gifts she has acquired, or honors she has received. No asset can be taken more than once, unless stated otherwise in its description.

A character may also take up to two liabilities, representing significant drawbacks and obstacles that are difficult to avoid or overcome. For each liability taken, the character gains another asset. Through hard work, characters can sometimes overcome their liabilities. If, through gameplay, and with the approval of the Narrator, a character is able to resolve the cause of a liability, she can spend seven experience points to permanently remove it from her character.

Narrators may also assign temporary assets and liabilities throughout the course of a game to represent the positive or negative ramifications of story events and character choices. When a Narrator grants a temporary asset to a character, that asset will remain for a set time period determined by the Narrator to fit the story. Any time a character has a temporary asset, it can be made permanent by spending seven experience points (see *Character Advancement*, p. 172). If a temporary asset is granted and there is no expenditure of experience points to make it permanent, it will be used up or fade over time. For example, if a character worked hard over the course of a campaign to woo, propose, and wed someone of a higher *Class* and *Means* than themselves, immediately after the marriage they would enjoy the temporary benefits of higher *Class* and *Means*. If no experience is spent to make those changes permanent, however, the benefits will fade. What was at first viewed as the character "marrying well" would come to be regarded as the new spouse "marrying poorly" and both of them being looked down upon by those of the higher *Class*; meanwhile their resources would deplete due to lack of management, gradually forcing them to slip intto a lower *Means*.

If the Narrator assigns a temporary liability it will normally be resolved naturally over the course of a book as the plot develops: a rival emerges and is defeated, the theft of an heirloom is discovered and the item is retrieved, and the like. If a character is assigned a temporary liability and wishes to make it permanent they can do so to immediately gain five experience points. Though a dire choice, the bump in experience points may provide valuable short-term assistance. Once a liability is permanent it could potentially be resolved as described above, but this would cost seven experience points to do so.

ASSETS

ADDITIONAL AFFINITIES

You are deeply vested in the world, and have more strong connections and deep cares that help drive you. You have four additional ranks to spend on Affinities.

ADDITIONAL AUGMENTATION

Beastfolk only. This asset may be taken more than once.

The madman experimenting on you seemed hell-bent to see just how much a human body could be altered, and subjected you to even more surgeries than other beastfolk. You have one additional augmentation. Extensive augmentations can only be taken by heavily augmented beastfolk as detailed in the bloodline description (see *Bestial Augmentations*, p. 113).

ALCHEMICAL REACTION

This asset may be taken more than once.

You have studied the nuances of alchemy—the New Science— and have mastered one alchemical reaction. Remember a specified minimum *Science* rank must be met in order to learn a reaction. (see *Alchemy*, p. 221).

CHARISM

Purebloods only. This asset may be taken more than once.

You have been blessed by the Clockmaker with the use of a miraculous ability; gain one charism for which you have the minimum required *Composure* rank (see *Charisms*, p. 226).

DANGEROUS FRIENDS

This asset may be taken more than once.

You are known to be close associates with others that are widely viewed as dangerous, either socially or physically. Others hesitate to cross you for fear of retaliation by your friends, but this will only remain true so long as your association with those friends remains strong.

Players should work with the Narrator to define the dangerous friends, the nature of their association, and the expectations to maintain the relationship. Dangerous friends have a reputation for a reason, and the character will likely be expected to do favors or provide dangerous or unsavory assistance to them from time to time.

Each time this asset is taken, these associates are willing and able to provide support in the form of a Threat 3 individual or group to engage in intimidation or physical violence on the character's behalf once per book so long as the relationship is maintained. More frequent assistance is only available at the Narrator's discretion and will likely incur debts and obligations owed to your dangerous friends.

DEVOTED COMPANION

You have formed an almost unshakeable bond with another person or creature who loves you deeply, and is willing to do almost anything for you. Almost any type of relationship is available, and the companion could be a friend, lover, mentor, ideological disciple, pet, or particularly devoted servant. Your companion will try to help and assist you, but they have their own life, goals, desires and responsibilities, and if you do not support and maintain the relationship with them their devotion will fade over time.

Players should collaborate with the Narrator to develop the companion's personality and the nature of the relationship, but the Narrator has final say over the build and will control the companion during play. Use the Ally creation system in *Chapter 9: Allies & Antagonists* to construct the devoted companion. The companion should be no higher than Threat 2, must begin play with a rank 3 Affinity *Aid and Support [your character]*," and her *Class* and *Means* cannot exceed those of the character taking this asset.

EAGER

You are always ready to engage in conflict, and can take action quickly. During the first sequence of a conflict, you draw one additional initiative card. You still retain the normal number of initiative cards (e.g. normally three, two if you have a single Wound, etc).

ESTATE

Through inheritance or shrewd investment, you own a property that would normally befit an owner with one more rank of *Means* than you have. This estate generates enough money to maintain itself through rents, tenant taxes, and land rights, but does not include the household servants or furnishings that higher *Means* would provide, and that are expected for such a dwelling.

EVER-READY

Your have nerves of steel and lightning-quick reflexes. The first time you take a turn in a physical conflict you may choose to replace your move with a maneuver, even if you are reacting.

EXPERTISE

This asset may be taken more than once, but only once for a given skill.

Through great effort and dedication you have achieved an exceptional understanding of a skill: choose one skill currently at rank three, and raise it to rank four.

FAULTLESS REPUTATION

You are known to be so steadfast in your beliefs and reliable in your behaviors that it is incredibly difficult for others to damage your Reputations, even temporarily. The first time in a scene anyone attempts to lower your Esteem, their test suffers an automatic -2 penalty. If that test is a failure the attacker's Esteem will immediately move one step towards *Hostile*, as others in the room take the assault on your good character poorly.

FAVORED

The Clockwork itself seems to work to protect you from danger. Once per installment, you may avoid an outcome or take narrative control as though you had spent a point of *Purpose*, without spending that *Purpose* yourself. The benefit from *Favored* may be used in a sequence in which you have already spent potential.

GLAMOUR

Changeling only. This asset may be taken more than once.

Your fey blood is particularly strong, and you may take one extra glamour for which you have the minimum *Guile* rank (see *Glamours*, p. 229).

GOOD REPUTE

This asset may be taken more than once.

Your endeavors have earned respect and admiration. You may gain a new Reputation at rank 2, or raise any of your existing Reputations by two ranks to a maximum of rank 3, or you may choose a single Reputation currently at rank 3 and raise it to rank 4. If your Reputation is raised to rank four, you have gained prestige throughout the Empire for a great accomplishment. Work with the Narrator to establish what brought you to the attention of the Empire; perhaps you were instrumental in a scientific breakthrough, were the hero of a great military action, saved the life of a member of the royal family, or were the voice of the downtrodden that spoke to the newspapers and the nation as the leader of a strike.

GRIMOIRE

This asset may be taken more than once.

You possess a book that contains mystical writings and one or more magical rites (see *Ritual Magic*, p. 233). In the ritual system, the power and utility of a rite is measured by its Difficulty to perform. The character's grimoire will contain a number of rites whose combined Difficulty equals 7. For each additional time this asset is taken, add 7 to the combined Difficulty. Work with the Narrator to detail how you came by the book—was it inherited, given to you by a mentor, or stumbled upon by accident? Have you ever performed the rituals before?

HIGHER CLASS

Either your family is of higher station than that of the background you have chosen, or you have gained social acceptance through a lifetime of hard work or an especially advantageous marriage: increase your *Class* by one. Note that unless you have a *Means* at least equal to your new *Class* you will be hard-pressed to maintain the social activity and presentation expected of someone of your station. This is a minor hindrance for *Class* 2, but at *Class* 3 or higher you are expected to display a certain amount of material wealth, and failing to do so could threaten to reduce your *Class* over the course of the game.

INVENTOR

This asset may be taken more than once.

You have the true spark of inspiration and are constantly abuzz with designs for new and wonderful creations. Inventors such as yourself can use skill in *Artisan*, *Engineering*, and *Science* to do far more than simply produce the designs of others—you can design your own unique inventions. The item creation system (p. 198) allows for the crafting of fantastic inventions by choosing and combining the functions of which that invention is capable. Each time this asset is taken, choose one of the options below and gain access to all of its related functions, which are delineated in *Chapter 6: Accoutrements & Technology*.

- *Fabricator:* When creating a new invention, you gain access to the most robust and widely used set of functions that allow you to make a variety of helpful tools, accoutrements, weapons, and armor. Items that use *Fabricator* functions require the *Artisan* skill to design and build.
- *Machinist:* You specialize in building clockwork items and complex machines that take full advantage of new technology. A grounding as a *Fabricator* or a colleague with such ability helps make these inventions practical. Items that use *Machinist* functions require the *Engineering* skill to design and build.
- *Innovator:* You turn to the study of chemistry, biology, and the forces of nature such as electricity to give function to designs. An *Innovators'* creations can be incredible, and require the *Science* skill to design and build.

With Narrator approval, characters who begin play with an *Inventor* asset may already have created several inventions. In the Item Creation system, an invention's utility is measured by the Difficulty of the test used to make it. An inventor may enter the game with a number of inventions whose total Difficulty to make is equal to three times the number of *Inventor* assets that character has. For example, a character with both *Inventor: Fabricator* and *Inventor: Innovator* may begin play with two Difficulty 3 inventions or one Difficulty 6 invention. Such inventions may only use a limited list of restrictions: *Crew Operation*, *Dangerous Use*, *Reload Time*, *Setup Time*, and *Single Shot*.

LIBRARY

This asset may be taken more than once.

You own a personal library of note. It may consist of a small collection of rare and seminal works that cover the essentials of one topic, or a wider selection that provides general knowledge in several areas. When taking this asset, choose to gain either a single topic with a remarkable collection or two topics with basic collections from the list of topics (see *Libraries and Research*, p. 139). Provided you have access to your library and time to research, you may use it to make *Reason + Academics* tests for research as detailed in the *Academics* skill description. Each time this asset is taken, choose one new remarkable or two new basic topics to add to your library.

Collections gained from this asset will never include books with magical rituals. To gain access to rituals, you must take the *Grimoire* assets, opposite page.

MAGICAL WORD

This asset may be taken more than once.

Your studies of ritual magic have borne fruit, and you have mastered either one magical verb or two magical nouns for which you have the minimum required *Mysteries* rank (see *Ritual Magic*, p. 233). Mastering words of power is necessary to develop your own custom rituals. You may master one verb or two nouns each time you take this asset.

MECHANICAL MARVEL

This asset may be taken more than once.

Through genius, inspiration, luck, or the expenditure of fantastic sums of money, you possess a unique masterpiece of clockwork design that is at the absolute pinnacle of human craft. Mechanical marvels can be almost any type of device, and the few that exist defy expectations—the analytical engine that Tesla boasts of designing uses electricity instead of cards, tape, or vacuum tubes; the mechanical orchestra at Neufchatel; or the clockwork hand of cardsharp and gunslinger "Teak" Avery.

In the item creation system, an invention's utility is measured by the Difficulty of the test used to make it (see *Item Creation*, p. 198). A character with a mechanical marvel may begin play with any item that would not be harder than a Difficulty 6 to make. The only restrictions that can be taken for the design are *Crew Operation*, *Dangerous Use*, *Reload Time*, *Setup Time*, and *Single Shot*. With the Narrator's permission, multiple players may take this asset and pool the results together to allow them to build large-scale marvels such as airships, trains, submarines, or other fantastic inventions.

MEMBERSHIP

This asset may be taken more than once.

You are a recognized, active member of an organization, and gain access to special authority, opportunities, privileges, Reputations, or training as a result. Organizations typically have several ranks, with higher ranks providing more benefits. In order to take the asset you must meet the minimum requirements of the first rank; if you also meet the requirements for higher ranks, you may take the asset additional times to increase your membership rank and gain additional benefits. A list of prominent organizations is given immediately following this section on p. 160.

POLYGLOT

This asset may be taken more than once.

Choose two mortal languages: you are now fully fluent in those languages and partially fluent in all languages within their language group (see *Literacy and Language*, p. 138). If you have at least one rank in the *Academics* skill you can also read and write these languages.

PRIZED POSSESSION

You own an item of great value. In addition to any accoutrements or living arrangements you have as a result of your *Means*, you also have a single item of your choice that can be purchased with a *Means* of 4. With Narrator approval, you may have enough accessible cash to make a *Means* 4 purchase instead of beginning play with an item.

This asset usually represents a family heirloom, an unusual or esoteric item of curiosity, or a windfall of cash from an inheritance. Discuss this item with the Narrator, how you came by it, and what it means to your character.

SENSITIVE PALATE

Nephilim only. This asset may be taken more than once.

You are able to absorb memories by ingesting far less blood or flesh than other nephilim. A rare gift, those with a sensitive palate view it either as an easy way to benefit from their birthright, or a ghoulish temptation to use it more often than they should. Some degenerate nephilim families or their allies willingly share blood with those who have sensitive palates as a way to pass secret knowledge or bolster skills.

Each time this asset is taken, it halves the amount of blood or flesh necessary to activate the *Knowledge in the Flesh* blessing. Taking *Sensitive Palate* once allows the use of *Knowledge in the Flesh* after consuming 4 ounces of blood or flesh; taking it twice allows use after ingesting 2 ounces, etc. Losing less than 8 ounces ounces of blood is not enough to cause a Wound, and makes it at least somewhat plausible to use this birthright with the spilled

blood from a fight or medical procedure. Narrators have final say over how frequently a character could lose small amounts of blood before suffering a Wound.

SKILLED

This asset may be taken more than once.

You have spent much of your free time pursuing your interests and putting them into practice, giving you more practical ability than many others with similar experiences. Gain two ranks to assign into any skill(s) of your choice. These ranks cannot be used to raise a skill above rank 3—for that you need to take the *Expertise* asset listed above.

SYMPATHETIC REACTION

Not available to purebloods.

Although marked by your unnatural bloodline, the way you carry yourself in spite of your origins is a testament to your strength of spirit and inherent determination. Such poise is noticeable to others and there are times when it softens or even overcomes the social stigma you usually suffer. At the beginning of any scene you may test *Presence + Composure* against a Difficulty equal to the Tenor of the scene. If successful, the automatic Esteem penalty you usually suffer is lessened by 1. There is no penalty for failure, as you cannot stand out any more than you already do.

TITLE

Requires Class 2+

You have been given a title and all the rights and responsibilities that come with it. For *Class 2*, this will be a nonhereditary title, normally a knighthood. Sometimes this honor is called a "life peerage." *Class 3* individuals may be awarded a baronetcy—a hereditary title similar in status to a knighthood but that passes from generation to generation. For those of *Class 4* or 5, a *Title* denotes that they are the titled individual at the center of a noble family. Normally this is an earldom or barony for *Class 4*, and a duchy for *Class 5*.

VICTORIAN VERSUS MODERN SENSIBILITIES

Victorian society had a very different understanding of challenging physical or mental conditions than we do today, and treated people living with them differently than what is acceptable now. The presentations for liabilities are meant to reflect the ideas and attitudes of the time in the setting, and are not value judgments or denigrations of anyone dealing with such issues in real life.

Each group should discuss with their Narrator how any social implications of a given liability will come up in gameplay to ensure that no player has their enjoyment ruined, or

that Narrator characters might treat a character with prejudice or hostility in a way that gives offense to any of the real people playing the game. *Clockwork: Dominion* games should be exciting, memorable, funny, terrifying, and all manner of other experiences, but they should never make any of the people playing the game feel shamed, belittled, or excluded. Player characters are exceptional individuals that can do extraordinary things, regardless of any liabilities, and playing the game should be an enjoyable experience for all.

FORMS OF ADDRESS

Title	Minimum Class	Entitled Man	Entitled Woman	Spouse	Child
Duke or Duchess	5	The Duke of [Duchy] • Your Grace	The Duchess of [Duchy] • Your Grace	Mr. [S] • The Duchess of [Duchy] • Your Grace	Boys: The Honourable [F] [S] Girls: The Lady [F] [S]
Earl or Countess	4	The Earl of [Earldom] • Earl [S] • Lord [S] • Lord [Earldom] • My Lord • Your Lordship	The Countess of [Earldom] • Countess [S] • Lady [S] • Lady [Earldom] • Your Ladyship	Mr. [S] • Lady [S] • Lady [Earldom] • Your Ladyship	Boys: The Honourable [F] [S] Girls: The Lady [F] [S]
Baron or Baroness	4	Baron or Lord [S or Barony] • My Lord • Your Lordship	Baroness or Lady [S or Barony] • Your Ladyship	Mr. [S] Lady [S] • Baroness [S] • Your Ladyship	The Honorable [F] [S]
Baronet or Baronetess	3	Sir [F]	Dame [F]	Mr./Lady [S]	Master/Miss [S]
Knight	2	Sir [F]	Dame [S]	Mr./Lady [S]	Master/Miss [S]

F = [Forename] • S = [Surname]

Whenever a titled individual attends an event whose *Class Tenor* is equal to or less than their *Class* rank, she enjoys a +1 bonus to Esteem. All titled persons are referred to by special forms of address in conversation. Failing to use the proper form of address is normally a faux pas. The *Forms of Address* table, this page depicts common forms of address. A forename is a person's given name or first name, while the surname is the last or family name. Widows of a Duke, Earl, Baron, or Baronet are referred to as Dowager Lady [Surname].

TOUCHED

Pureblood only.

While not a changeling yourself, you have some fey blood in your ancestry, or have had an experience with one of the feyfolk that has left you changed. Learn a single glamour for which you have the minimum required *Guile* rank.

WELL-OFF

Either your family's wealth is greater than your chosen background would normally suggest, or you have amassed greater material resources through hard work, canny investment, a large inheritance, or ill-gotten gains. Increase your *Means* by one. With higher *Means* comes greater comfort and quality of life, but be careful to mind that differences in *Class* will still affect your interactions.

WORKSHOP

This asset may be taken more than once.

You are the proud owner of a well-supplied personal workshop, complete with a selection of specialized equipment that enables the construction of objects with Bulk or Complexity of 5 and higher (see *Item Creation*, p. 198). Confer with the Narrator to determine how you came by the shop, its location, and other details. If two assets are spent, it is instead a very well-equipped professional workshop, and you have one apprentice who works there with two ranks in an appropriate *Vocation* skill. The extra labor and array of equipment allows you to build projects as though you had +1 *Means*.

The Narrator designs and plays the apprentice, but the apprentice will always begin the game with a rank 1 Affinity for the character to show their good relationship. The apprentice is skilled enough to staff the shop in your absence and help perform work to keep money and business active, but the apprentice and business do require some direct involvement from you, otherwise it will become a drain on your funds.

ORGANIZATIONS

A Character that takes the *Membership* asset is an active part of an important group at work in the Clockwork. Each organization has its own particular structure and goals to which its members will ascribe and resources to which they will have access. Organizations will frequently have hierarchies of membership, which is measured in ranks. Each rank of membership must be taken sequentially as an individual asset. A character wishing to take a certain rank of membership must qualify for it by possessing all of its prerequisites. A character with a given rank of membership will be granted all the benefits of that rank as listed in the following organizational descriptions. There are many other organizations that exist in the setting, and Narrators should feel free to create their own using the examples provided for reference.

BRITISH ARMY

The Army gives British subjects the opportunity to show their love of Crown and country by taking up a life of adventure, duty, and meaning. Those with few prospects sometimes join in the hope of increasing their station in life. To those of higher birth, martial service has long been seen as a mark of good character and an appropriate continuation of a long tradition of battlefield service among the aristocracy and gentility. Military service in the officers' ranks is a respected path for second sons of well-bred families to make a name for themselves on their own merit. Given this tradition, it is an unspoken prerequisite for anyone to rise high in the ranks, and common soldiers are rarely promoted past the ranks of non-comissioned officers.

The British Army is a rigid hierarchy, where upper echelons bear responsibility for the actions of their dependents and lower echelons have little say in where they are deployed or garrisoned. Men purchase commissions or enlist for a period of years and are assigned to a regiment. Regiments are usually kept together to encourage camaraderie among those who rely on each other for their very lives. Some regiments are moved from foreign front to foreign front, while others are semi-permanently garrisoned in particular areas of concern regarding invasion, civil unrest, or increasing Pontus activity. Garrisoned individuals are often envied by those abroad as they are afforded the ability to engage in local society including balls and even courtships. Women are not legally allowed to join the Army, but history has recorded several who fought in the ranks while pretending to be men.

All soldiers are provided with their daily necessities of food, shelter, and clothing, along with the best military training and standard military kits in the world. All on-duty soldiers wear the distinctive uniforms of their regiments. Most English units are clothed in matching khaki trousers and a jacket with rank insignia on sleeves and epaulettes, and a high, rounded helmet bearing the regimental badge. Great variety exists among regiments from other areas of the Empire. The Highland regiments are instantly recognizable in their tartan kilts, sporrans, and glengarry or balmoral caps with bright feathered cockles. Foreign regiments also incorporate their own cultural touches, such as the gurkhas with their heavy-bladed kukris or the sikhs with their distinctive turbans. In short, all British soldiers will be immediately recognizable as part of the Army, but civilians may not be able to identify exactly which regimental uniform they're seeing.

Additional gear may be issued as required by the mission at hand, and could include anything from special environmental gear to experimental weapons and alchemically-treated field armor.

Army Membership Rank 1

Requires *Grace 2, Vigor 2, Athletics 1*.

You are an enlisted soldier or non-commanding officer such as a corporal, lance-corporal, or sergeant.

- **Opportunity:** You are qualified to purchase the *Well-off* or *Higher Class* assets with experience points to increase your *Class* and *Means* up to a maximum of rank 1
- **Privilege:** Soldiers carry weapons while on duty, and authorities often look the other way when they are not.
- **Reputation:** Gain "British soldier" at rank 1
- **Resources:** Enlisted soldiers are granted full field and dress uniforms, boots, foul weather gear, a rifle, bayonet, combat knife, and first aid kit.
- **Training:** Increase your rank by 1 (to a maximum of rank 2) in one the following skills: *Engineering, Firearms, Melee, Riding, Survival,* or *Vocation: Soldier*

Army Membership Rank 2

Requires *Academics 1, Athletics 2, Command 1, Firearms 2, Tactics 2, Vocation: Soldier 1* or *Class* or *Means 3*

You are a non-commissioned officer such as a lieutenant or captain.

- **Authority:** Command over Army members of lower rank (the Narrator may provide allies for you to command depending on the circumstances of the game)
- **Opportunity:** You are qualified to purchase the *Well-off* or *Higher Class* assets with experience points to increase your *Class* and *Means* up to a maximum of rank 2
- **Reputation:** Gain "British Army officer" at rank 2—this replaces "British soldier"
- **Resources:** Officers at Sandhurst military academy and well-established bases have access to books and information equivalent to a library with a remarkable collection in both military history and geography. You are issued a sword and a reinforced field uniform that provides Armor 1.
- **Training:** Increase your rank by 1 (to a maximum of rank 3) in one of the following skills: *Academics, Command, Engineering, Fencing, Firearms, Tactics,* or *Vocation: Soldier*

Army Membership Rank 3

Requires *Class 3, Bureaucracy 2, Command 3, Refinement 2, Riding 2* or *Class* or *Means 4*

You are a commissioned officer such as a Major, Colonel, or Brigadier.

- **Authority:** Command over Army members of lower rank
- **Opportunity:** You are qualified to purchase the *Well-off* or *Higher Class* assets with experience points to increase your *Means* up to a maximum of rank 3
- **Reputation:** "British Army officer" at rank 3
- **Training:** Increase your rank by 1 (to a maximum of rank 3) in one the following skills: *Academics, Bureaucracy, Command, Engineering, Refinement, Riding, Tactics,* or *Vocation: Soldier*

Army Membership Rank 4

Requires *Class 3, Academics 2, Refinement 3,* and either *Bureaucracy 4* or *Tactics 4*

You are a Major General, General, or Field Marshal.

- **Authority:** Command over Army members of lower rank
- **Opportunity:** You are qualified to purchase the *Well-off* or *Higher Class* assets with experience points to increase your *Class* and *Means* up to a maximum of rank 4
- **Reputation:** "British Army officer" at rank 4
- **Training:** Increase your rank by one (to a maximum of rank 5) in one of the following skills: *Bureaucracy, Command,* or *Tactics*

CONSTABULARIES

Since the establishment of paid police force for Glasgow in 1800, Britain has embraced the idea of a permanent, professional civic constabulary. Sir Robert Peel made policing a priority with the Metropolitan Police Act of 1829 to establish an organized London constabulary. Other policing acts passed in the 1830s and '40s, and eventually set a nationalized standard in the 1850s. By the 1890s policing has become well-established throughout the Empire, and every municipality employs dedicated constables to uphold the law.

While on duty, members of the constabulary wear official uniforms consisting of trousers, shirt, jacket, and a hat or helmet, and all officers bear a badge worn on their uniform jacket, or a device pinned or stitched onto its epaulettes that shows an officer number and their rank. Most departments have police horses and bicycles to aid them getting about, and larger towns and cities have wagons to transport criminals. Metropolitan constables are issued keys to police call boxes so they can quickly call for aid or communicate with their station house. All constables are entitled to basic medical care for injuries suffered in the line of duty.

Constabulary Membership Rank 1

Requires *Vigor 2, Athletics 1, Command 1, Composure 1, Investigation 1, Melee 1, Streetwise 1*

You are a constable or court officer.

- **Authority:** Legal authority to conduct inquiries, make arrests, provide evidence to court
- **Privilege:** Limited protection from civil liability for damage to property or injury to persons when performing your duties as a constable
- **Reputation:** Gain "[Location] constable" at rank 1

- **Resources:** You are issued an uniform including reinforced greatcoat (Armor 1), helmet, and rain cape, as well as a truncheon, handcuffs, and whistle. If applicable, you may have use of transportation and a call box key
- **Training:** Increase your rank by one (to a maximum of rank 2) in one of the following skills: *Athletics, Bureaucracy, Composure, Investigation, Melee, Parley,* or *Streetwise*

Constabulary Membership Rank 2

Requires *Bureaucracy 2, Athletics 2, Command 2, Composure 2, Investigation 2, Melee 2, Streetwise 2*

You are the head of a rural constabulary, or a Sergeant or Inspector in a metropolitan department.

- **Authority:** Command over constables of lower rank in your jurisdiction
- **Opportunity:** You are qualified to purchase the *Well-off* or *Higher Class* assets with experience points to increase your *Class* and *Means* up to a maximum of rank 2
- **Reputation:** Gain "Police Officer" at rank 2—this replaces "[Location] constable"
- **Resources:** You have access to any firearms owned by your department, and are issued a gun license
- **Training:** Increase your rank by one (to a maximum of rank 3) in one the following skills: *Athletics, Bureaucracy, Composure, Investigation, Melee, Parley,* or *Streetwise*

Constabulary Membership Rank 3

Requires *Class 2, Bureaucracy 3, Command 3, Composure 3, Investigation 3, Parley 3, Refinement 1*

You are the Chief Constable or Commissioner in charge of a metropolitan station house or department.

- **Authority:** Command over constables in your jurisdiction of lower rank
- **Opportunity:** You are qualified to purchase the *Well-off* asset with experience points to increase your *Means* up to a maximum of rank 3
- **Reputation:** Gain "Police Officer" at rank 3
- **Training:** Increase your rank by one (to a maximum of rank 4) in one the following skills: *Bureaucracy, Command, Investigation,* or *Tactics*

THE ROYAL SOCIETY

The Royal Society was established by Charles II in 1660 to create a group of learned advisors for the government and burnish Britain's scientific achievements. Now the Royal Society represents hundreds of Fellows throughout the Empire in almost all fields of inquiry. The Society's periodical, *Philosophical Transactions*, is the oldest and longest-running scientific publication in the world, and has established a system of peer review that has become the standard for the scientific community around the globe.

The current members of the Royal Society hold an annual vote to select new Fellows for membership, and to elect the council and president. Foreign, non-British members have been included for some time, yet no women have been voted in. However, unofficial female members have gained access to Royal Society resources as daughters or wives of male members, some even retaining their access long after the actual member has died (unofficial rank 1 membership of this sort grants the same benefits and is acquired through the same asset). Council positions are generally pursued by Fellows that are already well-established in their fields. The presidency is often awarded to older members that are already very accomplished, or to younger members who are deeply involved in the internal politics of Society or British government.

Royal Society Membership Rank 1

Requires *Class 2* and a total trait combination of *Reason* + one of *Academics, Engineering,* or *Science* at 7

You are a Fellow of the Royal Society

- **Opportunity:** You are qualified to increase a Reputation related to research or your standing in the scientific community up to a maximum of rank 3
- **Resources:** Access to the Royal Society offices at Burlington House in London, including the library and workshops. The library houses extraordinary collections of geography, medicine, and technical material. Use of the laboratories and Royal Society workshop and staff must be approved by the council and is available once per year. Use of the workshop includes help from up to four other assistants with total *Reason + Artisan/Engineering/ Science* of 5, and *Means* 3 of material support to cover expenses for an experiment or project using the item creation rules (see p. 198).

Royal Society Membership Rank 2

Requires *Class 3,* popular election by Royal Society Fellows, a Reputation related to research or standing in the scientific community of at least rank 3, *Academics 3, Bureaucracy 2, Refinement 2,* and at least one of *Bureaucracy, Engineering,* or *Science* at 4

You are a council member or president of the Royal Society

- **Authority:** You and other council members have editorial control of Royal Society publications, peer review assignments, and approval for all use and funding requests for the workshop at Burlington House
- **Opportunity:** You are qualified to increase a Reputation related to your research of your standing in the scientific community up to a maximum of rank 4
- **Resources:** You are granted a small but elegant apartment and private office at Burlington House. Once per year you may use the workshop for a personal experiment or project as described above, but with up to 10 assistants and *Means* 4 of material support.

THE SEE OF CANTERBURY

In the strictest sense, any faithful man or woman who attends mass in an English church is a member of the See of Canterbury, but membership in the Church's hierarchy requires training and dedication. Once a man has been ordained to the priesthood, he devotes his life to the Maker and to doctrine and discipline of the English Church. For most clergy, this involves serving as a parish priest, called a vicar, and teaching, pastoring, and performing sacraments for a congregation. Other ordained clergy live more itinerant lives as colonial, hospital, or military chaplains. However, it is possible to serve as a priest in a great many capacities, including a small few who are also members of the Witchfinders serving in the Order of the Canons.

Monastic communities, which had been largely abolished during the Reformation, have seen a resurgence in the last century. Rather than serving in a parochial capacity, these faithful men and women live in sexually segregated monasteries or to serve in a particular community—usually in hospitals or schools. Some religious orders have come to serve in battlefield hospitals or in foreign missions at the fringes of the Empire. These communities are seen as a stabilizing agent helpful in thwarting Pontus activity and are welcome even by those who do not share the Christian faith.

Clergy are visibly marked by their archaic garb. For mass, clergy will wear all manner of medieval-style vestments. Formalwear for priests is a full-length black garment called a cassock, worn with a clerical collar. Canons line their cassocks in red trim and higher officials simply wear red cassocks. Modern times have seen the informal wear of priests turn to that of any other gentleman, but with a black shirt and broad white acetate collar to designate them as clergy. Monks will wear robes of a color that signifies their order and nuns add a headcovering to this attire. However, as the duties of clergy take them toward the fringes of society, the guidelines for special clothing becomes less rigid.

More information on the See of Canterbury can be found in *Chapter 2: Clockwork Society* on p. 32.

See of Canterbury Membership Rank 1

Requires the *Sacred Vows* liability, *Academics 2, Composure 1, Intuition 1, Mysteries 1, Parley 1, Refinement 1.*

You are an ordained vicar, priest, monk, or nun

- **Opportunity:** You are qualified to purchase the *Well-off* or *Higher Class* assets with experience points to increase your *Class* and *Means* up to a maximum of rank 2
- **Privilege:** You receive the *Bless* charism, even if you are not of pure blood. You are entrusted to bless on behalf of the Church and perform any magical rite sanctioned by the See of Canterbury (including the hearing of confessions through the Rite of Reconciliation). These privileges are reserved for the clergy and protected by law. This often allows for lawful study of *Mysteries* available to few other Imperial subjects
- **Reputation:** Gain "Cleric of the See of Canterbury" at rank 1
- **Resources:** Your parish or order provides you with vestments appropriate to your role and unrestricted access to parish or monastery grounds. You have access to religious texts equivalent to a remarkable religious library. You gain routine access to rank 1 magical reagents. The church provides you a stipend equal to your *Means* and simple room and board.
- **Training:** Increase your rank by one (to a maximum of rank 2) in one of the following skills: *Academics, Bureaucracy, Intuition, Parley*

See of Canterbury Membership Rank 2

Requires *Class* 3 or *Bureaucracy 2, Composure 2, Parley 2, Refinement 2.*

You are the Dean of a cathedral or college of canons, or the presiding priest at a large city church

- **Authority:** You have official administrative oversight of lower-ranked clerics in your parish, and unofficial authority over lower-ranked clerics in your diocese.
- **Privilege:** Your position is assumed to require a deeper knowledge of spirituality and those forces that act against it. Occult research that would normally be considered questionable or even illegal is overlooked as long as it can be explained.
- **Reputation:** Increase "Cleric of the See of Canterbury" to rank 2
- **Resources:** You gain access to religious and magical writings equivalent to a basic occult library. You have access to a subordinate clergyman who can occasionally take on your clerical responsibilities while you see to concerns within your jurisdiction. The church provides you a stipend equal to your *Means* and comfortable room and board.
- **Training:** Increase your rank by one (to a maximum of rank 3) in one of the following skills: *Academics, Bureaucracy, Composure, Intuition, Mysteries, Parley,* or *Refinement*

See of Canterbury Membership Rank 3

Requires *Academics 3, Bureaucracy 3, Composure 3, Mysteries 3, Parley 3, Refinement 3*

You are a Bishop.

- **Authority:** You have authority over all lower-ranked members of the See of Canterbury within your diocese, including the ability to appoint exorcists and assign clergy to all manner of posts.
- **Opportunity:** You are qualified to purchase the *Well-off* or *Higher Class* assets with experience points to increase your *Class* and *Means* up to a maximum of rank 3. If you become a member of Parliament, you join the House of Lords regardless of your *Class.*
- **Privilege:** You have immunity from most civil suits, and all moderate criminal offenses related to property crime for damages of *Means 2* or less.
- **Reputation:** Gain "Bishop of [Location]" at rank 3—this replaces "Cleric of the See of Canterbury"
- **Resources:** You have access to additional missals and religious writings in your diocese, which act as the equivalent of an extraordinary religious collection and a remarkable occult collection.

See of Canterbury Membership Rank 4

Requires appointment by the Crown, *Mysteries 4, Refinement 4*

You are the Archbishop of Canterbury.

- **Authority:** You have a mixture of official and unofficial authority over all lower-ranked members of the See of Canterbury, and are recognized as the chief spiritual authority for all doctrinal decisions.

- **Opportunity:** You are qualified to purchase the *Higher-Class* asset with experience points to increase your *Class* up to a maximum of rank 4
- **Reputation:** Gain "Archbishop of Canterbury" at rank 4—this replaces "Bishop of [Location]"
- **Resources:** You have access to various missals filled with magical rites composed of pure words (provided by the Narrator), unlimited access to rank 1, 2, and 3 reagents, and one use of rank 4 reagents once per month.

THE WITCHFINDERS

The Witchfinders were originally sanctioned by King James in 1647 as an organization to stand against the dangers posed by witches, magic, and the Pontus, and have continued to serve the Empire ever since. Today, members of the Order of the Star Chamber are frequently recruited from military and police forces to serve as enforcers, investigators, and tacticians. Members of the Order of the Canons are pulled from the clergy of the See of Canterbury. to serve as advisors, magi, and lore keepers. Individuals with unique gifts such as charisms, augmentations, or glamours are also brought into the organization, even if they are not empowered as full Witchfinders or assigned to a specific order (membership is not required for individuals to work under Witchfinder supervision).

For over three-hundred years, these vigilant protectors have worked together as the Witchfinders to keep the Empire safe from supernatural threats. However, times have changed and the organization has adapted to keep pace. The wonders of technology have caused magic to be increasingly viewed as a novelty to be dabbled in for curiosity or even entertainment. It is harder than ever to oversee the growing numbers of spiritualists and cunning folk, and those with more advanced knowledge are even more dangerous as they can find easy access to true magical rites reprinted in special editions of historical grimoires run off by London booksellers. Pontus events occur with increasing regularity, and there is much moral debate regarding whether or not the Empire would be better served by dealing with those who instigate these events before they have the opportunity to do so. Incredible advancements in technology have offered new tools to better protect the realm from supernatural menace, but also threaten the safety and secrecy of this organization. Even at the approach of the twentieth century, the Witchfinders are never short of work to do, and if someone is skilled enough and willing to face the challenge, the Witchfinders will make use of them.

While in service, all Witchfinders wear unmistakable leather longcoats and high peaked hats, both cut in a deliberately archaic style meant to evoke their history. The coats have high collars and a mantlet that drapes down above the elbows, and a long straight body that stops halfway down the calf. The jacket is slit up the back to the waist, and buttons from the neck to the knees, so it can easily be adjusted for comfortable wear and protection while on foot or horse. The hats have a wide, flat brim and a high crown that comes to a flat top some three to four inches above the head. All leathers are a deep black and alchemically treated to offer protection and remain supple no matter the conditions they endure.

All Witchfinders are also issued and trained in the use of a basket-hilted backsword and a pistol. The backsword is a lethal and surprisingly versatile close combat weapon in the hands of someone familiar with its use, and firearms are simply a must in the modern world. Most Witchfinders will also carry an assortment of other accoutrements as fits their individual skills and methods, as well as a few magical reagents and one or more magical rites that aid them in their work.

More information on the Witchfinders can be found in *Chapter 2: Clockwork Society* on p. 30.

Witchfinder Membership Rank 1

Requires *Purpose* 2, a conflict skill at rank 3, *Academics* 1, *Investigation* 1, *Mysteries* 1

If you also have *Membership: See of Canterbury*, you are a Witchfinder Canon; otherwise, you are a Witchfinder Star.

- **Authority:** All rights and authorities granted by the Witchfinder Charter: the right to bear and use arms without hindrance or license; the ability to arrest and detain anyone suspected of witchcraft or involved in aiding a witch; local authorities are required to jail and guard any prisoner you have taken into custody; any subject of the crown is required to give you food and shelter for one day if no other accommodations are available
- **Opportunity:** You are qualified to purchase the *Well-off* or *Higher Class* assets with experience points to increase your *Class* and *Means* up to a maximum of rank 2
- **Privilege:** You are exempt from prosecution from normal civil and criminal courts for your activities while in pursuit of a witch or combating a Pontus event. Any complaints against you are lodged with your superiors, who will pass judgment and handle any punishments as magistrates of the Star Chamber.
- **Reputation:** Gain "Witchfinder" at rank 2
- Resources: You are issued a set of Witchfinder leathers (Armor 2), a badge of office, a basket-hilted backsword, a revolver. Access to Witchfinder occult, religious, and historical libraries may be granted at the discretion of the Archdeacon or Warden oversee-ing your activities. For each assignment, Witchfinder Canons are issued three uses of rank 1 reagents, two uses of rank 2 reagents, and a single magical rite of the Narrator's choice—you may be granted additional reagents or rites as may be fitting to your current assignment.

Witchfinder Membership Rank 2

Requires *Purpose* 3, a conflict skill at rank 4, *Academics* 2, *Bureaucracy* 2, *Composure* 3, *Investigation* 3, *Mysteries* 3

You are an Archdeacon in the Canons, or a Warden in the Stars

- **Authority:** Command over all Witchfinders of lower rank, and the right to take command of constabulary and military members of rank 2 or lower during emergencies
- **Opportunity:** You are qualified to purchase the *Well-off* asset with experience points to increase your *Means* up to a maximum of rank 3

- **Privilege:** Immunity to prosecution in civil and criminal courts—any complaints against you must be lodged with the Witchfinder General, and the Star Chamber is the only court with jurisdiction to prosecute you
- **Reputation:** Increase "Witchfinder" to rank 3
- **Resources:** For each assignment, Canons are issued three uses of rank 2 reagents, two uses of rank 3 reagents, and one use of a rank 4 reagent. They are also taught magical rites for "*Commune Self* with *Mortal*", "*Restore* the *Body* of *Mortal*", "*Reveal Mortal* to *Self*", "*Restore* the *Boundary* of *Location*", and "*Ward Location* from *Chimera*". The Narrator determines the specifics of each rite and each should have a Difficulty of no higher than 6. Stars gain a talisman based on one of these rites at the beginning of each assignment. Both orders gain access to the organiza-tion's stores of seized technology, reagents, rites, and magical texts. The stockpile is controlled independently by Parliament-appointed managers, so materials captured must be reported and turned in, and use of materials is limited to situations of clear need as moderated by the Narrator.
- **Training:** Increase your rank by one (to a maximum of rank 3) in one of the following skills: *Academics, Fencing, Firearms, Mysteries,* or *Parley*

Witchfinder Membership Rank 3

Requires appointment by the Crown, *Purpose* 4

You are the Witchfinder General of the British Empire

- **Authority:** Command over all Witchfinders of lower rank, and the right to take command of constabulary and military members of rank 3 or lower during emergencies
- **Opportunity:** You are qualified to purchase the *Higher Class* asset with experience points to increase your *Class* up to a maximum of rank 3
- **Privilege:** Immunity to prosecution in civil and criminal courts—only the reigning Monarch sitting in judgment as head of the Star Chamber has jurisdiction to prosecute you
- **Reputation:** Gain "Witchfinder General" at rank 4—this replaces "Witchfinder"
- **Resources:** You have access to all resources granted to both Canons and Stars, and expanded access to the store of material seized by the Witchfinders. This includes unlimited access to rank 1 and 2 reagents, access to rank 3 reagents once per week, access to rank 4 reagents once per month, and a rank 5 reagent once per year. Further, the Witchfinder General's badge of office serves as the talisman for a "*Protect* the *Body* of *Mortal*" rite with a conditional activation keyed to a phrase you set. When acti-vated, the magic endures for a scene and will prevent the next two Wounds or persistent conditions that you would otherwise suffer. After the effect is spent other Witchfinders will perform the rite again and the effect will be refreshed at the beginning of the next book.

LIABILITIES

ABERRANT AUGMENTATION

Beastfolk only.

The surgeries performed on you were especially heinous. One of your augmentations uses material transplanted from a chimera or aberration, and as a result you are now afflicted with one permanent and irremovable rank of *Corruption*. Furthermore, the unnatural origin of the flesh makes you a powerful conduit for Pontus events. Whenever you trigger a Pontus event and draw a card to determine the nature of the event, subtract five from the card number before comparing it to the table of Pontus effects (see *Triggering Pontus Events*, p. 281).

AFFLICTION

You suffer a serious weakness that hobbles many of your endeavors. Reduce a single aptitude from rank 1 to rank 0, and place that rank into another Aptitude. Victorian society looks poorly on those that are so clearly imperfect, so you often face condescension or obsequious displays of shallow concern for your well-being. You suffer a -1 penalty to Esteem. The nature of the character's affliction is determined by Aptitude chosen to be reduced in rank.

It is possible to remove the affliction over time by improving the aptitude; you may spend 12 experience points to attain the first rank of the lost aptitude. If the aptitude is increased, the liability is removed and you will no longer suffer the penalty to Esteem.

Aptitude	Affliction
Grace	Crippled or paralyzed limb
Vigor	Extreme ill health and weakness
Reason	Cognitive impairment
Focus	Near blindness and/or deafness
Presence	Facial birth defect or significant speech impediment
Will	Poor impulse control

BAD REPUTATION

You have been publicly labeled a criminal, murderer, adulteress, or some other social stigma, and now suffer the consequences. Create a new, exclusively negative rank 2 Reputation. This Reputation is so firmly believed by others that it cannot be reduced or removed unless it is publicly and irreproachably proven false. Your bad reputation is always used when calculating Esteem, as even your brightest accomplishments are shadowed by this stain on your honor.

BLACKMAILED

There is something about you the world must never know, but somebody does, and they are using this knowledge to force you to do things you would never otherwise consider. The secret—and perhaps the blackmailer—pose a serious threat to the social and physical safety of you and your family, and will not hesitate to use this leverage. You can always choose not to give them what they want, but that may have terrible consequences. Money, favors, and other demands on your time and resources will continue until your secret is out, or you can somehow escape from under the thumb of your oppressor.

Collaborate with the Narrator regarding the nature of the secret, the form of the blackmail, and one or two serious consequences that would occur if the truth came to light. This liability pairs well with *Nemesis*.

DECLASSE

Maybe you made a poor marriage or your family lost its land. Maybe you suffered from scandal or squandered your fortunes in gambling and licentious behavior. Whatever the reason, you have fallen so far into public disfavor that you cannot keep up with social demands. You remember a time when your family was more highly regarded, but that time is gone. Reduce your *Class* by one.

FAINT-HEARTED

Whenever physical danger threatens you are thrown off-balance and freeze up. It is not a question of courage, but of reaction—you have the grit to stand and face danger, but you'll never be the first to meet it. During the first sequence of a physical conflict you must discard the initiative card you draw with the highest card number. However, you may retain the Fate card if it is drawn.

GULLIBLE

You are not stupid, but you are easily taken with new ideas or suggestions, and throughout your life you have been talked into far more than your fair share of trouble. It is very important you mind the company you keep, lest you be used as a patsy. During each social conflict, the first time your Disposition is changed against your will, it is changed by two steps rather than one.

HAUNTED

You or something dear to you is the tether for an unquiet spirit, and its presence and interference in your life condemns you to unhappiness and woe. Whether the spirit is a strange and unfamiliar presence that moves objects, or the remainder of a departed loved one, it does nothing but cause fear and complicate your life. Your only hope of being free from it is to find a skilled magus or priest, or discovering its attachment to you and releasing it from this world.

The player should tell the Narrator what story elements they want to explore with the haunting, but the Narrator should not tell the player the exact nature of the tether. Then, the Narrator creates a Threat 3 shade that plagues the character. Most of the shade's actions are small intrusions that occur only a few times per installment. If the character acts against the tether or threatens the shade, it will respond in a more intrusive or aggressive manner.

HORRIFIC AUGMENTATION

Beastfolk only.

One of your augmentations, while functional, is exceptionally gruesome, and even other beastfolk find you repulsive. You always suffer an additional -1 penalty to Esteem in all circumstances. The specifics of the horrific augmentation should be discussed and outlined with the Narrator, but in order for this to qualify as a liability the disfigurement must be noticeable at all times and cannot be concealed.

ILL LUCK

Throughout your life you have been plagued by all manner of misfortune. You lose keys, tear clothes, and drop coins more often than most. However, these annoyances are minor compared to the occasional spectacular examples of ill luck such as tripping and falling when making an entrance at a grand party, saying exactly the wrong thing in a crucial conversation, or having a gun jam at precisely the wrong time. Whenever *Ether* is used to force a character with *Ill Luck* to draw a new card, use the worst of all drawn results regardless of which was the most recent draw.

IMPAIRED SENSES

Your senses have been seriously damaged in a way that cannot be entirely overcome through the use of medicine or by restorative ritual magic. Any *Focus* tests that rely primarily on sensory input (sight, hearing, touch, taste, and smell) suffer a -2 penalty and you cannot score a remarkable (DoS 4+) or phenomenal (DoS 8+) success unless the Fate card is drawn. This liability can represent any sort of severely limiting sensory problem. It could be caused by a degenerative disease, exposure to an industrial accident, the confusion of a fey curse, or even the Pontus.

MEDDLESOME PARENT

Changeling only.

The parent or ancestor that is the source of your fey blood takes an unusual interest in your life. The capricious nature of feyfolk and their lack of understanding with regard to mortal life means that even the kindest intentions of a fey ancestor will, at best, end in bizarre events and, at worst, involve sadistic amusement. The Narrator creates a fey ancestor as a Narrator character. At least once per book, the ancestor will interfere in the character's undertakings in a highly disruptive way, or the ancestor's plans directly involve the character in a manner that introduces risk and complication into her life. These events need not be malicious, but they should always be troublesome and extremely difficult to explain away or hide. For example, when the character courts someone, the ancestor may step in to place some charm upon the suitor to force him to return the character's affection under magical duress, or the meddlesome parent might kidnap an unsuitable love interest.

MISSING LIMB

This liability may be taken more than once.

Whether from birth or through misadventure you have lost an extremity below the knee or elbow. Ritual magic cannot restore the loss of function, but the use of prosthetics will allow improved physical activity. Standard prosthetics can restore only basic functionality, but articulated clockwork prosthetics can return much more. The only way to regain complete functionality would be to possess a mechanical marvel-quality prosthetic. A missing leg makes walking without a prosthetic difficult, so corresponding uses of the *Athletics* skill should have a -2 penalty, or may even be impossible to perform as determined by the Narrator.

NEMESIS

You have crossed paths with an implacable foe, who now stands opposed to your happiness and all your endeavors. No matter what your pursuits, or where they may take you, your foe will always be lurking and plotting your downfall.

Players should work with the Narrator to establish the nature of the antagonistic relationship. After collaborating on the backstory, the Narrator will create the nemesis as a Threat 3 Narrator character with a rank 4 Affinity for "Seeing [the character's] life come to ruin." Narrators will play the nemesis and are encouraged to give the nemesis experience points at a similar rate as the character so she remains a worthy foe over the course of the campaign.

OBSESSION

To the shame and disappointment of your family, and most likely yourself, you are in thrall to an abominable vice such as alcoholism, opium addiction, reckless gambling, philandering, or blasphemy. You begin the game suffering from a persistent *Obsessed* condition for your chosen self-destructive behavior. See the rules for the regular effects of the condition on p. 100, but unlike incidental obsessions this is deeply ingrained. You can only rid yourself of this depravity if you abstain from your obsession for a full story and then spend seven experience points to remove this liability.

OBSESSIVE WATCHER

Nephilim only.

All nephilim are descended from the Grigori, the watcher angels that were assigned by the Clockmaker to observe humanity. You, however, are burdened with a consuming need to watch a specific person, family, or inhabited region. You don't necessarily care what happens to them, but the need to know and see what occurs is almost impossible to resist. If you are unable to observe the subject of your fixation daily you become so distracted that it is hard to behave normally. You *must* know what's happening!

An obsessive watcher has a person or location which she must spend at least one hour per day observing, and she cannot replenish potential unless she has done so. Some compulsive nephilim have kidnapped or locked away the target of their obsession to guarantee this observation can be at their leisure.

OBVIOUSLY INHUMAN

Changelings and nephilim only.

Those afflicted with this liability are indelibly marked as inhuman and are shunned even in liberal societies. Although not necessarily ugly, your features and presentation mark you as something outside the normal order of things. No matter the care and obfuscations you employ, any trickery short of supernatural illusions is incapable of hiding your inhuman nature. Anyone seeing you will treat you with fear or disdain at best, open hostility at worst; you always suffer a -1 penalty to Esteem in addition to all other penalties imposed by your bloodline.

PAUPER

Requires Means 0.

You are currently destitute and own only the shabby clothes on your back. You have no starting accoutrements and are afflicted with the rank 2 Reputation "Penniless wretch." Discuss with your Narrator how you came to be in such a low place, and how you may improve your lot. The Reputation cannot be reduced until after you have acquired a permanent *Means* rank of at least one.

PONTUS INFECTION

Due to an overwhelming or prolonged exposure to the Pontus, some part of your spirit has been warped beyond repair. Perhaps you witnessed a rain of fire which decimated your home or you were severely mauled by an aberrant beast. Whatever the cause, you now carry a seed of chaos inside you and nothing you've done or refrained from doing seems to help. You are forever marked by your exposure to the Pontus, and your *Corruption* rank can never drop below 2.

POOR

Requires Means 1 or higher. May be taken more than once.

Whether the result of financial mismanagement, a gambling addiction, or laziness, you have seriously damaged your financial standing compared to others of your background: reduce your *Means* by 1. Discuss with your Narrator what events forced you closer to the poor house.

SACRED VOWS

Sacred Vows are most often taken as part of formal investiture or ordination in a particular religious organization, but some individuals take them on as an expression of devotion. Regardless of the specific circumstances behind your *Sacred Vows,* it is widely known that you have voluntarily pledged yourself to abstain from or faithfully observe certain activities.

The exact combination of *Sacred Vows* varies between institutions and individuals, but the character must choose at least three of the following for this liability:

- **Chastity:** the character must avoid sexual activity and cannot marry

- **Obedience:** the character is subject to the direct authority of any superiors in her religious order, and they govern where she lives and works
- **Pacifism:** the character must never physically attack another
- **Poverty:** the character forswears ownership of all physical property and must rely on the organization to provide her housing and accoutrements
- **Ritual Cleanliness:** the character must always maintain observance of cleanliness standards defined by her religion, including restrictions on what food and drink are allowable, and possibly on what company she may keep
- **Service:** the character must spend the majority of her time working for and serving her religious and secular communities without any benefit to herself
- **Silence:** the character cannot speak outside of extremely limited proscribed times such as one hour at dinner, or during religious observances

Any time the character violates any of her vows—even accidentally or unknowingly—she immediately loses a point of *Purpose* and gains a point of *Corruption* for oathbreaking. Multiple or serious violations of *Sacred Vows* risks punishment from her religious organization, which may include the temporary or permanent sanction or being barred from the organization altogether and gaining the rank 2 Reputation "Disgraced Nun/Priest/Rabbi/Imam/etc." This liability may only be removed if the religious group the character belongs to formally releases her from her *Sacred Vows*.

SOCIAL CLIMBER

You have become a member of a social *Class* higher than the one into which you were born, and this information is readily apparent. Perhaps you are a dancing girl turned Countess by marriage, a soldier promoted from the ranks, or a former street urchin who struck it rich in India and has returned to Britain a wealthy nabob. Whatever the circumstance, many members of your new *Class* don't consider you to *really* be one of them. They will refer to you as "lowborn" or "ill bred" behind your back. Even those from the lower *Class* you left behind don't treat you with the same deference they would a "natural" member of your current social rank.

Since you were not born to your current station, you have never internalized the etiquette and social codes that are expected behavior. You are prone to gaffes and missteps that are improper or offensive, and given the nature of your circumstance, your peers are unforgiving. Whenever you use the *Refinement* skill in a test you draw two cards and must use the worst to determine the result. In order to get by, you very likely have to rely on other social skills such as *Guile, Parley,* or *Command,* which only proves to others of your *Class* that you are not really one of them and are unworthy of your current social standing.

TROUBLESOME WARD

A family member or legal ward for whom you are responsible is a constant source of irritation and disappointment to you. Recently, this person's poor decisions and bad behavior are beginning to subject you to shame and scandal. You and the Narrator should determine the general nature and proclivities of your ward, but these are only the most frequent and survivable offenses. Throughout the campaign your ward will be a source of terrible vexation, and expose you and your endeavors to unnecessary risk and complication. This liability can only be overcome if you reform your charge personally and in the eyes of the public, or find some socially acceptable way to sever all connections with her.

UNKNOWN BANE

Nephilim only.

You have no knowledge of which substance or circumstance can cause your true and ultimate death, nor do you know the severity of the Bane. This presents a huge risk to you as you do not know against what or when you must be on your guard. You are still entitled to the usual *Intuition* test when in the presence of your Bane, and if successful you will have a sense of uneasiness, but discovering your Bane may well end your life. When taking this liability the Narrator decides the particulars of your Bane, including its severity.

UNSKILLED

Perhaps you were a terrible student, never truly applied yourself, or are simply careless and unaware. As a result, you've learned less in your time on this earth than you should have. Lose two skill ranks that were already assigned.

AFFINITIES: CHARACTER CREATION STEP SEVEN

Affinities are the motivating goals, loyalties, and affections that drive a character's decisions. Her list of Affinities is not a list of everything she cares about, but rather a list of those things she cares for so much that they define who she is.

All characters begin play with three ranks distributed among at least two different Affinities. On the character sheet, each Affinity is recorded as a brief phrase that describes a single motivating affection. Each Affinity is then assigned a rank. Low ranks represent prominent interests or deep affections that motivate a character, while higher ranks are life-defining passions.

DEFINING AFFINITIES

Affinities are single short phrases that describe the subject of the Affinity, define a clear relationship to the setting, and suggest avenues for deeper connections. A character who has religious teachings as a core value could choose 'Christian' as an Affinity, but this is too broad and lacks context. A more specific description such as 'Devotee of the Order of Carolingians' shows an allegiance to the Christian faith while also describing a context within Christianity that informs the character's beliefs and, in this case, describes an organization that may make real demands on the character. Likewise, 'Honorable' is an Affinity without context, but 'Honorable as befits the name of York' provides a relational background for this Affinity that ties the character to her family and the history of the setting. Ideal Affinity descriptions can tell the story of why the character cares about her Affinity and how it manifests in her life in just a few words.

Affinities can be as broad or as narrow as the player and Narrator agree upon, but their breadth impacts how often they are used in the

AFFINITY RANKS

Rank	Description
1	**Fondness:** A character will endure some inconvenience to pursue or support the object of her fondness when possible. A character with a fondness for gambling will always sit down at a table when cards are being played. A character with a fondness for a person will always attend them when she enters the room.
2	**Love:** A character will actively seek to engage her love at all times. A character in love with a person will pine in their absence and constantly try to be near them or care for them. A character in love with an idea will constantly try to discuss it and share her enthusiasm with others. A person in love with an activity will engage in that activity as often as she is able.
3	**Passion:** A character will suffer horribly for her passions. A character passionate about her faith is willing to undergo ostracization, imprisonment, or even torture to maintain her beliefs. A character who is passionate about an activity will engage in it even if causes loss of wealth, damaged health, or some other suffering.
4	**Devotion:** A character will change their whole life to follow a devotion. Those who are devoted to the Clockmaker give up their current lives to become priests or missionaries. A noble may sacrifice heritage, wealth, and all the benefits of their position to be with someone to whom she is devoted.
5	**Martyrdom:** There is nothing a character will not sacrifice to serve and promote the object of this Affinity. Even her own life pales in comparison to its importance. A character may never have more than one Affinity at rank five.

game. Broadly defined Affinities will come up more frequently than narrow ones. In social conflict, Affinities can be used as weapons against the character or Armor to protect her, so managing the breadth of Affinities can have serious impact on the story (see *Social Weapon Potency*, p. 87 and *Affinities as Armor*, p. 92).

Players should take care when choosing how many Affinities they assign to their character, and the ranks of each. A character with two mid-rank Affinities has strong motivations that noticeably govern her life but may come into conflict. A character with many rank one Affinities may come across as fickle, constantly bouncing between interests as they come up. Few people in the Clockwork have Affinities higher than rank three. If a player character develops an Affinity above rank three it becomes her defining trait. Characters with Affinities of rank five are seen as zealots, and find it difficult to associate with people who do not share their obsessions.

ERODING AND STRENGTHENING AFFINITIES

Affinities are variable traits, and thus have both a current and a fixed value (see *Traits and Variable Traits*, p. 69). The ranks chosen at character creation are fixed, but the actions of a character during play can alter the temporary values of Affinities, either by force or by choice. The rank of the Affinity determines what kind of action is needed to harm it (see *Eroding Affinity* table). Any single action a character performs, by free choice or by persuasion, that significantly threatens one of her Affinities will cause the temporary rank of that Affinity to lower by one. If the temporary rank of any Affinity is ever reduced to zero, its fixed rank is reduced by one. Affinities that have suffered temporary damage will normalize to their fixed rank over time (see *Normalizing Affinities*, p. 103).

A character who consistently acts as though her Affinity is of a higher rank may increase its temporary rank. At any time, the Narrator may declare that a character's pattern of behavior over the course of a chapter or book dictates that an Affinity should be of a higher value. In such an instance, raise the temporary rank of the Affinity by one. Affinities that have been granted a temporary bonus will normalize to their fixed rank over time.

If the temporary rank of a character's Affinity has been increased or reduced from its fixed rank, she may pay experience points equal to twice the temporary rank of the Affinity to make the change permanent. If this is done, the temporary rank becomes the new fixed rank for the Affinity (if the temporary rank is more than one

ERODING AFFINITY

Permanent Rank	Action That Erodes Affinity
1	*Disregard:* Ignoring the subject of the Affinity or repeatedly showing a true lack of interest.
2	*Rejection:* Actively disregarding the subject's well being in favor of other things.
3	*Selfishness:* Putting one's own safety, needs or desires above the well-being of the Affinity.
4	*Autonomy:* Acting without serious thought for how it will affect the subject of the Affinity or not acting when the Reputation or well-being of the Affinity is at stake.
5	*Treasonous Thoughts:* Doubting the worth and sanctity of the Affinity, or seriously considering any action that could harm it or betray its interests.

rank different from the fixed rank, each change in fixed rank must be purchased separately). At any time, a character may also spend a single experience point to redefine any single Affinity, changing the phrase that describes it. The new phrase should be discussed with the Narrator before being finalized, and must have a connection to the spirit of the original Affinity, even if it changes its breadth or focus.

THE EFFECTS OF AFFINITIES ON GAMEPLAY

Affinities can be used as weapons and Armor in social conflict. If one character is attempting to persuade another concerning a matter favorably related to one of her Affinities, the temporary rank of that Affinity may be used as the Potency of the social attack. If the persuader is attempting to coerce the player into doing something that would injure or act against one of her Affinities, the temporary rank of the Affinity may be used as Armor against the attack. If a persuader's argument would relate to two Affinities, only the one most beneficial to the defender is used. The rules for this are fully described in *Chapter 4: Rules & Systems*.

AFFINITY EXAMPLES

Duties:
Dedicated Brother of the
    Franciscan order
God, Queen, and country!
Captain of the ship *Serenity*
Protect Anabelle with my life
Sworn servant of Lady Wiltshire

Goals:
Become as rich as I am clever
Find Rebecca, no matter what
Ireland will be free!
Master the secrets of alchemy
Restore the honor of my
    family name

People/Relationships:
As the East India Club rises, so
    shall the Atheneum fall
Cabar feidh gu brath!
See my enemies brought low
My dove, Thomas Harding
Provide a better life for my children

Behavior:
Beauty is all that matters
Chase the next horizon
Eat, drink, and be merry
Gambling is an honest trade
In vino veritas

REPUTATIONS: CHARACTER CREATION STEP EIGHT

Reputations are traits that define the things for which a character is known in society. Perhaps a character is known as "Mad, bad, and dangerous to know," or perhaps as someone who "Never forgets a debt." Player characters begin with three ranks to allocate into at least two different Reputations, as they are all noteworthy enough to have gained some notice for themselves before the game begins.

When a character takes a Reputation, the player and Narrator mutually agree on a relevant backstory behind how and why the character acquired it as well as a short description to note it on the character sheet. This description should ground the reputation in the Clockwork world. "Honorable man" is a good reputation, but "Honorable as befits the House of York" is better.

The fixed rank of the Reputation reflects how likely other people are to be familiar with her Reputation. Reputations of rank 1 are generally only known in certain social circles in a small geographic area. Rank 2 Reputations spread among a profession or in a close community like a city, neighborhood, or country village. Rank 3 Reputations denote regional fame, and Reputations of rank 4 and 5 can be known across the whole of Britain or throughout the Empire. Reputations precede a character, and figure prominently into determining one's Esteem during social events and conflicts. The right Reputation can create social opportunities or severely limit them.

Reputations are usually positive, but any Reputation can be negative depending on the situation. Being a "Notorious criminal" will carry great clout in the back alleys of London, but will not help when being questioned by the police. During the game, the Narrator determines whether a given Reputation is beneficial, harmful, or irrelevant to the current situation.

ORGANIZATIONAL REPUTATIONS

Characters that belong to a publicly-recognized organization via the *Membership* asset often gain a Reputation through their known membership in that organization. Depending on the organization and the character's known position within it, they will be assigned a Reputation such as "Edinburgh Constable" or "Lord Mayor of Chichester." These Reputations are a function of the character's position within the organization, and only apply to the character while that position is held. The Reputation's rank is permanently fixed, and cannot be increased or reduced unless the character's position in the organization is raised or lowered by gaining or losing ranks in the relevant *Membership* asset. Organizational Reputations are otherwise handled like any other Reputation for calculating Esteem.

ERODING AND STRENGTHENING REPUTATIONS

Reputations are variable traits, and thus have both a temporary and a fixed value (see *Traits and Variable Traits,* p. 69). The actions of characters during play can alter both the temporary and fixed values of Reputations, either through their own actions or those of others. A character or group who performs an amazing deed worthy of retelling can be awarded a one-rank Reputation for that deed. The fixed rank of this Reputation is considered to be 0, so unless the character spends experience points to make the Reputation permanent it will fade over time (see *Normalizing Reputations,* p. 103). At the Narrator's discretion, characters who achieve great renown regarding deeds for which they already have a Reputation, may increase the temporary rank of that Reputation by one. If a Reputation is permanently altered through the spending of experience points, its description may be changed by the Narrator or player to reflect its new scope.

Reputations are not undone by the actions of a character, but rather by people talking about those actions. Slander and gossip are what destroy public image. Malicious rumormongers may attack a character's Reputations, reducing their temporary value; and they may even spend their own experience points to make an opponent's change in Reputation permanent. The full rules for this sort of intricate social conflict are given under *Intrigues,* p. 92.

REPUTATION EXAMPLES

A killer in silk and lace
Always the first to laugh
The brazen brawler of Brady's pub
Ever a Queen's man
Fastest draw west of the Mississippi
Fearless explorer of the Sundarbans
Hero of the Battle of Elandslaagte
Honorable as befits the House of York

Jumps from bed to bed with the frequency of a wireless telegraph
Life of the best parties in Edinburgh
Mystic medium for the nobility
More lovers than regrets
Never forgets a debt
Once a criminal, now the best preacher in Liverpool

Prima ballerina in all of London
Staunchest Conservative in Essex
Survivor of the Battle of Blood River Poort
A voice to soothe the savage masses
Wisest woman in Berkshire

WEALTH AND ACCOUTREMENTS: CHARACTER CREATION STEP NINE

A character's *Means* determines what types of expenditures she can support without impacting her standard of living. At this step, you may choose any of the accoutrements from *Chapter 6: Accoutrements & Technology* listed with a Cost rank equal or lower than your *Means*. Players should review their selection of accoutrements with their Narrator, both to ensure they are covering any basic items that would be helpful for their character to have at the beginning of play, as well as to help establish the resources and standard of living for the character. Narrators may place certain limits on the number and type of accoutrements chosen. For example, it is unlikely that a character would have hundreds of outfits, even if they are all individually low-Cost items.

Describing a character's home and other property can be a wonderful way to illustrate who they are as people. For instance, a noble fallen on hard times could be living in the slowly crumbling ruins of an ancestral home; however, he may still devote funds to the care of a prized piano kept in an immaculate music room because of his happy memories playing childhood recitals for his now-deceased parents. This establishes the character as part of a broader world and history, and suggests other behaviors and goals for the character during play. It could also easily be the inspiration for an Affinity. Characters focused on engineering and item creation, ritual magic, or their role as members of certain organizations could all have accoutrements and lodgings that are an integral part of their overall character concept, and fleshing them out with the Narrator during this step can be a great way to involve those elements in the game.

FINISHING TOUCHES: CHARACTER CREATION STEP TEN

Now it's time to finish creating your character by calculating all of her derived traits, determining her potential, adding a physical description, a name, and fleshing out her personality—all based on the creation process so far. Reread your pursuit, bloodline, and background descriptions and consider how these templates may be put together. Add the spark of your own imagination and get ready to tell your character's story.

DERIVED TRAITS

These are traits and combinations kept on your character sheet. Many of them can be calculated once and simply referenced as needed. Others, such as Esteem, are calculated each time they are used.

Physical Defense

Vigor + Athletics or other relevant skill

This is your character's ability to reflexively protect herself from physical attacks by dodging, rolling with the punches, and enduring damage through sheer grit. While her Guard can be whittled away, a character will only be denied her physical Defense if she is rendered absolutely helpless (p. 82). Physical Defense is used as the Difficulty for all physical attacks made against a character.

Guard

½ Focus (rounded down), +1 for weapon

When a character puts her Guard up, she drops into a combat stance and is better able to protect herself. Guard represents combat awareness and the ability to respond to attacks by parrying blows or advantageously using the environment. Guard has a base value of one half your character's *Focus* aptitude rounded down. If she is wielding a weapon capable of parrying (or using a defensive accoutrement like a shield) the she receives a +1 bonus to Guard so long as the accoutrement is being used. The base value plus the weapon bonus is her maximum Guard. During physical conflict, a successful attack made by an opponent may lower your character's Guard; if her Guard is dropped to zero, she can be afflicted with Wounds and other terrible outcomes.

Social Defense

Will + Composure or other relevant skill

Social Defense is your character's ability to protect herself from social attacks through discourse, self-control, and social awareness. So long as a character is conscious she is never without her social Defense.

Esteem

Status Trait – Tenor +/– ½ relevant Reputations' rank

Esteem represents the attitude of others in the scene towards your character, and is tracked as a Disposition from *Hostile* to *Favorable*. It has no permanent value, so do not mark one on the character sheet. Instead, Esteem is calculated at the beginning of each encounter where social conflict is likely to occur. A full discussion on Esteem and how to calculate it occurs under *Conflict Specific Traits* beginning on p. 73.

Morale

Your character's Morale measures how confident she is within a given conflict and determines how likely she is to flee if things get rough. It has no permanent value, so do not mark one on the character sheet. In fact, Morale does not have a place of its own on the character sheet, but is recorded as a Disposition toward running away. Morale is calculated at the beginning of each physical conflict in which the Narrator wishes to use it. A full discussion on Morale and how to calculate it occurs under *Conflict Specific Traits* beginning on p. 73.

POTENTIAL

The choices made for your character's bloodline, pursuit, and background have contributed a total of four fixed ranks towards *Purpose* and *Ether*. Although the circumstances of birth and life have a major influence on how much a character fits into their intended role in the Clockwork or strays from it, some of that balance is simply a matter of free will: assign your character one last fixed rank into your choice of either *Purpose* or *Ether*. This should bring the total of these traits to five fixed ranks. The full mechanics for using *Purpose* and *Ether* are listed under *Potential*, beginning on p. 71.

Starting characters do not normally have any ranks of *Corruption* unless they have taken one of several specific assets or liabilities.

Altering Fixed Purpose and Ether Ranks

Over the course of a campaign, a character's actions may put them more at odds or in harmony with the Clockwork. Patterns of orderly behavior, and actions that support a character's Affinities move them towards greater *Purpose*, while erratic behavior and selfish actions in spite of one's obligations or against one's Affinities move them towards *Ether*. If the player and Narrator agree that the character's behavior merits a change in potential, one fixed rank of *Purpose* may be moved into *Ether* or vice versa. This should not happen more than once per book.

Corruption has no fixed ranks, and cannot be altered by spending experience points. Only a character's choices can change her ranks in *Corruption*.

DESCRIPTION & PERSONALITY

In order to play the role of a character, you must be able to conceptualize her as a three dimensional being. All of the decisions in character creation lead up to this moment when you put all the pieces together and make a full person. Affinities and Reputations tell you what she cares about and how other people feel about her. Her aptitudes and skills tell you what tasks she excels at and what she may have trouble with. Assets and liabilities can offer personality quirks and unique situations. Cobble these elements together into a cohesive backstory for your character. Describe how she looks and acts. Name her, her family, and those with whom she spends time. Let the character come alive and get ready to take on her role in the game.

CHARACTER ADVANCEMENT

As characters progress through a story, they will grow, learn new things, and continue to develop their skills and abilities by earning and spending experience points. At the end of every installment, all characters are awarded a certain number of experience points by the Narrator. Once earned, a player can spend her character's experience points at any time, even in the middle of an installment, to achieve a higher trait rank or acquire an ability. However, the advancement must be congruent with her behavior or training. If a character has never picked up a gun, it makes little sense that she would miraculously acquire a rank in *Firearms*. However, if one of her compatriots had showed her the basics of shooting or she had been practicing on her own, acquiring a single rank in this skill is wholly appropriate. The Narrator has the final say in what character advancement is possible given the story and circumstances, but is encouraged to be generous. Also, some assets and liabilities offer guidelines for story requirements in their descriptions.

ADVANCEMENT COSTS

Advancement	Cost
Increasing an aptitude	5 x new rank
Increasing a skill	2 x new rank
Increasing Reputation	2 x new rank
Increasing Affinity	1 x new rank
Gain an Asset	7 points (Consult with Narrator)
Lose an Asset	Gain 5 experience (Consult with Narrator)
Gain a Liability	Gain 5 experience (Consult with Narrator)
Lose a Liability	7 points (Consult with Narrator)
Partially Fluent Language	2 points
Fully Fluent Language	5 points to take new, 3 points to raise partial to fully fluent

Experience points can be spent to advance a character according to the Advancement Table.

Affecting a Narrator Character's Traits

When a character participates in increasing or reducing an NC's Affinity or Reputation, she may spend her own experience points to make that change permanent. If a character wishes to change a Reputation or Affinity by more than one rank, each individual rank must be purchased separately.

CHARACTER CREATION WALKTHROUGH

This walkthrough reviews how all the parts of character creation come together. As an example, we'll translate one of *Clockwork: Dominion's* iconic characters, the brilliant young alchemist Abigail St. George. Before building the character it helps to have a clear idea in mind. The concept behind Abigail is that she is exceptionally intelligent, is fascinated with the applications of alchemy, and wants to blaze new trails in that field. She has devoted herself and her education to becoming one of the finest alchemists in the Empire, and wants to use her intelligence and skill to become a member of the Royal Society.

All aptitudes begin at rank one, otherwise the character sheet is blank.

STEP ONE: BLOODLINE

Mechanically Abigail could work with any bloodline, but the supernatural ties that come with changelings and nephilim don't fit well with the scientific focus. Beastfolk are intimately linked with science and experimentation, but the animal augmentations and social ramifications don't fit with the character concept. Abigail is a pureblooded mortal, just like most people in the world. The benefits of the blessings are a natural fit, as the additional skills and free mastery will be especially useful for making sure she has plenty of options to support her interests. We'll make note of the skills bonus and mastery for now, and fill them in once we get to the allocating skills step.

Adding in her bloodline benefits gives the following:

Bloodline	Potential	Aptitude	Skill Bonus
Pureblood	*2 Purpose*	*Will*	+1 to any 2 skills

Blessings	Curses
Protected, Purposed, Talented	None

So Abigail now has:

Bloodline: Pureblood
Potential: *Purpose 2*
Aptitudes: *Grace* 1, *Vigor* 1, *Reason* 1, *Focus* 1, *Presence* 1, *Will* 2
Skills: +1 to any two, and one free mastery
Blessings: *Protected, Purposed, Talented*
Curses: None

STEP TWO: PURSUITS

Abigail cares first and foremost about using scientific inquiry and her own intelligence to understand the world. Reading over the descriptions, Discovery makes the most sense, both for the ideals and the mechanical benefits.

Adding in her pursuit benefits gives us the following:

Pursuit	Potential	Aptitude Bonuses	Professions
Discovery	*Ether*	*Focus, Reason*	Academic, Alchemist, Explorer, Magus

So Abigail now has:

Bloodline: Pureblood
Pursuit: Discovery
Potential: *Purpose 2, Ether 1*
Aptitudes: *Grace* 1, *Vigor* 1, *Reason* 2, *Focus* 2, *Presence* 1, *Will* 2
Skills: +1 to any two, and one free mastery
Blessings: *Protected, Purposed, Talented*
Curses: None

STEP THREE: BACKGROUND

The name alone makes it a clear choice: the *Scientist* background is a great fit for Abby's interests and covers exactly the type of skills she'll need to pursue her career as an alchemist. The *Class* and *Means* place her squarely in the middle class, which explains her educational opportunities and gives her a comfortable quality of life. The availability of three assets gives lots of flexibility for choosing assets later on, and will be noted for now.

Adding in her background gives us the following:

Backgrounds	Potential	Class	Means
Scientist	*Ether*	2	2
Skill Bonuses			**Assets**
Academics x2, Bureaucracy, Composure, Engineering, Science x2			3

So Abigail now has:

Bloodline: Pureblood
Pursuit: Discovery
Background: *Scientist*
Status: *Class 2, Means 2*
Potential: *Purpose 2, Ether 2*
Aptitudes: *Grace 1, Vigor 1, Reason 2, Focus 2, Presence 1, Will 2*
Skills: *Academics 2, Bureaucracy 1, Composure 1, Engineering 1, Science 2, +1 to any two, and one free mastery*
Blessings: *Protected, Purposed, Talented*
Curses: None
Assets: 3 available

STEP FOUR: APTITUDES

In this step we get to add five ranks of attributes to those already provided by the bloodline and pursuit. Abigail's intelligence is going to be her major focus, but we don't want her to be noticeably weak in any other areas. We'll put one rank each into *Grace, Vigor,* and *Presence* to make sure all her aptitudes are at least rank 2, then put the remaining two unspent ranks into *Reason* to raise it to 4. She's a very smart woman.

So Abigail now has:

Bloodline: Pureblood
Pursuit: Discovery
Background: *Scientist*
Status: *Class 2, Means 2*
Potential: *Purpose 2, Ether 2*
Aptitudes: *Grace 2, Vigor 2, Reason 4, Focus 2, Presence 2, Will 2*
Skills: *Academics 2, Bureaucracy 1, Composure 1, Engineering 1, Science 2, +1 to any two, and one free mastery*
Blessings: *Protected, Purposed, Talented*
Curses: None
Assets: 3 available

STEP FIVE: SKILLS

All characters get twelve ranks of skills to allocate. Abigail can also increase two additional skills by one rank each, and gain a mastery. After reviewing the skill descriptions there are several skills associated with observation, understanding, and discovery that are natural fits, and Abigail is assigned one more rank to each

of *Composure, Engineering, Medicine,* and *Science,* and two ranks to *Investigation.* That covers about half her available skill ranks, so the others will be placed into skills that help round her out and make sure she can survive and be successful in both physical and social conflict. She is assigned two ranks each to *Athletics, Fencing,* and *Firearms,* and the two bonus ranks from her blessing are placed into *Parley* and *Refinement.* Since *Science* is her best skill at three ranks, and used for alchemy, it is the best candidate for her mastery ability, and *Expert Alchemist* is a natural fit.

So Abigail now has:

Bloodline: Pureblood
Pursuit: Discovery
Background: *Scientist*
Status: *Class 2, Means 2*
Potential: *Purpose 2, Ether 2*
Aptitudes: *Grace 2, Vigor 2, Reason 4, Focus 2, Presence 2, Will 2*
Skills: *Academics 2, Athletics 2, Bureaucracy 1, Composure 2, Engineering 2, Fencing 2, Firearms 2, Investigation 2, Medicine 1, and Science 3 with the mastery Expert Alchemist.*
Blessings: *Protected, Purposed, Talented*
Curses: None
Assets: 3 available

STEP SIX: ASSETS AND LIABILITIES

So far Abigail is coming along splendidly, and her concept is being fleshed out well. Perhaps giving her a *Nemesis* could add to her story. The Lady Bathurst is an affluent duchess who spent her life working with her husband at the Royal Society, but could never gain admission because she was a woman, even upon her husband's death. Now, overtaken by bitterness, she scorns Abigail's aspirations for membership. If the duchess cannot be a member of the Royal Society, then no woman should! Now Duchess Bathurst spends copious time and money working to slander and undermine Abigail. Taking the *Nemesis* liability grants Abigail one more asset, for a total of four.

It would greatly help Abigail to be a gentleman's daughter, as the higher social station will help her when dealing with the blue bloods at the Royal Society and the extra money will help her afford the chalks used in more difficult alchemical reactions. She will have to take the *Higher Class* and *Well-Off* assets.

As an alchemist, Abigail should spend her remaining two assets on *Alchemical Reactions.* Thus ensures that Abigail has a variety of ways to use alchemy immediately. Checking out the alchemy options lets us see she qualifies for almost all of them. Taking *Transmutation Reaction* is extremely versatile and is a classic idea in alchemy. For her last asset, Abigail will take *Caustic Reaction* as it offers versatility and can be used offensively.

So Abigail now has:
Bloodline: Pureblood

Pursuit:	Discovery
Background:	*Scientist*
Status:	*Class 3, Means 3*
Potential:	*Purpose 2, Ether 2*
Aptitudes:	*Grace 2, Vigor 2, Reason 4, Focus 2, Presence 2, Will 2*
Skills:	*Academics 2, Athletics 2, Bureaucracy 1, Composure 2, Engineering 2, Fencing 2, Firearms 2, Investigation 2, Medicine 1,* and *Science 3* with the mastery *Expert Alchemist.*
Blessings:	*Protected, Purposed, Talented*
Curses:	None
Assets:	*Alchemical Reaction x2 (Caustic Reaction, Transmutation Reaction)*
Liabilities:	*Nemesis: The Duchess Bathurst*

STEP SEVEN: AFFINITIES

All characters have three ranks to assign to Affinities. Abigail's concept already centered around alchemy and using that as her means to joining the Royal Society, so those are both great options to convert into Affinities. Studying alchemy is fascinating for Abigail, but it's also a means to an end, so her desire to "Join the Royal Society" is assigned two ranks, and her wish to "Discover the secrets of alchemy" is given one rank.

So Abigail now adds:

Affinities:	"Discover the secrets of alchemy" 1, "Join the Royal Society" 2

STEP EIGHT: REPUTATIONS

All players have three ranks to assign to Reputations. Abigail's skill in science and alchemy puts her well ahead of most others in the Empire, so it makes sense that she would gain a Reputation for her talent. As she went to the girl's school on Oxford University campus, but outclassed the men at the main school, she's given two ranks for "Most brilliant alchemist Oxford has ever seen." Expanding on her concept a bit, she had to work hard to pursue her education and her independence is a bit unusual, so it makes sense that she is also known as a "Self-made woman" 1. These Reputations reflect what she cares about and how she presents herself to the world; many people will respect that and be impressed by her skill and accomplishment, but if she is in staunchly conservative or anti-scientific company those Reputations could hurt her Esteem.

So Abigail adds:

Reputations:	"Most brilliant alchemist Oxford has ever seen" 2, "Self-made woman" 1

STEP NINE: ACCOUTREMENTS

Abigail's traits are essentially complete, but she still needs to have the details of her daily environs fleshed out and the player and Narrator both need to know what gear she uses and has access to regularly. After discussing basic matters of Abigail's home—a small townhouse in Oxford where she continues her research, including a small lab space she's put together in an unused second bedroom—and how many purchases at her *Means* of 3 the Narrator considers appropriate to start the game, it's time to go shopping. After perusing the available accoutrements the key items are an alchemist's satchel with plenty of alchemical chalks, a sword-cane with a chalk mount in the tip so it can be used for writing alchemical channels or in a fight as needed, a small pistol, and a set of alchemically treated clothing that provides some Armor.

STEP TEN: FINISHING TOUCHES

The only mechanical decision at this step is assigning a final point of potential, which is put into *Ether* so Abigail has plenty of opportunity to use alchemy. Other than that, all that's left is filling out the derived traits for physical and social Defense.

Bloodline:	Pureblood
Pursuit:	Discovery
Background:	*Scientist*
Status:	*Class 3, Means 3*
Potential:	*Purpose 2, Ether 3*
Aptitudes:	*Grace 2, Vigor 2, Reason 4, Focus 2, Presence 2, Will 2*
Skills:	*Academics 2, Athletics 2, Bureaucracy 1, Composure 2, Engineering 2, Fencing 2, Firearms 2, Investigation 2, Medicine 1,* and *Science 3* with the mastery *Expert Alchemist.*
Blessings:	*Protected, Purposed, Talented*
Curses:	None
Assets:	*Alchemical Reaction x2 (Caustic Reaction, Transmutation Reaction), Higher Class, Well-Off*
Liabilities:	*Nemesis: The Duchess Bathurst*
Affinities:	"Discover the secrets of alchemy" 1, "Join the Royal Society" 2
Reputations:	"Most brilliant alchemist Oxford has ever seen" 2, "Self-made woman" 1
Defenses:	Physical 4 (*Vigor + Athletics*), Social 4 (*Will + Composure*)
Armor:	1
Guard:	1 base, +1 when wielding sword-cane
Attacks:	Sword-cane, *Grace + Fencing* +4, *Potency 2*, Close, Bleeding
	Holdout pistol, *Grace + Firearms* +4, *Potency 2*, Load 2, Extended, Bleeding
Accoutrements:	Alchemically treated clothing (Armor 1), Alchemist's satchel with 5 uses each of rank one and rank two alchemical chalks, holdout pistol with two reloads of ammunition, sword-cane with chalk mount tip.

Now that you've seen all the various pieces of character creation and how they work together, you should be ready to start making your own. Abigail and several other sample characters are presented on the following pages.

Abigail St. George, Alchemist

"All things change. To manage the process, we need to understand how and why."

Edison's discovery and codification of modern alchemy shocked the world, and captured Abigail's imagination. Since her childhood, she is bent her impressive intellect towards science, and alchemy in particular. Her efforts and education have paid off, and she is establishing herself as one of the foremost practitioners of the New Science in England. Abigail is determined to become a member of the Royal Society, and the only way to do that is to pursue her own research and make her own discoveries.

Thanks to her impressive *Reason*, skill in *Science* and her *Expert Alchemist* mastery ability, Abigail is able to perform extremely difficult reactions reliably. This allows her to create dramatic effects combining multiple reactions, or especially powerful individual transmutations. In order to make her mark on the world, she will have to venture into new and possibly dangerous circumstances, so she has also learned how to handle herself in both physical and social conflict.

Bloodline:	Pureblood
Pursuit:	Discovery
Background:	Scientist
Status:	Class 3, Means 3
Potential:	Purpose 2, Ether 3
Aptitudes:	Grace 2, Vigor 2, Reason 4, Focus 2, Presence 2, Will 2
Skills:	Academics 2, Athletics 2, Bureaucracy 1, Composure 2, Engineering 2, Fencing 2, Firearms 2, Investigation 2, Medicine 1, and Science 3 with the mastery Expert Alchemist.
Blessings:	Protected, Purposed, Talented
Curses:	None
Assets:	Alchemical Reaction x2 (Caustic Reaction, Transmutation Reaction), Higher Class, Well-off
Liabilities:	Nemesis: The Duchess Bathurst
Affinities:	"Discover the secrets of alchemy" 1, "Join the Royal Society" 2
Reputations:	"Most brilliant alchemist Oxford has ever seen" 2, "Self-made woman" 1
Defenses:	Physical 4 (*Vigor + Athletics*), Social 4 (*Will + Composure*)
Armor:	1
Guard:	1 base, +1 when wielding sword-cane
Attacks:	SWORD-CANE: Grace + Fencing (4), Potency 2, Close, *Bleeding*
	HOLDOUT PISTOL: Grace + Firearms (4), Potency 2, Load 2, Extended, *Bleeding*
Accoutrements:	Alchemically treated clothing (Armor 1), alchemist's satchel with 5 uses each of rank one and rank two alchemical chalks, holdout pistol with two reloads of ammunition, sword-cane with chalk mount tip.

popular spiritualists by posing as a credulous lady, or infiltrating the households of suspected witches under the guise of a member of staff. Her talents and remarkable luck for pulling herself out of dangerous situations were put to good use, and she was inducted as a Star after repeatedly proving her skill and reliability.

Last year, though, her luck ran out. An especially cautious magus was able to pierce her deceptions and lured her into a trap. In the midst of fighting for her life against the magician a terrible Pontus event occurred. She barely survived, but was forever marked by the encounter and has borne a stain of chaos ever since. Given the already high risk of solo infiltration work, the added danger of her pontal infection put an end to her undercover activity. Now, Ivy has been assigned to a new region and a new team of Witchfinders. For the first time, she can proudly wear her arms, leathers, and badge for all the world to see.

Ivy's social skills are best put to use chasing rumors, handling informants, and questioning suspects, but her hard-earned skill in a fight and willingness to push her luck serve her well when the time for talking is past.

Ivy Star, Witchfinder

"It matters not who you are, my lord, only that you are a witch, and I have found you out."

Growing up as a changeling in a working-class family was a hard start to Ivy's life. Her father's strong blood and inhuman appearance made it difficult for him to hold work, and her parents struggled to care for Ivy and her younger siblings. Even though changelings born to poor families were often given up for orphans or sent to work-houses, her parents kept all three of them close and raised them to be good children and loyal subjects of the empire that gave them more welcome than they would find in many other nations.

As soon as she could, Ivy began work to help her family. Using her wits, charm, and glamours, she won a place as a housemaid to a prominent family, and by the time she was sixteen she was one of the house staff that directly attended the lady and her daughter. This close position let Ivy see that the lady had become entangled with a spiritualist who meddled in real and dangerous magic. Circumspectly, Ivy brought proof of this to the Witchfinders. Although Ivy was not ungrateful for her position with the family, she knew that witches pose a threat to society as a whole. Even though it brought her employer's family to ruin, she exposed the lady, the magician, and a circle of others they had involved in witchcraft.

Her unflinching action and significant assistance during the case began Ivy's career with the Witchfinders. Though it meant breaking contact with the family she loved, it was a chance for Ivy to make a difference in the world and she took it without hesitation. She became something of a specialist, investigating

Bloodline:	Changeling (weak-blooded trickster)
Pursuit:	Dominion
Background:	Agent
Status:	*Class 2, Means 2*
Potential:	*Purpose 2, Ether 3, Corruption 2*
Aptitudes:	*Grace 2, Vigor 2, Reason 2, Focus 2, Presence 3, Will 3*
Skills:	*Academics 1, Athletics 2, Bureaucracy 1, Command 2, Composure 3, Firearms 1, Guile 3, Intuition 2, Investigation 2, Melee 3, Mysteries 1, Parley 2, Refinement 1, Stealth 1*
Blessings:	Glamours: *Beguile* and *Second Chances*
Curses:	Unnatural: may suffer a -1 penalty to Esteem in social encounters with those who look down on changelings
Assets:	*Favored, Membership: Witchfinders, Skilled x2*
Liabilities:	*Pontal Infection*
Affinities:	"Care for my family" 2, "Folklore and fairy stories" 1
Reputations:	"Witchfinder" 2, "The Devil's own luck" 2, "Never shies from danger" 1
Defenses:	Physical 4 (*Vigor + Athletics*) or 5 (*Vigor + Melee*), Social 6 (*Will + Composure*)
Armor:	2
Guard:	1 base + 1 when wielding sword
Attacks:	SWORD: Grace + Melee (5), Potency 3, Close, *Bleeding*
	REVOLVER: Grace + Firearms (3), Potency 3, Short Range, *Bleeding*
Accoutrements:	Witchfinder Leathers (Armor 2), badge of office, sword, revolver, copy of the "Magical Healing" rite (see p. 254), three uses of rank 1 reagents, and two uses of rank 2 reagents

Panth, Army specialist

"I am not the man I was, but I will never be the beast some think me to have become."

Taihal Singh was born into the kshatriya caste of an old Punjabii family with a long history of military participation. His family was not prominent or wealthy enough to have him enter as an officer, but Taihal's own ability and his caste background did enable him to enter the Punjab Frontier Force, a special battalion under the direct command of the British chief magistrate of Punjab tasked with stabilizing and maintaining the border. The PFF had none of the parade drill required of other Indian regiments, and instead focused on developing excellent survival, pathfinding, and small-group tactics that would be useful for patrolling and acting along the edge of colonial control. The PFF had very few British officers, and most promotion was handled from within, so Taihal had all the makings of a bright career in front of him, even with the presence of some rumors among his cohorts about the company he kept while off duty.

Taihal's skills as a pathfinder and excellent service record brought him some renown with his superiors, and so it was that he was invited on a tiger hunt in the Sundarbans with several senior officers. None returned, and all were presumed dead. That was the end of Taihal Singh.

Six years later, rumors of an unnatural creature stalking the wilds of the Sri Lankan coast began to circulate. With concern that it may be a chimera, hunting parties of the Ceylon Defense Force were dispatched to investigate. For days they chased it with little luck, for even when it was seen for a fleeting moment, it always managed to elude them. More hunters were dispatched, and the search was more aggressive. Tragedy was avoided when the trackers found a note scraped into tree bark stating that they were hunting no beast, but a man who had been altered to resemble one. Ensuing messages left in bits of bark or scratched out on stone coordinated a meeting, and the beastman calling himself Panth made contact with the world again.

His extensive augmentations make him look more animal than man: large ears from a flying fox, piercing golden eyes from an Indian eagle-owl, and the snout of a golden jackal create an inhuman visage. Extensive surgeries to replace and rebuild his musculature coupled with large patches of grafted rhino hide have left his body a patchwork of rough skin and scar tissue. The only links to his former life are a tarnished steel locket and well-honed skills. Unwilling to reclaim his history as Taihal, Panth has done what he can to start making a new place for himself in the world. Shunned by many civilians for his appearance, he re-enlisted in the Army. Although he has lost much, he is unwilling to surrender to the burdens of his new reality, and the Army is not so short-sighted as to turn away someone of his skills, or fail to make use of his new gifts.

Bloodline:	Beastfolk (heavily augmented)
Pursuit:	Discovery
Background:	Soldier
Status:	Class 1, Means 1
Potential:	Purpose 1, Ether 4
Aptitudes:	Grace 2, Vigor 3, Reason 2, Focus 4, Presence 1, Will 2
Skills:	Academics 1, Athletics 2, Command 2, Composure 3, Firearms 2, Intuition 1, Investigation 1, Melee 2, Mysteries 1, Streetwise 1, Stealth 3, Survival 3, Tactics 2
Blessings:	Animal Augmentations (Echolocation, Enhanced Smell, Low-Light Vision)
Curses:	Immunosupressed, Monstrous
Assets:	Additional Augmentations x2 (Hide, Muscular Structure), Membership: British Army
Liabilities:	None
Affinities:	"Xenotransplantation must stop!" 2, "Find a true home" 1
Reputations:	"Relentless Hunter" 2, "Tamed beast" 1, "British soldier" 1
Defenses:	Physical 5 (*Vigor + Athletics*) or 5 (*Vigor + Melee*), Social 5 (*Will + Composure*)
Armor:	2
Guard:	2 base +1 when wielding a bayonet or knife
Attacks:	RIFLE: Grace + Firearms (4), Potency 4, Long Range, *Moribund*
	FIXED BAYONET: Grace + Melee (4), Potency 3, Extended, *Bleeding*
Accoutrements:	Field uniform, dress uniform, foul weather gear, rifle, bayonet, combat knife, first aid kit, field rations, firestarting kit, bedroll, silver locket with picture of a well-dressed man

Silas' new life began when he realized that although he had been treated unfairly at times due to his bloodline, the worst of his troubles were the result of his own poor choices. He found a new community in the other nephilim families of Sydney, and won new opportunities through his own hard work. He returned to work as a ranch hand, working sheep and cattle, building up skills and savings for years before buying land and a small herd of his own. The ranch runs well, and Silas views those who helped him build it up as family.

Now, almost twenty years after arriving, Silas has found success and stability through his work, but never forgets the lessons he learned along the way. He works to maintain balance in his own life and avoid the excesses that led him to trouble and strong manifestation in his youth. He uses his new stature and success to keep fighting for fairer treatment of nephilim, changelings, and beastfolk, so they might have a better chance of making their way in the world. Most importantly, Silas is increasingly concerned with the problems of Pontus events in Australia and what can be done about it. Now that he has more invested in the world, he has much more to lose.

Silas Toyne, Rancher

Silas has had several lives already. The first was a quiet one in rural Ireland, where his family was one of only a few in his village. His parents taught him that he must be always be careful and balanced in his thoughts and actions, lest their nature as nephilim become too pronounced and risk their place in the community. As he grew up, though, Silas grew wild, and didn't care for a quiet life of family and routine. He started his nest life when he left home and took to roving, working as an itinerant moving from farm to farm, and town to town. Over the course of several years his life and habits became unfocused, and he began to turn to petty theft and casual criminality rather than hard work to support himself. Always a big lad, he began to manifest the traits of his Rephaim line, growing near seven feet tall and becoming ever more belligerent. That came to a close when he was caught, hauled in front of a judge, and sentenced to ten years transportation to Australia.

Transportation was hard on Silas. The worst parts of his temperament came to the fore, he slipped further into anger and recklessness, and it showed in his huge frame and increasingly taurine features. By the time he arrived in Sydney, his nature as a nephilim was clear for all to see, and his brutish behavior constantly embroiled him in trouble. What surprised Silas, though, was to find so many other nephilim, and their reaction to him. Due to the decades Transportation catching up nephilim and changelings the city had a noticeable and well-established population of inhuman bloodlines, but the rapid growth of Australia and great wealth that had come out of the colonies there allowed anyone willing to work for it a real chance at success. Other nephilim - even those that were clearly manifesting - were not relegated to the shadows.

Bloodline:	Nephilim
Pursuit:	Industry
Background:	Laborer
Status:	Class 1, Means 2
Potential:	Purpose 2, Ether 3
Aptitudes:	Grace 3, Vigor 3, Reason2 , Focus 2, Presence 2, Will 2
Skills:	Academics 1, Artisan 2, Athletics 2, Burglary 2, Composure 2, Firearms 2, Guile 2, Melee 2, Mysteries 1, Parley 2, Riding 1, Survival 1, Temptation 1, Vocation: Rancher 2
Blessings:	Angelic Immortality, Knowledge in the Flesh
Curses:	Abomination, Bane, Fluid Mien
Assets:	Dangerous Friends, Estate, Skilled, Well-off
Liabilities:	None
Affinities:	"Family first" at rank 2, and "The Sydney nephilim" at rank 1
Reputations:	"A nephilim made good" at 2, and "Once a drover, always a drover" at rank 1
Defenses:	Physical 4 (*Vigor + Athletics*), Social 6 (*Will + Composure*)
Armor:	0
Guard:	1 base +1 when wielding a close combat weapon
Attacks:	SHOTGUN: Grace + Firearms (5) Potency 3, Short Range, *Crippled*
Accoutrements:	Shotgun, knife, riding horse

5

Henry stood from his workbench, groaning as his muscles stretched and flexed for the first time in hours. He noticed a chill in the room and cursed softly as he went about re-lighting the potbelly stove that had gone cold while he was absorbed in his work. Once the spark ignited into a steady flame, he warmed his fingers and ticked through the adjustments he had made, considering if there was anything else he could check, yet could think of nothing. He turned back to his workbench and smiled. There, on the black velvet workcloth, the collection of finely-milled clockwork and lenses had come together into what Henry hoped would be the final version of the sensor he had been agonizing to perfect.

He donned a pair of cotton gloves and gingerly lifted the sensor to return it to its proper place in the device. As he approached, Henry studied it thoughtfully. At a glance, it could perhaps be mistaken for a camera. The housing was a sturdy leather-bound box, barely larger than the Flat Folding Kodak which sat beside it on the mounting platform; once the case was opened, though, the difference was unmistakable. The machine's interior was an elegant nest of gearwork, tightly packed around a tiny analytic engine no larger than a small book, a reel of punched tape, and the currently empty brackets to hold the sensor. Henry delicately placed the eye in its housing and used a fine pair of tweezers to reconnect it to the miniature analytic engine. He carefully refit the cover, and as he had before each test these past months, unlatched the rear of the box and peered within. Ensuring there were no obstructions among the eye's complex assemblage of gears and that the paper rings of the analytical engine's instruction tapes remained untorn was vital. The eye's mechanisms moved so quickly that even a minor fray at the paper's edge or a misfeed could shred the entire tape in seconds. As proud as he was of the sensor mechanism, the analytical program contained in the hand-punched paper was the the true heart of Henry's work, and what made the eye so special.

Content in his examination, Henry sealed the case, opened a small side panel and replaced the photograph there with another, plucked at random from a pile—politicians, famous performers, and the like—on the work table. He glanced down and saw the bushy beard and serious countenance of the Prime Minister, Lord Salisbury. He closed the photo slot, lifted the mounting platform's locking lever, flicked a toggle to give power to the eye, and stood aside as gears whirred into action.

The case shifted and began to turn side to side, scanning the far wall where Henry had tacked scores of photographs, different pictures of those personages on the work table interspersed with landmarks, advertisements, and other people entirely. Light flickered within the eye, accompanied by a soft hum. He waited, picturing the analytical engine cycling through its instructions, seeking a match. Henry counted under his breath. One, two, thr—

With an audible clack, the locking lever fell and the platform froze in place. A second release snapped sharply an instant later, triggering the Kodak, not that it held any film. Henry peered through the camera, though, and sure enough, the eye had located Lord Salisbury.

"Lowery's Analytical Eye," Henry mused, letting it roll off his tongue. So much faster, so much more discerning than anything out there…he and Kelly would make a fortune. Henry smiled broadly, but the corners of his mouth turned down as he settled his hand on the edge of the mounting platform. So heavily built and firmly braced, it wasn't pleasing at all. But Kelly had insisted, and the man seemed to value function over form. Henry had often said that the eye could be mounted on a light stand like those used for cameras, but Kelly had insisted it be built on a heavy frame that could be mounted on a carriage, ship, or building. He'd been clear enough in that respect, however vague he remained otherwise. Since Kelly was the investor paying for Henry's work this past year there was no point in fighting over such a trivial matter. The thought passed from his mind as he returned to testing the eye with new photographs to ensure its performance was reliable. A dozen times more the picture was replaced, and a dozen times more the eye whirred and clicked as it unerringly found its targets.

With barely suppressed glee, Henry returned to his workbench to clear away his tools and take out a fresh sheet of stationery. At last he had good news to share. At last he could redeem himself. He thought of the last time he had seen his sister, how much had changed for the worse, and how much it might now change for the better.

"I've spoken to William, and we'll support you as best we can. It's all we have to spare, Henry," Laura had said, ever confident, ever generous. "Make us proud."

As he clutched the heavy purse to his chest, William's hand had fallen heavily on his shoulder. His brother-in-law had still been virile then, before the sickness took hold. "I wish you all the best, Henry, but let this be the end of it. I've no doubt that Laura loves you dearly, but my generosity has limits."

The money gave Henry enough to make his first prototype of the eye, and paid for travel and lodgings in London that he might find investors, but it was not enough. After two years of work and travel Henry had found no investors and was reduced to taking a position as a machinist to pay for a cramped flat, only tinkering on the eye when he could. In the same time, disease had torn away William's vigor and his and Laura's fortunes, and he had grown bitter in his infirmity. "I want him out of my house, Laura," was all he'd said when Henry had last visited. His eyes had fallen judgmentally on Henry's shabby topcoat, seeing only failure in the disgraced inventor's appearance. After that shame, Henry threw everything he had into one last demonstration. Then, at last, he met Kelly and got the investment he so desperately needed.

With a rough shake of his head, Henry cast the painful memories away. He leaned forward and lifted pen to paper.

Dearest Sister,

The world turns, and 'tis finally on the upturn for us. I found a backer last summer. Mr. Kelly was at my demonstration (yes, that one) but he saw past the debacle of it and recognized the merits of my work. I haven't been able to say much before now, as he's a great proponent of secrecy in his dealings, but I've made amazing strides with my analytical eye over the past few months. The device works far better than my previous hopes! Now it can pick a face out of a crowd at a distance, and with a click it can snap a picture!

As soon as he wrote it, Henry realized his statement was false: it could not take a picture at a distance. The eye could recognize a target, move the platform to keep it centered, and trigger the camera, but someone would still need to focus the camera. He'd been so obsessed with miniaturizing the analytical engine, writing the program, perfecting the sensor, and dozens of other problems and improvements that he never thought to ask who would focus the camera. It was pointless to even use the eye if a photographer were present.

He shivered and stared at the machine clearly, without the burdens of finance and technical problems clouding his thoughts. His eyes darted from the camera's protruding lens to the far wall, and he only saw targets there. He turned back, staring at the sturdy frame, the clamps on the camera. Sturdy enough to absorb recoil, to hold a rifle steady.

And Kelly—all the secrecy, the predatory eyes, the sheer pressure of the man—it made sense. The strange little workroom tucked in the forgotten corner of a shipping warehouse, the fact the entrance to this section of the warehouse was always under watch by one or two of Kelly's men…When Kelly first made his offer he leaned in too close and said, "You'll be working in total privacy, you understand? I can't have anyone finding out what we're about before it's ready." There was a peculiar glint in his eyes, but at the time Henry had written it off as the natural suspicion of a businessman previously stung by industrial espionage, and the money was too good to question. Now, Henry had no further doubts. "Lowery's Analytical Assassin," he muttered, disgusted. He sank back into his chair, mortified at his achievement.

His eyes cast about the room, looking anywhere but at the device. The stove, the bales of cotton stacked across the room, his workbench and the letter for Laura, barely begun.

"Make me proud," she had said.

He snatched the letter from the table angrily and strode towards the stove to throw it into the flames. "Make me proud," he echoed his sister's request aloud. He drew a new sheet of paper from the stack.

Dearest Sister, he began again, a fire growing in his eyes.

ACCOUTREMENTS & TECHNOLOGY

This chapter covers the breadth of equipment and technology in the Clockwork. First, it describes how a character's *Means* is put to use during the game. Next, it covers the basic attributes of accoutrements and objects that might come up during gameplay, then offers accoutrement tables with details on scores of goods and services commonly available in the Empire. Lastly, it provides a system that characters with the proper assets can use to create their own unique inventions.

MEANS AND PURCHASES

The *Means* trait is an abstraction of a character's available wealth and resources. A character is considered to own or be able to purchase any accessible good or service she desires so long as its Cost rank is less than or equal to her *Means* rank. Using *Means* to purchase items represents spending disposable income or making larger purchases via credit or promissory agreement.

Purchasing an item with a Cost rank less than or equal to a character's *Means* rank does not affect her financial situation. Making several Cost 1 purchases daily is common for most people, though purchases of higher Cost are usually only made several times per week. It is assumed that Narrators will moderate

character acquisitions and help players understand the frequency and types of purchases their *Means* can support. Narrators always have final say on what is a sustainable amount of expenditure for a given *Means*.

Making purchases beyond one's *Means* can financially hinder or even bankrupt a character. A character may purchase an item of one Cost rank higher than her *Means* (but never two ranks higher). For each purchase made in this way, her temporary *Means* rank is reduced by one. Her fixed *Means* rank remains the same, and the character can roughly maintain her usual standard of living by spending less of what would normally be discretionary income.

MEANS

Means	Typical Property and Resources
0	You have almost nothing: the clothes on your back, an empty belly, and perhaps access to a shared shack or occasional stays in a "coffin house" or shelter.
1	You rent a home in the tenements or on a Lord's land, and have rough, functional furniture. Personal items are limited to the tools of your trade and a few changes of simple clothes.
2	You own a modest townhouse or small home filled with quality furniture and home decorations, maintained by a house servant to act as cook and maid. You have a few sets of both simple and formal wear, and small amounts of fine jewelry, heirlooms, and other small objects of interest.
3	You have earned or inherited a small country estate and a townhouse in the city, each with lavish furniture and home decorations, maintained by a handful of skilled servants. You can dress for many occasions in simple, formal, or lavish clothing. You have several sets of fine jewelry and collections of art and curios. Your family has access to a carriage when the horses are not needed in the fields.
4	You live on a large family estate and have access to several other holdings, each lavishly decorated with furniture, art, and symbols of wealth. You are served by a staff of highly recommended house servants, and can adorn your body with many sets of formal and lavish clothing and lavish jewelry. Your family has wide ranging collections of art and antiquities, access to a carriage at all times, and perhaps an automobile.
5	You live in a castle and travel to several other estates owned by your family in both the city and country. Each is decadently ornamented. You own many sets of formal and lavish clothing, extravagant jewelry, and most anything else desired.

To represent this, her ability to make purchases is reduced to the temporary *Means* rank.

A character may continue to spend herself into bankruptcy in this way, because her ability to purchase simple things that were once within her reach quickly diminishes as her temporary *Means* continues to fall. If a character's current temporary *Means* is ever reduced to zero, the character's fixed *Means* is reduced by one. When this happens, she must sell off possessions and permanently lower her standard of living to avoid a trip to the poor house. This stabilizes her finances and her temporary *Means* is reset to the new, lower fixed rank.

If a temporary *Means* rank is changed, it will normalize over time, eventually returning to its fixed value. One rank of reduced *Means* will recover in one month; a second in three months, a third rank in one year, and a fourth in three years. *Chapter 8: Narrating the Story* describes how Narrators can reward player characters with financial windfalls, which can be used to resecure or even raise one's *Means*.

For example, a gentleman of *Means* 3 wishes to buy a simple carriage, a Cost 4 purchase. He could acquire the carriage, but his temporary *Means* rank would become 2 and until it returned to normal, he must make purchases as though his *Means* rank were 2. After one month, his temporary *Means* rank will move one rank toward his fixed *Means* rank. In this case, it returns to 3 and his finances have fully recovered from his large purchase.

DON'T LEAVE HOME WITHOUT IT

Everyone has things they always have on them. Sometimes this is due to personal preference, but cultural norms also dictate what a person of a given *Class* and *Means* is like to carry with her.

A GENTLEMAN'S ACCOUTREMENTS

Daytime: a light-grey three-piece suit consisting of sack coat, a matching waistcoat, and matching or contrasting trousers; a four-in-hand or bow tie; a bowler hat

Evening: a black dinner suit, ascot, and top hat; a dark top coat for cold weather

Always: a silver or gold pocket watch, a white pocket-handkerchief; a silver case of calling cards with the gentleman's name, rank, and address; a billfold

Perhaps: snuff box, a cane or umbrella, cigarettes

In the Country: a tweed jacket, a rugged cloth belt, breeches, high socks

A LADY'S ACCOUTREMENTS

Daytime: a corset, a "mutton-sleeved" dress with a tailored fit at the wrists and cinched at the waist to promote an hour-glass figure, a large hat decorated with ribbon or flowers, silk stockings. The hair is worn is lavishly swept on top of the head in the "Gibson girl" fashion.

Evening: an evening gown, long white gloves, jewels—young upper and middle class woman are permitted to wear gowns that bear the shoulders and the top of the bust.

Always: a silver case of calling cards with the lady's name, rank, and address

Perhaps: a three-quarter length jacket with wide revers and very large sleeves above the wrists, a shawl of fine material; an ostrich-feather fan; a warm cloak of brocade, satin, and velvet for cold weather

A WORKING CLASS MAN'S ACCOUTREMENTS

Daytime: a baggy button front cotton shirt, a waistcoat in light brown or dark earth tones showing signs of wear, baggy cotton pants in a dark color showing wear, a tweed cap or bowler hat.

Special Times: a second-hand three-piece suit and bowler hat, but if he is especially poor he will just wear the cleanest clothes he has in the best repair.

Always: tools of his trade, if he is working

Perhaps: a crude clay pipe and tobacco, a strip of cloth worn as an improvised neck tie: in white if he is understated, in bright red or another loud colour if he is assertive of his working class identity (dock-workers are known for this), suspenders, a worn or ill-fitting top coat or sports coat

A WORKING CLASS WOMAN'S ACCOUTREMENTS

Daytime: a corset, an old dress fitted at the waist and wrists, high wool socks—if she is selling wares in the street, she will wear a many-skirted petticoat, a bright scarf, and a hat bedecked with flowers or ribbon.

Special Times: a simple evening dress, probably second hand. Unlike the gowns of her upper class counterparts, a lower-class woman's dress must be modest, usually covering her all the way to the neck.

Perhaps: a simple shawl

ANATOMY OF ANY OBJECT

All accoutrements and objects in the game have some common use that requires no particular rules: a pocket watch tells time, a blanket keeps someone warm, and that's that. It is easy for Narrators and players to understand how they can be used within the game. When the anatomy of an object is irrelevant to its current use in play, no further detail is needed. However, the events of a series and the actions of player characters are rarely so mundane, and there will be times when questions come up about how big an object is, how tough it is to break, or how it could be affected by a special ability or transcendent power. In these circumstances it is important to be able to define an object more thoroughly. For these detailed mechanical considerations there are several key traits shared by all objects and accoutrements presented in this chapter. Each trait is detailed below, and attributes are listed as part of the entries in the accoutrement tables for easy reference during play.

OBJECT ATTRIBUTES

Similar to the way that a character's inherent qualities of are represented by six aptitudes, the qualities of objects are represented by three attributes: Bulk, Complexity, and Structure. Each attribute determines a Difficulty for a particular way to use or overcome an object. This is described in detail under each attribute below,

but when in doubt, the Narrator can always use an object's most relevant attribute as a Difficulty for a test to interact with it.

Throughout this chapter, all objects listed as accoutrements are assigned a trait code. The code for a silver pocket watch, for example, is 'B1, C4, S3;', which means a silver pocket watch is an object with Bulk 1, Complexity 4, and Structure 3.

Bulk

Bulk is an abstraction of an object's size and weight. Each rank represents a broad category of objects. When determining the Bulk of an object that is not listed in the rules (or when doing so during the game when there is no time to look up an object), simply choose a rank whose approximate longest dimension or weight is closest to the object in question. This is not an exact science. For example, an Enfield infantry rifle is forty-four inches long, which is closer to three feet (36") than it is to any other rank's approximate dimension, so the Enfield is Bulk 3. The categories are usually broad enough that there is little room for overlap; however, if the Bulk of an object is unclear the Narrator has final say.

The higher of an object's Bulk or Structure is used as the Difficulty when attacking an object (see *Attacking Objects*, p. 85). If using the optional rule for encumbrance, Bulk also determines

BULK TABLE

Bulk	Approx. Dimension	Approx. Weight	Notes
0	3"	—	A tiny object that fits in a pocket and has negligible weight. Examples: coins, pebbles, grain, bullets
1	6"	1 lb.	A small, lightweight object that can be held in one hand. Examples: apple, pocket knife, derringer
2	12"	5 lb.	A larger and heavier object that can be held in one hand. Examples: book, pistol, combat knife
3	3'	20 lb.	An object that takes two hands to carry or a longer object that is specially crafted for balanced use in one hand. Examples: picnic basket, bread box, rucksack, broadsword, rifle
4	6'	200 lb.	An object that is roughly the size or weight of an adult man. Examples: bolt of cloth, door, icebox, grandfather clock, motor-bicycle, steamer trunk
5	12'	1 ton	An object that can contain a few people. Examples: carriage, shed, small boat
6	30'	10 tons	A vehicle, living or gathering space that can contain a small family or crew. Examples: a cottage, a train car, a coastal fishing boat
7	60'	20 tons	A very large vehicle, storage facility, living or gathering space that could comfortably house a large family. Examples: townhouse, train station, chapel
8	120'	N/A	A very spacious living or gathering space or a massive vehicle that could house many dozens of people. Examples: country manor, town church, schooner
9	300'	N/A	Palatial estates and grand monuments. Examples: Buckingham Palace, Big Ben, cathedral, construction dry dock
10	600'	N/A	The grandest buildings or monuments or the most enormous vessels built within the Empire. Examples: LZ-1 zeppelin, ocean liner, Westminster Abbey

Bulk continues to grow using the same scale according to dimension: Bulk 11 = 1,200', Bulk 12 = 3,000', Bulk 13 = 6,000', Bulk 14 = 12,000', etc.

how easily an object can be carried (see the Optional Rule: Encumbrance sidebar).

Complexity

Complexity is a measure of the extent and sophistication of the work needed to produce it from raw materials and the intricacy of an object's inner workings. Higher Complexity allows for more sophistication and a wider range of what an object can do, but also imposes greater difficulty in production and maintenance. An object's Complexity is also used as the Difficulty to use or overcome it. For example, the Complexity of a lock is the Difficulty to pick it (the *Baffling* function can be given to a device to raise the Difficulty it provides).

Structure

Structure represents an object's physical integrity and its ability to withstand damage. The higher the Structure of an object used to make weapons and armor, the more damage they can inflict or protect against. The *Structure Table* offers some guidance as to what Structure different materials should have, but verisimilitude should always be the deciding factor. An aluminum door might have Structure 5, but an aluminum can has Structure 2. Let common sense govern instances where there is doubt, and the Narrator always has final say.

The higher of an object's Bulk or Structure is used as the Difficulty when attacking an object. An object is also considered to possess an Armor rank equal to half its Structure, rounded down. This rank is reduced by one for fragile or hollow materials and increased by one if the object is reinforced. Objects with Structure 2 or less are always considered fragile and thus never have an Armor rank (see *Attacking Objects,* p. 85).

FUNCTIONS AND RESTRICTIONS

Functions define what an item does and how it can be used for special tasks such as making attacks in conflict, or to serve as transportation. The functions of most accoutrements do not need to be referenced during play, because they create the standard statistics and uses for items covered under the normal rules presented in Chapter 4. Restrictions are the operating considerations for accoutrements, such as how long it takes to reload a pistol. Like functions, most restrictions deal with situations and uses that are part of the standard rules. Some functions and restrictions, however, offer slight modifications or special features. In the accoutrement tables any functions or restrictions with special considerations are named so they can be referenced in the *Item Creation* section that begins on p. 198.

COMPLEXITY TABLE

Complexity	Material	Notes
1	Raw Material	Natural objects, unworked by human hands Examples: hay, rocks, sticks
2	Worked Material	Raw material that has been worked through human artifice into different shapes Examples: cloth & clothing, hammer, shovel, wooden planks
3	Refined Material, Moving Parts	Raw material that has gone through complex treatments and multi-staged processing to give it notably improved performance over worked material, and/or any object that uses moving parts to operate Examples: blended brocade, waterwheels, wheelbarrows, ship's rigging, a tempered high carbon steel sword
4	Complex Machine, Chemical Reactions	Not just an object, but a machine with moving parts that all work synchronously as part of its overall operation, or any object that requires chemical reactions to operate Examples: basic clockwork devices, looms, typewriters, steam engines
5	Powered Machine	Any object that is powered by combustion or electricity, requires complex chemical processes to function, or that use electrical or chemical power to operate Examples: automobile engine, light bulb, radio, telegraph
6	Computational Machine	A machine that can be programmed to perform specific tasks Examples: analytic engines, programmable and independent clockwork automata
7+	Unknown	Beyond the boundary of current science

STRUCTURE TABLE

Structure	Material	Notes
0	Gases	Any object that offers negligible physical resistance Examples: air
1	Liquids	Liquids and weak or semi-solids incapable of supporting more than a few ounces of weight at most Examples: mud, water
2	Flexible or Fragile Solids	Flexible solids capable of supporting some weight, soft materials that can be deformed and shaped by hand, or exceptionally fragile materials Examples: glass, heavy cloth, leather, rope
3	Rigid Solids	Inflexible solids used for construction Examples: hardened plaster, wood, stone
4	Durable Solids	Extremely dense natural materials, processed metals and or hardened alloys, or any Structure 3 material that has been reinforced and secured through construction Examples: Refined steel, fitted stone, reinforced wood
5	Dense Solids	Ultra-dense natural metals and Structure 4 materials that have been heavily refined or reinforced Examples: aluminum alloys, titanium, hardened fortifications
6+	Unknown	Objects this enduring are unknown to science and exist only through alchemical treatment

ACCOUTREMENTS

Gentlemen need proper attire. Adventurers need proper gear. Combatants need proper weaponry. The tables in this chapter should cover most accoutrements needed to tell a story in the Clockwork, but are not meant to be an exhaustive list. Historical catalogues, many of which can be found online, can be a more exhaustive resource for what would be available in the British Empire of 1896. These lists focus primarily on those items with specific rules needed for play, those inventions more common in the Clockwork than in history, and an array of other common accoutrements needed for Victorian adventurers.

CLOTHING AND PERSONAL EFFECTS

Cheap cotton from the United States and the industrialization of clothing manufacture have revolutionized clothing in England; people of all social classes are able to own more garments than they would have in previous centuries. Most clothing and personal items can be purchased at department stores or specialty shops in any major British city. Those who live in the country, or who want a more unusual item, can often order from a catalog.

ANALYTICAL ENGINES

These rare and expensive computing devices are used to quickly and easily solve sophisticated computations. They are primarily used for producing astronomical and mathematical tables, artillery range calculations, global commerce, and engineering; however, some of the excessively rich will display engines in their homes as signs of wealth. Their construction must be specially commissioned.

Each analytical engine requires a *Program* to be of use. The engine will supply a *Reason* aptitude and the program will supply a skill rank. When running the program, the engine may test *Reason* + skill to retrieve, collate, and calculate information. For example, a basic analytical engine (*Reason* 1) is running a basic *Bureaucracy* program (rank 1); it would be able to test with a combination of 2 to process data for business or industry. Refer to the *Analytical* (p. 200) and *Program* (p. 207) functions for details.

ANALYTICAL ENGINES AND PROGRAMS

Item	Ranks	Description	Cost
Analytic engine, basic	Reason 1	The simplest available analytic device, primarily a novelty. B3, C6, S3	4
Analytic engine, advanced	Reason 2	Universities, militaries, and banks have analytical devices of this caliber to handle complex equations. B4, C6, S3	5
Analytic engine, exceptional	Reason 3	A handful of the most advanced analytic machines in the world are this powerful. B5, C6, S3	6
Analytic program, basic	[Skill] 1	Simple programs encapsulate basic knowledge on a topic, good for checking work and little else. B2, C5, S2	3
Analytic program, advanced	[Skill] 2	More robust programs can be almost as good as a clerk, if run on the best analytical engines. B2, C5, S2	4
Analytic program, exceptional	[Skill] 3	The brightest minds might be able to produce programs of this sophistication. B3, C5, S2	5

CLOTHING AND PERSONAL EFFECTS

Item	Description	Cost
Clothing		
Clothes, *Class* 1	Clothes are an outward expression one's *Class* and place in society, so most individuals will wear the best quality clothing their *Means* can provide, even if those clothes represent a higher *Class* than they truly have. Clothes may also reflect one's profession (e.g. a lawyer's wig), or vocation (e.g. a blacksmith's apron), or a particular social circumstance (e.g. a ball gown). For more detailed information about clothing see *Don't Leave Home Without It* (p. 184). B3, C2–3, S2	1
Clothes, *Class* 2		2
Clothes, *Class* 3		3
Clothes, *Class* 4+		4
Armored Clothes	Reinforced clothing for workers in hazardous environments: the thick leather apron that protects a blacksmith, the helmet that protects a miner, and other safety gear needed for heavy manual labor and industrial work. B3, C2, S2, Armor 1	2
Protective Clothes	Goggles, a work apron, gloves, or any piece of clothing that protects the wearer, but not enough to grant Armor.	1
Reinforced greatcoat	A greatcoat is a wool topcoat that extends to the lower leg almost to the ankles, reinforced with hardened leather or caning to protect vital areas—popular with the police and military. It is treated to be *Weather-Resistant* (p. 210) and can be worn over any other clothing. B3, C3, S2, Armor 1	3
*Alchemical treatment	Any clothing can be reinforced and protected via alchemical transmutation to provide Armor 1, but this increases the Cost of the clothing by 1.	+1
Witchfinder leathers	The distinctive leather longcoat and high-peaked hat issued to all Witchfinders is heavily altered by alchemical transmutations to grant enough Armor to protect against multiple weapons. It is also *Weather-Resistant*. It is illegal for non-Witchfinders to possess. B3, C3, S4, Armor 2	Not for sale
Jewelry		
Jewelry, *Class* 2	Jewelry ranges from tiny adornments with some silver or semi-precious stones to intricate pieces designed to feature unusually large and expertly cut stones. The quality and type of jewelry is often used as an outward expression of *Class*. In addition to necklaces, rings, and earrings; hair adornments, watch-chains, and bracelets are common; coronets are not unheard of among aristocrats for occasions of state. B1, C3, S2–3	2
Jewelry, *Class* 3		3
Jewelry, *Class* 4		4
Jewelry, *Class* 5		5
Lady's Timepiece	A dainty wrist watch or other piece of jewelry with a timepiece enclosed—add 1 to the cost of jewelry to make it a timepiece. B1, C4, S3	+1
Pocket watch, gold	An ornate men's pocket watch suitable for the well-to-do. B1, C4, S3	3
Pocket watch, silver	A gentleman's timepiece, usually worn in the lower front pocket of the waistcoat with the chain exposed. B1, C4, S3	2
Wristwatch	Made popular among soldiers in the Boer War for tactical timing, these timepieces have some small popularity among the working classes.	2
Beauty		
A visit to a ladies' beauty salon	The new ladies' salons that have opened in recent years focus mainly on hair and other visible efforts of a lady's daily toilette.	2
Perfumes, colognes, hair & skin tonics	Any of a variety of scents, creams, salves, and oils used to maintain a healthy and pleasing appearance. B1, C3, S1	2
Shave & haircut	A quick visit to a common barber for a lather and cut.	1
Shaving kit	Safety razor, badger-hair brush, and a bar of shaving soap. B2, C2, S3	1

COMMUNICATION AND MEDIA

Although books and newspapers are the most effective ways of disseminating general information, most interpersonal communication happens through the royal mail, which is delivered several times a day in London. Those who need to communicate frequently with others during the course of a single day often rely on sending servants or hiring working class boys to deliver their handwritten messages. Telephones are available in upper class homes and there are a few payphones in upscale hotels and gentlemen's clubs, but unless one is calling an individual, business, or government office well funded enough to have a telephone, the device is of limited use. Telegraph machines are a more economical way to send short notes almost instantaneously over a long distance. All cities and most modest townships have telegraph offices. Messages are received and hand delivered or mailed as notes called telegrams.

COMMUNICATION AND MEDIA

Item or Service	Description	Cost
Media		
Book, simple	A chapbook, novel, or magazine printed in black and white on cheap paper with a few illustrations. B2, C3, S2	1
Book, fine	A well-made hardbound book printed on quality paper, frequently including multiple color plates. B2, C3, S2	2
Book, lavish	A beautifully-made, custom-bound book on heavy paper, suitable as a display piece in a library or drawing room. B2, C3, S2	3
Calling cards	Printed cards with your name, title/profession, and possibly a contact address. B1, C3, S2	2
Newspaper	A daily newspaper purchased from a street vendor. B2, C3, S2	1
Mail		
Postage, regional	Letter or small parcel delivery within the country.	1
Postage, international	Letter or small parcel delivery to another country. The cost is the same for both land and sea shipping, but overseas shipping takes much longer.	2
Postage, international air mail	Rapid delivery of letters and small packages on one of the international zeppelin lines. Currently unavailable in much of Africa and Asia.	3
Postage, large freight	Larger items cost more to ship. Bulk 4 items increase the Cost by +1; Bulk 5, +2. Larger items cannot be shipped by Royal Mail.	+1 or more
Telegram		
Telegram, local	A telegram is a written message transmitted almost instantaneously by electric wire or radio broadcast from one telegram office to another. Such offices exist in every major city and town in the Empire and most other powerful nations. The message can be hand delivered at the receiver's end for an additional fee. Hand delivery may take several hours longer in the countryside.	1
Telegram, regional or international		2
Telegram, hand delivery		Up to +1
Telephone		
Personal telephone	A home telephone set, including installation. Only useful in cities and towns with local or regional telephone exchanges. B2, C5, S3	3
Phone call	A call from a phone booth or shop to another person in the same local exchange. Only cities and certain wealthy neighborhoods have exchanges.	2
Phone service	Arrangement with a local phone shop to have one of their clerks write out the messages from any calls that come in to you.	2

ENTERTAINMENT

As in all ages past, food, drink, spectacle, and time spent with friends provide most of the entertainments society has to offer. Members of the working classes might enjoy a meal in a public house and several rounds of beer. They also attend carnivals and circuses when those come to town, or visit theatre halls to see plays, ventriloquists, magicians, and musical performances. In the countryside, picnics are well-loved. Public lectures and religious revivals are also popular, and literate people of all classes can enjoy the reading of novels—although some civil and religious authority figures worry that the reading of fiction will degrade public morals. Sailors and other dissolute individuals may visit gin-sinks, brothels, and opium dens.

Members of the upper classes attend symphonies, operas, and talks given at various social clubs by acclaimed academics, scientists, and explorers. The very wealthy fill their time by paying one another social calls or gathering at the exclusive social clubs to which they belong. Both men and women with the disposition to be athletic and a little extra money can enjoy cycling, tennis, and lawn games. The upper classes ride horses for exercise and pursue sports like fencing and polo. Upper class men of less resolute moral character may seek membership in hellfire clubs where absinthe and gambling are popular.

ENTERTAINMENT

Item or Service	Description	Cost
Carnival	Admission and a day of entertainments/refreshment at a carnival, arcade, or resort boardwalk.	2
Carousing	Cheap gin and ale can be had at home for less, but a proper night of revelry and inebriation at a public house will set you back a pound or two.	2
Instrument, simple	A penny whistle, fife, hand drum, or similar small instrument. B1–2, C2, S2–3	1
Instrument, fine	A bugle, guitar, flute, or most drums. B2–3, C3, S3	2
Instrument, lavish	Well-crafted instruments such as concertinas, fiddles, banjos, concert stringed instruments, brasses, harps, or bagpipes. B2–3, C3, S3	3
Instrument, extravagant	Symphony-quality orchestral instruments, harpsichords, autoharps. B2–4, C3–4, S3	4
Meal, simple	Meals range from portions of roasted meat or nuts purchased from street vendors,	1
Meal, fine	through simple servings of roast beef with potatoes as found in many public houses,	2
Meal, lavish	to the sophisticated fare of restaurants and hotels that provide wealthy patrons with the best imported wines and multi-course meals of wild-game.	3
Moving picture show	Admission to see short film novelties, usually about 30 minutes.	1
Music hall ticket	Admission to a music or dance hall for an evening.	1
Orchestral/opera ticket, gallery	A treat for professionals, and an opportunity to enjoy some of the finer culture of the upper class.	2
Orchestral/opera ticket, dress circle	Seating with a good view of the performance, and a chance to be seen among the ranks of the well-heeled. This is a must during the Season.	3
Orchestral/opera ticket, private box	Private booths with excellent views, acoustics, refreshments, and capable attendants to cater to a lavish evening of art.	4
Photograph	Sitting for a single shot and print as a memento, or the film to take such a photograph.	1
Photography session	A scheduled sitting at a photography studio, suitable for family pictures, professional portraits, or to use trick photography.	2
Prostitute	A throw with a working girl. Even after the Ripper murders and despite the efforts of reformers, many young women and some young men are still lured or tricked into the booming sex trade in cities.	1–3
Theater ticket, gallery	Admission to the cheap seats, possibly standing room.	1
Theater ticket, dress circle	Seats with an excellent view and some separation from the gallery.	2
Theater ticket, private box	Exclusive seating for the well-off found in large, metropolitan theaters.	3
Zoo or botanical garden	A single entry ticket for a stroll through a menagerie or public garden. Popular for courting or family outings.	1

ESOTERIC EFFECTS

In every major city in the Empire, there are mediums, true magi, and charlatans who perform rites for a fee or sell the strange artifacts that serve as objects of superstition or magical reagents. A few of these practitioners are genuinely capable of providing these services, but only those with some occult knowledge or connections will be able to reliably tell the illusion of mysticism from its reality. Unlike mystics and mediums, all alchemists are professionals capable of enhancing objects through transmutation, and exclusively provide authentic albeit expensive services.

MEDICAL SERVICES

In the last century, hospitals have transformed from being places where the sick are isolated to either die or recover, to institutions of medical care. Most medical or dental concerns are addressed by making an appointment with a doctor or dentist in town. The level of care available often depends on the patient's ability to pay, and those who cannot pay receive only a minimal level of support.

MEDICINES AND DRUGS

All entries in this category are Bulk 1, Complexity 5, and Structure 1 or 2. For the full effects of drugs, see see *Medicines*, p. 101.

SECURITY EQUIPMENT

The more one has to lose and the closer one lives to the criminal elements, the more necessary security equipment becomes. Simple locks and personal safes can be ordered from catalogs or purchased from local shops; more complicated security mechanisms might need to be specially ordered from a highly skilled locksmith.

Those seeking to circumvent such security measures can obtain lockpick sets from a crooked locksmith, or, if using *Streetwise*, from a fellow criminal in one of many flashouses, (public houses known to be congregating places for gang-members and highwaymen) in the less law-abiding quarters of any major city. All locks can be picked or otherwise opened by testing *Grace + Burglary* against a Difficulty set by the lock.

SURVIVAL GEAR

Survival gear, usually purchased through mail-order catalogs and specialty shops, is no longer strictly the property of military personnel and intrepid explorers. A number of prominent naturalists, including John Muir, have popularized the idea of leaving the city by rail to spend a few days in nature; it is no longer unheard of for middle class individuals to indulge in such adventures. Wealthy men may send servants with military experience on ahead to set up so the canvas tents and camp will be ready when they arrive.

ESOTERIC EFFECTS

Item	Description	Cost
Alchemical chalks	Metallic chalks of many different elements. The Cost is equal to the quality rank of the chalk. Ex: A single piece of rank 3 chalk—one that's capable of channeling a Strength 3 alchemical reaction—is a Cost 3 item (see *Alchemy*, p. 221). B0, C3, S2	1–5
Alchemists satchel	A satchel used for safely transporting alchemical chalks and supplies. The satchel holds up to twelve pieces of chalk. When first purchased, this may be any combination of chalks, each with a quality rank less than or equal to the purchaser's *Means*. B2, C2, S2	2
Fortune telling	Whether by palmistry, astrology, or via a tarot deck, the credulous waste their money on all manner of tricksters and charlatans supposedly telling their futures.	1
Holy water	Used in many rites of the Church and by some magicians, as well as the faithful in the hope it will protect them from harm at the hands of unnatural things, or to protect their health. B0, C1, S1	1
Magical reagents	If a magus is able to purchase reagents, the Cost of each use of a reagent is equal to their rank when used in a ritual. Ex: Buying grave-mold scraped from the coffin of a king would have a Cost of 4 if it was a rank 4 reagent (see *Ritual Magic*, p. 233)	1+
Magical rite	A written copy of a magical rite, frequently included as part of a broader writing. Rites with a Puissance of 3 or higher will usually sell for at least Cost 3, though price varies depending on the nature of the rite. Rites may be illegal to sell or own depending on the nature of the effect.	2+
Visit to a medium	A session with a supposed professional who can talk with spirits. It is a growing fad among spiritualists and others intrigued by popular mysticism. True mediums may demand a higher price or more unique payment.	2

MEDICAL SERVICES

Service	Description	Cost
Care from a Physician		
Dental Care	Visit and temporary treatment for toothache, have a tooth pulled, or be fitted with dentures.	2
Doctor or hospital visit	Basic diagnostic visit or checkup.	2
Long term care at a hospital	Any service that requires the patient to stay in the hospital for more than one day, including food, bed fees, and any basic supplies or anodynes used while in the hospital.	+1 to Cost of service
Surgery	Any invasive surgery. This includes the anesthetics and other material supplies used during the operation and for immediate aftercare.	3
Medical Devices		
Medical device, simple	A plainly made and mass-produced aid, such as an unadorned wooden cane, brace, or pair of crutches. Such devices cannot help the user avoid any test penalties, but do allow basic functionality that would otherwise be lost. B1–3, C2–3, S2–3	1
Medical device, fine	A well-made and possibly complicated device, such as a wheelchair or articulated corrective brace. Such devices usually reduce or remove test penalties in some circumstances. B2, C3, S2–3	2
Medical device, lavish	Beautifully-crafted objects made with valuable materials and that are often decorated to make them either unobtrusive or aesthetically pleasing such as clockwork prosthetics. Devices of this quality often allow the user to ignore penalties entirely. B2, C3–5, S3	3+

MEDICINES AND DRUGS

Medicine	Strength	Duration	Effect	Side Effect	Treats	Cost
Antifebrin	1	Day	Reduces Wound Penalties by 1	*Fatigued*	Pain, Fever	1
Antiseptic	0	Day	Prevents infection of open Wounds	None	Infection	2
Chloroform	4	Scene	*Incapacitated*	*Incapacitated* for 1 additional scene	None	2
Cocaine	5	Chapter	Halves Wound Penalties, regain one initiative card lost to Wounds.	-2 on *Composure* tests and Social Defense, *Obsessed*	Pain	2
Laudanum	4	Chapter	Reduces Wound Penalties by 2	*Dazed, Obsessed*	Pain	2
Mercury	3	Day	+1 to Defense against diseases	*Disoriented*	Malaria, Syphilis	2
Morphine	6	Scene	Reduces Wound Penalties by 4	*Dazed, Incapacitated, Obsessed*	Pain	3
Opium	5	Scene	Reduces Wound Penalties by 3	*Dazed, Delirious, Obsessed*	Pain	3

SECURITY EQUIPMENT

Item	Description	Cost
Handcuffs	Simple iron cuffs, locked with a key. Difficulty 4 to pick. B1, C3, S3	2
Lock, basic	The simplest door or hasp style lock with a single simple tumbler. Difficulty 3. B1, C3, S3	1
Lock, advanced	A more advanced lock requiring a complicated key. Difficulty 4. B1, C3, S3	2
Lock, exceptional	A finely crafted lock with multiple pinsets and a reinforced installation that makes it extremely difficult to pick, or a multi-tumbler combination lock. Difficulty 6. B2, C4, S4	3
Lockpick set	A set of well-made tools, including a torsion wrench and various picks and rakes. Necessary for picking locks, otherwise *Grace + Burglary* tests suffer a -2 penalty. B2, C3, S3	2
Personal safe	A small reinforced iron safe commonly used by businesses or wealthy individuals to store valuables and important documents, secured with a fine key lock or a combination lock. Difficulty 5. B3, C4, S4	3
Vault	A strongroom fit for a bank or treasury secured with a heavily reinforced metal door that incorporates both key and combination locks. Difficulty 7. B5, C4, S5	4

SURVIVAL GEAR

Item	Description	Cost
Bedroll	A thinly padded mat, small pillow, and thin coverlet. This *Collapsible* mat is Bulk 2 when packed up. B3, C2, S2	1
Camp cooking kit	A small griddle, pan, kettle, set of 2 steel plates, 2 forks, 2 spoons, and a canteen. B2, C2, S3	2
Camp stove	A short iron stove that can be used for cooking, or to help keep campers warm by burning coal, wood, or charcoal. B3, C3, S3	3
Camping or military pack	Based on military designs, camping packs are *Weather-Resistant* to protect their cargo, and can carry gear as though they were Bulk 4 thanks to their high *Capacity*. B3, C3, S2	2
Climbing kit	A pick/hammer, 10 pitons, set of crampons, and 100' of rope. A climbing kit is needed in order to make *Athletics* or *Survival* tests without penalty. B3, C2, S3	2
Doctor's kit	A doctor's bag including four uses of first aid supplies and antiseptics to stabilize a patient and prevent infection, a dose of laudanum, plus medical instruments to examine and perform dentistry, advanced wound care, and set bones. B3, C3, S2	3
First aid kit	A small bag including two uses of first aid supplies and antiseptics to stabilize a patient and prevent infection. B2, C3, S2	2
Firestarting kit	Safety matches, flint, steel, and tinder in a small waterproof case. B1, C3, S3	1
Fishing rod & tackle	A *Collapsible* fishing rod that packs up as Bulk 2, complete with a reel, line, hooks, sinker, and bait. B3, C3, S2	2
Foul weather gear	Waxed and waterproofed coat, hat, and boots with additional insulation. *Weather-Resistant*. B3, C3, S2	2
Tent, small	A canvas tent for 1 occupant, with a few *Collapsible* metal poles that allow it to pack up as Bulk 2. B4, C2, S2	1
Tent, large	A heavy canvas wall tent that has been sealed to keep out wind and water, making it *Weather Resistant*. It is large enough to sleep two to four and still have room for a small stove (separate item), but is *Collapsible* and packs up as Bulk 3. B4, C3, S2	2

TRAVEL

Item	Description	Cost
Fares		
Airship travel, local	Brief flights in balloons, blimps, or zeppelins. Usually more for sightseeing and the experience than for long-distance travel.	3
Local travel, simple	Movement within a city, or around the environs of a small town or country village via cart, ferry, or the common cars on the Underground. Uncomfortable but effective.	1
Local travel, extravagant	Travel within a city, or the environs of a town or village via a hansom cab, rented carriage, or private boat.	2
Regional travel, simple	A train ticket in a passenger car, seat on a coastal steamer, or spot on a carriage line; includes some room for luggage.	2
Regional travel, lavish	A ticket for second class passage by train or ship, usually with access to a separate dining or club area at specified times.	3
Regional travel, extravagant	A first class ticket that grants exclusive and luxurious accommodations with dedicated service, kept wholly separate from passengers travelling in more meager circumstances.	4
International travel	Increase the Cost of regional travel by one to cover the cost of international passports and fees, due to the longer distance traveled.	+1
Horses		
A draft horse	A workhorse used for farm work or to pull carts and carriages. *Speed* 1, moves once per turn.	2
A fox hunting horse	A muscular horse over 16 hands especially adept at jumping; riders need only a single successful skill test to successfully clear all the jumps in a scene. *Speed* 3, moves twice per turn.	3
A polo pony	An extremely agile horse trained for polo, under 15.2 hands. *Speed* 3, moves three times per turn.	3
A riding horse	A trained riding horse in good health; a mount for all occasions. *Speed* 3, moves twice per turn.	3
Riding tack	Saddle, bit and bridle, saddle blanket, and bags. B3, C2, S2	2
Stabling	Stabling, feed, and basic care by a groom or stablehand	2
Vehicles		
Automobile	Popular among the modern elite, automobiles give fast passage for up to five passengers. Distance trips must be planned in advance to avoid running out of gas. B5, C5, S4. *Speed* 3, *Handling* 1. Combustion *Power Supply*.	4
Bicycle	A new bicycle, including tools for basic maintenance. B3, C3, S3. *Speed* 2, *Handling* 2.	2
Carriage, simple	A four person carriage with a finished interior, modern springs and suspension, and a two-person driver's bench: good for both short and long distance travel. B4, C3, S3. *Speed* 2, *Handling* 1. Physical *Power Supply, Capacity, Passengers/Personnel*.	4
Carriage, lavish	Quality worthy of the nobility: a beautifully-appointed carriage that is the height of craftsmanship. It can comfortably seat up to 6 inside, and has room for the driver and up to 2 additional footmen. Storage space for several pieces of luggage. B4, C3, S3. *Speed* 2, *Handling* 2. Physical *Power Supply, Capacity, Passengers/Personnel, Opulent*.	5
Cart	A simple cart used to haul goods. B4, C3, S3, *Speed* 1, *Handling* 1. Physical *Power Supply, Capacity*.	2
Motor-bicycle	A heavy-frame bicycle with an attached motor, including tools for basic maintenance. B4, C5, S3. *Speed* 3, *Handling* 2. Combustion *Power Supply*.	4
Trap and harness	A one or two-person trap, used for leisure travel. B4, C3, S3. *Speed* 2, *Handling* 2. Physical *Power Supply*.	3
Fuel		
Gasoline	One rank of fuel for automobiles, motor-bicycles, and other combustion engines. B3, C3, S3	2

6

GUN LAWS AND LICENSES

Due to restrictions put in place by the Gun Licence Act of 1870, it is illegal to carry or use a firearm outside of your property without a valid licence. The price for an annual license is only ten shillings (Cost 2) and can be easily procured at any Post Office. Licensure is easily afforded by professionals, but it is a significant expense for most workers. As those of *Means* 1 are extraordinarily unlikely to own any land at all, this Act makes gun ownership and use for the majority of British subjects a de facto criminal action. The presence of a gun during the commission of a crime—even if it is never discharged—is enough to raise the charge to a capital offense for all involved, and results in executions each year.

For all of these reasons, players and Narrators are encouraged to discuss how strictly these laws will be enforced in their games. Games focusing on high society and social intrigues will likely use the laws to their fullest, whereas games taking place in the far reaches of the Empire, or those that are going for a pulp style of play may ignore them entirely.

CLOSE COMBAT WEAPONS

Weapon	Potency	Condition	Reach	Notes	Cost
Bayonet	2	*Bleeding*	Close	If fixed to a rifle, the bayonet has a Reach of *Extended*. B2, C2, S3	1
Blackjack	1	*Incapacitated*	Touch	Though tricky to use well, a good hit can knock out a foe. B2, C2, S3	1
Brass Knuckles	2	*Staggered*	Touch	+1 on all *Burglary* or *Streetwise* tests to conceal this weapon. B1, C2, S3	1
Bullwhip	2	*Disoriented, Unbalanced*	Extended	Useful for controlling opponents. B2, C2, S2	2
Cavalry Lance	4	*Undone*	Extended	Long bamboo or ash spears used by mounted military units. If used unmounted, reduce Potency to 2 and no weapon condition. B4, C2, S3	2
Hatchet	2	*Bleeding, Overwhelmed*	Close	Axes are rarely used, but can cause grievous injuries. B3, C2, S3	1
Horsewhip	2	*Disoriented*	Close	Good for driving horses and scattering street traffic. *Non-lethal*—cannot inflict Wounds. B2, C2, S2	2
Improvised Weapon	2	-	Close	Most common weapon on the streets, often taking the form of shivs or clubs.	-
Knife	2	*Bleeding*	Touch	*Quick.* Simple and effective. B2, C2, S3	1
Naval boarding pike	3	*Unbalanced*	Extended	A long, hooked and bladed polearm used in military or boarding actions and piracy. +1 on *Grace* + *Athletics* tests to board adjacent sea or air vessels. B4, C2, S3	2
Smallsword	2	*Bleeding*	Close	*Quick.* Any type of slim dueling sword. B3, C3, S4	2
Stiletto	2	*Moribund*	Touch	+1 on all *Burglary* or *Streetwise* tests to conceal this weapon. B1, C2, S3	1
Sword	3	*Bleeding*	Close	Any broadsword or longsword. B3, C3, S4	2
Sword-cane	2	*Bleeding*	Close	A blade hidden within a gentleman's cane, used among the upper classes. B3, C3, S3	2
Tesla Taser	2	*Incapacitated*	Touch	*Single Use.* A device that delivers a powerful electric shock but is otherwise *Non-Lethal* and cannot inflict Wounds. B2, C5, S3	3
Truncheon	2	*Dazed*	Close	Any club, cane or similar object. B3, C2, S3	1

TRAVEL

Among the privileged, international travel remains an essential aspect of a young person's education. Time spent in Paris and Rome suggest sophistication, while adventures in Africa imply a daring spirit. The lower classes generally only experience international travel if they join the army. Most Britons, however, travel when circumstances necessitate it, rather than for amusement. Long-distance domestic travel is achieved by train, regardless of social class, although more luxurious train carriages can be purchased by those who wish to avoid the *hoi polloi*. When traveling locally, the poor walk, even if the journey is many miles. Lower middle class people can hire hackney carriages in cities, while wealthy individuals have elegant horse-drawn carriages of their own. Horses for riding are essential among the wealthy, although carriages are the preferred mode of transport because they leave one's clothing unmussed upon arrival. Only the wealthiest can indulge in air travel aboard the few commercial airships that have recently come into service, and such trips are prized for both their speed and the stories they provide for the club.

Mounts and Vehicles in Conflict

Mounts and vehicles move just like characters with a few exceptions. Vehicles have two extra attributes that govern how fast and far they can move: *Speed* and *Handling*. In chase situations, a vehicle with a higher *Speed* rank may choose to flee at the end of the first conflict sequence and vehicles of lower *Speed* cannot follow. A vehicle's *Handling* rank is how many times it can move per turn in conflict. This is an abstraction of how deftly the vehicle can move around or through terrain, quickly alter its direction, and deal with the ever changing layout of a conflict. See the *Speed* (p. 209) and Handling (p. 203) functions for more information.

Mounts use Speed in the same way vehicles do, but as they are organic creatures, they are created as Narrator characters rather than as objects. Thus, they use the Extra Move asset from Narrator character creation rather than the Handling function from item creation. However, for the purposes of movement in conflict, these traits are used interchangeably (see the Extra Move asset, p. 301).

WEAPONS

Most people in Britain do not own weapons. Only in the industrial slums is violence common enough for weaponry to be a regular part of life and these tend to be improvised: clubs, blackjacks, and iron spikes constitute the majority, knives are frequent, while brass knuckles or short swords are more uncommon. Guns are extremely rare because of the stiff legal penalties associated with carrying them without an expensive license or using them to commit a crime. Among the more privileged classes, and those living in the country, the cane is the preferred improvised weapon.

FIREARMS & RANGED WEAPONS

Weapon	Potency	Condition	Reach	Notes	Cost
Accoutrements					
Ammunition	—	—	—	1 Load of ammunition for any firearm listed below. B1, C3, S3	1
Gun license	—	—	—	Required to use firearms when off your property. B1, C3, S2	2
Ranged Weapons					
Longbow	3	*Overwhelmed*	*Long Range*	Single Shot, maneuver to reload. B4, C3, S3	2
Revolver	3	*Bleeding*	*Short Range*	The Colt New Service, Enfield Mk II. 6 round Load, maneuver to reload. B2, C3, S3	2
Rifle	4	*Moribund*	*Long Range*	Lee-Enfield, Winchester. 10 round Load, maneuver to reload. B3, C3, S3	3
Shortbow	2	*Staggered*	*Long Range*	Single Shot, maneuver to reload. B3, C3, S3	1
Shotgun	3	*Crippled*	*Short Range*	2 round Load, action to reload. +1 to hit targets at *Extended* Reach or closer. B3, C3, S3	
Small Pistol	2	*Bleeding*	*Extended*	Derringer, Pepperbox, Zig-Zag. 2 round Load, maneuver to reload. B1, C3, S3	2
Thrown Weapons					
Grenade	3	*Crippled*	*Short Range*	Area of effect (1 zone of control), ignores Guard. Illegal. B2, C3, S3	3
Throwing Knife	2	*Bleeding*	*Extended*	*Quick*. A balanced throwing blade. B2, C3, S3	1

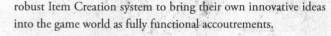

ITEM CREATION

"An inventor is a person who makes an ingenious arrangement of wheels, levers and springs, and believes it civilization." —Ambrose Bierce

A steampunk world is full of astounding creations utilizing clock-work and chemicals, electricity and steam. Some of these items are found throughout the Empire, and are produced by tradesmen using well-known, reliable patterns. Other items are unique curiosities manifested in steel and steam through the hard work of ingenious inventors.

Making most common objects does not require use of the Item Creation system: any character with a single rank in a relevant skill can follow patterns to create common goods and everyday objects. In fact, tradesman who create ordinary items that they sell for their livelihood are simply assumed to do so successfully, as long as they have the necessary time and skill. Additionally, quick and straight-forward fabrication such as cutting a reed to make a breathing tube or tearing cloth into strips for bandages is covered under the basic use of applicable skills. Item Creation is not necessary in these and similar circumstances.

There are, however, inspired men and women who see far beyond the ordinary boundaries of day to day fabrication. By taking one or more of the *Inventor* assets (see *Assets*, p. 155), exceptional individuals can step beyond the norm, and harness the inspiration necessary to create their own unique designs. For those wanting to explore cutting edge technology and test bold new ideas, the Item Creation system provides a vast array of exciting possibilities, allowing for the creation of everything from custom clockwork automata to airships and submarines. *Inventors* use the

robust Item Creation system to bring their own innovative ideas into the game world as fully functional accoutrements.

CREATING ITEMS FROM PATTERNS

All characters who have ranks in the necessary skills can create any item for which they have a pattern. A pattern can be something as formal as a blueprint or as informal as a set of memorized instructions passed from artisan to apprentice. The Narrator has final say in what can be used as a pattern.

Each pattern will supply a required trait test using the *Artisan*, *Engineering*, or *Science* skill and its Difficulty. It will also provide the Cost required for raw materials and the Time production will take. Some complicated items can require more than one trait test. If the character has the time, can supply the raw materials, and successfully make the necessary trait tests, then she makes the item described in the pattern. The complete process of constructing an item is described in detail in *Constructing Items* beginning on p. 213.

Making Patterned Items as an Occupation

Most tradesman across the Empire make their living creating items from patterns. They buy raw materials, manufacture goods, and sell them to provide the income by which they subsist. None of these activities need to be tracked or tested. It is assumed that the characters who work a trade for their livelihood are producing related items, re-investing in buying raw materials and tools, paying their fees and taxes, and generally getting on with their lives when not engaged in the events of the game. This is what sustains their *Means* and provides their weekly income. No extra monies are gained through these pursuits.

DESIGNING NEW ITEMS

The creativity of *Inventors* far exceeds the limited patterns designed by their forebears. Characters that take one or more of the three *Inventor* assets may design and create their own unique designs by following these steps:

1. **Choose Functions:** Each *Inventor* has a goal for what her invention is meant to do. Functions describe what an object does, and help define its attributes and how time consuming and difficult it is to make. To design an invention, the *Inventor* first chooses one or more functions she desires from the list—all items must have at least one function. These functions define how the item will be used in gameplay. Describing the item's appearance and operational minutiae are left to the player and Narrator to finalize, as these aspects add flavor to the created item and do not affect its utility. The functions chosen also influence the skill used to build the design. The list of functions begins on the next page.

2. **Choose Restrictions:** Restrictions are drawbacks or complications that place some limitation on the production or use of an object. Giving an invention restrictions reduces the Difficulty to create it. Restrictions can be crucial inclusions to ensure a design can be reliably produced at a reasonable Difficulty. The list of restrictions begins on p. 211.
3. **Determine Difficulty:** Add up the Difficulty ranks of all chosen functions and subtract the reductions from restrictions to yield the final Difficulty for the trait test made to produce the item.
4. **Determine Attributes, Time, and Cost:** Review all the chosen functions and restrictions to look at the minimum or maximum required attributes of Bulk, Complexity, and Structure. Your finished item may have attributes of any rank between the minimum and maximum.
   a. The Time needed to construct the item is based on its total attribute ranks. Add together the item's ranks in Bulk, Complexity, and Structure. This sum determines the ranks of Time needed to build the design. See the Time chart on p. 214 for the duration of each rank of Time.
   b. The Cost rank of the project is equal to the highest attribute –2. You must have *Means* equal to the Cost, or have access to material equal to that rank of *Means* in order to build the design.

5. **Production Test:** Building an item from a completed design requires a production test of the builder's *Reason* + the skill associated with the functions chosen for the device. Designs that use *Fabricator* functions can be produced with *Reason + Artisan* tests, those that use *Innovator* functions can be produced with *Reason + Science* tests, and those that use *Machinist* functions can be produced with *Reason + Engineering* tests. If a design uses functions from multiple disciplines, the test is made with the lowest applicable trait combination. Success on the test produces the device, while failure yields nothing. Full details on production tests and their Time and Costs are detailed on p. 213.

Separate Parts

If an invention is created with a *Power Source*, it will require a *Power Supply*. If one is created with a *Weapon Mount*, it may house a weapon. If an invention is created with the *Analytical*, *Applied Force*, or *Sensors* functions, it may run *Programs*. Weapons, *Power Supplies*, and *Programs* are created as separate items that are then used with the invention. These separate parts may be swapped out for others of a like kind during play.

FUNCTIONS

Clockwork: Dominion uses abstraction to keep play focused on the story and player actions, and the Item Creation system is no exception to that approach. The list of functions is not meant to represent every possible idea, and the function and restriction descriptions will not exhaustively catalogue every possible scenario or interaction. When an unusual circumstance arises, the Narrator always has the final say over how it is handled in the game.

Before producing an item or device, the players and Narrators should discuss how the combined functions in a design will work together. The rules cover what the object does, but the creator should have an idea of how the device would work and describe it in a way that makes sense. This ensures everyone is clear concerning how the invention works, what it can do, and how it will impact the game. It also ensures that players do not create items that could not exist simply by putting a series of functions together, and that the Narrator knows what to expect as the invention is used in the story.

Airtight Seal

Asset: *Inventor: Fabricator*
Requires: Bulk 1+, Structure 2+
Difficulty: +1

Function: The item provides an airtight seal for the space it encloses. All or part of the object is sealed against the exchange of gases or passage of liquids between the airtight object and anything outside.

Common Uses: This is useful when creating gasmasks or protective clothing for working with or in noxious substances, as it

can preventing the wearer from coming in contact with them in a harmful way. If applied to a vehicle with the *Submersible* function, it would allow the vessel to safely carry crew members underwater.

Ammunition/Consumables

Asset: *Inventor: Machinist*
Requires: Complexity 3+, Structure 3+, *Reload Time* restriction
Difficulty: +1 per standard Load

Function: The item requires ammunition or some other consumable resource to use, and this function allows multiple uses of the consumable to be loaded into the item itself so it may be used multiple times before it needs reloading. The standard Load is based on the Bulk of the item: Bulk 1 can contain a maximum Load of 1 consumable; Bulk 2, up to 6; Bulk 3, up to 10; Bulk 4, up to 50; Bulk 5, up to 100. An object may be made to house an additional Load of consumables for each rank the Difficulty of this function is raised. For example, a Bulk 2 item designed with *Ammunition/Consumables* for +2 Difficulty has a maximum Load of 12 consumables, a Bulk 2 item with *Ammunition/Consumables* for +3 Difficulty has a maximum Load of 18, etc. At the Narrator's discretion, consumables that do not have functions themselves can be produced with a relevant trait test, considered to be part of the characters occupation (see *Making Patterned Items as an Occupation*, opposite page), or simply purchased.

Common Uses: Firearm designs use this function for ammunition, but it is also put to use in domestic items such as cameras that use this function to determine how much film they can hold.

Analytical

Asset: *Inventor: Innovator*

Requires: Complexity 6+, Structure 3+, Bulk 2 + 1 Bulk per rank of *Analytical*, *Power Source* function

Difficulty: +2 per rank of *Reason*

Function: Analytical engines are the great computational powerhouses of our generation. Any item given this function contains an analytical engine, a machine used for information retrieval and complex mathematical computation. For each +2 Difficulty taken with the *Analytical* function, the resulting device will gain a rank of *Reason*. For example, a design that uses *Analytical* at +4 Difficulty produces an engine with *Reason* 2, whereas one that uses *Analytical* at +6 Difficulty produces an engine with *Reason* 3, etc.

Any device created with the analytical function may make passive trait tests regarding information to which it has access. To do this, it requires a program and data. Programs are designed as separate items with the *Program* function. The analytic engine provides the *Reason* aptitude rank and the program provides the skill rank. Data may come from user entry, punched paper tape archives (treat as a library), or through the *Sensor* function. The device may then make passive trait tests to respond to stimuli, collate or calculate information, or simply answer questions based on the data. The Difficulty for the test is determined normally.

Since the Analytical device has only the *Reason* aptitude, the passive trait tests it makes must be those that a character would use her *Reason* to accomplish; however, an analytic engine can perform in an action what would take a person one scene to accomplish. Regardless of the skills known by the user, the device can only make trait tests using the skill provided by the program(s) it is currently running. An analytical machine can run a maximum of one program at a time per rank of *Reason*.

Common Uses: Some of the best and brightest innovators are working in analytics, and have produced wonderful mechanical computing machines for use in scientific research in physics and natural phenomena, finance and banking, and military endeavors. Academic institutions, major banks, government agencies, and the Navy all have collections of analytic machines to perform complex calculations. Some of the truly wealthy have also purchased them for private use to pursue their own interests. See the *Program* function for program examples.

Applied Force

Asset: *Inventor: Machinist*

Requires: Complexity 4+, Structure 3+, *Power Source* function, *Refined Materials* restriction

Difficulty: +2 per rank of aptitude

Function: This function grants the device either a *Grace* or *Vigor* aptitude of its own. For each +2 Difficulty to the design the function grants one rank of the chosen aptitude. A design that included *Applied Force: Grace* at +2 Difficulty produces an item with *Grace* 1, and one that included *Applied Force: Vigor* at +4 Difficulty produces a device with *Vigor* 2. This function may be included twice in the same design to grant a device ranks in both aptitudes. If so, the

Difficulty modifiers are tracked separately and both are added to the final Difficulty of the creation test. If the two examples above were both used in the same design, it would have *Applied Force: Grace* at +2 and *Applied Force: Vigor* at +4 for a total modifier of +6 Difficulty, and would produce a device with *Grace 1* and *Vigor 2*.

The device requires a *Power Source* with an output equal to its highest aptitude rank in order to work, otherwise it is inert. For example, a device with *Grace* 2 and *Vigor* 3 would require a *Power Source* with an output of at least 3.

If the device is an accoutrement worn and used by a character, the character may use the device's aptitude instead of her own for any trait test that uses that aptitude. Characters using such devices, or vehicles that have *Vigor* scores to do heavy moving, can use the granted score as part of passive tests.

Devices with the *Applied Force* function can run a single program at a time. Programs are created separately with the *Program* function. When the program is used, it adds a skill to the device, allowing it to make its own trait tests. See the *Program* function, p. 207.

Common Uses: This function is most commonly used in the newest industrial machines such as those used in major railroad and canal projects. These machines move vast quantities of earth and stone, depending on a high *Vigor* to do their work. A few gifted machinists have produced some clockwork prosthetics that are incredibly deft, or automatons that are able to labor on their own, but such wonders are few and far between. The future may hold more promising uses of this function: penny dreadfuls posit unbelievable futures where men wear machines like suits to perform incredible feats of strength.

Area of Effect

Asset: *Inventor: Innovator* or *Machinist*

Requires: *Explosive*, *Poison*, or *Potent* function

Difficulty: +2 per zone of control affected

Function: When the item is used, it targets everyone and everything in an area. Including this function with +2 Difficulty lets the device affect all targets in a single zone of control when it is used. Each time the Difficulty is increased by a further +2, it expands the area affected by its use to an additional, adjacent zone of control. For example, an item built from a design that includes *Area of Effect* for +4 Difficulty will affect two adjacent zones of control, taking it for +6 Difficulty allows it to affect three adjacent zones of control, etc.

Common Uses: All manner of *Explosive* weapons depend on having an *Area of Effect* to injure multiple targets simultaneously. *Gaseous* and *Contact Poisons* can likewise be packed into containers that will detonate or release them to spread them across an area.

Armor

Asset: *Inventor: Fabricator*

Requires: Bulk 3+, Structure 2+

Difficulty: +2 per rank of Armor

Function: Objects will naturally have ranks of Armor (see *Attacking Objects*, p. 85), but will not provide that protection to people wearing or using them unless this function is used. An item with *Armor* is designed to protect its user, and grants her a physical

Armor value. Items that are worn or carried must be hollow or thin and light, and so cannot provide more ranks of Armor than half the object's Structure, rounded down. For example, a wooden shield with a Structure of 3 could only use this function to create Armor 1, since ½ of 3 = 1.5, rounded down is 1. A chestplate made of alchemically hardened steel with a Structure of 6 could take this function to create Armor 3, since ½ of 6 = 3. This function will increase the difficulty of the production test by +2 for each point of Armor it creates.

Common Uses: The widespread use of firearms in war has drastically reduced the use of armor on the battlefield, but as police forces have become better-established, many employ reinforced greatcoats and helmets as standard uniforms to provide basic protection for officers. With the growing practice of alchemy allowing for the production of phenomenally strong materials, there is also the renewed possibility of creating armor that protects against small arms fire.

Baffling

Asset: *Inventor: Fabricator* or *Machinist*
Requires: Complexity 3+, Structure 3+
Difficulty: +2 per rank of *Baffling*

Function: Many devices that require tests to use or overcome have a standard Difficulty equal to their Complexity. Including the *Baffling* function when creating a device increases the Difficulty to decipher, operate, overcome, or repair that device. An item designed with the *Baffling* function at +2 Difficulty increases the Difficulty to use or overcome the item by 1, a *Baffling* design at +4 Difficulty increases the Difficulty to use or overcome the item by 2, etc.

Common Uses: This function is almost exclusively used with locks and other devices using the *Secure* function to make them harder to overcome. Some paranoid inventors deliberately design their machines to be needlessly complex so that only they or other specialists can operate or repair them.

When paired with functions that record or transmit information *Baffling* can be used to design encoders/decoders that encrypt and translate information being transmitted by the device. Successfully unscrambling information encoded by such a device tests *Reason + Academics* against a Difficulty equal to the Complexity of the device plus the increases from the *Baffling* function.

Bespoke Design

Asset: *Inventor: Innovator* or *Machinist*
Requires: Bulk 2+, Complexity 2+, Structure 2+
Difficulty: +1

Function: The item is specially sized and shaped for use by a specific person. By carefully accounting for their unique physique and kinesthetics, anyone else attempting to use the device finds it awkward and uncomfortable, suffering a −2 penalty on tests to use the device. The Narrator has final say over whether or not an item can be designed with this function.

Common Uses: Made-to-measure clothing with a *Bespoke Design* is the standard for those of *Means* 2 or higher, but is most useful when applied to more utilitarian accoutrements. *Prosthetics,*

backpacks with the *Capacity* function, pieces of armor, or other special gear frequently incorporates this function to ensure comfortable wear and to make objects less desirable to thieves.

Camera

Asset: *Inventor: Innovator* or *Machinist*
Requires: Bulk 3+, Complexity 3+, Structure 3+, *Ammunition/ Consumables* function
Difficulty: +2

Function: The item is able to take photographs. To operate, film must be loaded into the camera as a consumable. The film must be developed separately outside the camera.

Common Uses: Photography has been a celebrated addition to Victorian culture for years, and advances in the art and science of taking and developing pictures have led to wonderful new cameras. Most frequently a stand-alone object, there is much speculation as to what amazing images it may be possible to capture in the future with advances to optics and if anyone ever managed to produce a camera that was also *Submersible*.

With the state of foreign diplomacy what it is, discreet cameras that were *Collapsible* would be welcome tools for the Foreign Service. Such tiny items could potentially record all sorts of valuable information, but would be limited by their small access to film *Consumables* and the *Reload Time* required to change them out.

Capacity

Asset: *Inventor: Fabricator* or *Machinist*
Requires: Structure 2+
Difficulty: +1 to establish *Capacity* equal to Bulk, additional +1 to increase it by one.

Function: The item is capable of housing people, goods, and cargo. An item with this function has a usable space for cargo equal to its Bulk. Taking this function at Difficulty +2 allows the item to have a *Capacity* as though its Bulk were one higher. Buildings and vehicles that house or carry people will use the *Capacity* function to cover cargo and usable space, but require the *Passengers/Personnel* function to accommodate people with any degree of comfort.

Common Uses: Vehicles and personal packs depend on the *Capacity* function to carry cargo and accoutrements, and almost every means of transit needs to take this function. Those that carry passengers or provide accommodations for crew will likewise need the *Passengers/Personnel* function. See the *Bulk* table on p. 185 for examples of items, structures, and vehicles of various Bulk ranks.

Collapsible

Asset: *Inventor: Fabricator*
Requires: None
Difficulty: +1

Function: While not in use the item can be collapsed to take up less space, making it easier to transport. Treat the object as though its Bulk were 1 lower when it is not in use. Getting the item in a working state always requires one maneuver in addition to any other time needed as defined by other design restrictions.

Common Uses: Many accoutrements used in travel and exploration make use of this function so they are more portable—everything from telescopes with cutting edge optics, to camping gear, and even full writing desks are often made *Collapsible*. Those who travel for more clandestine purposes can also benefit from having a few cleverly-hidden *Collapsible* weapons that make use of the *Potent* and *Weapon Condition* functions. The smaller the Bulk of an item, the harder it is to detect with *Focus* tests.

Communicator

Asset: *Inventor: Innovator* or *Machinist*
Requires: Bulk 2+, Complexity 4+, Structure 3+
Difficulty: +2

Function: The object can communicate spoken or written language in an analog format across a hardwire line to another machine with the *Communicator* function. A separate machine with this function must exist on both ends of the communication, otherwise the signal will be lost and no messages can be deciphered. A machine that also takes the *Wireless Transmission* function may communicate without the use of hardwires.

Common Uses: The telegraph system is by far the most widespread implementation of devices with this function, but many metropolitan cities have built modest telephone networks. Promising work is being done to develop wireless communicators, but such radio devices are still rarities. If a communication device includes the *Baffling* function, the transmissions themselves can be scrambled and encoded by the machine. If the same design is used to create a paired device the second machine can decode the the data automatically without requiring a test. Otherwise decoding the information tests *Reason + Academics* against a Difficulty of the device's Complexity, +1 per rank of *Baffling*.

Cover

Asset: *Inventor: Fabricator*
Requires: Bulk 3+, Structure 2 provides light cover, Structure 3+ provides heavy cover
Difficulty: +1

Function: At bulk 3 the item is capable of acting as cover for those that are carrying it, or provides cover for those that are on the item's exterior if it is Bulk 4+. The Bulk and Structure also determine whether it provides light or heavy cover as described above. This function is the result of the item including additional screens or plating extending from its exterior to provide cover to those carrying or riding on it. The function is not necessary to provide protection to anyone inside the item. See *Cover and Aiming*, p. 82.

Common Uses: The crenels and merlons of castles and fortifications are the classic example of *Cover* being incorporated into a design, but modern military ships will often include *Cover* so their topdecks allow gun crews to work without directly exposing them to enemy fire. Early prototypes of new field artillery are refreshing the medieval idea of a mobile mantlet to provide *Cover*, while a *Weapon Mount* allows them to use it as a platform to operate a heavy weapon.

Explosive

Asset: *Inventor: Innovator*
Requires: Bulk 1+, Complexity 4+, *Area of Effect* function, *Potent* function, *Single Use* restriction
Difficulty: +2

Function: The item causes an explosion at its point of use: the blast hits all people and objects as determined by its *Area of Effect*, wounding living things and damaging objects if the blast is *Potent* enough to overcome their Armor. To determine whether an explosion places any conditions, make a test of the item's Bulk + Potency against the physical Defense of all targets.

Grenades and similar objects are thrown by testing *Grace + Athletics*, Difficulty 3. Success places the grenade where the thrower wants, failure indicates it lands in a different zone of control in a random direction. A remarkable or catastrophic failure causes the thrower to fumble the device and drop it within their own zone of control.

Common Uses: Weapons of war make use of this function, and as such, it is always found in items that are *Potent*. The ability to affect a large area also greatly benefits devices that inflict weapon conditions such as *Burning*.

Filter

Asset: *Inventor: Fabricator*
Requires: Bulk 2+, Structure 2+, Complexity 3, *Airtight Seal* function
Difficulty: +1 liquid filtration, +2 for liquid and gas filtration

Function: The invention incorporates a filtration device that can remove particles from their surroundings. If taken at +1 Difficulty to the design, the filters can strain material out of liquids and flowing solids such as mud. If taken at +2 Difficulty, the filters is capable of removing much smaller particles and can filter both liquids and gases. The designer specifies what the filter will remove: it can sift out material by size, be built to remove toxins, poisons, allergens, or a specific substance. Using a device with appropriate filters makes characters at least ill-prepared for *Extreme Environments* (p. 96) with smoke and poisonous gases, and may provide other bonuses at Narrator discretion.

Common Uses: Simple filters have long been used in mining, dyeing, medicine, and brewing, but industry is always making more use of rarified materials that require filtration for purity and safety. Workers, physicians, and pharmacists may need specialized filters to do their work safely, and those travelling in the wilds or as part of military service may take liquid filters to clean their water and hopefully avoid disease.

Flight: Powered

Asset: *Inventor: Machinist*
Requires: Complexity 4+, Structure 2+, *Handling*, *Power Source*, and *Speed* functions
Difficulty: +3

Function: The item can fly under its own power. In addition to the amount of lateral movement provided by its *Handling* and *Speed* functions, the vehicle can climb at a speed of approximately

10' (one zone of control) or descend at a speed of 20' (two zones of control) during each move.

Movement while flying is automatic and cannot be stopped unless the object is rendered *Nonfunctional* or is *Destroyed*. If a flying device is engaged in a conflict, no characters in the device need to use a move for the vehicle to keep flying, it will move constantly. If all characters in a conflict are aboard the same flying vehicle, the actual movement of the vehicle through the air is irrelevant. If conflict involves multiple flying devices they will only move relative to each other. At the end of each sequence, the pilot flying the device with the highest *Speed* may choose to outrun his opponents and leave the conflict.

Common Uses: To date, powered flight is limited to lighter-than-air craft like blimps and zeppelins, but a number of *Inventors* have already made extensive studies of heavier-than-air craft and are testing prototypes. Blimps generally only have *Handling* and *Speed* ratings of 1 although their *Capacity* often allows them to carry large amounts of cargo or even take *Passengers/Personnel*. Zeppelins use the same functions, but tend to move much faster and have additional ranks of *Speed*. Since most airships fly at altitudes of only a few thousand feet they do not need to pressurize their cabins and don't need an *Airtight Seal* to remain comfortable, but any vessel travelling near or above 8,000 feet will want to include it.

As airships have begun seeing more frequent use—especially in the South China Sea and over Polynesia—there have been reports of pirates taking to the air as well. Though their balloons and blimps can often be chased off with small arms fire, some airships that expect to risk combat may need to be designed with *Weapon Mounts*.

Handling

Asset: *Inventor: Fabricator* or *Machinist*
Requires: Complexity 3+, *Speed* function
Difficulty: +1 per movement increment

Function: Devices that are meant to move nimbly in short distances or in conflicts rely on their *Handling*; devices without *Handling* are too ponderous to cover any ground quickly enough to matter in conflict. For each +1 Difficulty added to the production test, the *Handling* function allows the device to traverse up to one zone of control each time it takes a move as part of a turn in conflict. Increasing the Difficulty increases the maximum number of zones of control it can traverse as part of a single move. For example, an item built from a design including the *Handling* function for +2 Difficulty can travel up to two zones of control each time it takes a move during conflict, whereas a device including the *Handling* function at +3 Difficulty could traverse up to three zones of control in a single move, etc.

Common Uses: Since vehicles need to have some *Handling* to be useful, this function is found with several others common to almost every vehicle: *Speed*, a *Power Source*, and frequently *Capacity* and *Passengers/Personnel*. Modern inventions that allow for the mechanization of small, nimble vehicles like motorized bicycles or automata are notable for their *Handling*.

Wheeled vehicles dependant on user-propelled power usually have a *Handling* rating of 1 or 2. Those that use a mechanical *Power Source* often have a *Handling* of 3. No modern vehicle can be built with higher than *Handling* 4.

Huge

Asset: *Inventor: Fabricator, Innovator,* or *Machinist*
Requires: All items with a Bulk of 6+ must take this function and must take the same level of *Crew Build* as a restriction.
Difficulty: +1 per every two Bulk over 4

Function: Especially large items are challenging to build, and the *Huge* function must be included in the design for every item with a Bulk greater than 5. The function Difficulty is +1 for Bulk 6 items, +2 for Bulk 7–8, +3 for Bulk 9–10, etc.

Common Uses: The construction of buildings and large vehicles is the only regular use of this function, as other designs gain little from their size alone. Large items can potentially have a very high *Capacity*, and are often built expressly to house large amounts of goods or to provide temporary or permanent housing for occupants with the *Passengers/Personnel* function. As building techniques continually improve, many modern objects of this size are also treated to be *Weather-Resistant* so their users/occupants are comfortably protected from the elements.

Increased Reach

Asset: *Inventor: Fabricator* or *Machinist*

Requires: Bulk 1+, Complexity 2+, Cannot be combined with the *Reduced Reach* restriction.

Difficulty: +1 for *Extended*, +2 for *Short Range*, +3 for *Long Range*

Function: All items begin with a base Reach of *Close*. Objects designed with *Increased Reach* at +1 Difficulty will have a Reach of *Extended*; at +2 Difficulty, they have a Reach of *Short Range;* and at +3 Difficulty, they will have a Reach of *Long Range*. If Reach is increased to *Short Range* or *Long Range*, the item design must also include the *Ammunition/Consumables* function.

Common Uses: Firearms rely on their *Increased Reach* function to be effective, though polearms, whips, and other archaic weapons also incorporate this function. A rare few designs for new industrial machines also use this function to operate across a large area despite being stationary.

Non-Lethal

Asset: *Inventor: Fabricator, Innovator,* or *Machinist*

Requires: *Potent* function

Difficulty: +1

Function: A *Non-Lethal* weapon cannot inflict Wounds apart from a malfunction or use as an improvised weapon, as it incorporates design features to minimize the damage done to its targets.

Common Uses: Although exceedingly rare, some arms manufacturers or independent designers have begun to test new designs intended for use by police forces that can effectively subdue their targets, but minimize the chance of Wounding them.

Optics

Asset: *Inventor: Innovator* or *Machinist*

Requires: Bulk 2+, Complexity 3+,

Difficulty: +1 per magnification category

Function: A device with this function uses magnification to allow the user to view objects more clearly even if they are far away or very small. Items designed with *Optics* at +1 Difficulty can see small objects clearly, or over long distances via a 10x magnification factor. For +2 Difficulty up to 50x magnification is available, +3 Difficulty allows for up to 100x magnification. Including *Optics* at +4 Difficulty enables up to 200x magnification.

Many designs using *Optics*—such as telescopes or microscopes—use this as the only function. It is possible for a single design to incorporate more than one option from the list, in which case the total Difficulty from this function is the sum of all included options. A microscope capable of 100x, and 200x magnification would add 3 + 4 = 7 Difficulty to a production test.

Common Uses: Optics have a wide variety of uses. When used with a *Projectile Weapon* with a Reach of *Long Range*, an optic scope will increase the visible range by the magnification amount. 10x optics are also used for binoculars and small telescopes. 50x magnification is used for astronomy, and is the minimum necessary to see details on the Moon. Any device with magnification ratings of 100x or higher is likely to be found in the labs and observatories of universities: this level of magnification is required to be able to study microorganisms and planets in our solar system. Meanwhile, 200x magnification is needed to study the structure of individual cells or to see details of most of the distant planets and large satellites in the solar system.

Passengers/Personnel

Asset: *Inventor: Fabricator*

Requires: Bulk 4+, *Capacity* function

Difficulty: +1

Function: The item is capable of accommodating people. This includes all furnishings, sleeping quarters, toilet facilities, and personal necessities required to comfortably house the number of people for which the *Capacity* allows and other functions of the item may require. Vehicles with this function can carry additional passengers beyond those expressly required to operate it. Buildings or structures with this function are furnished and welcoming to inhabitants or workers.

Common Uses: All buildings meant to house people have this function. Also, almost all vehicles have this function, and it is necessary for ships, airships, and land vehicles that require both operators and other crewmembers who are sleeping/residing on the vehicle while not actively participating in its operation. Crew, *Passengers/Personnel*, and all other cargo is limited by *Capacity*, but without the *Passengers/Personnel* function, there is no way for them to be in or on the vehicle without getting in the way of the operator, inflicting a minimum –2 penalty on tests to use the vehicle.

Poison: Contact

Asset: *Innovator*

Requires: Complexity 2+ (see below), Structure 1+, *Potent* function

Difficulty: +2

Function: The item is a natural or synthetic poison, capable of inflicting maladies to those with which it comes in contact. Each production test makes one dose of poison. To have any effect, the poison must make contact with the skin of the victim. It may be applied directly to a *Subdued* or *Incapacitated* target, or smeared on any weapon to be delivered on the next successful penetrating attack. When the poison makes contact with a target, it attacks using its Complexity + Potency vs. the target's *Vigor*, ignoring Guard and Armor. If the poison's attack succeeds with a remarkable success (DoS 4+) it inflicts a condition: if the penetrating attack that delivers the poison does not inflict a Wound the poison inflicts a temporary condition, but if the delivering attack inflicts a Wound the poison inflicts a persistent condition.

If no *Weapon Condition* function is taken the poison's Complexity is 2. If the *Weapon Condition* function is taken with a standard condition the poison's Complexity is 3. Special conditions cannot be taken as *Weapon Conditions* with this function.

Common Uses: In order to be efficacious, contact poisons must be smeared on the cutting edge of a weapon, or used to coat a projectile. Some hunters and trappers that live in the wilderness use poisons to aid their pursuits, and may concoct them to increase their *Potency* and add any type of *Weapon Condition.* Otherwise, the only time poison sees much use in the Empire is among the ratcatchers, sewermen, or groundskeepers that employ it to exterminate vermin.

Poison: Gaseous

Asset: *Innovator*

Requires: Bulk 1+, Complexity 2+ (see below), Structure 0, *Area of Effect* function, *Potent* function, Cannot be combined with the *Explosive* function

Difficulty: +2

Function: A poisonous gas that ignores Guard, Armor, and physical Defense to directly harm those exposed to it. Each production test creates enough gas to fill the area of effect of the design for one sequence. Unless captured in some type of canister during production, it will immediately fill that area of effect when created, most likely poisoning the creator. If stored in a container, it will fill the area of effect around the container for the remainder of the sequence in which it is opened or otherwise breached. A character in the same zone of control as the gas and not wearing a gasmask with the *Filter* function to remove poisonous gases is subject to an attack of the poison's Complexity + Potency against her *Vigor*. If the attack succeeds with a remarkable success (DoS 4+) it inflicts a temporary condition. Poisonous gas ignores Guard and physical Armor.

If no *Weapon Condition* function is taken the poison's Complexity is 2. If the *Weapon Condition* function is taken with a standard condition the poison's Complexity is 3. Special conditions cannot be taken with this function.

Common Uses: Poisonous gases are sometimes the byproduct of industrial activity, and only exterminators put them to any domestic use. The Hague Convention of 1899 banned the use of all projectiles "the sole object of which is the diffusion of asphyxiating or deleterious gases." Sadly, this has not eliminated their use entirely.

To safely store or transport any noxious gases a container with the *Capacity* and *Airtight Seal* functions is needed. Weaponized gases may be used in grenades or artillery shells with high *Potency* and one or more *Weapon Conditions.*

Poison: Internal

Asset: *Innovator*

Requires: Bulk 1+, Complexity 2+ (see below), Structure 1, *Potent* function

Difficulty: +3

Function: A successful production test creates a single dose of poison. This poison must be ingested or injected into the victim in order to have any effect. If the victim is *Subdued* or *Incapacitated*, it may be injected from a syringe as a standard action, or the poison

may be ingested if it has been added to food or drink. Anyone eating or being injected with the poison has a brief window before the poison takes effect; at the beginning of the next sequence the poison makes an attack of its Complexity + Potency vs. the target's *Vigor*, and the attack ignores Guard and physical Armor. If the attack succeeds with a remarkable success (DoS 4+) it inflicts a persistent condition.

If no *Weapon Condition* function is taken the poison's Complexity is 2. If the *Weapon Condition* function is taken with a standard condition the poison's Complexity is 3. If a special *Weapon Condition* is taken, the poison's Complexity is 5.

Noticing a poisoned dish before eating it is a passive test of *Focus + Composure* (*Survival* or *Medicine* may be substituted for *Composure*) against a Difficulty equal to the poison's Complexity + Potency. If successful, the eater realizes there is something off about the dish before they consume it. On a marginal success, they notice something is wrong, but only stop themselves after they have begun to consume the poison: the poison's attack against them suffers a –2 penalty. On a failure, the target does not notice the poison at all and consumes the full dose, allowing the poison to attack normally.

Common Uses: Thankfully, in the civilized world, there is little deliberate use of internal poisons. There are, of course, always rumors of foul play or some dark political intrigue whenever a dignitary or other notable person dies of sudden sickness, and the more sensational newspapers are only too happy to report such stories.

Potent

Asset: *Inventor: Fabricator, Innovator,* or *Machinist*

Requires: Bulk 1+, Structure 2+ or any *Poison* function

Difficulty: +1 per additional rank of Potency

Function: Simply put, *Potent* items are designed to inflict harm. Designs that include the *Potent* function at +1 Difficulty produce weapons with a Potency of 2. Increasing the Difficulty of the *Potent* function further increases the Potency of the produced weapon: +2 Difficulty produces a weapon with Potency 3; +3 Difficulty, Potency 4, etc.

There is an upper limit to how *Potent* a device can be, however. The increased Difficulty modifier cannot exceed the highest of the item's Bulk, Complexity, or Structure. For example, an item with B2, C4, S3 can only include a maximum of *Potent* +4 since that equals its highest attribute.

Common Uses: Weapon designs use *Potent* at least once so they are better able to defeat a target's Armor, and may include a *Weapon Condition.* Cannon and other artillery designed to damage large objects and buildings need additional punch to be effective, and will often include the *Potent* function at +3 or +4 Difficulty. With some alchemists now producing unnaturally strong materials there are some in the military arguing for a return to using protective clothing for combatants, it is a certainty that all manner of new, ever-more *Potent* weapon designs will make use of this function to remain effective.

Power Source

Asset: *Inventor: Fabricator, Innovator,* or *Machinist*

Requires: The item must be paired with a separate *Power Supply,* see below

Difficulty: +0

Function: Many designs require a *Power Source* to provide energy for other functions. A separately designed and built item with the *Power Supply* function must be mounted to the device in order for it to function. Without a working *Power Supply,* any item that requires a *Power Source* is inoperable.

Common Uses: Vehicles and automatons need a *Power Source,* and some pieces of advanced clockwork technology such as *Analytic* engines of items that incorporate *Sensors* do as well. Some major metropolitan centers have stable domestic electric grids with a power output of 1 or 2; devices with the *Power Source* function may use such a domestic *Power Supply* as long as they are plugged in to it via the *Connected* restriction.

Power Supply

Asset: Varies, see below

Requires: Varies, see below

Difficulty: Varies, see below

Function: Power Supplies provide energy and operating power for other devices. Each *Power Supply* is designed and produced as a separate item with its own production Time and creation tests, then incorporated into another device with the *Power Source* function. The requirements and performance of a *Power Supply* vary based on the type of energy being used.

Most *Power Supplies* will require fuel. For everyday use, the consumption and resupply of fuel is not tracked: it is assumed to be part of the normal lifestyle of the character as defined by their *Means.* When fuel is scarce or excessively costly, operating an item consumes units of fuel equal to the highest of the item's *Handling, Potency,* or *Speed.* So an item requiring 5 power consumes 5 units of fuel to operate for one installment.

Common Uses: Vehicles of all shapes and sizes have and always will rely on *Power Sources* to enable *Handling* and *Speed.* The large industrial machines that have enabled the march of progress into modernity likewise depend on many different *Power Supplies.* Thanks to the brilliant work of Mr. Tesla, electricity has been tamed for widespread use, and designs incorporating this function are likely going to become increasingly common.

POWER SUPPLY: CHEMICAL OR ELECTRICAL FUEL CELL

Asset: *Inventor: Innovator*

Requires: 1 Bulk +1 per 2 ranks of power output, Complexity 5+

Difficulty: +1 per power output

These power cells or batteries contain a set power output before they must be replaced. If fuel is being tracked, a fuel cell will provide power for one installment before expiring. So long as there is another *Power Supply* to create the energy, recharging a fuel cell can be done by testing *Reason + Science,* Difficulty equal to half the power output of the fuel cell. Fuel cells require no other fuel source while in use.

POWER SUPPLY: CLOCKWORK ENGINE

Asset: *Inventor: Machinist*

Requires: 1 Bulk +1 per rank of power output, Complexity 4+

Difficulty: +2 per power output

This type of *Power Supply* can be mobile or immobile. A *Clockwork* device uses no fuel, but a mobile device will require a person to wind it, and an immobile *Clockwork* device will require a weight/pendulum and the *Immobile* restriction. The pendulum/weight used must itself have a Bulk equal to the ranks of power output. For devices that are wound, the power output is both the number of winders required as well as each winder's minimum *Vigor* (a power output of 3 requires at least 3 people or animals with a *Vigor* of 3 to wind). Resetting the weight or rewinding the spring takes a full turn and requires no test.

POWER SUPPLY: COMBUSTION OR STEAM ENGINE

Asset: *Inventor: Machinist*

Requires: 1 Bulk per 2 ranks of power output, Complexity 4+

Difficulty: +1 per power output

Combustion and Steam *Power Supplies* require the constant consumption of fuel (coal, gasoline, or similar combustible) to operate. Any interruption of the fuel supply causes the engine to cease all power output and the item to stop functioning at the end of the current sequence. When tracked, fuel is used per installment as previously described.

POWER SUPPLY: PHYSICAL LABOR, WATER, OR WIND

Asset: *Inventor: Fabricator*

Requires: Complexity 3+

Difficulty: +1 per 3 ranks of power output

This is not a *Power Supply* in its own right, but rather a device that that captures the energy provided by water, wind, people, or animals to power a device. The item requires no other fuel source other than the continued dedication of the water, wind, people or animals. Power output equals that average *Vigor* or average water or wind *Speed* rounded down, up to the cap set by this function (3 rank maximum if taken once, 6 rank maximum if taken twice, etc).

Production: Quick

Asset: *Inventor: Fabricator*

Requires: None

Difficulty: +1

Function: Reduce the total Time required to produce the item by one rank.

Common Uses: Any design can benefit from the reduced Time to produce, but simple designs that are meant to be mass-produced benefit from it the most.

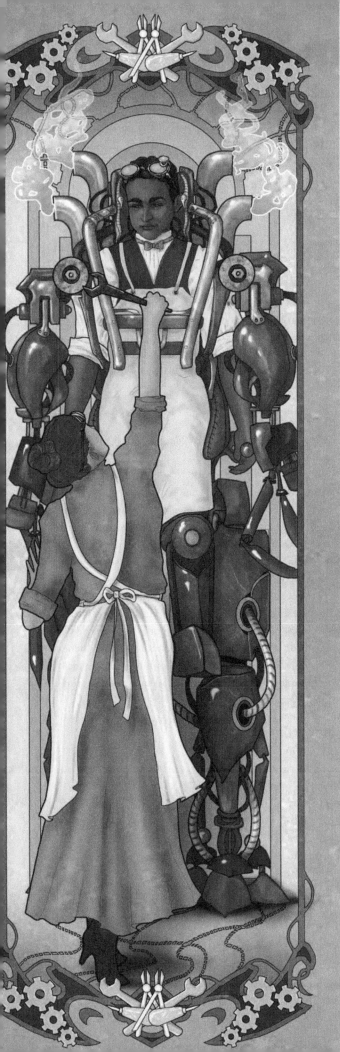

Program

Asset: *Inventor: Innovator*
Requires: Bulk 1+, Complexity 5+, Structure 2+
Difficulty: +2 per rank of skill

Function: A program is a separate item, usually created solely with the *Program* function. Each program provides a skill of the designer's choosing to a device that is able to run programs. So long as that device has a function that grants it an aptitude (*Analytical, Applied Force,* or *Sensor*), the program will allow the device to make trait tests. The designer chooses one skill in which she has ranks to be the basis of information used in the program. At +2 Difficulty *Program* will grant the skill at rank 1 rank; at +4 Difficulty, rank 2; at +6 Difficulty, rank 3, etc. The program cannot be written to grant more skill ranks than are possessed by its designer. Every skill rank beyond the first also increase the minimum Bulk of the design by 1, as the needed punch cards, vacuum tubes, or other media needed to store and run the program becomes cumbersome and requires a larger housing.

Common Uses: Programs are used in industrial automation and analytical engines. Banks will use analytic engines with *Bureaucracy* programs for the purposes of calculating interest, tracking balances, and printing paper trails. Scientists will use them with *Science* programs to make complex numerical and astronomical charts, run scientific models, or simply crunch numbers with higher speed and accuracy. Soldiers use *Science* programs for artillery range finding and *Survival* programs for navigation.

Programs can also be used with devices that possess the *Applied Force* or *Sensor* function to create automated machines that make their own trait tests.

Projectile Weapon

Asset: *Inventor: Fabricator, Innovator,* or *Machinist*
Requires: Bulk 2+, Structure 2+, *Increased Reach* function,
Potent function
Difficulty: +2

Function: The weapon launches a projectile as an attack. This will require the *Increased Reach* function to determine the Range of the attack. Projectile attacks always ignore the target's Guard and are always subject to all rules for *Aiming* and cover. If the *Ammunition/Consumables* function is taken, the item is a ranged weapon that fires consumable projectiles (like bullets or arrows). Otherwise the item is designed to be thrown itself (such as a spear or throwing knife) and must be retrieved between uses.

Common Uses: Firearms depend on this function for their efficacy, and are the overwhelming majority of the designs for *Projectile Weapons,* though bows and some exotic ranged weapons make use of it as well. Any *Projectile Weapon* design almost always includes multiple instances of *Potent, Weapon Conditions,* and benefits from multiple uses of the *Ammunition* function to make sure they can be used repeatedly.

Projector

Asset: *Inventor: Innovator* or *Machinist*

Requires: Bulk 3+, Complexity 4+, Structure 3+

Difficulty: +2

Function: The device is able to project the images captured on film onto any clean white or silver surface, but such images can only be seen clearly in low lighting or darkness. Such a device may be designed to project still or moving images as chosen by the designer.

Common Uses: A relatively new technology, some entertainers are employing *Projectors* to put on moving picture shows for the delight and amazement of paying spectators. More seriously, such items could be a boon to academic and educational work, as it allows the rapid dissemination of news and information with the added impact of pictures.

Prosthetic

Asset: *Inventor: Fabricator* or *Machinist*

Requires: Complexity 2+ for basic or 4+ for clockwork (see below), Structure 3+, *Bespoke Design* function

Difficulty: +1 for basic, +2 for clockwork

Function: The item replaces or assists one limb or feature, custom fitted to its intended user.

Basic prosthetics allow the user to recover some of the missing function and have at most two points of articulation, letting them perform rudimentary tasks such as walking, holding objects, and other activities of daily living related to personal care normally. More sophisticated tasks (anything that would normally require an active trait test for everyone attempting them) are performed at a –2 penalty.

Clockwork prosthetics allow for finer manipulation that equals or exceeds that of a natural limb. Those with clockwork prosthetics may take the full range of passive tests, and active tests are taken without penalty. In unusual or especially physically demanding circumstances the Narrator may impose a –2 penalty to tests made with this prosthetic.

Common Uses: In the Empire's struggles around the globe many have suffered grievous injuries, and the fighting in Crimea and Afghanistan both sent home many soldiers missing limbs. The increased need for prosthetics has greatly improved their quality, and new technologies allow those with resources access to amazing clockwork replacements. Designs for *Prosthetics* are often very straightforward, only incorporating this function and the necessary *Bespoke Design* for their intended user.

In rare cases, truly exceptional pieces can be built that might even exceed natural performance by including the *Applied Force* function and the necessary *Power Source* to operate it. If the popular stories of the American West or South China Sea are to be believed, some go further still, incorporating weapons into their replacement limbs. Though difficult, adding the *Potent* and *Weapon Condition* functions could make a fearsome hand-to-hand weapon, or by including *Ammunition* and a *Reload Time* it

is possible to incorporate a *Projectile Weapon*. Creators that wish to allow for weaponization but wish for more flexibility may opt instead to provide a *Weapon Mount* for their prosthetic and design the attachments separately.

Quick

Asset: *Inventor: Fabricator*

Requires: Bulk <4, *Potent* function, cannot include the *Unwieldy* function

Difficulty: +1

Function: The weapon is light and agile, and all attacks made benefit from +1 advantageous circumstance for determining Attack Priority.

Common Uses: Lightweight weapons that depend on speed and finesse are often able to land a hit on an opponent first, and sometimes dealing the first Wound in an exchange can make a difference between leaving an exchange uninjured or grievously harmed. Dueling weapons like smallswords almost always include this function so they can retain an edge against slower—but often more *Potent*—weapons.

Recorder

Asset: *Inventor: Innovator* or *Machinist*

Requires: Bulk 2+, Complexity 4+, Structure 3+, *Ammunition/Consumables* function

Difficulty: +2 each for either sound or video

Function: The device is capable of making audio recordings of the sounds around it, or film recording of images in black and white. It requires wax recording cylinders or acetate platters for sound, or film rolls for motion pictures, as a separate consumable to create a physical recording.

Common Uses: A quintessential part of the process for making records or moving pictures, recording devices are most often standalone pieces. Some gramophones combine this with the *Speaker* function so tinkerers and audiophiles can entertain themselves. More seriously, easily portable sound or film recorders could be a boon to explorers, naturalists, and academics documenting their experiences and research.

Seaworthy

Asset: *Inventor: Fabricator*

Requires: Structure 3+

Difficulty: +1

Function: The item is capable of remaining afloat and performing its functions above water.

Common Uses: For thousands of years this design has allowed humanity to fish, travel, and explore. All watercraft will also need to take *Capacity* to safely carry anything and the *Handling, Power Source,* and *Speed* functions to be able to navigate. Vessels meant for sea travel will also require the *Passengers/Personnel* function to have room for off-duty crew and other travellers. Rarely, especially valuable cargo might be shipped in containers (relying on their

Capacity to store things) that are also *Seaworthy*, so the cargo will survive any potential disaster. Some vessels also carry safety equipment with the *Capacity* and *Seaworthy* functions that can be worn to keep oneself afloat.

Secured

Asset: *Inventor: Fabricator* or *Machinist*
Requires: Complexity 3+, Structure 3+
Difficulty: +1

Function: The object includes a keyed or combination lock, requires a keyed ignition, or has some other security feature to begin operation. Without the required key or combination, the object will not function unless someone successfully tests *Grace + Burglary* against a Difficulty equal to the item's Complexity to overcome the security.

Common Uses: This function is often paired with *Baffling*, as that will increase the Difficulty of the test to overcome the *Secured* device. By far the most common use of this function is to create locks, but some automatons, vehicles, and dangerous industrial devices also use the function to ensure that they aren't used by those the inventor feels are unqualified or untrustworthy.

Sensor

Asset: *Inventor: Innovator*
Requires: Bulk 3+, Complexity 5+, *Power Source* function,
             Refined Materials restriction
Difficulty: +2 per rank of *Focus*

Function: This device is equipped with sensors that allow it to perceive its surroundings, granting it the *Focus* aptitude. If this function is included in a design with a +2 Difficulty, the device has *Focus* 1; +4 Difficulty, *Focus* 2, +6 Difficulty, *Focus* 3, etc. This bestows the device with the ability to to respond to outside stimuli.

A device with the *Sensor* function has the ability to run one program at a time. Programs are created separately with the *Program* function. When the program is used, it adds a skill to the device, allowing it to make its own trait tests. The device may only make trait tests that use the *Focus* aptitude and the skill provided by the program.

The exact means of detection are abstract and do not need to be exactly analogous to human senses, but it is limited to approximately human sensory ranges. No one has yet honed ways to observe and understand extreme ends of light spectra, or how to translate inaudibly-pitched frequencies into ranges intelligible to humans. Players and Narrators should discuss to ensure a common understanding of what types of information the *Sensor* can perceive.

Common Uses: By far, the most common uses of *Sensors* are in automated devices such as doors that open when someone approaches or an automobile that turns on when someone sits in the driver's seat. However, the most cutting edge experimental uses of *Sensors* are in fully functioning automata who can perceive and respond to their surroundings. Such free-functioning automata

would often also incorporate the *Analytical* and *Applied Force* functions. Given the extremely high Difficulty of such plans, automata including the full suite of related functions will often rely on many other restrictions to make the designs feasible.

Speaker

Asset: *Machinist*
Requires: Bulk 2+, Complexity 4+, Structure 3+
Difficulty: +1 for speaking volume, +2 for performance/public
             address volume

Function: The design incorporates a small phonograph or music box that is capable of producing sound: music, recordings of voices, or any other noise the creator desires. For +1 Difficulty the device can emit sounds at a normal speaking volume, while at +2 Difficulty it is loud enough for public performances to to serve as an amplified public address system.

Common Uses: Aside from directly creating phonographs or artificial music for entertainment purposes, some automaton designers have played with including *Speakers* and a set of wax cylinders with recorded answers to make it more pleasant to interact with them. Scientists and explorers—as well as some vainglorious nobles—also combine this function with *Recorder* so they can document their observations and experiences.

Speed

Asset: *Inventor: Fabricator* or *Machinist*
Requires: Complexity 3+, *Power Source* function
Difficulty: +1 per 10 miles per hour of maximum speed

Function: The item can move using the energy provided by its *Power Source* to move up to a maximum speed of 10 mph for each rank of *Speed*. This function can be taken more than once, but even the most advanced modern machines rarely exceed 5 ranks. If designing automata that walk on legs this function can only be taken once. Vehicles normally accomplish locomotion using wheels, tracks, sails, or propellers, and will require the appropriate *Power Source* to operate. Items with *Speed* can only move in straight lines or on tracks unless they also have at least one rank of *Handling*.

Common Uses: Vehicles of all types and sizes depend on the *Speed* function to travel. Steam engines are the preferred *Power Source* for modern transit, but teams of horses and mules are still commonly used in the country, and many sailing ships still ply the ocean. Vehicles also depend on *Capacity* and their ability to carry *Passengers/Personnel* to be of much use.

Most carriages and sailing ships have a *Speed* of 2, while mechanized transport via steamers, trains, or on the new motor-bicycles or automobiles have 3 ranks. The fastest trains and airships sometimes manage a *Speed* of 4 while working, but only the most powerful locomotives running under full steam and with light cargo, or brilliant new zeppelin designs have attained a *Speed* of 5 or even higher.

Submersible

Asset: *Inventor: Machinist*
Requires: Bulk 2+, Complexity 3+, Structure 2+
Difficulty: +2

Function: The item is capable of operating while completely below the water. It cannot take any cargo unless it has the *Capacity* function, and requires the *Airtight Seal* and *Passengers/Personnel* functions in order to safely transport any living crew while submerged. The item cannot control its travel under the water unless it takes the *Handling, Power Source,* and *Speed* functions. Sail power cannot be used for underwater movement, and steam power requires an exhaust snorkel be extended above the waterline at all times.

Common Uses: The oldest underwater devices are diving bells that use the *Airtight Seal, Capacity,* and *Submersible* functions, as well as the *Connected* restriction to haul them back up to the surface. Undersea diving suits protect only one person, and so don't need the *Capacity* function. Since the suits aren't rigid, they have the benefit of allowing their user to move under their own power.

The first moving submersible was the *Turtle* from 1775, an one-man machine designed to approach anchored vessels and affix explosives to them. Its designers dropped *Connected* and added *Handling* and *Speed* to the list of functions thanks to its occupant's pedal-driven *Power Source,* and made it *Seaworthy* and *Airtight* so it could function above or below the water.

With the availability of new, much more efficient *Power Sources* and *Sensors* that could allow for navigation not based on sight, it's possible to build undersea vessels that could be much more versatile. Any such vehicle would also likely be large enough to require multiple crew members, so would also need to be *Huge* and use the *Passengers/Personnel* function to accommodate its off-duty crew.

Weapon Condition

Asset: *Inventor: Fabricator, Innovator,* or *Machinist*
Requires: *Potent* function
Difficulty: +1 for a standard condition, +2 for a special condition

Function: The item gains a weapon condition of the designer's choice which can be applied to targets on any attack that yields a remarkable success (DoS 4+). See *Placing Physical Conditions,* p. 83

Standard conditions: *Aggravated, Bleeding, Dazed, Disarmed, Disoriented, Entrapped, Exposed, Staggered,* and *Unbalanced.*

Special conditions: *Burning, Crippled, Fatigued, Incapacitated, Moribund, Outmaneuvered,* and *Overwhelmed.* Special conditions can only be taken with Narrator approval.

Common Uses: Almost every weapon ever fashioned has been designed to include the *Weapon Condition* function so it can inflict harm in a particular way.

Weapon Mounts

Asset: *Inventor: Fabricator*
Requires: Bulk 4+, Structure 3+, *Capacity* function
Difficulty: +1 Difficulty for one mount/Bulk, +2 Difficulty for two mounts/Bulk, +3 Difficulty for five mounts/Bulk, +4 Difficulty for up to ten mounts/Bulk

Function: The item is capable of having weapons affixed to or carried aboard it. The Difficulty modifier for this function and the item's Bulk determine how many *Weapon Mounts* are created on the final device. For +1 Difficulty this function grants one weapon mount per Bulk of the final object, for +2 Difficulty two weapon mounts per Bulk, +3 Difficulty grants five weapon mounts per Bulk, and +4 Difficulty grants up to ten weapon mounts per Bulk. So if *Weapon Mounts* are included in a design at +1 Difficulty and the item is Bulk 6, it has six weapon mounts. If the function is included at +3 Difficulty on a Bulk 5 item, it has fifteen weapon mounts.

All mounted weapons must have a Bulk of at least two lower than the object they are mounted on, so a Bulk 5 item with this function can mount weapons up to Bulk 3, Bulk 6 items can mount weapons up to Bulk 4, etc. The weapons, ammunition and their related gear will fill the item's *Capacity.*

The benefit to using this function is that it allows any mounted weapons to be designed and produced as entirely separate items. If *Weapon Mounts* are not incorporated into a design, any weapons included in the design are permanently integrated into the physical structure of the item. If they are removed from the item they cannot work.

Common Uses: Warships all make use of this function to carry their cannon. No military force currently includes land or air vehicles with mounted guns, but it is likely only a matter of time until they do. Any vehicle will always need *Handling, Speed,* and a *Power Source,* and those bearing weapons will also need the *Capacity* to carry the guns and the *Passengers/Personnel* function as well to carry the crew.

Weather-Resistant

Asset: *Inventor: Fabricator*
Requires: Bulk 3+, Structure 2+
Difficulty: +1

Function: The item is particularly well-insulated or affords excellent protection from extreme environments, protecting those wearing it or inside it from severe storms, as well as from the designer's choice of either hot or cold extreme temperatures. While wearing or inside the item, the users are always considered prepared for moderate extreme environments of the designers choosing and cannot be less than ill-prepared for severe extreme environments of that type (see *Extreme Environments,* p. 96).

Common Uses: Most large camping and safari gear is *Weather-Resistant,* as otherwise it would be of little use. Tents and shelters often make use of the *Compact* function as well to make them easier to transport.

Wireless Transmission

Asset: *Innovator*

Requires: Complexity 4+, *Communicator* function

Difficulty: +1 per mile of range

Function: Any object that communicates information may be given this function to transmit its information over radio waves. The effective range of a wireless machine is equal to one mile for each +1 Difficulty of the function in the design. An item designed with a *Wireless Transmission* function at +4 Difficulty could transmit over four miles, an item designed with the function at +5 Difficulty could transmit over five miles, etc. Regardless of rank, *Wireless Transmission* is blocked by intervening lead, dense soil or rock, and anything with a Structure of 5 or more placed in its transmission path.

Common Uses: Since *Wireless Transmission* is still a new and experimental technology it has no truly common use, but it has great potential for use in designs with the *Recorder, Sensor,* and *Communicator* functions.

RESTRICTIONS

If restrictions are included in the design of an item, each will reduce the Difficulty of the creation test by the listed amount. Each restriction will limit the functionality of the final product.

Connected

Requires: Complexity 3+ and/or *Power Source* function

Excludes: *Speed* 3 or higher

Difficulty: –1

Restriction: The device's fuel or some other vital supply (such as air for submersibles) is provided through an exterior physical connection. If the connection is broken, the function of the device is compromised. Narrators have the final say on what that compromise entails, but it usually means that the devices that require tests to use or operate stop working after the next test, or by the end of the sequence or scene for items that require no tests to use.

Crew Build

Requires: Bulk 2+, Complexity 2+. This restriction is mandatory if the *Huge* function is included, and must be taken at the same rank.

Difficulty: –1 for 2–5 workers, –2 for 6–24, –3 for 25–99, –4 for 100–499, –5 for 500–999, –6 for 1000 or more

Restriction: The item's constructions requires multiple participants working simultaneously to complete vital tasks. Workers must have at least one rank of the skill being used for the production test, and must be present for the full Time requirement of the project. The test is made at a –1 Difficulty if it requires simultaneous work from 2–5 people, –2 Difficulty for 6–24 people, –3 Difficulty for 25–99 people, –4 Difficulty for 100–499 people, –5 Difficulty for 500–999 people, and –6 Difficulty for simultaneous work by 1000 or more people.

Crew Operation

Requires: Bulk 4+, Complexity 3+.

Difficulty: –1 for two operators, –2 for five operators, –3 for ten or more operators

Restriction: Operating the item requires multiple participants working simultaneously to complete vital tasks. The full complement of operators must all be present and physically able to perform their work in order for the item to work properly. The Difficulty reduction from *Crew Operation* determines how many crew members are needed: for –1 Difficulty the device needs two operators, –2 Difficulty for five operators, and –3 Difficulty for ten or more operators. At the Narrator's discretion, devices that are only partially crewed may be able to operate in some very limited fashion and with a –2 penalty on all tests and with a requirement of additional time and actions spent.

Dangerous Use

Requires: Complexity 3+, *Potent* function, the item must require an active trait test to use

Difficulty: –1 Difficulty for repair tests, –2 Difficulty if failure also inflicts a temporary condition on the user(s), and a –3 Difficulty if the failure inflicts a Wound on the user(s).

Restriction: The item will break or malfunction dramatically whenever someone using the item suffers a remarkable failure on an use test. If this restriction is included for –1 Difficulty the device requires a successful *Reason + Artisan* or *Engineering* test against Difficulty 3 to repair before it can be used again. If included at –2 Difficulty the item will require repair, and any character using the item or acting as crew to meet the *Crew Operation* restriction immediately suffers a temporary condition, ignoring Armor—either the device's *Weapon Condition* if it has one, or a random condition determined by a single card draw. If *Dangerous Use* is included at –3 Difficulty the item breaks and requires repair as above, but also immediately inflicts a Wound, ignoring Guard and Armor, on any character using the device or acting as crew to meet the *Crew Operation* restriction.

Delicate

Requires: Structure 2+

Excludes: Cannot be combined with the *Armor* or *Cover* functions

Difficulty: –1 per rank

Restriction: The object is especially fragile, and much easier to damage or destroy than others with the same Structure; reduce the Armor value of the object by one each time this restriction is taken, to a minimum of 0. Any failed test to use an object with an Armor of 0 will automatically apply the *Nonfunctional* condition.

Difficult to Use

Requires: Complexity 3+, the item must require an active trait test to use

Excludes: Cannot be combined with any other function or restriction that modifies Difficulty to use

Difficulty: –2

Restriction: At the best of times the item is very hard to use properly, and all tests to use it are made at an additional –2 penalty.

Multi-Disciplinary

Requires: Functions selected from at least two different disciplines of *Fabricator*, *Machinist*, or *Innovator*

Difficulty: –1 if it requires two separate production tests, –2 if it requires three different production tests

Restriction: Producing the item requires components created by several different disciplines, all of which must be well-made for the item to work properly. The components from each discipline must be made with separate production tests against the Difficulty of the design in order to complete the build. All tests are made at the beginning of the project. If one or more of the required tests fail they may be retried another full Time period for the build.

Production: Slow

Requires: None

Difficulty: –1

Restriction: The assembly and finishing process for the item is particularly painstaking, increasing the required Time to produce the design by 1.

Reduced Reach

Requires: Bulk 2+, *Potent* function

Excludes: Cannot be combined with the *Increased Reach* function

Difficulty: –1

Restriction: The item has some operational limit to its Reach; reduce the Reach to *Touch*.

Refined Materials

Requires: Complexity 3+

Excludes: Cannot be combined with the *Scavenged* restriction

Difficulty: –1

Restriction: Producing the item requires alchemically treated or otherwise unusual materials that are expensive and difficult to come by, and production is impossible without them. Unless the materials are acquired through gameplay or can be directly produced by character(s) fabricating the object, they must be specially purchased. Increase the required Cost to produce the item by 1.

Reload Time

Requires: Complexity 2+, either the *Ammunition/Consumables* function or *Single Shot* restriction

Difficulty: –1 for a maneuver, –2 for an action, –3 for a sequence (3 turns)

Restriction: The item can only function a set number of times before it must be reloaded or have its consumables replaced, as determined by the *Ammunition/Consumables* function, or after every use if it is a *Single Shot* item. The amount of time needed to reload the device is defined by this restriction. If *Reload Time* is included at –1 Difficulty for the design the item takes one maneuver to reload, at –2 Difficulty it instead takes an action to reload, and at –3 Difficulty it requires three separate actions to reload.

This restriction can be combined with the *Setup Time* restriction, but the time requirements must be met separately while operating the item. If this restriction is included for a device that also requires *Crew Operation*, all crew members must perform the activity in order to complete the reload.

Scavenged

Requires: None

Excludes: Cannot be combined with the *Refined Materials* restriction

Difficulty: –1

Restriction: The item is made of found and scavenged material that has been significantly repurposed: the item will function—barely—for a single scene. At the end of the scene, it will fail utterly and the components will be unusable for item creation thereafter.

Setup Time

Requires: Complexity 3+

Difficulty: –1 for a maneuver, –2 for an action, –3 for a sequence (3 complete turns)

Restriction: The item requires active setup and adjustment between each use such as resetting mechanisms, charging power, running calculations, and the like. The amount of time needed to prepare the device before each subsequent use is defined by this restriction. If this restriction is included in a design at –1 Difficulty the item takes one maneuver to set up, at –2 Difficulty it instead takes an action to set up, and at –3 it requires three separate actions to set up.

This restriction can be combined with the *Reload Time* restriction, but the time requirements must be met separately while operating the item. If this restriction is included for a device that also requires *Crew Operation*, all crew members must perform the activity in order to complete the setup.

Single Shot
Requirements: *Ammunition/Consumable* function, *Reload Time* restriction
Difficulty: −1

The item requires ammunition to function, but is incapable of having more than one shot ready at a time, and therefore must be reloaded between each use.

Single Use
Requires: None
Difficulty: −2

Restriction: The item is irreparably destroyed after a single use, regardless of the success or failure of the attempt. No usable material may be salvaged from the broken item.

Two-handed
Requires: Bulk 1 or 2
Difficulty: −1

Restriction: Although an item of this Bulk would normally require only a single hand to use and manipulate properly, the design makes an item that is too complicated or imbalanced to use correctly one-handed and instead requires both hands for proper use. Any attempt to use the item with only a single hand suffers a −2 penalty.

Unwieldy
Requires: Bulk 3+, *Potent* function, cannot include the *Quick* function
Difficulty: −1

Restriction: The shape, weight distribution, or operation of this weapon is cumbersome, making it awkward to use in a fight. While using the object in conflict the wielder is always subject to 1 disadvantageous circumstance when determining Attack Priority.

CONSTRUCTING ITEMS

TOOLS

In order to produce an object, you need the equipment to get the job done. To make sure players do not need to keep exhaustive lists of particular equipment and raw materials, the kit needed to make items is abstracted as requiring either tools or a workshop.

Tools are portable and can produce items up to a Complexity or Bulk of 4.

Workshops are dedicated work areas that house a wide array of non-portable equipment and supplies necessary to produce items with a Complexity or Bulk of 5 and higher

Tools are available for purchase and managed as standard accoutrements. So long as a character carries her tools with her, she can work wherever she happens to be. Due to the size and significant investment needed to own and maintain a workshop, this is acquired by taking the *Workshop* asset (p. 159). Workshops are stationary, and can only be used when the character is able to get to the physical location of the shop.

TIME

The Time required to produce the item is equal to its Bulk + Complexity + Structure, modified by any design parameters or special results from the design or build quality that alter production speed. So creating a silver pocket watch with Bulk 1, Complexity 4, and Structure 3, requires a Time rank of 8, which equals 48 hours of continuous work time.

COST

To determine the Cost of a build, find the highest of the design's Bulk, Complexity, or Structure, then subtract 2. The result is the Cost of the build. The silver pocket watch with Bulk 1, Complexity 4, and Structure 3, has a final Cost of 4 − 2 = 2.

If the Cost is equal or less than the *Means* of the character attempting the build, she can manage one project at a time. If a build has a Cost beyond the *Means* of the character attempting it, she either cannot pay for it and must abandon the build, or must go into debt to fund the project and reduce her temporary *Means* as described on p. 183.

PRODUCTION

Production tests are made at the beginning of a project because the results may impact the overall Time needed to complete the work. When a character decides to start building a design she will need to make a *Reason* + skill test against the Difficulty of the design. The skill needed will vary based on which type of functions were utilized: *Fabricator* functions use the *Artisan* skill, *Innovator* functions use the *Science* skill, and *Machinist* functions use the *Engineering* skill. If a design has multiple skills for its component functions, only a single test is made using the lowest applicable trait combination. If only one character is making the item, she makes a single test using the lowest applicable trait combination. Alternatively, multiple inventors may participate, each making one

TIME

Time Rank	Continuous Work Time	Possible Regiments (Subject to Narrator Approval)
1	30 minutes	NA
2	1 hour	NA
3	2 hours	NA
4	4 hours	NA
5	8 hours	1 hour per day for eight days
6	12 hours	1 hour per day for two weeks
7	24 hours	2 hours per day for two weeks, 1 hour per day for one month
8	48 hours	8 hours per day for a week, 2 hours per day for a month, 1 hour per day for a season
9	1 week	8 hours per day for two weeks, 4 hours per day for a month, 2 hours per day for a season, 1 hours per day for a year and a day
10	1 month	8 hours per day for three months, 4 hours per day for six months, 2 hours per day for a year and a day
11+	2+ months	Double the previous entry's hours per day up to 8 hours, add one year. Ex: 8 hours per day for 6 months, 4 hours per day for a year, 2 hours per day for 2 years

of the required skill tests. The Difficulty for multiple tests will always be the total Difficulty for creation of the invention, not just for those functions covered by that skill.

A marginal success with a DoS of 0 on the creation test produces the item, but more slowly and at greater expense than it should: increase the production Time by 1. Success (DoS +1 to +3) produces the item in the expected Time. Remarkable success (DoS +4 to +7) shows excellent work by the builders, and the build takes -1 Time to complete. If there is an extraordinary success (DoS +8 or more) it is completed in -2 Time.

Failure (DoS -1 to -3) shows that the project should be abandoned after half the standard amount of Time has been spent in vain. A remarkable failure (DoS -4 to -7) indicates that the majority of the build was completed, but the device failed at the very end and all the Time was wasted. An extraordinary failure (DoS -8 or worse) is plagued with delays before being ultimately abandoned after the normal Time +1 worth of effort.

SAMPLE ITEM CREATION

Jim's character Professor Baker is an inventor that wants to design a new weapon. First, Jim thinks about what he wants to accomplish so he can get a good idea for the design and find functions that fulfill that purpose. He knows he wants a weapon that can be used in physical conflict to help him and his comrades quickly overpower enemies, and it would be ideal if it could impact multiple enemies at once. The character Professor Baker abhors unnecessary violence, so the weapon should be non-lethal if at all possible. Since the Professor isn't the greatest physical combatant, it would also be nice if the weapon allowed for him to stay out of close quarters fights.

In order to turn this idea into a working item design Jim needs to proceed through several steps.

1. Choose functions
2. Choose restrictions (optional)
3. Determine final Difficulty and check minimum requirements
4. Determine final production parameters of the design
5. Finalize item description

Choose Functions

With these ideas in mind Jim reads through the list of available functions and finds several that catch his eye, and so notes their effects as well as the design Difficulty and any requirements:

- *Area of Effect* can hit multiple targets (+2 Difficulty, requires *Explosive* and *Potent* functions)
- *Explosive* ignores Guard and is an efficient way to get straight to placing outcomes (+2 Difficulty, requires Bulk 1+, Complexity 4+, *Area of Effect* and *Potent* functions, and *Single Use* restriction)
- *Non-Lethal* avoids dealing out Wounds and eliminates the risk of manslaughter (+1 Difficulty, requires *Potent* function)
- *Potent* is needed for any weapon design to ensure it can reliably inflict outcomes, and since *Explosives* are more effective the more *Potent* they are Jim decides to take this function at a high level (+4 Difficulty, Bulk 1+, Structure 2+)
- A good *Weapon Condition* like *Overwhelmed* provides options to debilitate enemies (+2 Difficulty for choosing a special condition, requires the *Potent* function)

With the list of functions determined Jim adds up the Difficulty so far so he can get a good sense of how many restrictions he wants to include in the design to make sure the production won't be too hard. Right now the Difficulty is 2+2+1+4+2 = 11, so he'll definitely need to bring that down.

Choose Restrictions

From the functions selected, the design must include the *Single Use* restriction, but Jim finds several more that make sense and help bring the final Difficulty down so it can be produced reliably by Professor Baker.

- *Dangerous Use* makes sense for inclusion on weapons, and since the device is focused on inflicting a condition it seems reasonable to take this twice so remarkable failures when using the weapon inflict the condition on the user instead of the targets (-2 Difficulty, requires Complexity 3+, the *Potent* function, and the completed device must require an active test to use)
- *Production: Slow* is not ideal for turning out the design rapidly, but since Jim plays Professor Baker as a meticulous person it makes sense to him and helps bring the Difficulty down (-1 Difficulty, no requirements)
- *Refined Materials* will increase the final Cost of the design, but Professor Baker is a man of *Means* and can handle the expense (-1 Difficulty, requires Complexity 3+)
- *Single Use* is a mandatory restriction from the *Explosive* function, and must be part of the design (-2 Difficulty, no requirements)

Determine Final Difficulty and Check Requirements

Starting with the Difficulty of 11 from the chosen functions, Jim subtracts the adjustments from the restrictions to find the final Difficulty for the design; 11–2–1–1–2 = 5. Those restrictions bring the final Difficulty back down to a point where Professor Baker should be able to succeed on the test reliably, so Jim stops there. Next, he needs to determine the minimum Bulk, Complexity, Structure, and any other special considerations dictated by the functions he's chosen. Based on his selections, the final design needs a minimum Bulk 1+, Complexity 4+, Structure 2+, and must require an active test to be used. Those are the minimums, and Jim could increase the Bulk, Complexity, and Structure if he wished, but decides not to. As they stand now, those attributes describe a small, easily portable device that is quite sophisticated, which fits his idea for the design nicely.

Determine Production Parameters

Jim must determine the production Time needed to build the design, and how much it will Cost. To determine the Time he adds the attributes of the design plus any modifiers for functions and restrictions; Bulk 1 + Complexity 4 + Structure 2 + 1 from the *Production: Slow* restriction = Time 8. Consulting the Time table (opposite page) he sees that will take forty-eight hours of production time. For the Cost he finds the highest attribute and subtracts two, then adds any modifiers for functions and restrictions; Complexity 4 – 2 + 1 from the *Refined Materials* restriction = Cost 3. While he is working on this build Professor Baker will need to have *Means* 3 to cover the expense without penalty.

Finalize Description

These functions describe a powerful, single use weapon that targets everything in a zone of control, and can inflict the *Overwhelmed* condition to immediately start working through opponents' Guard. Jim thinks the best description for this item would be some type of grenade, and decides that the reason it can drop Guard and why it is *Non-Lethal* is because it emits a deafening, high pitched whistle. The source of the whistle could be superheated gas, so he imagines that it depends on an energetic chemical reaction contained inside the grenade that creates a blast of expanding gas that is pushed through tuned apertures in the shell and creates a deafening chorus of shrill tones. Looking forward to upcoming sonic shenanigans, Jim presents the design to his Narrator and has Professor Baker set to work in his shop.

BAKER'S BANSHEE

B1, C4, S2   Cost: 3

Functions:	*Area of Effect* (one zone of control), *Explosive*, *Non-Lethal*, *Potent* (Potency 5), *Weapon Condition* (Overwhelmed)
Restrictions:	*Dangerous Use* (Overwhelmed condition on a remarkable failure), *Production: Slow*, *Refined Materials*, *Single Use*
Weapon Statistics:	Reach *AoE Close*, Potency 5, Load -, Weapon Condition *Overwhelmed*

Description: A small, round grenade made of brass sheeting with a series of irregular protuberances with carefully shaped openings and a removable priming pin. When the pin is withdrawn it shatters a small glass vial in the grenade that kicks off a chemical reaction. The reaction releases a large amount of gas, which is forced through the holes and emits a near deafening keening wail for several seconds. The piercing tones cause physical pain in the ears and sinuses of people and animals nearby, and is very likely to *Overwhelm* them temporarily.

As with all grenades, it is thrown to a target zone of control by testing *Grace + Athletics*, Difficulty 3. The grenade makes an attack against all targets in the zone of control by testing its Bulk + Potency against targets' *Vigor + Athletics*.

I had no need to turn around to know something was amiss. It was written plain as day on Silas Folwell's face when he stopped speaking mid-sentence and stared out into the pounding rain.

I looked, of course, though I almost wish I hadn't. A two-headed crow-thing, all beaks, talons, and glowing eyes, crashed into a window in the middle of the Pullman car. Through the fractured glass a trickle of blood red rain ran down the inside of the pane. As others saw strange shapes fluttering outside the sounds of conversation died and we knew that the worst was surely yet to come. Another crash followed, then another, and another, and I heard glass shatter and a chorus of justified screams—the sounds of panic from the other passengers.

Silas pawed at his coat pockets before triumphantly producing a distinctive glass flask, but his face fell when he realized it was empty. "We need to get to the baggage carriage," he muttered. "The Pontus rises."

Despite having just met Mr. Folwell on the train an hour before, I was inclined to accept his logic and at least temporarily throw in my lot with him, as he was keeping his head better than most. A windowless baggage carriage seemed a prudent alternative to the wrecked windows of a dining car. Furthermore, we'd each just discovered the other was heading to Oxford at Professor Cavendish's request, and I have always regarded my alchemy instructor as an excellent judge of both character and capability.

At any rate, the train had nearly come to a halt, the ferocity of the storm having forced us to a standstill lest we jump the track, which meant we were stuck with these creatures. I had the presence of mind to collect Professor Cavendish's invitation from the table and tuck it into my satchel. We made for the door at the rear of the car, but it was locked. A few other passengers had made their way to us, and a heavyset Scotsman joined Silas in trying to force the door open. Even then, it refused to budge.

Hoping to see a porter that might have keys, I looked back down the length of the car and saw that the situation was deteriorating quickly. More of the aberrations squirmed through broken windows, shrieking in fury as glass tore at their flesh. A woman thrashed on the ground beneath one of the creatures. A beak darted at her eye, while the bird-thing's second head met my gaze with a sinister fixation. I could feel the room grow oppressive, weighing down on me, pushing, squeezing. My breath caught in my throat, and a flash of lightning through the blood-soaked windows painted the whole cabin red. The crows' first victims had gone still. Bloody, Janus-beaked faces turned toward us and the other passengers crowded toward the far ends of the car. Red rain whipped through the air from the shattered windows.

I heaved at a table, then grabbed Silas' shoulder and he helped me flip it over. Dimly aware of the men brandishing broken chair legs and positioning more tables as a barricade, I studied the dining car, picturing the placement of the wheels, and crouched down, digging in my satchel for the proper chalk. With a sweeping circle, I began to draw my channel on the carpet.

"What are you doing?" Silas asked.

"Science," I muttered in annoyance, rushing through my process. I didn't have time to explain my calculations if he wasn't skilled enough to keep up. Surely another of Cavendish's students could see a basic caustic channel for what it was? Even so, Silas' doubt made me hesitate. I looked at the completed pattern. I could still feel the strange pressure upon me. Had I done something wrong? Had the Pontus upwelling affected my perceptions? I lifted my chalk, studied it for a moment. No time for hesitation. I gave my channel that last little push. Sure enough, the entirety of the circle began to bubble and hiss, the floor sagging where I'd made the carpet corrosive.

Time was of the essence, though, and the reaction was taking too long to eat through the undercarriage by itself. Flipping a nearby chair onto its back, I pushed it into the circle, eliciting a round of fresh sputtering. I planted a foot squarely against its seat and shoved. Foolish of me. A clean circle of the dining car's floor creaked and collapsed, and I barely managed to spring free and avoid tumbling onto the acidic floor. My skirts were not so lucky; a swath of fabric sizzled and burned where it brushed the edge of the circle.

As the reaction subsided, I looked back at Silas and flashed a smile. "This way to the baggage car."

A few other passengers scrambled out after us, the big Scotsman coming up last, joining the rest of outside the baggage car, having done something clever with the tables to bar pursuit, at least for the moment. "Weel dain, lassie." He clapped a hand on my shoulder as if I were his drinking companion. Fresh slashes and gouges riddled his forearms.

"Are you alright?"

"Aye, lassie. Man's both body an' breath, an' A'm aye breathin'."

He flashed a grin and the lot of us walked to the baggage car. Silas, who had run ahead was persuading the panicky baggage handler to open up and let us inside. As the others hurried into the safety of the carriage, I pulled Silas aside. "You're no alchemist."

"I never said I was."

"You studied under Cavendish?"

"Oh. No. I've worked with him. We approach things from…different traditions."

A magus? But he'd spoken of the professor like a fellow scientist. And to think I'd put my life in this fool's hands! "What's in here?" I demanded, gesturing at the baggage car.

"I have…talismans. Items of power."

I jabbed his topcoat pocket. "Like the flask?"

He nodded. "But relevant to the situation at hand. I should be able to—"

One of the creatures dove at him out of the darkness, slamming him down into the mud. I batted at the creature with my satchel, knocking it aside. Someone pulled Silas to his feet and we scrambled through the door with screeching sounds at our backs. The Scotsman had found a fallen branch somewhere and was swinging it wildly to drive the crows back as the other passengers made it through. After what seemed an eternity, we pulled the door closed behind us, all eight of us alive, and several of the others pushed a heavy trunk in front of the door.

Beaks banged at the wood, starting to splinter it. Silas, flat on his back and bleeding from a nasty chest wound, gasped, "My trunk. Find it!"

I gave him a helpless look, having no idea where to start. "Silas…"

"Sorry…flat top steamer, black bands…should be with my Gladstone. J.S.F. monograms."

The baggage handler grunted and pushed past me. He seemed to know what he was on about, and just as well. I had more important matters to attend to. I turned my attention back to the splintering wood of the door and dug into my satchel for another piece of chalk. Centering myself, I ran through quick calculations and drew another channel around the door. As soon as I finished I could already see the cracked and splintered wooden door reacting to my transmutation, growing heavier and more solid as it became as dense and strong as steel. The furious thumps of beaks on wood turned to ringing metal sounds, then died away.

Some minutes later, how many I cannot say, I rested against a pile of luggage, breathing hard and heart pounding, but safe. Nearby, Silas sat cross-legged beside his open trunk, chanting softly in some tongue unknown to me. Before my eyes I saw the bloody ruin of the claw and puncture wounds in his chest restored, and the flush of health come back to his features. When he ceased his incantations, he slumped down beside me, obviously exhausted. The other passengers—even the doughty Scot—regarded us both with a mix of awe, gratitude, and disquiet. We huddled down to wait, and I was pleased to note the others gave Silas and me as much room and privacy as they could in the cramped interior of the baggage car.

"So, Miss St. George, have you read Becquerel's papers?"

"What?"

"The physicist. Found some new energy in pitchblende extracts. Salts. It's why Cavendish sent for us. He thinks there's something there." Silas paused and gestured towards his trunk. "There's a copy of them in my Gladstone."

"Physics? You?"

"Yes, well. Oh, mind the eye of newt."

TRANSCENDENT POWERS

There exist within the Clockwork gifts and powers that transcend what most people see as natural. Some of these powers are gained through an advanced knowledge of the sciences, others through a study of arcane mysteries, and still others are gifted from the Maker or flow from the supernatural taint of inhuman bloodlines. Characters who meet the requirements can acquire these powers through the *Alchemical Reaction*, *Charism*, *Glamour*, or *Magical Word* assets.

Those who wield transcendent powers can affect the Clockwork and its inhabitants in profound ways. Their use can be a vital piece to either maintaining or destroying the frail orderliness the world. While some people are fascinated that these abilities exist at all, there are others who view these powers as sacrilegious at best and a sign of the Pontus at worst. Precisely because of this, many who have learned transcendent powers do their best to keep their abilities a secret.

Alchemy alone is well-regarded by the public. This so-called "New Science" has already been vitally important to the development of new technologies, and it promises to be even more important in the years ahead. Its transition from mythology to an accepted scientific reality has been a topic of much discussion, and the reliability of its modern practice places it firmly in the realm of industry rather than arcane study. The practice of alchemy is governed by a system of reactions that can be triggered, either alone or in combination with one another, to affect change in a given piece of matter.

Magic has fallen as alchemy has risen. Magic is performed by weaving together mystical words and the selection of several arcane parameters. It is a complex and time consuming art, but it can yield great power and knowledge. The popular opinion of magic has greatly diminished in recent centuries. Most view it as a real force, although less reliable and efficient than modern scientific practices. Magi are often respected as skilled, at least by those without religious grievances toward them, but there is always the question of why magical practitioners would waste their efforts on an art whose time has come and gone. Today, the most common performance of magical rites occurs within the sacraments and official religious ceremonies of the Church. This orderly use of magic is sanctioned by the state; however, both religious and secular authorities are wary and watchful of those magi who practice magic for their own purposes. All who study such mysteries must beware lest they run afoul of the Witchfinders or Inquisition.

Charisms are individual powers granted by the Clockmaker, but those blessed with them are viewed with a mixture of praise

WHICH TRANSCENDENT POWERS TO CHOOSE

Transcendent powers are quite rare in the Clockwork and by no means required for player characters. However, for adventurous individuals who want to explore these mystical abilities, the Clockwork Roleplaying Game provides four separate transcendent power sets: charisms, glamours, alchemy, and ritual magic. These sets have varying levels of complexity and utility, making some easier for players to master than others. Thus, a player who wants her character to explore transcendent powers must consider not just which abilities are right for her character concept, but also which rules systems are a good match for her own gaming preferences. This ensures that the players will enjoy the characters they create.

Charisms and glamours offer the easiest powers to use. Each charism or glamour asset is a powerful self-contained ability that doesn't require knowledge of an integrated subsystem. For players who are new to roleplaying games or simply wish to avoid crunchy mechanical rules, one or more abilities from these power sets are a good choice.

Alchemy offers opportunities for more flexible creativity. Alchemical reactions have a wider range of uses, and can be used alone or in combination with each other. However, the accommodation for this adaptability requires more character assets, some bookkeeping, and a familiarity with object attributes.

Ritual magic offers the most complex system and requires the most assets to master, but it is also the most versatile of the transcendent powers. It allows characters to create custom effects from scratch. If players and their characters are willing to invest themselves in pursuing magic extensively, it can become much more powerful than the other transcendent abilities.

and suspicion. Charismatics are most often seen as holy men and women, but their supernatural powers can still be viewed as inscrutable or even frightening to others. There are many records of prophets killed for speaking the truth to those unwilling to hear it, or faith healers persecuted if they fail to heal the "right" person. The Church is usually the greatest protector of charismatics if they seek a place within her ranks, and their greatest adversary if they reject her institutional hierarchy.

Glamours are the illusory magics that flow from the fey blood of changelings and other fey creatures. Although changelings are seen as socially acceptable in most cosmopolitan areas, glamours are widely viewed with fear and suspicion. No one truly knows how glamours work, but everyone knows that they can trick, manipulate, and deceive others. The use of glamours is a large part of why changelings are stereotyped as untrustworthy and dangerous.

THE EMERALD TABLET (as translated by Sir Isaac Newton)	DERIVED UNDERSTANDING
Tis true without lying, certain and most true.	
That which is below is like that which is above and that which is above is like that which is below to do the miracles of one only thing.	**The Law of Divinity**: All matter on the earth is a reflection of the divine will in Heaven.
And as all things have been and arose from One by the mediation of One: so all things have their birth from this one thing by adaptation.	**The Law of Unity**: All matter is derived from one primordial substance and was created by one God, the Clockmaker. From this primordial substance, all things can be made.
The Sun is its father, the Moon its mother, the wind hath carried it in its belly, the earth is its nurse.	The Clockmaker set creation in motion, and now creation continues to care for itself.
The father of all perfection in the whole world is here.	Alchemy has its origin in the creative power of the Clockmaker, the creator of Heaven and Earth.
Its force or power is entire if it be converted into earth.	Etheric force is the essential power behind the practice of alchemy, and is found everywhere.
Separate thou the earth from the fire, the subtle from the gross sweetly with great industry.	**The Law of Polarity**: Manipulating matter's opposing qualities allows an alchemist to change its properties. Old Alchemy saw this as balancing the four elements of creation. New Alchemy views this as balancing atomic structure and charges.
It ascends from the earth to the heaven and again it descends to the earth and receives the force of things superior and inferior.	Matter is manipulated by use of etheric force.
By this means you shall have the glory of the whole world and thereby all obscurity shall fly from you.	The use of etheric force grants the alchemist a clear understanding of both the Clockwork and herself.
Its force is above all force. For it vanquishes every subtle thing and penetrates every solid thing.	*Etheric force* exists in all things, and may be harvested from any piece of matter.
So was the world created.	Alchemy was the means by which the Clockmaker created the world, by channeling etheric force to mold the Pontus into creation.
From this are and do come admirable adaptations whereof the means (or process) is here in this. Hence I am called Hermes Trismegistus, having the three parts of the philosophy of the whole world.	By emulating the act of divine creation, the alchemist can give any piece of matter the properties of a different piece of matter.
That which I have said of the operation of the Sun is accomplished and ended.	

ALCHEMY

Alchemy is one part science and one part philosophy. It is the art of changing the natural properties of matter by exposing it to carefully channeled quantities of etheric force, an ambient energy that seems to be the medium through which all other forces flow. Its practice is an odd paradox that seems both theological and heretical, both scientific and superstitious. It has thus suffered scorn among scholars, scientists, and theologians for many centuries. Only within the past few decades has the distinction between Old Alchemy and New Alchemy been made. Old Alchemy is relegated to the history books as a semi-reliable pseudo-science and a fumbling precursor to chemistry, but New Alchemy has been accepted by the scientific community as a methodical practice by which the Clockwork can be more deeply understood and its very substance be made subject to human will.

OLD ALCHEMY

The earliest record of alchemy comes from the Emerald Tablet, an inscribed gemstone manuscript, itself a product of alchemy. The Tablet is said to predate the Flood, and was allegedly composed by Hermes Trismegistus, a man legend says is none other than the Egyptian god Thoth. This Emerald Tablet contains thirteen verses of script. They are a lens through which to see all of matter, and perhaps even the alchemist herself. These philosophical axioms governed the practices of Old Alchemy, and still provide a more metaphorical understanding to the New Alchemists of our modern day. At left is Sir Isaac Newton's translation of the Emerald Tablet with notes on its derived meaning.

From this text comes the basic understanding of alchemy: all matter is composed of a single substance the ancients referred to as "One" or "Primus." It is argued by many that this primordial substance is actually a reference to the Pontus. Harnessing etheric force allows the alchemist to purify portions of matter into this primordial substance. From this substance, the alchemist can harness power or recreate the matter to make it manifest different properties. In Old Alchemy this process was wrapped in mysticism and heavily linked to magical practices, a methodology that led to fantastic but unreliable results.

The Decline of Old Alchemy

The practice of Old Alchemy was unreliable for two reasons: its lack of understanding the composition of matter, and its inability to properly and consistently harness etheric force.

Old Alchemy's understanding of matter was simply an oversight in popular opinion. An ancient alchemist named Democritus claimed that matter was constructed of invisible particles composed of the same substances. He named these particles 'atoms' and taught how each type of atom had different qualities, and that by changing these qualities, one could transmute the matter. Although Democritus' teachings held brief popularity, they were eventually dismissed in favor of Aristotle's simpler four-element

THE SALE OF ALCHEMICALLY ALTERED GOODS

With Old Alchemists' ubiquitously rumored pursuit of turning lead into gold, the possible threat posed by alchemy to global economies has been a consistent fear to those in power. In the late thirteenth century, the Magisterium commissioned alchemist Thomas Aquinas to answer the question of whether alchemically created gold could be sold on the open market. To the surprise of many, Aquinas concluded that any substance that had all of the properties of gold could be sold as gold. His answer held authority for half a century, and is often cited by alchemists who argued against the decrees that came later. In 1317 Pope John XXII published *Spondent quas non exhibent*, a papal bull that harshly criticized the dishonesty and lack of credibility of alchemists and their trade. He stressed the fact that alchemically created materials are *not* identical to naturally occurring ones. All sale of alchemically altered products ceased. It is highly debated whether this bull was motivated by theological, financial, or political agendas. Whatever the cause, this papal precedent holds power to this day.

Even within the Empire and in other lands that now exist outside the Magisterium's purview, the sale of alchemically altered products in the guise of natural goods is treated as forgery and punishable by local law, usually by hanging. Dealers of precious goods will typically screen their purchases to avoid this fate, using scientific processes to detect alchemical alteration. Thus, alchemically created gold, gems, and other objects of value are now largely worthless on the open market. There is still money to be made in industry, where the functionality of goods is of more concern than their authenticity, but for now, the days of independent alchemists creating objects of extreme value in their own laboratories are over.

reality which claimed that all matter was made up of earth, air, fire, and water. Who knows what would have happened had the alchemical community sided with Democritus and the factual nature of matter as we understand it today, but as they did not, alchemy pushed down the superstitious path of balancing the elements. This error in understanding was not corrected until the mid-nineteenth century when the publication of the first periodic tables forced Old Alchemists to reevaluate their work.

Etheric force was always a mystery. Old Alchemists treated it with divine reverence. Much of alchemical work was performed by trial and error, but without a full understanding of how to measure and control etheric force, even tried and tested alchemical reactions were just as likely to fail as to succeed. This inconsistency in results paired with steady advancements in the field of chemistry caused the practice and credibility of Old Alchemy to rapidly decline throughout the Age of Enlightenment.

OUT WITH THE OLD AND IN WITH THE NEW

In November of 1875, Thomas Alva Edison made a startling public announcement that he had discovered a force that differed markedly from heat, light, electricity, or magnetism. He named it 'etheric force,' citing previous investigation and evidence in the experiments of German alchemist Baron Karl von Reichenbach. Edison improved upon Reichenbach's theories and produced a method for quantifying etheric force in a unit he referred to as the "Od" (a name taken from Reichenbach's work and derived from the norse god "Odin"). The quantification of etheric force allowed for the birth of New Alchemy, a measurable and reliable science that has achieved great popularity in academia across the world.

Tradition Versus Progress

The truths expressed in the Emerald Tablet have held throughout the transition from Old Alchemy to New, but the understanding of their true meanings has undergone significant reinterpretation. As far as New Alchemy is concerned, Old Alchemy is dead and its practice is folly. However, the ancient traditions run deep, even if unspoken, in the minds of those who remember the old ways that dominated the practice until just a few decades ago.

Thus, while the science of alchemy has reached a consensus, the theology of alchemy has not. For some, alchemy can become its own religion, and that is why it is looked upon with suspicion by both the See of Canterbury and the Magisterium. Some have even called alchemy a cult that makes an idol of the Pontus. Debate and hostility exists between those with respect for the ancient mystical and reflective art of alchemy and those who treat it solely as a scientific method for harnessing the intrinsic power of matter.

THE PRACTICE OF ALCHEMY

An alchemist performs reactions which pull at the atomic bonds of matter and either harvest its natural energies or transmute it into a different state or type of matter. These reactions are fueled by etheric force, believed to be the medium through which all other forces flow. The understanding of how these amazing scientific phenomena occur is still nascent, but the reliability of their effects is affirmed.

Alchemical reactions harness the energy inherent in a piece of matter to produce desired results. An alchemist can use alchemical reactions to pull electricity from water, agitate atoms to force a material to produce heat or light, change the physical properties of matter, and many other reactions. Each reaction an alchemist learns will have its own unique effects.

Alchemical reactions require that the alchemist create a channel, a circular pattern of meticulously placed markings and lines drawn in conductive material (usually chalks made of specific types of metal), that harnesses and directs ambient etheric force into the target object. The channel is a drawn equation that is one part calculation and one part instruction. Once it is complete, the channel will direct the etheric force into and around the target object, drawing out its energies to create the alchemist's desired effect. To complete a channel, the alchemist must follow four steps:

- First, the alchemist must select a piece of matter.
- Secondly, the alchemist must choose which reactions will be performed. This will determine the Difficulty of the final test and the quality of the chalk needed to draw the channel.
- Next, the alchemist must draw the channel itself. This will consume one piece of conductive chalk and will take one or more maneuvers to complete.
- Finally, the alchemist must initiate the alchemical reaction by spending a single point of *Ether* and using an action to test *Reason + Science* against a Difficulty determined by the Bulk of the object and the reactions chosen in the second step. The total Difficulty of the parameters chosen cannot exceed 10. Any reaction with a Difficulty of 11 or higher automatically fails.

Step One: Selecting Matter

An alchemist must first select any single non-living object or a portion of a larger non-living object. The Bulk rank of the affected piece of matter will be added to the Difficulty of the alchemy test.

Step Two:
Selecting Reactions and Transmutations

Once the matter has been selected, the alchemist must decide what she wants to do to it. She may select any number of reactions she has acquired through the *Alchemical Reaction* asset. The alchemist must then determine the Strength level of each reaction to be performed. For each Strength level of the reaction, the Difficulty it provides will be increased by the amount listed in its description. The total Difficulty for the alchemy test will equal the sum of the reaction Difficulty plus the Bulk of the target object.

Step Three:
Designing and Drawing the Channel

A channel is a set of instructions that tell the alchemical process how to function. The outer shell of a channel is a two-dimensional circle drawn around the object. This circle defines the circumference of a three-dimensional sphere, which must wholly contain the affected matter. The internal lines of a channel are used to direct etheric force in much the same way that copper wire conducts electricity. The pattern conducts the energy through the object to

facilitate its alteration. The resulting channel can sometimes look like an ancient magical sigil, but is actually the product of specific scientific computations.

If a channel is made of the wrong type or amount of conductive material, or is drawn improperly to the specific context of the object, it will not alter its target. In such instances, the etheric force will escape and the object will remain unchanged. Most modern alchemists will draw their channels with conductive metallic chalks referred to as 'alchemist's chalk.' Each stick of chalk has a quality rank to represent the types of materials used to make it. Drawing a channel will consume a single piece of chalk with a quality rank equal to the Strength level of the most complicated reaction used.

Step Four: Initiating the Alchemical Reaction

Once the channel is complete, the alchemist spends a point of *Ether* to initiate the reaction and tests *Reason + Science* against the Difficulty defined in step two. If the test is successful then all of the chosen reactions and transmutations occur immediately. If the test fails nothing happens. Remember that tasks with a Difficulty higher than 10 cannot be attempted.

TRAIT TEST FOR ALCHEMICAL REACTIONS
Reason + Science – Difficulty of Reaction + Card Value
= Degree of Success

Duration of Alchemical Reactions

Any given alchemical reaction continues for a period in Time ranks equal to twice the Strength level of the reaction. That means that a level 1 alchemical reaction can last up to two ranks of Time (1 hour). Alchemists can draw their channels to end a reaction at any time before this deadline or simply let the reaction run its course for the entire continuous reaction Time. More information on Time can be found on the *Time* table on p. 214.

REACTION DURATIONS

Reaction Strength	Time Rank	Duration
1	2	1 hour
2	4	4 hours
3	6	12 hours
4	8	48 hours
5	10	One month

ALCHEMICAL REACTIONS

Different alchemical processes are learned by taking the *Alchemical Reaction* asset. A new reaction is learned each time the asset is taken. However, the alchemist may only choose to learn reactions for which she has the required *Science* skill rank. An alchemist may only use reactions that she has learned by taking the asset.

Caustic Reaction

Requires: *Science 3*

Difficulty: +1 Difficulty per Strength level of the reaction

For the duration of the reaction the affected object becomes highly caustic. If the alchemist wishes the object to have a container that it will not corrode, that container must be declared and placed within the channel before the reaction is initiated. Apart from this optional container, the caustic object will damage everything it touches.

In industry, this reaction is used to create dangerous solvents when needed so that hazardous chemicals needn't be stored long-term. Alchemists with more daring lives can use this reaction to cause a door to corrode its own frame, create caustic floor panels to entrap trespassers, or make weapons whose caustic properties inflict severe damage on opponents.

When a caustic item comes into contact with an object or person other than its container, it will make a passive attack against it using the alchemist's *Reason + Science* against the target's physical Defense. The attack has the *Undone* weapon condition and a Potency rating equal to the Strength level of the reaction. A successful penetrating attack will cause a Wound to a living being or a rank of Damage to an object. An individual who willingly picks up a caustic item or an object that rests on one will automatically suffer a Wound for each turn they remain in contact.

If the caustic object is actively used as a weapon, it has the *Undone* weapon condition and a Potency rating equal to the Strength level of the reaction. A successful penetrating attack will deal two Wounds to a person or two ranks of Damage to an object, one from the weapon and one from its causticity.

Caustic weapons require the use of a container to be effective. A caustic hand weapon must have a container such as a glove or it cannot be held. A caustic projectile must have the weapon that fires it declared as its container or it will damage that weapon, rendering it *Nonfunctional* after a single attack.

The caustic object can inflict a total number of Wounds or ranks of Damage conditions equal to the Strength level of the reaction, after which the object becomes inert.

Electrical Reaction

Requires: *Science 2*

Difficulty: +1 per Strength level of the reaction

Pioneered by Edison himself during his research into electricity, this is one of the first codified reactions in New Alchemy. It may be used to power any object that runs on electricity, to generate light, or to electrocute a person or object.

When used to generate power, this reaction creates one rank of power output for each Strength level of the reaction. The target object can serve as an electrical *Power Supply* for the duration of the reaction. Creating alchemical batteries from scavenged materials is a common use of this reaction (see *Power Supply,* p. 206).

If the electrified object is touched without proper shielding, the object will make a passive attack on the handler using the alchemist's *Reason + Science* against the target's physical Defense. The attack has the *Incapacitated* weapon condition and a Potency rating equal to the Strength level of the reaction. A successful penetrating attack will cause a Wound to a living being or the Nonfunctional condition to any object uses an electric Power Supply. An individual who willingly picks up an electrified item will automatically suffer a Wound for each turn they remain in contact.

If an electrified object is actively used as a weapon, it has the *Incapacitated* weapon condition and a Potency rating equal to the Strength level of the reaction. A successful penetrating attack will deal two Wounds to a person or two ranks of Damage to an electronic object, one from the weapon and one from electrocution.

The electrified object can inflict a total number of Wounds, ranks of Damage, or *Nonfunctional* conditions equal to the Strength level of the reaction before the power is fully discharged.

This reaction can also be used to harness electromagnetic energies from an object, producing an eerie light. The radius of this light is measured in Reach increments equal to the Strength of the reaction: 1 = *Touch*, 2 = *Close*, 3 = *Extended*, 4 = *Short Range*, 5 = *Long Range*. Alternatively, the alchemist may choose to reduce the radius of this light source in order to increase the duration of the reaction. For every Reach increment decreased, increase the Time increment by one rank. Luminescent objects are safe to touch.

Explosive Reaction

Requires: *Science 4*

Difficulty: +2 per Strength level of the reaction

Although discovered accidentally, even the New Science has been bent toward military applications in these uncertain times. Should an alchemist turn her talents to wanton destruction, this reaction is almost assuredly her favorite.

The target object of this reaction will become wildly unstable and explode at a predetermined time during the duration of the reaction. When the object explodes, a single test of the alchemist's *Reason + Science* is made against the physical Defense of all objects and characters in the object's zone of control. If the targets have cover, they benefit from the rules for *Blocking Terrain* and *Cover and Aiming* (see p. 82). The explosion has a Potency rating equal to the Strength level of the reaction. If the attack is successful, it will bypass Guard and inflict one Wound to a living object or one rank of Damage to a non-living object. A remarkable success will inflict two Wounds or two ranks of Damage.

The alchemically altered object can be set with a trigger for an additional +1 Difficulty to the reaction. Instead of a set time, a triggered explosion will be set off with a named impetus, such as exposure to fire, electricity, or sharp physical contact such as being struck by an attack or thrown against a hard surface. When the trigger occurs, the object explodes as normal.

- If combined with *Thermal Reaction*, the explosion will take on the form of fire. Any target successfully hit by the blast will be on fire, suffering an additional attack as per the *Thermal*

Reaction, and the attack gains the weapon condition *Burning* (p. 98).

- If combined with *Electrical Reaction*, the explosion will take the form of an electrical burst. Any target successfully hit by the blast will suffer an additional attack as per the *Electrical Reaction*.
- If combined with *Caustic Reaction*, the explosion will spread caustic material. Any target successfully hit by the blast will suffer an additional attack as per the *Caustic Reaction*.

Thermal Reaction

Requires: *Science* 2
Difficulty: +1 per Strength level of the reaction

Only recently formalized by members of the Royal Society and entering general practice, *Thermal Reactions* allow a reaction to give off or take in prodigious amounts of heat. The early discussions of further Arctic and Antarctic exploration have garnered momentum as the presence of a skilled alchemist could make such ventures much safer. On a more mundane level, cooled transportation of perishable goods is leading to a revolution in the food industry.

The target object of a *Thermal Reaction* can serve as a source of heat or cold. This is commonly used for climate regulation, powering of steam engines, and weaponry. For each Strength level of the reaction, a certain amount of heat is given off or taken in by the object. With a level 1 reaction, an alchemically heated object can warm a room to a comfortable temperature. Furthermore, each Strength level of the reaction allows one person to sustain comfort in the equivalent level of an extreme environment (see *Extreme Environments*, p. 96).

A thermally altered object can also boil the water of a steam engine, creating a *Power Supply*. This allows the steam engine to create power output equal to the Strength level of the reaction up to the maximum output of the engine. This power will last for the duration of the reaction (for more information, see *Power Supply*, p. 206).

If the heated or cooled object is touched without proper insulation, the object will make a passive attack on the handler using the alchemist's *Reason + Science* against a Difficulty equal to the target's physical Defense. The attack has a Potency rating equal to the Strength level of the reaction. A successful penetrating attack will cause a Wound to a living being or a rank of Damage to an object. An individual who willingly picks up a alchemically heated or cooled item or an object that rests on one will automatically suffer a Wound for each turn they remain in contact.

If a weapon is heated or cooled via this reaction, the attack has a Potency rating equal to the Strength level of the reaction. A successful penetrating attack will deal two Wounds to a person or two ranks of Damage to an object, one from the weapon and one from heat or cold.

Heated objects will have the *Burning* weapon condition which can be placed on any combustible materials (see *Attacking Objects*, p. 85), but cooled objects inflict no further effects. The heated or cooled object can inflict any number of Wounds or ranks of Damage during the duration of the reaction.

Transmutation Reaction

Requires: *Science* 3
Difficulty: +2 per Strength level of reaction

The alchemist can draw and execute channels that transmute a target object into another type of matter. In game terms this is abstracted into altering the object's Structure or Complexity, or adding or removing a physical property. A target object's Structure may be increased or reduced by a number of ranks equal to the reaction's Strength level. The object will not change in Bulk when its Structure is altered. In this way, an alchemist can transmute wood into brick or paper into steel. The description of the change is left to the player and Narrator: the system is only concerned with the attributes of the object she creates and how it can be used in the game. *All Transmutations are permanent*, so once an object has been transmuted it will remain in its new form, unless it is transmuted again.

While an object is being transmuted, it can be molded by the alchemist controlling the reaction. This requires an alchemist to use other skills to shape a substance as it is being changed by a *Transmutation Reaction*. For example, the *Artisan* skill could be used to sculpt a statue from water as it is being turned into titanium, producing a solid titanium statue that could never be sculpted by normal means. The use of this skill must be completed before the duration of the *Transmutation* ends, at which time the object is only as malleable as its new substance would dictate.

A *Transmutation Reaction* may also be used to reduce the Complexity of an object by transmuting its component parts into other types of matter. An object's Complexity can be reduced by a number of ranks equal to the reaction's Strength level, but no object's Complexity can be reduced below 2 in this way (the alchemical reaction cannot produce a natural material). Objects whose Complexity is reduced to 2 will receive the *Nonfunctional* condition. Complexity 1 objects can be transmuted into Complexity 2 objects with a level 1 *Transmutation Reaction*, but no object may have its Complexity raised above rank 2 by a reaction. An alchemist can refine and purify, but she cannot create moving parts or finished products.

Transmutation Reactions can also be used to violate the normal bounds of an object's natural properties. The following material properties can be given or removed from the targeted object: combustible, electrically conductive, magnetic, translucent, or reflective. Other properties may be allowed at Narrator discretion. A number of physical properties equal to the level of the reaction can be added or removed. Added properties will not change the attributes of an object (i.e. making a brick translucent does not make it glass and easily shatterable, it is simply a translucent brick). Many unnatural items may be created in this way.

The Great Clockmaker is known to bless his people with spiritual gifts called charisms. These abilities are extremely rare and it is unknown why certain individuals are gifted while others are not. Even more perplexing is that most commonly the men and women who receive these abilities are simple people of faith rather than those of noble birth or those of high station within the Church. In fact, it is a source of consternation to the Magisterium that cloistered monks are much more likely to manifest these abilities than Cardinals.

Faithful men and women who manifest a charism are a great boon if they are within the Church hierarchy, but are perceived as a possible threat to its power if they are outside of it. Charisms show the power of the Maker and can only be used by those of pure heart. Thus, charismatics can quickly become popular folk religious figures or even revered as living saints. Those whose whereabouts become known are usually sought out and confirmed by Witchfinders or Inquisitors, often to be drafted into the ranks of those organizations, or placed elsewhere in the religious or political power structure. However, some can go their whole lives using their gifts to serve remote villages, forever escaping the notice of religious authorities.

Nearly all recorded accounts of charisms occur in adherents of one of the Abrahamic faiths, and no charism has ever been seen in those polytheists that worship false gods. However, there have been rare individuals from other monotheistic or non-theistic faiths that have manifested these powers. The response to those of "foreign faiths" who manifest charisms ranges widely, but has improved over the centuries. The Magisterium labels all non-Christians with charisms as anathema, but is apt to attempt to convert them rather than kill them. Long ago, the See of Canterbury would have hung such people as witches, but their continued exposure to indigenous beliefs in Africa and on the Indian sub-continent has softened their xenophobia into a frightened confusion mixed with tolerant disdain. Local response to such individuals can differ greatly based on the practices of their regional religious institutions. Sometimes agents of the Church have been known to appear and protect foreigners from their own religious brethren.

Each charism is a separate ability, and most of the gifted seldom possess more than one or two. Although, very rare cases have been recorded where many more witnessed charisms manifested in an individual. Each time a character takes the charism asset, she acquires a charism of her choosing. Pureblood characters may acquire any charism for which they meet the minimum *Composure* rank, but may only use these abilities if they remain pure of heart. If a character with one or more charisms receives even a single rank of *Corruption*, she will no longer be able to use them until she is purified.

USING CHARISMS

A character who has taken the charism asset is called a charismatic and may use any of the charisms to which she has access. All charisms require one point of *Purpose* to be spent at the moment of their use. The effect of a charism may not be counteracted, including through the expenditure of potential; it is as if charisms express the will of the Clockwork itself.

Banish

Requires: *Composure 2*

A banisher may call upon the divine Name to drive away outsiders. An outsider is any being who resides somewhere other than its intended place in the Clockwork. For example, the souls of the dead are meant to go on to the heavens, they are considered outsiders while they are anywhere else. A full description of outsiders is starts at *Natives and Outsiders,* p. 55.

Banishing is most commonly used for malevolent shades and chimera. The banisher uses an action to make a *Presence + Composure* social attack against a Difficulty equal to the target's *Will.* If successful, the target must leave the sight and presence of the banisher and may not, willingly or unwillingly, return until the following sunset. There are no circumstances where a banished entity may enter or target anything within the banisher's zone of control.

If the entity to be banished is incorporeal and tethered to an object or living person, it will automatically return to its tether after sunset. The destruction of tethers can only be accomplished through an exorcism.

Bless

Requires: *Composure 2*

This charism is gifted to all who receive the sacrament of holy orders within the Church. In addition to priests, it has been found among many faithful believers from London to Hong Kong. It is the most commonly found charism and the least likely to draw attention from religious authorities. It is most often used to prevent the restless dead from creating tethers to the material world, bolster objects and reagents used against spirits, and to create holy weapons for use against the creatures of the Pontus.

Blessing something is the act of setting it aside for a specific and holy use. Charismatics with this gift may bless any object they can touch with a successful *Presence + Composure* test, Difficulty 0. This action will take a full minute/sequence to complete. The Clockwork actively protects and bolsters blessed objects in the following ways:

- Blessed items cannot be used as tethers for incorporeal beings such as shades, wyldlings, or demons. Objects currently being used as tethers cannot be blessed until the tether is broken.

Outsiders will find blessed items disconcerting and uncomfortable to touch, making it impossible to effectively use them as weapons or tools.

- The blessed object's intended use cannot be impeded in any way through the use of potential. Thus, a targeted creature can neither spend *Purpose* to avoid outcomes caused by blessed objects nor spend *Ether* to force a character to draw again for a trait test to use a blessed object for its designated purpose.

- Blessed weapons receive a +1 to Potency when used against outsiders, and can make physical attacks against incorporeal creatures even though they have no body. A physical attack made against an incorporeal being in this way will change Morale instead of reducing Guard. A penetrating attack will force the entity to flee instead of Wounding or subduing it.

- Blessed locations are considered consecrated and are less likely to suffer from Pontus events (see *Environmental Stability*, p. 281).

Once something is blessed it will retain that blessing until it is profaned. An object is profaned the moment it touches a character with at least one point of *Corruption* or the object is used for any purpose other than the specific one for which it was blessed. For example, a holy symbol blessed to remind people of their faith will become profaned if it is taken by someone else and disfigured. A weapon blessed for the destruction of chimera will be profaned if used to attack a wylding or to prop open a door. An object may never be blessed for any sinful purpose or for violent use against mortals (purebloods, beastfolk, and changelings). Any object used to make a physical attack against a mortal is immediately profaned.

Discernment of Spirits

Requires: *Composure 3*

This charism allows a character to perceive incorporeal beings such as shades, demons, and spirits. Although these beings are not usually visible, the charismatic will see, hear, and interact them as though they were corporeal, subject to all the usual rules for sight and speech. This can often be a terrifying experience, especially for those not exposed to teachings that would give context to this ability. The *Discernment of Spirits* has driven many such charismatics mad from exposure to the rantings of the dead. A trained charismatic can avoid this fate by making a successful *Focus + Composure* test against a Difficulty of the incorporeal being's *Presence*, which allows her to completely ignore the incorporeal being.

A charismatic with *Discernment of Spirits* may also sense the passions and drives of any corporeal or incorporeal entity with whom she interacts. A successful *Focus + Intuition* test against a Difficulty of the target's *Will + Composure* allows the charismatic to know the target's strongest Affinity. A remarkable success (DoS 4+) will additionally discern an additional Affinity. An extraordinary success (DoS 8+) will tell the character all of the target's Affinities.

Exorcism

Requires: *Composure 3*

With increasing regularity, incorporeal entities such as shades and demons seek to find a home in the mortal world. Shades often bind themselves to objects or people that will serve as their tether to keep them from being pulled toward the heavens. Demons seek to tether themselves to mortals, allowing them access to a body through which they may fulfill their lusts. Exorcism is the art of destroying these tethers so that these entities are no longer bound to the world.

The charismatic begins an exorcism by engaging the tethered being in a social conflict. The targeted entity will begin with a Disposition of *Favorable* toward being exorcised, minus one step for each rank of its Affinity to its tether. Each successful *Presence + Composure* attack against a Difficulty of the entity's *Will + Composure* will move its Disposition back toward *Favorable*. If the exorcist delivers a successful penetrating attack, the bond with the tether is destroyed and the entity can no longer use it to remain in the mortal world. The entity will keep its Affinity, although it can no longer be used as a tether.

Exorcisms can be very dangerous. A possessing entity will do anything, including self-inflicted physical harm to its hosts or her loved ones, to persuade an exorcist to stop. Even when successful, an exorcism will not banish the entity and it may attempt to possess a new host immediately.

A charismatic with *Exorcism* receives divine advantages when performing an exorcism. This charism allows the charismatic to ignore any social Armor provided to the targeted entity by its Affinity to its tether and gives all of her social attacks against the entity the *Undone* weapon condition. This makes a charismatic exorcist much more effective at breaking tethers, and those who also have the *Banish* charism are even more fit for this sort of service. Rare individuals with both of these gifts are usually sought after by the Witchfinders and the Inquisition.

Faith Healing

Requires: *Composure 3*

Faith Healing is not the most common charism, but it is the most widely spread of the gifts. Like all charisms, it is largely found among adherents of the Abrahamic faiths, but it has also been discovered in believers of every monotheistic religion the Empire has encountered. Perhaps the Maker sees the havoc wrought in the world by the Pontus, and takes pity on us through the beautiful gift of healing.

A faith healer may target a wounded individual and take an action to test *Presence + Composure*, Difficulty 0. This test is considered a standard recovery test on behalf of the wounded character and can be made in addition to all normal recovery tests. On a remarkable success (DoS 4+), the next recovery or *Medicine* test to be performed by or on this character will be performed against a Difficulty of 0, regardless of the target's Wound Penalties. On an extraordinary success (DoS 8+) all recovery or *Medicine* tests of any kind made by or on the target will use a Difficulty of 0 until all current maladies are healed.

Greater Miracles

Requires: *Composure 5*

Whenever the charismatic plays the Fate card, regardless of how it is played, the character may spend a single point of *Purpose* to invoke a completely impossible event. If the Fate card is drawn for a trait test, this charism may be activated immediately. If the Fate card is drawn as an initiative card, it may be activated whenever that initiative card is used to take an action. Activating this ability ignores the usual restriction of only spending a single point of potential in a given sequence. *Greater Miracles* include raining fire, resurrecting the recently deceased, turning water into wine, or walking on water.

Lesser Miracles

Requires: *Composure 4*

Any time the charismatic could normally spend a point of *Purpose* to create a *plausible* event, she may instead spend two points of *Purpose* to create a single *possible* event. Activating this ability ignores the usual restriction of only spending a single point of potential in a given sequence. The created effect must be within the bounds of physics and natural law, but may otherwise be well outside the bounds of likelihood. *Lesser Miracles* include rain in the desert during the dry season or cutting open the fish you just caught to find your wife's engagement ring, which she had lost while swimming in that lake one year ago.

Prayer

Requires: *Composure 2*

All believers pray, but there are some that have the ear of the Clockmaker in a special way. These charismatics receive what they ask for in very real and immediate ways. Characters with this charism usually dedicate a great deal of their free time to prayer, not just in those moments when they are in need. A combination of this obvious piety and the plausibility of the Clockmaker's response makes these charismatics almost undetectable to the religious and secular authorities who would seek to recruit them.

A character with the *Prayer* charism may spend a point of *Purpose* before any trait test as she says a prayer. The action being attempted cannot be a sin, cause the character or the action's target to take *Corruption*, or be an attack against a mortal of pure blood. So long as the action meets these criteria, no card is drawn and the test is considered to succeed with a DoS of 1.

Prophecy

Requires: *Composure 3*

Prophets proclaim the divine plan and have an intrinsic understanding of the ramifications of people's choices on the Clockwork. Spending one point of *Purpose* and making a successful *Presence + Intuition* test against a situational Difficulty set by the Narrator will allow a character to prophesy about one event. What this prophecy contains is completely determined by the Narrator, but it will always involve speaking a truth regarding the Clockwork that the character did not know before. This may be the impending ramifications of a given action, a looming threat to someone's safety, the location of something needed by the prophet or for which she is looking, or other piece of information that aids the prophet in navigating the Clockwork. A prophecy will always contain at least one piece of information that is useful to one of the listeners, but a prophet can never prophesy about his own individual life or desires. This information will often be cryptic, must be spoken aloud by the prophet as it is received, and will often bear critical words against the Pontus and those who are actively or ignorantly working against the divine plan. The Narrator should speak on behalf of the prophet character when prophecies are given.

At times, the Clockwork may require an intermediary to convey a message to the people and attempt to use a prophet as its instrument. In such an instance, the character need not pay the *Purpose* cost to speak the prophecy, but may spend a point of *Ether* to remain silent.

Tongues

Requires: *Composure 2*

This is often considered the least of the charisms because it is commonly used in self serving ways or to intentionally speak in languages unknown by the listener. Such arrogant use of this charism is condemned in the holy texts, but this gift is still a great blessing to diplomats and missionaries who spread peace and unity across the Clockwork.

The charismatic may spend one point of *Purpose* to gain partial fluency in the native language of her listener for the duration of a chapter. If more than one character is conversing with the charismatic, all will hear her words as if they were spoken in their native tongue. If the character already has partial fluency in a given language, she will gain full fluency in that language until the end of the chapter, and may then engage in social conflict with any conversational partner who is also fully fluent in that language (even if it is not their native language). No trait test is necessary.

Although against the intent of this charism, the charismatic may also speak in any language she wishes regardless of what would be understood by her listeners. This can be done to speak

in code to a single individual or to perform the gift of *Tongues* in a showy display of nonsensical gibberish. Such practices are upheld by the Church as personal meditative practices, but are frowned upon when they occur in public.

Word of Knowledge

Requires: *Composure 4*

The world is a dangerous and confusing place, and many within it are not aware of the true nature of the Clockwork or its Maker. Charismatics with the *Word of Knowledge* can share information regarding the Clockwork that extends far beyond their own personal understanding. The information is gifted by the Maker for the preservation of the Truth.

When this charismatic engages in a social conflict where she is convincing or persuading another regarding something that is true and good, she may spend a point of *Purpose* to use the *Word of Knowledge* ability. For the remainder of the current conflict, her opponents' Defense is equal to their *Will* only (in lieu of the standard Defense of *Will* + skill). This charism may never be used to convince someone of something that is not true, even if the charismatic believes it is. It may also never be used to convince or persuade someone of anything sinful or against the will of the Maker.

Word of Wisdom

Requires: *Composure 3*

Charismatics can inspire a great deal of fervor in the hearts of those who hear them. Those gifted with the *Word of Wisdom* can very easily create great love and desire in others, provided they are working toward a noble purpose and do not use any kind of deceit.

At the end of a social conflict, after the charismatic has successfully convinced or persuaded another character, she may spend a point of *Purpose* to place a temporary Affinity on that character. This Affinity must be directly related to their new conviction or belief. A basic success (DoS 1+) will place a rank 1 Affinity; a remarkable success (DoS 4+) will place a rank 2 Affinity; an extraordinary success (DoS 8+) will place a rank 3 Affinity. This Affinity will normalize over time in the standard manner of social recovery.

GLAMOUR

Glamours are the illusory magics that flow in the blood of the fey. As such, they are only available to fey and their descendents: changelings, purebloods who take the *Touched* asset (p. 159), wyldlings, or feyfolk. These abilities are powerful distortions that can alter the senses, manipulate the unstable energies of the Clockwork, and even rewrite fate itself.

While other transcendent powers have a clear place in the workings and history of the Clockwork, the exact nature and source of glamours is barely understood. Of the few magi and mystics who have seriously studied fey, most agree that fey creatures somehow originate in the Borderlands. The residual creative energy from

the making of the Clockwork still infuses that strange place, and perhaps the fey maintain a link with this creative power which lets them project illusions and temporary passions. Yet, unlike charisms, magic or alchemy, which can enact real and lasting change in the world, glamours are only echoes and reflections.

Even with that limitation, glamours should not be taken lightly. Unless a target is exceptionally strong-willed or perceptive, the illusions and false beliefs that glamours forge can seem more real than the world around them. Many glamours are quite subtle and can only be perceived by their intended target, if at all. The only evidence they leave is the memories of those they deceive, which makes their use virtually impossible to prove. The uneasiness many people feel around changelings stems from their fear of being deceived in such ways.

Awe
Requires: *Guile 2*

The Tuatha Dé Dannan, an ancient race of feyfolk, were known for a fierce beauty and commanding presence that would cause many to love, envy, or cower before them. Like them, fey imbued with Awe can spend a point of *Ether* to increase their own Esteem by one step, increase the Morale of an ally or group by one step, or decrease opponents' Morale by one step. With this mystical bearing the fey may inspire people toward love or fright, but such powerful beauty can also inspire jealously, envy, and spite.

Befriend
Requires: *Guile 2*

A common glamour among changelings, *Befriend* allows them to make serious connections with others quickly and easily. Some use the ability to build genuine friendships and close ties, but more often than not this glamour is used for convenience or more selfish reasons.

The changeling may take an action to target a single person with whom they are in physical contact or with whom they have made eye contact, and make a subtle social attack using *Presence + Guile* against a Difficulty of the target's *Will + Composure*. If the attack is successful, the target immediately gains a temporary rank 1 Affinity for the attacker that lasts until the end of the scene. The use of this glamour does not require the expenditure of *Ether*.

This connection is strong enough that the target will treat the changeling as a friend. The befriended character is subject to all of the effects of a rank 1 Affinity, including a social Armor 1 against those trying to convince her that her feelings are not genuine. This Affinity may not be made permanent through the spending of experience points.

Beguile
Requires: *Guile 3*

Fey creatures with this gift can ensure that no matter the distrust or vitriol between themselves and another, their conversation partners must give a fair hearing to whatever they have to say. At the beginning of a social conflict, before initiative cards are played, the fey can spend a point of *Ether* to nominate a single target they can see that is part of the social conflict. If the target's starting Disposition towards the fey's position is *Hostile* or *Guarded*, it immediately becomes *Indifferent*. For the duration of the conflict that Disposition cannot drop below *Indifferent*. However, if any of the fey creature's social attacks yield a remarkable failure (DoS –4) or worse, the glamour is immediately broken and social conflict continues without its effects.

Captivate
Requires: *Guile 2*

Some fey creatures have the ability to *Captivate* those to whom they speak. Something about the fey is compelling, and it is almost impossible to draw oneself away. All social attacks made by a fey creature with this glamour have the *Entrapped* weapon condition, which can be applied any time a social attack yields a remarkable success (Dos 4+).

Charm
Requires: *Guile 3*

A fey with this glamour may spend a point of *Ether* to charm another character with whom they have made physical or eye contact by making a subtle test of *Presence + Guile* against a Difficulty of the target's *Will + Composure*. If successful, the target immediately gains a temporary rank 2 Affinity towards the fey which lasts for the rest of the scene. The target will view her with love and affection; however, even lovers can disagree or come to blows. The target will gain the normal things associated with a rank 2 Affinity: a social Armor 2 against those trying to convince her that her feelings are not genuine, and Potency 2 is granted to all of the fey's social attacks made against the victim while she is charmed. This Affinity may not be made permanent through the spending of experience points. Clever fey are very deft with this glamour and use this Affinity as a way to more easily convince or persuade the target using social conflict.

Curse
Requires: *Guile 4*

With spite and anger, a fey with this glamour perverts the designs of the Clockwork and ensures her target's next failure will punish them. By taking an action and spending a point of *Ether*, the fey taints and disrupts the fortune of one character they can see. The next time this character fails a test during the same scene, the results will be determined as though the failure were one category worse. Marginal successes (DoS 0) will be treated as failures, failures (DoS –1) will be treated as remarkable failures, and remarkable failures (DoS –4) will be treated as extraordinary failures. Extraordinary failures (DoS –8) are treated as though the target played the Doom card with all the consequences thereof. Once the curse has exacerbated a failure, the glamour ends. If the scene ends before the targeted character fails any tests, the glamour has no effect.

Doppelgänger
Requires: *Guile 5*

A fey with the *Doppelgänger* glamour may spend a point of *Ether* to take on the appearance of another person for the duration of one scene. The impersonated target must be within sight of the fey at the time the glamour is enacted. A photograph or accurate drawing may be used for this purpose, but when the glamour ends such an image will be irreparably distorted.

This glamour mimics complete physical appearance including basic mannerisms and voice, making it difficult for even close associates of the target to notice the impersonation. No test is necessary for the fey to pass as the target unless there is a specific reason for suspicion (e.g. seeing both the fey and her target together simultaneously). If someone suspects the imposture, they can make a *Focus + Intuition* test against a Difficulty equal to the fey's *Presence + Guile*. If successful, they will see the fey as she truly is. If they fail, they are unable to pierce the glamour and must rely on other means to prove that the fey is not as she appears.

Enthrall

Requires: *Guile 5*

Stories of those with fey blood being silver-tongued manipulators stem mainly from this glamour's ability to temporarily trick a target into adoring the fey. This glamour may only be attempted against a specific target once per scene, but it may be attempted on multiple targets over the course of a scene. The fey selects a single target with whom they are in physical contact or with whom they have made eye contact, and spends a point of *Ether*. She then makes a subtle social attack using *Presence + Guile* against a Difficulty equal to the target's *Will + Composure*. If successful, the target immediately gains a temporary rank 3 Affinity for the fey that will last until the following sunrise. If the test fails, the enthrallment does not occur. Remarkable failure (DoS –4) will instead instill unease and discomfort in the target. Extraordinary

failure (DoS –8) creates outright enmity towards the fey that lasts until the following sunset.

If the fey wishes to continue a successful enthrallment beyond the following sunrise, she must spend another *Ether* and take an action to attempt the test anew before dawn. If successful, the enthrallment continues without interruption for another day.

While enthralled, a character is subject to all of the effects of a rank 3 Affinity. This includes a social Armor 3 against those who would try to convince her that her feelings are not genuine, and Potency 3 granted to all of the fey's social attacks made against the victim while she is enthralled. This Affinity may not be made permanent through the spending of experience points.

Players and Narrators should remember that the sudden and overwhelming devotion of the target for the fey could very easily seem unnatural to others. This is a potent glamour to be sure, but one that must be used with caution and subtlety. The Empire considers supernatural coercion a capital offense, punishable by hanging.

Fey Stroke

Requires: *Guile 5*

The least subtle, and arguably most dangerous glamour, is the *Fey Stroke*. This glamour renders its victim completely senseless and unresponsive. Before making a physical attack, the fey must specify that they are attempting a *Fey Stroke*. They then spend a point of *Ether* to test *Presence* combined with their choice of *Fencing, Firearms, Fisticuffs,* or *Melee*. This test is made against their target's *Vigor + Will*. The Reach of the attack is equal to the weapon used to make the attack. If the attack is successful it does not reduce Guard or inflict any Wounds. Rather, the victim gains the *Incapacitated* condition that will persist for a number of sequences equal to the DoS of the attack, or for the remainder of the scene if there are no further sequences of conflict. The condition is placed regardless of the target's Armor and cannot be removed via any means unless the fey herself willingly dismisses it.

While a victim is *Incapacitated* as a result of a *Fey Stroke* they are utterly helpless and insensate, and they have no awareness of anything that is done to them. Though some fey with this power only ever use it in self-defense, folk tales abound of this glamour being used for abductions or thievery.

Geas

Requires: *Guile 5*

A fey creature may invite or persuade others to enter into a pact. An oath needn't be spoken, but can be inferred through the exchange of services, gifts, food, or other commodities, and may occur without the complete understanding of the second party. This process requires participation in a customary exchange with unspoken but culturally understood ramifications. Depending on local customs, this could include sexual intercourse inferring a promise to marry, an invitation into the home inferring a three-day stay, the acceptance of a valuable coin inferring enlistment into an army, or any other cultural expectation. An arrangement may also be the result of persuasion, or to the fey creature holding a person to something that was said even if it wasn't meant. However it happens, a deal is struck and an oath is made.

The fey must then spend one point of *Ether* to finalize the contract. After the contract is sealed, the victim subject to the *Geas* must make consistent progress toward the contract's goal or she will suffer a −2 penalty to all actions that do not directly relate to the contract's successful completion. These penalties will continue until the character fulfills her oath.

Hex

Requires: *Guile 2*

Many who find themselves at odds with a fey are plagued with all manner of unfortunate happenstance. With a *Hex*, a fey can sometimes bring what should be successful endeavors to frustrating ends. Whenever a character makes a trait test, a fey creature with this glamour may spend a point of *Ether* to force that character to draw two cards instead of one. The test is then resolved with the worse of the two cards.

Phantasm

Requires: *Guile 2*

Some fey may, with a moment's effort, fool the senses of a single target and trick them into perceiving an illusion. By spending an action to concentrate on a single visible target, the fey may make a subtle test of *Presence + Guile* against a Difficulty equal to the target's *Will + Composure*. If the test succeeds, the target experiences an illusion with a single sense for just a moment (one turn while in conflict). The hallucination can affect any of the target's senses: hearing a gunshot, feeling a frigid breeze, seeing a strange face peer out of a window, tasting blood, or smelling a sumptuous Christmas goose are all fair uses of this glamour.

Using this glamour on the same target more than once in a short period is difficult, though, as their credulity is tested. During a scene, all subsequent uses of this glamour that choose the same target are made with a cumulative −2 penalty on the test.

Any use of this ability that yields a remarkable failure (DoS −4) will immediately alert the target to the fact they are being manipulated, and an extraordinary failure (DoS −8) will also immediately alert the target that the acting fey is the source of the illusions.

Phantasmagoria

Requires: *Guile 4*

Potent and versatile illusions can be created with this glamour. The fey spends one point of *Ether* and makes a subtle attack against one or more visible targets. This attack is made once using *Presence + Guile*, and is resolved as an individual attack against each target's *Will + Composure*. All of the targets against whom this attack is successful will experience full sensory illusions for the remainder of the scene. These illusions can be as simple or grandiose as the the fey desires and can affect all five physical senses.

The illusions created by this glamour may depict people, events, or even whole panoramas. They may talk, move, act, make attacks, or do anything else the fey wishes. The fey dictates the motions, speech, and other actions of the illusions. In conflict scenes, she will use her own initiative cards to determine the turns for her illusions. No matter the activity, all actions taken by an illusion are performed with the fey's *Presence + Guile −2* and made against a Difficulty of the targets' *Will + Composure*. If the action is an attack, use the most appropriate social Defense of the target. Successful attacks can convince, persuade, reduce Guard, and place conditions normally. The effects of physical attacks will look and feel real to the victims; however, an illusion cannot place physical outcomes and cannot Wound or subdue an opponent.

The illusions fade for any target that leaves the fey's line of sight and for all targets if the fey makes any tests other than to control the illusions, loses her last point of Guard, suffers a condition, takes a Wound, or if any action the fey takes to control the illusions yields a remarkable failure (DoS −4). Worse, if such a control test ever yields an extraordinary failure (DoS −8), or if the Doom card is drawn, the illusions immediately end and all targets of the glamour know that the fey was the source of their delusion. Even if all goes well, at the end of the scene, all illusions will fade away. If the fey wishes to continue the illusions beyond a single scene, she must spend one point of *Ether* at the start of each subsequent scene.

Second Chances

Requires: *Guile 2*

All fey have a connection to the disruptive and unstable energies of *Ether*, but some develop a propinquity which allows them to manipulate this force to their benefit. Whenever a fey with this glamour spends a point of *Ether* to draw a new card for herself during a trait test, she uses the better of the two cards to resolve the test, rather than whichever she drew last.

Weaken Purpose

Requires: *Guile 4*

If a fey witnesses someone acting against one of their Affinities, she may use *Weaken Purpose*. The fey immediately spends one point of *Ether* and makes a subtle attack against the individual using *Presence + Mysteries* against a Difficulty equal to the target's *Focus + Will*.

Success on the test drains the target's temporary *Purpose*. A basic success (DoS 1) will drain 1 point; a remarkable success (DoS 4+) drains 2; and an extraordinary success (DoS 8+) drains 3. Failure, however, has dire consequences for the fey as her *Ether* is drained instead: she loses 1 point of *Ether* on a remarkable failure (DoS −4) or 2 points of *Ether* on an extraordinary failure (DoS −8).

The surest way to be present when a target violates an Affinity is to be the one convincing or persuading them to violate it. Canny fey will often create circumstances where they can trick or manipulate someone into violating an Affinity in some minor way, then use this glamour to rob them of any protection they are afforded by their *Purpose*.

RITUAL MAGIC

Ritual magic is the path to a deeper understanding of the cosmos and the hidden connections between all things, and to power of which science cannot dream. It is also a secret and subtle art that can be used in many ways for both good and ill. To the uninitiated, it is a threat to the expected routines of their daily lives, and is at best barely understood and terrifying. To some, it is one tool among many to be used in their own schemes, or for the great struggle to save the Clockwork from the rising threat of the Pontus. To many in the modern day, however, it is something that is not well understood.

Science has never been able to refute the existence or efficacy of ritual magic. It simply views magic as an inefficient and imprecise practice with too many uncontrollable and unforeseeable variables. To most within the Empire it is unfathomable why someone would spend so much time in study and research to learn a dangerous art with few legal uses, and even fewer reliable outcomes. Science is heralded as the true way to study and understand the fundamental nature of the Clockwork. However, even with all the progress of recent decades, science cannot explain the broader cosmology of creation as a whole, nor can it accomplish or understand the effects of ritual magic. Magi know that it never will.

THE ORIGIN OF MAGIC

"You see what Azazel has done; how he has taught all forms of oppression upon the earth. And he revealed eternal secrets which are performed in heaven so that man has learned them."

—*1 Enoch 9:6*

When the angels known as the Grigori fell, they took mortal wives and came to live in the land of Canaan. There they built communities and taught the mysteries of Heaven to the mortals with whom they lived. The fallen Grigori disclosed the secrets of the

7

SANTIAGO

earth that led to advanced agriculture and metallurgy, the secrets of the night sky that led to navigation and astronomy, and the secrets of vegetation that led to medicine and pigmentation. However, not all lessons were simply for the betterment of mundane life. Azazel, the most malevolent of the Grigori, took the mystical arts given to the angels by the Clockmaker and taught them to mortals. Thus magic entered the world of men.

Azazel taught the language of Heaven, now called Enochian, to humankind. The holy words used by the Clockmaker to call forth the world from the Pontus were now on the lips of men, and their power that was once spoken to maintain the Clockwork was now spoken to manipulate it. The Fallen and their descendants discovered new words of power that could be used to perform magic, allowing them to use this once holy power for their own personal gain. Magic became corrupted and men became powerful.

Today, there are dozens of words of power, pure words handed down from the Enochian tongue and impure words discovered from the languages of mortals. These words are woven together to call forth magical power that can be channeled through reagents and rituals. The results are limited only by the caster's skill and imagination. Such power was never meant to fall into the hands of men. Ritual magic has long been abused, and even among modern mystics there is fear that misuse of this power intended to hold the Clockwork together is now slowly tearing it apart and giving the Pontus yet another foothold in the world.

THE PRACTICE OF RITUAL MAGIC

Ritual magic is performed through special combinations of words, materials, and movements that harness supernatural energies to produce magical effects. A magus prepares and performs a ritual by following the instructions described in a written set of directions called a rite. After the ritual is performed, the magus will spend one point of potential: *Purpose* to perform a pure ritual, *Ether* for an impure one. She then tests *Will + Mysteries* against the Difficulty of the rite. If the test succeeds, the ritual will produce its intended effect. The potential must be spent even if the test fails.

TRAIT TEST FOR RITUAL MAGIC

Will + Mysteries – Difficulty of Rite + Card Value = Degree of Success

USING EXTANT RITES

Any character with at least a single rank in the *Mysteries* skill can perform a rite composed by someone else. To do this, the magus needs to acquire a copy of the rite. Next she must perform it as written. Unless the rite uses one of the *Mandatory* restrictions, the magus may meet the ritual requirements (Participants, Reagents, and Time) in whatever way is most convenient to her resources. If the rite does have a mandatory clause, the mandatory requirement must be exactly as the rite prescribes. After the rite is performed,

the magus will spend one point of potential. If the rite is pure, she spends *Purpose*. If the rite is impure, she will spend *Ether*. Finally, the magus must succeed on the ritual performance test described above.

The convenience of not having to do the immense amount of study and research required to compose one's own rite makes these heirlooms a valuable commodity among magi. Also, as there can be many methods to achieve the same magical effect, more efficient rites are highly prized. Some rites are commonplace and available to anyone who can buy a book. Others, especially those of questionable morality, are subject the ever present threat of Witchfinders or Inquisitors with a propensity for burning magical texts and hanging those who utilize them.

The disadvantage of extant rites is their specificity. Magic is a chaotic force and it needs to be directed properly or unforeseen results may occur. The more precise the rite, the more likely it is to have the intended effect. Thus, many magi create highly specialized rites with little room for error. This makes many extant rites less convenient for the magus who wishes to use them in a different context. A rite composed specifically to heal Thomas Whitaker of scarlatina could not be used to heal Richard Upton's leg wound even though mechanically the rites could be otherwise identical. On the other hand, room left for flexibility can be room left for chaos. A rite meant to harm five people can be used to harm one, but the extra energy called forth by the ritual will harm

MAGIC AND BLOODLINES

Pureblood mortals are fully bound to the Clockwork and benefit from its protection, while each naphil is an abomination before the Maker and actively shunned by the Clockwork. This makes pure bloods partially resistant to magical effects and nephilim more vulnerable to them. Whenever a ritual would affect any pureblood character, the Ritual Magic trait test will be performed at +1 Difficulty. Whenever a ritual would affect only nephilim characters, it will be performed at –1 Difficulty. The desirability of the effect does not matter; these modifiers are a reflection of the characters' integration within the Clockwork.

RITE COMPOSITION

REQUIRED STEPS

Constructing a Magical Sentence
Choose one verb and two nouns; form a magical sentence. This will define the magical effect and to what or whom it will be done.

Shaping the Intent
Choose ranks in the three components of Intent: Scope, Puissance, and Duration. This will define the power of the effect, how long it will last, and how much or many it will affect.

Fueling the Intent
Choose ranks in the three components of Requirements: Participants, Reagents, and Time. This will define what items, people, and time are necessary. These ranks must equal or exceed ranks in Intent.

Complete the Rite
Record the magical sentence and all chosen components. The Difficulty of the rite will equal the total ranks of Intent minus any exessive Requirement ranks.

OPTIONAL STEPS

Select Features
Choose any number of Features. Each will add to the magical effect, and counts as one rank of Intent.

Select Restrictions
Choose any number of Restrictions. Each will limit the magical effect. Each Restriction counts as one rank of Requirement for the purposes of Fueling Intent.

---

other random things if possible. Although only a single rank in *Mysteries* is required to perform an extant rite, the majority of these rites are too specific or too dangerous for many would-be magi. This preserves magic as a rare practice, approachable only by those with the right connections.

COMPOSING NEW RITES

The ability to compose one's own rite is what allows a magus to use her resources in ways that best match her intentions. Any character that has mastered at least one verb and two nouns through the *Magical Word* asset is capable of composing her own rites.

Constructing a Magical Sentence: What do you intend the magical effect to do? Combine one verb and two nouns you have mastered into a sentence which describes what the ritual will do and who or what will be affected. A list of words of power and instructions on how to create sentences with them begins on the next page.

Shaping the Intent: The general effect described by the magical sentence is given shape by the intent of the magus. The three components of intent (Duration, Puissance, and Scope) provide mechanical parameters for the magical sentence: defining how long the effect will last, how strong the effect is, and how many targets are affected. Choose a rank in each component that corresponds with your desired magical effect. A detailed description of intent begins on p. 244.

Select features (optional): features may be chosen to add special enhancements to the effect. Each feature has its own unique effect and adds one rank of intent. A detailed description of features begins on p. 247.

Fueling the Intent: Intent determines how much mystical energy is required to fuel the spell. This energy is generated by requirements, objects and actions that tap into the essence of the Clockwork itself. There are three requirement components: Participants, Reagents, and Time. These components define how many magi are required to perform the ritual, the needed materials, and how long the ritual will take to complete. To properly fuel a ritual, you must choose a number of ranks in requirements that equal or exceed the number of ranks chosen for intent. If ranks of requirements exceed ranks of intent, reduce the Difficulty of the rite by the excess amount. Remember that no one can attempt a task can with a Difficulty above 10. A detailed description of requirement components begins on p. 248.

Select Restrictions (optional): Restrictions may be chosen to limit the effect of the ritual, thereby reducing its consumption. Each restriction will reduce the functionality or versatility of the rite in a unique way, but counts as fulfilling one additional rank of requirements to be used in paying for intent. A list of restrictions begins on p. 250.

Complete the Rite: Record the magical sentence and all the components of the rite. Record the purity of the rite, which is the same as the purity of the chosen verb. Make sure that the number of ranks in intent (Duration, Puissance, Scope, and features) is matched by the total requirements (Participants, Reagents, Time, and restrictions). The rite's Difficulty equals the total ranks of intent, less any reductions in Difficulty from excessive requirements. A rite can only be attempted if its final Difficulty is 10 or lower. You may also name the rite if you desire.

WORDS OF POWER

Words of Power are used to produce the magical sentence at the heart of a rite. One verb and two nouns are required to do this. The verb will create the action and determine how the nouns are used. The nouns will define the objects or entities upon which the ritual is focused (the targets) and other things that are subjected to the magical effect (the subjects). When combining the verb with the nouns, the magus may use whatever articles (a, this, the, etc.) and prepositions (of, with, from, to, etc.) she wishes to create a simple magical sentence that describes her desired result.

Each verb in the list that follows supplies a sample sentence representing the most common method in which it is used. For example the magical verb *Expel* provides this sample sentence: "*Expel* [subject] from [target]." In this instance, the term [subject] is replaced by a magical noun that will represent the object or entity to be expelled; and the term [target] is replaced with the magical noun that describes the container or space from which the subject is to be expelled. With this sentence structure, the magus could compose the following magical sentences: "*Expel Shade* from *Body*" (to drive a remnant spirit out of the body of a person) or "*Expel Object* from *Place*" (to have a pocket watch fall off of a shelf). Examples in the text will often supply the most common nouns to be used in various sample sentences, but a magus can use whatever nouns make sense to the situation and her character's intent.

The description for each magical verb will explain how the target noun and subject noun are to be used in conjunction with it. So long as players follow these rules, many sentence forms are possible, and Narrators should be generous when players find ingenious ways to string words together. As long as a magical sentence abides by the rules for subject nouns and target nouns given in the description of the chosen verb and does not conflict with the cosmology of the Clockwork, creative combinations should be encouraged.

THE PURITY OF VERBS

The verb of power utilized will decide the purity of the rite. Pure verbs make pure rites and impure verbs make impure rites. Magical nouns are neither pure nor impure. The purity of the rite will determine which type of potential must be spent to perform it, and whether or not the rite risks exposure to *Corruption*.

Pure rites use verbs of power from the Enochian tongue, the language of the angels. Their use can only protect and support the Clockwork. Pure rites require all Participants to spend a point of *Purpose* when the ritual begins, and there is no risk of *Corruption* if the ritual fails.

Impure verbs of power are either perversions of pure words, or new ones developed by the Fallen and their human students. Rites that use impure verbs break the divine intention for magic and, even when they do good, work against the will of the Maker. Impure rites require Participants to spend a point of *Ether* when the ritual begins. Furthermore, if the ritual test fails, all Participants gain a point of *Corruption* as they are tainted by the dangerous and chaotic energies they failed to control.

THE SPECIFICITY OF NOUNS

The nouns of power are broadly focused. A magus who masters a noun learns how to affect a vast array of things that fall under that noun's purview. The word *Animal* grants a magus access to birds, mammals, insects, fish, and any creature in the Animalia Kingdom. The word *Feyfolk* grants a magus access to the embodied fey that slip into the mortal world, but also changelings and the fey who manifest as nature spirits. If there is confusion about what a noun may cover, more information on creature types and what is included in them may be found in *Chapter 3: Cosmology*. All of the nouns of power have this kind of breadth, but it can often be useful to a magus to tighten the focus of a noun when she uses it.

When a magus constructs a magical sentence for a rite, she may replace any noun she has mastered with any specific example that falls under that noun's purview. Someone who has mastered the word *Object* could instead use the words "book," "sword," or "rock." A noun that depicts a type of creature can always be replaced by that creature's name, family, or other group. A magus who could construct the magical sentence "*Degrade* the *Body* of *Mortal*" could also construct the sentences "*Degrade* the *Body* of Enemies," "*Degrade* the *Body* of Englishmen," or "*Degrade* the *Body* of Michael Donahue." Likewise the word *Body* could be narrowed to 'Heart' if causing a wound, or 'Brain' if applying the *Dazed* condition.

The practice of using more specific words than absolutely required is incredibly common in all magical traditions. Sometimes this is done to make the rite too specific to be useful to one's enemies. However, it is most often used to reign in the chaotic energies of magic and ensure the proper targeting of the ritual (see *Choosing Specific Targets within Scope*, p. 246). For these reasons, most extant rituals that a character will find or be taught will use highly restrictive nouns.

MASTERING WORDS OF POWER

Although anyone with a single rank in the *Mysteries* skill can speak the words of power written by another magus, most magi aspire to master words of power so they may compose their own rites. The noun *Self* is automatically mastered by all characters with at least a single rank in the *Mysteries* skill. Mastering other words of power requires the *Magical Word* asset. Each time the asset is acquired the character may choose either one magical verb or two magical nouns to master. Some words are easier to learn than others. To represent this, each word is assigned a minimum *Mysteries* rank, and a magus cannot master that word until her ranks in that skill meet or exceed this prerequisite. A list of magical words and their requirements are listed in the *Words of Power by Rank* table, this page.

WORDS OF POWER BY RANK

Words that appear in white are pure. Words that appear in black are impure.

Rank 1— nouns: Self (gained with first rank of *Mysteries*)

Rank 2— verbs: **Bind**, Commune, **Obscure**, **Reveal**
nouns: Animal, **Object**, Place

Rank 3— verbs: **Degrade, Evoke,** Expel, Restore
nouns: Body, Demon, Feyfolk, Mortal, Shade

Rank 4— verbs: Ward
nouns: Boundary, Chimera

Rank 5— verbs: Ban, Protect
nouns: Angel, Fallen, Wyldling

NOUNS

When a rite is composed, two nouns are used to define the persons, places or things affected. One noun will describe where the magical energies will be focused or contained. This is the target of the ritual. The other will describe will describe what will be affected by those energies. This is the subject of the ritual. It's not the grammatical subject to the magical sentence, but the thing subjected to the magical effects (much like the subject of an experiment or a test subject). For example, one might assume that the target of a *Ban* would be the entity being banned, but this is not so. The magus actually targets an area which will contain the energies of the *Ban*, and the entities or objects subjected to the effect are banned from that area. Thus, in a *Ban*, whatever is being kept safe is the target and whatever is being kept at bay is the subject.

Angel

Requires: *Mysteries* 5

A magus who masters this word may compose rites to affect celestial angels, a dangerous prospect indeed. Even the least of the heavenly host are strange and powerful entities well beyond the means of most ritualists to safely control. Interacting with an angel in any way that interferes with its appointed task in the Clockwork may incur both *Corruption* and heavenly wrath. Out of fear and caution, even devout magi rarely attempt to target angels. This word can be used within a rite to affect angels of any power or choir, and those rare nephilim who achieve a *Purpose* 5.

Animal

Requires: *Mysteries 2*

This noun governs all non-sapient living creatures in the Animalia Kingdom: birds, beasts, and all creatures that creep or crawl. Ancient rites exist that turn animals into messengers, allies, or guardians. Other rites use the *Animal* word for protections against aberrations, and it has recently been discovered that this word may be used to affect beastfolk.

Body

Requires: *Mysteries 3*

All physical things have a body. This word refers to the corpus, the tangible manifestation, be it a bookshelf, a tree, or a changeling. It cannot refer to entities without a corporeal form. This word can be used as a target word in conjunction with a subject word that describes the type of body. For example "*Body* of *Mortal*" or "*Body* of *Chimera*." *Body* is particularly useful when combined with verbs that create physical outcomes such as *Degrade*, *Restore*, and *Protect*.

Boundary

Requires: *Mysteries 4*

The Clockwork is comprised of many realms, each distinct from the others. Heaven, the Borderlands, the Outer Darkness, and the Pontus are separated from one another by mystical boundaries. This word of power is exclusively used as a target noun alongside the subject noun *Place* to allow a magus to affect these demarcations. This word combination can only be used with verbs that create physical outcomes (*Degrade*, *Restore*, and *Protect*), and are used to change the environmental stability of a location. While the uses of this word are somewhat restrictive and limited, the skilled magus who learns to effect the boundaries between realms can mend the weak places from where the Pontus emerges or punch holes to allow travel from one realm to the next.

Chimera

Requires: *Mysteries 4*

This word allows magi to create rituals to affect chimera. Many rites of the Witchfinders and Inquisition depend upon this word to keep their practitioners safe when dealing with these hybrid monstrosities which emerge from the depths of the Pontus.

Demon

Requires: *Mysteries 3*

A demon is the disembodied soul of a dead naphil. These entities always hunger to fulfill their lusts, and some amass great power. Only the most daring or depraved magi deal with demons. Brave magi with mastery of this word may combine it with *Expel* to compose rites of exorcism. Combined with *Ward or Ban*, rites can be composed to hinder a demon. Some cults and madmen seek to pact with demons in a bid for power, and master this word to *Commune* or perhaps *Evoke* and then *Bind* them. This word can affect any soul of a dead naphil, but it may also be used to target living nephilim, so long as the demon that is their soul is still within them.

Fallen

Requires: *Mysteries 5*

Once an angel falls, it is ontologically changed. It retains all angelic power, but becomes corrupted and even more fearsome. The Fallen are the most dangerous entities a mortal can encounter. At the height of his authority and backed by the labors of a kingdom, King Solomon is reputed to have bound fallen angels to imprisonment or service. Yet even among the most dark and deluded, few have ever claimed to match his mystical prowess. This word allows rites to affect any type of fallen angel as well as their offspring, the nephilim.

Feyfolk

Requires: *Mysteries 3*

Britain has a long folk tradition describing the use of magic to mediate dealings with feyfolk. This word of power allows a rite to affect any fey who has made a home in the mortal world. This includes both embodied feyfolk, those posing as nature spirits, and changelings. Ironically, dealing and even pacting with feyfolk is often done through mundane means, and given the proclivity of feyfolk to hold grudges, most rites that deal with them are written to prevent their capricious revenge.

Mortal

Requires: *Mysteries 3*

This word governs all mortal sapient beings who live on the Earth. It can be used to affect purebloods, beastfolk, and changelings. It cannot, however, target nephilim; they are simply too unnatural for this word to reference them. Rites that target multiple people, or that are designed to have blanket effects, can use this word to affect a large number of targets.

Object

Requires: *Mysteries 2*

Humanity is utterly dependent on the material things it builds to make life easier, so it is little wonder that many magi quickly learn to target objects of all sorts. This word may be used to affect any inanimate object, including living ones such as plants. Due to their usefulness, rites that *Obscure*, *Reveal*, *Protect* against, or *Ban* objects are among the most commonly handed down within a magical tradition.

Place

Requires: *Mysteries 2*

Being able to affect places is critical for a wide variety of spells, especially those that defend a given area from attack or egress. Including *Place* in a rite enables much finer control when defining Scope. Magi who know both *Place* and *Object* can be extremely versatile with as little as one or two known verbs.

Self

Requires: *Mysteries* 1 (automatically learned)

Use of this word allows the magus to compose rites that affect herself. All who attain even a rudimentary study of *Mysteries* begin with contemplation and understanding of themselves before gaining enough knowledge to master any other words of power. This word of power is automatically learned by all magi with *Mysteries* 1 or higher.

Shade

Requires: *Mysteries* 3

This word allows the magus to compose rites that affect shades, the souls of the restless dead. Shades are often dangerous, but being able to *Commune* with, *Bind*, or *Expel* them can be critical for a priest, Inquisitor, or Witchfinder. Through communing with a shade, a magus may be able to determine its tether to the mortal world, and then use that knowledge to release the shade from its entrapment. Expelling a shade from its haunt, or a possessed victim, can be crucial to protecting others. This word of power has no effect on living beings; it may only affect a soul once it has been separated from its original body.

Wyldling

Requires: *Mysteries* 5

Mastery of this word allows a magus to affect the fey beings that inhabit the Borderlands. This may be of use to those magi who use the Borderlands for travel, exploration, eavesdropping on dreams, or gathering reagents. Defending themselves from these capricious monsters can be of the utmost importance for safe egress in the unintended realm. Cunning magi may also use this word to *Commune*, *Bind*, or even *Evoke* wyldlings, but such attempts can have highly unpredictable results. This word can also be used to affect objects that originate in the Borderlands, a confusing truth that some magi often ponder.

VERBS

When a rite is composed, one verb is used to define the action that takes place between the two nouns. A magus must master a verb of power through the *Magical Word* asset (p. 157) to be able to use it within a rite. The exact effects that the verb will produce are controlled by the Duration, Puissance, and Scope of the rite. These are described generically under *Shaping Intent* later in this chapter, but more specific or unique uses of these intent components are given with the descriptions below.

Ban

Requires: *Mysteries* 5
Purity: Pure
Sentence: "Ban [subject] from [target]."

A ban prohibits a subject (one location or type of object/entity) from physically interacting with a target (another location, or type of object/entity) in any way. The subject of a ban can be whatever the magus wishes hold at bay. Often this is a type of entity (Chimera, Feyfolk, Mortal, etc.), but it could just as easily be an unwanted Object (bullets, rain, a knife, dirt, etc.). The target of the ban is whatever is being protected. Usually this is an Object or a Place, but bans can also be placed directly on Mortals or Animals. The sentence "Ban Object(dagger) from Wyldling" can create a dagger no wyldling may touch. The sentence "Ban Animal(dog) from Place(my bedroom)" can prevent your pet dog from entering your sleeping chambers. A banning rite can never affect a subject that was within the area of effect when the ritual was performed; such an entity will ignore the ritual effect unless it leaves the area and attempts to enter once again during the Duration of the effect. The Puissance of a banning rite must equal or exceed the Highest Threat or Attribute of the subjects that are to be banned.

No physical barrier is created by a ban. The target and subject will simply physically avoid one another in all ways possible. This

EXTENDING RITUAL EFFECTS

Extending a ritual effect already in place requires a new ritual to be performed using the exact same magical sentence. If successful, the amount of time from the Duration of the new rite is added on to the amount already established. As long as the new rite is successfully completed before the previous effect expires, the effect will persist unbroken. This allows a magus to manifest lengthy effects by serially performing several easier rituals.

For example, Solomon originally performed a banishment with a Duration of 6 (one week). During the following 5 days he spent time composing and successfully performing a much more powerful rite using the same magical sentence, but with a Duration of 8 (a year and a day). There were two days left in the original banishment, which are now added to the time period from the new rite, for a total of one year and three days. Now he has plenty of time to plan and perform further rituals to extend the banishment, or to prepare as he wishes to face the possible return of the entity he banished.

Magi that engage in evocation are likely to benefit from performing this type of serial banishment, lest the entities they summon be given an opportunity to enact revenge. Religious groups and secret societies have been known to organize their members, allowing for repetition of specific rites to maintain bans, wards, and obscurations.

manifests as subtly as the circumstances will allow. If a weapon is banned from an opponent, it will miss. If a tool is banned from a specific person, that person will constantly fumble, unable to ever touch it, move it, or pick it up. If an object is banned from a room, it will fall out of a pocket before it can enter. If a person is banned from another person, both will stumble and fail to touch or strike the other. When subtlety cannot be maintained, the magic will manifest in more vulgar ways, such as impassible boundaries and untouchable objects. This avoidance does not prevent perceiving or communicating with the target. A ban will only prohibit the banned target from directly or indirectly touching or interacting with the subject; any non-physical contact is permissible.

Bind

Requires: *Mysteries* 2
Purity: Impure
Sentence: "Bind [target] to [subject]."
A binding rite tethers a target to a subject, trapping it within a given place, object, or structure. If the target is corporeal, the subject must be something that can contain or surround it. If the target is incorporeal, the subject can be any physical object. Extant rites use sentences such as "*Bind Demon/Shade/Wylding* to *Place*(binding circle)/*Object*." The target will be unable to leave the chosen object or area for the Duration of the effect. If the subject is mobile, the target will remain bound to its container during relocation. The Puissance of a banning rite must equal or exceed the Total Threat or Attribute of the targets that are to be bound.

Commonly bindings are used in tandem with rites of evocation. Entities who are summoned into the presence of a magus are free to do as they will, and may attack or leave unless a binding effect imprisons them. Thus, many summoners will evoke an entity into an already active binding vessel and then bargain with it for some service in exchange for its freedom. Such bargaining is done through normal social conflict. Other binding rites can be performed serially to keep entities safely imprisoned indefinitely.

Other binding rites are meant to create homes rather than prisons. Incorporeal entities such as wyldlings, shades, or demons have only a few ways by which they can interact with the world physically, but should they be bound to a body, automaton, or other device capable of movement, they may possess that device and control it.

Commune

Requires: *Mysteries* 2
Purity: Pure
Sentence: "Commune [target] and [target]."
Rites of communion allow the magus to create an avenue of communication between the two targets that lasts for the Duration of the effect. While the targeted entities are in communion, they may communicate with one another in whatever way they are capable. If the communication is spoken, the recipient will hear a voice; if the communication is written, she will see text appear. This can occur in whatever way the author of the rite desires.

Uses of *Commune* may involve reagents such as steamy mirrors upon which words may appear or gramophones from which a voice may emerge. Without specific reagents, the communication may take the form of a 'voice on the wind.' Communicants may also test *Will + Composure*, Difficulty 5 to share sensory information directly.

The Puissance of a communion rite must equal or exceed the Highest Threat or Attribute of the targets that are to communicate (the attribute only being used in the rare instance that objects are communicating, such as with telegraphs). However, the ritualist needn't account for her own Threat rank if she participates as a target. Scope is determined by the total number of targets in the communion and the maximum distance between them.

Rites of communion are frequently used by magi to contact supernatural beings with whom they cannot normally communicate. However, targets can include anything from a forest dryad to a chimpanzee to an elder demon. No common language is necessary; although, the communicants are always limited by their ability to form rational thought. A magus could commune with a squirrel, but it would speak in broken thoughts and have little to say apart from the location of the best nuts in the forest. Commune rites may be performed to seek favors, hidden information, or in preparation to summon powerful entities through a separate rite of evocation. Careless magi who attempt to commune with powerful beings can find themselves in significant trouble, as the entities they contact may persuade them to do their bidding. Any entity in the communion may initiate social conflict normally, but the magus who performed the rite will always have Attack Priority. More cautious magi will often incorporate the *Circumstantial Cancellation* feature into rites of communion to ensure they can end the effect prematurely and walk away from any unexpected social conflicts.

Degrade

Requires: *Mysteries* 3
Purity: Impure
Sentence: "Degrade the [target] of [subject]."
Rites of degradation are used to inflict harm and decay. No physical or social Defense is available against magical attacks, and the target immediately suffers the effect of any successful ritual. When used to cause damage to a living entity, degradation rites will use a magical sentence such as "*Degrade Body* of *Mortal/Feyfolk/Animal*." When used to damage an object, degradation rites will use a magical sentence such as "*Degrade Body* of *Object*." In such rites, the target noun will always be *Body* and the subject is that body's owner. These rites will use Puissance to produce Outcomes. Puissance 3 grants the ability to place temporary conditions. At Puissance 5, living beings can be subject to wounds, lingering conditions or other maladies. Also at Puissance 5, objects can be subject to Damage or the *Non-functional* condition.

Rites can also be designed to "*Degrade* the *Boundary* of a *Place*." Degrading the boundary of a location weakens it against the Pontus, and can thin the borders between realms. A rite with a

Puissance 5 can permanently make a Stable location Compromised, or a Compromised location Breached (see *Environmental Stability,* p. 281). A Puissance 3 will make the degradation last for as long as the Duration prescribes. Degrading an area that is already Breached allows for the barrier between realms to be temporarily removed, creating a thin space ((see *Thin Places,* p. 54). The Scope of such a rite must account for the size of the area affected.

Evoke

Requires: *Mysteries* 3
Purity: Impure
Sentence: "Evoke the [target] to [subject]."

Evocation rites are used by magi to summon objects or entities to a specific location. "*Evoke Mortal to Place*" will summon a mortal to the location subjected to the magical effect. Likewise, "*Evoke Shade/Demon/Wyldling to Place*" will summon an incorporeal entity. Summoned entities will feel inexplicably compelled. Treat this as a rank 5 Affinity for traveling to the subjected location, but the entity may otherwise think and act normally and will not realize they are under a compulsion until after the Duration of the ritual expires.

The Duration of the rite must account for the travel time it will take the target to arrive at the specified location. For shades, demons and other incorporeal entities who move at the speed of thought, this is never more than Duration 1. For mortals who rely on more mundane locomotion, this can be much higher. If the trip is neither perilous nor particularly dramatic, usually Duration 3

A TREACHEROUS ROAD

All impure rites are condemned by the Inquisition and the Witchfinders, but given the many risks of interacting with outsiders, rites of evocation are deemed especially dangerous. Although reckless publishing houses have made magical writings more available, extant rites of communion and evocation are still difficult to find. Most magi learn these rites by discovering lost grimoires or through the direct tutelage of others.

Hidden knowledge and powerful servants can be gained through contact with outsiders, but to avoid the fate of Faust, it is essential to understand the strategies to best protect oneself. Bindings are the first and most sensible precaution. Before making any attempt at evocation, establishing a strong binding will lock the summoned entity to a place or object. This provides the magi with protection from any direct attack by the entity, as well as a powerful bargaining tool: the promise of freedom for services rendered. Once freed, an entity could seek vengeance on the magus, so rites of expulsion and banishment are practical ways to remove the entity and prevent its return. It is usually preferred to enact a ban, expel the entity, and then engage in renewal of the ban to prevent the target from returning with malicious intent.

Some whispers suggest that there are cabals of magi—or even whole religious orders—that exist to stand guard against baleful outsiders. These groups endlessly teach and perform rites to keep particular entities at bay. With the general decline of magical practitioners, who knows how many of these ancient banishments may have lapsed, or what malevolent terrors wait patiently outside our world, ready for a chance to return.

(one chapter) will cover the travel time from one place to another. The Puissance of an evocation rite must equal or exceed the Total Threat or Attribute of the targets that are to be summoned.

If the specified location is an *Object* that can be moved the targeted individual will continue to follow it for the Duration of the ritual effect. The target of the ritual may itself be an *Object* as well. So long as the target has the ability to move of its own power (such as an automobile or automaton), the ritual effect will guide it to the desired location.

Once the target arrives in the specified location, it may remain at its own discretion and interact as it wishes—including instigating physical or social conflict. Entities that require tethers to remain in their current realm will be forced to leave when the Duration expires, unless they become tethered or subject to a binding ritual.

Expel

Requires: *Mysteries* 3
Purity: Pure
Sentence: "Expel [subject] from [target]."

Rites of expulsion remove a subject from a target area, container, or structure. If a rite expelled a *Mortal* from a *Place*, the target mortals would flee from the location subjected to the magical effect. If a rite expelled an *Object* from a *Place*, the affected object would leave the area by any means available to it (e.g. an automobile might drive itself away, while a book might fall off a shelf and slide out of the room, and a gun may fall from its owners hand). Subjected objects will never disappear; they must utilize a mundane form of movement that appears as coincidental as possible.

The Scope of the rite must account for the total area from which the subjects are to be expelled (i.e. expelling a spirit from a pocket watch would take Scope 1, expelling a man from Derbyshire county would take Scope 6, and expelling a demon from the mortal realm would take Scope 10). The magus does not have control over where the subjects go, only that they leave the targeted location. Also, an expulsion rite can never affect a subject that was outside the area of effect when the ritual was performed, even if the Duration is ongoing.

The Duration of the rite must account for the travel time it will take the subject to leave the specified location. For shades, demons and other incorporeal entities who move at the speed of thought, this can be ast little as Duration 1. For mortals and others who rely on more mundane locomotion, this can be much higher. If the trip is neither perilous nor particularly dramatic, usually Duration 3 (one chapter) will cover the travel time from one place to another, but the Narrator should provide players with an idea of the likely required travel time. The Puissance of an expulsion rite must equal or exceed the Total Threat or Attribute of the subjects that are to be expelled.

When the rite is completed, all subjects affected by the expulsion immediately act to leave the area in the fastest way possible and by whatever means available, and will continue to do so for the Duration of the expulsion. Treat this urge to flee as a rank 5 Affinity and assign any trait test that does not directly contribute to leaving a penalty equal to the Puissance of the rite. Once outside the Scope of the expulsion, the Affinity ends, but will return if the subjects venture back into the affected area. If the Duration of the effect ends before the targets have been able to flee the area, they lose the Affinity and may act as they wish.

Obscure

Requires: *Mysteries* 2
Purity: Impure
Sentence: "Obscure [target] from [subject]."

Mages concerned about keeping their activities secret, or who wish to make things difficult to discover, will frequently employ rites of obscuration. Magical sentences such as "*Obscure Self/ Animal/Mortal* from *Mortal/Feyfolk/Demon*" can make it difficult for a target to be noticed by others and can be a great help for those sneaking and skulking. Magical sentences like "*Obscure Object/Place* from *Mortal/Chimera*" offers indirect protection by making an object or location difficult to find. In both cases, the Puissance rank of the rite must equal or exceed the Highest Threat or Attribute rank of the subjects, and is also applied as a penalty on any Focus test that anyone makes to notice the target. For example, "*Obscure Object(sword cane)* from *Mortals*" with Puissance 4 would affect all mortals of Threat 4 or lower, giving them a –4 to all *Focus* tests to see the sword cane. This penalty would last for the Duration of the effect. Characters who are not actively looking for something and have no other cause to make a *Focus* test will simply never actively notice the obscured object, even if it is in plain sight.

Protect

Requires: *Mysteries* 5
Purity: Pure
Sentence: "Protect [target] from [subject]."

After a protection ritual is successfully performed, the target will be protected from outcomes caused by the objects or entities subjected to the magical effect. With the Magical sentence "*Protect Self* from *Chimera*," a magus could prevent a chimera from wounding her. The Magical sentence "*Protect Object*(door) from *Mortals*," a magus could make it much more difficult for the police to kick in a door. The protection manifests against the subject, not the weapon. Thus, protection from mortals will prevent outcomes created by guns, swords, fists, or any other weapon so long as its wielded by a mortal.

Mechanically, these rites will use Puissance to prevent Outcomes. The rite can define which outcomes are to be prevented (a lingering condition, a wound, *Staggered*, etc.) or leave the effect undefined and allow the Puissance rank to soak up as many outcomes as it can. Each outcome requires a certain rank of Puissance (e.g. a temporary condition requires Puissance 3, a wound or rendering an object *Nonfunctional* requires Puissance 5). Add together all Puissance requirements to create the necessary Puissance rank for the rite. For example, a protection rite with a Puissance 5 could prevent one wound; with a Puissance 10, it could prevent two wounds. A single rite of Protection can grant its effects to multiple individual targets, as defined by Scope. For example, "*Protect Mortals*(friends) from *Mortals*(enemies)" with a Puissance 3 and a Scope 3 could protect up to five friends from one temporary condition each.

The magical effect will conclude when the maximum number of outcomes per target are prevented or the Duration concludes, whichever occurs first. Rites of protection often use the *Circumstantial Activation* feature to allow greater flexibility.

Restore

Requires: *Mysteries* 3
Purity: Pure
Sentence: "Restore the [target] of [subject]."

Rites of restoration return the targets to their proper, natural states. This can eliminate wounds, damage, lingering conditions and other maladies. When used to heal a living being, restoration rites will use a magical sentence such as "*Restore Body of Mortal/Feyfolk/Animal.*" When used to repair an object, restoration rites will use the magical sentence "*Restore Body of Object.*" In such rites, the target noun will always be *Body* and the subject is that body's owner. The restoration is instantaneous and requires only Duration 1.

Mechanically, these rites will use Puissance to remove outcomes. An object with the *Nonfunctional* condition will have this condition removed when a single rank of Damage has been repaired, whether the damage is removed through ritual or by mundane repairs (see *Repairing Objects,* p. 86).

Restoration rites can also be designed to "*Restore the Boundary of a Place*" to restore the barrier against the Pontus. Such a rite can make a Compromised location Stable, or a Breached location Compromised (see *Environmental Stability,* p. 281). Puissance 3 will make the change temporary, lasting for the Duration of the rite. Puissance 5 will make the change permanent, and will only require Duration 1. If the *Place* is a thin space, any restoration will eliminate this. The Scope of such a rite must account for the size of the area affected.

Reveal

Requires: *Mysteries* 2
Purity: Impure
Sentence: "Reveal [target] to [subject]."

Rites of revelation allow the magus to see and know things she would not otherwise, taking the form of either answered questions, perceiving something that is magically or mundanely hidden, or even remotely viewing a target. Magical sentences may be constructed with "*Reveal Mortal/Place/Angel to Self/Mortal.*"

If a rite of revelation is simply used to find something that is hidden, the Puissance will grant a bonus to the trait test used to discover the target. If a rite of revelation is used to see something that is invisible, the Puissance must equal or exceed the Total Threat or Attribute rank of the revealed objects or entities. Duration must be used to cover the length of time an object can be seen or searched for.

If the target of the revelation is beyond the visual range of the magus, this type of rite can grant remote viewing. The magus will mystically see the object, person or place. The vision centers on the target and provides clear visual and audible information, but that is all. If viewing a place, the vision begins by showing the entire area covered by the defined Scope. A magus may focus in on anything within the defined Scope so long as the Puissance of the rite equals or exceeds the Highest Threat or Attribute or what is being viewed. Rites of revelation used for remote viewing are notoriously difficult to target, so a precise targeting noun, such as a name, may be necessary to keep the magical effect from accidently targeting something unintended.

If the rite is used to gain information, one yes or no question may be asked by the magus for each rank of Puissance. The subject is the entity who receives the information and the target is the source of the information. information is learned instantaneously and requires only Duration 1.

FORTUNE-TELLING AND DIVINATION IN THE EMPIRE

Technically, magic cannot perceive the future. Such glimpses are only available to those blessed with the *Prophecy* charism. However, a quick wit and the ability to read people has earned a living for many a charlatan claiming to be a fortune teller. Aside from these tricksters, there are also those who use a supernatural knowledge of the present to predict what is likely to come. This is the art of divination: one part mystical revelation and one part critical problem solving.

Both the See of Canterbury and the Magisterium have long held that divination is a violation of the divine plan, and English statutes have specifically listed prognostication through the use of revelatory magical rites as criminal offenses. Despite this, the appeal of fortune-telling has grown over time, and it is mixed up in the current popular trends of spiritualism and mysticism. Carnival workers turn tarot cards in tents and on boardwalks, and men and women of quality gather in their parlors at dinner parties to speak with alleged seers and visionaries. Witchfinders are occupied with the serious threats of more harmful witchcraft, so those that do perform these rites of revelation are usually ignored unless they become too conspicuous.

Other cultures around the world have a wide range of history with the issue, and indeed many African and Asian societies accept or even revere divinatory practices. In Lagos or Shanghai, any number of local wise women, religious figures, or even market-stall seers can be found to read the bones, tell your future from a drop of blood, or consult the I'Ching to find answers to your questions. Most Englishmen write such activities off as heathenism, while thinking nothing amiss with having their palms or tarot cards read at the carnival at Brighton. Though there are certainly frauds abroad just as there are at home, there are also assuredly some magi performing revelatory rites with different reagents than their English counterparts.

Ward

Requires: *Mysteries 4*
Purity: Pure
Sentence: "Ward [target] against [subject]."

Wards sap the vitality and capability of the entities they oppose. A rite using a magical sentence such as "*Ward Place/Object* against *Chimera/Animal/Demon*" would hinder the subject creature type as soon as they entered the *Place* or touched the *Object*. The Scope of the rite determines the area being warded, and the maximum targets it can affect. The Puissance determines both the Highest Threat or Attribute of the entities or objects that the ward will affect, and the penalty that will be applied to all entities of that type affected by the rite. If a magus places a Puissance 3 ward against *Shades* over her sanctum, and a shade of Threat 3 or lower enters the space, all of the shade's tests and Defenses would suffer a –3 penalty. Any entity affected by a ward will become listless, confused, weak, and generally miserable, and if given the option will often attempt to leave the area as soon as possible.

Due to the efficacy of placing wards across large areas, magi seeking to make the best use of this word often use the *Exclusionary Clause* (p. 247) feature if placing a ward that could affect themselves. Those who excel in evocation and have the resources to spare may lay wards against the entities they summon instead of, or in addition to, binding rites, because the penalties they inflict may make it possible to strike a favorable bargain with even powerful entities.

SHAPING INTENT

While the magical sentence gives a narrative description of a rite's magical effect, the components of intent provide the mechanical effects within the game. Most of these effects are universal and described below, but some verbs have unique uses for one or more components and these will be listed in the verb's description. In all other instances, the descriptions below determine how each rank of Duration, Puissance, Scope and features will play out during a magical effect. All effects must have at least one rank in Scope, Duration, and Puissance.

DURATION

Duration measures the length of time the effect of a ritual will last. The number of assigned ranks in Duration will set a specific amount of time as defined in the following table.

In most circumstances, the ritual effect will begin upon the successful completion of the ritual and ends when the Duration has elapsed. If a second rite using an identical magical sentence is cast on the same target prior to the lapse of the prior rite's Duration, then the time remaining on the older rite adds to the Duration of newer rite. A magus may further manipulate Duration through the use of features (see below).

As long as a ritual effect is ongoing, it cannot be hindered except by an opposing ritual effect of a higher Puissance. Thus, a person that has been wounded by a *Degrade* rite cannot heal that Wound or have it treated with *Medicine* until the Duration of the effect has ended. However a *Restore* rite of a higher Puissance could heal the wound even during the ongoing opposing effect. Restoration rites never require more than Duration 1 to be effective. They instantaneously return things to their natural state of wholeness and no benefit is gained by increasing the Duration of this effect.

The Duration of some effects can be nebulous and better thought of in narrative terms. An evocation ritual may require a corporeal being to travel during the Duration of the ritual effect. Any journey that lacks drama or danger can be said to require a Duration 3 (one chapter). Shorter effects that last for a single conversation, such as with *Commune*, can be said to require Duration 2 (one scene). However, the Narrator always has final say as to how long a segment of narrative time (scene, chapter, or book) will last.

RITUAL DURATIONS

Rank	Effect Duration
1	Instantaneous
2	1 hours / 1 Scene
3	4 hours / 1 Chapter
4	12 hours
5	1 day
6	1 week / 1 Book
7	1 month
8	1 year and a day
9	10 years
10	100 years

PUISSANCE

Puissance measures the power of the ritual effect. It is used to define the strength of the effect, the strength of the target that can be affected, or both. Depending on the chosen magical verb this will manifest in one of three different ways. Some verbs also have unique ways in which Puissance is used and these are listed with the description of those verbs.

Highest Threat or Attribute Verbs:

Ban, Commune, Obscure, Reveal, Ward

Verbs that use Puissance in this way affect everyone or everything the magical sentence of the rite will allow, up to a particular level of strength. For characters and antagonists, this is measured by Threat. For example, "*Ban Mortal* from *Place*" with a

REQUIREMENTS BY OUTCOME

Target	Subject	Outcome	Puissance Required
Body	Any object, living creature, or place	Inconsequential narrative effect with no mechanical ramifications: hives, dampness, rust & wear, etc.	1
Body	Any living creature: Animal, Chimera, Feyfolk, Mortal, etc.	Temporary condition	3
		Any persistent condition, Wound, or other malady	5
Body	Any inanimate thing: Object	Temporary condition	3
		One rank of Damage, any persistent condition such as *Nonfunctional*	5
Boundary	Place	Temporarily move one step in stability: Stable to Compromised to Breached	3
		Permanently move one step in stability	5

Puissance 3 would would ban all mortals of Threat 3 or less for the Duration of the effect. If uncertain what a target's Threat truly is, treat PCs as Threat 3 and inconsequential NCs as Threat 2. An object's strength is measured by the object's most relevant attribute. Weapons will use Potency, a non-threatening object might use its Bulk, and an inconsequential object (such as rain or dust) is affected by Puissance 1. For example, "*Ban Object(blades)* from *Mortal*" with a Puissance 2 would would prevent all edged weapons from striking the target for the Duration of the effect so long as they had a Potency of 2 or less. Usually, rites will only have one noun where strength will apply. However, in those rare instances where both the target and subject both have Threat or relevant attributes, Puissance need only account for the larger of the two.

Total Threat or Attribute Verbs:

Bind, Evoke, Expel

Unlike the verbs that use Puissance as a threshold, these verbs use it as a sum total. When measured this way, Puissance becomes the total number of ranks in Threat or Attribute to be affected. For example, "*Bind Mortal* to *Place*" with a Puissance 4 would would bind a number of mortals with a total Threat of 4. This could be two Threat 2 mortals or one Threat 4 mortal. "*Expel Object*(weapons) from *Place*" with a Puissance 6 would expel a number of weapons whose total Potency equaled 6. This could be three Potency 2 weapons, two Potency 3 weapons, etc. If the magical sentence did not specify who or what was to be affected, the results will be random within the parameters of the magical sentence and the rite's Scope. Usually, rites will only have one noun where strength will apply. However, in those rare instances where both the target and subject both have Threat or relevant attributes, Puissance must account for the total of all relevant Threat or relevant attributes.

Outcomes

Degrade, Protect, Restore

Rites that create, remove, and prevent outcomes use Puissance to determine both the strength and quantity of the outcomes.

For example, "*Restore Body* of *Mortal*" with a Puissance 3 could cure a temporary *Staggered* condition, while the same rite constructed with Puissance 5 could remove a Wound. If it was constructed with Puissance 8, it could do both. "*Degrade Body* of *Object*" with a Puissance 5 could inflict one rank of Damage on the object or place the *Nonfunctional* condition on it. When affecting *Boundaries*, Puissance 5 can shift *Environmental Stability* (p. 281) by one level. A magus may also place, remove, or prevent a narrative effect that has no mechanical impact with Puissance 1. For example, "*Restore Body* of *Object*" with a Puissance 1 could be used to restore the color of a piece of clothing.

Puissance in Countermagic and Multiple Effects

Whenever the effect of one rite directly contradicts the effect of another, the rite with the higher Puissance will have its full effect and the rite with the lower Puissance will be completely negated. For example, rites of obscuration oppose the effects of rites of revelation. If both were performed on the same target, whichever rite has the higher Puissance prevails, while the rite with the lower Puissance does not occur. For example, a magus enacts a rite of obscuration with Puissance 5 on her grimoire. Meanwhile, a rival has broken into her home attempting to locate the grimoire and is benefitting from a rite of revelation with Puissance 4. The rite of obscuration takes precedence, and the rival suffers a –5 penalty on all *Focus* tests related to finding the grimoire. The rite of revelation is neutralized and has no effect. When rites with an identical magical sentence are cast on the same target, the ongoing effect will use the highest Puissance rank available, unlike Duration which is cumulative.

SCOPE

Scope defines what can be targeted by a ritual. The chosen rank of Scope will limit the the maximum number of individual targets and as well as the distance between them. This is detailed in the *Effects for Magical Rituals* table (below).

In all of the example sentences given for verbs in this chapter, Scope governs what is affected by the [target] word. If *Place* is used, the Scope must cover the total area it contains. For example, Scope 4 would be one large estate or village. If targeting any human-sized individuals (*Mortal*, *Feyfolk*, etc.) or incorporeal entities (*Demon*, *Shade*, etc.), Scope must cover the number of targets and the distance between them. For example, a rite with Scope 3 can affect up to five individual targets within the same large building. Larger targets, such as buildings themselves or gigantic creatures, are limited by their Bulk attribute. For example, a rite with Scope 3 could not target a number of objects with a total Bulk of greater than 7.

Line of sight and distance between the magus and targets are not required, so it's possible to target an individual on another continent with Scope 1. However, the distance between targets always applies. Thus, if a magus wanted to use a single rite to target two individuals on two separate continents she would need at least Scope 9. If the magus targets herself and others, such as with a communion rite, the Scope would have to account for the distance between the magus and the other target(s).

Choosing Specific Targets within Scope

A ritual will target exactly what the rite prescribes. If the rite leaves any ambiguity at all, the ritual will randomly target whatever the chosen magical noun will allow within the specified Scope. The more narrow the Scope, the less likely a ritual is to go awry. Rites composed with Scope 1 affect a single target and leave little room for misdirection. However, the wider the Scope of a rite, the more possible targets there are and thus a greater possibility of error.

For example, a magus composes a healing rite with which she wants to heal two individuals on opposite sides of a village. She constructs the magical sentence, "*Restore Body of Mortal*" and uses the necessary Scope 4. Scope 4 allows the ritual to target up to ten individual targets within an area the size of a village. Thus, if there are ten or less mortals within the chosen village, the ritual will target them all. If there are more than ten mortals within the village, this ritual would target ten of them at random. The subject noun, *Mortal*, restricts the effect to mortals and the Scope of 4 restricts the effect to ten targeted *Bodies* within the village. The rite offers no further specificity, and the effect will occur within these parameters.

Narrowing the magical noun is the best way to more directly target a ritual. The magus composing the above rite may narrow the noun *Mortal* into specific names, constructing the sentence "*Restore the Bodies of Daniel Donovan and Philip Greystone.*" This greatly limits the utility of the rite by others, but completely specifies who will be healed. This would also limit the effect to two targets, as only two individuals are named. A similar but more versatile sentence could be, "*Restore the Bodies of friends.*" At Scope 4, this sentence would heal up to ten people in a village-sized area whom the magus considers to be her friends. The ability to narrow the focus of the nouns gives great specificity to rites. However, once the sentence is constructed, the noun may not change. A rite cannot be altered once it has been completed.

The only exception to the randomness of magic is when the magus has a direct and unbroken line of sight to her targets. This must occur sometime either during the performance of the ritual itself or at the moment of *Circumstantial Activation* (opposite page), and all targets must be seen simultaneously. If the magus can see her desired targets, she can direct the magical effect at them. However, this is an all or nothing prospect.

When rites with an identical magical sentence are cast on the same target, the ongoing effect will use the highest Scope rank available, unlike Duration which is cumulative.

EFFECTS FOR MAGICAL RITUALS

Scope Rank	Number of Targets	Distance or Area of Effect	Total Bulk
1	1	A single person, beast, or object known to the magus and anywhere on the globe	5
2	2	One grand room, one small cottage	6
3	5	One large building	7
4	10	Within one neighborhood, large estate, or village	8
5	25	One metropolitan city: ex. London, New York	9
6	50	One County: ex. Essex, Derbyshire	10
7	100	One Region: ex. Scottish Highlands, The Rhine Valley	11
8	250	One Country: ex. England, France, Annwn	11
9	500	One Continent or Empire: ex. Europe, The British Empire, all territories of a nation	12
10	1,000	One Realm: ex. Earth, The Pit, The Borderlands	12

FEATURES

Features may be added to a rite to give it more utility or flexibility. Each feature will add a conditional clause to the magical sentence, modifying the description of the ritual effect. This added description may cause the ritual effect to begin at a future time, end early, stop and then reactivate, or selectively affect targets. Examples of conditional clauses include "when the magic circle is broken" and "until the door of this room opens." Intentionally fulfilling a conditional clause should take at least a single maneuver. The feature chosen will determine what kind of conditional clause can be added, and how it can be worded. Every feature included in a rite increases its total intent by 1 rank.

No conditional clause should ever necessitate additional magical nouns or verbs. The clause may focus on things normally covered by magical words (such as the door in the example above), but these are only parameters and are outside the true effect of the ritual. For every feature, the Narrator has the final say on whether the clause, and magical sentence overall, is sufficiently clear.

Circumstantial Activation

The effects of the ritual will not begin until a special triggering circumstance is met, at which point the effect is activated and the planned Duration begins. This circumstance must be clearly and unequivocally described by the magus in the conditional clause. Examples of such clauses include "When I am being watched," "On May 1, 1897 at 5:00," and "After an attack is successful against me." The ritual effect will trigger the moment this circumstance occurs.

A *Circumstantial Activation* clause may also be added to focus a ritual on an object called a talisman. The underlined clause in the magical sentence "*Ward* the *Mortal* who wears this pendant against *Demons*," causes the wearing of the pendant to be the *Circumstantial Activation*. If the pendant changes persons, the magical effect will transition to the person wearing the pendant rather than the person originally targeted by the rite. The art of talismanic magic uses this feature to create magical items that may be passed from person to person. This may be combined with other features such as *Multiple Activations* to create magical artifacts whose power can be released on unspecified individuals long after their creation.

Circumstantial Cancellation

The rite's effect ends automatically and immediately when a certain circumstance is met. This circumstance is defined in a conditional clause placed at the end of the magical sentence such as "until the sun sets," "until she no longer believes this lie," or "until I say stop." Provided it has already begun, the ritual effect will end when this circumstance is met or when the Duration of the effect ends, whichever occurs first.

Exclusionary Clause

The rite is composed so that a particular circumstance will grant a person or object exclusion from its effects. This is done by adding a conditional clause modifying one of the nouns in the magical sentence. For example, "*Ward* this *Place* against *Shades* except for those of my own ancestors" or "*Obscure* this *Object* to *Mortals* except for other members of the Order of the Golden Dawn." Individuals can be marked by visible tokens such jewelry ("except for someone wearing a bronze brooch in the shape of a peacock"), specific affinities ("except for those who love the queen"), or any specific identifier that separates someone from the general populace. Exclusions for objects can be based on color, size, shape, composition, or any other quality that clearly distinguishes it.

Multiple Activations

This feature must be combined with both the *Circumstantial Activation* and *Circumstantial Cancellation* features, resulting in a minimum increase of 3 in intent.

The Duration of the effect may be paused each time the cancellation circumstance is met and restarted each time the activation circumstance is met. This can occur a number of times equal to the Duration rank, essentially breaking up the Duration into several discrete instances. The total period of active effect is still limited by the rite's total Duration. The person composing the rite determines the conditional clauses that pause and restart the effect. Pausing and restarting may be instigated in any way the composer desires, and requires no further tests. For example, "Ward this Place against Shades while this candle burns, but not when its light is extinguished." If this rite was composed with a Duration 2, the candle can be burned on up to two separate occasions, and will be effective up to a maximum of one total hour of warding. After the total number of activations or the total Duration has been reached, the ritual ends normally.

FUELING INTENT

A properly composed rite will harness enough magical energies to fuel the intent of the ritual. This means it contains a number of ranks in requirements that equal or exceed its number of ranks in intent. If a rite's requirement ranks are fewer than its intent ranks, the ritual will always fail. Fulfill this need by choosing ranks from the three requirement components: Participants, Reagents, and Time. At least one rank must be placed in each component, since all rituals require at least one magus, at least some magical items, and some time to perform.

When a rite contains requirement ranks in excess of what is needed to properly perform the ritual, it is easier to perform. For every rank of requirements above the rite's ranks in intent, lower the Difficulty of the rite by one. This is commonly done bring rites that would otherwise have impossible Difficulties (11+) down into the realm of human ability. However, excessive requirements cannot be added to an extant rite after it is composed. Excessive requirements must be written into the rite at the time of its composition.

PARTICIPANTS

At their most basic, all rituals require at least one Participant, but the involvement of additional others can produce greater effects. In order to count as a Participant in a ritual a person must have at least one rank in *Mysteries*, be present throughout the ritual's entire performance, and expend one point of potential (the same type as the magus leading the ritual). The additional power garnered through added Participants is one significant factor that leads to the forming of cabals and cults.

RITUAL PARTICIPANTS

Participant Rank	Number of Participants	Magus Notes
1	1	Magus is alone
2	2	Leads one other
3	5	Leads four others
4	10	Leads nine others
5	25	Leads twenty-four others
6	50	Leads forty-nine others
7	100	Leads ninety-nine others
8	250	Two magi, each leading 124 others
9	500	Four magi, each leading 124 others
10	1,000	Eight magi, each leading 124 others

Starting at rank 8, the large number of Participants requires extensive coordination with multiple magi leading the group. Each magus must make the *Will + Mysteries* test, and the lowest result is used to determine the success or failure of the entire ritual. Also, any interruption that causes at least one necessary Participant to cease ritual activity during the performance causes the ritual to fail. Savvy magi often lead more Participants than are actually required by the rite, safeguarding the performance even if one or more Participants are interrupted.

REAGENTS

Reagents are objects or materials within the Clockwork whose inherent power can be tapped to fuel magical effects. The power of each Reagent is measured in ranks. Reagents commonly take the form of burning candles or incense, and expending chalks or powders to draw magical sigils and mark boundaries. At other times, an object can be imbued with immense power from the passions of those who care for or covet it. These reagents are powerful not because of their substance, but because of the relationship the object has to a community, culture, or the magus who uses it. Rather than physically destroying the object, the magus simply severs her relationship to the object and reaps the energy that results from this. In either case, no magus may ever use the same reagent twice. It will either be destroyed or rendered spiritually inert to the magus.

When a magus composes a rite and assigns it a number of ranks in the Reagent requirement, that rite will require a Reagent of that rank to be used during the performance of the ritual. For example, a rank 1 Reagent can only be used to fulfill a Reagent 1 requirement; a rank 2 Reagent can be used to fulfill a Reagent 1 or 2 requirement; etc. Note that Reagent ranks are not cummulative. No matter how many rank 2 Reagents a magus uses in a ritual, it will only fulfill a Reagents 2 requirement. Reagent ranks can never be added together to make more powerful Reagents.

When fulfilling the Reagent requirement of a rite, any material with a sufficient Reagent rank can be used (see the *Magical Reagents* table). Players may wish to define the specific reagents for roleplaying purposes, but this is not required by the rules. It is assumed that most rites require similar low rank Reagents (candles, chalk, etc.), and that magi can fuel intent with energies harnessed from similar objects and materials. This means that magi characters needn't track the specific reagents they carry, only their rank values. Thus, there is no need to note how many white candles or bundles of dried bay leaves a magus has in store. A character can simply record how many uses of each rank of Reagent she possesses, and reduce these values as she uses them in rituals. As the Cost rank of a Reagent is equal to its Reagent rank, magi may quickly acquire common reagents ranked below their *Means*.

MAGICAL REAGENTS

Reagent Rank	Description	Examples
1	Ubiquitous materials of Cost 1 or less; easy to obtain.	Holy water, common herbs, candles, small amounts of the magus' own hair, blood, etc.
2	Common materials which are largely available at Cost 2+, or unusual materials that are difficult to obtain.	Uncommon fresh seasonal flowers or herbs, lock of hair or small amount of blood from the target.
3	• Unusual items with a Cost 3+ • Items that require specialized knowledge to acquire or produce (trait test, Difficulty 3+). • Items whose acquisition creates an outcome on the magus.	A silver ring engraved with angelic script, feathers from a rare bird fashioned into a talisman, a liturgical candle blessed by a bishop, enough blood or flesh from the magus or target to cause a Wound.
4	Rare items of Cost 4+, highly illegal materials, or artifacts with emotional weight that are extremely difficult to acquire.	Lavish jewelry, a sigil drawn on lambskin vellum with ink made from powdered silver, a vial of tears from 100 mothers whose sons died in battle.
5	Very rare items revered by many that are extremely expensive (Cost 5+) and dangerous to obtain.	The coronation crown of a former king, vestments made of cloth-of-gold produced from coins of every European nation, the true relic of a saint, locks of hair from the last 7 generations of the target's family.
6+	Unique, priceless, and storied items that are revered or despised by entire cultures.	The Ark of the Covenant, the Lance of Longinus, the Stone of Scone, the mummified heart from the body of Azazel.
+1	Special Reagents from ranks 1–4 can receive an additional rank if possessing the item is a capital offense, there is an extremely narrow window to acquire or use them, or it possess irreplaceable sentimental value to the magus.	An heirloom from a beloved departed parent, an object robbed from a grave, fresh petals from a flower that blooms for only a few days each decade.

The *Mandatory Reagents* restriction requires the Reagents to be specified within the rite and must be recreated exactly. For these rites, uncommon or unique reagents should be recorded by both specific kind and rank. Even when this restriction is not involved, it can be fun to record unique and more powerful reagents such as heirlooms and holy relics, as this adds to the flavor of the story.

PERFORMANCE TIME

All rituals require an investment of time to focus and perform the necessary manipulations of the reagents. Even the weakest rituals often require hours of preparation and execution, and grand undertakings may necessitate participants reorganize their lives for months to iterate ritual observances. Small increments of Time can be the easiest factor to control when designing a ritual, but larger Time requirements can be difficult to manage. Performance Time requires strict observance of ritual activity, and interruption that causes even one necessary Participant to cease ritual activity during the observance will cause the ritual to fail. For this reason, performance Time can be divided into equal regiments over the course of many days. As long as the regiment is planned and Time divided equally across days, many regiments are possible. Examples are provided in the *Ritual Performance* table.

RITUAL PERFORMANCE

Time Rank	Continuous Activity	Possible Regiments
1	30 minutes	NA
2	1 hour	NA
3	2 hours	NA
4	4 hours	NA
5	8 hours	1 hour per day for eight days
6	12 hours	1 hour per day for two weeks
7	24 hours	2 hours per day for two weeks, 1 hour per day for one month
8	48 hours	8 hours per day for a week, 2 hours per day for a month, 1 hour per day for a season
9	One week*	4 hours/day for a month, 2 hours/day for a season, 1 hour/day for a year and a day
10	One Month*	4 hours/day for six months, 2 hours/day for a year and a day

* It is impossible for any human to perform a ritual for more than two continuous days, but inhuman entities might be able to do so.

RESTRICTIONS

While features add beneficial flexibility and greater utility to rites, restrictions help meet a rite's requirements at the expense of increased rigidity. Many extant rites are written with multiple restrictions as a way to achieve powerful effects with much-reduced costs.

Each restriction written into a rite contributes 1 rank towards fueling the intent.

Draining

The rite is especially taxing, and draws much more heavily on potential than other rites. When beginning the rite, the magus and all other Participants must spend two points of potential rather than one. Rites using pure verbs require *Purpose*, and those with impure verbs require *Ether*, as usual.

Mandatory Location

A rite with this restriction is designed to work in a specific location, and unless the rite is performed in the predetermined location it automatically fails. This restriction is frequently used by magi with great personal resources who have established their own *sancta sanctorum*, or who are part of a particular order or cult with temples and other sacred spaces devoted to their art.

Mandatory Participants

This restriction requires the magus and all Participants to share a *Membership* asset in one organization, a shared Affinity of rank 3+, or some similar mechanical designation. Using the *Mandatory Participants* restriction is the most common method to ensure that a rite cannot be used by one's enemies as in many cases it would be impossible to perform.

Importantly, there must be more than one person who can meet this requirement, so it cannot be used to specify only the writer of the ritual. "Ordained Anglican priests" or "Members of the Esoteric Order of the Black Bull" are valid restrictions, whereas "Alfred Beauchamp" or "The Head of the Esoteric Order of the Black Bull presiding since the June of 1894" are not.

This restriction may be taken up to 3 times, but each time it is taken it increases the requirements of the level of *Membership* asset, or Affinity rank of the person specified. Taking it twice would require someone with 2 ranks of *Membership* in an organization, or an Affinity of 4. Taking it 3 times requires 3 ranks of *Membership* or an Affinity of 5.

Mandatory Reagent

The ritual is written in such a way that it clearly specifies the exact material reagents necessary for completion. The reagent used can only be the one specified in the rite, not any generic reagents or substitutions. Rites with the *Mandatory Reagent* restriction must require Reagents of rank 3 or higher, as less powerful reagents simply lack the magical power to provide this benefit. This restriction is most commonly found in extant rituals from the ancient or medieval period.

Mandatory Timing

The ritual is written in such a way that it can only be performed at a specific time—most often during an event of some astrological

CLARIFICATIONS ON THE BEHAVIOR OF MAGIC

The following rules apply to magical effects. Any circumstances not clearly addressed are resolved at the Narrator's discretion:

- The magus performing a ritual may choose to exempt themselves from the effects of the rite. Once made, the choice is irrevocable.
- Unless a target is clearly and specifically identified by the magus during the performance of a rite, the magic will affect a random eligible target within the Scope. This will continue until the maximum number of targets are affected by the rite.
- When a rite has a Duration longer than instantaneous, it will affect additional targets at the beginning of each sequence (if in conflict) or each minute (if in narrative time) until it is affecting the maximum number of eligible targets defined by Scope.
- When a target is invalid because a rite's Puissance is insufficient to affect it, there is no impact on the target whatsoever.

There are no partial or incidental effects from magic; it is successful or it is not. Those unaffected by magic can still observe and interact with any physical changes in the environment caused by the ritual.

- All targeting criteria and exemptions for a rite that include the *Circumstantial Activation* feature are made at the time the ritual is performed. Once made, the choices are irrevocable.
- If a rite using the *Circumstantial Activation* feature produces a physical object that serves as the focus for the rite's effect (a talisman), any character bearing the object may activate the effect by meeting the circumstances defined in the feature's clause. Bearers have no control over the targeting or exclusions for the effect.
- Rites using the *Sympathetic Connection* restriction can only affect those targets whose sympathetic ties were used in the performance of the ritual.

significance or in relation to a date of personal significance to the target, such as a birthday or wedding anniversary. Unless the ritual is performed and completed at the right time it will automatically fail, even if all other aspects of the ritual are correct. The period of time in which the ritual can be performed cannot be available more than once per month, as everyday occurrences have no special significance and do not contribute any additional power to the rite.

This restriction can dramatically limit the usefulness of extant rites, as it might require research to discover the right time, or the timing could depend upon knowledge or references known only to the magus who first composed the rite. Further, rituals with *Mandatory Timing* often limit the flexibility of using Time as a requirement as it cannot extend beyond the duration of the occurrence. For example, a ritual that must be performed "on the night of a full moon" would automatically fail if the Time to perform the ritual was longer than the period between sundown and dawn.

Sympathetic Connection

The rite is written in such a way that it necessitates a reagent that has an intimate personal connection to its target. For physical beings, this is almost always a piece of their body: blood, hair, fingernails, tears, etc. It may also be a treasured possession to which the target has an Affinity 2+. The item required is in addition any and all other items used as Reagents, and does not contribute as an additional or separate Reagent, or change the Reagent rank of other materials used.

EXAMPLE OF RITUAL COMPOSITION

As a practical example of ritual composition, let's walk through the process of designing the rite to reproduce a piece of folklore featured prominently in the demo adventure *Idle Hands*, a hand of glory.

First, we'll look at the inspiration from folklore and how its effects can be reflected in-game. In folklore, hands of glory were the hands of hanged criminals made into special candles prized by thieves because they could cause all people in a building to have dulled senses, and anyone in its immediate presence to become unconscious. The easiest reflection of that is the *Incapacitated* condition, which will make its targets helpless and insensible. Now we have enough information to start following the steps outlined above to compose the rite.

1. Constructing a Magical Sentence

Placing conditions on a person is handled by the verb *Degrade*. Our rite is placing a physical condition, so we want to use the noun *Body* for the target word. We could use any of several words for the second—*Animal, Mortal, Demon, Feyfolk*, or a few others— but *Mortal* will be the most likely to affect possible subjects, as almost everyone in the world is a mortal. Now we have the magical sentence: "*Degrade* the *Body* of *Mortals*." *Degrade* is an impure word, so beginning the rite costs the magus and each Participant a point of *Ether*, and it will give the magus and all Participants a point of *Corruption* if the *Will + Mysteries* test for ritual magic fails. That will be an important consideration when balancing the final Difficulty of the rite, as failure comes at a price.

2. Shaping the Intent

We now choose rank values for the three intent components: Duration, Puissance, and Scope. For Duration, one hour/one scene should give the bearer time to steal whatever they like, so it has a Duration of 2. Placing the *Incapacitated* temporary condition requires the Puissance to be at least 3. A Scope of 3 should impact everyone in a house, and subjecting up to five targets to the effect should be enough to allow the magus to carry out any nefarious deeds they had in mind.

Since it would be impractical to have the effect start immediately when the ritual is complete, we'll also include the *Circumstantial Activation* feature. Thinking about the lore, a hand of glory is used like a candle, so lighting the flame makes sense as the way the effect will be started. Thus, we'll add the phase "when the hand is lit on fire."

Now we add all these ranks together to determine the intent and initial Difficulty for the rite. Duration 2 + Puissance 3 + Duration 3 + 1 feature = 9. The Difficulty for the rite will be 9.

So far, the first part of the ritual description looks like this:

Hand of Glory, Impure rite, Difficulty 9
"*Degrade* the *Body* of *Mortals* when the hand is lit on fire."
Intent: Duration 2, Puissance 3, Scope 3.
Features: Circumstantial Activation

3. Fueling the Intent

Now we choose rank values for the three requirement components: Participants, Reagents, and Time; and add any restrictions we may want to use. The rite must meet significant requirements and will be very difficult to perform, so we'll have to very carefully manage choices to make it workable.

Needing only one Participant would be ideal for a criminal undertaking using the hand, and there are few ritualists willing to assist in a ritual this vile. It makes sense to use Participants 1. Since there is much ground left to cover in the requirements, the Reagents and Time will need to be high.

Seeking out a rare Reagent will help, and the folklore calls for the titular hand to come from a hanged murderer or thief that is still fresh enough to have flesh and fat on it to burn. This is a good fit. Given the illegality, rarity, and short time-frame to acquire the Reagent it has a rank of 5.

Going along with the solitary and time-sensitive nature of the ritual the Time can't be too long or the risk of discovery is high. To keep things relatively brief the Time is set at 3. This gives us nine ranks in requirements so far.

The total ranks for the requirements and restrictions must equal the total ranks chosen for the intent and features, so we could stop now. However, we have built a ritual at Difficulty 9, a very daunting undertaking. Remember that if the ranks in requirements exceed the ranks in intent, the rite's Difficulty is reduced by the difference. If we add some restrictions to our rite, that will help to make it easier to perform. There are several options that make sense:

- *Draining*: Requires 2 points of *Ether* to begin the rite.
- *Mandatory Reagent 5*: Hand of a recently-hanged murderer or thief.
- *Mandatory Timing*: Night of a new moon.

Choosing three restrictions adds three ranks to requirements. This brings our total to 12 ranks of requirements, which exceeds our rite's ranks in intent by 3, reducing the Difficulty of the rite by 3. This makes the final Difficulty: 9–3 = 6.

4. Complete the Rite

Record the final Difficulty, ranks of both intent and requirements, all features and restrictions, and the description of the rite's effect. Be creative when writing out how the ritual is performed and what it does. Our final rite would look like this:

Hand of Glory

Impure rite, Difficulty 6

"*Degrade* the *Body* of *Mortals* when the hand is lit on fire."

Intent: Duration 2, Puissance 3, Scope 3

Features: *Conditional Activation*

Requirements: Participants 1, Reagents 5, Time 3

Restrictions: *Draining*

Mandatory Reagent: Hand of a recently hung murderer or thief.

Mandatory Timing: Night of a new moon.

The severed hand of a recently-hanged criminal is the *Mandatory Reagent*, and will become the talisman storing the power of the effect. The rite can only be performed on the night of a full moon. Over the course of the ritual, the hand will be treated with wax and oils so it can be used as a candle. If the ritual is successfully performed, the hand of glory can be activated by lighting the fingers. When active, up to 5 mortal targets in the area suffer from the *Incapacitated* condition for the Duration of the effect as long as they are in the Scope of the effect.

SAMPLE RITES

Beastblind

Impure rite, Difficulty 6

"*Obscure Self* from *Animal* when the basilisk's eye is crushed."

Intent: Duration 5, Puissance 3, Scope 1

Features: *Conditional Activation:* When the basilisk's eye is crushed.

Requirements: Participants 1, Reagents 4, Time 6

Restrictions: *Mandatory Reagent:* A basilisk's eye.

An old Norse rite from ancient times, beastblind allows one person to go unnoticed by most animals for one day. If anyone is able to acquire a copy of this rite and a basilisk's eye, they could use it to prepare the eye as a talisman to store the effect until needed. Preparing the eye requires the magus spend one hour per day for a fortnight brushing the eye with the blood or urine of various wild animals from the region. Each day the eye grows more plump and moist, until by the end of the rite it again looks like a fresh, living eye. If the rite is successful, the eye will hold the effect in abeyance until it is crushed in the hand of the bearer and its juices smeared on her clothing. For a full day thereafter, all animals of Threat 3 or lower will not be able to see the user, though they will still be able to notice physical signs of her passage. Variations on this rite supposedly also exist using different Words that allow it to affect chimera, feyfolk, mortals, and others.

Bind the Unquiet Dead

Impure rite, Difficulty 6

"*Bind Shade* to *Object* when the object is sprinkled with drops of blood."

Intent: Duration 4, Puissance 3, Scope 1

Features: *Conditional Activation:* When the target object is sprinkled with drops of blood.

Requirements: Participants 1, Reagents 3, Time 5

Restrictions: *Mandatory Participants:* Member of the Esoteric Order of the Black Bull.

Mandatory Reagent: Grave dirt from a grave at least 100 years old mixed with special oils and salts packed in a small clay vessel.

Mandatory Timing: Night of a new moon.

Written in Theban and employing several cryptic references to the ritual observations of the Esoteric Order of the Black Bull that are completely opaque to the uninitiated, copies of this rite occasionally surface in spiritualist circles. When performed correctly during the night of a new moon, the rite establishes a powerful binding effect that lays dormant, so it may later be triggered to trap a shade.

especially when the demons themselves actively teach such rites to their servitors. This rite is most likely meant to be used by a magus already cooperating with a demon, as the excessive Time required would make it difficult to pair with a binding rite. The magus attempting the rite must engage in 8 hours of fervent supplication and ceremonial bloodletting to summon the target demon. If a specific demon is being called, the rite must use that entity's name. It can also be performed by calling out generally, in which case the nearest demon of Threat 3 is summoned.

Expellere a Ritu Mundi

Pure rite, Difficulty 7

"*Expel Demon* from *Place*."

Intent: Duration 1, Puissance 4, Scope 10

Features: None

Requirements: Participants 6, Reagents 5, Time 7

Restrictions: *Draining*

Mandatory Participants rank 3: Archbishop of the Magisterium

Mandatory Reagent: A pure gold medal of St. Benedict, blessed by the Pope.

The *expellere a ritu mundi* is among the most powerful magical tools used by the Inquisition, and only a few highly placed Inquisitors know of its existence. When performed correctly, this ritual can expel powerful demons from the world entirely. Such a powerful effect is incredibly draining and difficult for even a master ritualist to perform: It requires a carefully choreographed mass that lasts a full 24 hours, fifty total Participants skilled in *Mysteries* (each of whom must spend two points of *Purpose*), a large golden medal of St. Benedict blessed by the Pope for use in the mass, and the names of any demons targeted by the rite must be known and used throughout. If performed properly, this ritual will expel a Threat 4 or weaker demon into the Borderlands.

Curse of Lethargy

Impure rite, Difficulty 3

"*Degrade* the *Body* of *Mortal*."

Intent: Duration 1, Puissance 5, Scope 1

Features: None

Requirements: Participants 3, Reagents 3, Time 4

Restrictions: *Sympathetic Connection: Blood.*

Only grimoires of black magic are likely to contain such a pernicious rite. A curse of lethargy deadens the limbs and drains the vitality of the target, inflicting *Fatigued* as a persistent condition. Although the rite is relatively easy it does require the blood of the target and a number of Participants to perform, so there are some hurdles to putting it to use.

Demonic Call

Impure rite, Difficulty 2

"*Evoke Demon* to *Place*."

Intent: Duration 1, Puissance 3, Scope 1

Features: None

Requirements: Participants 1, Reagents 2, Time 5

Restrictions: None

Dangerous rites of evocation are frequently confiscated by the Witchfinders and Inquisition, but even those organizations cannot seem to fully stamp out the knowledge of summoning demons,

The Iron Ban

Pure rite, Difficulty 6

"*Ban Feyfolk* from *Place*."

Intent: Duration 7, Puissance 3, Scope 2

Features: None

Requirements: Participants 2, Reagents 3, Time 8

Restrictions: *Draining*

Mandatory Reagent: Four iron sigils with silver filigree of Enochian characters that must be kept at the cardinal points of the area of the ban.

Mandatory Timing: The performance must begin each day at dawn.

The iron ban is an ancient rite of the Magisterium meant to guard monasteries and churches established in pagan lands from the feyfolk that often inhabited such areas. The magus and at least one other acolyte must perform a lengthy series of chants and prayers beginning exactly at dawn for two hours every day for a month. Upon the completion of the rite, a ban is enacted around the sanctuary that prevents fey creatures of Threat 3 or lower from entering the protected area.

Magical Healing

Pure rite, Difficulty 5

"*Restore* the *Body* of *Mortal*."

Intent: Duration 1, Puissance 5, Scope 1

Features: None

Requirements: Participants 2, Reagents 3, Time 4

Restrictions: None

Perhaps the most sought-after rites are those those that provide physical healing. As mortals have always known physical danger, a flexible healing rite can be found in every magical tradition. This version requires the magus and one assistant spend several hours preparing the target's Wound, then applying ritually purified poultices and balms specially prepared from rare herbs gathered at times of astrological significance. Though the reagents are somewhat costly to acquire and prepare, being able to instantaneously heal the target of one Wound at the end of the successful rite is thought to be worth the expense.

Repair the Breach

Pure rite, Difficulty 6

"*Restore* the *Boundary* of *Place*."

Intent: Duration 1, Puissance 5, Scope 3

Features: None

Requirements: Participants 2, Reagents 4, Time 4

Restrictions: *Mandatory Participants*: Witchfinders.

Mandatory Reagent: A white linen shroud stitched with thread-of-silver.

This rite is used by those Witchfinders tasked with repairing the damage done by especially foul acts or powerful Pontus events. The rite begins with a series of call and response verses chanted by two Witchfinder magi over a white linen shroud stitched with angelic sigils in silver thread. After two hours of chants and prayer, the shroud is torn in two and dragged around the periphery of the *Place* being *Restored*. When the magi meet again after one perambulation, they spend the remaining two hours repairing the shroud with silver thread, intoning words of blessing and protection with each stitch. When the rite is completed successfully the environmental stability of the *Place* is moved one step towards Stable (see *Environmental Stability*, p. 281).

Those serving dark powers use an inverted version of this rite with the formulation "*Degrade* the *Boundary* of *Place*" to damage the environmental stability of an area and make it easier for their masters to cross into the world. Such foul rites require membership in a cult, and instead of the prayers and use of a shroud a picture of the location is drawn in exotic inks and ritually defaced while the magi beseech fell powers of the Outer Darkness to weaken the Clockwork. If the rite is successful the environmental stability of the *Place* moves one step towards Breached.

A Rite Purported to Allow Communication Over Any Distance

Pure rite, Difficulty 6

"*Commune Mortal* with *Self* until I clap my hands."

Intent: Duration 2, Puissance 3, Scope 1

Features: *Circumstantial Cancellation*: When the magus claps her hands.

Requirements: Participants 1, Reagents 2, Time 3

Restrictions: *Sympathetic Connection*: A lock of hair.

An extant rite that can be found printed as an appendix to a Cambridge-printed monograph *An Consideration of the Superstitious Mind: Irrationality, False Beliefs, and Madness*. Should any magi read the work, they would find an effective rite that allows them to mentally contact any individual from whom they have a lock of hair. The performance of the rite is also very straightforward, requiring 2 hours of meditation and concentration and the burning of the target's hair. Once the ritual is successfully performed, the magus may communicate freely with the target, and vice versa. Should the magus wish to end the communion before the Duration expires, she is able to do so by clapping her hands.

Seeking Visions

Impure rite, Difficulty 4

"*Reveal Self* to *Self*."

Intent: Duration 1, Puissance 3, Scope 1

Features: None

Requirements: Participants 1, Reagents 3, Time 1

Restrictions: Mandatory Reagent: *Natem* tea.

The Shuar people of the Amazon and Andes in Peru have brewed a special tea of the *caapi* vine and other amazonian plants to produce natem, but outsiders have become familiar with it through the Portugese and know it as *ayahuasca*. Drinking it can inspire powerful visions in anyone, but it is also a useful reagent for revelatory rites. This rite was brought back to Portugal by a jungle explorer decades ago, and has since made its way into the hands of some more mystically-inclined spiritualists in Europe. If one is able to acquire the caapi root to brew the tea, the rite is a simple matter of brief meditation to call to mind three questions about her own life that the magus seeks to clarify with mystical insight, and then experiences the visions brought on by the tea and shaped by the rite to bring understanding. The effect of the rite provides knowledge, but does nothing to blunt the physical effects of the tea, which will often leave the magus suffering the *Fatigued* and *Dazed* conditions for a scene after drinking it.

تبدیل پره از دشمنان من
("Turn the blades of my enemies")

Pure rite, Difficulty 5

"*Protect Mortal* from *Object* (blade) when the amulet is first worn."

Intent: Duration 2, Puissance 5, Scope 1

Features: *Conditional Activation*: When the amulet is first worn.

Requirements: Participants 2, Reagents 3, Time 6

Restrictions: *Draining*

Sympathetic Connection: Blood and tears.

As long as mortals have known ritual magic it has seen use in times of conflict, and all magical traditions have included rites designed to protect their targets from injury. This modern translation of a classical-era Persian rite produces an amulet engraved with sigils of protection that, when worn, will prevent a single Wound from any bladed weapon. Performing the rite requires the magus to intone blessings and beseech angels to protect the target, who must assist throughout the rite as the amulet is being prepared and marked with her blood and tears over the course of 12 hours. If successfully completed, the amulet will store the protection effect as a talisman until the target puts it on. Then the target will benefit from the protection for one scene. Once the scene is over or a Wound from a bladed weapon is prevented the amulet becomes brittle and dull. A more modern variation of this rite also exists that protects against bullets rather than blades.

Ward Against Chimera

Pure rite, Difficulty 5

"*Ward Place* against *Chimera*."

Intent: Duration 3, Puissance 3, Scope 2

Features: None

Requirements: Participants 2, Reagents 4, Time 2

Restrictions: *Mandatory Reagents*: A strip of heart muscle taken from a slain chimera of Threat 5 or higher.

Mandatory Participants rank 2: A Witchfinder Archdeacon.

A copy of this rite is shared with all Witchfinder Canons when they are promoted to the rank of Archdeacon. As their elevated position requires them respond to the worst reports of Pontus activity, the rite affords them a powerful tool to aid them in dispatching chimera. The archdeacon performing the rite places a strip of heart muscle from a potent chimera into a container of any liquid, then, with the help of the other Participant begins to intone blessings in Enochian, the language of angels, meant to reinforce the intended order of the world in that place. When the ritual is complete, the strip of muscle will have dissolved into the liquid, which is then sprinkled about the area to be defended. If performed correctly, the rite will subject any chimera in that area to a –3 penalty on all tests for the next scene. Since the effect only covers a small area, the rite is most often used to bolster the defenses of a particular location, or to set up an ambush for chimera that are being lured there.

RITE OF RECONCILIATION

There are magical words beyond human ken that can only be understood by angels, the Fallen, and the Clockmaker Himself. Rites made from these words were not composed by mortal hands. They were gifted to humanity from on high and handed down among the faithful within the rites of the Church. Among these is the rite of reconciliation, a powerful and ancient sacrament that allows for the forgiveness of terrible sins. Performing it requires neither a trait test nor the expenditure of potential. It simply works so long as its requirements are met.

The rite of reconciliation can be performed by any cleric of the See or Canterbury or Magisterium, and many of the Denominationalist sects. There are certainly similar rites in other religious traditions, but they are even less understood by Imperial scholars. The cleric performs this rite on behalf of a person afflicted with Corruption that was gained through sinful behavior. If the corrupted individual is honestly contrite and is willing to disclose the full nature of her sin to the cleric, she will be forgiven and the Corruption that was gained through that sin will be removed. The corrupted individual may confess multiple sins and be freed from the Corruption acquired through each of them.

Receiving this rite does not require the individual character to have any sort of faith or belief in the Church. However, this rite requires a character to be sincerely sorry and have the honest intention of never performing the confessed behavior again. This is treated as an oath. If a character does perform the sin again, she incurs one point of Corruption from breaking her oath and another from the newly committed sin. Most clergymen will recommend an act of contrition at this point, as reconciliation will do no more good.

"Warden Reed of the Witchfinders to see you, sir."

With that simple introduction the footman conducted the visitor into the office and withdrew, closing the door behind him. The Witchfinder came into the center of the room in long strides, the tread of his boots and swish of his ankle-length black leather longcoat was the only sound he made as he moved. Even without sword and pistol, the man cut an intimidating figure and looked every inch the scarred survivor of dire battles that the public imagined. In contrast, his host seemed of a softer sort, more fit for a garden party in his crisp linen suit in dove gray, gold rings on his fingers, and some exotic bloom in his lapel. The two men met each others' eyes for a moment, then the host inclined his head slightly in greeting, gestured towards an over-stuffed leather chair for his guest, then settled himself into the well-worn seat beside his desk before he spoke.

"You're late."

"I'm not sure I take your meaning, Mr. Adebayo."

That the Witchfinder was uncomfortable and taken off-guard was plain to see. Adebayo considered the man while he formulated his response. Even in the heat of the day, this man had insisted on wearing that heavy leather longcoat, and the high hat that marked him as a Witchfinder. He must have assumed that it would present an imposing facade. In reality, it made him sweat and look uncomfortable, and the unexpected opening of their conversation had not helped matters. If the Warden wished to play a game of bluster and appearances, Adebayo would be more than happy to oblige.

"What I mean, Warden Reed, is that members of the Inquisition were here an hour ago. I imagine they have already asked me the very same thing which you are about to." He flashed a grin before continuing. "Since your question will not be novel, I am interested to see how the rest of the conversation might be different."

"I didn't realize you were friendly with the Magisterium."

"I'm not," Adebayo said flatly. "However, they are friendly with the Yoruba tribe. We have venerated a single Godhead in three manifestations since before European contact. Thus, we are more… familiar to them… than are our Muslim Fulani neighbors." He smiled again. "I am one of the more influential Yoruba in Lagos, Warden Reed. So, yes. The Magisterium come to me quite often."

A glare entered the Witchfinder's eyes. "If you already know about the *HMS Argenta*, then I assume you also know what went down with her. People are going to die. This is no time to play one bid against another."

Adebayo's jovial arrogance was gone now, replaced by a shrewd pragmatism. "Careful, Warden. This is not England, and the Empire does not rule in Nigeria as it does in other places. Such dictates among friends are not always well-received."

"There are other places we can go. You are not the only man with ships in this port."

"And where will you go? To whom? You know well, I am the only man in this city with a ship capable of maintaining atmospheric diving suits and a crew you can trust to use them. Best of luck finding another to retrieve your… cargo… quickly and discreetly." He paused to see if the Warden would persist in his bluff, or acknowledge the truth by his silence.

The clock on Adebayo's desk ticked.

The corners of Reed's mouth turned down as though he tasted something foul. "Money is no object. I have the full support of the Crown."

Adebayo waved his hand around the room, drawing the Witchfinder's attention to the collection of expensive furnishings and near-priceless memorabilia. His drawing room was paneled in imported European hardwoods, carpeted with oriental rugs, and decorated with unique artifacts from across the globe. In the corner of the room was an analytical engine of a size and complexity Reed had never seen, one that would be the envy of any counting-house or university. It was such an ostentatious display it was hard to say if the machine was used to manage his shipping business or if it was just to impress his guests. "Money is such a vulgar topic between gentlemen, is it not? It seems highly prized only by those without it."

The Witchfinder furrowed his brow. "The fact that we're continuing this conversation at all means there must be something that the Crown can offer you that the Magisterium cannot. What is it that you want? Think carefully before you answer, though. The Witchfinders are, above all, in service to the order of the Clockwork and the Empire. We will not be drawn into the petty politics of this city, nor serve as catspaws for the removal of rivals. If such are your expectations, you will be disappointed."

Adebayo leaned back in his chair and looked at the Witchfinder over steepled fingers. "I want membership in the Atheneum."

Reed's guarded disposition dropped in surprise. "Your price is membership in a gentleman's club?" The Witchfinder gripped the arms of his chair in white-knuckled indignation and leaned towards his host, nearly spitting his words in frustration. "The Pontus rises, and if you know half so much as you pretend about what brought down the *Argenta* you know as well as I the risks facing us all. Still, you haggle over the lives and fortunes of many for entrance into a club?!"

Ignoring the outburst, Adebayo responded plainly. "I need no reminders from the Witchfinders or the Magisterium concerning the dangers of the Pontus, sorcerers, demons, feyfolk, or any other type of monster, Warden Reed. These things are not so rare on 'the Dark Continent.'" A hint of scornful bemusement crossed his face as he uttered those words the British newspapers liked to use for his home. "We simply do not share the same fears, in the same proportions, as you."

"The Atheneum is one of the most prestigious clubs in London, and counts among its members some of the brightest minds and most prominent names in the Empire. The wait list for new members is over three years long, even with sponsors. I am not by nature one who waits. I'd like my application to receive an attentive eye, and I'm sure that with your organization's connections to the Crown, it would receive a great deal of attention." Adebayo leaned back comfortably in his chair, and dropped his hands onto his lap. "It's a simple request, and well within your power to grant. If you give me what I want, then I will give you what you want, and you won't even have to spend a shilling."

The men locked eyes, the Warden's cold stare against the calm gaze of the businessman. Reed was doubtless a terror in a fight, but this was not his type of battle. Adebayo was a veteran of half a hundred negotiations more fraught than this, and Reed had already lost whether he realized it or not. No matter what he did next, it would cost him. If he rebuffed the simple offer, he would lose the prize of the *Argenta* and drive Adebayo to closer ties with the Inquisition over a trifling price. If the Warden agreed, then he made himself a client of Adebayo, and such a relationship could be grown and deepened, making it an easy choice for the Witchfinders to return to him in the future for favors. Word would spread that Adebayo had such powerful friends—his trusted staff would see to it—and everyone in Lagos would come to know what shipping office the Crown came to for its work.

The clock on the desk ticked, and chimed softly to mark the quarter hour.

Warden Reed let out a slow exhalation, and rose to his feet. Reflexively, his left hand dropped to rest on the hilt of a sword that wasn't there. He loomed.

"I'll need to send a telegram."

A warm smile returned to Adebayo's face, and he rose to shake the Witchfinder's hand. "I'm pleased we can be of service to one another. I'll have your ship ready by the time you return."

NARRATING THE GAME

When a host plans a dinner party, there are certain expectations that must come to pass if the endeavor is to be successful. Such a gathering can be a positive experience overall, but without a meal, it would flop. It is also necessary to have guests that are willing to share polite discourse according to the proper etiquette. It is the job of the host to make certain these things occur, and to step in and intercede if they do not. Beyond these basic things, each party will be different. Depending on the social class of those gathered, such an event may also involve singing, games, dancing, cocktails, or even a brawl. It is ultimately up to the guests to decide if the night was a pleasant experience.

A tabletop roleplaying game is much the same. The Narrator plays the part of the host, and it is her job to provide the main course: the story. The players are the guests; they interact with one another and the Narrator, engaging each other and adding to the story. Ideally, the Narrator and the players will collaborate to spin a tale that is engaging and fun. Beyond these basic things, each story will be different. Depending on the desires of the players, games can focus on high society and social mobility, beat cops taking

down organized crime, impoverished street urchins making ends meet, killing the big bad evil about to destroy the world, or anything in between. It is ultimately up the the Narrator to provide the skeleton of the story, while the players provide the flesh.

As the host to a story, the Narrator has responsibilities that extend beyond simply providing the story's framework. To ensure everyone's enjoyment, a dutiful host must listen attentively, speak so as to make others feel comfortable to contribute, intervene when interaction begins to lag, and mind the rules. When conflict arises in the story, or at the table, the Narrator must step in, manage the conversation, and make sure that all is resolved fairly and in a way that is engaging and purposeful.

This chapter provides guidelines and advice to help Narrators of all levels of experience. The first portion of this chapter looks at writing and telling stories, developing plot to engage players, and portraying Narrator characters. The latter portion covers mechanical concerns such as how to effectively run conflicts, assign *Corruption*, use Pontus events, and reward player characters.

WRITING AND TELLING STORIES

Stories told in *Clockwork: Dominion* depict exceptional individuals struggling against, and hopefully overcoming, dramatic threats. Well-written stories provide characters with the means and motivation to participate in the drama, and provide the Narrator with ongoing inspiration and enthusiasm for running the game. There are many types of stories to be told.

Using Prewritten Modules

Narrators may use published adventures to serve as complete stories or as a starting foundation from which to build an unique, ongoing series. Published adventures are built from clearly defined story elements to highlight a central theme or aspect of the setting, and are meant to be picked up and played by anyone. New Narrators can use published adventures to familiarize themselves with the game, and as examples to help write their own stories. Experienced Narrators can find inspiration and a ready source of story elements, Narrator characters, and material they can repurposed for inclusion in their own series. The first *Clockwork: Dominion* adventure, *Idle Hands*, is included in the Quick Start Rules available for free download from ReliquaryGameStudios.com.

Writing Your Own Stories

For Narrators with a story idea that interests them, writing adventures from scratch can be a very rewarding way to explore the setting and shape the play experience for the players at your table. This may seem daunting for new Narrators, so planning the general framework before working on all the particulars can be a helpful way to start. There are five primary elements in an engaging Clockwork story: themes, locations, protagonists, an agent of chaos, and drama. As long as a story is written with some thought given to these elements, it should work well at the table.

- **Themes:** The Clockwork Dominion setting has strong strains of steam, punk, Victorian, and gothic horror. Deliberately focusing on one or more themes helps the Narrator build on the setting to give the story shape and mood. Having a primary theme and occasionally modifying or tweaking it by the inclusion of a secondary theme can turn a flat and linear story into a vibrant one.

- **Location:** This the place and time at which your story occurs. A location can have a large effect on a story. If you want to tell a horror story about bodysnatchers living beneath an urban metropolis, the undercity of the Edinburgh vaults might work best. If you want to tell a Victorian story about rival families waging a social war over political constituencies, London during the Season is best. Choose a location that fits the story you want to tell.

- **Protagonists:** The protagonists are the player characters. Before the game begins tell your players the themes you want to use in the story and also ask them what themes they wish to explore so the story can be created with them in mind. If the story will highlight specific skills, *Memberships*, and other assets, share this information with your players so that the created characters can have access to these abilities and their character concepts fit with the story to be told. Relevant characters are key for a cohesive story and help the players stay engaged with the themes that interest them.

- **Agent of Chaos:** This is what drives the story, and it can manifest as a person, organization, circumstance, or crisis. The agent of chaos is whatever threatens and opposes the player characters and their goals. Depending on the nature of the agent of chaos and the type of story being told it may threaten the characters physically, socially, emotionally, economically, politically, or even spiritually.

- **Drama:** The interaction of the protagonists with the agent of chaos creates the tension in the story. The chance to resolve this tension motivates the protagonists to take part in your story. Without opportunity and motivation, the players will not act and the story falls flat. Some drama is overcome using the structured mechanics of social or physical conflict, but at other times it can be averted entirely or brought to a head through clever roleplay. Present the players with a variety of situations where they can choose how to engage the drama of the story.

All of these elements are discussed in detail in their own sections below, but can be worked on in any order. Sometimes good story idea starts with a theme, while others begin with an idea for a memorable antagonist.

THEMES

All the major themes in Clockwork Dominion are encapsulated in the tag line: "Steampunk roleplaying in a Victorian world of gothic horror." When writing a story, it's best to consistently focus on one primary theme throughout, and use one or more secondary themes as inflection points for important parts in the series. Mixing in complementary themes keeps the feel of the plot consistent, but using contrasting themes prevents it from becoming stale.

Steam: Technology, Innovation, and Wonder

Steam stories highlight the changes wrought by new technology and the incredible possibilities it brings for both good and ill. Modern innovations in transportation, power, and communication enable grand adventure. International travel is faster than ever, allowing global escapades. Governments, universities, and militaries are competing for the best and brightest minds in the Empire. Patent disputes create bitter rivalries between inventors. The threat of war is a horrible prospect as great powers arm themselves with weapons undreamed of a generation ago. Everywhere, technology is simultaneously making the world more wonderful and more terrifying.

The use of fantastic technology lends itself to pulp adventure—airships, undersea travel, automatons, and incredible gadgetry can make regular appearances in this sort of adventure. Characters can use astounding devices to perform larger-than-life feats. For example, duels might be settled with steam-powered exoskeletons rather than swords.

Steam games can also have a strong social component. Victorian society respects great intelligence and those who put it to good use. The accomplishment and public notice that comes with great skill and invention could open the doors of high society and intrigues well removed from the labs and workshops characters might be used to occupying. Innovators can sometimes bypass the poor circumstances of their birth to achieve great heights of prestige. The social response to disruptions caused by new technology can also have serious social ramifications. If a genius inventor worked to minimize the casualties of war by inventing more efficient automatons to take the place of soldiers, how is it received when the working poor try desperately to prevent their factory jobs from being taken over by the same mechanical men. How do foreign powers react if they fear that such mechanized soldiers means that the Empire is preparing to go to war? Thinking about and planning for the social side of a steam campaign can add a great deal of depth and provide characters plenty of opportunities to engage with the world.

In a steam story, players characters will often be the ones advancing science and technology or putting it to good use pushing the boundaries of human knowledge and accomplishment. They could be the alchemists or inventors who create fantastic technology, pirates or spies working to steal or destroy those inventions, or the scholars and entrepreneurs who research and market them. They can be motivated to join the Royal Society, or work together as part of an airship crew, in an elite military unit, or for a global corporation. Characters with assets such as *Alchemical Reaction* or *Innovator*, ranks in the *Science* or *Engineering* skills, or *Membership* in a relevant organization all have abilities and connections to draw on that exemplify the theme and provide plenty of plot hooks.

You can engage players by providing challenges that let the ingenuity and unique talents of their characters shine. Include a variety of encounters that feature advanced technology, puzzles that can be overcome with clever use of gadgets, or even the debate of scientific ideas through social conflict. Since technology is part of the defining theme for player characters, rewards that grant access to unique accoutrements and opportunities to use them can be great motivation. Be careful not to grant access to too much advanced technology, though, as blasting through waves of enemies with a lightning cannon is not exciting if it becomes commonplace.

Moving the story along through use of time or plot pressures is especially critical. Steam stories can lose momentum and the sense of drama if player characters spend too much time in their workshops churning out fantastic inventions instead of engaging with the plot. It is also possible for the characters to become so well-equipped that only the most deadly encounters pose a real challenge. Including some situations that deprive characters of access to their gear can manage this, but must be handled carefully. Robbing characters of the advantages they have worked hard to develop can spoil the fun and lead to frustration. Keeping the series focused on some clear goal or endpoint avoids this problem entirely. A race against time to develop some particular technology capable of thwarting a disaster, overcoming a known rival, or breaking some boundary of human knowledge through exploration or experimentation are all worthy goals that can provide satisfying closure to your story.

Punk: Change, Disruption, and Defiance

Civilization is often unjust. Throughout the Empire there are massive inequalities between those born into privilege and those who have almost no hope to attain wealth, education, or equal treatment under the law. Games with a strong punk element don't shy away from these social problems; they build stories around them. Punk plots highlight double standards and inequality, putting the player characters at the center of the ongoing struggle against the status quo.

Including plots designed to allow the player characters to step outside the social norm is a great way to highlight that they are playing extraordinary individuals. Many punk-themed stories focus on the ideal of social justice or even revolution, and provide player characters a chance to create real change for themselves and for others. These stories can be as personal as a character that defies class and gender norms to pursue their own goals and desires, or as sweeping as the abolitionist work that successfully ended slavery in the Empire. Other punk stories can be frivolous and subversive, showcasing social dissidents who embarrass the pompous, point out the absurdity of Victorian social artifice, or who are simply ridiculous or lewd. The mechanics for social conflict, propaganda, and Reputations are perfect tools for any punk game, and give players a chance to make waves. Player characters with a distinctly lower *Class* than other major characters in the story, and those that use social conflict and skills such as *Guile*, *Parley*, and *Streetwise* will have many opportunities to make their opinions heard, whatever they may be.

All games with a punk theme must confront the fact that the Clockwork itself is held together by order, not justice. Thus, there are always forces in the setting who believe that social institutions must be kept in place, even when they cause harm. It is

THE YEAR OF THE GAME

The default year of a story within the Clockwork world is 1896, but it need not always be so. The Clockwork: Dominion setting draws on the events and society of 1890–1913, and a story can easily take place at any time in that range. The Victorian era begins in 1837, and games in this earlier period can be handled with a few adjustments to the setting such as the removing zeppelins and automobiles, a lack of beastfolk, and the formal methods of alchemy being yet undiscovered. Series taking place in the 1900s would make some technology more prevalent, such as analytic engines, automatons, and flight. Stories set after 1914 take place during the rapid technological and social change of the Great War, and lie beyond the scope of *Clockwork: Dominion*, but will be addressed in future supplements.

countered by those who cry out to eradicate the suffering that goes against the Clockmaker's will for humanity. Player and Narrator characters will have differing ideas about what traditions and behaviors must be maintained because the order they provide keeps us safe from the Pontus, and which new ideas and changing mores are important because justice is the will of the Maker. No one faction or ideology truly understands how to hold the Clockwork together, so there is always room for the clash of ideas, even within a single organization or political group. Including punk-themed Narrator characters allows you to show glimpses of the world's clashing ideologies from in-game viewpoints, which can be a powerful tool for bringing the setting to life.

Be very careful when including charged social issues as part of a plot, especially instances of discrimination based on race, gender, sexuality, religion, or ability. Having players confront and overcome those hurdles can be rewarding, but must be handled thoughtfully and will only work if due respect is given to the feelings and experiences of everyone at the table. Communicate with players *before* running stories that feature these types of punk elements, then listen carefully and respectfully to any concerns or objections raised by players. It's the best way to be sure that everyone enjoys the game. If used carelessly or too frequently, such events can be hurtful or alienating to the real people playing the game. Inequality and bigotry are still problems in the world today, and players may have encountered them in real life. Engaging inequality in a fictionalized way, such as by dealing with the bigotry experienced by corrupted bloodlines like beastfolk or nephilim might be a way to introduce social adversity in a manner that is more comfortable for players than directly facing bigotry centered on real-world issues.

Victorian: Culture, Tradition, and Stability

Victorian-themed stories allow the players and their characters to explore the glory of the Empire at its zenith, featuring the culture, standards, and social traditions that brought it there. These stories immerse players in the intricacies and aesthetics of Victorian culture. High society games can focus on dinner parties, ballrooms, the politics of marriage arrangements, and the social intricacies of life within the Empire. A Victorian story could just as easily focus on the working poor trying to make ends meet and surviving the streets of London. The context of the characters will define the aspects of Victorian culture with which they come in contact. The key to a good Victorian story is to help the players feel like their characters could be in a tale written by Jane Austen, Charles Dickens, Sir Arthur Conan Doyle, or H.G. Wells.

Characters in a Victorian story are often focused on improving their station, which creates many opportunities for drama. Socialites may wish to better their Reputations or climb the ranks of an organization. Scientists and inventors may try to gain fame from their achievements and technological innovations. Politicians may pursue an elected office. Bellicose characters may attempt to increase their status through distinguished military service. Anyone can benefit from the traditional route of marrying well. Focused as they are on social structures, Victorian campaigns usually require player characters to have ranks in *Refinement* and other social skills, and might center around a relevant organization or a certain rank of *Class*.

Narrators who tell Victorian stories should familiarize themselves with the contents of *Chapter 2: Clockwork Society*, and may consider seeking out additional sources of information on Victorian life such as the book *What Jane Austen Ate and Charles Dickens Knew* by Daniel Pool. Including tidbits from period culture can add authenticity and enhance the feel of the setting, but beware of becoming too rigid when implementing these customs within a story. While subjects of the Empire might live and breathe these behaviors, players do not. Be lenient with players who are still learning the intricacies of the setting. Introduce situations and characters that illustrate the information and let the characters participate. A grand ball, tea party, or session of Parliament can be a great way to help players understand how Imperial society works.

Another angle of approach for Victorian games is including elements that touch on matters of national pride such as British achievements in technology, military might, wealth, and politics that support Imperial dominance. Including Narrator characters and plots that focus on military expeditions, daring explorers, and brilliant inventors working to expand Imperial knowledge, strength, and borders shows the vastness of the Empire, and including characters in such action shows their importance. Pitting characters against the threats posed by foreign armies, dissenting colonies, espionage, ritual cults, and the ever-present hazard of the Pontus lets players feel like their characters are making a difference on a grand scale—these are not just threats to the characters, but threats to the Imperial way of life! The grit and danger they endure enables the genteel society at the heart of the Empire. Hence, Victorian stories can run the gamut from the social clubs of London's elite to the trenches of a foreign battlefield.

Horror: Fear, Loss, and Alienation

Horror-themed stories revolve around the supernatural and mundane terrors in the Clockwork. The ability of the Pontus to unmake and reform reality, spawn monsters, and the risk that it could manifest at any time makes it a perfect source of otherworldly menace, but the Pontus only enters the world as a consequence of mortal actions. Sometimes the most disturbing horror comes from the evil that people do of their own volition, and sadly there is no shortage of human evil in the Clockwork. Mad scientists perform surgical experiments on unwilling subjects. Technological advances are co-opted into weaponry capable of causing unrestrained destruction. Fanatic ideologues strive to cleanse the world of "unworthy" people or ideas. Cultists are the active or unwitting instruments of terrible otherworldly beings. The Empire itself expands through bloodshed, conquest, and theft. Even those who stand against this wickedness may find themselves engaging in atrocities in the name of combating the darkness threatening to consume the world.

Characters who deal with the horrors of the setting will be pushed to their limits facing down black-hearted evil and senseless madness, and must call on any benefit at their disposal to endure. They may have access to supernatural powers such as ritual magic, charisms, and glamours, belong to inhuman bloodlines, or hold *Membership* in religious institutions, hermetic orders, the Witchfinders, or the Inquisition. Skills such as *Investigation, Mysteries,* and *Intuition* can play a vital role alongside physical and social conflict skills. Most horror-themed stories are written with the expectation that the player characters have skills and assets to deal with the dangers they face, but some stories depend on the characters being outmatched and struggling to survive.

Managing the sense of constant tension and risk critical to a good horror series requires finesse as a Narrator. To elicit a fear response from players, some encounters may have to be truly daunting or terrifying. Make retreat or escape available at a cost, and when necessary clarify this option for players who think they must fight to the death every time. This ensures that a story can continue even if players suffer from bad decisions or bad luck. You can also create this tension by introducing a major antagonist early on in the series, well before the characters are capable of confronting it directly. This lets the players know the scope of the danger they face, but gives them time over the arc of the story to explore the extent of the horror they must face, learn its secrets, and strengthen themselves enough to overcome it.

When running a horror game you must know the capabilities of the player characters and be especially careful when planning and balancing combat encounters to present real risks. It is critically important that horror stories have consequences. Victory is never assured. Relationships strain and fail, and characters die. If the players believe their characters or allies are not truly in danger, the story will fall flat. It is not an easy genre to run for a long series, and best suits those groups that can pull together in the face of shared danger, rather than each trying to pursue their own ways forward. Perhaps most importantly, you must understand the comfort levels of the players in order to tell a good horror story. It can be fun—even thrilling—to be scared and push boundaries, but making people personally uncomfortable or upset at the table is a quick path to unhappy players and an abandoned storyline. To manage the experience for everyone, have a frank discussion with players about their comfort levels for descriptions of graphic violence and elements such as personal fears or traumas that players may desire to keep out of the game. If players feel strongly that particular events or topics are "off the table," it is up to you to find out ahead of time and, if needed, adjust the plot accordingly. It's also important to include occasional breaks in the tension through humorous moments or by including positive aspects of other themes. This keeps the game enjoyable, and can remind players of the good things their characters are risking it all to protect.

LOCATIONS: PUTTING THE STORY IN ITS PLACE

Where a story takes place has a huge impact on the player experience, and it is important to consider the way the setting influences the action as play unfolds. The right location can enhance the theme and feel of a scene, or provide an opportunity for a surprising twist. A graveyard at midnight is a perfect setting for a scene involving clandestine activity or interaction with a shade. An old country church that the characters seek out for safety, but is actually the the profaned sanctuary of the cult they were fleeing, subverts player expectations and adds tension. These are simple examples, but given the incredible variety of locations available in the Clockwork world—everything from the halls of Parliament to the panoply of strange Realms in the Borderlands—Narrators have access to any setting they need for any scene.

Describing locations can be just as important as the choosing them. Good description allows for a great deal of indirect world-building, provides players with relevant information without breaking immersion, and can generate interactions and opportunities during play. To that end, plan at least a few details for a location before the storytelling begins. A ballroom is just a huge room if there's no further description. However, if it is described as being "a grand room capable of hosting all the cream of London Society in style, decorated in beautiful paintings and huge mirrors that reflect the softly glowing gaslight from a chandelier overhead, and graceful silver candelabras set on lacquered tables along the walls" there are many useful details that can be pulled out. The room itself speaks of wealth and power, helping establish the *Class* and *Means* of the owner and those whom it is meant to host. It points out useful features of the scene to set on fire, take cover behind, or even use as a weapon that can come crashing down from the ceiling. Well-described locations give both Narrators and players more to work with during a game.

PROTAGONISTS: CREATING THE PLAYER CHARACTERS

Before a story begins, help the players understand the dominant themes of the planned series so they can build their character to be successful. Making sure all players have the same idea of what to expect in the story helps to ensure player engagement and party cohesion. It's not fun for anyone if one player is excited about playing a battle-scarred Witchfinder eager to face the horrors of the Pontus when the rest of the group desires to play members of a group of country gentry intent on marrying up. Ensuring everyone has a clear idea of the type of story being planned *before* characters are made helps to avoid problems that arise from incongruous character concepts, disparate *Class* and *Means* among characters, and conflicts of interest.

Incompatible character concepts are a frequent source of friction at the table. Loner characters only out for themselves with no relation to other player characters will be difficult to include in the story. Lone heroes are great protagonists for books or movies,

STORIES AND STATUS

Status in Story	Class and Means	Example
Nobleman's story	4–5	*Downton Abbey* (BBC TV Series)
Gentleman's story	3–4	*Pride and Prejudice* by Jane Austen
Middle class story	2–3	*Brideshead Revisited* by Evelyn Waugh
Working class story	1–2	*Treasure Island* by Robert Louis Stevenson
Lower class story	0–1	*Oliver Twist* by Charles Dickens

but make poor roleplaying companions. Similarly, characters who have already secured prestige, wealth, and accomplishment, or that have no goals or desires are unlikely to have any motivation to participate in an adventure.

Social standing can also have dramatic effects on character interaction. If all of the characters live in the same area and are of similar *Class* and *Means*, they are likely to be at least casual acquaintances or share interests and experiences. Wildly different ranks of *Class* and *Means* can have the opposite effect, causing friction or isolation in the game. Sometimes this can be a way of adding a punk element to the story, but it can easily cause an upstairs/downstairs split in engagement with the plot. Discussing the typical *Class* and *Means* for a series at the beginning lets players know the standard social setting for the story. If a character is made outside that norm, at least the concept can take that into account and hopefully adds interest and excitement to the game.

It is also a good idea to encourage player characters to share a common interest, ideal, or profession. This could be the affection of a lifelong friendship, a shared *Membership* in an organization, or a similar Affinity or Reputation. These similarities can justify pre-existing acquaintanceships or allow for smooth introductions. Creating these links between player characters promotes a situation where they are more likely to have a cause and a desire to work together. Building from these connections it is easier for characters to be built that complement each others' skills and abilities, and it is easier for Narrators to relate the particulars of each character's background to early plot points. Treat each character's Affinities, assets, liabilities, and what they do professionally as easy

GIVING PLAYERS WHAT THEY WANT

Different gamers come to the table with different expectations of what constitutes a good game and a good time. What satisfies some players may frustrate others, so balancing different types of experiences during play is required to keep everyone engaged. Below are five common archetypes of players, each detailed with some typical gaming expectations. Being mindful of the blend of archetypes at the table will help you tell a story that everyone will enjoy.

The Actor: This type of player loves to roleplay. She will get bored if conflicts are focused only on the rules and do not provide the opportunity for well described actions and banter. Give this player the opportunity to have in-character conversations and act out interesting parts of the story even if they are not central to the larger plot.

The Explorer: An explorer wants to know more about the setting and what it contains. Quickly pushing past interesting characters or intriguing locales in the game world will frustrate them. Give this player the opportunity to discover new things and see new places.

The Hero: This player wants to overcome adversity, defeat the villain, and save the day. Too much time spent talking rather than acting will frustrate her. Give this player the opportunity to engage in conflict, rescue those in distress, and other daring feats. Do not let the rules of the game inhibit this player's creativity. If a character would be able to run across the room without penalty, what's the harm in letting her cover the same distance by swinging on a chandelier?

The Tactician: A tactician wants to solve problems, build interesting things, strategize, and use the rules of the game to her best advantage. She will get bored if the story doesn't offer enough puzzles to solve or if there is never time to prepare for conflicts before they occur. Give this player an opportunity to plan and solve plot related problems through creative use of her skills and abilities.

The Companion: Most gaming groups have at least one person who isn't really a gamer, but is a good friend to gamers: someone's sister, brother, significant other, or anyone who is primarily at the table to spend time with friends. Give her time to banter with the other players out-of-character. It is important to not let this player slip into the background of the story, while at the same time not demanding a level of participation that would make her uncomfortable. To draw her in, give her moments to shine, such as problems that only her character is equipped to solve.

opportunities to motivate them. Including such personal hooks builds player engagement and enthusiasm. Likewise, include a variety of encounters and trait tests that allow each character a chance to shine.

The one notable exception to the above advice is that certain styles of horror begin by throwing complete strangers into terrible danger with the expectation that standing together in a time of crisis will forge a cohesive group. That approach can be very successful, and is easy to drop into almost any circumstance due to the ever-present risk of Pontus events. By including at least a few hooks to keep the characters together once the immediate danger has passed you give yourself and the players time to form a cohesive group.

AGENTS OF CHAOS

Protagonists must face a clear call to action—an obstacle to overcome, a villain to defeat, a crisis to survive, or a mystery to solve. Whatever it is that disrupts their lives and spurs them to act is the agent of chaos. It is the element of the story that provides adversity and motivates the player characters to respond.

You will use many different agents of chaos over the course of your story to keep the plot moving and the players engaged. A series of books is likely to have one overarching villain or grand mystery that will not be dealt with once and for all until that series is concluded. Before reaching the final confrontation, however, the characters will need to face other, less powerful agents of chaos tied to the main threat. Designing the central antagonist first can help inspire other, secondary agents of chaos, related mysteries, and important challenges that the player characters must overcome as part of major plot arcs that close out each book in the series. Facing and overcoming these lesser agents of chaos allows you to introduce new dramatic tension and moments of resolution throughout the series, and gives players a sense of accomplishment as each victory brings them closer to the conclusion.

On a smaller scale, each installment will need one or more minor agents of chaos to keep each scene and chapter moving. Minor agents might be the active or unwitting pawns of the overarching villain, or other obstacles. Overcoming them should provide information or some other opportunity to advance the plot towards the next agent of chaos, and ultimately, the main villain or mystery at the heart of the larger story. Occasionally including minor agents of chaos unrelated to the grand narrative can be a nice palate cleanser, but use them sparingly. Changing the pattern of a story keeps it interesting, but too-frequent diversions can quickly make a game lose focus and energy. Any such incidental agents of chaos should at least be related to the theme and mood of the series, even if they are not directly tied to the central plot.

Sometimes the easiest way to design an agent of chaos is to determine what kind of conflict or mystery you want in a portion of your story, and choose an agent that best facilitates that conflict. In a Victorian-themed story where social conflict and intrigue are the norm, conflict could be instigated by a group of highly-placed socialites, a corrupt city official, or a romantic rival. In a horror-themed story with supernatural elements the players could be facing an ancient cult tearing a rift in reality through which chimera are emerging, or realize that a vital clue to defeating a major foe is only known by a half-mad shade that the characters must placate. Finally, try to vary the agents of chaos you use. If they are all too similar, the players will quickly become bored. Instead, use a mixture of concepts to keep things fresh and engaging. If one book's major antagonist is a charismatic charlatan with a crew of thieves as henchmen that is well and good, but if every book has the same charlatan and interchangeable henchmen players will know what to expect and find little to excite them.

Possible Agents of Chaos

FOR A SCENE

- aberrations or chimera attack the protagonists
- a lone cultist gets in the players' way, revealing a mysterious plot
- a single clue needs to be found

FOR A BOOK

- a rift in the boundary of the mortal realm is spewing forth chimera and must be closed
- a cult of sorcerers attempting to raise a greater demon from the Outer Darkness
- a major plot point must be puzzled together from clever references scattered throughout a library

FOR A SERIES

- an outcast Fallen, wyldling lord, or Grigoros is attempting to carve a hole in the boundary between realms so it can enter the mortal world
- a greater demon is manipulating a cult of sorcerers into performing a dire rite
- an eccentric academic learned a terrible truth that threatens great change, and hid knowledge of her findings in the hope later generations may put it to better use

8

INSPIRATION

For those unfamiliar with the process, writing your own stories can be daunting. Narrators may worry about how to get the mood right, construct interesting agents of chaos, or how to incorporate proper Victorian elements. A good way to overcome these hurdles is to draw inspiration from existing stories or other works that come from or evoke the period and themes of the game. Reading period fiction or watching film and television based in the Victorian era can inspire great ideas and help illustrate how the society of that time functioned. Here are some inspirational media to get you started.

BOOKS

- Jane Austen, Charles Dickens: Any novel by these authors details social politics, marriage customs, as well as the etiquette and interaction of different classes.
- Charlotte Brontë, Sir Arthur Conan Doyle: These authors explore mystery in the social and criminal spheres of the Victorian world.
- Edgar Allen Poe, Mary Shelley, and Bram Stoker: These authors helped define gothic horror and mystery as genres.
- William Gibson, *The Difference Engine*. A key piece of early steampunk fiction, this novel explores an alternate history of Charles Babbage's mechanical computer.
- The Brothers Grimm: *Fairy Tales*. These are excellent source material for horror, fey lore, drama, monsters, and the consequences of bad choices.
- Cherie Priest, *Boneshaker*. A great example of a grungy steampunk aesthetic and exploration of the severe societal responses to dramatic and unexpected change.
- Jules Verne and H. G. Wells: Works by Verne and Wells show a Victorian take on themes of exploration, advanced technology, and society.
- Mystical and Holy Texts. A great deal of the inspiration for the cosmology of the Clockwork came from the Bible, the Talmud, the Book of Enoch, and Francis Barret's *The Magus*.

TELEVISION

- *Downton Abbey* (2010). The first season of this fantastic show takes place directly in the time period of Clockwork: Dominion, and while the subsequent seasons push the end of the era, they still provide immense detail on *Class* 4 life and drama.

- *North & South* (2004). This BBC miniseries talks about the differences between British regions and social classes, depicts period industrialization, and frames it around a love story.
- *Pride and Prejudice* (1995). This BBC miniseries is widely regarded as an excellent adaptation of Austen's novel. It is a story of Victorian love, marriage politics, and petty social intrigue.
- *Ripper Street* (2012). A compelling crime drama set in Whitechapel in 1889.

MOVIES

- *From Hell* (2001). A period crime drama with horror and mystical elements.
- *The Ghost and the Darkness* (1998). Based on the true story of Lieutenant-Colonel John Henry Patterson's hunt to kill the aberrant lions that were devouring workers on an African rail line.
- *The Prestige* (2006). A fantastic example of bitter social rivalry and the possible horrors of technology. Plus, David Bowie plays Nikola Tesla.
- *Sherlock Holmes* (2009). This film and its sequel (2011) are excellent examples of the Victorian sense of mystery and conspiracy involving fantastic technology and a touch of the occult.

MUSIC

- *Edward Elgar*: A popular Victorian composer of everything from opera to choral and chamber music. Elgar would have been playing on the gramophones of many English gentry.
- *Eli August, Emilie Autumn*, and *Rasputina* are examples of modern groups that draw on Victorian styles and topics for an interesting take on aesthetics and culture both then and now.
- *English Folk Artists:* There are a wide variety of English folk and folk revival acts that play music that was popular in dance halls and pubs throughout the Empire. Some great examples include Cliff Haslan, Eliza Carthy, Mumford & Sons, Steeleye Span, and others.

CRAFTING DRAMA: PUTTING IT ALL TOGETHER

An overarching idea of what will happen is all that is needed to start a story, but it takes work to finish one. As you define each of the story elements described above conceptualize where the story begins, what needs to happen to progress the plot, and a possible conclusion. Story ideas can be completely original, but don't be afraid to draw inspiration from books, movies, or television. Sometimes a good idea is worth stealing, especially if you can adapt it to meet your needs.

Once you have the basic framework of a story in your head, consider how long it might last. If your story involves one or two main conflicts and one main location, it is likely to fit into a single installment. If your story has multiple agents of chaos and spans multiple locations, it is likely to be a book. In a series of books, each in the series will likely focus on an overarching story bound by a significant agent of chaos or particular location. Will your story be small enough to be a single installment? Can it support an entire book or series of books? If you want your story to be longer, consider adding an extra mystery, side plot, or an extra layer of villains. If you want your story to be shorter, simplify it. The discussion of what makes up a book, series, or installment is included at the beginning of *Chapter 4: Rules & Systems*.

Writing a Book or Series

A book is a collection of installments that fit together to tell a larger story over the course of multiple gaming sessions. A series is a collection of books that constitute a single long and epic adventure. When conceptualizing the overarching plot for a book or series, think about the story elements on a macro level. If the book is a mystery, the plot will tell how the players uncover the truth. In a drama, the plot will revolve around how the players will overcome the villains.

Once you have the larger story idea, separate the overarching plot into individual plot points and use them to form a storyline. A plot point is a key event that moves the story forward. Map out the plot points that will take your story from start to finish. You can start with very broad points and then refine them. Adding clues and specific scenarios is a great way to refine a broad plot point. If the book is a police mystery, perhaps the broad plot points could be:

- discover an artifact by happenstance
- a cult of villains tries to steal the artifact
- players uncover truths about the artifact
- players discover the cult's plot concerning the artifact
- players confront the cult to prevent them from achieving their goals.

After some thought, a more refined set of plot points for a single installment could take 'discover an artifact by happenstance' and turn it into:

- notice a burglary in progress and intervene
- the investigators discover the burglar was attempting to steal an heirloom music box
- the burglar attacks the investigators, risking his own life to get the music box
- after the conflict, the investigators find a strange tattoo on the burglar (the cult's sigil)

Notice how the agent of chaos-the burglar-works to give the players motivation to participate in the story. As the story flows, two new agents of chaos are introduced: the mystery of the music box and the cult that wants it. The players find themselves enveloped in a growing mystery, but they also have clear questions they can investigate.

Make sure each plot point contains an agent of chaos that is likely to motivate the player characters to participate. Use a mixture of villains, situations, and mysteries. If you can get one agent of chaos to flow into the next, that keeps the story moving. For example, think of a hierarchy of antagonists, each opposing the players in one or more installments and leading them up the chain to the major villain or discovery. Be mindful to build the plot points and agents of chaos around the themes you chose to include so the story feels cohesive.

Lastly, consider several ways the book might end and have a clearly defined goal for the players. This goal will encourage your players to develop ways of interacting with the agents of chaos. An enjoyable story allows for several plausible successful endings based on character choices, a few endings that are only partially successful, and the possibility of failure. It is generally best to help the players to succeed when it is possible and to allow partial success when feasible, but actions must be allowed to have undesirable consequences if they are failures.

Writing Installments

Individual installments of a book are written to provide enough story for one session's worth of play. Most of the time, one installment will cover about three refined plot points from your storyline. Usually, each plot point will be anywhere from a scene to a chapter in length. Determine how many chapters or scenes each plot point needs to be in order to accomplish its task within the story. These chapters and scenes are used to compose a storyline at the installment level in much the same way you used plot points to create a storyline at the book level. You may discover that a plot point you originally constructed at the book level is too broad and can be refined into two or more plot points at the installment level. Simply readjust your storyline accordingly. Acting as the Narrator is an art, not a science.

When designing the individual scenes of an installment, assign each scene a location, an agent of chaos, and determine how each one can produce drama that will be exciting and motivating to the players. Each scene will likely require several Narrator characters, so make sure you have these created and ready. Sometimes it's helpful for new Narrators to record the elements of a scene on note

EXAMPLE STORYLINE

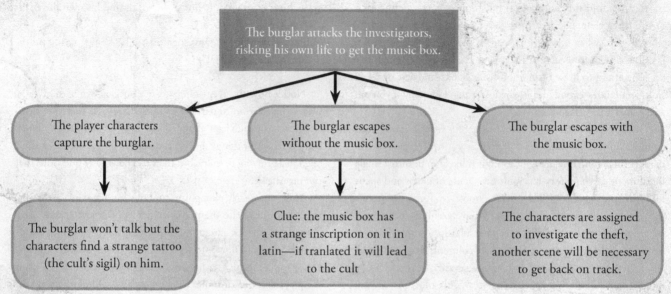

The burglar attacks the investigators, risking his own life to get the music box.

The player characters capture the burglar.

The burglar escapes without the music box.

The burglar escapes with the music box.

The burglar won't talk but the characters find a strange tattoo (the cult's sigil) on him.

Clue: the music box has a strange inscription on it in latin—if tranlated it will lead to the cult

The characters are assigned to investigate the theft, another scene will be necessary to get back on track.

•cards as a visual reminder of what you are trying to accomplish with each scene.

At the installment level, your storyline needs to be dynamic. Think of a *Choose Your Own Adventure* novel. Each page in such a novel is like a scene in your story. There will be some scenes in your storyline that will never take place because the players choose a path that takes them in a different direction. You may also have to invent new points when they do something unexpected (and they invariably will). This sort of flexibility is necessary for the players' choices to have impact on how the story unfolds. Thus, your installment's storyline may look more like a flowchart when you are finished. Each scene on the flowchart is a piece of story that occurs and then expands into another scene based on player choices.

Account for as much player choice and variance as you can foresee. Player choices can and should influence the story, but if they begin to wander too far be prepared to bring them back into the main plot of your story. This way, they will eventually arrive at the culmination of your story, even if the path they took to get there was different than the one you laid out. At a minimum, have multiple ways to reach whatever endings you have in mind, including at least one path that does not necessitate overt violence.

Make sure each installment has *at least* one truly exciting scene: a big conflict, a major reveal, or a step forward toward player goals. Just like no one would like to watch an episode of a television show where nothing significant happens, no one wants to play an installment of a story where there is no surprise or change. Do your best to help your players feel like they are making progress toward a goal, even if that goal is not realized in the current installment.

SAMPLE STORYLINES

Understanding how to write a storyline and coming up with an idea for the plot are two very different things. To get your creative juices flowing, we've provided several sample storylines. These encompass a number of plot points and hooks that, once fleshed-out, will help you create an experience filled with adventure and provide a model for what an original completed storyline can look like.

SAMPLE SERIES: CANON AND STAR

The Witchfinders are an insular and much-feared organization working directly for the Crown, and they wield broad authority to guard the Empire against the harmful use of magic and the worst eruptions of the Pontus. There is always justified concern that the organization may abuse its power for personal or political gain, but a far graver threat would be if its power was subverted for a darker purpose.

Drama

Warden Shale, the senior Witchfinder overseeing the characters and assigning them missions, is possessed by a powerful demon. Unbeknownst to the characters, the early missions in the series appear to be normal cases, but are in fact helping the demon gather the rites and materials it requires to conduct a powerful ritual, which will certainly further its own nefarious plan. As the characters' suspicion grows, they will need to somehow convince other Witchfinders that their fears are real or take action against the possessed Warden directly and face the consequences.

Theme

Gothic Horror: The player characters face the terrors of Pontus events, aberrations, chimera, mortal cults, and the insidious threat of a demonically possessed Witchfinder. The characters will learn to suspect everyone and everything around them of serving some darker purpose.

Location

Various locales throughout Britain. Key chapters and books take them into a small town in the English countryside harboring a witch cult, they scour the undercities of Edinburgh and London for the resources desired by the Warden, and the secluded heaths of the Kirkwall islands provide a setting for the final confrontation.

Protagonists

The players' characters are Witchfinders and their allies, commissioned to do the work of the Church and Crown. Most should take the *Membership* asset for the Witchfinders and ranks in the *Mysteries* skill. *Magical Word* and *Charism* assets will be extremely helpful when resolving certain plot points. Access to extant rites and other special resources will be made available through the course of the game.

Agents of Chaos

- The witch cult of Pendle Forest is the focus of the characters' first assignment. They are the latest manifestation of a long history of covens in the area, and are using magic to harm and extort their neighbors. The demon wants to disband them and acquire their grimoires so that their powerful rites can be used in its ultimate plan.
- Various Pontus events around Britain cause the characters to explore thin places, or confront dangerous aberrations and chimera.
- The greater demon possessing Warden Shale manipulates the player characters secretly for as long as it can. Once the characters grow suspicious, it will attempt to eliminate them by sending them on dangerous missions or discredit them.
- As soon as the players begin to act against the demon, its hidden allies and cultists will render it aid.

Plot Points

- The characters are sent on a series of missions by the demon. Each is episodic, and is resolved in one or two books. Every mission brings back resources that the demon can use to further its own plans.
- Over several books, the characters find threads of commonality between the material they're bringing back to Warden Shale, notice odd behavior, and slowly come to suspect he isn't what he appears.
- The characters confront Warden Shale directly in conflict, or indirectly by bringing their concerns to other Witchfinders. Either way, he is able to escape.
- At the culmination of the series, the most powerful of the demon's servants are gathered in an ancient set of standing stones in the Kirkwall islands, preparing the final ritual required to put the demon's vile plan into effect. The characters race to stop them, and face hazards along the way.
- Finally, after confronting the demon on Kirkwall—either killing its host, exorcising it, or expelling it magically—it flees to the Borderlands. If the players wish to deal with the demon permanently, they must find a way into the Borderlands for one final battle.

SAMPLE SERIES: AIRSHIP PIRATES

In 1896–98, the Philippines gained independence from Spain with last-minute help from the Americans, but then the Treaty of Paris turned the islands over to American control. Soon thereafter, the Filipinos began fighting for their freedom again, this time against the Americans. Hoping to bring the insurrection to a swift close, the Americans have brought the U.S.S. *Eagle*, their first combat-ready zeppelin, to the islands. Whoever controls that airship controls the skies, and there are many forces hoping to use it for their own ends.

Drama

The characters have an opportunity to seize the U.S.S. *Eagle*, and must then decide how they will put her to use. They will immediately gain notoriety and and earn the enmity of the Americans, but will they choose to leave with their zeppelin to plunder the skies or will they choose to stay and make a difference in the war?

Theme

Steam and Punk: The characters' access to advanced technology sets them apart from all others, but how they decide to use that technology comes down to their own political and personal views.

Narrators can also bring in a horror theme by focusing on the devastation of war: tens of thousands of troops died in the three years of fighting, but hundreds of thousands of civilians died from starvation and a cholera epidemic. Battlefields and stricken villages are a ripe setting for shades, Pontus events, aberrations, and chimera.

Location

The Philippine islands, with emphasis on Manila and Luzon as major centers of conflict, and the U.S.S. *Eagle* herself. If the characters decide to go farther afield, other southeast Asian locations are all fair game. Cuyo island serves as a refuge and base of operations for the player characters.

Protagonists

The player characters can be a mixture of mercenaries, freedom fighters, and local folk caught up in the war. From wherever they come, and for whatever reason they came, the Philippines are now their home. Player characters should have Affinities for people or institutions in the region, especially if they wish to see its liberation.

Agents of Chaos

- The war itself is a major disruption to daily life, and battles are devastating to both the population and infrastructure.
- War profiteers on all sides—arms dealers, pimps, criminal syndicates, and greedy opportunists are eager to price-gouge, hoard food and medicine, and reap any benefit they can through the theft and sale of arms, supplies, and information.
- The United States military has not given up on its flagship zeppelin, and while they prefer its recovery, its destruction is better than its desecration by pirates. The Filipino freedom fighters may act in the same way, wanting the ship for themselves and desperately wanting to keep it from returning to the Americans.

Plot Points

- Circumstances align to offer the party an opportunity to steal the U.S.S. *Eagle*.
- Once they control the zeppelin they will need to secure contacts who can provide fuel and ammunition. This requires them to deal with war profiteers who may have their own designs for the *Eagle*, or be willing to sell them out.
- Fully equipped and able to pilot the fast U.S.S. *Eagle*, the characters may choose to plunder defenseless merchant vessels, run contraband and supplies within the war zone, or acquire needed goods from nearby countries. Allow players to enjoy their time aboard the zeppelin, and see where their interests lay.
- The players are increasingly aware of the devastation caused by the war and may be drawn in to help bring it to a close. Friends and associates will beg their aid for various personal causes.
- Eventually, the American Navy tracks them back to Cuyo and brings the war to their doorstep through occupation of the island.
- The characters must engage in a decisive battle to save Cuyo from the fate of the other Philippine islands, or to abandon their home and save themselves.

SAMPLE BOOK: HIGH SOCIETY INTRIGUE

The estate of Pembrook has recently changed hands after the death of the much respected Lord Bingham. You know who the intended heir was meant to be and it is not the man who claimed the inheritance. Can the players restore this great estate to its rightful heir?

Drama

After the death of a wealthy relative, a wicked uncle has falsely claimed the estate that should rightfully pass to one of the player characters. When the story begins, the uncle has already moved into the estate and established himself there. It will take months, or even years, to address the matter through the courts; but perhaps the characters can resolve it themselves.

Theme

Victorian: The player characters are working to restore the family estate to the rightful heir and right the social and legal order of a region.

Location

The estate and a nearby village; while this can be located anywhere in Britain, the English countryside works best to limit the action to a few easily-defined venues. The villagers will have strong opinions on the inheritance because the estate controls land and taxes in the village, and they may have lingering feelings about the noble family itself for good or ill.

Protagonists

The player characters should include family members of the heir, such as siblings or cousins, loyal friends of the family, servants, and perhaps the heir himself. They may also include prominent villagers that know the family well, such as the vicar, town doctor, or clerk. If the heir is not a player character, perhaps he is a child (aged 6–10) who depends on the characters to act in his interests.

Mr. Anthony Grace, the former valet of the recently deceased, bears no love for the uncle, has been a loyal servant to the family for years, and secretly supports the claim of the true heir. Mr. Grace has limited access to the uncle's personal dealings and effects, and while he can provide the characters with valuable information, his continued position at the estate depends on secrecy and discretion. He is an honorable man who believes in the integrity of his station and therefore refuses to go so far as stealing, even to serve a just cause.

Agents of Chaos

- The wicked uncle who usurped the inheritance claim and his accomplice, the county sheriff, Simon Waumsey. Sheriff Waumsey used his authority as a court officer to enforce a painfully distorted reading of the will to give the estate to the uncle. The sheriff's term expires soon, and the characters may be able to appeal to local members of high standing in the county to support another appointee who may be more sympathetic to the rightful heir's claim.

Plot Points

- It becomes known that Sheriff Waumsey's support has caused the estate to pass to the wicked uncle.
- The characters must build their Reputations to gain the support of both the villagers and area gentry, as well as find evidence of malfeasance to discredit the wicked uncle's claim on the inheritance.
- A series of formal and informal gatherings allow the characters to hobnob with the upper and middle classes. Helping the local villagers with disputes, and perhaps a Pontus event, can gain their favor as well.
- Mr. Grace discovers that the wicked uncle signed a document ceding a portion of the estate's revenues to Sheriff Waumsey. It was only after this that Waumsey backed the uncle's claim. How can the characters prove this with Mr. Grace unwilling to steal the document or tell others what he's discovered?
- The story culminates in a grand ball thrown by the wicked uncle for those returning from the Season in London. The local lords will decide the appointee for sheriff soon thereafter. Can the characters garner enough reputation, good will, and hopefully a few favors owed by the right people, to get the local gentry to turn on one of their own and restore the estate to its true heir?

SAMPLE INSTALLMENT: THE PONTUS RISES

Pontus events can occur anywhere, and range from minor oddities to life- and sanity-threatening horrors. When serious events occur, circumstances throw normal relationships and roles into disarray, and how well people react and organize themselves may mean the difference between life and death. Inserting Pontus events to interrupt the action or alter the mood of a game can be an effective way to shake up an ongoing series. Alternately, having the characters meet and work with each other for the first time during a Pontus event is an opportunity to bring together people of diverse backgrounds.

Drama

The everyday life of the characters is dramatically interrupted when they are caught in an ever-worsening series of Pontus events. The only hope of escape is to identify who among them is the vector of *Corruption* fueling the events, and to put a stop to his or her activities.

Theme

Punk: Although there will be moments of horror from the rising Pontus, the main thrust of the session is that when the normal social order is toppled by extreme events, the stricken participants must recognize and value the best people for the new situation.

Location

When the action begins, a Pontus event isolates several buildings and prevents the characters from interacting with their normal surroundings. This can be any town or city large enough to have a hotel and an active commercial district.

The chief locations are the Brass Post livery stable, the Leffingwell Hotel with its attached restaurant, the surrounding alleys, and the water cistern and sewers to which both are connected. Within the hotel there is a restaurant, kitchen, main lobby, guest rooms, and storage areas. The livery stable includes a horse barn, carriage house, office, and storage area. The street in front of both buildings, as well as the alleys that run between them are open. All locations in this session are considered Breached (see *Environmental Stability*, p. 281).

Protagonists

- The player characters who become trapped at the scene
- Donnel Rouncy, an elderly drunkard and ostler at the livery stable
- Jonas White, a porter at the hotel

Agents of Chaos

- The cause of the Pontus event and source of the ongoing problems is the charlatan Toby Plimpton. He recently murdered and robbed an injured Witchfinder he encountered by chance, and is the unwitting bearer of a magical talisman. During his confrontation with the police, he and the talisman trigger the Pontus event that begins the session. Use the hardened criminal on p. 319 for Toby Plimpton.

- Throughout the session many aberrant animals will attack the characters. Use the statistics for hellhounds and rat kings on p. 307 and p. 308.
- Sir Julian Husting. Although Sir Julian is a well-respected man and has enjoyed a legal career of some note, his attempts to control the situation are counterproductive and dangerous. Use the influential politician on p. 320.

Storyline

CHAPTER 1: THE EVENT

- **Scene 1:** The characters are either staying at the hotel, having lunch in the restaurant, or are at the livery stable. Their day is interrupted when they hear a gunshot outside and the sky suddenly goes dark. A moment later, Toby Plimpton crashes into the room, engaged in a mortal struggle with the constable he just shot. Toby claims he is a Witchfinder, while the constable instead calls him a murderer. Give the characters one initiative card to act in the round. No other NCs will act. Toby shoots the Wounded constable (physical Defense 2, one remaining Wound, tests at a base of +2) and encourages the characters to help kill him. The constable gasps out "impostor" before he passes.

- **Scene 2:** After the fight, Toby displays the badge of the Witchfinder he slew and introduces himself as Onyx Star; he claims the constable was a witch whose black magic caused the darkness and killing him prevented further destruction in the town. As the characters and NCs explore, they discover they cannot leave the area—when they walk in the darkness they simply come back to the area from another angle. In the confusion, Sir Julian insists that it is everyone's duty to do as the Witchfinder says, which is to wait and do nothing.
- Characters may test *Focus + Intuition* against Toby's social Defense to detect that he is nervous about the situation. Testing *Reason + Mysteries*, Difficulty 3 tells characters that what Toby is saying makes no sense: what is happening is not ritual magic, it is a Pontus event. Testing *Focus + Burglary*, Difficulty 5 notices Toby sneaking the constable's notebook from the corpse into his own pocket. If the characters protest, Toby and Sir Julian will use social conflict to convince the crowd to respect Toby's authority.

CHAPTER 2: THE INVESTIGATION

- **Scene 1:** The characters' suspicions are raised, and there is no sign of the event ending. They may search for clues and talk to staff and guests. The guests saw nothing, but the porter Jonas White knew the dead officer. The constable was a stand-up man making him an unlikely witch, and Jonas further offers that he always took copious notes, which may provide clues. Donnel, the ostler, has a terrible reputation as a drunk—and he's been drinking today—but he saw the constable chase Toby down, heard him say Toby was under arrest for suspicion of murder and impersonation, and then Toby shot him.
- **Scene 2:** The ongoing Pontus event is worsening, and has begun warping the animals caught inside it. As they wrap up their investigations, the characters are attacked by several rat kings and/or hellhounds. At the same time elsewhere, NCs are attacked, causing several casualties and inciting panicking. Toby proclaims that there must be another witch present, and accuses someone: either a person who rendered aid to the constable, or if no one did, one of the player characters.

CHAPTER 3: THE CONFRONTATION

- **Scene 1:** The characters confront Toby socially or physically. If the players can get the room to be *Hostile* towards him the bystanders will assist, and Toby will openly attack the players Otherwise, he and Sir Julian will try to shift the attitude of the room regarding the players to *Hostile*.
- **Scene 2:** If the players search Toby, they may be able to identify the amulet as the focus of a *Degrade* the *Boundary* of *Location* effect; destroying it will end the Pontus event. Otherwise, have the Pontus effect subside shortly.

PERSONALITY TRAITS	REPUTATIONS	AFFINITIES
97–100 Compassionate	Godly	A good parent lives for her children
93–96 Idealistic	Loyal friend	A pious man is an honorable man
89–92 Generous	Soul of kindness	Criminals must face justice!
85–88 Pious	In the know	I will attain [rank] in [organization]
81–84 Romantic	Musical prodigy	Defending the weak is our obligation
77–80 Brutally honest	Brilliant inventor	Find true peace
73–76 Eccentric	Proper lady/gentleman	God, Queen, and Country
69–72 Overbearing	Dauntless explorer	Happiness is in service to others
65–68 Absent-minded	Gracious host	Honor the memory of the fallen brethren
61–64 Secretive	Bon Vivant	I must go where no mortal foot has trod
67–60 Shy	Eligible Bachelor	Irish independence!
53–56 Naive	Daring pilot	I will rise above the circumstances of my birth
49–52 Anxious	Upright citizen	I will make my enemies fear me
45–48 Arrogant	Well-connected	I will see my foes brought to ruin!
41–44 Judgemental	Skilled _____	Anything for my one true love
37–40 Distrustful	Social campaigner	My honor is my life
33–36 Depressed	Reliable in a fight	My name will live on in song and story
29–32 Jealous	Free spirit	My word is my bond
25–28 Manipulative	Never forgets a debt	We are only free if we are all equal
21–24 Obsessed with something	Never lost a fight	Perfection comes from constant training
17–20 Contrary	Slave to fashion	Plumb the mysteries of the Pontus
13–16 Spreads gossip	Card sharp	Reason is the only path to Truth
9–12 Bigoted	Louche	Restore honor to my family name
5–8 Licentious	Mad inventor	The world must know the Maker's love
1–4 Violent	Religious zealot	Women and men must be equal!

PORTRAYING NARRATOR CHARACTERS

Every character that is not controlled by the players is controlled by the Narrator. These are referred to as Narrator characters (NCs). There are several different types of NCs: minor characters, allies, antagonists, and other threats. Minor characters are those incidental characters that flow in and out of a story. Allies are those characters who support and fight alongside the player characters. Antagonists are rivals and foes who fight against them. Creating these characters is covered in detail in *Chapter 9: Allies & Antagonists*. Here, we will address how to effectively portray these characters as believable and engaging people within the story.

MINOR CHARACTERS

Sometimes you don't need a character with a complete life story and a full character sheet. Maybe you just need someone to sell a player character a horse or rent her a hotel room. For characters not destined for conflict and who are unlikely to exist in your story for more than a scene, you can make a minor character. Most minor characters are the socialites, merchants, and incidental friends that come up in your story; they recur with irregularity or are made on-the-fly to fill a bit part in a scene.

To design a minor character, choose a name and record any traits you think are necessary. For example, an Indian tea merchant named Adharma has a *Presence + Parley of* 5. Simply treat any trait combinations not directly linked to the character's reason for being as a 3. That's enough to complete a scene for a player character who wants to haggle over the price of tea.

If you want to make these characters more interesting, you may wish to choose a personality trait from the box above or draw a card and use the card number to select one randomly. Making Adharma a brutally honest tea merchant will make the scene much more interesting. Of course, coming up with your own personality traits can allow you to choose something that perfectly fits your scene and the current temperament of your players.

Minor characters can provide the Narrator with an excellent tool to explore and develop the world from within the context of the game. Rather than describing politics to players in the abstract, having a few NCs at a pub loudly expressing different views on a particular issue or event can give players the same information, but in a more natural manner that builds their engagement with the setting.

If a minor character recurs with some frequency you may want to add extra details or traits—perhaps a *Class* or *Means* rank, one Reputation, and one Affinity. If you foresee this character fighting the PCs or aiding them in conflict, make sure to assign their most relevant trait combinations and Defenses. If you find that a minor character is making frequent trait tests or notice she is becoming a larger part of the story, it is likely worthwhile to create her as a full ally or antagonist using the system in *Chapter 9: Allies & Antagonists*.

ALLIES

Any recurring NCs who are important to the story and sympathetic to the player characters are considered allies. Allies frequently interact with the PCs and thus need to be more complex than minor characters. Create them using the system provided in *Chapter 9: Allies & Antagonists*. When building an ally, try to keep her trait combinations within two ranks of the average trait combinations of the player characters. Larger disparities than this between trait ranks of NCs and PCs can create significant problems during conflicts and other interactions. Keeping a master list of traits for all of your ally characters can be extremely helpful for quick reference during play.

Ally Personalities

Allies should have unique personalities, appearances, and motivations, which help immerse the players further into the story. The unique personalities of your allies will derive from their Affinities. If Adharma the brutally honest tea merchant were to become an ally, the players would start to wonder why she became so brutally honest. Perhaps she has the Affinity *"Mother always said, 'Honesty is the best policy.'"* Affinities hint at a character's backstory and depth and she becomes more interesting with ongoing interaction. You may choose an Affinity from the table or draw a card and use the card number to select an Affinity randomly, but it is best if you come up with your own ideas for Affinities that enhance the ally's role in your story.

A character's personality can be given further depth by using a Reputation. This immediately tells the characters what they already know about the ally before they meet, and what they might expect from them. You can choose a Reputation from the table or select one randomly. If you can contextualize your chosen Reputation into the specifics of your plot, it will add more to the story. You'll also find that making up your own Reputations is simple and often gives you exactly the reaction and expectation you wish from your players.

Remember that NCs are characters in their own right, which means they act according to their own desires and rationale. Even if an NC loves and supports the player characters, that does not mean that she will always behave exactly the way the players want. Sometimes friends and lovers fight. Including occasional disagreements or social conflicts with an NC can offer a sense of realism and provide an unexpected change of pace in the game.

Ally Motivations

Answering one question is often the difference between a believable ally and an unbelievable one: why does this person want to be an ally to the player characters? Any NC that wants to help the player characters should have a reason for doing so. Even if this reason is secret or hiding below the surface of conversation, knowing it can help you portray the character more effectively. You can choose a motivation from the *Ally Motivation* list or draw a card and use the card number to select a trait randomly; however, designing your own custom motivation for the allies you portray will make them seamlessly fit into your story.

ANTAGONISTS

Every story needs enemies and obstacles to overcome, and tales told in the Clockwork are no exception. How antagonists are used can be the difference between a flat or predictable scene and an engaging and exciting one. When designing and portraying antagonists, try to think about how and why they are opposing the characters, what they are trying to achieve in an encounter, and how they will respond to player choices.

Designing antagonists to serve a purpose in the story allows conflict to influence the plot and moves the storyline forward. Captured enemies can provide information and accoutrements. Social conflicts can deal with whatever matter is at hand, but can also be used to introduce details about the world, and new friends or foes as interlocutors. At the bare minimum, any conflict should serve to heighten or resolve the tension around achieving one particular goal.

Describing Antagonists

Description alone can go a long way to setting expectations and crafty Narrators will use this to their advantage. Even weak enemies that are painted as fearsome beasts might make the characters approach with caution, whereas a brief description of a powerful foe may belittle it. For example, "an enormous swine, covered in thick bristles of discolored hair and pockmarks of ruptured skin glistening wetly from some unwholesome discharge; atop its back, a pulsing pseudopod of ropy, distended muscle" and "a pig, with a tentacle coming out of its back" both describe the same thing, but the latter isn't likely to inspire much trepidation.

Antagonist Motivations

Each antagonist has feelings, desires, and needs. These should be represented by Affinities and Reputations in the same way that allies use them. You can pick them from the table in the prior section or design your own. These will help your antagonists feel like real people rather than two-dimensional obstacles. For extremely minor antagonists, a motivation may be enough.

Antagonists have reasons for doing what they are doing. Even if the players don't know what it is, you should. It will help you make believable choices for the antagonists as they progress in the story. You can choose a motivation from the *Antagonist Motivation* list or draw a card and use the card number to select a trait randomly;

ALLY MOTIVATIONS		ANTAGONIST MOTIVATIONS
Altruism	1–7	Idealism
Duty	8–14	Preserving personal honor
Friendship/Love	14–20	Duty
Shared goal	21–28	Guarding something you want
Satisfying a debt of honor	33–34	To gain acceptance or admission
Mutual Benefit	40–41	Social Advancement
Shared enemy	46–47	A yet undetected misunderstanding
Access to something the PCs control	53–54	Self Preservation
Social advancement	59–60	Wants something you have
Along for the ride… for now	61–67	Territorialism
Payment	68–73	Desperation
Fears the PCs' enemies	74–80	Paranoia
Pity	81–86	Retaliation or Revenge
Emotional desperation	87–93	You are just collateral damage
Revenge	94–100	Sociopathy

however, designing your own custom motivation for the antagonists you portray will make them seamlessly fit into your story.

Antagonist Tactics and Options

Different antagonists will use different tactics in a conflict. An animal aberration may fight fiercely with little regard for its own safety. Gang members may mix in taunts with physical attacks, trying to throw an opponent off balance or bully them into surrender or retreat. Even with such bluster, an individual may fear for her life and retreat if she takes a single Wound. Such differences in decision making add wide variety to the mood of encounters, and help keep the game lively and challenging.

USING NON-CHARACTER THREATS

Not every risk the characters face will be some silver-tongued schemer or dangerous beast that can only be handled by direct conflict. Indeed, if a story only presents challenges that require directly squaring off against an antagonist it will quickly become stale. When planning stories, include puzzles, environmental risks, and difficult situations. Challenging the characters outside of conflict ensures that a wide variety of character concepts and player personalities can be engaged. Any of the different options below can also be placed into a story to add variety.

Hostile Physical Environments

From braving the wilderness to racing through a collapsing building, placing characters in situations where their surroundings pose a risk is a sure way to increase the tension of a game. Outside of conflict, extreme environments will require characters to make thoughtful use of accoutrements and the *Survival* skill (see *Extreme Environments*, p. 96). If there is a chance to prepare, well-funded characters can make meaningful contributions to their peers. If unexpectedly dropped into extreme environments, characters with high *Survival* skills can even become the difference between life and death for their group.

In conflict, environmental hazards such as burning buildings, volcanic eruptions, or violent storms can add a sense of urgency. They can be a narrative tool to create a clear motivation for the players to leave a specific area, but beware of forcing the players' actions too heavily or too often as it can feel overbearing. Likewise, penalties from exposure to environmental dangers can stress player vulnerability, but it can also quickly overwhelm the characters. A balanced use of extreme environments can add excitement and drama to a story.

Hostile Social Environments

Hostile social environments are those that are so charged with prejudice or filled with propaganda that they negatively affect characters. Mechanically, those who are the subject of scorn from hostile environments will suffer an Esteem penalty set by the Narrator; this allows a way to represent the hostility without requiring roleplay that could be uncomfortable for the real people playing the game. In extreme cases, this may result in an entire room being hostile towards a certain person or group. Esteem penalties also create vulnerabilities for player characters, as their Reputations can be easily attacked, and they may face hurdles to raise their Esteem before they can effectively interact with important NCs. Narratively, specifics regarding the prejudice may also provide the players with information about the setting and the values of the NCs in the scene. This can be a powerful narrative tool, especially for punk-themed stories. However, keeping characters in hostile social environments for long periods of time risks alienating the players.

Ignorance

The protagonists can certainly dash headlong into any situation, but they might find themselves without the knowledge or tools needed to resolve it in they way they wish. The characters may need to defeat a nephilim antagonist, but they may not know the Bane that can kill him. They could want to bargain with a spirit, but don't know any weaknesses to exploit. In situations such as these, player character ignorance enhances the threat of a situation and adds a sense of mystery.

Narrators can introduce ignorance by including challenges that are impossible to perfectly resolve without special information. When a particular piece of knowledge exposes the weakness of a foe or creates a unique opportunity, it becomes a reward. When players see that gaining information helps them succeed more easily and completely, it will be a powerful incentive to more fully immerse themselves in both the plot and the setting.

Ignorance can also allow certain characters to shine. When a lack of information is established as a threat, characters with ranks in Reason and various knowledge-based skills are able to prove their value. Specialized assets such as *Library*, *Ritual Book*, and certain transcendent powers are also great sources of solutions for ignorance-based concerns, and validates players who invest resources in those areas.

Threats from ignorance work best in games with a strong horror or technological component. Introducing dangerous obstacles or foes that must be avoided or ignored until special knowledge is gained is a classic approach to such stories. Otherwise, ignorance of any situation will make it more dangerous, and it exacerbates all the other non-character threats listed here.

Time

The drama of your story can be increased with the use of time constraints. Impending extreme environments, Pontus events, and character vulnerabilities are all made more frightening when each tick of the clock signals the forthcoming danger. Many Victorian and punk games have a heavy social component, so tasks which need to be completed at tonight's concert or before the anticipated election of an opponent can keep drama high and players on their toes. Survival horror will often have a strong time component, requiring the characters to endure for a set period before help

HANDLING THE DECK

One of the signatures of *Clockwork: Dominion* is the use of the custom card deck throughout play. Having a common deck that all players share not only allows for wonderfully balanced mechanics, but it can also shape the play experience at the table. Narrators are encouraged to try several different ways of dealing cards to see what works best for their group.

Common Deck: Everyone shares a single deck that is kept in the center of the table. Whenever someone needs a card, they draw from the deck and place it face up on the table for everyone to see. This works best in small groups where everyone can easily reach the deck.

Dealer: The Narrator controls the deck and deals cards face down to whomever needs them. The player then reveals the card for everyone to see. In this style, the Narrator can control the precise moment trait tests are resolved, allowing for longer descriptions and player engagement. The Narrator can also control pacing by dealing cards languidly during relaxed scenes and more quickly in conflict or other fast paced scenes.

Distributed: The deck is cut into two or more stacks that are placed around the table. Whenever someone needs a card, they draw from a stack of their choice and reveal it for everyone to see. If you have lots of players or a table whose shape makes it difficult for everyone to reach a common deck, this is probably the best method. Players will generally draw from the stack nearest to them, but they may draw from whichever stack they choose.

Magician: Pick a card, any card. The Narrator holds the deck out to allow players to take any card they want. The player then reveals it for everyone to see. You can manage the deck with whatever degree of theatricality desired: you might fan out the cards to allow the player to choose any they wish, let them draw from the bottom of the deck, cut it, shuffle it, or employ any other artifice you like. This is especially useful to heighten the tension during dramatic moments. When used well, this presentation can do wonders for investing the players in the action of the game.

Multiple Decks: Two complete decks are used during the course of play. The Narrator will use one deck and the players will use another, keeping each deck separate from the other. Additionally, for groups that have frequent or long physical conflicts, using an additional deck can be a significant time saver. In these instances, everyone shares one deck and the alternate deck is swapped in whenever the current deck needs to be shuffled so play can continue immediately.

Regardless of what method is used most often, using different techniques during the course of an installment can help keep up the energy at the table. For story-defining encounters—especially during critical draws, or when Ether is being used—a sudden change of style highlights the moment and heightens the drama. One of the great pleasures of any role-playing game are those times of shared anticipation, triumph, and heartbreak when an important test succeeds or fails. Don't hesitate to put on a show when the opportunity presents itself.

SIMPLE CHANCE

There will be circumstances that may influence the story in a minor way but are not involved in advancing the plot, or don't tie directly into the action at hand. When a player wishes to know an incidental detail— the availability of an item, the presence of a Narrator character in a crowded scene, a feature of a room, etc.—chance can be used to determine the answer. Characters always have the option to spend *Purpose* to take narrative control and establish their own answer. However, if the player wishes to hold on to their potential, the Narrator can either decide the answer or can let a card draw determine fate. The Narrator assigns each possible answer a percentage chance of being true, then

the asking player draws a card and checks the card number against the ranges given by the Narrator.

For example, Jack wants to know whether the house the characters are in uses gaslight or electricity for illumination. The Narrator, Samantha, hasn't defined it, and doesn't know what Jack has in mind, so she is willing to leave it up to chance. Jack doesn't want to spend potential to define it, and accepts the random determination. Samantha gives it a 50/50 split, assigning 1–50 as gaslight and 51–100 as electric. Jack draws card number 71, and the scene is now defined as using electric lighting. Once a detail is defined this way, it can no longer be changed by spending *Purpose*.

---

arrives or until a foe is vulnerable. Technology-focused games more typically have time restrictions on the research and construction time necessary to produce new items, which requires characters to carefully choose when and how they are created. If the characters are aware that they are ignorant regarding a particular foe, the scramble to find the needed information before time runs out is a great way to keep the game moving.

Vulnerability

Many player characters will want to face their enemies head on, but the most resourceful antagonists have no interest in direct confrontation. Usually, every player character has a weakness that can be exploited: a spouse or child, something with which they are *Obsessed*, a daily routine, or some other vulnerability. When antagonists indirectly target player characters through their loved one, allies, and resources, it can evoke real concern or fear. Going after

"innocent" victims is also a good way to express the villainy or inhumanity of antagonists, and reminds players that just because their characters are special in the game doesn't make them invulnerable or immune to consequences. Looking beyond the player characters themselves to find ways to strike at them indirectly is a great technique for mixing up the conflict in a story and reinforces that the player characters are part of a broader world.

It is vital to balance this approach with fun and engaging gameplay. Narrators should never completely remove or permanently invalidate anything that players have spent experience points to acquire. Such actions upset players and can cause a mechanical disadvantage that sets them behind. Taking something away, but allowing players a chance to recover it, seek retribution, or gain closure, are story opportunities that can excite and engage players and make them more fully appreciate what they have.

NARRATING A CONFLICT

The full rules for conflicts of every type are provided in *Chapter 4: Rules & Systems*. This section is meant to help Narrators decide when and how they should include different types of conflict and how to effectively narrate them. There are very specific guidelines given below, but at its most basic, a physical conflict is used when characters want to physically hurt or restrain one another, a social conflict is used when a character wishes to convince or persuade another without violence, and an intrigue is used when one character wants to boast or discredit another character. Almost all stories will favor one form of conflict over the others, but every story will likely have opportunities for each.

Quick Conflict Resolution

Physical or social conflicts with minor narrative impact can be resolved with roleplay and a single trait test. Trying to haggle over

the price of a pistol, or kicking down a door, could each take multiple trait tests and a lot of game time to accomplish. Since neither of these circumstances is usually narratively significant enough to merit a full conflict, Narrators can and should resolve these minor situations quickly through roleplay and a single applicable trait test. Treat this test as a penetrating attack, and resolve the conflict based on its success or failure.

Some situations will involve two or more characters actively opposing or competing against one another. For example, several characters are running a footrace or two thugs in a pub are arm wrestling over who pays for their beer. In such instances, have all participants make the same trait test, Difficulty 0. The highest DoS wins the challenge. If it is important to know the succession of accomplishment for multiple characters, such as the order the racers cross the finish line, use the order from highest DoS to lowest.

PHYSICAL CONFLICT

Elaborate challenges or conflicts whose outcome will have significant effects on the story should use the full physical conflict system. If an entire pub is watching two thugs arm wrestle and the stakes are for an entire year's bar tab, that might be enough drama to justify a conflict. If the match escalates to a fist fight, it most certainly deserves the use of the conflict system.

Who Participates?

When a fight breaks out, the Narrator must decide to whom initiative cards are dealt. It is critical that player characters and their allies at the location be involved. They will always be dealt initiative cards even if they do not directly participate in the fight. Bystanders always have the option to flee from the scene when violence starts, and this can be described at the Narrator's discretion without initiative cards. If there are bystanders or observers that stay in the scene but are content to watch, such as in a formal duel or a brawl in a street, they are simply present as background dressing and are not dealt initiative cards unless they are drawn into the conflict.

When is the Conflict Over?

Physical conflict ends when no one is able or willing to make an attack. A conflict will immediately end if all participants on one side of a conflict are incapacitated, flee, or have surrendered. Conflict will also end if all combatants refuse to attack. If all participants in an initiative sequence pass and there is no acting character, conflict ends. Both sides have reached an informal end to hostilities. After physical conflict, the action will switch back to roleplay or may even transition to a social conflict.

Narrating Physical Conflict

With the high stakes of blood and honor in play, Narrators should do everything they can to help conflict flow smoothly. First and foremost, be familiar with the rules presented in *Chapter 4: Rules & Systems*, so you can address any questions that arise quickly and consistently. Try to have a clear goal and basic strategy in mind when using antagonists and Narrator characters so you set the pace of play. Generally, describing each action based on the test result is a great way to keep the scene vibrant and avoid becoming a boring back-and-forth of making tests and comparing numbers. Inviting players to describe their own actions also helps keep them engaged.

Include opportunities for all players and characters to be involved. If a player with a strong social character isn't good at melee, remind her that she can make social attacks to decrease a foe's Guard or Morale. Describe the scenery that surrounds the conflict so that players can move tactically, have details for possible uses of potential, and make effective use of cover. For new players learning the system, remind them of tactical possibilities. Ask if they're going to react when targeted and prompt them to see if they wish to use potential.

Lastly, enjoy the fight. Take risks. Throw yourself into description and roleplay, and use any trick of scene-setting and performance you can think of to make conflict more fun for the group.

SOCIAL CONFLICT

Social conflict may happen whenever one character or group wants to convince or coerce another. However, you do not need to use social conflict every time a character wants to persuade another person. Save social conflict for those times when a situation has high tension, high risk, or for those moments when social conflict would prove to be dramatic and fun. You do not have to run a full social conflict to haggle over the price of a night's stay in a hotel; use quick conflict resolution instead. However, social conflict may add excitement to a scene where the entire party is attempting to convince Lord Buckingham to fund their expedition to the Dark Continent, or the scene where the succubus serving girl is seducing a character back to her lair. Don't be afraid to simplify minor social exchanges.

Who Participates?

Initiative cards should be dealt to all interested characters within earshot of the social conflict. However, the actual participants in social conflict are determined by the available avenues of attack. Only a single avenue is available for defender (or group of like-minded defenders), so only the first character to attack on each side of social conflict may fill an avenue of attack. However, this character may take an *Elicit Aid* maneuver to ask supporters for help. Any character who agrees to help may participate in the social conflict, sharing an avenue of attack with the asking character. Characters who are not invited to assist may talk and roleplay within the social conflict, but cannot impact how the conflict resolves.

When is the Conflict Over?

The most important thing to remember about narrating a social conflict is that no social conflict will last longer than a single sequence. This means that once the initiative cards dealt for the first sequence are spent, the conflict is over. If no outcome was reached, then the other party was simply not completely receptive to the attacker's argument. However, any altered Dispositions should be roleplayed beyond the end of the conflict.

If an outcome is reached while one or more characters still have unspent initiative cards, the conflict may continue. Outcomes may not be removed, but Dispositions can still be changed. Additional outcomes may be inflicted, but only one outcome can be placed through each avenue of attack.

The second most important thing to remember is that any participant may leave a social conflict at any time. In many cases, this will constitute a faux pas; however, if a character is willing to endure the loss of Esteem this might cause, she can simply walk away. No character is ever forced to participate in a social conflict unless they are literally tied down or somehow *Entrapped*.

Narrating Social Conflict

The pace of social conflict greatly differs from that of physical conflict. Social conflicts are more conversational, and characters rarely act at their earliest opportunity to do so. Instead, the argument or debate is roleplayed and attacks are made as persuasive words are spoken. If one player wishes to attack before another, consult the initiative cards and allow the character with the highest card to go first. Try to keep the flow of a social conflict as relaxed as the conversation it represents.

The instigating character will make the first social attack, filling the avenue of attack of her target(s). The instigating character may take an *Elicit Aid* maneuver to ask those around her for help. Within the story, this means the characters are joining in the debate and working with one another to make a stronger argument. All characters who choose to participate in this way may make their social attacks alongside the acting character. The highest DoS achieved by any single participant will be the DoS for the collaborative attack for that turn.

The first character to act on the other side of the argument may also *Elicit Aid* and make similar collaborative attacks in retaliation. Remember that each defender within an argument can only have a single avenue through which they may be attacked, and the first character to fill this avenue will occupy it until the end of the conflict. The only exception to this rule is through browbeating, described in *Chapter 4: Rules & Systems*.

INTRIGUE

An intrigue is a deliberate attempt to either build up or tear down someone's Reputation and social standing. A character can build her own or another's social standing, maneuvering from a social nobody to a person of note, or she can make a rival lose all credibility with their peers. The Narrator should only employ an intrigue when these types of intentions have been declared.

Who Participates?

Most intrigues are very fluid endeavors. Intrigue attacks to affect Esteem or Reputation are made as they arise during the course of roleplay, and are not subject to a regimented initiative system. Thus, no initiative cards are dealt for intrigues and the number of attacks are not limited. The only participants in an individual intrigue attack are the character(s) making the attack and their target.

When is the Conflict Over?

No intrigue will last longer than a single chapter. When a new chapter begins, Esteem is recalculated. If a socialite did not achieve her goals by the end of the chapter, then the rumor mongering simply didn't take. However, even though an intrigue may not have permanent effects on a character's Reputation, it may have narrative consequences. If any gain or loss in Esteem was particularly memorable or dramatic, it may continue to be talked about even if there are no mechanical ramifications.

Narrating an Intrigue

As each intrigue attack represents an entire conversation, they should not be made in rapid succession, but rather spaced throughout the scenes of a chapter. Manipulating someone to make an affront to civility, or working a room to change its opinion of someone, takes time. The mechanics provided in *Chapter 4: Rules & Systems* prevent abuse through the use of Armor and the limitation of affecting only a single rank of a single Reputation per character per chapter. However, verisimilitude and immersion require that intrigues be roleplayed over time. Encourage your players to get into character, and allow the collaborative narrative to tell you when attacks should be made.

CORRUPTION

A character who directly opposes the will of the Maker will slowly fall out of the Clockwork. Unspeakable acts, such as murder and betrayal, are measured by the *Corruption* trait. They have such a significant effect on a mortal's integration into the Clockwork that the level of *Corruption* can influence the Pontus when it manifests.

GAINING CORRUPTION

Different gaming groups will use *Corruption* differently. As the Narrator, you must decide what constitutes an unspeakable act of chaos in your group. Some actions, such as those listed below, should always incur *Corruption*, but beyond these, it is up to each group to determine how they want to use this mechanic.

Murder and Manslaughter

If a character willfully kills another mortal—a pureblood, changeling, or beastfolk—or is somehow complicit in the death of a mortal, she will always gain a rank of *Corruption*. The character needn't have intended or even directly caused the death. A gunslinger who shoots another character intending to wound her will still gain a rank of *Corruption* if the shot accidentally kills her instead. A character who hires an assassin to kill her rival, even though she was not even present, will gain *Corruption*. A character who has the opportunity to save a man from drowning, but opts not to help, will incur a point of *Corruption*. The will of the Maker is to preserve life. Anyone who by action or inaction allows a mortal to die will suffer the consequences.

Slaying creatures other than mortals never incurs *Corruption*. There are no spiritual ramifications for the killing of fey, chimera, aberrations, nephilim, or any other creature in the Clockwork. This does not mean that such actions are favorable to the Maker, only that that are not so vile as to cause *Corruption*.

Acts of Chaos

At its core, an act of chaos is exemplified by the breaking of oaths. If a man swears an oath of marriage to his wife and then sleeps with another woman, he takes a rank of *Corruption*. If a soldier swears fealty to the crown but flees the country to avoid military service, he takes a rank of *Corruption*. Any formal oath that is broken will have the same results. Every individual act of chaos will incur a rank of *Corruption*.

Beyond oathbreaking, the Narrator may define what constitutes an act of chaos. However, this decision should have firm boundaries. A broad example might be breaking any of the Ten Commandments. Any time a character breaks one of these ten rules, she takes a point of *Corruption*. A narrow example might simply include a handful of truly heinous sins such as betrayal, torture, and severe emotional brutality. The Narrator can define an act of chaos however she wishes, but she needs to define it rigidly enough so that the players know what to expect. It is also helpful to warn players when they are about to do something that will incur *Corruption*.

Be mindful to narrate a setting where the spiritual ramifications are believable and acceptable to your players. Their personal beliefs will play a role in what will create a fun time at the gaming table.

Profound Exposure to the Pontus

Not every way of accumulating *Corruption* is linked to behavior. The unintelligible chaos of the Pontus can corrupt the human body and breath just by encountering it. Certain chimera and aberrations can inflict *Corruption* on those they touch. Severe Pontus events that swallow a character or completely encapsulate her can have this effect as well. Prolonged exposure to demons, such as being possessed, or remaining in thin places can also leave a person tainted.

Optional Rule: Permanent Corruption

Some people believe that there are certain sins you can commit that will forever taint you. If you would like to use this optional rule in your story, choose a very small number of truly heinous sins. Examples might be willful murder, betraying a friend, or breaking an oath sworn in the divine Name. When a character does any one of these things, she receives a single point of *Corruption* from which she can never be free. No contrition or reconciliation will remove it. It is an eternal brand on her soul. A character should never receive more than a single rank in permanent *Corruption*.

RECOVERING FROM CORRUPTION

While gaining *Corruption* is a truly terrifying thing, in most instances it can be undone. Characters who wish to rid themselves of *Corruption* can seek out ways to cleanse their souls. While the *Corruption* mechanics are deliberately open ended, Narrators should be extremely cautious about allowing players an easy out. The cleansing circumstances below are harsh, restrictive, and demanding, and while Narrators can add to this list, all situations should be similarly difficult.

Acts of Contrition

A character can remove a single rank of *Corruption* by undoing the consequences of the action that created the *Corruption*. If a character can make reparations, such as returning a stolen object or paying back a debt, this will remove the *Corruption*. In situations where one's soul was tainted by something that cannot be taken back, such as adultery or murder, the character must make amends through a formal and sincere apology, and also refrain from the behavior for a year and a day. At the end of this time the *Corruption* is removed.

Rites of Reconciliation

The Church offers the rite of reconciliation whereby a person can visit with an ordained clergyman, confess her sins, and ask for forgiveness. If a character is honestly contrite and is willing to disclose the full nature of her sin, she will be forgiven and the *Corruption* gained through that action will be removed. The rite of reconciliation is described in further detail on p. 255.

Profound Exposure to the Orderly Workings of the Clockwork

Just as exposure to the Pontus can inflict *Corruption*, exposure to the Clockwork can cure it. Being present for a *Greater Miracle* or prolonged exposure to angels or the heavenly realms will remove a rank of *Corruption*. Also, spending three months participating in the orderly systems of a Stable area can remove a rank of *Corruption*. This could be participating in monastic life with the brothers of a monastery or living off of the land in a virgin wilderness. This sort of intentional healing is likely to take place during down time between installments.

THE PONTUS

CRACKS IN CREATION

Every game of *Clockwork: Dominion* has the ever-present threat of the Pontus lurking in the background. Even in stories where player characters diligently keep themselves free of *Corruption*, there will be instances where the story moves to a Compromised location and someone will draw the Doom card. The Pontus can only touch the Clockwork through the cracks in the order of creation. For characters in the game, this is represented by ranks of *Corruption*. For places, this is represented by one of three states of environmental stability: Stable, Compromised, and Breached. The ranks of character *Corruption* and the stability of a location both determine what occurs during a Pontus event, and Narrators must be ready to handle Pontus events whenever they occur.

Environmental Stability

The Clockmaker's creation is inherently stable, but when corrupting acts occur in a place, or when a location is subject to a Pontus event, that stability may be weakened or destroyed, leaving it more susceptible to the Pontus in the future. Locations are considered to be Stable, Compromised, or Breached. The category descriptions provide the standard for determining which status is appropriate for a given scene.

TRIGGERING PONTUS EVENTS

Pontus events are triggered in two ways. Any time the Doom card is played, the character that played it triggers an event. Alternately, if a character that already has Corruption 5 acts in a way that would incur a sixth rank of Corruption, the corrupted character triggers an event. Regardless of the cause of the event, the triggering character draws a number of cards equal to the highest Corruption rank of all characters present in the scene, including all NCs. The lowest card number drawn is checked against the Pontus Events table for the current location's environmental stability to determine what type of event occurs.

Once the effect has been determined, use the event descriptions to resolve the event. Narrators are strongly encouraged to describe the strangeness and danger of these effects in detail. Every time the Pontus touches the world it should leave its mark, both in its effects and on the lives of witnesses.

After the Pontus activity is resolved, the triggering character loses one rank of Corruption, as it has bled off to fuel the event. However, if the triggering character already had Corruption 5 and caused the event by acting in a way that would have caused a sixth rank, it is the sixth rank that fueled the event, and the character remains at Corruption 5.

The listed effects are only a few of many possibilities. Narrators should feel free to use the listed examples to determine the severity of the effect and then alter or replace the particulars as they see fit.

Blind Rage

The meaningless chaos of the Pontus is momentarily revealed to all in the scene, and even that flashing glimpse is enough to drive many into a brief fit of blind rage. All characters in the scene test *Reason + Will*, Difficulty 3 + the triggering character's *Corruption* rank. Success allows a character to maintain control over herself until the madness passes, but she struggles to do so and must discard her highest unused initiative card.

Those that fail succumb to blind rage, and strike at the nearest person. Characters must use all their remaining initiative cards as soon as possible to make close combat *Grace + Melee* attacks against the nearest character, using actions to Run if no target is available within a single move. These enraged characters cannot use maneuvers, and can only attack with whatever accoutrements they had in their hands when the event occurred. No transcendent powers, Mastery abilities, blessings, assets, or any other special abilities may be used by enraged characters. At the end of the sequence the event subsides and all characters return to sanity.

Breach!

The Pontus begins to tear at the very fabric of reality, rending asunder the boundary between the mortal world and the Borderlands. The physical environment immediately becomes blurred and undefined, and objects begin to vanish. At the end of the sequence, all characters who have not fled are pulled from the world entirely and deposited at a random location on the Broken Road in the Borderlands.

Cacophony

Sounds become ceaseless, and the crescendo builds into an overpowering and potentially deadly cacophony that could deafen or madden those in the scene. The effect endures for a number of sequences equal to the *Corruption* rank of the triggering character. It is immediately noticeable because speech becomes garbled, as each sound in a word continues and renders any speech a mess of incomprehensible tones. By the beginning of the next sequence, even the sounds from clothes and accoutrements rustled in movement, the motion of the air, and any other sound in the scene mounts on itself to become confusing and physically painful. All characters in the scene are temporarily subjected to the *Outmaneuvered* condition as long as the effect persists.

ENVIRONMENTAL STABILITY

STABLE

Untouched nature, places of great beauty and peace, consecrated ground, and areas that are very sparsely settled or only lightly travelled through, represent creation as it is meant to be in the Clockwork. This bulwark against the Pontus is weakened by the chaotic activity of mortals, so it is rare for areas to remain stable once there is a population beyond that of a small town. Pontus events are rare in one of these Stable areas, but those that do occur are often severe.

COMPROMISED

Any location that has either been dramatically altered from its natural state or exposed to *Corruption* becomes Compromised, and these places are more vulnerable to the influence of the Pontus. Towns and larger population centers often despoil nature, and large populations always bring crime, disease, suffering, and the stain of corrupt behaviors. Once an area becomes Compromised only powerful rituals of cleansing magic or other transcendent powers can restore it to a Stable state. Compromised locations will suffer more frequent and severe Pontus effects, including incredible weather, impossible occurrences, disappearances, and the creation of aberrations.

BREACHED

These unholy locations only arise through exposure to the worst atrocities. They are the scenes of repeated torture and murder, battlefields, and sites used for the practice of impure magic and sorcery. Breached locations often have ill reputations, both for the terrible events that happened there, as well as for the deep sense of unease and disquiet that permeates them. Even outside of an active Pontus event, Breached locations seem subtly off. Many people report fleeting hallucinations, odd qualities of the light, and an unfocused sense of tension. Animals tend to stay away from Breached areas if possible, and even people travelling through these areas will feel ill-at-ease.

Areas marked with such dark history are at great risk for Pontus outbreaks, and when the Pontus rises in Breached locations, anything can occur. Massive storms of impossible weather, the physical warping of the location, disappearances, and chimera spawnings are all possibilities.

UNDERGROUND AND OVERSEA

Certain locations simply do not hold back the Pontus as well as others. For reasons, unknown, traveling under the earth or sailing over deep waters seem to incur a greater danger from the Pontus. If a Pontus event is triggered in such an area, draw an additional card when determining the event.

CONSECRATED GROUND

Ground that is set aside for a holy use through the *Bless* charism is considered consecrated. In addition to usually being Stable, these holy places are less likely to suffer the most drastic effects of the Pontus. If a Pontus event is triggered in such an area, draw one fewer cards when determining the event. If this reduces the number of cards to zero, no Pontus event will occur. This is the reason most people of faith have their homes blessed by the local priest and then refuse to invite evil into them.

Pontus Events in Stable Areas	
Result	**Stable Effects**
1–5	The location is now *Compromised*. Draw again on the Compromised table.
6–15	Disappearance
16–35	Spawn Chimera
36–45	Spawn Aberrations
46–55	Impossible Event: Major
26–75	Impossible Weather: Major
76–100	No effect

Pontus Events in Compromised Areas	
Result	**Compromised Effects**
1–5	The location is now *Breached*. Draw again on the Breached table.
6–10	Wave of Corruption
11–20	Compression
21–30	Cacophony
31–40	Unnatural Angles
41–50	Blind Rage
51–55	Spawn Chimera
56–70	Spawn Aberration
71–80	Hallucinations
81–85	Potential Leech
86–90	Impossible Weather: Minor
91–100	Impossible Event: Minor

Pontus Events in Breached Areas	
Result	**Breached Effects**
1–5	Dissolution
6–10	Breach!
11–20	Disappearance
21–30	Translocation
31–50	Spawn Chimera
51–60	Synaesthesia
61–75	Impossible Event: Severe
76–89	Impossible Weather: Severe
91–100	Wave of Corruption

Especially loud noises such as gunshots, explosions, and screams become dangerous. Whenever such a sound occurs, the Narrator makes a penetrating area attack against all characters who can hear the cacophony. Instead of using a combination, the attack's Strength is equal to 2 + the triggering character's *Corruption* rank, and has a Potency 2 and the *Dazed* weapon condition. Afflicted characters Defend with their *Will + Vigor*. The attack can inflict Wounds in the form of burst eardrums, perforated sinuses, and shattered blood vessels in the eyes and head. The characters can only escape the cacophony by leaving the location.

Compression

Some fundamental aspect of physics is momentarily undone by the Pontus, crushing and collapsing all physical matter in the scene. The Narrator immediately deals the Pontus event a number of initiative cards equal to 2 + the *Corruption* rank of the triggering character. The Narrator must play these initiative cards as soon as she is able. When the Pontus plays an initiative card, all characters must test *Will + Vigor*. For the first card, the test is at Difficulty 3. The Difficulty for tests forced by each additional card will raise by one cummulatively. If a character succeeds she is able to withstand the compression without ill effect. The first time a character fails, she suffers a -2 penalty on all actions for the remainder of the sequence. The second time she fails, she immediately loses an unused initiative card. Third and subsequent failures inflict a Wound. Fleeing the scene allows characters to escape the effect.

Disappearance

Sometimes the Pontus devours parts of the Clockwork. The Narrator deals a number of cards to each PC and NC equal to their *Corruption* rank, and a single card to any other people, animals, or significant objects in the scene. A number of people or objects equal to the *Corruption* rank of the triggering character simply disappear. Those with the lowest card numbers on the cards dealt to them are those who vanish. The only evidence of their existence is perhaps a scorch mark on the ground or a lingering acrid smell.

Player characters and important NCs who disappear are assumed to emerge at some random location on the Earth or in the Borderlands. Other characters and objects are swallowed by the Pontus and may eventually emerge as part of a chimera.

Dissolution

The worst of all possible risings, the chaotic nothingness of the Pontus touches the world and unmakes it. The Narrator immediately deals a number of initiative cards to the Pontus event equal to 1 + the *Corruption* rank of the triggering character. The Narrator must play these initiative cards as soon as she is able. When an initiative card is played, randomly determine a character in the scene: characters in that zone of control immediately suffer one Wound and all unattended objects are immediately *Destroyed*. The characters' accoutrements affixed upon their person are not destroyed unless the character is killed by the effect. Characters killed and objects destroyed by this effect are utterly unmade, and leave no physical remains behind.

Hallucinations

Characters begin experiencing a confusing barrage of hallucinations as the chaotic energies of the Pontus overwhelm their senses. All characters immediately test *Will + Composure*, Difficulty 2 + the *Corruption* rank of the triggering character. Those that succeed are initially distracted and immediately lose one point of Guard. They also suffer the *Outmaneuvered* temporary condition for the remainder of the sequence, but are able to effectively ignore the hallucinations thereafter. Characters that fail the test lose all sense of what is real and what is imagined, and are incapable of reacting effectively to physical reality. They immediately lose one point of Guard, cannot regain Guard, and suffer the *Outmaneuvered* temporary condition for the remainder of the scene.

Impossible Event

When the Pontus rises, anything is possible, as even the laws undergirding reality itself can be suspended or temporarily re-written. The Narrator can describe any manner of event she wishes, and is encouraged to be both imaginative and creepy. The following rules provide guidelines for mechanical effects.

- **Minor:** This event creates an effect that is centered on the triggering character and her zone of control. Minor impossible events usually require the triggering character to make a single aptitude + skill test against a Difficulty of 1 + her *Corruption* to avoid a temporary condition. For example, the ground in her zone of control turns into a viscous ichor, requiring a *Grace + Athletics* test to escape the *Entrapped* condition. These events may also disable a single accoutrement for a number of sequences equal to 1 + the *Corruption* rank of the triggering character. For example, all the bullets in a gun spontaneously decay into filth requiring it to be cleaned out and reloaded.

- **Major:** These events impact an entire location for the remainder of the scene. Major impossible events automatically place a temporary condition on everyone within the immediate vicinity which can only be removed by a trait test, Difficulty of 2 + the *Corruption* rank of the triggering character. For example, the gaslights on the street begin to absorb light rather than provide it, giving everyone in the location the *Blinded* condition until they can make a *Focus + Composure* test to adjust to the darkness. Alternatively, the Narrator may choose more serious effects such as penalties on all tests, Wounds or other outcomes that can be avoided by a passive test, Difficulty of 2 + the *Corruption* rank of the triggering character. For example, maddening voices persuade the characters to attack their own bodies unless they can make a *Will + Composure* test to ignore them.

- **Severe:** These dangerous events radically and permanently alter the physical conditions of the location or temporarily create an extreme environment that is best handled by fleeing. Those who do not flee will be subject to a variety of conditions, Wounds, and other outcomes can only be avoided by active tests, Difficulty of 3 + the *Corruption* rank of the triggering character. Examples might be the earth begins to swallow up the city and characters must test *Grace + Athletics* to navigate the collapsing buildings without being hit by debris, or all of the dead in the graveyard rise from their graves to attack the player characters, who must make *Vigor + Athletics* tests to avoid them as they flee, or stand their ground to fight them.

Impossible Weather:

Freak weather occurrences are the most widely reported manifestations of the Pontus. Tempests and unnatural rain will sometimes occur in Breached areas even if no Pontus event has been triggered.

- **Minor:** Transient but severe weather begins immediately and endures for the remainder of the scene. Minor impossible weather may require characters to make a single aptitude + skill test against Difficulty 1 + her *Corruption* to avoid a temporary condition. If so, these tests must be made immediately and then during the character's first turn in each sequence for the remainder of the scene. Reported effects include:

  - The temperature instantaneously becomes frigid or swelteringly hot. Characters must test *Vigor + Will* or be subjected to the *Fatigued* condition.

  - The earth quakes. Localized seismic activity immediately forces everyone to test *Grace + Athletics* or be knocked to the ground and suffer the *Unbalanced* temporary condition.

- The calm air suddenly becomes a raging wind storm and the tempest hurtles loose objects through the air. All characters must test *Vigor* + *Athletics* to avoid being blown down and suffer the *Dazed* condition.
- The sky immediately above darkens or turns red. A disturbing rain of animals or objects fall from the sky, pelting everyone in the immediate vicinity. Characters must test *Will* + *Athletics* or suffer the *Disoriented* condition.

- **Major:** These events are clearly caused by the Pontus; the effects break natural laws and last for one scene. Major impossible weather may require characters to make a single aptitude + skill test against Difficulty 2 + the *Corruption* of the triggering character to avoid a temporary condition or other penalty. If so, these tests must be made immediately and then during the character's first turn in each sequence for the remainder of the scene. Possible effects include:
  - The rain is pure darkness, coating everything in a thick black liquid that makes normal sight impossible. After the rains begin, all targets outside an affected character's zone of control are considered to have light cover. Characters must test *Focus* + *Composure* or suffer a -2 penalty to all physical attacks and tests that involve sight.
  - The light from the sun or moon in the sky abruptly intensifies and the incandescence causes all exposed flesh to rapidly blister and burn. Characters test *Vigor* + *Will* to avoid an immediate -1 Wound Penalty (although no Wounds are caused). Characters fully protected by hats, gloves, and clothing gain a +1 bonus to these tests.
  - A forceful gale descends upon the area and counteracts every attempt to move. Speech is impossible over the howling gusts, all loose objects are immediately blown away, and it is impossible to *Aim* in the whirlwind. Any character attempting to move must succeed on a passive test of *Vigor* + *Athletics*.
  - The sky immediately darkens a sinister red. An unnatural rain of blood, animals, or other strange objects falls upon everyone in the vicinity, inflicting a -2 penalty on all Defenses as the characters are battered, blinded, and confused. Characters must test *Will* + *Composure* or their Morale will reduce by one step.

- **Severe:** Weather manifestations in Breached locations are dangerous and the only safe option is to flee. The effects include a variety of penalties including automatic temporary conditions. Major impossible weather may require characters to make a single aptitude + skill test against Difficulty 3 + the *Corruption* of the triggering character to avoid an outcome. If so, these tests must be made immediately and then during the character's first turn in each sequence for the remainder of the scene.
  - A dense, opaque fog the consistency of molasses quickly rises from the ground and begins to fill the entire area. All characters immediately gain the *Staggered* temporary condition until the end of the scene. The characters must test *Vigor* + *Athletics*

or suffer a Wound. Additionally, any character attempting to wade through the fog must test *Vigor* + *Athletics* to move (this may be done passively).
- Crackling spheres of ball lightning erupt from the skies overhead and hurtle towards the ground. A number of lightning balls equal to the *Corruption* rank of the triggering character are created. The first appears in the zone of control of the triggering character, the second appears in the zone of control of the character with the highest *Corruption*, the third appears in the zone of the person with the next-highest *Corruption*, etc.

The lightning balls are treated as antagonists who attack with a trait combination equal to 3 + the *Corruption* of the triggering character. These attacks have Potency 4, the *Incapacitated* weapon condition, and ignore Guard. All characters and objects in the same zone of control as a lightning ball are immediately targeted for an attack. At the beginning each subsequent sequence, each lightning ball moves up to twenty feet towards the closest character and attacks if anything is in its zone of control. During a sequence, anything that moves through any lightning ball's zone of control is immediately attacked as though the ball lightning had just seized the initiative to attack. At the end of each sequence, after the first one of the balls disappears. The ball lightning is immaterial and cannot be attacked or killed, and is immune to all conditions and penalties.

Potential Leech

As the destabilizing energies of the Pontus rise, the connection of all characters to their broader role in the Clockwork is disrupted. Characters must spend two points of potential whenever they would normally spend one, or three points if they would normally spend two. The effect endures for the remainder of the sequence, plus a number of sequences equal to the *Corruption* of the triggering character.

Spawning Aberrations

The event spawns one or more aberrations with a total Threat of 2 + the *Corruption* rank of the triggering character. The event usually warps and twists creatures or plants that are already present in the scene, but may bring aberrations from any other place touched by the Pontus. Once these aberrations enter the world, they remain until destroyed.

Spawning Chimera

Chimera with a total Threat of 3 + the *Corruption* of the triggering character are spawned. Chimera are spawned immediately, and are either created from creatures and objects that are already present in the scene, or they can rise from the depths of the Pontus itself. Once these chimera enter the world, they remain until destroyed.

Synaesthesia

As the Pontus rises, the senses of all characters in the scene are hopelessly scrambled, leaving them awash in a confused rush of sensations. The event persists for a number of sequences equal to 1 + the *Corruption* rank of the triggering character. All characters immediately lose an initiative card and must test *Reason + Intuition* against a Difficulty of 3 + the triggering character's *Corruption*. If successful, they suffer the *Dazed* and *Unbalanced* temporary conditions until the Pontus event subsides. Failure is even more debilitating, as the characters suffer a -2 penalty on all actions in addition to the *Dazed* and *Unbalanced* temporary conditions for the duration of the event.

Translocation

The surging energies of the Pontus unmoor the scene from its proper place in the world, immediately and permanently depositing the physical space that contains all characters in the scene somewhere else in the world. The distance covered by the translocation increases with the *Corruption* of the character that triggered the event:

There is also a 5% chance per rank of *Corruption* (5% at *Corruption* 1, 10% at *Corruption* 2, etc) that the new location will present some immediate environmental hazard, such as being in a physically precarious position at risk of falling or collapse, all or partially in water, in a wildly different climate, or any other situation the Narrator desires. It will never result in a situation that is immediately fatal, such as appearing midair and falling, submerged in lava, or at the bottom of an oceanic trench.

Corruption	Distance
1	1 mile
2	10 miles
3	100 miles
4	1000 miles
5	Anywhere else on Earth, or in another realm.

Unnatural Angles

It must be a trick of the eyes, because all movements are happening in random directions and at impossible angles. As the rising Pontus warps perception and perspective, the character's visual perception and sense of space is rendered useless for the number of sequences equal to 1 + the *Corruption* rank of the triggering character. All characters are incapable of effective physical activity unless they use an action and succeed on a *Reason + Athletics* test, Difficulty equal to 2 + the *Corruption* of the triggering character. Success allows them to act for the remainder of the sequence, any attempt to *Aim* is still impossible. Failure leaves characters flailing helplessly in place, unable to take any moves or maneuvers.

At the beginning of each subsequent sequence characters must achieve another successful *Reason + Athletics* test before they are able to move normally.

Wave of Corruption

The *Corruption* that triggered the effect washes over everything in the location, immediately increasing the *Corruption* score of all characters in the scene by one. Every character in the scene that already has a *Corruption* of 5 before the effect will immediately trigger a new Pontus event.

USING THE PONTUS THEMATICALLY

Creative use of Pontus events will go a long way to establishing and enhancing the themes of your game. Imaginative description of impossible events, and the various effects that impact characters' perceptions are a huge opportunity for creating atmosphere and inspiring unease in players. Make an effort to familiarize yourself with the types of Pontus events, keep track of how much *Corruption* the characters have, prepare possible events ahead of time, and bear in mind the limits of the characters' abilities. We also recommend having a stable of pre-made aberrations and chimera of various threat levels. This way, you will be ready to place even unexpected Pontus events right into your story.

You can use the Pontus events described above, but feel free to also create your own. Preparing Pontus events that are appropriate

to your story or even using them as planned set-pieces for a scene are a good way to include this core aspect of the setting. Some suggestions to consider how to incorporate Pontus events into different themes are as follows:

Steam

Steam games rely on the rational order of technology and science. Allow the Pontus to be a constant threat to this rational order, and at times completely unmake it. Pontus events in steam-themed stories should violate or subvert physical laws and cause players to question reality itself. If science and technology make the players feel safe, use the Pontus to show them that safety is an illusion. They are always merely one step away from oblivion, and even the rationality of science and ingenuity of technology are powerless against the rising chaos.

Punk

The punk theme will either focus on stabilizing the status quo or tearing it down to build something better. In these stories, the Pontus is the ocean of chaos lapping at the crumbling barriers of society. If the players want to uphold social structures, vividly show them how evil oppressive structures can be and how desperately they need to be dismantled. If the players want change, allow that change to invoke Pontus events. Remind them that if the Pontus were capable of want, it would crave the destruction of evil because

destruction of any kind makes the cracks through which it can enter the world. This is an impossible scenario where even the most noble player characters must choose between fighting evil or fighting chaos.

Victorian

Victorian stories focus on the structure and aesthetics of Imperial culture. Pontus events in such a story should distort and corrupt the aspects of Victorian society that are beautiful: the intricacies of etiquette, fashion, art, and architecture. If there are players who are fans of particular aspects of Victorian society, directing the Pontus against those will immediately motivate and involve them. Depicting how 'Society' reacts to such events, and behaves in their aftermath, can open up many new stories to explore.

Horror

Horror stories can find many uses for the Pontus and the disturbing results of its rising. The Pontus is most effectively used as a consequence to human behavior. Show the players that evil begets evil, and that their choices can have deadly ramifications. A feeling of horror can be rooted in fear, so make the players fear the Pontus. Once Pontus events are linked to the horrible things they do, player characters will start to get nervous about doing bad things, and fearful about sitting idly by as bad things happen. Nurture this fear slowly over the course of a story and you will build a wonderful foundation for horror.

REWARDS

Even when players are thrilled with every aspect of a plot and enjoying their characters, they will always be happy to receive something in return for their time and engagement with the game. Rewards are an important tool for the Narrator to control the pacing of character development, manage the difficulty of a game, and provide the players with some tangible benefit for the growth and activity of their characters. Use different types of rewards and vary their use over the course of a story; the rules and setting of *Clockwork: Dominion* offer multiple possibilities.

EXPERIENCE POINTS

The most common reward in the game is experience points. Players will use these to advance their characters' skills and abilities. Thus, the rate at which they are given out by the Narrator will determine the power levels the characters can achieve and how quickly they will achieve them. A Narrator can use any of the methods below, but rewards should average out to about two to four experience points per installment.

Installment Experience Rewards

Many Narrators will simply give a set reward to all players who participated in the installment, usually an average of two to three experience points. This allows characters to pick up the basics of a

new skill, advance a developed skill, or gain a new asset once every two or three installments. If you want player characters to advance quicker than this, simply raise the standard reward level.

Awarding experience points in this fashion should be done in addition to any experience points awarded by the rules for certain situations that came up during the game. For example, if a character received a permanent liability in gameplay for which the rules state she should receive five experience points, these five points are in addition to those given to everyone for the installment.

Individual Experience Awards

Some Narrators prefer to give individualized awards in lieu of a standard number of points given to everyone. As long as all participating players receive roughly equivalent experience awards over time, the Narrator may choose any method she wishes to award them, spotlighting certain characters and players at different points in the story. For each installment, Narrators should consider the following criteria and award accordingly:

- 1 experience point for each character that participates
- 1 experience for each character that makes progress toward a personal goal
- 1 point for each character who took significant risks to further their Pursuit or roleplayed their Affinities

- 1 experience point for each character who was convinced or persuaded of something during the course of a social conflict and accepted the outcome
- 1 experience point for the single character voted most valuable to the installment by the other players

Book Award Ceremonies

At the end of every book, all players are granted a single extra experience point for participating in the book. We also strongly recommend an experience award ceremony. If this option is chosen, the players and Narrator will vote to determine which single character best expressed each theme that was used throughout the book. Use all of the themes the book touched on, even if they were not the major themes you originally planned. If any theme seems irrelevant to your book, leave it out of the award ceremony. The character who is voted best in each theme receives one additional experience point. Ideas for how to judge each theme are below.

- **Steam:** the character most involved with discovering, creating, using, or learning about advanced science or technology.
- **Punk:** the character that most actively supported or threatened a social system or institution.
- **Victorian:** the character most involved in historical Victorian society: politics, romantic entanglements, fashion, etc.
- **Horror:** the character most involved in uncovering hidden knowledge, most impacted by Pontus events, chimera and/or aberrations, or surviving some form of personal horror.

Pacing Experience Rewards

This reward scale is designed for games that will run for dozens of installments, allowing the characters to mature over the course of a long series of books. If you are running a shorter story or wish to speed up advancement so characters can fight more powerful antagonists, you might increase the standard number of experience points awarded at the end of each installment and book. If you wish to run an epic story that will last for hundreds of installments over the course of many years, consider reducing the amount of experience points granted at the end of every installment.

The rules for spending experience points are given in *Chapter 5: Character Creation*.

WEALTH

Wealth rewards represent a temporary windfall allowing a character to make a certain number of purchases with a Cost that is higher than her *Means*. For example, if the characters caught a wanted criminal and turned them in for a reward, they may all be given a payment that would allow them to make a single purchase of Cost 2. For professionals and gentry, that may not mean much of anything, but it represents a significant benefit for a worker of *Means* 1. Even for characters who don't get much use from a particular wealth reward, compiling them may allow for a permanent increase in Means, which is a very significant benefit. Full details on using rewards to acquire new assets is discussed in the *Opportunity* section.

Temporary wealth can be of any value the Narrator wishes to give, but it is recommended that it be no more than two ranks higher than the party median, and never more than Cost 5. Rewards beyond this would be the period equivalent of winning a modern lottery jackpot, and could disrupt the story.

ALLIES AND ACCOUTREMENTS

Giving player characters new or unusual accoutrements is an excellent way to mark them as special within the setting, and to make sure that they are appropriately equipped to handle the demands of the story. Likewise, gaining the assistance of allies with specialized skills that the players lack can ensure that the party has appropriate traits for the tasks at hand without forcing players to develop skills that they don't want or won't need later in the story.

You control what special accoutrements or unique skill sets are introduced. Make sure they are balanced for their intended role in the story. Allowing the players to retrieve a powerful weapon from a defeated foe gives them a memento of their success and a unique tool; however, the weapon needn't have stats far better than other options, or use ammunition that the players can easily acquire. The benefit of this accoutrement is that the themes of the story are enhanced and new options for the players and Narrator open up. Will the authorities outlaw the weapon? Will the players study it in hopes of recreating the technology? Skill sets provided by NCs are likewise easy opportunities for story development. As the players and their characters get to know and build relationships with the NCs it creates ties to the game world, as well as other voices and viewpoints. And though it is not a technique to overuse, NCs can be a way for the Narrator to give the players information or introduce new leads in the story.

KNOWLEDGE

Giving the players and their characters access to additional information about the setting and the plot of the story enables them to make more informed choices, and increases their play possibilities. Special knowledge goes beyond the normal plot points and should give them an edge if they choose to exploit it. Finding out that a group of cultists intends to break into a university library to steal a manuscript that has a particular rite they desire, is a necessary plot element that allows the story to move forward. Rewarding clever play by giving the characters the opportunity to interrogate a cultist regarding the details of the theft lets them influence how the scenario will proceed. Perhaps they set an ambush, blackmail the cultist, or steal the manuscript before the cultists are able. Giving the players more agency increases their engagement, and can make the storytelling more collaborative.

Extraordinary successes, excellent roleplay, and clever or unusual approaches to problems are all good opportunities to give out special information. When preparing an installment, include pieces of information that are not necessary to progress the plot but which can dramatically change player options. Giving players the opportunity to ferret out this information is a great way to reward them for exploring your world.

AFFINITIES AND REPUTATIONS

Affinities and Reputations play an important role in Clockwork society. Rewarding a character with temporary bonuses to these traits can greatly improve their effectiveness in social conflict. Dramatic choices and consistent roleplaying qualifies a character to change her Affinity scores. Great deeds of renown or infamy merit new temporary ranks in a Reputation. These changes to Affinities and Reputations are given at the Narrator's discretion. Both create new development opportunities if the players decide to make these temporary changes permanent by spending experience points. They also inspire satisfaction and morale by showing players that their choices will mechanically impact their character. In highly social and intrigue-focused games, Reputations are important, so they make an excellent companion piece to experience rewards. The reactions of NCs to Reputations can also provide players with more roleplaying hooks to work with.

If a group is not engaging much with the social aspects of the game and the Narrator wishes to encourage this, changing Affinities and Reputations based on especially noteworthy roleplay may create interest among the players.

OPPORTUNITY

All the other rewards taken together allow the player characters to have unique opportunities in the game and grow over time. Aptitudes and skills can be advanced whenever a character has enough experience, but other traits such as *Class, Means,* potential, and some assets and liabilities are significant changes to her identity and abilities and should be supported by actions within the story. The Narrator may reward players with temporary changes to these traits, which can then be made permanent by spending experience points.

Granting a temporary asset is usually the only way that a player will have a chance to acquire that asset permanently. A character who marries above her station may gain a temporary boost to *Class* and/or *Means,* which she could then make permanent with experience. Liabilities such as an *Obsession* may be fought off through roleplaying, *Will* tests, and suffered consequences. In

such an instance, the Narrator may allow the character to buy off the *Obsession* liability. Character exploits may also be able to grant them an invitation to join an organization, or saving an NC could create an opportunity to gain a *Devoted Companion.* Using rewards like this ties directly into player actions, the story of her character, and reinforces that her actions in the world do matter.

INCREASED CHARACTER THREAT

Unlike the other options described above, this reward is reserved for the final climax of a series. After the player characters have each received at least 100 experience points, the Narrator may opt to elevate them to Threat 4. Just like antagonists of this Threat level, player characters who reach Threat 4 will increase their collective Conflict Assessment score and retain an additional initiative card in each conflict sequence (the standard rule is that players can only retain three initiative cards, since they are considered Threat 3).

If this option is used, it should come as an exciting surprise, not an expected right for the players. This might be awarded just before the grand finale, when the characters have become skilled and hardened individuals. This should make the players feel as though an important threshold has been crossed. Allowing them to enjoy their newfound capability for a book or so prior to the finale of the story gives you the opportunity to gauge their effectiveness and scale up the difficulty of the finale appropriately. Remember that the increase in Threat will significantly increase the characters' Conflict Assessment scores, and should allow them to face powerful foes for a suitably epic close to a long series.

Given the large mechanical impact of this reward if used it will change the tone of the game, making the players more confident and aggressive. It works best with pulp heroic stories, and shows the characters are clearly among the best in the world at what they do. Horror stories often use a sense of helplessness to good effect, but an increase in player Threat can represent the characters finally being able to stand up and face the terror or give them a fighting chance against foes that would otherwise be impossible for them to deal with.

Constable Rooker was in a foul mood. He hadn't been happy in weeks, not since too many complaints were made about graft on his last beat and he'd been transferred to the East End. He was especially surly tonight as he finally put his finger on what he hated most about the East End: the smell. Too many people, not enough room. The dockworkers, ragmen, and street hawkers were stacked atop each other like cordwood, and the side streets and alleys hosted those too poor for shelter. Everywhere was ankle-deep muck in the street from night soil and all the damn horses that no one cleaned up after. Even in a tavern, the smell of it came in on people's boots. It curled in Rooker's nostrils and soured the taste of the free beer he was drinking at the Doe.

Rooker drained the last of his mug and banged it down on the bartop. "It's packed in here like rats tonight Falwell."

His partner looked at him askance before replying. "Hardly surprising. Folk are upset, worried. Last night was the fifth time in as many days that people saw that devil dog, but no sign of progress on tracking it down. And after that poor girl going missing, well, they think the streets ain't safe. Weren't you paying no attention earlier?"

The sergeant had gone on about the same thing before they watch began, nagging them to look out for strange dogs and any sign of that girl they were supposed to be looking for. As far as Rooker was concerned, when a teenaged girl goes missing in the East End it means either she has enough sense to try to run away for anywhere else, or that she was working in an alley or a flash house somewhere and something went sour. She'd either come crying back home in a few days or some mudlark would find her body somewhere along the river. Neither process would be sped along by him trudging about through the stinking streets asking after her, whatever her name was.

Well, if he was supposed to be looking for a girl, he was going to find one. Might be that a quick throw with one of the ladies by Lower Chapman would put him in a better mood.

Leaving the Doe, Rooker strode through the narrow streets quickly, mainly to make Falwell miserable. The man was a ball of suet, shapeless and fatty. Falwell's puppy-like concern for the East Enders irked Rooker to no end, and so he visited what petty cruelties he could on the man. "Keep up now Falwell, we're on the hunt."

"If you'd slow down a little…we should…be looking for….anything unusual. The streets… getting narrow. Oughtta be careful."

Barely a fast walk and the man was wheezing like a bellows. Shameful.

"A fair point Falwell. Why don't you stand here at the corner to catch your breath and keep a look out. Since we're at Lower Chapman I think I should check to make sure that all the girls around are alright, and ask them if they've seen anything. It should only take ten, fifteen minutes."

Leaving his winded partner behind, Rooker headed off, peering into the alleys and side streets that cut away into the darkness. He flashed his electric torch down each, trying to see if anyone was out working, but saw no one. Frustrated, he was just about to head back when the beam of light swept over the hunched form of the hellhound slinking along a wall towards him. As soon as it was revealed the beast let loose a chilling howl and burst into motion, and Rooker broke into a run back the way he came.

"Falwell! Falwell!"

As he raced forward his partner hove into view. "What on earth was that noise? What's happening?"

Rooker didn't say a word and raced past him. Falwell stopped and turned after Rooker, never seeing the hellhound. Just as he was about to call after his partner, the beast leapt from the shadows onto his back, knocking him to the ground. As the hellhound wrestled against the constable, Falwell managed a few moments of terrified screams before they were cut short. For a moment, the instincts of the dog it once was urged the hellhound to eat what it could from its prize, but the bloodlust instilled by the warping energies of the Pontus won out, and drove it after more prey. After tearing off a mouthful of fatty flesh and gulping it down the hellhound bayed, and was back on the trail of more athletic prey.

Rooker slowed his mad dash and rested against a wall to catch his breath. Falwell's screams still echoed in his ears, but, he thought, at least the fool finally did something useful. Hopefully it would take even that monstrosity a while to eat such a big man. Rooker began collecting his thoughts and formulating the lies he would tell the watch sergeant when he heard the howl again. He began to walk faster, then he began to run. Its guttural barks were quickly growing louder, and Rooker wondered how fast a thing like that could move, and how well it could keep his scent in the stench and squalor of the East End. Although Rooker's grip on rationality was slipping, he knew that he was dead if he stayed in the tight alleys and side streets. He needed to make it to one of the main streets where he might find others to help him confront the beast, or at least provide enough distraction for him to escape.

Rooker turned one last dark corner and ran free of the maze of back alleys and dead ends onto the wide thoroughfare. Most of the shops were closed, and even the cramped apartments above them had their windows shut against the chilly night air, but here and there people were still visible on the street. For a moment relief fluttered through him as he saw a few carters loading goods into a shop a few doors down. He fumbled for his whistle and blew to get their attention. As they turned he slowed to a stop and waved them over to him. "You men, I've got the bloody hellhound cornered in this alley, come help!" One of them started forward, but the other clapped him on the shoulder and said something Rooker couldn't hear, then both men quickly began drawing the loading door shut to close themselves inside. Rooker raced towards them shouting, but it was too late. The door rumbled closed. He pounded on it, to no avail. "Help me, you spineless, feckless cowards! For God's sake let me in!" The only answer was another otherworldly howl, getting perilously close.

He looked about, but the few others on the street had vanished into nearby doorways. He was alone.

"Blast you all, you worthless guttersnipes! Bloody animals, to turn on a man like this!" Rather than yell for the assistance that he knew in his heart would never come, Rooker began running again. He needed shelter, or at least an open door he could force his way through. With the hellhound closing on him—God, already on the street!—he began venting his hatred of the area's negligent meat packers, slovenly factory workers, and miserable beggars who would neither open their doors nor offer themselves as a distracting second-course for the creature.

Approaching another intersection, Rooker knew he had to make a choice, quickly. He couldn't continue down Cable Street. It offered no cover or shelter for several blocks. If he stayed his course he had no hope of outrunning the hellhound.

To the right he'd only find himself in the warrens of the tenement houses again, and was just as likely to find a dead end as an escape route.

To the left? A glimmer of hope: the fountain in Prince's Square. He could, perhaps, scale the large structure and stay out of the reach of the beast until it tired and left, or at least wait until a passer-by provided an easier meal and a chance for escape.

Left it was. Rooker made a mad dash toward his last hope of survival. The street opening into the square was almost in sight. Hope surged and Rooker knew he would indeed survive this night. He swore to himself that he would find the bastards who denied him sanctuary and make them regret it. He heard the hound round the corner a few seconds behind him, barking. Almost on his heels, but not close enough—the fountain was only a few strides away.

Rooker never saw the clod of dirt that was thrown at him from the shadows, he only felt its impact as it crashed into his temple, causing him to stumble.

It was all the advantage the hellhound needed to be upon him.

Over the snarls of the beast and his own screams Constable Rooker heard a voice call out from the shadows, "That's for Matilda, you bastard!." As the hellhound tore his windpipe from its fleshy sheath his last thought before darkness claimed him was "Who the bloody hell is Matilda?"

ALLIES & ANTAGONISTS

The greatest heroes take their measure, in part, from both the quality of their friends and the opposition of their foes. Thus, memorable Narrator characters (NCs) are a critical part of every good story. Suggestions and ideas for how to narratively portray NCs as allies and antagonists was covered in detail in *Chapter 8: Narrating the Chapter*. This chapter details the mechanics of using Narrator characters within the game, how to assess their power levels when compared to PCs, and how to create them using a streamlined system that is much faster than the comprehensive player character creation system detailed in *Chapter 5: Character Creation*. Lastly, a series of templates and ready-to-run antagonists are also provided.

ANATOMY OF A NARRATOR CHARACTER

While Narrator characters use the same rules as every other character in the game, they will often be recorded on a Narrator sheet rather than a character sheet. This truncated record sheet has simplified and abstracted statistics, allowing NCs to be referenced and used with ease.

Threat

Threat is an abstraction that broadly measures how powerful a character is. The higher its Threat, the more impact an entity is expected to have on any given situation. The average player character is considered to have Threat 3, but Narrator characters can be anywhere from Threat 1 to Threat 10, or even higher.

When creating Narrator characters, a Threat score is the first thing to be chosen. It will determine the number of ranks and character elements an NC receives at all stages of its creation. In play, it will determine the number of initiative cards an NC is dealt in conflict, in addition to several other effects (see *Allies and Antagonists in the Initiative Sequence*, p. 76).

Conflict Assessment (CA)

A character's Threat, skills, and other important traits are factored together in order to assess how effective she is likely to be in a given type of conflict. These numbers are plugged into the equations provided (p. 295) to yield a character's Conflict Assessment score. This CA score can be used alone, or the CAs of several characters can be added together to determine the overall strength of one side of a conflict. The CAs of two sides can be compared to show how challenging one side of a conflict will be for the other side. This number is imperative for balancing conflict encounters and making sure that the PCs are never in over their heads.

Name _____

~ Aptitudes ~

Grace [1] [2] [3] [4] [5]
Vigor [1] [2] [3] [4] [5]
Reason [1] [2] [3] [4] [5]
Focus [1] [2] [3] [4] [5]
Presence [1] [2] [3] [4] [5]
Will [1] [2] [3] [4] [5]

~ Potential ~

Purpose ○ [1] [2] [3] [4] [5]
Ether ○ [1] [2] [3] [4] [5]
Corruption [1] [2] [3] [4] [5]

~ Skills & Traits ~

Physical [1] [2] [3] [4] [5]
Mental [1] [2] [3] [4] [5]
Social [1] [2] [3] [4] [5]
_____ [1] [2] [3] [4] [5]
_____ [1] [2] [3] [4] [5]
_____ [1] [2] [3] [4] [5]
_____ [1] [2] [3] [4] [5]
_____ [1] [2] [3] [4] [5]
_____ [1] [2] [3] [4] [5]
_____ [1] [2] [3] [4] [5]

Threat
Social CA
Physical CA
Wounds
Penalty

~ Guard ~

1/2 **Focus** +1 for Weapon

○ ○ ○ ○

~ Defenses ~

— Physical — — Social —

Defense *Armor* *Defense* *Armor*

~ Disposition ~

Hostile Guarded Indifferent Agreeable Favorable
(H) (G) (I) (A) (F)

~ Weapon, Damage, Reach, Condition ~

~ Abilities & Notes ~

UNIVERSAL SKILLS

Universal Skill	Standard Skills Covered
Physical	*Artisan*, Athletics, Burglary, Fencing, Firearms, Fisticuffs, Melee, Riding, Stealth, Survival**
Mental	*Academics, Artisan*, Bureaucracy*, Engineering, Investigation, Medicine, Mysteries, Science, Survival*, Tactics, Vocation*
Social	*Bureaucracy*, Command, Composure, Guile, Intuition, Parley, Refinement, Streetwise, Temptation*

Aptitudes and Skills

Aptitudes and skills work exactly as they do in character creation, but to keep antagonists easy to use, ranks are not recorded for every individual skill. Instead, universal skills are an abstraction that provide their rank value for every skill in an area of endeavor—physical, mental, or social. Antagonists are presented with a few universal skills that cover their general capabilities, and are only assigned ranks in individual skills that are developed beyond the level of their universal skills. The breakdown of which specific skills each universal skill covers is shown in the *Universal Skills* table, above.

Those skills marked with an asterisk (*) appear in multiple lists; Narrators should use their judgment as to whether or not they would be appropriate for the Antagonist. If an Antagonist has universal skills for both categories that cover a given skill, the Narrator should use the ranks from whichever grouping seems most applicable. Attempts to use the skill actively in the world should be based off the physical value, attempts that require thought and planning or depend on specialized knowledge should use the mental value, and attempts to convince or persuade should use the social value.

If an Antagonist has ranks in both a universal skill and an individual skill that would cover the same task, use the highest rank. This is most common with skills directly used in conflict. In the antagonist entries listed at the end of this chapter, the aptitude names are truncated to use only their first letter (i.e. *Grace* is listed as G; *Vigor* as V; etc.).

Potential

Most Narrator characters have a very limited pool of potential. NC potential ranks are meant to show how much *Purpose* and *Ether* they have available at a given time, not their full unspent potential. Refresh this amount for each installment, but NCs do not otherwise regain *Purpose* and *Ether* through roleplaying like player characters. NCs spend *Purpose* and *Ether* exactly like player characters.

Narrator characters that have been touched by the Pontus or engaged in acts of villainy will also possess *Corruption*, which functions the same as it does for player characters.

Conflict Information

Narrator characters have and use Guard, physical and social Defenses, Armor, Disposition, and attacks just as player characters do, and they follow the same rules for conflict. However, NCs may have special modifiers to their derived conflict information as a result of assets or liabilities not available to player characters.

Narrator Character Assets and Liabilities

Assets and liabilities function similarly to those for player characters, but are chosen from a different list. Full details and lists begin on p. 300.

Affinities and Reputations

Since the vast majority of antagonists will only appear briefly in the the course of a series, their cares, worries, and motivations usually do not need to be spelled out in as much detail as those of player characters. For games that focus more on social conflict and intrigues, however, antagonists making even brief appearances might need to have those aspects defined. Any antagonist may be given ranks in Affinities and Reputations equal to their Threat. For example a Threat 3 antagonist would have three ranks to spend on Affinities, and three on Reputations.

Class, Means, & Accoutrements

For NCs who take part in Clockwork society, the Narrator can set their *Class* and *Means* as needed for the story. A general guideline is that the *Class* and *Means* are typically no higher than the NC's Threat +1. Animals, aberrations, chimera, and inhuman feyfolk generally do not have *Class* or *Means*. They are unable to use accoutrements unless they have an anatomy that allows them to do so, and Reason 1 or higher. Intelligent supernatural entities such as angels, demons, or shades will be familiar with how to use accoutrements and may do so as circumstances warrant, but will never have *Class* or *Means*. The only ways such beings have access to those traits is through possession or indirectly through their mortal servitors. Accoutrements are given to NCs for free, but if an accoutrement grants *Armor* or a *Penetrating Attack* the NC must have the corresponding asset.

CONFLICT ASSESSMENT

Conflict Assessment is used by the Narrator to gauge the effectiveness of a character in a conflict and it is a critical tool to help balance encounters. Conflict Assessments can be calculated for both player characters and Narrator characters, and they are calculated differently for physical and social conflict. Assess a character by combining a few key traits and multiplying the total by her Threat:

Physical Conflict Assessment = (Grace + Vigor + best physical conflict skill + Guard + modifiers) x Threat

Social Conflict Assessment = (Presence + Will + best social conflict skill + modifiers) x Threat

The traits needed for these equations are taken directly from the character sheet. The "modifiers" are listed on the *Conflict Assessment Modifiers* table and are used to take into consideration special abilities and powerful effects that characters might use in a conflict. Add all traits and modifiers that apply to the calculation and multiply the total of all traits and modifiers by the entity's Threat. For NCs, use their listed Threat as the multiplier. For beginning player characters, use Threat 3. If any character is Wounded or *Fatigued* before the conflict, reduce their Threat by one for each initiative card lost due to these effects.

The average physical Conflict Assessment score for a starting player character is 30. The average social Conflict Assessment score for a starting player character is 20. Narrator characters can vary widely.

CHALLENGE LEVELS FOR ENCOUNTERS

It is important for the Narrator to provide encounters that are appropriately challenging to the player characters. To do this, start by comparing the total Conflict Assessment of all antagonists against the total Conflict Assessment of the player characters. The difference between these numbers will show how challenging the encounter will be, and can be compared using the *Encounter Challenge Levels* table.

For example, the player characters make up a hunting party of three adventurers: William, with a physical Conflict Assessment of 36; Harold, 36; and John, 33. The player characters have a total physical Conflict Assessment of 105. They come across two hunting cats (p. 309), each with a physical Conflict Assessment of 52, for a total of 104. The total antagonist CA of 104 is just below the party's total CA of 105. The *Encounter Challenge Levels* table classifies this as a standard encounter.

This challenge level will be increased if an antagonist has a particularly high CA compared to the player characters. This ensures opponents with stronger skill combinations and powerful attacks do not overwhelm the player characters. If any single antagonist has a higher CA than 1½ times the party's average CA, the encounter's challenge level is increased by one step. If any single antagonist has a CA higher than twice the party's average CA, the challenge level will increase by two steps. In the above example, the player character's average CA is 35 and the antagonist's average CA is 52. 52 is just below 1½ times the player average (which would be 53). The *Encounter Challenge Levels* table indicates this is not enough of a discrepancy to necessitate changing the challenge level of the encounter.

Periodically, perhaps every three or four sessions, the Narrator should recalculate the Conflict Assessment of the player characters, as their scores will change over time. Having current and accurate information makes it much easier to design balanced and varied encounters that are interesting and appropriately challenging for the player characters. This may also be done during an installment if the PC's are significantly Wounded or lose access to penetrating attacks, as this will greatly change their Conflict Assessment.

CONFLICT ASSESSMENT MODIFIERS

+1	The character has an attack, mastery, or transcendent power that bypasses normal Guard/Disposition, or prevents an outcome that can be used a single time in the conflict.
+1	The character uses an area of effect physical attack (physical Conflict Assessment only).
+1	The character has the *Strong Guard* or *Strong Morale* asset (physical Conflict Assessment only).
+1	The character has the *Strong Defense* asset or Armor usable in the type of conflict being assessed.
+2	The character has the *Materialize* or *Psychokinetic* asset (physical Conflict Assessment only).
+2	The character has an attack, mastery, or transcendent power that bypasses normal Guard/Disposition, or prevents an outcome that can be used more than once in the conflict.
-1	The character has the *Weak Guard* or *Weak Morale* liability (physical Conflict Assessment only).
-1	The character has the *Weak Defense* liability for the type of conflict being assessed.
-X	Apply the total negative modifier of any Wound Penalties the character is suffering before conflict begins.

FIREARMS IN CONFLICT

"One man with a gun can control one hundred without one."
—Lenin

The presence and number of firearms (or any other penetrating attack) will have a major impact on the way physical conflicts play out, as the side with the most guns can potentially dominate the encounter. If the characters have this advantage, they might blast their way through encounters too easily. If antagonists have too much firepower, there is a serious risk of killing player characters or relegating them to weeks of bed-ridden recovery. By adjusting the setup of encounters where player characters and/or the NCs have multiple penetrating attacks, they can still be tense, memorable affairs without overwhelming one side. Some things to consider:

- Guns are not commonly carried inside the borders of Great Britain. Among the poorer classes, guns are rare because gun licenses are prohibitively expensive and penalties for gun crimes and unlicensed use are severe (see the *Gun Laws and Licenses* sidebar, p. 196). Also, while there are no legal restrictions against carrying guns in polite society, it is certainly a social faux pas if noticed. Narrators and players should be realistic about when guns would actually be carried.

- Building an encounter with several weaker antagonists alongside one or more stronger enemies creates plenty of targets for player characters to shoot. Characters can make meaningful contributions and enjoy the impact of their weapons by taking out weak enemies quickly. These weaker enemies can provide a distraction and absorb fire while the stronger ones have time to be effective.

- Setting encounters in close quarters or areas with plenty of cover helps negate the impact of firearms. Needing additional maneuvers to *Aim* will slow down shooters. Also, shooters with opponents within their zone of control cannot take maneuvers to *Aim*, and suffer a -2 penalty on their *Firearms* test. Fast enemies or large numbers of them can overrun shooters and mitigate their advantage.

- Seizing the initiative can allow targets to quickly dive for cover, or allow combatants to enter a zone of control to interfere with a foe's ability to *Aim*.

ENCOUNTER CHALLENGE LEVELS

Challenge	Antagonists Total CA	Narrative Impact
Harmless	½ PC total	The encounter will be little more than a brief hindrance for the player characters.
Easy	¾ PC total	The antagonists present some risk, but unless the players are unlucky or sloppy there is little chance that the characters will suffer Wounds or social outcomes.
Standard	PC total	There is a significant chance the characters will suffer Wounds or social outcomes. The characters will likely need to use potential and special equipment to complete the encounter without suffering harm.
Taxing	1½ x PC total	The characters will need all their skill and a little luck to be victorious. It is almost certain that characters will suffer Wounds or social outcomes. These scenarios may render a character ineffective to continue in the story. Save taxing encounters for the climactic finale of a chapter or story.
Deadly	2 x PC total or higher	Serious social manipulation and character death are a distinct possibility. Make sure characters have the opportunity to flee, negotiate, or be taken captive rather than be killed.
+1 step	One antagonist's CA is more than 1½ x the PC average	
+2 steps	One antagonist's CA is more than 2 x the PC average	

SAMPLE CONFLICT ASSESSMENT

Kiera is preparing a series for new players, and wants to have the first session end with a fight between the player characters and a pack of hellhound aberrations that were spawned by a Pontus event. She has four players, so she starts off running a Conflict Assessment on their characters to get a sense of what they can handle.

She begins with the best physical combatant in the group, Jacob Miller, an ex-soldier. Checking his sheet she records his *Grace, Vigor*, best conflict skill (*Melee* in this case), and default Guard. So far his assessment is:

(*Grace* 3 + *Vigor* 4 + *Melee* 3 + Guard 1)

but now she needs to check for any modifiers for special abilities, accoutrements, and unusual circumstances. He has a 6-shot revolver, which is a firearm that ignores Guard and can be used more than once in a fight, so that's a +2 modifier, and his reinforced greatcoat provides physical armor, so that's an additional +1 modifier. All together he has a +3 modifier for a base score of:

(*Grace* 3 + *Vigor* 4 + *Melee* 3 + Guard 1 + modifiers 3) = 14

Kiera now multiplies that times his Threat 3 (for being a player character) and comes to a final physical assessment of:

14 x 3 = 42!

Jacob Miller is a very dangerous physical combatant.

Even though the fight is physical, Kiera also decides to run a social Conflict Assessment so she has it on hand when planning social conflicts for later scenes. Jacob is built to be a great physical character, but his social capabilities are weaker. Looking at his sheet for *Presence, Will,* and his best social conflict skill he has:

(Presence 2 + Will 2 + Command 2)

Jacob has no special abilities or assets that give him any modifiers, so his final assessment is:

(Presence 2 + Will 2 + Command 2 + no modifiers) x Threat 3 = 18

Jacob will have to watch out if he's around anyone persuasive, lest he be wrapped around their finger.

Kiera completes Conflict Assessments for the three other player characters, and comes up with the following for the entire party:

Jacob Miller:	Physical 42, Social 18
Iphigenia Bartlett:	Physical 33, Social 24
Taylor Spratt:	Physical 24, Social 30
Victoria Beauchamp:	Physical 21, Social 27
Party Total:	Physical 120, Social 99

Since Kiera is working with new players she doesn't want to go too hard on them for the first session, and decides to keep it a standard encounter. This means she'll need to keep the physical conflict assessment score for her custom hellhounds close to 40 each, so she stays very close to the party total and doesn't exceed 1 ½ times their average of 30. She goes through the custom NC creation system and comes up with the following final stats and physical assessment for her hellhounds:

(*Grace* 4 + *Vigor* 3 + *Melee* 3 + Guard 1 + 1 for Armor) x Threat 3 = 36 each

Using 3 hellhounds creates a total CA score of 108, which keeps the pack in a standard encounter range, so Kiera is confident that the characters will face some risk but can handle it.

CREATING NARRATOR CHARACTERS

The following section presents a quick and comprehensive system that can build everything from minor annoyances like London street urchins to potentially world-changing entities such as the Fallen or Pontus-spawned monstrosities. The unifying standard that runs throughout Narrator character design is Threat. The more ranks in Threat a character possesses, the bigger the impact it will have on the game. Threat determines how many turns the Narrator character will have in conflict, its number of trait ranks, its number and maximum value of skills, and any special assets.

Many ready-to-run NCs are available at the end of this chapter as well as in *Idle Hands* and other prewritten modules. It is strongly recommended that all Narrators have some actual play experience

with the *Clockwork: Dominion* rule set before creating their own NCs. The Narrator character creation system promotes good NC design, but the insight gained from running even a few sequences of conflict will help any Narrator identify and achieve the type of performance they want from any NC they build.

When creating a Narrator character, first choose a creature type and a Threat rank. The creature type will provide a template that includes all the basic attributes a Narrator character of that type will have. The Threat rank of the character will determine how many extra trait ranks and abilities can be added to this template. A basic template is considered to be a Threat 0 character of that creature type. Additional ranks of Threat will add to this value.

All creatures are blessed and cursed by their current role in the Clockwork. The creature type chosen for a Narrator character grants the aptitudes, universal skills, assets, and liabilities as listed in the *Creature Type Templates* table. All listed bonuses are recorded prior to any bonuses granted by the assigned rank of Threat. The assets and liabilities listed do not count towards the total allowed during NC creation, but do count toward any restrictions on being able to take each asset or liability more than once, unless specifically stated otherwise.

After selecting a creature type template and recording its bonuses, assets, and liabilities, use the following steps to complete the character. Each rank of Threat will grant additional trait ranks and abilities.

- **STEP 1:** For each rank of Threat, gain: 1 aptitude rank, 1 universal skill rank, 3 skill ranks, 1 NC asset.
  - Aptitude ranks can be assigned freely, and may exceed five.
  - Universal skill ranks in a category cannot exceed the NC's Threat.
  - Skill ranks cannot exceed the NC's Threat unless they take the *Exceptional Skill* asset, but are not otherwise limited to an upper maximum.
- **STEP 2:** Assign a total number of ranks in *Purpose* and *Ether* equal to ½ Threat, rounded down.
- **STEP 3:** Optionally, NCs may be assigned ranks of Affinities and/or Reputations equal to their Threat.
- **STEP 4:** All NCs have any number of physical attacks with the same starting stats:
  - Physical attack: *Grace* + skill, Potency 1, Reach: *Touch*
  - Additional effects may be added to an attack through the use of accoutrements or through the use of *Special Attack* assets (p. 303).

BALANCING APTITUDES AND SKILLS

It may be tempting to design antagonists that are heavily skewed towards being powerhouses in physical conflict and weak in social, or vice versa. If an antagonist is too physically-focused, though, it can often be easily overcome by players attacking its Morale, or by dropping its Guard using feints. Similarly, foes that have strong social capabilities shouldn't be physically helpless, even if they primarily depend on social mores or legal ramifications to keep themselves safe.

Managing the distribution of aptitude and skill ranks so there are no major weaknesses in physical or social defense scores is a good standard for antagonists of any Threat, but this becomes especially important when designing those with Threat 4 or higher. There are few things more disappointing for a Narrator than having a major antagonist too easily overcome.

- **STEP 5:** All NCs have any number of social attacks with the same stats:
  - Social attack: *Presence* + skill, Potency 1, Reach: *Audible, Social*
  - Additional effects may be added to a social attack through the use of *Special Attack* assets or transcendent powers.

CREATURE TYPE TEMPLATES

Type	Aptitudes	Skills	Assets	Liabilities
Animals				
Aberrations	Grace 2, Vigor 2, Reason 1, Focus 2, Presence 1, Will 2	Physical 1, Mental 0, Social 0	*Special Attack* (Condition, Potent) *Special:* Immune to Pontus effects	*Corrupt, Fixed Potential: Ether*
Animals	Grace 2, Vigor 1, Reason 1, Focus 2, Presence 2, Will 2	Physical 1, Mental 0, Social 0	*Special Attack* (Condition, Potent, Quick), Strong Guard	*Potential Penalty, Skill Penalty*
Automata				
Automata	Grace 1, Vigor 3, Reason 0, Focus 2, Presence 1, Will 2	Physical 1, Mental 0, Social 0	Armor, Mindless, *Special Attack* (Potent)	*Potential Penalty*

CREATURE TYPE TEMPLATES

Type	Aptitudes	Skills	Assets	Liabilities
Celestials				
Angels	Grace 0, Vigor 0, Reason 2, Focus 3, Presence 4, Will 4	Physical 0, Mental 2, Social 3, *Command* 5, *Composure* 5, *Mysteries* 5	*Fount of potential:* Purpose, Limitless Potential, Terrifying Presence *Special:* Minimum Threat of 11, Angelic Immortality	*Fixed Potential:* Purpose, Skill Penalty x2, Unskilled
Demons	Grace 0, Vigor 0, Reason 1, Focus 1, Presence 3, Will 3	Physical 0, Mental 0, Social 1	*Incorporeal, Possession, Potential* (+1 Ether), *Special Attack* (Potent)	*Corrupt, Fixed Potential:* Ether, *Repelled:* Crosses
Fallen	Grace 0, Vigor 0, Reason 2, Focus 3, Presence 4, Will 4	Physical 0, Mental 2, Social 3, *Composure* 5, *Mysteries* 5, *Temptation* 5	*Fount of potential:* Ether, Limitless Potential, *Magical Word* (one verb or two nouns), *Special Attack* (Condition, Potent x2), Terrifying Presence *Special:* Minimum Threat of 11, Angelic Immortality	*Corrupt, Fixed Potential:* Ether, *Repelled:* Enochian sigil of their original name, *Unskilled*
Nephilim	Grace 1, Vigor 1, Reason 2, Focus 3, Presence 2, Will 1	Physical 0, Mental 1, Social 0	*Special:* Angelic Immortality, Fluid Mien, Knowledge in the Flesh	Bane (rank 1) *Special:* -2 Esteem if known to be a naphil
Chimera				
Chimera	Grace 2, Vigor 1, Reason 1, Focus 2, Presence 2, Will 2	Physical 0, Mental 0, Social 0	*Potential* (+1 Ether), *Special Attack* (Condition, Potent, Reach) *Special:* Immune to Pontus effects	*Corrupt, Fixed Potential:* Ether, *Unskilled*
Fey				
Feyfolk	Grace 1, Vigor 1, Reason 2, Focus 2, Presence 2, Will 2	Physical 1, Mental 0, Social 0	*Glamour, Potential* (+1 Ether), *Special Attack* (Potent)	Bane (rank 1), *Special:* Ether must be higher than *Purpose*
Nature Spirits	Grace 0, Vigor 0, Reason 1, Focus 1, Presence 3, Will 2	Physical 0 Mental 0 Social 1	*Glamour x2, Incorporeal, Potential* (+1 Ether)	Aptitude Penalty, Tethered
Wyldlings	Grace 1, Vigor 1, Reason 1, Focus 2, Presence 4, Will 1	Physical 0 Mental 0 Social 1	*Glamour x2, Limitless Potential, Potential* (+2 Ether)	Aptitude Penalty, *Fixed Potential:* Ether, *Unskilled*
Mortals				
Beastfolk	Grace 1, Vigor 2, Reason 2, Focus 2, Presence 2, Will 2	Physical 1 Mental 0 Social 0	*Augmentation x2*	Vulnerable, *Special:* -1 Esteem if known to be a beastman
Changelings	Grace 1, Vigor 1, Reason 2, Focus 2, Presence 3, Will 1	Physical 0 Mental 0 Social 1	*Glamour, Potential* (+1 Ether)	None
PureBloods	Grace 1, Vigor 1, Reason 2, Focus 2, Presence 2, Will 2	Physical 0 Mental 0 Social 1	*Skill Bonus, Potential* (+1 Purpose)	None
Souls				
Shades	Grace 0, Vigor 0, Reason 2, Focus 2, Presence 2, Will 2	Physical 0 Mental 0 Social 1	*Incorporeal, Special Attack* (Condition, Social Attack)	Tethered

NARRATOR CHARACTER ASSETS

Narrator characters can display many unusual abilities or terrifying attacks, and so have a special list of NC assets. Many of these assets are directly related to conflict, as that is where an NC's capabilities matter most in a game. Unless otherwise specified in the description, each asset can only be taken once. Some powerful options count as more than one asset choice. Additional assets beyond those provided by creature type and Threat can be gained by taking liabilities. A number of entries reference various conditions, Wounds, Wound Penalties and other particulars of conflict. Conditions are covered beginning on p. 96, Wounds and Wound Penalties on p. 84, and Conflict on p. 73.

When building an antagonist, make sure she has all the assets she needs to present a viable challenge to the players. A dangerous social foe may be terrifying when she has someone cornered, but if she has no means of maintaining engagement (such as an attack with an *Entrapped* condition), players will simply leave the conversation. Likewise, a dangerous physical combatant can be thwarted by an opponent shooting to kill from a distant location. The foe would be more effective if she could close that distance by using the *Extra Move* asset. A lack of proper assets can render an antagonist feeble, while the right assets can create opportunities to play to the antagonist's strengths. Think through how the antagonist should behave in conflict and how the PCs are likely to respond. Make sure your antagonists have the right assets to be notable threats to your protagonists.

ALCHEMICAL REACTION

The NC knows an alchemical reaction for which she meets the minimum skill requirements (see *Alchemy*, p. 221). This asset may be taken more than once. For the purposes of using alchemy, the NC is considered to have any necessary alchemical chalks to perform any reactions that come up in gameplay. The Narrator can always decide to expand or limit the number and rank of chalks available as she sees fit, but should generally provide at least a number of chalks of a rank equal to the NCs Threat: so a Threat four NC would have four chalks of rank four, etc.

ALTERNATE FORM

The NC can shapeshift into an alternate physical form. Create both the character's primary form and the *Alternate Forms* as separate and complete Narrator characters, each with the *Alternate Form* asset. The character must spend an action to switch between forms. *Alternate Forms* have no access to any of the accoutrements or attacks of the primary form. Each form can have a different allocation of aptitudes, skills, and universal skills, as well as make separate choices for assets and liabilities that only apply to that form. However, the *Potential* asset and *Corrupt* liability must be the same for every form. Wounds are shared across all forms, but Wound Penalties may vary if one form has the *Painless* asset and others do not. This asset may be taken once to create antagonists

such as werewolves. This asset may be taken more than once to create even more bizarre skinchangers.

APTITUDE BONUS

Gain one additional aptitude rank. This asset may be taken more than once.

AQUATIC

The NC can breathe normally underwater, makes passive *Athletics* tests for swimming and underwater movement, and does not suffer any penalties to *Focus + Composure* tests to sense her surroundings while underwater.

ARMOR

Increase the physical or social Armor of the NC by 1. This is an inherent quality of the NC or a worn accoutrement. Armor values from multiple sources do not stack: a NC's Armor rating will always be the highest single value from all available sources. This asset may be taken more than once.

AUGMENTATION

The NC gains the benefits of one augmentation (see the *Beastfolk* bloodline description, p. 112). This asset may be taken more than once.

BURROWING

The NC is able to tunnel through sand, earth, and rocky soil with ease, and can create tunnels through solid rock if given enough time. By taking a maneuver to begin digging, she may move through most ground at her normal movement speed. Returning to the surface requires another maneuver. While so moving, she burrows quickly through the ground, does not leave behind any stable tunnels, and cannot be followed by non-*Burrowing* characters. While underground, she cannot physically attack or be attacked.

Burrowing characters can only move through solid rock with great time and effort. For each hour the NC spends digging through rock it can clear a five foot section of rock as a stable tunnel.

CHARISM

The NC gains a charism for which she meets the minimum skill requirements (see *Charisms*, p. 226). This asset may be taken more than once.

DURABLE

The NC is remarkably tough; she can reliably survive Wounds without medical treatment and automatically stabilizes after being Wounded. This is usually found only on very large, resilient natural animals, but occurs with distressing regularity in Pontus-touched beasts and chimera.

EXCEPTIONAL SKILL

Choose a skill already at a rank equal to the NC's Threat and increase its rank by one.

EXCEPTIONAL TEAMWORK

If there are two or more NCs with this asset in the same zone of control and they both engage the same target, that target automatically suffers from the *Overwhelmed* temporary condition as long as the NCs remain engaged.

EXTRA MANEUVER

Through extraordinary manual dexterity, having multiple limbs, or some other exotic circumstance, the NC gains the ability to trade one move for a maneuver as part of her turn. This means that normally she can take up to two maneuvers if she foregoes her move, and even when she is afflicted with a Wound or is reacting she can still take a maneuver by exchanging her move.

EXTRA MOVE

This ability costs two assets. The NC can cover great distances quickly, and always has an additional move action as part of her turn. Even if this is combined with *Extra Maneuver*, it does not allow an NC to trade more than one move for a maneuver in a single turn.

FLIGHT

The NC is capable of flight at her normal movement speed, either naturally or through the use of an accoutrement. During her moves she may fly, ignoring terrain, and may choose to stay aloft between moves.

FOUNT OF POTENTIAL

This ability costs three assets, and is only available to NCs with Threat 6+. Choose *Purpose* or *Ether* when taking this asset: the NC regains one point of the chosen type of potential at the beginning of each sequence.

GLAMOUR

The NC possesses a glamour for which she meets the minimum skill requirements. This asset may be taken more than once.

IMPLACABLE

The NC will never flee or surrender from losing Morale. She may retreat voluntarily, and may be convinced or persuaded normally in social conflicts unrelated to Morale.

INCORPOREAL

The NC has no physical form: her *Vigor* and *Grace* is always 0, she can neither inflict nor receive physical damage or Wounds. *Incorporeal* NCs can move through solid matter without effort. They may also augment this ability by taking the *Materialize*, *Possession*, or *Psychokinetic* assets.

KEEN

When drawing initiative cards at the beginning of a sequence draw one additional card for each NC with *Keen*, then choose and discard down to the current Threat of the group. If a group of NCs contain both *Keen* and *Hesitant* members, the effects cancel each other on a 1:1 basis before cards are drawn.

LIMITLESS POTENTIAL

The NC may spend an additional point of potential each sequence beyond the usual cap of one per sequence. This asset may be taken more than once, and increases the total possible potential to spend in a sequence by one each time it is taken (a maximum of two per sequence if taken once, three per sequence if taken twice, etc).

MAGICAL WORD

The NC masters one verb or two nouns of power for which she meets the minimum *Mysteries* skill requirements (see *Words of Power*, p. 236). This asset may be taken more than once.

MASTERY

The NC gains a mastery ability for a skill in which she has 5 or more ranks. This asset may be taken more than once, but must be taken for a different qualifying skill each time.

MATERIALIZE

Requires: *Incorporeal.*

The NC can briefly cohere into a physical form by taking a maneuver: doing so grants it temporary ranks of *Vigor* and *Grace* equal to 1/2 Threat, rounded down. The NC remains material until the beginning of its next turn, when it must either use another maneuver to remain material, or automatically reverts to being *Incorporeal*. Becoming *Incorporeal* at the start of a turn or reaction is immediate and automatic, and occurs before all other parts of the turn or exchange. Unless the NC also has the *Extra Maneuver* asset, there is no way for it to remain material when it reacts as it does not have a maneuver to use.

While material, the NC may be targeted by physical attacks, and can suffer conditions and Wounds. If the NC becomes *Incorporeal* it automatically stabilizes. Wound Penalties suffered while physical continue to affect it while *Incorporeal*, and it will heal at the standard rates outlined in *Healing and Recovery* (starting on p. 100).

MINDLESS

The NC is incapable of conscious thought. Its *Reason* aptitude is always 0 and it cannot be convinced or persuaded. Its Morale cannot be changed, but the NC is still subject to feints to lower its Guard. If it can attack, it only does so only by instinct. It cannot use accoutrements of any type, and may only use weapons that are part of its body. This asset is almost exclusively found in automata, animals, and chimera.

PAINLESS

This ability costs two assets. The NC is less susceptible to pain and is barely aware of even grievous injuries: the penalty from Wounds is –1 instead of –2.

PARTING BLOW

When the NC loses her last initiative card due to Wounds she has an immediate, free reaction, ignoring all Wound Penalties and condition effects. This free reaction includes an advantageous circumstance for determining Attack Priority (see *Attack Priority*, p. 79).

PENETRATING WEAPON

The NC has an accoutrement with an attack that ignores Guard, such as a gun.

POSSESSION

Requires: *Incorporeal.*

Through possession, an *Incorporeal* entity may enter or control the body of any creature that draws breath, or even a corpse from whom the breath has gone. To initiate a possession attempt the *Incorporeal* entity must enter the prospective host's zone of control and spend a point of *Ether*. Normally, the host is unaware of the attempt, and the entity may make a number of subtle social attacks equal to its Threat. If the targeted host or anyone in the host's zone of control becomes aware of the attempted possession

a social conflict begins immediately, but initiative cards are only dealt to those who can perceive the possessing entity.

If the targeted host is *Mindless* or otherwise has a *Reason* or *Will* of 0, the possession occurs automatically, and requires no successful attacks. Otherwise, the attacking entity tests *Will + Mysteries* against the host's *Will + Composure*. The target host begins with a *Hostile* Disposition towards being possessed. Each successful attack moves the target's Disposition one step toward *Favorable*. Once the Disposition is *Favorable*, any subsequent successful attack completes the *Possession*.

Once possessed, the possessing entity has full access to all of the host's senses and may communicate with them telepathically—this may be used to initiate social conflict normally, but the host is always treated as *Entrapped*. A possessing entity may also attempt to take direct control of the host's body by testing *Will + Mysteries* against the host's *Will + Composure*. Success gives the possessing entity total control of the host's body for one turn. A remarkable success (DoS 4+) on this test allows the entity to control the host's actions for the remainder of the sequence (or about one minute outside of conflict). An extraordinary success (DoS 8+) allows control for the remainder of the conflict or scene.

Long-term control of the host is possible, but the possessing entity must declare the attempt and spend a point of *Ether* before testing. If successful, the control lasts until the host falls asleep or otherwise becomes unconscious. A remarkable failure (DoS –4) prevents the entity from attempting to take control for the rest of the sequence, or one minute outside of conflict. An extraordinary failure (DoS –8) prevents further attempts for the remainder of the conflict or scene.

POTENTIAL

The NC has one additional point of *Purpose* or *Ether*. The total of all potential cannot exceed the Threat of the NC. NCs with 3 or more total potential often take the *Limitless Potential* asset. This asset may be taken more than once.

PSYCHOKINETIC

Requires: *Incorporeal.*

The *Incorporeal* entity may spend a point of potential at the beginning of a sequence to be able to affect physical objects as though she had a *Vigor* equal to her Threat. Any and all objects and persons in her zone of control can be interacted with, but since most tests used for attack require *Grace*, this asset offers little use in physical combat. For example, a typical attack of *Grace + Melee* would only use the entity's *Melee* skill, as her *Grace* would still be zero. Instead, psychokinesis is often used outside of conflict to move objects, touch targets, or otherwise make the entity's presence known through some physical interaction. Use of this ability does not negate the entity's immateriality.

SKILL BONUS

The NC gains two additional skill ranks. These ranks cannot increase a skill above the NC's Threat. This asset may be taken more than once.

SMALL TARGET

This ability costs two assets, and can only be taken if the NC is no more than three feet long in its longest dimension. This NC has up to two physical avenues of attack available, rather than the typical three.

SPECIAL ATTACK

The NC has an attack that is part of her being, or access to some special accoutrement that grants her an extraordinary means of attack. *Special Attack* is not an asset, but rather a collection of features that may each be taken as a separate asset. A *Special Attack* can then be built by adding these features together. All *Special Attack* assets other than *Penetrating Attack* and *Social Attack* can be taken for both physical and social attacks. The features below may be taken more than once if they apply to different *Special Attacks*.

Area of Effect

The attack hits all targets within its Reach. This feature costs one asset for attacks with a Reach of *Touch* or *Close*, and an additional asset for each Reach category beyond *Close* (so two total assets for *Extended*, or three for *Short Range*). *Long Range* cannot be used with *Area of Effect* attacks. This can be either an area of effect centered on the NC or applied to a ranged attack. If applied to a ranged attack, the area of effect is centered on the target of the attack.

Condition

The attack gains one weapon condition. The *Crippled* or *Undone* conditions cost two assets, and all others cost one asset. *Damaged* cannot be chosen. This asset may be taken more than once.

Font of Corruption

Requires: *Corrupt* liability.

Whenever the NC's attack scores a remarkable success, or hits a target whose Guard is down, the target gains one point of *Corruption* in addition to all other effects of the attack.

Overpowering

This ability costs three assets. When drawing cards for this attack, draw one additional card and choose which card value is used to resolve the test. If an *Overpowering* attack is made against a target in cover, the number of extra cards drawn for cover is reduced by one instead.

Penetrating Attack

This is a physical attack that ignores the target's Guard but is subject to rules for aiming and cover (see p. 73 and p. 82).

Potent

Increase the Potency of the attack by +1. This asset may be taken more than once.

Quick

The attack can be performed with blinding speed and always counts as having +1 advantageous circumstance when determining Attack Priority (see *Attack Priority*, p. 79). This asset may be taken more than once.

Reach

For each asset taken, the attack's Reach is extended one step: from *Touch* or *Close* to *Extended*, then to *Short Range,* and then to *Long Range*. This asset may be taken more than once.

Reactive

This ability costs two assets. The first time each sequence that an attacker in the NC's zone of control fails on a non-projectile physical attack against the NC, the NC can choose to make a reactive attack against the foe without needing to spend an initiative card. The reactive attack is made after all other effects of the failure are resolved. The reactive ability is lost whenever the NC has a Wound.

Social Attack

A social attack that has a Reach of *Audible* or *Visual,* and can affect anyone who can hear or see the NC. The attack cannot cause Wounds.

Unusual Attack

An extremely rare asset only found in chimera, Pontus-touched, or supernatural beings. This attack depends on some strange skill and/or aptitude as part of the trait combination used for the attack rather than the usual *Grace + Athletics/Fencing/Firearms/ Melee.* This asset may be taken up to two times per attack: the first time lets you change the skill used in the attack combination, the second time lets you change the aptitude used in the attack combination as well.

Unusual Defense

Found only in attacks that attempt to affect their targets in strange and specific ways, the attack can only be defended against using an unusual trait combination rather than the default combination of *Vigor + Athletics* for physical attacks, or *Will + Composure* for social attacks. This asset may be taken up to two times per attack: the first time lets you change the skill used in the defense combination, and the second time lets you change the aptitude used in the defense combination as well.

STRONG GUARD

This ability costs two assets, and can only be taken by those with a Guard lower than their Threat. The NC is almost impossible to beat in a fight, either from an enhanced ability to dodge and deflect attacks, or due to an anatomy that is resistant to injury. Increase their calculated Guard by one; this change increases the Conflict Assessment score.

STRONG MORALE

Shift the target's initial Morale one step towards *Hostile* at the beginning of a conflict. Cannot be taken with *Cowardly, Mindless,* or *Weak Morale*. This asset may be taken more than once.

STRONG PHYSICAL DEFENSE

The NC is a skilled and cautious combatant: increase her calculated physical Defense by one.

STRONG SOCIAL DEFENSE

Words have little effect on the NC: increase her calculated social Defense by one.

TERRIFYING PRESENCE

This ability costs two assets, and can only be taken by those with a Threat of 6+. The NC gives off an aura of terror, pushing all those nearby to panic. At the beginning of the conflict, all characters opposing the NC have their Morale set to *Indifferent* and it cannot become *Guarded* or *Hostile* to fleeing. The effect persists so long as the NC is present in the scene.

UNNATURAL PERCEPTION

Through some bizarre sensory apparatus, the NC doesn't rely on normal physical senses for perception. She never suffers any environmental penalties to *Focus* tests (though she is still subject to Wound Penalties) and can make *Focus* tests passively. This can make it impossible for them to be evaded or caught unawares in most circumstances.

NARRATOR CHARACTER LIABILITIES

Unless stated otherwise, each liability taken allows the NC to take one additional asset, and each liability can only be taken once. NCs of Threat 1–10 can gain up to five extra assets by taking liabilities; additional liabilities may be taken but provide no benefit. NCs of Threat 11–20 may gain up to ten extra assets by taking liabilities.

APTITUDE PENALTY

Remove one already-assigned aptitude point. This liability may be taken more than once.

ATTACK RESTRICTIONS

One or more of the NC's natural attacks suffers from an unusual limitation. These modifications cannot be applied to any attacks gained through accoutrements. Each restriction applies to a single attack and counts as one liability unless otherwise specified; the assets gained from the liability can only be used to modify the *Special Attack* for which this liability was taken. Each restriction cannot be taken more than once for a given attack unless specified.

All-Consuming

Gain two assets. The attack requires all the NC's attention, and uses her entire turn (move, maneuver, and action). The attack cannot be used as a reaction. If the NC becomes Wounded, she can still perform this attack even though she can no longer take maneuvers.

Clumsy

The attack is graceless and slow and always counts as having a disadvantageous circumstance when determining Attack Priority (see *Attack Priority*, p. 79).

Follow-up

Select one *Special Attack* possessed by the NC to be the primary attack, and then choose a different attack to receive the *Follow-up* liability. Only a successful primary attack can provide the opening for a *Follow-up* attack. If this primary attack is successfully used while in combat, then the *Follow-up* attack may be made on the NC's next action against the same target.

Harmless

The attack cannot inflict Wounds. This liability cannot be taken with *Social Attack*.

Limited Use

The attack can only be used once per sequence.

Potential Trigger

Gain two assets. The attack requires the expenditure of a point of potential to use. The potential is used regardless of the success or failure of the attack, and counts against the limit of potential spent in a single sequence.

Self-Defeating

After the NC succeeds on a test for this attack she automatically suffers one temporary condition. Draw two cards to check for conditions, and the target of the attack chooses which condition is applied.

Self-Destructive

Gain two assets. After the NC succeeds on a test for this attack she automatically takes one Wound. Taking the Wound cannot be avoided through the use of *Purpose*.

Single Use

Gain two assets. The attack can only be used once per conflict.

Underwhelming

Gain two assets. When drawing cards for this attack, draw one additional card and use the lowest result to resolve the test.

BANE

Gain one asset for a rank 1 Bane, or two assets for a rank 2 Bane. Similar to the bloodline curse for nephilim (see p. 121), the NC has some substance which spells her doom. A rank 1 Bane causes distress: the NC automatically suffers the *Disoriented* temporary condition whenever she is in the same zone of control as her Bane, and attacks against the NC using the Bane gain +1 Potency.

Rank 2 Banes can cause severe injuries and are greatly feared. In addition to all the effects of a rank 1 Bane, any successful attack with a Bane substance doubles its DoS (so an attack that would normally yield DoS 2 instead yields DoS 4, etc).

This liability is almost exclusively found on supernatural creatures or things that have been changed by exposure to the Pontus. Many creatures with a Bane are *Repelled* by their bane substance, and may have that liability as well.

CORRUPT

The NC is touched by the Pontus or stained by her own unconscionable acts, and has a *Corruption* score equal to her Threat (maximum 5).

COWARDLY

Gain two assets. The NC always begins the conflict with a Morale *Favorable* to fleeing. *Cowardly* may only be taken by NCs of Threat 3+, and cannot be taken with *Mindless*, *Strong Morale*, or *Weak Morale*.

FIXED POTENTIAL

Gain 0 assets. Choose *Purpose* or *Ether*: the NC can only have potential of that type.

HESITANT

When drawing initiative cards at the beginning of a sequence draw one additional card for each NC with *Hesitant*, then choose and discard the highest value card for each of them. If a group of NCs contain both *Keen* and *Hesitant* members, the effects cancel each other on a 1:1 basis before cards are drawn.

IMMOBILE

Gain two assets. The NC cannot use move actions to change location.

LARGE TARGET

The NC has up to four physical avenues of attack available. This asset cannot be taken with *Small Target*, and the NC in question must be at least six feet long in at least one dimension.

NO CONTROL

Gain two assets. The NC has no zone of control. Reactions can only be made with a Reach of *Touch*. Cannot be taken with *No Reactions*.

NO INTERRUPTION

The NC cannot seize initiative. This liability can only be taken by NCs with Threat 3+.

NO MANEUVERS

The NC is awkward and uncoordinated, and cannot use maneuvers during her turn.

NO REACTIONS

Gain two assets. The NC cannot use initiative cards for reactions. Cannot be taken with *No Control*.

PERSISTENT CONDITION

The NC begins the conflict already suffering one persistent condition of the Narrator's choice.

POTENTIAL PENALTY

Lose one potential. This liability may be taken more than once, but it cannot reduce potential to less than 0.

REPELLED

The entity is repelled by a symbol or substance, and cannot bear to be in its close proximity. Choose any item or symbol: whenever the NC is in the same zone of control as that item or symbol she becomes distraught and uncomfortable, and immediately begins suffering from the *Outmaneuvered* temporary condition. The *Outmaneuvered* condition will endure as long as the entity is in the same zone of control. An NC who is *Repelled* by something cannot willingly touch it, though she may use tools or other implements that allow her to manipulate it indirectly. If the object or symbol is forced upon her and touches her involuntarily it is physically painful. Many creatures that have Banes are also *Repelled* by them. Many evil supernatural beings are *Repelled* by holy symbols such as the cross.

SKILL PENALTY

Lose two skill ranks. This liability may be taken more than once, but cannot reduce available skills ranks below 0.

TETHERED

There is a person, item, or location that the NC is intimately connected with and cannot bear to be apart from. Choose one person, item, or location: the NC gains an Affinity for it equal to her Threat (maximum rank 5). If the NC cannot directly observe or interact with her tether for at least one scene each day she becomes distraught and weakened, suffering a −2 penalty on all tests and Defenses. Spending more than one day away from the tether also violates the Affinity, reducing its temporary rank. Each further day away from the tether counts as another violation, and will continue to reduce the temporary value of the Affinity. Prolonged periods away from a tether can erode the Affinity entirely.

All shades and some fey are only anchored to the Clockwork through their tether. If the fixed value of the tether is ever reduced to zero, the entity will lose that connection entirely. For shades, this means they will go on to their proper place in the afterlife and leave the world. Untethered fey will immediately cease to be. Very rarely, chimera or aberrations will also form a tether, and if the Affinity is completely eroded they will die.

UNARMED

Gain two assets. The NC cannot have any physical attacks other than a single unarmed attack with a Potency of 1, without an associated condition, and cannot use accoutrements to gain physical attacks.

UNSKILLED

Gain two assets. The NC is far less skillful than others of similar Threat and has one fewer universal skill ranks.

VULNERABLE

The NC is unusually susceptible to conditions. All attacks made against the NC gain +1 Potency. This is most commonly found with abberations as their Pontus-twisted bodies are more susceptible to injury, but those of the lower classes who have lived with deprivation and sickness might also display such frailty.

WEAK GUARD

Gain two assets. The NC fights recklessly and leaves herself unusually exposed. Her calculated Guard is reduced by one, to a minimum of zero.

WEAK MORALE

Shift starting Morale one step towards *Favorable* to fleeing or surrender. Cannot be taken with *Cowardly*, *Mindless*, or *Strong Morale*.

WEAK PHYSICAL DEFENSE

The NC fights sloppily, and allows her opponents unnecessary openings to attack. Her calculated physical Defense is reduced by one.

WEAK SOCIAL DEFENSE

Due to either a weak will or gullibility, the NC is more easily swayed than most. Her calculated social Defense is reduced by one.

WOUNDED

Gain two assets. The NC is already wounded; she suffers a –2 penalty on all tests and cannot take maneuvers. This neither changes the NC's starting Threat nor reduces her number of dealt initiative cards.

NARRATOR CHARACTER TEMPLATES

The following pages provide further detail on different types of Narrator characters, grouped by creature type. Each entry lists some general information on the creature type, how they can be best used as NCs, the template on which to base custom builds, and samples of complete, ready-to-run NCs.

ANIMALS

All manner of beasts great and small populate the world. Domesticated animals are those most frequently encountered, and pose little danger to player characters. When venturing into the wild, though, there are many beasts that can present a great risk to life and limb. Also, the influence of the Pontus can take even the tamest of animals and turn them into fierce monsters.

CREATING ABERRATIONS

Physical traits and attacks are the most prominent features for aberrations, and many are notably weak socially and mentally. Their deficiencies in these areas stem from their animal origins and the shattering experience of becoming so dramatically changed by the Pontus. In rare instances, the opposite occurs, and even plant aberrations could be raised to genius-level intelligence.

Aberrations are a common sign of Pontus activity, and appear frequently in sewers and undercities, jungles, or areas of the countryside where strange and terrible things have occurred. Since almost anything can become aberrant, their abilities vary wildly from specimen to specimen. Using many different assets is the easiest way to make the most of this variety, which usually requires taking several liabilities. Although aberrations are often physically powerful and very dangerous, their liabilities are often also physically-oriented due to the destructive influence of the Pontus.

Hellhound

Dogs are among humanity's oldest companions, and as a result are often exposed to Pontus events and *Corruption*. When a dog is warped into an aberration it loses its socialization and reverts to a feral beast, usually turning on its owners first before fleeing. Hellhounds on the loose can be a major problem, as they tend to quickly establish dominance over local feral dog packs and become a vector for spreading *Corruption* that may result in more Pontus events and more hellhounds. In cities, constables are often the ones tasked to deal with them, and it is a risky affair. In the country, the skill of fox hunting has been recapitulated to ensure hunts for hellhounds are quickly called and brought to a bloody close.

HELLHOUND

Threat: 3

Conflict Assessment: Physical 36   Social 18

Potential: Ether 1, Corruption 3

Aptitudes: G 3   V 3   R 1   F 4   P 1   W 2

Universal Skills: Physical 3   Mental –   Social 1

Skills: Command 3, Composure 3, Tactics 1

Attacks:

CLAWS AND TEETH: Grace + Melee (6), Potency 3, Touch, *Bleeding*

CHILLING HOWL: Presence + Command (4), Potency 1, Audible, *Fatigued*

Defenses: Physical 6   Social 5

Armor: Physical 1   Social –

Guard: 2

Morale: Guarded

Assets: Armor x1 (Physical), Special Attack: Chilling Howl (Condition, Social Attack), Special Attack: Claws and Teeth (Condition, Potent x2)

Liabilities: Corrupt, Fixed Potential: Ether

Special: Immune to Pontus effects

Hunger Bramble

The hedgerows of the British countryside are a visible symbol of the stability and constancy of life in the Empire. Many have stood where they are for hundreds of years, marking out the same roads, fields, and boundaries. It is often joked that an ancient hedge is a better roof in a storm than a farmer's cottage, and to this day travellers will still use them for occasional shelter. These same hedges have hidden lovers' trysts, highwaymen lurking in wait, the occasional stash of stolen goods, or the occasional corpse. In the unfortunate circumstance that a Pontus event occurs during such an act, the hedges themselves can become suffused with the sinister energies of the Pontus and take on a bloody activity of their own. Aberrant plants such as the hunger bramble are no longer

sessile: instead, they mindlessly attack anything that comes within reach of their grasping vines. Once they strike a victim with their vines, they wrap and bind them with snaring brambles, hoping to immobilize them while they are crushed to death. The bodies of those they kill are dragged back to the base of the bramble, where they rot and give it sustenance. Brambles that are undiscovered can grow rapidly, choking out all other plant and animal life.

HUNGER BRAMBLE

Threat: 3

Conflict Assessment: P 39   Social NA (Mindless)

Potential: Ether 1, Corruption 3

Aptitudes: G 3   V 4   R 0   F 2   P 1   W 2

Universal Skills: Physical 3   Mental –   Social –

Skills: Composure 3, Melee 4, Stealth 3

Attacks:

REACHING VINES: Grace + Melee (7), Potency 1, Extended Follow-up

SNARING BRAMBLES: Grace + Melee (7), Potency 3, Extended, *Unbalanced*

Defenses: Physical 7   Social 5 (vs. feints only: Mindless)

Armor: Physical 2   Social –

Guard: 1

Morale: Guarded

Assets: Armor x2 (Physical), Exceptional Skill: Melee, Mindless, Special Attack: Reaching Vines (Potent, Reach), Special Attack: Snaring Brambles (Condition, Reach, Potent x2)

Liabilities: Attack Restriction: Snaring Brambles (Follow-up), Corrupt, Fixed Potential: Ether, Immobile, Large Target, No Interruption

Special: Immune to Pontus effect; cannot use move actions to change position; cannot seize initiative; cannot be convinced or persuaded, cannot convince or persuade

Rat King

Rats can be found almost anywhere in the world, and often congregate in cities, sewers, and along docksides: all places with frequent minor Pontus activity. It is hardly a wonder, then, that they fall prey to having their bodies twisted and reformed into aberrations. A rat king occurs when a mass of rodents is joined together and partially integrated into one coordinated being. The rodents are partially connected to one another through a web of flesh and fur, and their tails seem especially prone to becoming joined into one writhing

Aberration Template				
Creature Type	**Aptitudes**	**Universal Skills**	**Assets**	**Liabilities**
Aberrations	*Grace* 2, *Vigor* 2, *Reason* 1, *Focus* 2, *Presence* 1, *Will* 2	Physical 1, Mental 0, Social 0	*Special Attack* (Condition, Potent) *Special:* Immune to Pontus effects	*Corrupt,* *Fixed Potential: Ether*

mass. Popular folklore holds that this arises from the rats living so tightly packed and in such filth that they simply become hopelessly entangled with one another, but ratcatchers and sewerfolk know that they are both the symptoms and harbingers of the Pontus.

RAT KING

Threat: 2

Conflict Assessment: Physical 16   Social NA (Mindless)

Potential: Ether 1, Corruption 2

Aptitudes: G 3   V 2   R 0   F 3   P 1   W 2

Universal Skills: Physical 2   Mental –   Social –

Skills: Composure 2

Attacks:

SWARMING BITES: Grace + Melee (5), Potency 2, Touch, *Unbalanced*. Reactive

Defenses: Physical 4   Social 4 (vs. feints only: Mindless)

Armor: –

Guard: 1

Morale: Indifferent

Assets: Mindless, Special Attack: Swarming Bites (Condition, Potent, Reactive), Painless, Small Target

Liabilities: Corrupt, Fixed Potential: Ether, Hesitant, Unskilled, Skill Penalty x2

Special: Immune to Pontus effects; Wound Penalties –1 instead of –2; only two physical avenues of attack available; cannot be convinced or persuaded, cannot convince or persuade

CREATING NATURAL ANIMALS

Natural animals are straightforward physical NCs and are best used for allies, pets, or direct conflicts. The *Mindless* asset applies to most creatures, but not to highly social or intelligent animals such as dogs, horses, primates, and some birds. If a social animal has been trained and exposed to a particular language, characters may attempt to convince or persuade the animal to obey commands given in that language with *Presence + Command* tests. The Disposition of trained animals to commands is usually *Favorable* towards their owner or trainer, and *Indifferent* or *Guarded* to others. If the appropriate language is not used, the animal does not understand the command and the test automatically fails.

Unless the animal is an especially clever hunter, it will often only possess a single physical attack, which should be the focus of the majority of its assets. Adding in one or two other utility assets, such as *Exceptional Teamwork* or *Keen* can be a good way to make

sure the animals are effective and have a distinct feel in conflict without creating too much complexity. Animals that are notably faster than people should also be given the *Extra Move* asset.

Animals are unlikely to stay in a fight if they are seriously injured, so taking morale-based liabilities such as *Cowardly* or *Shaky Morale* is a good way to gain extra assets. A major drawback for animal of all types is that they tend to be easily outmatched by characters with firearms. Using animals in encounters where the players' mobility is limited and where there is plenty of cover can be a useful way to compensate for this vulnerability.

Horse

Throughout history, humanity has depended on horses as beasts of burden, for transport, for use in war, and they are still used in these capacities throughout the world. Horses can be encountered almost anywhere, and although they are generally well-kept by their riders and handlers there is always the chance to encounter one in the wild, one that has escaped, or a domestic animal may be provoked to violence by ill treatment. The statistics below are for a generic draft horse or a simply trained riding animal. Race horses and fine riding horses will be bred for speed and possess even more *Extra Move* assets. The heaviest draft animals and war horses will have a higher Threat and better physical aptitudes.

HORSE

Threat: 2

Conflict Assessment: Physical 18   Social 8

Potential: None

Aptitudes: G 2   V 3   R 1   F 2   P 2   W 2

Universal Skills: Physical 2   Mental 0   Social 0

Skills: Composure 2

Attacks:

POWERFUL KICK: Grace + Melee (4), Close, Potency 3, *Dazed*; Quick (+1 Attack Priority)

Defenses: Physical 5   Social 4

Armor: –

Guard: 2

Morale: Indifferent

Assets: Extra Move, Special Attack: Powerful Kick (Condition, Potent x2, Quick)

Liabilities: Potential Penalty, Skill Penalty x2

Special: When taking a move during a turn a horse may move up to two zones of control

Animal Template				
Creature Type	**Aptitudes**	**Universal Skills**	**Assets**	**Liabilities**
Animals	*Grace* 2, *Vigor* 1, *Reason* 1, *Focus* 2, *Presence* 2, *Will* 2	Physical 1, Mental 0, Social 0	*Special Attack* (Condition, Potent, Quick), *Strong Guard*	*Potential Penalty*, *Skill Penalty*

Striking Snake

This entry can represent a viper or any manner of mildly-poisonous snakes. They may pose some danger to people if they are foolish enough to engage them, and are best left alone. Exotic poisonous snakes are easily represented by taking additional assets to increase the Potency of the attack and change its *Dazed* weapon condition to a more a dangerous condition such as *Bleeding* or *Undone*. Constrictors are best represented by adding Threat, increasing *Vigor*, and changing the bite to a crushing attack with a higher Potency, and a Reach of *Touch*.

STRIKING SNAKE

Threat: 2

Conflict Assessment: Physical 18   Social NA (Mindless)

Potential: None

Aptitudes: G 4   V 1   R 0   F 2   P 2   W 2

Universal Skills: Physical 2   Mental 0   Social 0

Skills: Composure 2

Attacks:

VICIOUS BITE: Grace + Melee (6), Potency 2, Close, *Dazed*; Quick x2

Defenses: Physical 3   Social 4 (vs. feints only: Mindless)

Armor: –

Guard: 2

Morale: Indifferent

Assets: Mindless, Special Attack: Vicious Bite (Condition, Potent, Quick, Reach), Strong Guard

Liabilities: Potential Penalty, Skill Penalty, Unskilled

Special: Cannot be convinced or persuaded, cannot convince or persuade

Hunting Cat

Africa and India are both home to lions and tigers, and both will hunt large game and occasionally become man-eaters. Hunters on safari, unlucky explorers, locals defending their livestock, and poachers looking to turn a profit on the exotic animal market could all come into conflict with a big cat. The most important survival tip for going after hunting cats it to make sure that you remain the hunter the entire time. If they are able gain the advantage and ambush their pursuers, the hunter can quickly become the hunted.

Tigers are solitary hunters and more likely to have unusually dangerous adults that could easily creep into the Threat 5 or 6 range, which would be a challenge for an entire party. Lions are also group hunters, and encountering several females from a pride could be an exceedingly dangerous encounter.

HUNTING CAT

Threat: 4

Conflict Assessment: Physical 52   Social 28

Potential: 1 Purpose

Aptitudes: G 3   V 4   R 1   F 2   P 2   W 2

Universal Skills: Physical 4   Mental –   Social –

Skills: Command 3, Composure 3

Attacks:

POUNCE: Grace + Melee (7), Potency 3, Extended, *Overwhelmed*, Overpowering, Limited Use

CLAWS: Grace + Melee (7), Potency 3, Close, Bleeding; Quick (+1 to Attack Priority)

THREATENING GROWL: Presence + Command (5), Potency 1, Audible

Defenses: Physical 8   Social 5

Armor: –

Guard: 2

Morale: Hostile

Assets: Special Attack: Claws (Condition, Potent, Quick, Reach), Special Attack: Pounce (Condition, Overpowering, Potent x2, Reach), Strong Guard

Liabilities: Attack Restrictions: Pounce (Limited Use), Potential Penalty, Skill Penalty x3, Unskilled

AUTOMATA

An automaton is any machine that can operate on its own without a user to guide or instruct it. Programmable and miniaturized analytical engines have birthed automata developed to serve as very expensive and questionably useful domestic servants, often purchased as symbols of wealth and modernism. Advancements in hydraulics and power sources have allowed for automata to serve as effective machine labor to supplement human workers in especially demanding or unsafe work sites. While still rare, these mechanical marvels are slowly becoming more common as the new century approaches. Perhaps we will one day see a world where many tasks are taken over by these amazing machines.

Automata are mostly designed and built as individual creations meant for a particular use. When designing automata as NCs, Narrators should always keep in mind what they are meant to do and emphasize that intended role with thematic assets and liabilities. The *Vigor* aptitude tends to be quite high as it is easy to build machines that are physically strong, and many automata are also built with significant *Armor* to represent their rugged construction. Most automata meant to do their job around humans will be humanoid in appearance, but there are times when their function requires any of a number of more bizarre shapes and sizes.

Automaton Template				
Creature Type	Aptitudes	Universal Skills	Assets	Liabilities
Automata	Grace 2, Vigor 3, Reason 0, Focus 2, Presence 1, Will 2	Physical 1, Mental 0, Social 0	Armor, Mindless, Special Attack (Potent)	Potential Penalty

Auto-miner

Serret Bros. Steelworks in Manchester has produced a short run of heavy mining automata that are designed to work as primary tunnelers when extending branches of mines, and as supplemental labor to keep digging when conditions are unsafe for living workers. The first few were sent to mines in Wales and Cornwall, but new orders are slowly taking them to new job sites across Britain. Though not intended for combat, these beetle-backed machines can be extremely dangerous to careless workers who get in their way, or to everyone if they were ever given new programs that directed them to smash people instead of rocks. They are incredibly hard to damage, and their hammers and picks would strike for incredible damage.

AUTO-MINER
Threat: 2
Conflict Assessment: Physical 36   Social NA (Mindless)
Potential: None
Aptitudes: G 1   V 5   R 0   F 2   P 1   W 2
Universal Skills: Physical 3   Mental –   Social –
Skills: Vocation (Miner) 4
Attacks:
STEAM HAMMER AND PICK: Grace+Melee (4), Close, Potency 4
Defenses: Physical 7   Social 2 (vs. feints only: Mindless)
Armor: Physical 3   Social –
Guard: 1
Morale: NA (Mindless)
Assets: Armor x3 (Physical), Burrowing, Durable, Special Attack: Steam hammer and pick (Potent x3)
Liabilities: Hesitant, Large Target, No Maneuvers, Potential Penalty, Unskilled, Weak Physical Defense

CELESTIALS

The most powerful of the celestials are rarely active in the mortal realm. Angels reside in Heaven, guard the Pit, or run mysterious errands in the Borderlands. Many of the Fallen are bound in the Outer Darkness, and those that remain free try to find a home in the Borderlands, particularly Hell or Annwn. The concerns of mortals matter little to these celestials. Conversely, the mortal-hybrid descendents of the Fallen, the nephilim, attempt to fit into mortal society or create societies of their own. If a naphil dies, its soul becomes a demon that restlessly wanders the earth or other realms, constantly searching to feed its destructive desires.

CREATING ANGELS

At a minimum of Threat 11, even the least among the angels is an overwhelming entity that even battle hardened characters have little to no hope of overcoming in direct conflict. Angels should be used mainly as plot devices. For series that are focused on ritual magic and the supernatural, angels can be excellent long-term patrons working to guide the characters, or inuman obstacles whose heavenly duties performed for the greater good still manage to wreak havoc in the characters' lives.

Angel Template (Starting from Threat 5)				
Creature Type	Aptitudes	Universal Skills	Assets	Liabilities
Angels	Grace 1, Vigor 1 Reason 2, Focus 2, Presence 4, Will 3	Physical 0, Mental 2, Social 3, Command 5 Composure 5, Mysteries 5,	Fount of potential: Purpose, Limitless Potential, Terrifying Presence, Angelic Immortality Special: Minimum Threat of 11,	Fixed Potential: Purpose, Skill Penalty x2, Unskilled

Angels are usually uncomplicated beings, living only to perform their purpose in the Clockwork. As mortals are part of the Clockwork, an angel will almost never be found in conflict against them. An angel will never attack a character without *Corruption*; however, attacking an angel is akin to attacking the divine plan and will thus incur *Corruption*. The Narrator should only use angels in conflict at the culmination of a major story arc or at the end of a series. As allies, they are too powerful to be used with frequency, and as enemies they present the greatest risk of player death.

Asset and liability choices are the best ways to reflect how they carry out their particular role in the Clockwork. Most angels will know several pure *Magical Words*, and having them prepare or enact magical effects outside of conflict is an excellent way to give them involvement in a story without having them directly face player characters, or to provide limited support from afar. Angels also receive the blessing *Angelic Immortality* (p. 120). If they are ever physically slain, they will be restored to life on the third sunrise after their death, healed of one Wound and able to recover thereafter. Angels cannot be permanently killed unless they both become Fallen and acquire a Bane.

CREATING DEMONS

Unlike other incorporeal characters, demons are very likely to retain physical skills since they can be used whenever they possess a corporeal body. Universal skills are best assigned to mental or social pursuits, while specific skill ranks are used to develop useful trait combinations for physical action. Demons favor learning words of power, as they allow them to enact rites that can make even weak hosts very effective in conflict.

Their ability to possess any host allows them to appear in almost any form, from humans to animals or even aberrations and chimera. Possessing demons use the host's *Grace* and *Vigor*, but otherwise retain their own aptitudes and skills. If a demon does not care about its host, or if it is facing enemies that lack the resources to threaten it magically, it can be very cavalier about the safety of its host body. Forcing its foes to harm or slay hosts and deal with the consequences is a favorite tactic for malicious demons confronting characters that cannot bind or banish it.

When portraying a demon, plan for the long term and use every trick and resource at its disposal to whittle away at the player characters. Given the difficulty of trapping and containing a demon, they make excellent recurring villains in games as players must constantly peel back the layers of their plans and battle a changing cast of servitors, pawns, and hosts before a climactic confrontation.

Diminished Grigoros

Some of the Fallen can be killed using a Bane, then they too will become demons. The restless spirit of a dead Grigoros is a terrifying entity, but millennia of travails in the Borderlands, spiritual injury at the hands of other supernatural powers, and the grinding passage of time can erode even mighty beings. This demon realizes that it must either regain some measure of power or risk utter dissolution. Using its *Tempting Whispers* attack to foster a cult of devotees with promises of glory and rewards, it teaches them magic, and carefully cultivates the group to provide it with a powerful physical form. Soon it can once again walk in the world as a being of dread might.

Demon Template				
Creature Type	Aptitudes	Universal Skills	Assets	Liabilities
Demon	*Grace* 0, *Vigor* 0, *Reason* 1, *Focus* 1, *Presence* 3, *Will* 3	Physical 0, Mental 0, Social 1	*Incorporeal, Possession, Potential* (+1 Ether), *Special Attack* (Potent)	*Corrupt, Fixed Potential: Ether, Repelled:* Crosses

DIMINISHED GRIGOROS

Threat: 6

Conflict Assessment:

    Physical* (Use host's (Grace + Vigor + 6) × 6)   Social 84

Potential: Ether 4, Corruption 5

Aptitudes: G –   V –   R 3   F 4   P 4   W 4

Universal Skills: Physical 1   Mental 2   Social 4

Skills: Academics 3, Melee 4, Mysteries 5, Temptation 6

Attacks:

TEMPTING WHISPERS: Presence + Temptation +10,

    Potency 2, Audible

Defenses: Physical* (Host's Vigor + 4)   Social 8

Armor: –

Guard: 2*

Morale: Hostile

Assets: Aptitude Bonus, Incorporeal, Possession, Potential
(+1 Ether), Psychokinetic, Special Attack: Tempting Whispers
(Potent), Magical Word x 4 Words of Power (verbs: Bind,
Obscure; nouns: Body, Chimera, Mortal, Object, Self)

Liabilities: Corrupt, Fixed Potential: Ether, Repelled: Crosses

Special: All items marked with an asterisk (*) are only available
when the diminished Grigoros is possessing a host

CREATING FALLEN

The high Threat of the Fallen (11+) make them antagonists that
pose a dire challenge to even the mightiest player characters. Such
conflicts should only occur at the culmination of a major story arc
or the end of a series. Players may spend the entire series arming
themselves with the rites necessary to summon or banish one of
the Fallen, or a climactic fight could see the characters needing to
merely survive against a Fallen for a few sequences as they defend
others trying to complete such a rite.

The Fallen were once assigned roles in the Clockwork. The large
number of universal skills available to them should cover most
general skills required to support this role. Specific skills should
be used to build up inhumanly high ratings in several closely associated skills that directly relate to their original place in the divine
plan. All of the Fallen have high ranks in *Mysteries* as a result of
their limited understanding of the divine plan, and to reflect their
facility for working ritual magic. The Fallen also receive the blessing
(see *Angelic Immortality*, p. 120): if they are ever physically slain,

they will be restored to life on the third sunrise after their death,
healed of one Wound and able to recover thereafter. They can only
be permanently killed if they are acquire the Bane liability.

Asset and liability choices are the best ways to reflect how they
once carried out their particular role in the Clockwork, or how
they have abandoned that duty. Most of the Fallen will know
several *Magical Words*, which may be used to enact magical effects
against the player characters without having to directly face them.
Using the *Unusual Attack* and *Unusual Defense* assets can keep
characters on their toes. Special attack assets and liabilities are best
used to design two or three powerful attacks, rather than designing
many different weak attacks or create a wide array of lesser benefits.
Keeping design focus on a few powerful abilities makes any high-
Threat NCs easier to run.

CREATING NEPHILIM

Nephilim will often fill the same roles as mortals, as fitting into
mortal society is need for many of this bloodline. This can be a
very difficult endeavor as nephilim are rarely viewed with kindness,
and killing them doesn't even incur *Corruption*, so they can find
themselves in distress from religious and societal oppression. The
monstrous appearance that can come with a naphil's *Fluid Mein*
is often taken for a sign of sin, but it is almost as likely to manifest
from excessively orderly behavior. This allows manifested nephilim
to be used as both allies and antagonists in ways that can be surprising. Perhaps a naphil who at first appea2red to need the player
character's help is truly their nemesis, or a naphil lynched by their
village is actually a person of great faith and integrity.

There are also nephilim who do not concern themselves with
being a part of mortal society. They instead occupy their time
attempting to reacquire the power and authority of their Fallen
progenitors. These characters can be found gathering cults of worshipers, acquiring ancient magics and artifacts, or simply wreaking
havoc as a display of their strength. Naphil are effectively immortal, so some of these antagonists have been acquiring allies and
resources for generations. Such a naphil could make a high-Threat
antagonist that can serve as the major villain for a series.

When making a naphil NC, choose assets and liabilities in the
same way one would for a mortal ally or antagonist. The bloodline blessings listed in the template's asset list are described in the
Nephilim bloodline description on page p. 119.

Fallen Template (Starting from Threat 5)				
Creature Type	**Aptitudes**	**Skills**	**Assets**	**Liabilities**
Fallen	*Grace* 1, *Vigor* 1 *Reason* 2, *Focus* 2, *Presence* 3, *Will* 4	Physical 0, Mental 2, Social 3 *Composure* 5, *Mysteries* 5, *Temptation* 5	*Fount of potential: Ether, Limitless Potential, Angelic Immortality, Magical Word* (one verb or two nouns), *Special Attack* (Condition, Potent x2), *Terrifying Presence, Special:* Minimum Threat 11	*Corrupt, Unskilled, Fixed Potential: Ether, Repelled:* Enochian sigil of their original name

Nephilim Template				
Creature Type	Aptitudes	Universal Skills	Assets	Liabilities
Nephilim	Grace 1, Vigor 1, Reason 2, Focus 3, Presence 2, Will 1	Physical 0, Mental 1, Social 0	Special: Angelic Immortality, Fluid Mien, Knowledge in the Flesh	Bane (rank 1), Special: -2 Esteem if known to be a naphil

Old Soldier

The Empire is in a near-constant state of physical conflict at its borders and in its colonial territories, to say nothing of the fighting it conducts by proxy. As a result, there is a high demand for professional soldiers around the world. Those that survive can become highly skilled combatants.

Some lineages of nephilim have long been drawn to a life of fighting as their angelic immortality offers them significant protection. If they can conceal their physical manifestations, they can have long careers and hone their skills to exceptional levels.

OLD SOLDIER

Threat: 4
Conflict Assessment: Physical 56   Social 28
Potential: Ether 2
Aptitudes: G 3   V 3   R 2   F 4   P 2   W 2
Universal Skills: Physical 3   Mental 1   Social 1
Skills: Command 2, Composure 3, Guile 3, Firearms 4, Mysteries 2

Attacks:
RIFLE: Grace + Firearms (7), Potency 4, Long Range, *Moribund*
FIXED BAYONET: Grace + Melee (6), Potency 2, Extended, *Bleeding*
LARGE KNIFE: Grace + Melee (6), Potency 2, Close, *Bleeding*
Defenses: Physical 6   Social 5
Armor: –
Guard: 2 (rifle in firing position), 3 (rifle w/bayonet for close combat or other weapons)
Morale: Hostile
Assets: Aptitude Bonus x2, Penetrating Weapon, Skill Bonus
Liabilities: Bane, lv. 1 (linden wood)
Special: Angelic Immortality (unless killed with their Bane, rises after 3 days); Fluid Mien (change appearance based on potential balance); Knowledge in the Flesh (consume 8 oz. of flesh or blood from a living person to gain access to one memory or a +1 bonus to a skill they have at a higher rank than this character until the next sunrise)

CHIMERA

Any fantastic, impossible creature could be made into a chimera. The critical piece that sets them apart from aberrations is that it is immediately clear that they could never have been part of the natural world. Only the surreal influence of the Pontus can create chimera, and they are among its most dangerous manifestations in the world. Aside from the physical danger they pose, chimera are also nodes of *Corruption,* and can quickly lead to an outbreak of further Pontus activity if left unchecked.

Strange appearances, amalgamations of multiple or distorted animal features, and clearly unnatural behavior are excellent ways to capture the feel of chimera, and these can be reflected by taking unusual combinations of assets and liabilities. Chimera that have *Flight* but no visible or physically possible means of flying, those that are unusually *Large* or *Small Targets*, have *Extra Moves* or *Extra Maneuvers* available from their many limbs, or whose impossible anatomies leave them *Vulnerable* or subject to a bizarre *Bane* can all reinforce this strangeness.

Almost all chimera are *Mindless*, but a rare few are self-aware enough to interact socially. Their minds are alien and will almost never understand human languages, so there is almost no hope of using social conflict to convince or persuade them of anything, but intimidation based on physical danger is possible and may still change Morale. If an intelligent chimera were able to somehow gain regular exposure to mortal societies, it may learn language or other social trappings.

Chimera are dangerous, and should usually be at least Threat 4 or higher. As high-Threat antagonists they will also have high *Corruption*, so there is a very real risk that Pontus events could spring up during a fight with a chimera. It is recommended that a few likely possibilities for Pontus events are planned out and kept ready in case the need arises. As creatures of the Pontus, chimera can always choose to ignore any Pontus effects.

Bleeding Burrower

This vile monstrosity is known as the *Minhocão* by the natives who first reported it. The bleeding burrower is a long, sleek mass of skinless muscle with many sets of needle-like legs. The two forwards sets end in digging blades of bone and chitin that it uses along with its pointed head case to make its way through the earth. Although left vulnerable by its bizarre physiology, its muscles emit a thick, viscous discharge that looks like coagulated blood, but is actually a lubricant to protect it from irritation and smooth its passage underground. Although the jet of acidic bile it can spray at a distance is a deadly weapon, strikes from its claws are perhaps more fearsome as they spread *Corruption* to anything they touch.

BLEEDING BURROWER

Threat: 4

Conflict Assessment: Physical 52   Social 32

Potential: Ether 2

Aptitudes: G 4   V 3   R 1   F 2   P 2   W 2

Universal Skills: Physical 4   Mental –   Social –

Skills: Command 4, Composure 2

Attacks:

BILE SPRAY: Grace + Athletics (8), Potency 2, Short Range, *Staggered;* Limited Use

STABBING LEGS: Grace + Melee (8), Potency 3, Touch, Font of Corruption

TERRIBLE HISSING: Presence + Command (6), Potency 1, Audible

Defenses: Physical 7   Social 4

Armor: –

Guard: 2

Morale: Hostile

Assets: Extra Maneuver, Extra Move, Burrowing, Special Attack: Bile Spray (Condition, Potent, Reach x2), Special Attack: Stabbing Legs (Potent x2, Font of Corruption) Strong Guard

Liabilities: Attack Restriction: Bile Spray (Limited Use), Corrupt, Fixed Potential: Ether, Unskilled, Skill Penalty x3, Vulnerable,

Special: Immune to Pontus effects

The Stonecray

A tale making the rounds in the cheapest bars in Shanghai tells of a handful of islanders rescued at sea by an Australian steamer. The men were ranting about their families and villages being destroyed by "the angry earth." Sailors are always quick to imagine some sea monster rather than the much higher likelihood that it was an earthquake or some type of volcanic fissure, so the story is spreading fast. Tale is told that the stone and coral of the reef comes bursting up from the water like a living thing, attacking whatever is foolish enough to remain on the beach. Others described the beast larger than a carriage and something between a cuttlefish and a crab.

THE STONECRAY

Threat: 7

Conflict Assessment: Physical 119   Social 63

Potential: Ether 4

Aptitudes: G 2   V 5   R 1   F 4   P 2   W 3

Universal Skills: Physical 5   Mental 1   Social 1

Skills: Athletics 7, Composure 4, Melee 6

Attacks:

MASSIVE CLAWS: Grace + Melee (7), Potency 4, Extended, *Crippled*

Defenses: Physical 12   Social 7

Armor: Physical 4   Social –

Guard: 2

Morale: Hostile

Assets: Armor x4, Aquatic, Durable, Extra Move, Painless, Special Attack: Massive Claws (Condition, Potent x3, Reach)

Liabilities: Corrupt, Hesitant, Fixed Potential: Ether, Large Target, Unskilled, Skill Penalty x2

Special: Immune to Pontus effects; draws one extra initiative card and must discard the highest; automatically and immediately stabilizes if Wounded, Wound Penalties are –1 per Wound, rather than –2; four physical avenues of attack available

Chimera Template				
Creature Type	**Aptitudes**	**Universal Skills**	**Assets**	**Liabilities**
Chimera	*Grace* 2, *Vigor* 1, *Reason* 1, *Focus* 2, *Presence* 2, *Will* 2	Physical 0, Mental 0, Social 0	*Potential* (+1 *Ether*), *Special Attack* (Condition, Potent, Reach), *Special:* Immune to Pontus effects	*Corrupt, Fixed Potential: Ether, Unskilled*

FEY

The fey are alien to the world, refugees and castoffs from the strangest parts of the Borderlands, seeking to stabilize their own frail existence. In the Borderlands, they exist as capricious and constantly changing entities called wyldlings. In the thin places where the boundary between the Earth and the Borderlands is weakened, some wyldlings choose to slide through. Once in our realm, they take on a shape born from mortals' unrealized beliefs or fears. When the monster under your child's bed suddenly becomes real, that is a fey finding a home in the Clockwork. Such embodied fey are called feyfolk. Those who enter the Clockwork taking the form of incorporeal beings are referred to as nature spirits.

CREATING FEYFOLK

Feyfolk exist in bewildering variety, and express all behaviors from the terrifying to the ridiculous, which allows for incredible flexibility in their use during a game. As entities that exist just outside the proper order of the Clockwork, they can be used to introduce an element of the supernatural without requiring the players to have invested in supernatural abilities. Player characters can often deal with feyfolk effectively without magical rituals or other transcendent powers, although characters with these skills will certainly have an advantage.

Inspiration for feyfolk can come from the folk traditions of every culture in the world, and those that study these beliefs can often find useful information about the nature and habits of feyfolk they might encounter. This allows feyfolk to be used as a "known unknown," creatures that may at first seem bizarre, but that ultimately have some logic and consistency to their behavior, however strange. They can present puzzles for the characters to untangle, threats for them to overcome, or even provide comic relief by inserting mischief into a game as needed. All feyfolk should require some level of deciphering, as their origins, actions, and access to glamours all stem from fundamental deceptions whereby they manipulate the world. At their core, they are and will always be inhuman, and some aspect of that should always be hiding behind whatever mask they present.

Kishi

The two-faced kishi are spoken of throughout the Congo, and are a reason why men travelling alone are sometimes viewed with fear. A kishi appears most often as an athletic, attractive mortal man. When approaching a settlement he often claims to be a lone hunter, looking for new grounds, or tells a sad story about why he cannot find a bride in his own village. If welcomed, he will stay and quickly prove his worth as a hunter and tracker. As soon as he is able, he lures his real prey—a young woman—into a secluded space. Once alone, he reveals the hyena face hidden beneath the hair on the back of his head and devours the woman. The bite of a kishi is said to be stronger than any natural animal, and cannot be escaped. A kishi will frequently move on after consuming a single victim, but if a settlement isn't suspicious then he may stay and keep hunting.

KISHI

Threat: 3
Conflict Assessment: Physical 30   Social 24
Potential: Ether 2, Corruption 3
Aptitudes: G 3   V 3   R 2   F 2   P 3   W 2
Universal Skills: Physical 2   Mental –   Social 1
Skills: Composure 3, Melee 3, Temptation 3
Attacks:
RENDING BITE: Grace + Melee (6), Potency 4, Touch, *Crippled, Clumsy.*
SALAMPASU SWORD: Grace + Melee (6), Potency 3, Close, *Bleeding*
THROWING SPEAR: Grace + Melee (6), Potency 2, Short Range, *Bleeding*
Defenses: Physical 5   Social 5
Armor: –
Guard: 2 (while armed)
Morale: Indifferent
Assets: Enhanced Aptitude x2, Glamour (Fast Friends), Special Attack: Rending Bite (Condition, Potency x3)
Liabilities: Attack Restriction: Rending Bite (Clumsy), Bane (rank 1, bronze), Corrupt, Weak Morale

Feyfolk Template				
Creature Type	**Aptitudes**	**Universal Skills**	**Assets**	**Liabilities**
Feyfolk	*Grace* 1, *Vigor* 1, *Reason* 2, *Focus* 2, *Presence* 2, *Will* 2	Physical 1, Mental 0, Social 0	1 *Glamour, Potential* (+1 *Ether*), *Special Attack* (Potent)	Bane (rank 1), *Special: Ether* must be higher than *Purpose*

Kelpie

Northwestern European cultures have similar stories of shape-shifting fey that live in turbulent rivers and lochs. They go by many names, Alastyn in Ireland, Cabyll Ushtey in Scotland, Bäckahäste in Scandinavia, but in the Empire these water-horses are called Kelpie. Particulars vary, but it is widely agreed that these feyfolk can transform between a physically powerful horse and a beautiful man or woman. While in mortal guise a kelpie's true nature can be identified by some holdover of its aquatic aspect such as hair interlaced with seaweed or that is always damp, an unnatural green-shimmer of the mare's coat, webbed fingers and toes, or retained equine ears.

Their motivations are a mystery, but there are many stories of them pulling a surprised victim to a watery grave, posing either as a prospective mortal lover or as a mount waiting to be tamed. After the drowning, the corpses of those they kill are kept in some underwater grotto or weighted to remain submerged so the kelpie can return to eat them after they have become sufficiently bloated or brined. The hearts, lungs or liver is usually left uneaten, although the legends do not tell us why. These fey occasionally wander away from their aquatic habitat to hunt livestock or unwary travelers.

Some stories tell that if a kelpie is bridled as a horse, or has a necklace placed upon it as a mortal, that it will be bound to serve the one who placed the halter. Mystics aver that such service is not guaranteed, but it is most likely a misunderstanding of a binding rite some skillful magus once performed. If a kelpie were bound, it would make a powerful servant.

KELPIE (HUMANOID)

Threat: 4
Conflict Assessment: Physical 40   Social 40
Potential: Ether 3, Corruption 4
Aptitudes: G 2   V 3   R 2   F 2   P 4   W 2
Universal Skills: Physical 2   Mental —   Social 3
Skills: Athletics 4, Melee 4, Guile 4
Attacks:
POWERFUL STRIKE: Grace + Melee (6), Potency 2, Touch
STICKY HIDE: Grace + Melee (6), Potency 1, Touch, *Disarmed*, Reactive.
Defenses: Physical 7   Social 6
Armor: –
Guard: 1
Morale: Hostile
Assets: Alternate Form: Kelpie (Water Horse), Aquatic, Enhanced Aptitude, Glamour (Fast Friends, Phantasm), Special Attack: Powerful Strike (Potency), Special Attack: Sticky Hide (Condition, Reactive)
Liabilities: Attack Restriction: Sticky Hide (Harmless), Bane (rank 1, silver), Corrupt,
Special: Kelpies in humanoid guise will use any accoutrements at hand, and will often have additional attack options and an increased Guard through the use of weapons.

KELPIE (WATER HORSE)

Threat: 4
Conflict Assessment: Physical 44   S 28
Potential: Ether 3, Corruption 4
Aptitudes: G 3   V 4   R 2   F 2   P 2   W 2
Universal Skills: Physical 4   Mental –   Social 1
Skills: Composure 3, Guile 3, Parley 3, Temptation 3
Attacks:
FLAILING HOOVES: Grace + Melee (7), Potency 3, Touch, Staggered
STICKY HIDE: Grace + Melee (7), Potency 1, Touch, *Disarmed*, Reactive.
Defenses: Physical 7   Social 5
Armor: 0
Guard: 1
Morale: Hostile
Assets: Aquatic, Alternate Form: Kelpie (Humanoid), Enhanced Aptitude, Extra Move, Glamour (Fast Friends), Special Attack: Flailing Hooves (Condition, Potent x2), Special Attack: Sticky Hide (Condition, Reactive)
Liabilities: Attack Restriction: Sticky Hide (Harmless) Bane (rank 1, silver), Corrupt, Large Target, Weak Physical Defense

CREATING NATURE SPIRITS

Most fey that come to the world will manifest physically as feyfolk. Others, however, manifest not as tangible beings but as incorporeal spirits. Any animist spirit, local god, or elemental can be the inspiration for a fey nature spirit. The *Materialize* asset can add even more flexibility, allowing a nature spirit to switch from incorporeal to corporeal. These entities can be used as allies, antagonists, or interesting scenery. The spirit of a bridge may demand the solution to a riddle before it allows passage. The spirit of the forest may wander through the trees manifested as a giant hart. The presence of these entities can even be used simply to cause tension between worshipers of the Clockmaker and adherents of ancient or indigenous religions. After all, fey nature spirits definitely seem to aid those who pay them homage much more often than does the Clockmaker.

Magi who work as summoners often find nature spirits a much safer alternative to demons and shades. This is certainly the case with indigenous shamans. Nature spirits can sometimes have similar capabilities to shades, and are good resources for information gathering. Also, unlike demons and shades who often have violent and malicious intentions, fey nature spirits seem to benefit from the belief of mortals and can be much more easily swayed to help them.

Muldjewangk, Spirit of Lake Alexandrina

Aboriginal oral traditions tell of all manner of terror befalling those that intrude on the tranquil waters of what is now Lake Alexandrina. Giants with seaweed for hair, or made of algae, have long been associated with the lake. Parents have warned their children against playing near the shores, lest they fall victim to the powerful water spirits that inhabit its depths. Fishermen have stories of their nets being inexplicably pulled and damaged, or their boats suddenly being struck by some unseen, powerful force from below. Some even claim to have seen a great shape resembling half-man and half-fish, or monstrous hands reaching up from the deep, chasing their boats back to shore.

In truth, these tales refer to the last of the fey spirits the Australian Aboriginal people call the muldjewangk. As Adelaide expanded its settlement, the Witchfinders came and banished almost all the muldjewangk from the lake so they would die, separated from their tether. Those remaining are enraged and fear eventual banishment. This fear of being banished from the lake is the only thing preventing them from attacking the many boats now traversing it daily. Each net of fish pulled from the water, or noisy steamer chugging along atop it angers them. Soon, dragging down a lone swimmer or fouling the nets of fishers may not be enough to sate their quiet rage.

A muldjewangk uses its *Phantasmagoria* glamour to create images to frighten people away from the lake, or trick them into believing they face a physical threat. When they are discovered, the muldjewangk can use its *Psychokinetic* ability to attack foes, or, preferably, drag them into the water to drown while they are subject to a *Fey Stroke* glamour. Thanks to the continually renewing *Ether* of this strong fey spirit, it can use these powerful abilities near-constantly. For mortals, the best chance of safety is retreat: due to the strength of its tie to the lake it won't leave the waters voluntarily to follow. Banishing the remaining muldjewangk from the lake is the only hope of removing them permanently, but such a powerful banishing rite would be incredibly demanding to perform.

MULDJEWANGK, SPIRIT OF LAKE ALEXANDRINA

Threat: 6

Conflict Assessment: Physical 96   Social 96

Potential: Purpose 1, Ether 3

Aptitudes: G –   V (6)*   R 2   F 3   P 4   W 4

Universal Skills: Physical 3   Mental –   Social 4

Skills: Athletics 6, Guile 6, Melee 6

Attacks:

VIOLENT THRUST:* Grace + Melee (6), Potency 3, Touch

INVISIBLE CURRENT:* Grace + Melee (6), Potency 1, Short Range, *Entrapped*, Clumsy, Harmless.

FEY STROKE: Will + Melee +10, Touch: if successful, target is *Incapacitated* for a number of sequences equal to the DoS of the attack. This ignores Guard and Armor, and cannot cause Wounds

Defenses: Physical –   Social 8

Armor: –

Guard: NA

Morale: Hostile

Assets: Fount of potential: Ether, Glamour x2 (Fey Stroke, Phantasmagoria), Limitless Potential: Ether, Psychokinetic, Special Attack: Invisible Current (Condition, Reach x2), Special Attack: Violent Thrust (Potent x2)

Liabilities: Aptitude Penalty, Attack Restriction: Invisible Current (Clumsy, Harmless), Tethered (Rank 5 Affinity for Lake Alexandria "Keep the waters sacrosanct")

Special: *The use of Vigor and the physical attacks are only available when using *Psychokinetic*

Nature Spirit Template				
Creature Type	**Aptitudes**	**Universal Skills**	**Assets**	**Liabilities**
Nature Spirits	*Grace* 0, *Vigor* 0, *Reason* 1, *Focus* 1, *Presence* 3, *Will* 2	Physical 0, Mental 0, Social 1	2 *Glamours*, *Incorporeal*, *Potential* (+1 *Ether*)	*Aptitude Penalty*, *Tethered*

Wyldling Template				
Creature Type	Aptitudes	Universal Skills	Assets	Liabilities
Wyldlings	Grace 1, Vigor 1, Reason 1, Focus 2, Presence 4, Will 1	Physical 0, Mental 0, Social 1	2 Glamours, Limitless Potential, +2 Ether	Aptitude Penalty, Fixed Potential: Ether, Unskilled

CREATING WYLDLINGS

Wyldlings are usually only encountered within the Borderlands, where despite being incorporeal, they can act as though they had corporeal bodies. They will present themselves in two ways: as the semi-permanent fey lords of Annwn or as tormented wandering beings of flux. Within Annwn, the mightiest of the wyldlings rule over vast tracts of land given form by the mortals they lure and trap within their domain. These fey enjoy some degree of stability in identity, but as this depends on the hopes and fears of their captives, they are fearsomely protective of those mortals whom they have ensnared. Most of their skills, assets, and liabilities should center around their ability to lure and capture mortals, and retain them.

Wandering wyldlings are profoundly mutable beings. They have no true form of their own, but are instead shaped by the ambiance of wherever they are found and the beliefs of whoever finds them. These beings will serve as whatever is needed by the domain in which they are encountered, and may change as the player characters affect that domain with their own hopes and fears. The *Alternate Form* asset can be used to simulate this fluidity during a single encounter. It is even possible for a Narrator to recreate the same wyldling for each time the players encounter it, as this will clearly represent its existence of constant flux. The ceaseless change and precarious nature of their existence allows them to manifest in the game in myriad ways. Be creative. Use their mutability to show the abstract nature of the Borderlands.

MORTALS

The bewildering array of mortals in the Clockwork is hard to overstate. Different societies, experiences, and goals lead people down many paths, and mortal NCs can represent everyone from a local grocer to the Queen herself. All of the drama of a story plays out against the ever-present backdrop of the daily lives of people, so featuring mortal NCs is a vital part of any story.

Mortal Templates				
Creature Type	Aptitudes	Universal Skills	Assets	Liabilities
Beastfolk	Grace 1, Vigor 2, Reason 2, Focus 2, Presence 2, Will 2	Physical 1, Mental 0, Social 0	Augmentation x2	Vulnerable, Special: -1, Esteem if known to be a beastman
Changelings	Grace 1, Vigor 1, Reason 2, Focus 2, Presence 3, Will 1	Physical 0, Mental 0, Social 1	1 Glamour, Potential (+1, Ether)	None
Nephilim*	Grace 1, Vigor 1, Reason 2, Focus 3, Presence 2, Will 1	Physical 0, Mental 1, Social 0	Special: Angelic Immortality, Fluid Mien, Knowledge in the Flesh	Bane (rank 1), Special: -2, Esteem if known to be a naphil
Purebloods	Grace 1, Vigor 1, Reason 2, Focus 2, Presence 2, Will 2	Physical 0, Mental 0, Social 1	Skill Bonus, Potential (+1 Purpose)	None

CREATING MORTALS

All mortals NCs are tightly linked to the full bloodlines available for player characters, but are stripped down slightly to keep them easy to design and run. This works well for minor characters, but the primary recurring allies and antagonists may merit development with the full character generation system.

Mortals of any stripe have the most flexibility of any NC creature type for who they are and what they can do. Increasing skill ranks through *Skill Bonus* is a great way to reflect specialization as well as make them effective combatants, regardless of their Threat rank. *Special Attack* assets are uncommon, as most attacks are based on whatever accoutrements are utilized. Most accoutrements are free, but remember that any weapon with a *Penetrating Attack* does require the expenditure of an asset. Other than that, almost any asset or liability from either the player character or NC lists can be appropriate. Finding unusual combinations of assets and liabilities is a great way to add flavor to even low-Threat NCs. For example, a gang of orphan pickpockets may all be *Keen* to use their *Exceptional Teamwork* to steal from the unsuspecting, but they're also *Cowardly* and run away from any physical altercation.

Most purebloods in the world are Threat 2 or 3. Exceptional individuals may sometimes achieve Threat 4, but only the most extraordinary will ever rise beyond. Purebloods tend to make well-rounded NCs with a broad spread of skills and ability. Beastfolk and changelings are more likely to move into the higher Threat ranges due to their atypical natures. Nephilim, while not truly mortal, can often take on mortal roles within the game and can have an extraordinarily high Threat rank if they are truly old. The frequency of these corrupt bloodlines having unusual assets tends to make them more specialized, and so they are likely to be highly effective in some conflicts, but at a decided disadvantage in others.

Hardened Criminal

There are always those willing to take what they want from an easy victim. The hardened criminal is an all-purpose scofflaw that could be found anywhere in the world. Although generally content to steal from the unsuspecting or those weaker than themselves, hardened criminals are often part of gangs and pose a serious risk if encountered in numbers.

HARDENED CRIMINAL
Threat: 3
Conflict Assessment: Physical 33   Social 21
Potential: Purpose 1, Ether 1
Aptitudes: G 2   V 3   R 2   F 2   P 2   W 2
Universal Skills: Physical 3   Mental –   Social 1
Skills: Burglary 2, Command 2, Composure 2, Guile 2, Medicine 1, Streetwise 3, Tactics 1

Attacks:
KNIFE: Grace + Melee (5), Potency 2, Touch, *Bleeding*
PISTOL: Grace + Firearms (5), Potency 3, Short Range, *Bleeding*
Defenses: Physical 6   Social 5
Armor: –
Guard: 2
Morale: Guarded
Assets: Penetrating Weapon, Potential, Skill Bonus x2, Strong Social Defense
Liabilities: None

Changeling Hustler

The suspicion and mistrust that changelings face throughout their life is, ironically, what drives many of them to rely on their glamours and tendency towards strong social skills to overcome that prejudice through deception. Those changelings that embrace their gifts to the fullest can often find a lucrative though dangerous life in the genteel criminality of confidence schemes and hustles.

CHANGELING HUSTLER
Threat: 2
Conflict Assessment: Physical 10   Social 20
Potential: Ether 2
Aptitudes: G 2   V 2   R 2   F 2   P 3   W 2
Universal Skills: Physical 1   Mental –   Social 2
Skills: Academics 2, Guile 3
Attacks:
WALKING STICK: Grace + Melee (3), Potency 2, Close, *Dazed*
CRAFTY LIES: Presence + Guile (6), Potency 1, Audible, *Entrapped*
Defenses: Physical 3   Social 4
Armor: –
Guard: 2
Morale: Agreeable
Assets: Aptitude Bonus, Exceptional Skill, Glamour x2, Potential
Liabilities: Skill Penalty, Weak Morale, Weak Physical Defense
Glamours: Beguile (before conflict, spend 1 Ether to fix a target's starting disposition to Indifferent: their Disposition cannot drop below Indifferent); Captivate (all social attacks have the Entrapped condition)

Beastfolk Laborer

The Empire officially welcomes beastfolk, but the daily reality of social stigma drives many to take work out of the public eye, performing dangerous or thankless jobs. The physical hardiness that made beastfolk likely candidates for their surgeries dovetails with these demanding jobs, and the combination tends to further enhance their strengths.

The laborer presented here is extremely strong and tough, thanks to the *Hide* and *Muscular Structure* augmentations, but barely looks human. Exchanging the augmentations and moving even one or two aptitude ranks can greatly change how the NC is used in conflict. Choosing *Grace* 3, *Vigor* 3, and swapping *Hide* for *Claws* makes for a more aggressive attacker. Selecting *Grace* 4, *Vigor* 2, and taking *Brachiator* and *Prehensile Feet* would instead describe a nimble climber that would be at home on tall ships or zeppelins, or that could make a criminal career as a cat burglar.

BEASTFOLK LABORER

Threat: 3
Conflict Assessment: Physical 36   Social 21
Potential: 1 Ether
Aptitudes: G 2   V 4   R 2   F 2   P 2   W 2
Universal Skills: Physical 3   Mental –   Social 1
Skills: Academics 1, Command 2, Composure 2, Streetwise 2, Vocation 2
Attacks:
REPURPOSED TOOL (IMPROVISED WEAPON): Grace + Melee (5), Potency 3, Close
Large Knife, Grace + Melee (5), Potency 3, Close, *Bleeding, Quick*
Bare hands, Grace + Melee (5), Potency 2, Touch
Defenses: Physical 7   Social 4
Armor: Physical 2   Social –
Guard: 2
Morale: Hostile
Assets: Augmentation x2, Strong Guard, Strong Morale
Liabilities: Vulnerable
Augmentations: Hide (Physical Armor 2; cannot be concealed); Muscular Structure (All Athletics tests are passive; +1 Potency on close combat attacks)

Influential Politician

Those who pursue a life of civil service in the Empire can amass a great deal of social influence and attain positions of political power. This is easiest for the upper classes, but a few talented and determined professionals can reach positions of importance as well. Those in such positions often jealously guard and cultivate their power through all manner of social intrigues, and can be relentless foes if offended or threatened.

INFLUENTIAL POLITICIAN

Threat: 4
Conflict Assessment: Physical 24   Social 48
Potential: Purpose 2, Ether 1
Aptitudes: G 2   V 2   R 3   F 2   P 4   W 3
Universal Skills: Physical 1   Mental 1   Social 3
Skills: Academics 3, Bureaucracy 3, Fencing, 2, Parley 5, Riding 2
Attacks:
STIRRING ORATION: Presence + Parley (8), Potency 2, Social Attack, *Undone*
Walking stick, Grace + Melee (3), Potency 2, Close, *Dazed*
Defenses: Physical 3   Social 8
Armor: –
Guard: 2
Morale: Guarded
Assets: Aptitude Bonus x2, Exceptional Skill: Parley, Mastery: Parley (Closing Argument) Potential, Skill Bonus, Special Attack: Stirring Oration (Condition, Potent)
Liabilities: Hesitant, No Interruption, Weak Morale
Special: Draw one extra initiative card at the start of conflict then discard the highest; cannot seize initiative; when testing Parley against a target Favorable to your argument draw two cards and choose which is used to resolve the test

SOULS

Mortals are one part body and one part breath. When they die, their bodies are laid to rest in the ground until the Day of Resurrection. Their breath, also called the soul, leaves the body to slowly make its way toward Heaven. Some souls may get held up somewhere along this journey, and many don't even make it out of the mortal realm.

SHADES

Sometimes mortal passions and emotional ties are strong enough to bind the breath of a man to the world even after death. Tethering this fractured remnant of a complete individual to an emotion, object, place, or person, prevents it from moving on. A soul that is tethered to the world in this way is called a shade. All

Shade Template				
Creature Type	Aptitudes	Universal Skills	Assets	Liabilities
Shades	*Grace* 0, *Vigor* 0, *Reason* 2, *Focus* 2, *Presence* 2, *Will* 2	Physical 0, Mental 0, Social 1	*Incorporeal, Special Attack* (Condition, Social Attack)	*Tethered*

shades are defined by their tether, that all-consuming obsession that binds them to the mortal realm and is the center of every thought. Resolving that tether is the only way to release a shade to find its peace in the afterlife.

Their lack of physical form leaves few options for dealing with shades. They can be convinced or persuaded to act against their tethers, gradually weakening them enough to let the shade move on. They can also be exorcised or banished long enough that they lose their Affinity to their tether. These options can present a very unusual challenge to characters that take a predominantly physical approach to encounters, while giving social characters or those with some transcendent powers a moment to shine.

Creating Shades

When building shades, creating very strong social attacks with additional *Special Attack* assets is the easiest way to make them effective. Adding social Armor is a thematic way to represent their single-mindedness and help protect them from being tricked by clever characters. Sacrificing skills and aptitudes for liabilities is easier with shades than other antagonists, as they are narrowly-focused on social conflict.

A few of the oldest and most terrifying shades can grow to great power, as their obsession with their tether builds over the years and increases their strength. Powerful shades may even interact with the physical world directly through the *Materialize, Possession,* or *Psychokinetic* assets. Such entities can be extremely difficult to deal with, as they get to choose the terms of when and if others can even attempt to fight back.

Ancient Miser

A person obsessed with wealth, or unnaturally fixated on a particular item, will sometimes remain even after death if she is unable to part with her prized possession. Should anyone disturb the item or—worse yet—take it for themselves, the shade will harry them tirelessly until the treasured belonging is returned to its resting place. If such an object is destroyed, the shade will do everything in its power to punish those who defiled it. Graverobbers and criminals have always told tales of such specters, but with the growing field of archaeology increasing the number and reach of cultural expeditions around the world, a few academics and self-styled adventurers are telling them as well.

ANCIENT MISER

Threat: 5

Conflict Assessment: Physical 60*   Social 70

Potential: Ether 2

Aptitudes: G (4)*   V (4)*   R 2   F 3   P 4   W 4
   *when Materialized, see assets

Universal Skills: Physical 2   Mental 1   Social 3

Skills: Command 5, Melee 4, Stealth 3, Survival 3

Attacks:

PERILOUS COMMAND: Presence + Command (9), Potency 2, Audible, *Staggered*

CLUTCH OF THE GRAVE*: Grace + Melee (8), Potency 3, Touch, *Aggravated*

Defenses: Physical (7)*   Social 7

Armor: Physical –   Social 2

Guard: 1

Morale: Hostile

Assets: Armor x2 (Social), Flight, Incorporeal, Materialize, Special Attack: Perilous Command (Condition, Potent, Social), Special Attack: Clutch of the Grave (Condition, Potent x2)

Liabilities: Hesitant, No Interruption, Slow, Tethered (Rank 5 Affinity to "Guard my treasures forever!"), Weak Physical Defense

Special: All entries marked with an asterisk * are only usable while Materialized.

CLOCKWORK DOMINION: KICKSTARTER BACKERS

Imperial Sympathizers: amauri, Eric Babineau, Henry Bingham, Consorte Marketing, Karl Fenner, Anthony J. Gallela, Patrick Habegger, James, K Lennart Jansson, Jason Lee, Lovedart, MaJeStu, Dirk Manning, raven mimura, Pair-A-Dice Games, Raffaele Passarelli, Praemus, Proxy Army Games, Aaron Ramsby, Reed Raymond, scionofnyarlathotep, Benjamin Szymanel, Elise M. Tincher, Miranda Van Vliet, Kennan Ward, Michael Woycke, Erich Zann

Patrons of the Arts: Mallory Bram, Brian Crick, Alex Dingle, Thomas Egebak, Flashflood, Daniel Kratz, Dave McNally, Norton, Maria Piteros, Jordan Radomi, Valdimir Shotton, Rémy "Skuz974" Stieglitz

Émigré: Brett Anderson, Andreas, Robin Armstrong, Christopher Baerman, Kevin Bailey, Edward Bednar, Alex Blair, Ian Borchardt, Mike Brodu, Julie Brown, Josh Buschbacher, Gabrielle Campeau, Todd Carter, chapel, Daniel Chow, Eccles, Eclipse, Kristen Elkington, FaolchuDonn, Fernando, David Michael Finzi, Charles Fitt, Scott Fitzpatrick, Glenn Francis II, Javier Perez Garcia, Craig Hackl, Chua Chee Han, Cynthia Leigh Harris, Seth Hartley, Jane, Brian Rygaard Jensen, JoeyR, _Journeyman_, Riikka Kauppi, Jeremy Kear, Khadour, Log A Kin, David King, Daniel Lawrence, Marc Margelli, Mark, Michael "gleepism" McCormack, Daniel Medina, Michael, Mark Morrison, Matthew Blake Myslinski, Shawn Nichols, Philippe Niederkorn, David Nielsen, Thomas D Pairan, Ingrid Parena, Jens Kaaber Pors, Jamie Revell, Jaime Robertson, runester, Ian Schneider, Schnuffel, Travis Smith, chris stewart, TavernKeeper, Tealus, TechnocratJT, Tomas, Igor Toscano, JP Trudel, Mindy Tuan, David Turkington, Oscar Ulloa, Garou Verroq, Jeremy Wong, Stewart "Zoot" Wymer

Citizen: Stras Acimovic, Alexander, Geoffrey Allen, Marek Benes, Matthew Benson, Meg Blaha, Jason Blalock, Michael Blanchard, LeRoy Robert Brown, David Burwell, Camithril, Kevin Collins, Paul Counts, James E. Davis, John Desmarais, Stephanie L Dierker, John Dossa, Michael Duchene, John Eddy, Eiphah, James Enge, Erik Extrell, Michael Feldhusen, Johan Gärderud, Andrew Geneczko, Carl Gilchrist, Ira Gluck, Mark H, John C Hay, Damon Hochnadel, Gunnar Hogberg, Simon Hunt, Illyan, Chris Jahn, Tania Joyce, M Alexander Jurkat, Edward Kabara, kevin, Andy King, Robyn Kistemaker, Ian Kitley, Steve Klein, Ed Kowalczewski, Ted Leaman, Oliver Lind, Lil B's ghost, Steven Lord, Loxly, Conor MacSubine, Angela Manella, Matt, Robert W McElaney, Nathan Michael, Charles Myers, Pete Newell, Daniel Nissman, Quenton Edward Michaelis Oakes, oldstevo, Alex Perrault, Sara Peters, Primewave, Bradley Proper, Louise Prosser, Chris Quin, Paul Riddle, Jon Robertson, Mathew Sangraw, Caroline Schultheis, Andreas Sewe, Danielle Siler, Cerity "Legendary Bottlejak" Silverhawk, Justin Smith, Stephan Szabo, Janahan Thiru, Scott Tweedie, ken vennard, Vincent, Duncan Webster, Brook West

Esquire: christopher block, Kielo Blomqvist, Matt Bowerman, Brandon M Bonar, Kenneth Cockrell, Dylan Durrant, Evan Foulke, Brian M. Gray, William Hochella, Craig Huber, Mark Kilfoil, Josh Kroger, Jordan Lennard, Ben McCabe, Rod Meek, Regan Miller, Sarah Noe, Skeeter Panes, Teppo Pennanen, Sarah Perry, Robin, seith, Ryan Thames, TJ, Timothy Travis, David Waldron, Penni Walker, Kenneth J. Weir, Nichole Williams, Robert Wood

Gentry: Alfonso Abella, Nick Adams, Kimberly Akre, Albert, Alexandra, Amy, Svend Andersen, Chris Angelini, aragaer, Sethreich Ardestahdt, Ian Arentz, Chad Andrew Bale, Ben Balestra, J. D. Beers, Bigbywolfe, Ralph Bigio, Kevin Bortnick, mike bowie, Charley Brandum, Anne Brannen, Brennan, Brian, Sterling Brucks, Kyle Burckhard, Shaun Burton, Scott Carpenter, Robert Cavender, Andrew Chang, Daniel Chase, Cintain 昆游龍, Meredith Collins, Raechel Coon, Jason Corley, James Cruise, Jean-Christophe Cubertafon, D, Darren, Tim Davis, Doug Deck, Tod Detre, Matthew Dimalanta, Matt Dinep, Joanna Duncan, Bram Dyckmans, V. Dzundza, Paul Echeverri, Bob Edwards, Chris Edwards, Chris Emmerson, Todd Evangelista, James Folkerth, Geoffrey Ford, Phil Freund, K.B. Friesen, Lee Fuchs, Joshua Gammon, Anthony Garcia, Gabriel Garcia, Mark Gillings, john e graham, Bernard Gravel, Rebecca Grayden, Patrick Griffis, Keith H, Hectaimon, Jill Heller, herrold, Jonna Hind, Andreas Hoetzel, Brian Holder, Tom Huber, Hubnutzen, William Huggins, Alex Hunter, Eric Isbell, Glen Ivey, Jack, James, jlc, J T, Helen June, Lynlee Kaufman, E. King, Fred Koning, Daniel Krenzke, Thomas Krømke, K. Adam Kunst, Tom Lamb, Nat Lanza, Jason Larsen, Chris Lavin, Robert J. Lawrence, Michael Lonon, Lost And Found, Derek Lynch, Ignatius Magee, Chris Maggiolo, manika, Marianya, Jason Marks, Rich Martin, Will Martin, Andrea Martinelli, Mike Maxson, Patrice Mermoud, Christopher Merrill, Steve Morris, Michael Murphy, Anthony Nijssen, Christian Nord, William Nourse, Dawn Noyes, Oubliette, Glenn Overby II, Jason Pack, Lisa Padol, Joshua Pantalleresco, Matthew Peterson, Jonas Petersson, Genghis Philip, Clinton Pong, Bill Racicot, Ray, Cory Rewcastle, Gregg Q. Reynante, Matthew Richardson, John Riggle, Yaro Rohowsky, Seth Rollins, Rostow, Hardus le Roux, Robert T. Sagris, Sagital Games, Lai Cheong Sang, Kevin Schantz, James Schauer, marc schiermeier, Jacob Segal, Damien Serrano, Geoff Seymour, Jess Shively, daniel singhal, Sleet, Gary Smith, Jennifer L Smith, Timothy Sparks, Pineapple Steak, Angelo de Stephano, Suko, Nicholas Taylor, Ricardo Tijerina, Traiden, trenchcloak, David Turner, Rachel Ventura, Adam Waggenspack, Matt Wagner, stephanie wagner, Eric Walch, Lori Watson, Morgan Weeks, Bill Werring, Petri Wessman, Adam Whitcomb, Ron Wilhelm, Christopher Wong, Daniel Wood, Proton Wrangler, Gavin Wright, Jacob Yeager, Jeffrey A York, Y Y Zhed, Kristian Zirnsak, Adrian Zollinger, rebecca zumbrun

Nobility: Alloyed, Jose Antonio Nuá'ez Alvarez, Michael Baker, John Bellando, Calum, Andrew Carrick, Chechu, Bradford T Cone, corsair43, Arthur Dean, Cornelis DeBruin, Victoria Elizabeth-Francis DeMaria, Anthony DiNovo, Frank Donatelli, Mathew Duckwitz, Brett Easterbrook, Timothy David Elrod, Andrew Findlay, britt fitch, David Ford, Kiery Franklin, Martin Friedrichs, Alex Fux, KT Glitz, Beverly Gonzales, Aaron Grossman, Josh Hale, Franklin Hamilton, Richard Hansen, Will Harrison, Al Hartmann, Briar Jansons, Hui Jiang, Beth Karabin, Kathy, Kendall, Troy Kozee, Andrew Laffin, Matthew Le Blond, Tony Lee, Iain MacPhee, Hans-Joachim Maier, Liz Masterson, Matthew, Ian McFarlin, Timothy McGowan, Michael McLaughlin, Evan Miller, Troy B. Morgan, orlean, Stephan Pennington, Michael Pierno, Luke Platfoot, April Powers, David Richardson, David Rosenstein, Chris Satola, Richard Savage, Scott Schwarzwalder, Michael Smith, Chris Snyder, Robin Stirzaker, Shawn Stutzel, Matthew Williford, wouter

Persons of Note: Carissa Hill, Michael McGrath, Mathew Mills, Brian Smith

Witchfinders: Jim Baker, William Coughlin, Daniel Goldman, Brogan King, Kevin Ullrich

Immortals: Michael Butz & Courtney, Lisa Coughlin, Howard Fein, Ken Thronberry

CLOCKWORK DOMINION

Name: _____
Bloodline: _____
Pursuit: _____
Background: _____
Player Name: _____

STATUS

Class ○ 1 2 3 4 5
Means ○ 1 2 3 4 5

POTENTIAL

Purpose ○ 1 2 3 4 5
Ether ○ 1 2 3 4 5
Corruption 1 2 3 4 5

APTITUDES

Grace — 1 2 3 4 5
Vigor — 1 2 3 4 5

Reason — 1 2 3 4 5
Focus — 1 2 3 4 5

Presence — 1 2 3 4 5
Will — 1 2 3 4 5

SKILLS

Skill					
Academics	1	2	3	4	5
Artisan	1	2	3	4	5
Athletics	1	2	3	4	5
Bureaucracy	1	2	3	4	5
Burglary	1	2	3	4	5
Command	1	2	3	4	5
Composure	1	2	3	4	5
Engineering	1	2	3	4	5
Fencing	1	2	3	4	5
Firearms	1	2	3	4	5
Fisticuffs	1	2	3	4	5
Guile	1	2	3	4	5
Intuition	1	2	3	4	5
Investigation	1	2	3	4	5
Medicine	1	2	3	4	5
Melee	1	2	3	4	5
Mysteries	1	2	3	4	5
Parley	1	2	3	4	5
Refinement	1	2	3	4	5
Riding	1	2	3	4	5
Science	1	2	3	4	5
Stealth	1	2	3	4	5
Streetwise	1	2	3	4	5
Survival	1	2	3	4	5
Tactics	1	2	3	4	5
Temptation	1	2	3	4	5
Vocation	1	2	3	4	5

MEMBERSHIPS

○ 1 2 3 4 5

REPUTATIONS

○ 1 2 3 4 5
○ 1 2 3 4 5

AFFINITIES

○ 1 2 3 4 5
○ 1 2 3 4 5

BLESSINGS, CURSES & MASTERIES

ASSETS, LIABILITIES & TRANSCENDENT POWERS

WEAPONS & EVIDENCE

Name — Reach — Potency — Load — Weapon Condition

PHYSICAL CONFLICT

PHYSICAL DEFENSE
VIGOR + SKILL

Athletics _____
Armor _____

GUARD
1/2 FOCUS +1 for Weapon

○ ○ ○ ○ ○

WOUNDS
○ ○ ○ ○ ○

Wound Penalties [ ]

EXPERIENCE POINTS [ ]

Persistent Conditions

SOCIAL CONFLICT

SOCIAL DEFENSE
WILL + SKILL

Composure _____

DISPOSITIONS

Hostile	Guarded	Indifferent	Agreeable	Favorable
H	G	I	A	F
H	G	I	A	F

ESTEEM Indifferent + (Tenor-Status) +/- 1/2 Relevant Reputation

H	G	I	A	F

CPSIA information can be obtained at www.ICGtesting.com
Printed in the USA
BVOW10*0529090715

406721BV00002B/3/P